Cisco Networking Academy Program

IT Essentials II: Network Operating Systems Companion Guide

Cisco Systems, Inc.

Cisco Networking Academy Program

Cisco Press

800 East 96th Street

Indianapolis, Indiana 46240 USA

www.ciscopress.com

Cisco Networking Academy Program

IT Essentials II: Network Operating Systems Companion Guide

Cisco Systems, Inc.

Cisco Networking Academy Program

Course sponsored by Hewlett-Packard Company

Copyright© 2003 Cisco Systems, Inc.

Published by:
Cisco Press
800 East 96th Street
Indianapolis, IN 46240 USA

Printed in the United States of America   6 7 8 9 0

Sixth Printing June 2007

Library of Congress Cataloging-in-Publication Number: 2002105112

ISBN: 1-58713-097-1

Trademark Acknowledgments

Warning and Disclaimer

Feedback Information

At Cisco Press, our goal is to create in-depth technical books of the highest quality and value. Each book is crafted with care and precision, undergoing rigorous development that involves the unique expertise of members of the professional technical community.

Reader feedback is a natural continuation of this process. If you have any comments regarding how we could improve the quality of this book, or otherwise alter it to better suit your needs, you can contact us through e-mail at networkingacademy@ciscopress.com. Please be sure to include the book title and ISBN in your message.

We greatly appreciate your assistance.

Publisher	*John Wait*
Editor-in-Chief	*John Kane*
Executive Editor	*Carl Lindholm*
Cisco Representative	*Anthony Wolfenden*
Cisco Press Program Manager	*Sonia Torres Chavez*
Cisco Marketing Communications Manager	*Tom Geitner*
Cisco Marketing Program Manager	*Edie Quiroz*
Production Manager	*Patrick Kanouse*
Development Editor	*Karen Hicks*
Senior Editor	*Sheri Cain*
Copy Editor	*Gayle Johnson*
Technical Editors	*Jim Drennen, Arthur Toch, Arthur Tucker*
Assistant Editor	*Sarah Kimberly*
Cover Designer	*Louisa Adair*
Composition	*Mark Shirar*
Indexer	*Tim Wright*

CISCO SYSTEMS

Corporate Headquarters
Cisco Systems, Inc.
170 West Tasman Drive
San Jose, CA 95134-1706
USA
www.cisco.com
Tel: 408 526-4000
    800 553-NETS (6387)
Fax: 408 526-4100

European Headquarters
Cisco Systems International BV
Haarlerbergpark
Haarlerbergweg 13-19
1101 CH Amsterdam
The Netherlands
www-europe.cisco.com
Tel: 31 0 20 357 1000
Fax: 31 0 20 357 1100

Americas Headquarters
Cisco Systems, Inc.
170 West Tasman Drive
San Jose, CA 95134-1706
USA
www.cisco.com
Tel: 408 526-7660
Fax: 408 527-0883

Asia Pacific Headquarters
Cisco Systems, Inc.
Capital Tower
168 Robinson Road
#22-01 to #29-01
Singapore 068912
www.cisco.com
Tel: +65 6317 7777
Fax: +65 6317 7799

Cisco Systems has more than 200 offices in the following countries and regions. Addresses, phone numbers, and fax numbers are listed on the
Cisco.com Web site at www.cisco.com/go/offices.

Argentina • Australia • Austria • Belgium • Brazil • Bulgaria • Canada • Chile • China PRC • Colombia • Costa Rica • Croatia • Czech Republic
Denmark • Dubai, UAE • Finland • France • Germany • Greece • Hong Kong SAR • Hungary • India • Indonesia • Ireland • Israel • Italy
Japan • Korea • Luxembourg • Malaysia • Mexico • The Netherlands • New Zealand • Norway • Peru • Philippines • Poland • Portugal
Puerto Rico • Romania • Russia • Saudi Arabia • Scotland • Singapore • Slovakia • Slovenia • South Africa • Spain • Sweden
Switzerland • Taiwan • Thailand • Turkey • Ukraine • United Kingdom • United States • Venezuela • Vietnam • Zimbabwe

About the Technical Reviewers

Jim Drennen, CSSP, CCNP, CCDP, is an associate professor of information technology at Pensacola Junior College, Pensacola, Florida. Jim was instrumental in Pensacola Junior College obtaining the status of a Regional Cisco Networking Academy, as well as a Cisco CCNP Academy, and a Cisco Sponsored Curriculum Academy. Jim was the first director of the Institute for Information Technology at PJC. He has worked with the Cisco Worldwide Education team writing, reviewing, and editing assessment exams for the CNAMS curriculum. Jim is the owner of Drennen & Associates Consulting, and a partner in Gulf Coast Networking Technologies. He is currently completing his CSS1, Cisco Security Specialist certification, and a masters degree in Information Technology. You can contact Jim at Jim.Drennen@gulfcoastnettech.com or jdrennen@pjc.edu.

Arthur Toch, A+, CCAI, CCNA, CCNP, MCT, MCSE NT4, MSCE, Win2k, is a network and systems engineer for Venture Computer Systems and an Adjunct instructor for Rochester Community and Technical College. He is responsible for designing, installing, and maintaining networks, wide-area networks, and various types of network servers in medium and large enterprise clients for Venture Computer Systems. He also teaches the Cisco Networking Academy Program and Microsoft System Engineer classes at his local community college. Art has been in the networking industry for more than five years.

Arthur Tucker is a Cisco Certified Academy Instructor (CCAI) at West Virginia University for the CCNA and Web Design curricula. Arthur has a BS degree in Computer Science and is A+ certified.

Overview

Introduction xix

Chapter 1   Operating System Fundamentals 3

Chapter 2   Introduction to Networking 51

Chapter 3   Physical Components of a Network 99

Chapter 4   TCP/IP Networking 155

Chapter 5   Overview of Network Services 203

Chapter 6   Introduction to Network Operating Systems 263

Chapter 7   Installation and Boot Process Overview. 305

Chapter 8   Windows 2000 Professional 361

Chapter 9   Linux Installation Procedures 401

Chapter 10   Linux 453

Chapter 11   Advanced NOS Administration. 519

Chapter 12   Installing and Maintaining Hardware in a Linux Environment. . .595

Chapter 13   Troubleshooting the Operating System 653

Chapter 14   Network Security 719

Appendix A   Answers to Check Your Understanding Questions 763

Glossary of Key Terms 801

Index 831

Contents

Introduction xix

Chapter 1   Operating System Fundamentals 3

Operating System Basics 4
Overview of PC Operating Systems 4
PCs and Computer Networks 5
Operating System Components 7
Common Desktop Operating Systems 12

Microsoft Windows 14
MS-DOS 14
Windows 3.1 17
Windows 9*x* 19
Windows NT and Windows 2000 21
Windows XP 22
Windows GUI 24
Windows CLI 25
Windows Control Panel 27

UNIX and Linux on the Desktop 28
Origins of UNIX 28
Origins of Linux 29
Linux/UNIX GUI 31
Linux/UNIX CLI 32
Linux and UNIX System Configuration Tools 33

Network Operating Systems Overview 34
Common Network Operating Systems 34
Client/Server Model 38
Evaluating Customer Resources and Requirements 40

Summary 45

Check Your Understanding 46

Key Terms 48

Chapter 2   Introduction to Networking 51

Benefits of Networking 51
File, Print, and Application Services 51
Mail Services 52
Directory and Name Services 54
The Internet 55
Network Administration 55

Types of Networks 57
    Local-Area Networks 57
    Wide-Area Networks 59
    Peer-to-Peer Networks 63
    Client/Server Networks 65

Networking Standards 68
    Proprietary Versus Open Standards 68
    The OSI Reference Model 69
    The DoD Model 75
    The IEEE 76
    The ITU 77
    Other Standards 77

Networking Protocols 78
    Protocol Suite 78
    TCP/IP 78
    IPX/SPX 80
    AppleTalk 81

LAN Architectures 82
    Ethernet 82
    Token Ring 86
    Fiber Distributed Data Interface 87

Summary 90

Check Your Understanding 91

Key Terms 94

Chapter 3   Physical Components of a Network 99

Configuring a Network Interface Card 99
    What Is a NIC? 99
    Setting the IP Address 101
    DHCP Servers 102
    Domain Name System 105
    Default Gateway 108

Topologies 108
    The Network Topology 108
    Physical Versus Logical Topology 109
    Bus Topology 111
    Star Topology 112
    Ring Topology 114
    Mesh Topology 116
    Hybrid Topology 117

Media Types 117

   Networking Media 117

   Coaxial Cable 118

   Twisted-Pair Cable 120

   Fiber-Optic Cable 123

   Wireless 125

Devices 127

   Hubs and Repeaters 127

   Bridges and Switches 129

   Routers 132

Connecting to the Internet (WANs) 134

   Synchronous and Asynchronous Serial Lines 135

   Modems 135

   Dialup Networking, Modem Standards, and AT Commands 138

   ISPs and Internet Backbone Providers 140

   DSL 142

   Cable Modems 144

   Cable Modems Versus DSL Internet Technologies 145

Summary 147

Check Your Understanding 148

Key Terms 150

Chapter 4   TCP/IP Networking 155

History of TCP/IP 155

   Origins and Growth of TCP/IP 155

   The TCP/IP Network Model 157

   TCP/IP and Network Operating Systems 161

IP Addressing 163

   IPv4 Addressing 163

   IPv4 Addressing Overview 164

   Class A Addresses 167

   Class B Addresses 168

   Class C Addresses 168

   Class D and E Addresses 168

   The IPv4 Address Crisis 169

   Subnetting 173

Name Resolution 178

   Overview of Name Resolution 178

   Host Names and Host Tables 178

The Domain Name System 180
Name Services and the NOS 181
WINS 182

TCP/IP Protocols 183
Overview of TCP/IP Protocols 184
Address Resolution Protocol 185
Internet Control Message Protocol (ICMP) 186
Transmission Control Protocol (TCP) 188
User Datagram Protocol (UDP) 189
DHCP Services 189
Hypertext Transport Protocol 190
File Transfer Protocol (FTP) 192
Telnet 192
SMTP 193
POP3 195
IMAP 195

Summary 196

Check Your Understanding 198

Key Terms 200

Chapter 5   Overview of Network Services 203

Network Services 203

Remote Administration and Access Services 204
What Is Remote Access? 205
Telecommuting 206
Mobile Users 207
Terminal Emulation Services 207
Telnet Services 208
Configuring Remote Access for a Client 210
Controlling Remote-Access Rights 218
Remote Administration on a Linux System 223

Directory Services 226
What Is a Directory Service? 227
Directory Service Standards 229
Windows 2000 Active Directory 231
The Novell Network Directory Service 234
Network Information Service 237

Other NOS Services 238
    Mail 239
    Printing 240
    File Sharing 241
    FTP (File Transfer) Web Services 242
    Web Services 244
    Intranets 247
    Extranets 249
    Automating Tasks with Script Services 250
    Domain Name System 252
    DHCP 254
    Domains 254

Summary 256

Check Your Understanding 257

Key Terms 258

Chapter 6   Introduction to Network Operating Systems 263

Characteristics of a Network Operating System 263
    Overview of NOS Characteristics. 264
    Differences Between a PC and a NOS 265
    Multiuser, Multitasking, and Multiprocessor Systems 266
    NOS Server Hardware 267
    Choosing a NOS 268
    Types of NOSs 269

Windows NT/2000 270
    Windows Terminology 270
    Windows NT 4.0 271
    Windows 2000 Operating Systems 273
    Windows 2000's Family of Operating Systems 275

Linux 278
    History of Linux 278
    What Is UNIX? 279
    Linux Operating Systems 280
    Linux Clients 286

Determining Software Requirements for a Linux NOS 287
    Workstation Software and Programs 287
    Server Software and Programs 291
    Additional Software and Programs 293
    Verifying Software Compatibility .297

Summary 298

Check Your Understanding 299

Key Terms 301

Chapter 7   Installation and Boot Process Overview 305

Preparing for the Installation 305

Background: Installing a NOS 305

Planning the System 306

Planning Hardware Installation 307

Server Hardware Components 310

Hardware Requirements 317

Creating a Hardware Inventory 320

Identifying Hardware Using Device Manager 322

Checking Hardware Compatibility Lists 323

Verifying the Network 324

Verifying Network Connectivity 325

The Installation Process 326

Installation Media 327

BIOS Settings 328

The Installation Program 328

Disk Partitions 331

Partitioning a Disk 334

Swap Files 338

Formatting the Disk 342

Creating the Initial Administrative Account 343

Completing the Installation 344

The Boot Process 345

Steps of the Boot Process 345

Basic Files Required 346

BIOS Interaction 347

Detailed Steps of the Boot Process 348

Linux Boot Process 350

Troubleshooting NOS Installation 351

Unable to Boot from the Installation Medium 351

Problems During the Installation Process 352

Post-Installation Problems 353

Summary 354

Check Your Understanding 355

Key Terms 357

Chapter 8   Windows 2000 Professional 361

Installation 361

Installing the OS 361

Installing OS Add-On Options 368

Administrator/User Interface 369

Login Procedures 369

Graphical User Interface 370

Command-Line Interface 373

Windows Explorer Navigation 375

User Accounts 376

Adding Users 376

Managing User Accounts 377

Managing the File System 379

Creating and Sharing Folders 379

Creating Groups and Adding Users 380

Passwords and Permissions 381

Services 383

Hypertext Transfer Protocol 384

File Transfer Protocol 385

Telnet 387

E-Mail Server/Client Relationship .389

Printing in Windows 2000 390

Scripts 393

Summary 394

Check Your Understanding 395

Key Terms 397

Chapter 9   Linux Installation Procedures 401

Pre-Installation Tasks 401

Boot Method 402

Installation Medium 403

Selecting the Appropriate Parameters for Installation 404

Creating the Linux File System 406

Selecting Packages to Install 408

Installing and Configuring Linux 409
   Linux Hardware Requirements 409
   Starting the Installation 409
   Configuring Appropriate Security Settings 410
   Configuring Network Settings 412
   Other Configurations and Settings .413

X Server 416
   Video Card Chipset 416
   X Server Options 417
   Installing X Server 418
   Configuring X Server 419
   Hardware Configurations 423
   Window Managers 427
   Desktop Environments 429

Post-Installation Configuration and Tasks 433
   Red Hat Package Manager 434
   Debian Package Manager 437
   Tarballs 438
   Installing and Reconfiguring the Boot Loader 439
   Kernel Issues 442
   Environment Variables 444
   Verifying Proper Application Functioning and Performance .445

Summary 447

Check Your Understanding 448

Key Terms 449

Chapter 10   Linux 453

User Interface Administration 453
   Login Procedures 453
   Graphical User Interface 454
   Command-Line Interface 457
   Linux Shells 462
   vi Editor 464

User Accounts and Group Accounts 466
   User and Group Accounts in a Linux Environment 466
   Adding Users 469
   Managing User Accounts 471
   Creating Groups and Adding Users to Groups 472

File System and Services Management 474
   Creating and Sharing Directories 474
   Passwords and Permissions 475
   Mounting and Managing File Systems 477

File System Configuration Files 481
   User Configuration Files 482
   System Configuration Files 483
   Startup Configuration Files 483
   System Function Configuration Files 484
   Configuration Files for Specific Servers 484
   Editing Configuration Files 485
   Managing Runlevels 488

Documenting a Linux System Configuration 490
   System Maintenance Log 491
   Backing Up the /etc Directory 492

Daemons 492
   Introduction to Linux Daemons 493
   Starting, Stopping, and Restarting Daemons 494
   HTTP 498
   FTP 501
   Telnet 502
   Server Message Block Protocol 504
   NFS 505
   Mail Client 506
   Printing in a Linux Environment 506
   Scripts 511

Summary 512

Check Your Understanding 514

Key Terms 515

Chapter 11 Advanced NOS Administration 519

Backups 519
   Overview of Backup Methods 519
   Installing Backup Software 522
   Backup Hardware 525
   Backup Strategies 530
   Automating Backups 533

Drive Mapping 533
  What Is Drive Mapping? 534
  Mapping Drives in Windows Networks 534
  Mapping Drives in Linux Networks 537
  Mapping Drives in Novell Networks 537

Partition and Process Management .538
  Using fdisk, mkfs, and fsck 538
  Managing System Processes with cron Jobs 540
  Core Dumps 543
  Critical and Noncritical Processes 545
  Assigning Permissions for Processes 551

Monitoring Resources 552
  Disk Management 552
  Memory Usage 554
  CPU Usage 555
  Reviewing Daily Logs 556
  Checking Resource Usage in Windows 2000 and
    Windows XP 559
  Checking Resource Usage in Linux 561

Analyzing and Optimizing Network Performance 563
  Key Concepts in Analyzing and Optimizing
    Network Performance 563
  Determining Internet Connection Speed 571
  Network Monitoring Software 572
  Network Management Software 577
  Management Software for Small and Medium-Sized
    Networks 581
  Management Service Provider 582
  SNMP Concepts and Components 582
  SNMP Structure and Functions 584

Summary 589

Check Your Understanding 590

Key Terms 591

Chapter 12 Installing and Maintaining Hardware in a Linux Environment . .595

Hardware Terms, Concepts, and Components 595
  Overview of Hardware Components 596

CPU 599
Video Hardware 601
Miscellaneous Hardware and Components 602
Hardware Monitoring Devices 605

Hardware Installation, Configuration, and Maintenance 608
Locating Hardware Drivers for Linux 609
Configuring Hardware in a Linux System 610
Linux Kernel Modules 616

Checking and Confirming Hardware Configuration 621
Power Cables 621
IRQs, DMAs, and I/O Settings 624
EIDE Devices 626
SCSI Devices 627
BIOS Settings 629

Diagnosing and Troubleshooting Devices 631
SCSI Devices 633
Peripheral Devices 636
Core System Hardware 640

Laptop and Mobile Devices 641
Power Management 642
PC Card Devices 644

Summary 646

Check Your Understanding 647

Key Terms 649

Chapter 13   Troubleshooting the Operating System 653

Identifying and Locating Symptoms and Problems 653
Hardware Problems 654
Kernel Problems 655
Application Software 655
Configuration 656
User Error 657

Using System Utilities and System Status Tools 658

Unresponsive Programs and Processes 660
When to Start, Stop, or Restart a Process 660
Troubleshooting Persistent Problems 661

Examining Log Files 662
The dmesg Command 664

Troubleshooting Problems Based on User Feedback 665

LILO Boot Errors 667
   Booting a Linux System Without LILO 670
   Emergency Boot System 672
   Using an Emergency Boot Disk in Linux 673

Recognizing Common Errors 679
   Various Reasons for Package Dependency Problems 679
   Solutions to Package Dependency Problems 681
   Backup and Restore Errors 684
   Application Failure on Linux Servers 687

Troubleshooting Network Problems 689
   Loss of Connectivity 689
   Operator Error 689
   Using TCP/IP Utilities 690
   Problem-Solving Guidelines 695
   Windows 2000 Diagnostic Tools 696
   Wake-On-LAN 698

Disaster Recovery 698
   Understanding Redundancy, Clustering, Scalability, and
    High Availability 700
   Redundancy 700
   Clustering 704
   Scalability 706
   High Availability 707
   Hot Swapping, Warm Swapping, and Hot Spares 708
   Creating a Disaster Recovery Plan Based on Fault Tolerance/
    Recovery 709
   Testing the Plan 710
   Hot and Cold Sites 711

Summary 712

Check Your Understanding 713

Key Terms 714

Chapter 14   Network Security 719

Developing a Network Security Policy 719
   Accessing Security Needs 719
   Acceptable-Use Policy 722

Username and Password Standards 722
Rules for Network Access 723
Policy for Disposal of Materials 723
Virus-Protection Standards 724
Online Security Resources 724
Server Room Security 725
Antitheft Devices for Server Hardware 728
Securing Removable Media 729

Threats to Network Security 730
Overview of Internal and External Security 730
Outside Threats 731
Denial of Service 733
Distributed Denial of Service 735
Well-Known Exploits 736
Trojan Horse Programs 738
Inside Threats 738

Implementing Security Measures 740
File Encryption 740
IP Security 741
Secure Sockets Layer 742
E-Mail Security 742
Public/Private Key Encryption 744

Patches and Upgrades 745
Finding Patches and Upgrades 745
Selecting Patches and Upgrades 746
Applying Patches and Upgrades 747

Firewalls 747
Introduction to Firewalls and Proxies 748
Packet Filtering 751
Firewall Placement 753
Common Firewall Solutions 754
Using a NOS as a Firewall 756

Summary 757

Check Your Understanding 758

Key Terms 760

Appendix A Answers to Check Your Understanding Questions 763

Glossary of Key Terms. 801

Index 831

Introduction

Cisco Networking Academy Program IT Essentials II: Network Operating Systems Companion Guide supplements the online course and its corresponding classroom and laboratory instruction. Although IT Essentials I: PC Hardware and Software is not a prerequisite to taking this course, it provides the foundation on which this course builds. This book parallels the online course to provide support for the information and skills you need to pursue a career in information technology as a PC technician or network administrator. In addition to the Linux+ and Server+ certification objectives that are covered, this book provides information on Windows, UNIX, and the Linux network operating system.

The book introduces and extends your knowledge of operating systems, the benefits of networking, and types of networks. The physical components of a network are reviewed, including the NIC, types of media, and networking devices that provide Internet connections. The concepts covered in this book enable you to develop practical experience and skills related to TCP/IP networking, IP addressing, and name resolution and protocols. The importance of a hardware inventory list is stressed, as is verifying compatibility with the network. The steps to install a network operating system, including Windows 2000 and Linux, are described in detail.

This book introduces the responsibilities of a network administrator, including managing users and groups, and creating directories, passwords, and permissions. It also covers backup methods and strategies, partition and process management, monitoring server resources, and analyzing network performance. The book then discusses troubleshooting the operating system, including how to identify the type of problem and create an emergency boot disk, and the process of disaster recovery. It ends by highlighting security issues and how to assess security needs and develop an acceptable-use policy to prevent inside and outside threats.

Comprehensive explanations and descriptions, along with review questions and worksheets, provide a strong foundation for students who will be taking the Server+ certification exam and Linux+ certification exam. The CD-ROM included with this book further enforces such important topics as the floppy drive, the CD-ROM drive, the sound card, and other interactive elements.

This Book's Goal

The goal of this book is to lay a foundation of the basic information required for network operating system administration and other network administration tasks. It is designed to be used in conjunction with IT Essentials I: PC Hardware and Software to fully prepare students to pass the Server+ certification exam and, when studied in conjunction with the Fundamentals of UNIX course and its related titles, the Linux+ certification exam.

This Book's Audience

This book is intended for students who want to pursue a career in information technology or who want working knowledge of how a computer works, how to administer Windows 2000 and Linux Red Hat Network Operating Systems, and how to troubleshoot operating system issues. Students who will be seeking their Server+ or Linux+ certifications will find this book particularly useful.

This Book's Features

The features in this book help facilitate an understanding of computer systems and troubleshooting system problems:

- **Objectives**—Each chapter starts with a list of objectives that you should be able to master by the end of the chapter. The objectives summarize the concepts covered in the chapter.

- **Figures, examples, tables, and scenarios**—This book contains figures, examples, and tables that help explain theories, concepts, commands, and setup sequences, as well as help you visualize the content covered in the chapter. In addition, specific scenarios provide real-life situations that detail the problem and the solution.

- **Chapter summaries**—At the end of each chapter is a summary of the concepts covered in the chapter. It provides a synopsis of the chapter and serves as a study aid.

- **Check Your Understanding questions**—Review questions are presented at the end of each chapter to serve as an assessment. In addition, the questions reinforce the concepts introduced in the chapter and help test your understanding before you move on to new chapters.

- **Skill Builder**—Throughout this book are references to worksheet and lab activities found in CISCO NETWORKING ACADEMY PROGRAM IT Essentials II: Network Operating Systems Lab Companion. These labs allow you to make a connection between theory and practice.

How This Book Is Organized

This book is divided into 14 chapters and an appendix:

- **Chapter 1, "Operating System Fundamentals"**—This chapter covers the basics of the operating system, including the kernel, the user interface, and the file system. This chapter provides detailed information on Windows, and it covers DOS, Windows 9x, Windows 2000, and Windows XP. The origins of UNIX and Linux are discussed, including the GUI and the CLI.

- **Chapter 2, "Introduction to Networking"**—The benefits of networking are covered, including file and print services, mail services, directory and name services, the Internet, and administration. This chapter provides important information on the types of networks, networking standards, protocols, and LAN architectures.

- **Chapter 3, "Physical Components of a Network"**—To fully understand the network, you must understand the components that comprise it. You will learn about the network interface card (NIC), different topologies, the physical media or ways to connect, and the devices used, such as switches, hubs, and routers. This chapter also covers connecting to the Internet. It details ISPs and the Internet backbone, the different types of modems, and modem standards.

- **Chapter 4, "TCP/IP Networking"**—Starting with the origins of TCP/IP, this chapter discusses IP addressing, including the classes of addresses, the crisis in IPv4, and subnetting. Name resolution is a function of the NOS. This chapter details host names, host tables, and the domain name system (DNS). In addition, TCP/IP protocols are detailed in terms of their function and how they operate in the NOS.

- **Chapter 5, "Overview of Network Services"**—To offer the services provided by the NOS, the network administrator must have a thorough understanding of remote administration and directory services—specifically, for Windows and Novell. Other services include mail, printing, file sharing, FTP, intranet, extranet, and scripting to automate tasks.

- **Chapter 6, "Introduction to Network Operating Systems"**—This chapter provides an overview of NOS characteristics. Windows NT/2000 and Linux are detailed in preparation for the installation.

- **Chapter 7, "Installation and Boot Process Overview"**—To successfully install a NOS, you must understand the steps involved in preparing the system, as well as the actual installation. This includes the server's hardware requirements, creating an inventory, and using the Device Manager. The boot process also is detailed to provide maintenance and troubleshooting of problems.

- **Chapter 8, "Windows 2000 Professional"**— The Windows 2000 Professional NOS is covered in this chapter. When it is successfully installed, you will learn about administrative duties, including adding users, managing the file system, and security options to protect the network.

- **Chapter 9, "Linux Installation Procedures"**—The procedures specific to the Linux operating system are covered in this chapter, including determining the appropriate installation method and the steps to successfully prepare and install Linux on the server.

- **Chapter 10, "Linux"**—Network administration is performed in Linux just as it is in Windows, but the differences are significant. Although a network administrator creates user accounts and manages the file system, this is done in the Linux shells and the vi editor. This chapter also introduces the Linux daemon.

- **Chapter 11, "Advanced NOS Administration"**—Advanced administration in any NOS includes backing up the system, mapping the drive, and monitoring system resources. In addition, the ability to partition and manage the process is critical to system processes. An advanced administrator understands the key concepts of analyzing and optimizing system performance.

- **Chapter 12, "Installing and Maintaining Hardware in a Linux Environment"**— This chapter details hardware terms, concepts, and components specific to the Linux NOS. You will learn the proper procedure for installing, configuring, and maintaining hardware. Additionally, diagnosing and troubleshooting in Linux are discussed with regard to cabling, ERQ, SCSI devices, and the BIOS. Topics relating to laptops and mobile devices are provided to help you install Linux and manage power issues.

- **Chapter 13, "Troubleshooting the Operating System"**—The first step in troubleshooting is determining if a problem is hardware-, software-, or user-related. This chapter details how to identify and locate symptoms and how to use the tools available to implement a solution. Boot errors, network problems, and application failures are covered. Of particular importance to a network administrator is the ability to recover from disasters. You will learn how to create a disaster recovery plan based on fault tolerance.

- **Chapter 14, "Network Security"**—Network security is very important. Threats to the system come from the outside in the form of hackers, viruses, denial of service (DoS) attacks, and many others. Inside threats are also a concern. This chapter provides detailed information on assessing security needs and developing an acceptable-use policy. It also discusses implementing security measures, keeping the NOS upgraded and applying patches, and firewall placement and solutions.

- **Appendix A**—The appendix lists the answers to the Check Your Understanding questions that appear at the end of each chapter.

CompTIA Authorized Quality Curriculum

The contents of this training material were created for the CompTIA Server+ Certification exam and CompTIA Linux+ Certification exam covering CompTIA certification exam objectives that were current as of December 2002.

How to Become CompTIA Certified

This training material can help you prepare for and pass a related CompTIA certification exam or exams. In order to achieve CompTIA certification, you must register for and pass a CompTIA certification exam or exams.

In order to become CompTIA certified, you must

1. Select a certification exam provider. For more information, visit www.comptia.org/certification/general_information/test_locations.asp.

2. Register for and schedule a time to take the CompTIA certification exam(s) at a convenient location.

3. Read and sign the Candidate Agreement, which will be presented at the time of the exam(s). The text of the Candidate Agreement can be found at www.comptia.org/certification/general_information/candidate_agreement.asp.

4. Take and pass the CompTIA certification exam(s).

For more information about CompTIA's certifications, such as their industry acceptance, benefits, or program news, visit www.comptia.org/certification/default.asp.

CompTIA is a nonprofit information technology (IT) trade association. CompTIA's certifications are designed by subject matter experts from across the IT industry. Each CompTIA certification is vendor-neutral, covers multiple technologies, and requires demonstration of skills and knowledge widely sought after by the IT industry.

To contact CompTIA with any questions or comments, please call + 1 630 268 1818 or e-mail questions@comptia.org.

About the CD-ROM

A CD-ROM complements this book. The CD contains two test engines consisting of Server+ and Linux+ questions, interactive e-Lab Activities, high-resolution Photo-Zooms, and instructional video vignettes. These materials review and reinforce the content covered in this book. This CD also includes supplemental material on how to install and manage HP OpenView Network Node Manager and HP OpenView Customer Views for NNM, and certification maps that align chapters to Server+ and Linux+ certification exam objectives. Additionally, the CD provides the following:

- An easy-to-use graphical user interface
- Accurate and concise feedback
- Frequent interaction with content
- Support for guided and exploratory navigation
- Learner-direction and support
- Flexibility to learners at different levels of expertise

Objectives

After completing this chapter, you will be able to complete tasks related to

- Operating system basics
- Microsoft Windows
- UNIX and Linux on the desktop
- Network operating systems

## Chapter 1

Operating System Fundamentals

The first personal computers (PCs) were designed as standalone desktop systems. The operating system (OS) software allowed one user at a time to access files and system resources. The user had physical access to the PC.

As PC-based computer networks gained popularity in the workplace, software companies developed specialized network operating systems (NOSs). Developers designed NOSs to provide file security, user privileges, and resource sharing among multiple users. The explosive growth of the Internet compelled developers to build the NOSs of today around Internet-related technologies and services such as the World Wide Web.

Within a decade, networking has become centrally important to desktop computing. The distinction between modern desktop operating systems, now loaded with networking features and services, and their NOS counterparts has blurred. Now, most popular operating systems such as Microsoft Windows 2000 and Linux are found on high-powered network servers and on end users' desktops.

This course examines the components of the most popular NOSs in use today, including Windows 2000 and Linux. This chapter reviews desktop operating systems, including their components, their limitations, and their relationship to NOSs.

This chapter provides an overview of PCs, including the OS and computer networks. Microsoft Windows is detailed, from the beginnings of MS-DOS to the latest version of Windows, XP. The UNIX and Linux operating systems are also detailed, from their origins to the current configurations. Most network applications, including the Internet, are built around a client/server relationship. You will learn how this relationship works, along with the NOS's components and configurations.

Operating System Basics

This section covers the following topics:

- PC operating systems
- PCs and computer networks
- Operating system components: the kernel, the user interface, and the file system
- Common desktop operating systems

Overview of PC Operating Systems

Desktop microcomputers first became popular and widespread in the early 1980s. Users of these early desktop PCs put their systems to work performing a variety of tasks, including word processing, home accounting, and computer gaming.

Desktop PCs also appeared in the workplace, but their productivity was limited by their inability to share information easily with other systems. Figure 1-1 shows how these early desktop PCs were electronic islands, unable to efficiently communicate with other PCs and the powerful mainframes and minicomputers that housed mission-critical data.

Figure 1-1 Mainframe Computer

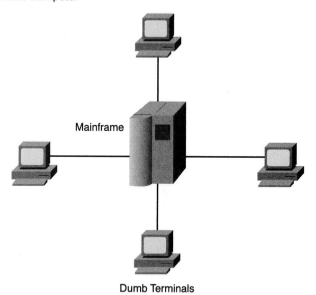

Mainframe

Dumb Terminals

For the most part, the operating systems of these early desktop PCs were designed for the standalone system. These operating systems assumed that only one user would access system resources at any given time. The concepts of file security and user privileges were not necessarily built in to desktop operating systems, because only one user could access the system at a time, and that user had to be physically present at the keyboard.

PCs and Computer Networks

As desktop computing matured in the workplace, companies installed local-area networks (LANs) to connect desktop PCs so that the PCs could share data and peripherals, such as printers. Installing network adapter cards in the PCs and then connecting the adapters using copper wire created LANs. Networking computers solved the problem of efficient communication, but new problems arose.

Early PC-based LANs needed a way to provide file security, multiuser access to resources, and user privileges. PC-based LANs also needed a way to communicate with the mainframes that were still the focal point of corporate computing environments.

One approach to solving these problems was to develop operating systems that were specialized to work in a networked environment. These so-called network operating systems (NOSs) required more computing muscle than their desktop counterparts. A new breed of powerful PCs was pressed into service as network servers. These computers ran NOSs and became the focal point of the PC-based LAN. In a server-based network, client machines connect to and access resources on the server. These client machines can run desktop operating systems, and the more powerful servers use a NOS. Software companies such as Novell and Microsoft designed their NOSs to control PC-based network environments.

As network servers became more powerful, they began to take on the functions once handled by mainframes and minicomputers. Companies such as Sun and HP modified the UNIX operating system to run extremely powerful servers. In the past, only expensive mainframes and minicomputers were trusted with mission-critical applications and data storage. But like the Novell and Microsoft NOSs, UNIX could run on microcomputers. Today, virtually all organizations rely (at least in part) on microcomputers to store mission-critical data and provide key applications and services.

Computer networking is not confined to the workplace. Most home users expect to connect to the largest network in the world, the Internet. Web browsing, e-mail, and other Internet-related applications are now the focus of home computing. To provide these Internet technologies, companies such as Microsoft have retooled their desktop operating systems. The desktop OS now includes many of the features and services that were once reserved for NOSs.

Figures 1-2, 1-3, and 1-4 show the evolution of networking.

Figure 1-2 Standalone Devices

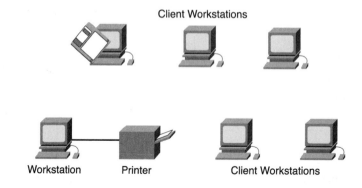

Figure 1-3 Networked Devices

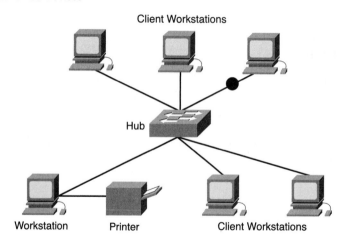

Figure 1-4 Mainframe Integration

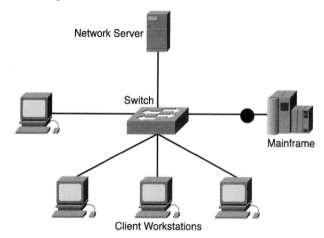

Operating System Components

Whether designed for a standalone desktop computer or a multiuser network server, all operating system software includes the following components:

- Kernel
- User interface
- File system

Kernel

Kernel is the most common term for the core of the operating system. The kernel is a relatively small piece of code that is loaded into memory when the computer boots. This computer code contains instructions that allow the kernel to manage hardware devices, such as disk drives. The kernel also manages and controls memory allocation, system processes, and other programs. Application software and other parts of the operating system rely on the kernel to provide basic scheduling services and access to the computer hardware and peripherals.

With a UNIX or Linux system, a file named "kernel" might be present. In some cases, the kernel code might have to be customized and compiled. If this file were to become corrupted, the system would no longer function.

On a Windows system, filenames that include the word "kernel" or "kern," such as kernel32.dll, might be seen. These are critical files that are used by the OS's core. Figure 1-5 shows the kernel32.dll file and where it is located within the Windows core system files.

User Interface

The *user interface (UI)* is the most visible part of a computer operating system. The UI is the component of the OS that the user interacts with. It acts like a bridge between the user and the kernel. The UI is like an interpreter, translating user keystrokes, mouse clicks, or other input for the appropriate programs. The UI can organize and display program output. On a UNIX or Linux system, a UI is typically called a shell.

User interfaces fall into two general categories:

- Figure 1-6 shows an example of the Windows command-line interface (CLI).
- Figure 1-7 shows an example of the Windows graphical user interface (GUI).

Figure 1-5 Windows 2000 Kernel File

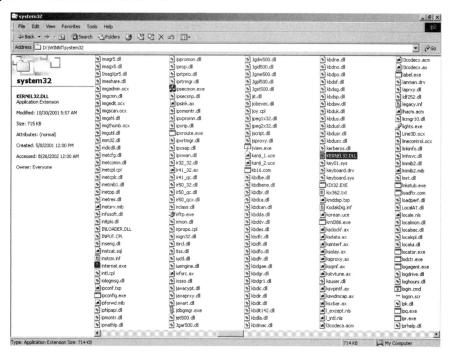

Figure 1-6 Command-Line Interface

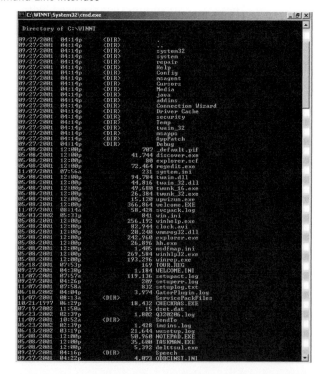

Figure 1-7 Graphical User Interface

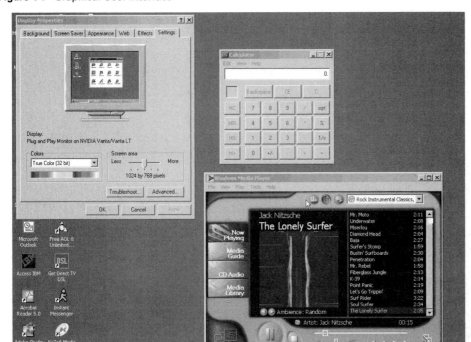

The first desktop PC operating systems used CLIs exclusively. The CLI provides the user with a visual prompt, and the user inputs commands by typing them. The computer outputs data to the screen typographically. In other words, a *CLI* environment is completely text-based. The user can get things done only by inputting commands with the keyboard.

UNIX and Linux users can choose from a variety of CLIs, or shells, such as the Bourne shell and the Korn shell. UNIX shells are discussed later in this chapter.

Today, all popular desktop OSs support GUIs. A *GUI* allows the user to manipulate software using visual objects such as windows, pull-down menus, pointers, and icons. The GUI allows the user to input commands via a mouse or other point-and-click device. End users prefer a graphical interface, because it makes operating the computer easy and intuitive. A user can perform simple operations using a GUI without even knowing how to read.

The trade-off for simplifying the user interface comes in performance. Some GUI software can consume more than 100 times the storage space that CLI software does. And because GUIs are more complicated than CLIs, GUI software requires significantly more memory and CPU time.

Because the average end user prefers and expects a graphical interface when using a computer, GUIs are now considered a requirement for desktop OSs. However, NOSs have not traditionally catered to the needs of inexperienced users. Several NOSs do not fully support GUIs. Today, most NOSs support GUIs as separate modules that can be loaded and used just as any other program that runs on the system. Most NOSs do not require these GUI modules to function, but these modules make the NOS easier and more attractive to the inexperienced user and more available to the public.

System administrators typically are comfortable working in CLI environments, so they might choose to preserve server resources by not loading the GUI software. For example, UNIX and Linux both support GUIs, but when deployed as NOSs, UNIX and Linux are often configured without GUI components. In contrast, Windows servers always include the GUI and therefore make heavier demands on system resources.

File System

An OS's file system determines how files are named and how and where they are placed on storage devices, such as hard disks. Windows, Macintosh, UNIX, and Linux OSs all employ file systems that use a hierarchical structure.

In a *hierarchical file system*, files are placed in logical containers that are arranged in an upside-down tree structure, as shown in Figure 1-8. The file system starts at the tree's root. UNIX and Linux call a container residing at the top level of the tree a *directory*. Containers inside each directory are called *subdirectories*. Windows and Macintosh OSs use the terms *folder* and *subfolder* to describe directories and subdirectories.

An OS's file system determines more than just how files and folders are logically organized. The type of file system the computer uses determines whether files can be secured from other users or programs. The file system also defines how data is physically arranged on the storage medium (such as a hard drive). Some file systems use disk space more efficiently than others.

One common type of file system is called a *file allocation table (FAT)*. FAT file systems are maintained on the disk by the operating system. The table contains a map of files and where they are stored on the disk. The FAT references *disk clusters*, which are the basic unit of logical storage on a disk. A given file may be stored on several clusters, but a cluster can contain data from only one file. These clusters might or might not be next to each other. The OS uses the FAT to find all the disk clusters where a file is stored.

Figure 1-8   File System

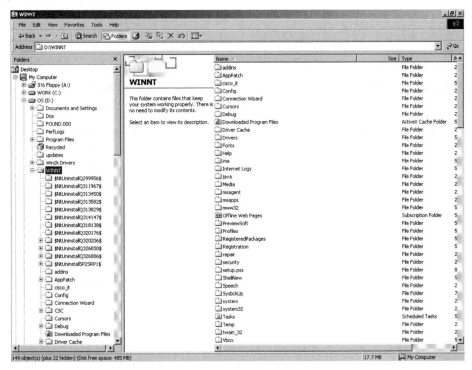

There are the three types of FAT file systems. The original FAT file system is called
FAT. The two other types, FAT16 and FAT32, are advanced and improved versions of
the original FAT file system.

The original FAT file system was used on the first versions of DOS. However, it couldn't
be used with the larger hard disks and more-advanced operating systems such as Windows 3.1, Windows 95, and Windows 98. The original FAT file system was limited in
various ways, such as recognizing filenames up to only eight characters long. Other limitations of FAT were that it was not be a viable option to use on the larger hard disks and
more-advanced operating systems that were rapidly being developed. The original FAT
file system could not make efficient use of space on these larger hard drives.

This inefficient use of space was the same problem facing FAT16 and was a major reason
why FAT32 was developed. FAT16 was created for use on larger partitions (up to 4 GB).
Although larger disks can be formatted in FAT16, doing so is an inefficient use of disk
space, because in the FAT file system, larger partitions result in larger cluster sizes. For
example, with a 512 MB partition, the size of the clusters (that is, the basic storage units)
is 8 KB. This means that even if a file is only 1 KB in size, it uses 8 KB of space, because
more than one file cannot be stored in a cluster; the extra 7 KB is wasted.

To overcome this problem, FAT32 was developed. This 32-bit file system uses smaller cluster sizes on large disks. It supports partitions up to 2 terabytes (TB) in size. Table 1-1 shows the file systems of operating systems.

Table 1-1   Operating Systems and Their File Systems

Operating System	Supported File System(s)
DOS	**FAT**
Windows 3.*x*	FAT16
Windows 95/98/Me	FAT16, FAT32
Windows NT/2000	FAT16, FAT32, NTFS
Windows XP	FAT32, NTFS
IBM OS/2	High-Performance File System (HPFS)
Linux	Ext2, Ext3, Journaling File System (JFS)

Different operating systems use different file systems, and some operating systems can use more than one file system. For example, although Windows 3.*x* can use only the FAT16 file system, Windows 2000 can use FAT16, FAT32, or the New Technology File System (NTFS).

The file system determines file-naming conventions and the format for specifying a path, or route, to the file location. These rules for naming files vary depending on the file system and include several issues:

- Maximum number of characters allowed in a filename
- Maximum length of file extensions or suffixes
- Whether spaces are allowed between words in a filename
- Whether filenames are case-sensitive
- Which characters are "legal" for use in filenames
- Format for specifying the path

Common Desktop Operating Systems

Over the past 20 years, desktop operating systems have evolved to include sophisticated GUIs and powerful networking components, as shown in Figure 1-9.

Figure 1-9 Desktop Operating Systems

Microsoft Disk Operating System (MS-DOS) is an obsolete OS that is still used to support legacy business applications. Windows versions prior to Windows 95 were essentially user interfaces for DOS.

Microsoft Windows includes Windows 95, 98, Me, NT, 2000, and XP.

Apple Macintosh OS (Mac OS) includes OS 8, OS 9, and OS X (OS 10).

Linux includes distributions from various companies and groups, such as Red Hat, Caldera, Santa Cruz Operation (SCO), SuSE, Slackware, Debian, and others.

UNIX includes HP-UX, Sun Solaris, Berkeley System Distribution (BSD), and others.

Today, OS developers and users alike recognize that the Internet is at the center of computing, confirming the Sun slogan, "The network is the computer." Because networking and the Internet have become such an integral part of using a computer, the desktop operating system is rapidly converging with the network operating system.

Microsoft Windows and MacOS can trace their roots to early desktop PCs. The latest versions of these OSs have powerful NOS components at their core. Windows XP is built on Microsoft NOS technology (NT and 2000), and MacOS is built around UNIX. UNIX is considered the first NOS. And like UNIX, the information technology (IT) industry has always considered Linux a NOS first and a desktop operating system second.

Are Windows, Linux, and UNIX desktop software or network server software? The answer to that question depends on several factors, including the specific OS version, the components installed, and the system configuration. In the following sections, Microsoft Windows and Linux are discussed as desktop operating systems. Windows 2000 and Linux are discussed in terms of NOSs later in this course.

Worksheet 1.1.6   Operating Systems Basics

This covers some of the basic topics universal to all operating systems and the types of files systems supported in various operating systems that are covered in this course.

Microsoft Windows

This section covers the following topics:

- MS-DOS
- Windows 3.1
- Windows 9*x*
- Windows NT and Windows
- Windows XP
- Windows GUI
- Windows CLI
- Windows Control Panel

MS-DOS

Microsoft released its first Windows product, Windows 1.0, in 1985. Figure 1-10 shows what the user interface looked like in this first version of Windows. Windows 2.0 was released in 1987. The earliest versions of Windows functioned as graphical user interfaces that ran "on top of" the native OS, which was called the Disk Operating System (DOS). Windows was a shell that allowed the user to manage the underlying DOS software.

Figure 1-10 Windows 1.0

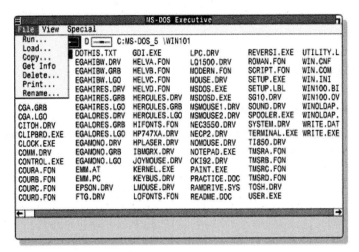

The Microsoft version of DOS (MS-DOS) was built on an OS called 86-DOS or Quick and Dirty Operating System (QDOS). Seattle Computer Products wrote QDOS to run on the Intel 8086 processor. IBM used the 8088 processor, a less-expensive version, in its new line of PCs. Microsoft bought the rights to QDOS and released MS-DOS in 1981. Figure 1-11 shows the MS-DOS user interface.

Figure 1-11 MS-DOS

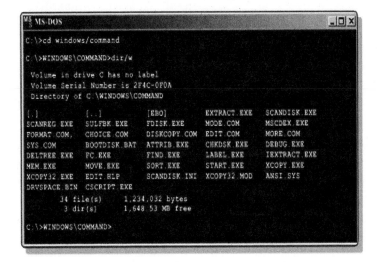

MS-DOS began as a simple operating system with a text-based CLI. Designed to run on the 16-bit (8-bit data bus) Intel 8088 processor, MS-DOS was a 16-bit operating system, which could process only 16 bits (2 bytes) at one time.

MS-DOS and 16-bit processing are obsolete in today's Internet-based and graphically-oriented desktop environments. Today, 32-bit operating systems are standard, and a handful of 64-bit operating systems are available for systems that have 64-bit processors. However, many corporations and small businesses continue to rely on MS-DOS to run legacy business applications in the workplace. A *legacy application* is outdated software that remains in use due to a previous investment. Some companies have made a significant investment in computer hardware, software, and training, and they find that MS-DOS and its related applications still get the job done.

There are several reasons for using MS-DOS:

- **MS-DOS is a simple, low-overhead operating system**—Memory and processor requirements are very low. DOS runs readily on outdated hardware.
- **MS-DOS is inexpensive**—Not only is the operating system itself inexpensive, but the cost of compatible hardware, as mentioned previously, also is low.
- **MS-DOS is stable and reliable**—Because it is not a multitasking operating system (that is, it runs only one program at a time), there is no need to worry about the conflicts and crashes caused by shared memory addresses.
- **MS-DOS is easy to learn and use**—Although it is not as intuitive as a GUI-based operating system, as soon as you master the command syntax, DOS is relatively simple to use.
- **Many programs are available for MS-DOS**—Because it was a standard for many years, a large number of programs were written to run on DOS. Some companies continue to run the operating system because proprietary programs, custom-written for their business to run on MS-DOS, do not work properly on the newer operating systems.

Of course, there are many disadvantages to continuing to use this old operating system. MS-DOS cannot run the sophisticated graphical programs written for modern 32-bit Windows operating systems. The MS-DOS FAT file system is insecure and ill-suited for today's privacy-conscious multiuser environments.

Networking with MS-DOS clients is problematic. In some cases, an MS-DOS user might be unable to connect to network resources that use long filenames (more than eight characters).

Finally, the most obvious shortcoming of MS-DOS is its intimidating CLI. As the desktop PC evolved, Microsoft set out to address the limitations of MS-DOS, particularly the user interface. Windows 1.0 and 2.0 were the first step toward this goal.

Windows 3.1

It was not until Windows 3.0 was released in 1990 that Microsoft established its user interface as a major force in the industry. In 1992, Microsoft released an upgrade to 3.0 called Windows 3.1. Shortly thereafter, Microsoft made available a free upgrade to Windows 3.1, called Windows 3.11. This family of products is known collectively as Windows 3.x. Figure 1-12 shows the initial screen that appears when Windows 3.1 and Windows 3.11 boot up.

Figure 1-12   Windows 3.x

Running MS-DOS with Windows 3.x addresses many of the MS-DOS shortcomings. The Windows 3.x shell provides a GUI and supports cooperative multitasking, which allows users to run more than one program simultaneously.

However, Windows 3.x still has significant disadvantages. Although multitasking is good, cooperative multitasking is not the best way to implement it. Also, Windows 3.x is a 16-bit operating system that does not provide the file security and built-in networking support that users now demand.

Cooperative and Preemptive Multitasking

Cooperative multitasking is an environment in which programs share memory addresses and exchange information. In a multitasked environment, applications share the use of the processor through a method known as *time slicing*. The application programs are written to give up the processor after a set amount of time so that other programs that are running simultaneously can use it. If the program is poorly written, it might monopolize the processor. If one program crashes, it might bring the other programs down.

A more efficient form of multitasking first used in Windows 9x is called *preemptive multitasking*, now used by newer versions of Windows as well. The operating system controls the allocation of processor time, and 32-bit programs run in their own separate address spaces. With preemptive multitasking, an unruly program cannot take over the system, and if one program crashes, it does not affect the others. Figure 1-13 shows the Windows Task Manager for Windows 2000. You can see that all the processes and programs running on the system have their own Process ID (PID) number, which the operating system uses to distinguish between running processes.

Figure 1-13 Windows Task Manager

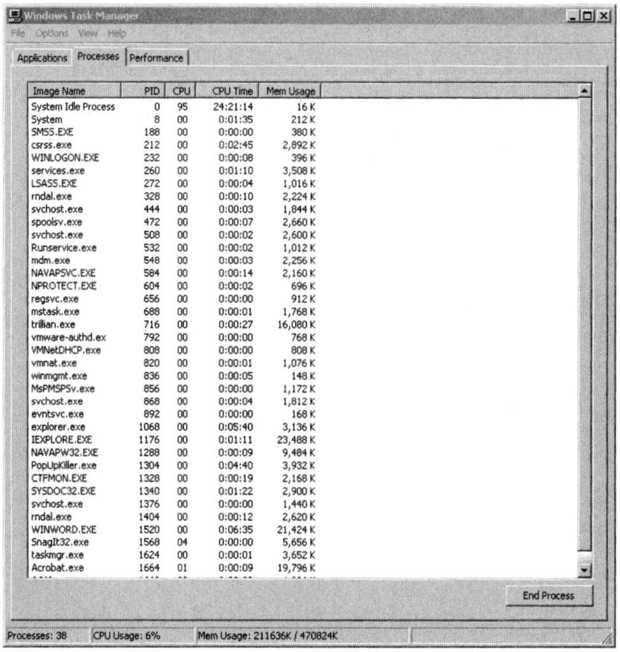

Networking with Windows 3.x

MS-DOS and Windows 3.1 require that additional network client software be installed before you can connect to a network. Windows for Workgroups 3.1 (released in 1992) was the first Microsoft operating system to have networking components built in. Microsoft released Windows for Workgroups 3.11 in 1993.

Windows for Workgroups was designed to allow users to share files with other desktop PCs in their workgroup. Figure 1-14 shows the network setup screen that is used to configure a Windows 3.11 system for network access. This kind of networking, in which every computer plays an equal role in the network, is called *peer-to-peer networking*. Built-in networking and peer-to-peer capabilities were important additions to Windows, but other operating systems, such as Apple Macintosh OS, provided peer-to-peer networking long before Windows for Workgroups.

Figure 1-14 Windows for Workgroups 3.11

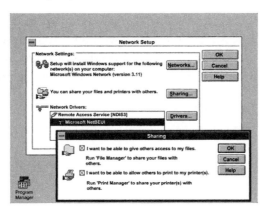

Today, Windows 3.*x* is considered obsolete. More recent versions of Windows offer significant advantages, including improved networking. Windows 3.*x* and MS-DOS can be used to connect to a modern Windows NT or Windows 2000 network, but in such cases, Windows 3.*x* clients are likely to receive limited services.

Windows 9*x*

Microsoft Windows 95 was designed for easy networking, and the tradition was carried on and enhanced in Windows 98. These operating systems are collectively called Windows 9*x*. Figure 1-15 shows an example of the Windows 9*x* desktop with the taskbar, which was a new feature that was added to the Windows 9*x* family of operating systems.

Figure 1-15 Windows 9x

Some of the other new features that were added to Windows 9x operating systems are listed here and in Table 1-2:

- **Windows 95a**—The original release of the first Microsoft 32-bit desktop operating system.
- **Windows 95b**—Also called OSR2. It included enhancements such as FAT32 support but was made available only to Original Equipment Manufacturers (OEMs) for installation on the computers they sold.
- **Windows 98**—An upgrade to Windows 95 that added the Active Desktop technology, the Advanced Configuration and Power Interface (ACPI), support for the Universal Serial Bus (USB) and TV-tuner cards, and setup and maintenance enhancements.
- **Windows 98 Second Edition** (**SE**)—Provided the Internet Explorer 5.0 web browser, stronger encryption for dialup networking, and added support for Internet Connection Sharing (ICS).
- **Windows Millennium Edition** (**Windows Me**)—An OS targeted specifically at home users. Because it builds on the Windows 9x code, Windows Me is generally recognized as part of the 9x family. Windows Me includes the following features:
  - Enhanced multimedia support, making it easy to work with movies and digital photos
  - Built-in disaster recovery features that let you restore the system to a predetermined state
  - Simplification of the configuration required to set up simple peer-to-peer networks
  - Faster startup and shutdown (when using new hardware that supports the FastBoot technology)

Table 1-2   Versions of Windows 9x

Version	Features
Windows 95a	32-bit OS, improved interface over Windows 3.x
Windows 95b	Added FAT32 support
Windows 98	Active Desktop, ACPI, USB
Windows 98 SE (Second Edition)	Internet Explorer 5.0, ICS
Windows Me (Millennium Edition)	Simplified and enhanced for home PCs, additional multimedia support, disaster recovery

Networking with Windows 9x

The Windows 9x operating systems include specialized networking client software. Client software allows the OS to participate in server-based networks. Clients take advantages of services that are offered by systems running NOS software, such as Windows NT or Novell Netware. These services include authentication, file sharing, printer sharing, directory/naming services, mail service, and web services.

Windows 9x includes client software for a variety of networks. Because of its connectivity features, Windows 9x is one of the most popular client operating systems in the business world. For several years, it has been the desktop operating system of choice for both small and large companies, for peer-to-peer networks, and for use as a client to Microsoft NT, NetWare, and UNIX servers.

32-Bit Processing and Preemptive Multitasking

Windows 9x supports 32-bit applications, but it also includes 16-bit code for backward compatibility with DOS and Windows 3.x programs. It uses Virtual File Allocation Table (VFAT) for long filename support, and Windows 95b and 98 can use FAT32 for more efficient disk use. Some advantages of Windows 9x as a desktop operating system and network client include the following:

- It is less expensive than Windows NT and Windows 2000.
- It runs a wide variety of DOS, 16-bit, and 32-bit Windows applications.
- Its interface is familiar to most PC users.
- Client software is available for Windows 9x to connect to most NOS types, such as Windows, NetWare, UNIX, and Linux.

Windows NT and Windows 2000

In the 1990s, Microsoft began developing an operating system that would meet the needs of a modern networked environment. The result was Windows NT. The NT stood for "New Technology." Microsoft first released NT as version 3.0 in 1993. Windows NT 4.0 was released in 1996.

Windows NT ran on an entirely new kernel. It did not rely on the old DOS-related code that other versions of Windows had been built on. The Windows NT software featured improved file security, stability, networking, and 32-bit support. To that end, Windows NT supported a new file system called NTFS.

From the start, Microsoft positioned Windows NT as an operating system for high-end servers and power users. Windows NT was the first Microsoft NOS.

Because of NT's superior features, Microsoft planned to unite its desktop OS (Windows 9*x*) with its NOS (NT) as a new family of products called Windows NT 5.0. The NT 5.0 project was eventually dubbed "Windows 2000" after the year in which it was finally released. Despite Microsoft's original intention to release a home user version of the software, Windows 2000 has remained an OS for power users, corporate desktops, and high-end servers. Figure 1-16 shows a timeline of the Windows operating systems from NT 3.1 to the release of Windows 2000.

Figure 1-16 From Windows NT to 2000

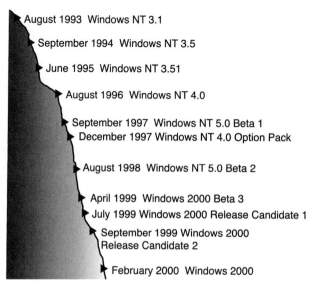

August 1993 Windows NT 3.1

September 1994 Windows NT 3.5

June 1995 Windows NT 3.51

August 1996 Windows NT 4.0

September 1997 Windows NT 5.0 Beta 1
December 1997 Windows NT 4.0 Option Pack

August 1998 Windows NT 5.0 Beta 2

April 1999 Windows 2000 Beta 3
July 1999 Windows 2000 Release Candidate 1
September 1999 Windows 2000 Release Candidate 2

February 2000 Windows 2000

Windows XP

Windows XP was released in 2001. It represents the first OS built on NT that was directly targeted toward home, as well as corporate, desktops. The Windows XP family is as follows:

- **Windows XP**—Targeted for home users
- **Windows XP Pro**—Targeted for power users and the corporate desktop
- **Windows .NET server**—Targeted for servers as a NOS

Although Windows XP and XP Professional share many components with their NT/2000 ancestors, they are still considered desktop operating systems. Despite this semantic distinction, Windows XP and XP Professional offer many of the key features associated with a NOS, including sophisticated file security and resource sharing, support for multiple user accounts, remote administration, and numerous networking components and services. Both Windows XP Home Edition and XP Professional support multiple user accounts, but only Windows XP Professional supports remote access. Figures 1-17, 1-18, and 1-19 show how different the Windows XP GUI is from the Windows 2000 GUI.

Figure 1-17 Launching Windows XP

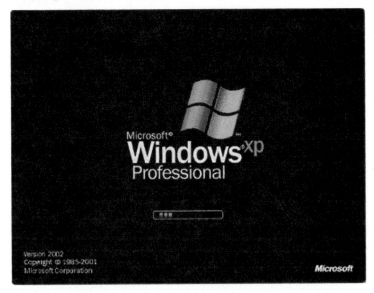

Figure 1-18 Logging on to Windows XP

Figure 1-19   Windows XP

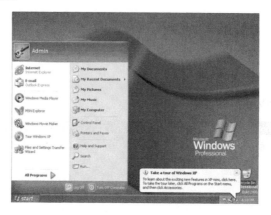

Windows GUI

The Windows GUI is perhaps the most recognizable user interface in the world. The Windows 9x, NT, 2000, and XP operating systems all share common elements in their GUIs. Figure 1-20 points out many of these similar features that all these versions of Windows have in common:

- Desktop
- Windows taskbar
- Start menu
- My Computer icon
- Network Neighborhood (also known as My Network Places)
- Recycle Bin

Figure 1-20   Elements of the Windows GUI

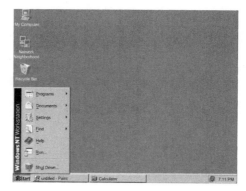

When you use the Windows GUI, right-clicking the **My Computer** icon and selecting **Properties** from the popup menu lets you check what version of Windows is currently installed in the system. The version of the OS software is displayed on the General tab of the System Properties window. Figure 1-21 shows an example of this window where the Windows version is displayed.

Figure 1-21 Windows Version

Windows CLI

All Windows operating systems include a command-line environment that lets you enter common MS-DOS commands. Figure 1-22 shows an example of the MS-DOS CLI interface.

Figure 1-22 Command Prompt Window

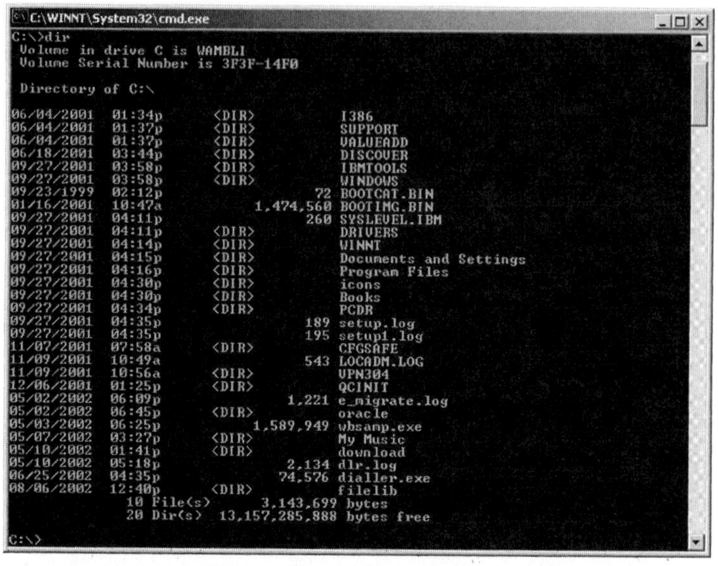

NOTE

With Windows NT, 2000, and XP machines, enter **cmd** instead of **command** to open a DOS box.

To access the command line in Windows *9x*, select **Run** from the **Start** menu and enter **command**, in the Run dialog box. This opens a window commonly called a *command prompt*. At the prompt, you can enter text-based commands and run programs. Output in the DOS box is also text-based.

Table 1-3 lists some common Windows CLI commands.

Table 1-3 Common Windows CLI Commands

Command	Result
dir	Lists the files in the current directory
cd *directory name*	Changes to a different directory
time	Displays or sets the system time
date	Displays or sets the system date
copy	Copies files to another location
diskcopy [*source*][*destination*]	Copies the contents of one floppy disk to another
attrib	Displays or changes file attributes
find *text string*	Searches for a text string in a file
help	Displays a list of other available commands and their functions

Windows Control Panel

The Windows GUI includes an important configuration tool called the Control Panel. The Windows Control Panel is a central location for making system configuration changes. Figure 1-23 shows an example of the various configuration tools that are available in the Control Panel.

Figure 1-23 Windows 2000 Control Panel

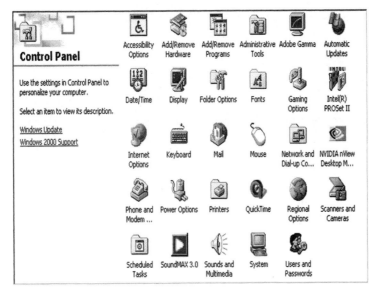

From the Control Panel, a user can perform the following key tasks:

- Install and remove hardware drivers
- Install and remove software applications and other components
- Add, modify, and delete user accounts
- Configure an Internet connection
- Configure peripheral device settings (modem, mouse, printer, and so on)

Worksheet 1.2.8   Microsoft Windows Basics

This worksheet covers the fundamental aspects of Microsoft Windows.

UNIX and Linux on the Desktop

This section covers the following topics:

- Origins of UNIX
- Origins of Linux
- Linux/UNIX GUI
- Linux/UNIX CLI
- Linux and UNIX system configuration tools

Origins of UNIX

UNIX is the name of a group of operating systems that trace their origins to 1969 at Bell Labs. UNIX was designed to support multiple users and multitasking. UNIX was also one of the first operating systems to include support for Internet networking protocols. The history of UNIX, which now spans more than 30 years, is complicated, because many companies and organizations have contributed to its development.

During the 1970s, UNIX evolved through the development work of programmers at Bell Labs and several universities, notably the University of California at Berkeley. When UNIX first started to be marketed commercially in the 1980s, it was used to run powerful network servers, not desktop computers.

Today, there are dozens of different versions of UNIX, including the following:

- HP-UX (Hewlett-Packard's UNIX)
- Berkeley Software Design, Inc. (BSD UNIX, which has spawned derivatives such as FreeBSD)
- Santa Cruz Operation (SCO) UNIX
- Sun Solaris
- AIX (IBM's UNIX)

Despite the popularity of Microsoft Windows on corporate LANs, much of the Internet runs on powerful UNIX systems. Although UNIX is usually associated with expensive hardware and is considered "user-unfriendly," recent developments, including the creation of Linux (described in the next section), have changed that image. Table 1-4 shows some of the various types of servers that UNIX and Linux systems are used for.

Table 1-4 Popular Network Uses of UNIX and Windows

Operating System	Popular Uses
UNIX	Web servers FTP servers DNS servers Firewalls Large file servers
Linux	Client workstations Corporate file servers Low-scale web servers

Origins of Linux

In 1991, a Finnish student named Linus Torvalds began work on an operating system for an Intel 80386-based computer. Frustrated with the state of desktop operating systems such as DOS, and the expense and licensing issues associated with commercial UNIX, Torvalds set out to develop an operating system that was "UNIX-like" in its operation but used software code that was open and completely free.

Although it was not his original intent, Torvalds' work led to a worldwide collaborative effort to develop *Linux*, an open-source operating system that looks and feels like UNIX. By the late 1990s, Linux had become a viable alternative to UNIX on servers and Windows on the desktop. Figure 1-24 shows a timeline of the major developments made with the Linux operating system. The popularity of Linux on desktop PCs has also contributed to interest in using UNIX distributions, such as FreeBSD and Sun Solaris, on the desktop. Versions of Linux can now run on almost any 32-bit processor, including the Intel 80386, Motorola 68000, Alpha, and PowerPC chips.

Figure 1-24 Linux Development Timeline

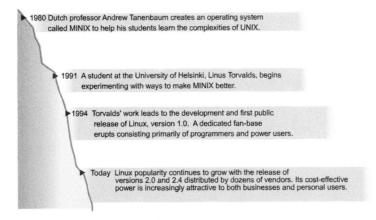

1980 Dutch professor Andrew Tanenbaum creates an operating system called MINIX to help his students learn the complexities of UNIX.

1991 A student at the University of Helsinki, Linus Torvalds, begins experimenting with ways to make MINIX better.

1994 Torvalds' work leads to the development and first public release of Linux, version 1.0. A dedicated fan-base erupts consisting primarily of programmers and power users.

Today Linux popularity continues to grow with the release of versions 2.0 and 2.4 distributed by dozens of vendors. Its cost-effective power is increasingly attractive to both businesses and personal users.

As with UNIX, there are numerous versions of Linux. Some are free downloads from the web, and others are commercially distributed. The following are a few of the most popular:

- Red Hat Linux, distributed by RedHat Software
- OpenLinux, distributed by Caldera
- Corel Linux
- Slackware
- Debian GNU/Linux
- SuSE Linux

Linux is one of the most powerful and reliable operating systems in the world today. Because of this, Linux has already made inroads as a platform for power users and in the enterprise server arena. It is less often deployed as a corporate desktop operating system. Although GUI interfaces are available to make it user-friendly, most beginning users find Linux more difficult to use than MacOS or Windows. Currently, many companies (such as Red Hat, SuSE, Corel, and Caldera) are striving to make Linux a viable operating system for the desktop.

NOTE

Although UNIX is more often implemented as a server operating system, UNIX machines can also function as network clients. In many cases, the configuration and commands for UNIX are the same as they are in Linux systems. However, because both UNIX and Linux come in many different versions, the instructions in the following sections might not apply to every distribution of UNIX or Linux. Generally, use the **man** command to access the manual for the specific version being used.

Application support must be considered when Linux is implemented on a desktop system. The number of business productivity applications is limited when compared to Windows. However, some vendors provide Windows emulation software (such as WABI and WINE) that lets many Windows applications run on Linux. Additionally, companies such as Corel are making Linux versions of their office suites and other popular software packages.

Networking with Linux

Recent distributions of Linux have networking components built in for connecting to a LAN and establishing a dialup connection to the Internet or another remote network. In fact, TCP/IP is integrated into the Linux kernel instead of being implemented as a separate subsystem.

Here are some advantages of Linux as a desktop operating system and network client:

- It is a true 32-bit operating system.
- It supports preemptive multitasking and virtual memory.

The code is *open-source* and thus is available for anyone to enhance and improve.

In this chapter, UNIX and Linux are discussed together because of their superficial similarities. Later chapters explain the differences between these two operating systems.

Linux/UNIX GUI

Both UNIX and Linux can run GUIs. Because there are so many different versions of both UNIX and Linux, there are literally dozens of popular graphical interfaces to choose from.

For example, the default installation of Red Hat 7.*x* installs the GNOME desktop environment and uses GNOME as the default GUI for all users (see Figure 1-25).

Figure 1-25 GNOME Desktop Environment

Although other desktop environments, such as the K desktop environment (KDE) (shown in Figure 1-26), can be configured and used with Linux, GNOME is rapidly gaining industry acceptance as a "standard" UNIX and Linux GUI.

Figure 1-26 KDE Desktop Environment

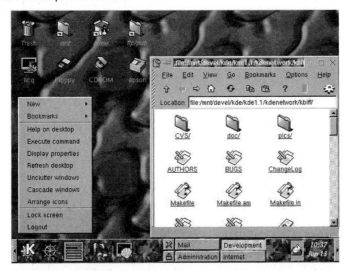

UNIX and Linux both rely on the X Window System to display the GUI. The X Window System is software that works with the system's hardware and graphical applications, including the window manager. The *window manager* is the software responsible for sizing, positioning, and rendering the graphical windows that programs run in.

Windows includes borders that you can drag to resize and graphical buttons that you can click to minimize, maximize, restore, and close the window. Because Linux supports dozens of window managers, and each window manager can be customized, there is no one way a window looks or acts. Table 1-5 lists some common window buttons and their functions.

Table 1-5 Common Linux GUI Windows Controls

Windows Button	Function
▢	Minimizes a window. You can restore a minimized window by clicking its title on the taskbar (the taskbar is part of the panel).
▣	Maximizes a window.
☒	Closes a window. If the window contains an application running in the foreground, this option terminates the application.

NOTE

GNOME stands for GNU Network Object Model Environment and is pronounced "guh-NOME." GNU stands for "GNUs, not UNIX." GNU is a software project devoted to producing free open-source software for Linux. GNU is pronounced "guh-NEW," which is why GNOME is pronounced with a "g" sound. Despite this, it is acceptable to pronounce GNOME as "NOME."

GNOME is not a window manager. In fact, GNOME can work with several different kinds of window managers. GNOME is a desktop environment. A desktop environment is a combination of programs, applications, and applets that make up part of the GUI.

GNOME provides the following:

- Graphical panels that can be used to start applications or display status
- A graphical "desktop" that can be used to place applications, files, and menus
- A standard set of desktop tools and applications
- A set of conventions that let applications work together

Linux/UNIX CLI

UNIX and Linux were designed to be extremely flexible and customizable. As a result, UNIX and Linux support dozens of user interfaces. The most common are the text-based interfaces called *shells*.

Users type commands that are interpreted by the shell, which in turn relays the user instructions to the operating system and other programs. UNIX (and Linux) shells are difficult to learn because they rely on abbreviations and complex command syntax. Commonly used shells include the following:

- Bourne shell
- Korn shell
- Bash shell
- C shell
- TC shell

The distribution and configuration of the PC running UNIX or Linux determine the shells that are available to users. Although dozens of GUIs are available for UNIX and Linux, the CLI environment is the only user interface available on many systems. If a UNIX or Linux GUI is being used, there might be several ways to access a CLI shell, such as opening a terminal window, or "term."

You can enter the UNIX command **uname** on most systems to find out what version of UNIX or Linux a computer is running.

Linux and UNIX System Configuration Tools

The various versions of UNIX and Linux offer a variety of configuration tools, similar to the Windows Control Panel. Some of these tools are text-based, for CLI environments. Others, such as linuxconf for Linux and admintool for Solaris, can be used in the GUI. Figures 1-27 and 1-28 show examples of the two main GUI configuration tools that are used with Linux and UNIX.

Figure 1-27 Linux GUI Tools: linuxconf

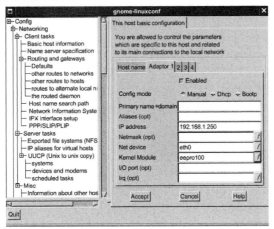

Figure 1-28 Solaris GUI Tools: admintool

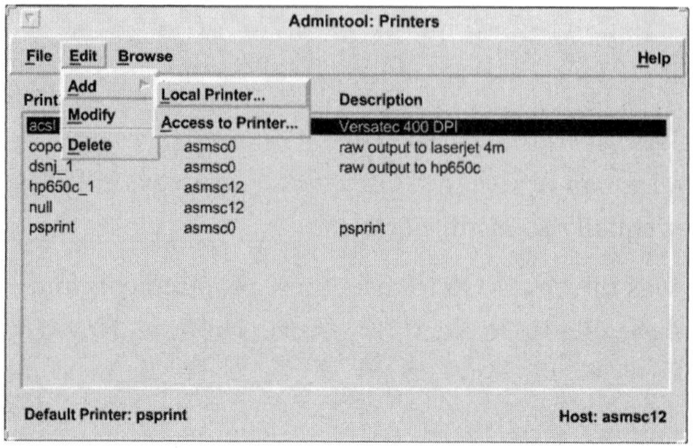

			Admintool: Printers		
File	Edit	Browse			Help
Print	Add	Local Printer...		Description	
acsl	Modify	Access to Printer...		Versatec 400 DPI	
copo	Delete		asmsc0	raw output to laserjet 4m	
dsnj_1			asmsc0	raw output to hp650c	
hp650c_1			asmsc12		
null			asmsc12		
psprint			asmsc0	psprint	
Default Printer: psprint				Host: asmsc12	

Using these configuration utilities, you can perform the following key tasks:

- Add, modify, and delete user accounts
- Configure an Internet connection and network services
- Configure peripheral device settings (modem, mouse, printer, and so on)

 Worksheet 1.3.5   UNIX and Linux on the Desktop

This worksheet covers the fundamental aspects of UNIX and Linux.

Network Operating Systems Overview

This section covers the following topics:

- Common network operating systems
- The client/server model
- Evaluating customer resources and requirements

Common Network Operating Systems

The limitations of early desktop OSs and the increasing demand to network PCs led to the development of more-powerful NOS software. In contrast to early desktop PC software, NOSs provide built-in networking components and network services, multiuser capability, and sophisticated file security and file-sharing technologies.

NOSs must have a robust kernel to prevent crashes and downtime. It is especially important that the NOS kernel schedule and manage multiple processes so that each program is prevented from crashing other parts of the system.

Because specialized administrators manage NOSs, they do not necessarily require resource-consuming graphical interfaces. NOSs have historically offered less-than-friendly user interfaces, especially when compared to their desktop counterparts. However, both Windows 2000 and Linux support fully featured GUIs and even web-based controls.

Finally, a NOS requires a sophisticated file system that allows for efficient storage and maximum security. Instead of FAT, a NOS typically employs NTFS, UFS (UNIX file system), or another equally robust file system.

Novell's NetWare was the first NOS to meet these requirements and enjoy widespread deployment in PC-based LANs in the 1980s. Since that time, Novell's software has lost its position as the top PC-based NOS.

Common NOSs in use today include those covered in the following sections.

Microsoft Windows

Figures 1-29 and 1-30 show examples of various Windows operating systems. Other types of NOSs offered by Windows are NT 3.51, NT 4.0, 2000, XP, and .NET. Keep in mind that NT 3.51 and NT 4.0 are being phased out as a result of the superior Windows 2000, XP, and .NET.

Figure 1-29 Windows XP

Figure 1-30 Windows 2000

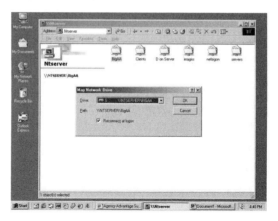

Novell NetWare

Figures 1-31 and 1-32 show examples of the Novell line of operating systems, which include NetWare 3.12, IntraNetWare 4.11, and NetWare 5.0 and 5.1.

Figure 1-31 Novell Login Box

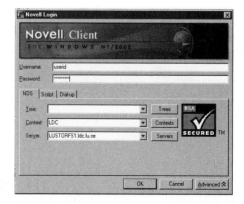

Figure 1-32 Novell Desktop

Linux

Figures 1-33 and 1-34 show various examples of Linux operating systems, including Red Hat, Caldera, SuSE, Debian, and Slackware.

Figure 1-33 Red Hat Linux

Figure 1-34 Caldera Linux

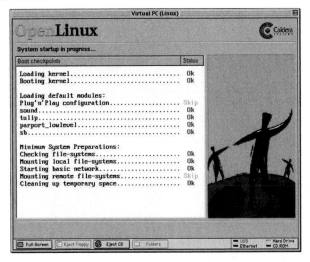

UNIX

Figures 1-35 and 1-36 show some examples of the various operating systems offered by UNIX, such as HP-UX, Sun Solaris, BSD, SCO, and AIX.

Figure 1-35 Sun Solaris

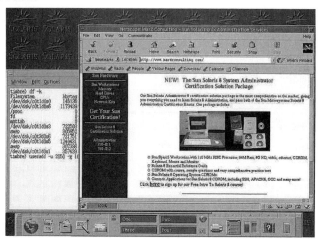

Figure 1-36 BSD UNIX Project

Client/Server Model

Most network applications, including Internet-related applications such as the World Wide Web and e-mail, are built around a client/server relationship.

A specialized program called a *server* offers network services such as e-mail to other programs called *clients*. (Server programs are typically called *daemons* in the UNIX community.) After it is enabled, a server program waits to receive requests from client programs. If a legitimate request is received, the server responds by sending the appropriate information back to the client. Figure 1-37 demonstrates how this interaction works.

Figure 1-37 Client/Server Interaction

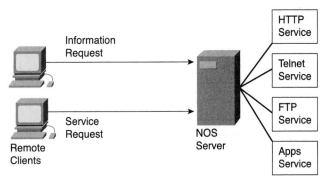

For example, as soon as a web server program is run, it waits for client requests. A web browser is an example of a client program. Web browsers send requests to web servers. When the browser requests data from the server, the server responds, and the browser program receives a reply from the web server. The browser then displays the Hypertext Transfer Protocol (HTTP) data it received in its window.

In theory, any computer can act as a server as long as it is connected to the network and is configured with the appropriate software. In practice, most organizations put all their key network services on high-end computers called servers running NOSs optimized for servicing remote clients. Figure 1-38 shows a typical logical arrangement of how servers would be placed in a network.

A typical server running a NOS can be configured to offer literally hundreds of services to clients. Moreover, most NOSs can communicate with various kinds of client platforms by following a universally understood set of rules or protocols.

The Internet is built around a set of rules collectively known as Transmission Control Protocol/Internet Protocol (TCP/IP). Because of the importance of the Internet, the majority of network services and client programs use TCP/IP to exchange data.

However, other protocols, such as Novell IPX, Apple AppleTalk, and IBM SNA, are still used today. Most NOSs can be configured to communicate using one or more of these protocols as well as TCP/IP.

One server running a NOS might work well when serving only a handful of clients. But most organizations find that they must deploy several servers to achieve acceptable performance. A typical design separates services so that one or two servers are responsible for e-mail, another server is responsible for file sharing, and so on.

High-end servers running a NOS are typically configured to use the Internet family of protocols, TCP/IP, and offer one or more TCP/IP services. Servers running a NOS are also used to authenticate users and provide access to shared resources.

Figure 1-38 Server Farm

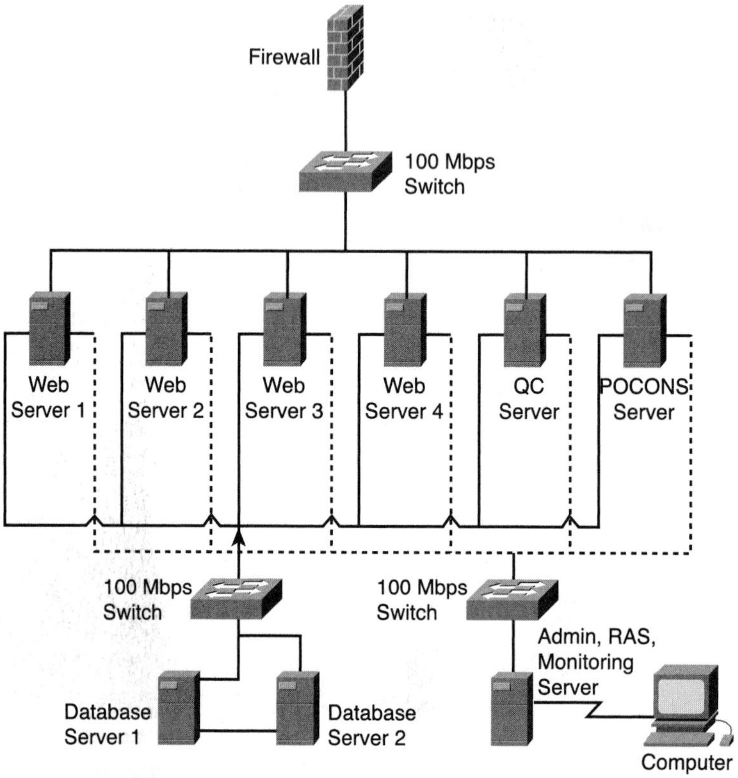

Evaluating Customer Resources and Requirements

One of the first things you must consider when buying or building a new computer are the requirements that are needed to allow the system to efficiently provide the service. Determining the customer's resources also helps you decide what type of system to build or buy for the customer.

Most computers that are sold are not designed to have Linux run on them. Therefore, evaluating certain requirements such as hardware and software helps in every other step of configuring Linux for the system. Other requirements, such as determining whether the system will be a workstation, server, or dedicated appliance, also help with subsequent steps of configuring Linux on the system. Careful planning of this step helps when you tackle other issues, such as installation, configuration, and administration (which are covered later in this course).

Workstations

A Linux *workstation*, which is also known as a desktop computer, is a system that is typically a standalone computer consisting of one monitor, keyboard, and mouse. Most often a workstation is configured with a network connection as well, but this is not a requirement for a workstation or desktop computer. Figure 1-39 shows an example of a typical workstation that Linux can run on.

Figure 1-39 Linux Workstation

When evaluating the proper requirements for a Linux workstation, you must keep in mind that this system is used by an individual who needs to have specific hardware and software installed on the system. For example, a low-end system, which an individual might need for only simple tasks, such as word processing, does not need a very fast CPU or large amounts of memory and hard disk space. However, the requirements for a high-end system that an individual needs to do more-complex tasks, such as video editing or heavy-duty scientific simulations, are much greater. In fact, this high-end system needs to have a very fast processor as well as large amounts of memory and hard disk space.

Other hardware requirements that typically are found on workstations are audio hardware such as a sound card and speakers. In some cases, a microphone might be needed as well. On a workstation you might also need some high-capacity removable media drives. These drives can be either zip drives or CD-R or CD-RW burners, and in some cases a DVD-ROM drive as well.

Servers

The requirements for a *server* are very different from those for a workstation. Figure 1-40 shows what a typical Linux server might look like. As you can see, servers generally look very different from workstation systems. Servers really have no need for user-oriented features such as large monitors, speakers, or a sound card. Servers need to consist of things such as very reliable and fault-tolerant hard disks. For this reason, servers have large, high-performance hard disks such as SCSI disks, as opposed to EIDE disks that would be installed in a workstation. This is because most servers make heavy use of their hard disk and therefore require disks that perform better. SCSI disks provide these features and are especially useful when multiple disks are installed on a single server.

Figure 1-40   Server

The size of the network that the server will support helps determine the server's CPU and memory requirements. For example, if you're installing a server in a large network environment that will handle a lot of requests and services, having a system with a fast CPU and a large amount of RAM is a necessity. This is not the case for a server that is in a small office that handles requests from a few users. With a Linux server, having large amounts of RAM can be more important, because the server has a feature that automatically stores in memory recent accesses to the hard disk. Therefore, Linux can read right from memory rather than going back to the hard disk when subsequent requests come in. This is called *buffering disk access.* For this reason, a Linux server with a lot of RAM can outperform a server with the same setup and less RAM.

Another aspect to look at when determining requirements is what type of server this system will be. Determining whether this server will be a web or FTP server, Usenet news server, database server, or time server is a pertinent consideration. For example, if the server will handle a web site that will be accessed numerous times and provide many services, you need to design a very powerful server. In some cases, you might need to have more than one server providing the web services.

Dedicated Appliances

It can be difficult to suggest requirements for a Linux system running as a dedicated appliance. A *dedicated appliance* can be a Linux system running as a router, print server, or firewall, for example. Figures 1-41 and 1-42 show examples of how a Linux server might be used as a firewall or a print server. When building a system that will be used as a dedicated appliance, you can often use recycled hardware that would be otherwise unusable. In some cases, these dedicated appliances can also require very specialized hardware, such as custom motherboards or touchscreen input devices.

Figure 1-41 Linux as a Firewall

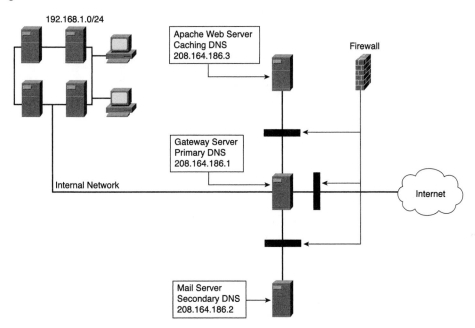

Customer Resources

Determining the customer's resources is also a very important step in evaluating the requirements that are needed and also that are available. These can include things such as whether any existing hardware can be used, budgetary constraints, and having the proper expertise available.

Linux provides an excellent means of reusing existing hardware and extending the life of old and otherwise unusable systems. One reason for this is that Linux can run without a GUI that can use up all the system's resources. This is especially helpful if you want a system to act as a firewall for a small or medium-sized network. For this firewall, you could install Linux on an early Pentium or 486 system, and it would serve as an excellent firewall. A Linux system running as a firewall would not require a lot of CPU power or memory and would consist of very little or no disk space. This type of system could also be used as a print server or file server if a small amount of RAM were added. Another instance where a system such as this might be used is as a terminal and even a graphical X terminal to other Linux or UNIX computers.

Figure 1-42 Linux as a Print Server

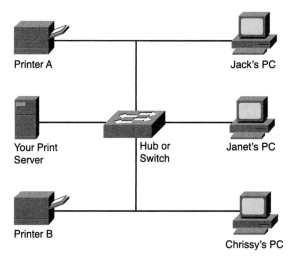

Budgetary constraints always come into question when you purchase new computers or hardware. One way to deal with these constraints is to decide which hardware you need to accomplish the job. For example, you can always add hard disk space later. It might be a good idea to start with an adequate-sized hard disk that is cost-effective. You can always add more hard drives later as needed. Another area where careful evaluation and planning can help meet a budget is CPU speeds. Today, the top-of-the-line CPUs are very nice, but that doesn't mean they are necessary for a user's needs. For example, it would be a waste of money to install a 2.4-GHz Pentium 4 processor on a system that will be used mainly for word processing.

Another factor you must consider in handling budgetary constraints is that after you have installed the computers or new hardware, you need someone with the proper expertise to provide support and training to the individuals using the new hardware and software. For example, the users might need to be taught how to access resources over the network if their system was integrated in to an existing network. In Linux, you access the floppy and CD-ROM drives differently than the way you might be used to in Windows.

Summary

This chapter covered PC fundamentals. Some of the important concepts to retain from this chapter include the following:

The NOS provides built-in networking components and network services, multiuser capability, and sophisticated file security and file-sharing technologies.

Kernel is the most common term used for the operating system's core. This computer code contains instructions that manage hardware devices, such as disk drives. The kernel also manages and controls memory allocation, system processes, and other programs.

The UI acts like a bridge between the user and the kernel. It acts as the interpreter by translating user keystrokes, mouse clicks, or other input for the appropriate programs. Program output can be organized and displayed by the UI. On a UNIX or Linux system, a UI is typically called a shell. User interfaces fall into two general categories: CLI and GUI.

An OS's file system determines whether files can be secured from other users or programs. The file system also defines how data is physically arranged on the storage medium (such as a hard drive). One common file system is called a FAT.

The Internet is built around a set of rules or protocols collectively known as TCP/IP. The majority of network services and client programs use TCP/IP to exchange data.

The next chapter is an introduction to networking. You will learn about the types of networks, the importance of the OSI reference model, and network protocols.

Check Your Understanding

The following review questions help you assess what you learned in this chapter. Answers can be found in Appendix A, "Answers to Check Your Understanding Questions."

1. What are three reasons to use MS-DOS?

   A. Simple, low-overhead operating system

   B. Inexpensive

   C. User-friendly

   D. Stable and reliable

   E. Runs on all platforms

2. Match each operating system with its description.

Operating System	Description
Windows 95a	IE 5.0 and stronger encryption and Internet connection sharing
Windows 95b	Added Active Desktop and USB support
Windows 98	Original release of Microsoft's 32-bit operating system
Windows 98 Second Edition (SE)	Built-in disaster recovery and faster startup and shutdown
Windows Millennium Edition (Me)	OSR2, FAT32 enhancement

3. Enter the command that accomplishes the result.

Command	Result
	Lists the files in the current directory
	Changes to a different directory
	Displays or sets the system time
	Displays or sets the date
	Copies files to another location
	Copies the contents of one floppy disk to another
	Displays or changes file attributes
	Searches for a text string in a file
	Displays a list of other available commands and their functions

4. Which of the following are distinguishing characteristics of a workstation?

   A. Standalone computer

   B. Must be configured for network access

   C. Runs a Graphical User Interface

   D. The system typically has speakers/sound card

   E. Multiple processors

5. What are the two most important features that a server must contain?

6. Give three examples of a Linux server that is considered a dedicated appliance.

7. Select all of the following that are a consideration in determining customer resources.

   A. Evaluating existing hardware

   B. Inexpensive

   C. User-friendly

   D. End-user support

   E. Budgetary concerns

8. Explain why most servers and other network operating systems are configured to use the TCP/IP protocol.

9. Whether designed for a standalone desktop computer or a multiuser network server, all operating system software includes which of the following components?

   A. Sound card

   B. File system

   C. Kernel

   D. Multimedia support

   E. User interface

10. Fill in the following chart with the appropriate type of file system that can be used on the operating system in the left column.

Operating System	Supported File System(s)
DOS	
Windows 3.*x*	
Windows 95/98/Me	
Windows NT/2000	
Windows XP	
IBM OS/2	
Linux	

Key Terms

buffering disk access   A feature that automatically stores in memory recent accesses to the hard disk. This lets Linux read right from memory rather than going back to the hard disk when subsequent requests come in.

command-line interface (CLI)   A completely text-based user interface in which the user can accomplish tasks only by inputting commands with the keyboard.

cooperative multitasking   An environment in which programs share memory addresses and exchange information. In a multitasked environment, applications share the use of the processor.

dedicated appliance   A Linux system running as a router, print server, or firewall, for example.

disk cluster   The basic unit of logical storage on a disk.

File Allocation Table (FAT)   The type of file system that is used on Windows operating systems.

graphical user interface (GUI)   Allows the user to manipulate software using visual objects such as windows, pull-down menus, pointers, and icons.

hierarchal file system   A system of arranging the directory and file structure so that they are placed in logical containers that are arranged in a tree structure. The file system starts at the tree's root.

kernel   The core of the operating system. This is a small piece of code that is loaded into memory when the computer boots. It contains instructions that allow it to manage hardware devices such as disk drives, memory allocation, system processes, and other programs.

Linux   An open-source operating system that looks and feels like UNIX. By the late 1990s, Linux had become a viable alternative to UNIX on servers and Windows on the desktop.

open-source   A noncommercial alternative means of software distribution in which the source code is open for anyone to copy or change. Usually open-source means that the software is distributed and available for free.

peer-to-peer networking   A set of calls for each network device to run both client and server portions of an application. Also describes communication between implementations of the same OSI reference model layer in two different network devices.

preemptive multitasking   The operating system controls the allocation of processor time, and 32-bit programs run in their own separate address spaces. With preemptive multitasking, an unruly program cannot take over the system, and if a program crashes, it does not affect the others.

server   Servers generally look very different from workstation systems. They have no need for user-oriented features such as large monitors, speakers, or a sound card. Servers consist of things such as very reliable and fault-tolerant hard disks.

UNIX   An operating system designed to support multiple users and multitasking. UNIX was one of the first operating systems to include support for Internet networking protocols.

user interface (UI)   The component of the OS that the user interacts with.

window manager   Linux and UNIX software responsible for sizing, positioning, and rendering the graphical windows that programs run in.

workstation   A system that is typically a standalone computer consisting of one monitor, keyboard, and mouse. Most often a workstation is configured with a network connection.

Objectives

After completing this chapter, you will be able to complete tasks related to

- Benefits of networking
- Types of networks
- Networking standards
- Networking protocols
- LAN architectures

## Chapter 2

Introduction to Networking

This chapter starts with an overview of networking. You learn about the types of networks used today, including LAN, WAN, peer-to-peer, and client/server. The benefits of an open system as opposed to a proprietary system are discussed. The OSI reference model represents an open system. As covered in this chapter, the OSI reference model divides network functions into seven layers that enable communication. You gain an understanding of protocol suites, including specific protocols used in TCP/IP, IPX/SPX, and AppleTalk. This chapter also explains LAN architecture, Ethernet, Token Ring, and FDDI.

Benefits of Networking

This section covers the following topics:

- File, print, and application services
- Mail services
- Directory and name services
- The Internet
- Network administration

File, Print, and Application Services

Computers can store, process, manipulate, and display vast quantities of information more quickly and efficiently than any previous technology. Because they are programmable, computers can take on many different tasks. They are multipurpose machines. The work accomplished with computers is of high value to users and organizations. The desire to share valuable information was one of the driving forces behind the development of computer networks. Figure 2-1 shows how the development of networks allowed multiple computers to connect to share files and communicate via e-mail. This figure also shows how network devices such as printers can connect to the network so that multiple users can all share one printer.

Figure 2-1 Common Network Components

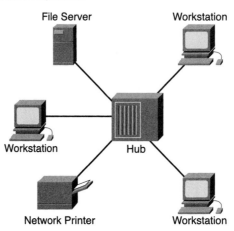

Although computer technologies continue to become more efficient and less expensive, there is still a substantial investment on the part of users and organizations. Along with the sharing of important information, networks enable the sharing of expensive devices. Rather than having a printer attached to each computer, a network can enable shared access by many systems concurrently.

Mail Services

From the earliest days, computer networks have allowed users to communicate by electronic mail. E-mail services work like the postal system, with some computers taking on the function of the post office. A user's e-mail account operates like a post office box. Mail is held for the user until it is picked up over the network by an e-mail *client* program running in the user's system. E-mail continues to be the single most widely used feature of computer networks.

E-mail works as a *storage-and-retrieval* application. Mail messages (along with identifying information such as the sender, receiver, and *time stamp*) are stored on an e-mail *server* until the recipient retrieves them. When an e-mail account is created for a user on the e-mail server, a *post-office box* is created for the user as well. When an e-mail is received, the e-mail server redirects the message to the user's post-office box, where it remains until the user retrieves it. Typically, e-mail messages are short communications. Current e-mail systems also allow users to *attach* longer files of many different types (documents, pictures, movies) to their messages. These attachments can be retrieved or *downloaded* along with the e-mail message. In this way, e-mail services blend into file-transfer services on the network.

Although e-mail systems have evolved along with networking technology, the Internet's rapid growth has allowed more and more people to connect online. This allows for immediate communication between users of the network. The storage-and-retrieval nature of e-mail systems does not require that the recipient be connected when the e-mail is sent. It can be picked up or retrieved at a later time. Besides e-mail, the Internet has spawned a variety of *instant messaging* systems that let network users *chat* with almost no delay in so-called "real time" as long as they are connected to the network at the same time. Figure 2-2 shows an example of the storage-and-retrieval process when an e-mail is sent. Figure 2-3 shows Microsoft's e-mail client, Outlook, which comes with the Microsoft Office suite software. This e-mail client can be used to retrieve e-mail from the post-office box on the e-mail server. Figure 2-4 shows the Linux e-mail client, K-Mail.

Figure 2-2 E-Mail Being Sent and Received

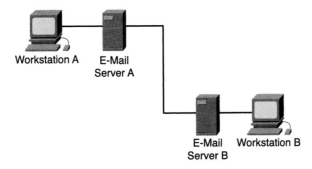

Figure 2-3 Microsoft Outlook E-Mail Client for Windows

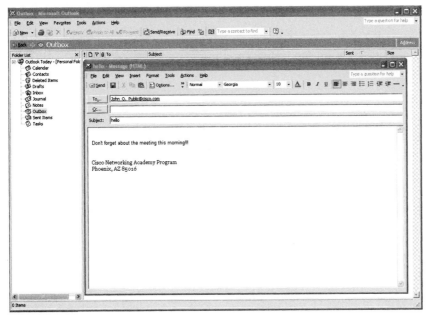

Figure 2-4 K-Mail E-Mail Client for Linux

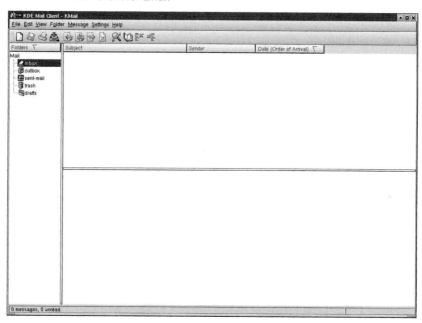

Directory and Name Services

Another important benefit of networks involves the ability to find resources and
devices wherever they are located. To help users and systems on the network find the
services they require, computer networks use directories and name services. Working
like the telephone directory, the network assigns names to users, services, and devices
so that they can be identified and accessed. Knowing the name of a service on the network lets users contact that service without having to know its physical location. In
fact, its physical location can change, and users can still find the service or device if
they know its name.

Directory and name services make a network easier for people to use. People work
more easily with names for services and other entities. They can rely on network directory and name services to translate those names into the addresses used to communicate with the desired service. After the initial setup of the directory or name service,
this translation takes place behind the scenes, or *transparently*. In addition to ease of
use, this makes the network more flexible. Network designers and administrators can
locate or move file, print, and other services with the assurance that users can still
locate them by name. The advantages of directory and name services are as follows:

- They offer a standardized means of naming and locating resources on a network
- Text names are easier to remember than numeric addresses
- Network resources are not bound to a physical location

The Internet

The *Internet* is a worldwide public network that interconnects thousands of other networks to form one large *web* for communication. Many private networks, some with thousands of users, connect to the Internet by using the services of Internet service providers (ISPs). These linkages enable long-distance access to network services for information and device sharing.

The Internet functions like a long-distance "pipe" to facilitate exchange between geographically separated users, organizations, and branches of companies. The term *information superhighway* was coined to describe the benefit of the Internet to business and private communication. The Internet enables the sharing of information around the globe almost instantaneously. Figure 2-5 shows a graph that represents the extremely fast-paced growth of the Internet in the past few years.

Figure 2-5 Exponential Growth of the Internet

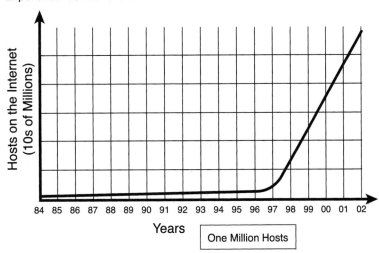

Network Administration

The benefits of new technologies bring with them certain problems, issues, and costs. Often, the designers of a new technology cannot foresee all the uses and implications of the new technology. Other major inventions, such as the internal combustion engine and the television, have brought social and economic costs along with their benefits. In the same way, computer networks generate new issues even as they open new possibilities for business and entertainment.

As businesses and individuals become more dependent on the use of computer networks for their daily activities, it becomes vitally important that these networks deliver the services that users expect. Even after engineers have completed the design and installation of a new network, the network requires attention and management to ensure that it continues to deliver a consistent level of service to its users. Computer networks need to be monitored and maintained to remain dynamic. They must also change and grow in response to new technologies and user requirements.

The ongoing task of maintaining and adapting the network to changing conditions falls to network administrators and support personnel. Responsibilities of network administrators range from setting up new user accounts and services to monitoring network performance and repairing network failures. Often, administrators rely on the skills of specialized support personnel to locate the sources of network problems and repair them efficiently. As networks grow, administrators must ensure that network availability is maintained while the network *migrates* to include new equipment and features that serve its users. Network administrators must be skilled in the use of a wide range of tools on a variety of devices and systems.

Network administrators face many decisions that often involve trade-offs or, as economists say, cost-benefit analysis. As they evaluate new technologies and requirements, administrators must measure their benefits against the issues, costs, and problems that the new features might introduce to the network. Table 2-1 lists some of the common issues for which a network administrator is responsible.

Table 2-1 Responsibilities of Network Administrators

Administration Issues	Responsibilities
Security	Computer networks and their data must be protected from unauthorized access. Such security violations can be either accidental or malicious.
User Administration	Network administrators grant access to a network by creating, maintaining, and deleting all necessary user accounts.
Troubleshooting	A network's daily operations typically result in technical issues that the administrator must resolve to keep the network running smoothly.
Upgrades	Computer technology is continually improving, and a successful network must stay abreast of these technological enhancements.
Backups	The data stored on network file servers is critical to its many users and must be backed up regularly to safeguard against potential disasters.

Types of Networks

This section covers the following topics:

- Local-area networks (LANs)
- Wide-area networks (WANs)
- Peer-to-peer networks
- Client/server networks

In the design and construction of every new tool, from hammers to hammocks, spatulas to space stations, engineers follow the general rule that "form follows function." The form or shape that a tool takes on is determined by its function. A hammer is shaped and built to bang in nails, a teapot to pour tea. Similarly, computer networks, as tools, take on different shapes and are constructed from different materials as a consequence of the different functions they perform.

Some networks are designed to interconnect many users and systems in a relatively limited geographic region and to enable high-speed communication among them. Other networks connect a smaller number of devices that are separated by large geographic distances. To meet the requirements of these two broad categories of users, different types of networks have been designed. Local-area networks (LANs) meet the requirements of the first group of users. Wide-area networks (WANs) satisfy the requirements of the second. Table 2-2 provides examples to help you understand the difference between LANs and WANs.

Table 2-2 LANs Versus WANs

	Scope	Example
LAN	Limited geographic area, usually within the same building	Schools, homes, small businesses
WAN	Larger global network with no physical boundaries	Large corporations, government organizations

Local-Area Networks

Local-area networks (LANs) connect many computers in a relatively small geographic area such as a home, an office, a building, or a campus. The network connects each computer to each of the others by using a separate communications channel. A direct connection from one computer to another is called a *point-to-point link*. If the network were designed using point-to-point links, the number of links would grow rapidly as new computers were added to the network. For each computer added, the network would need a separate connection to each of the other computers. This approach would be very costly and difficult to manage.

In the late 1960s and early 1970s, network engineers began designing a form of network that allowed many computers in a small area to share a single communications channel. By allowing computers to share a communications channel, LANs greatly reduce the network's cost. Point-to-point links are used to connect computers and networks in separate towns or cities, or even across continents.

A LAN's general shape or layout is called its *topology*. When all the computers connect to a central point, or *hub*, the network is a *star topology*. Another topology connects the computers in a closed loop, where a cable is run from one computer to the next until the last one is connected to the first. This forms a *ring topology*. A third type, called a *bus topology*, attaches each computer to a single long cable. Each topology has its benefits and drawbacks. Today, most LANs are designed using some form of star topology, although ring and bus layouts are still used in some installations.

Whatever the network's topology, all LANs require the networked computers to share the communications channel that connects them. The communications channel that they all share is called the *medium*. It is typically a cable that carries electrical signals through copper, or it might be a fiber-optic cable that carries light signals through purified glass or plastic. In the case of wireless networks, the computers might use antennas to broadcast radio signals to each other.

On a LAN, the rules for coordinating the use of the medium are called the *Media Access Control (MAC)*. Because the network has many computers, but only one of them can use the medium at a time, there must be some rules for deciding how they will take turns sharing the network. The MAC rules allow each computer to have its turn using the medium so that there is a fair and efficient way to share the network. In the case of conflicts, when more than one computer is contending for the medium, the rules ensure that there is an agreed-upon method for resolving the conflict. Later sections of this chapter review the major types of LANs, including their rules for sharing the medium (see Figures 2-6 and 2-7).

Figure 2-6 LAN Segmentation by Geographic Area

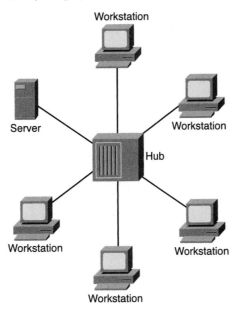

Figure 2-7 LAN Segmentation by Workgroups

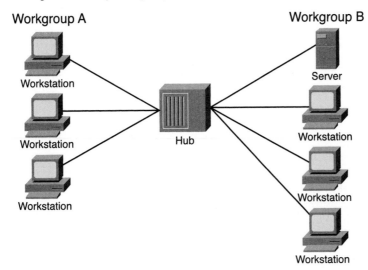

Wide-Area Networks

For economic and technical reasons, LANs are unsuitable for communications over long distances. On a LAN, the computers must coordinate the use of the network, and this coordination takes time. Over long distances, computers would take more time coordinating the use of the shared medium and less time sending data messages. In addition, the costs of providing high-speed media over long distances are much greater than in the case of LANs. For these reasons, *wide-area network (WAN)* technologies differ from LANs. Figure 2-8 shows how a WAN is usually segmented into multiple LANs that make up a WAN. You can also see that the WAN's different segments are still connected.

Figure 2-8   Characteristics of a WAN

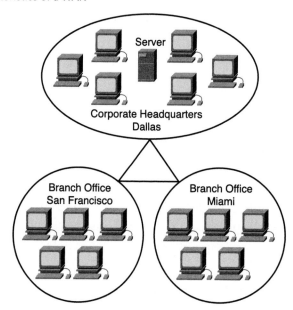

The WAN's different locations, as shown in Figures 2-8 and 2-9, use point-to-point serial communications lines. These lines are called point-to-point because they connect only two devices, one on each side of the line. They are called *serial lines* because the bits of information are transmitted one after another in a series, like cars traveling on a single-lane highway. Typically, individuals and companies do not build their own WAN connections. Government regulations allow only utility companies to install lines on public property. So WANs use the communications facilities put into place by the utility companies, called common carriers, such as the telephone company.

Figure 2-9 Point-to-Point WAN

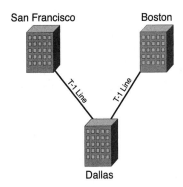

Connections across WAN lines can be temporary or permanent. Using a telephone with a dialup line, for example, makes a temporary connection to a remote network from a computer in a home or small office. In this case, the home or office computer calls a computer on the boundary of the remote network. The telephone company provides the connection, or circuit, that is used for the duration of the call. After data is transmitted, the line is disconnected just like an ordinary voice call. If a company wants to transmit data at any time without having to connect and disconnect the line each time, it can rent a permanent line or circuit from the common carrier. These leased lines are "always on" and operate at higher speeds than temporary dialup connections.

In both temporary and permanent cases, computers that connect over WANs must use special devices called *Channel Service Unit/Data Service Unit (CSU/DSU)* at each end of the connection. This is the connection point where the user's data coming from the computer or network interfaces with the WAN connection. The data that is sent from the user, which is in digital format, needs to be converted into a form that can be transmitted on the WAN link, which is analog. The CSU/DSU or modem converts the user data into an acceptable form that can be sent over the WAN link. Again, the same must be done on the destination WAN link so that the data can be converted into a form that the computer can translate. This device acts similar to a modem (modulator-demodulator). The transmitting end of the connection on a CSU/DSU or modem transforms digital computer signals into analog signals. On the receiving end, the reverse transformation is done. Figures 2-10, 2-11, and 2-12 show examples of how WANs can be connected. As you can see, WANs can be connected in several different ways.

Figure 2-10 WAN Ring

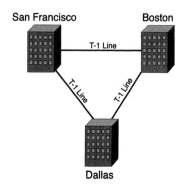

Figure 2-11 WAN Star

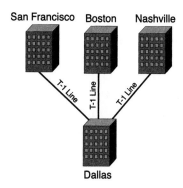

Figure 2-12 Multitiered WAN

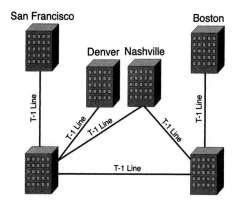

WANs normally operate at lower speeds than LANs. However, a WAN can provide the means for connecting a single computer or many LANs over large distances to allow networks to span whole countries and even the globe.

Peer-to-Peer Networks

By using LAN and WAN technologies, many computers are interconnected to provide services to their users. To accomplish this, networked computers take on different roles or functions in relation to each other. Some types of applications require computers to function as equal partners. Other types of applications distribute their work so that one computer serves a number of others in an unequal relationship. In either case, two computers typically communicate with each other by using request/response protocols, as shown in Figure 2-13. One computer issues a request for a service, and a second computer receives and responds to that request. The requestor takes on the role of a client, and the responder takes on the role of a server.

Figure 2-13 Peer-to-Peer Networks Request/Response

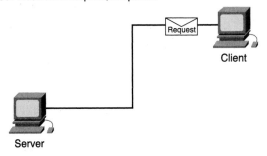

In a *peer-to-peer network*, the networked computers act as equal partners, or peers to each other. As a peer, each computer can take on the client function or the server function. For example, computer A might request a file from computer B, which responds by serving the file to computer A. Computer A functions as the client, and computer B functions as the server. At a later time, computers A and B can reverse roles. Computer B, as the client, makes a request of computer A, and computer A, as the server, responds to the request from computer B. Computers A and B have a reciprocal or peer relationship to each other.

In a peer-to-peer network, individual users control their own resources. They may decide to share certain files with other users. They may also require passwords before they allow others to access their resources. Because individual users make these decisions, the network has no central point of control or administration. In addition, individual users must back up their own systems to be able to recover from data loss in case of failures. When a computer acts as a server, the user of that machine might experience reduced performance as the machine serves the requests made by other systems.

Figure 2-14 shows that a user shares the Docs folder with the others. After sharing the Docs folder, the user who is connected to the server Constellation can browse the Docs folder from the network. Figure 2-15 shows how the folder appears over the network after it has been shared.

Figure 2-14 Creating a Shared Folder

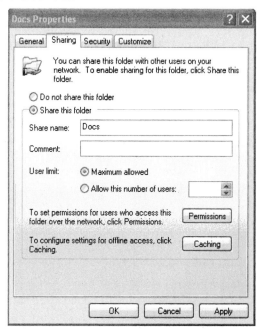

Figure 2-15 Shared Folder Available on the Network

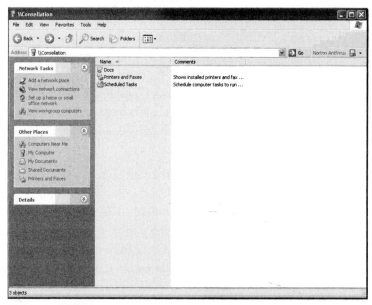

Peer-to-peer networks are relatively easy to install and operate. No additional equipment is necessary beyond a suitable operating system installed on each computer. Because users control their own resources, no dedicated administrators are needed. A peer-to-peer network works well with a small number of computers, perhaps ten or fewer.

As networks grow, peer-to-peer relationships become increasingly difficult to coordinate. Because they do not scale well, their efficiency decreases rapidly as the number of computers on the network increases. Also, individual users control access to the resources on their computers, which means that security might be difficult to maintain. The client/server network model can be used to overcome the limitations of the peer-to-peer network.

Client/Server Networks

In a *client/server* arrangement, network services are located on a dedicated computer called a server, which responds to the requests of clients. The server is a central computer that is continuously available to respond to a client's requests for file, print, application, and other services. Most network operating systems (NOSs) adopt the form of client/server relationships. Typically, desktop computers function as clients, and one or more computers with additional processing power, memory, and specialized software function as servers.

Servers are designed to handle requests from many clients simultaneously. Before a client can access the server resources, it must identify itself and be authorized to use the resource. This is done by assigning each client an account name and password that are verified by an authentication service acting as a sentry to guard access to the network. By centralizing user accounts, security, and access control, server-based networks simplify the work of network administration. Figure 2-16 shows three examples of client/server arrangements. Figure 2-17 demonstrates how the information that is stored on a server can be localized to one server or distributed across multiple servers.

The concentration of network resources such as files, printers, and applications on servers also makes the data they generate easier to back up and maintain. Rather than having these resources spread around individual machines, they can be located on specialized, dedicated servers for easier access. Most client/server systems also include facilities for enhancing the network by adding new services that extend the network's usefulness.

Figure 2-16 Client/Server Environment

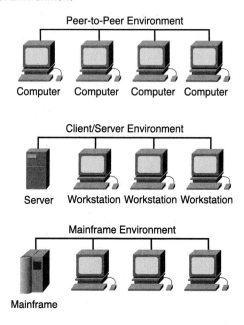

The distribution of functions in client/server networks brings substantial advantages, but it also incurs some costs. Tables 2-3 and 2-4 outline some of these advantages and disadvantages. Although the aggregation of resources on server systems brings greater security, simpler access, and coordinated control, the server introduces a single point of failure into the network. Without an operational server, the network cannot function. Servers require a trained, expert staff to administer and maintain. This increases the expense of running the network. Server systems also require additional hardware and specialized software that add to the cost.

Table 2-3 Advantages of Peer-to-Peer Versus Client/Server

Advantages of a Peer-to-Peer Network	Advantages of a Client/Server Network
Less expensive to implement.	Provides for better security.
Does not require NOS server software.	Easier to administer when the network is large, because administration is centralized.
Does not require a dedicated network administrator.	All data can be backed up on one central location.

Figure 2-17 Client/Server Environment

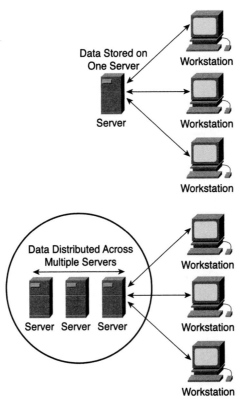

Table 2-4 Disadvantages of Peer-to-Peer Versus Client/Server

Disadvantages of a Peer-to-Peer Network	Disadvantages of a Client/Server Network
Does not scale well to large networks; administration becomes unmanageable.	Requires expensive NOS software such as Windows NT, Windows 2000 server, or Novell Netware.
Each user must be trained to perform administrative tasks.	Requires expensive, more powerful hardware for the server machine.
Less secure.	Requires a professional administrator.
All machines sharing the resources negatively affect performance.	Has a single point of failure if there is only one server; users' data can be unavailable if the server is down.

Worksheet 2.2.5   Types of Networks

Covers some of the basic principles that make up different types of networks.

Networking Standards

This section covers the following topics:

- Proprietary versus open standards
- The OSI reference model
- The DoD model
- The IEEE
- The ITU
- Other standards

Proprietary Versus Open Standards

Traditionally, computer vendors have attempted to keep customers to themselves by building proprietary systems. *Proprietary technologies* are owned by one company and generally are incompatible with equipment sold by other vendors. Even today, some companies with a large share of a particular market seek to establish private, *de facto* standards so that other companies have to follow their lead. De facto means that it has become the industry standard just because the majority has chosen to implement it. But with the proliferation of computer equipment and networking, it has become increasingly difficult for proprietary or de facto standards to survive. Computers from different vendors must communicate with each other and interoperate. Customers want flexibility and no longer accept systems that limit their choices to a single vendor. Public standards for networking systems ensure that equipment from different vendors will work together.

Networking standards are developed by a number of organizations that specialize in developing standards for networking technology. Companies send their engineers to the standards committees to design and agree on a specification for a particular networking function. These specifications are then made public so that all vendors can build their systems to conform to the standards.

Some people within the computer industry are unhappy with the limitations that proprietary standards impose, so they prefer to use the open-source standard instead. This was the main argument that Microsoft had to defend in its monopoly lawsuit. If you decide not to use proprietary software such as Dell, Compaq, and Microsoft, you have the option of choosing open source. Open-source software is free, and users are not bound to the copyright laws they might break when using proprietary software. Unlike most commercial software, the core code of open-source software can be easily studied and improved by other programmers. The only provision is that these improvements must be revealed publicly and distributed freely in a process that encourages continual innovation.

A leader in the open-source arena is Linux. It realized the potential and set standards for what open source can achieve. The Linux operating system is discussed more thoroughly in other chapters.

The debate about proprietary systems such as Microsoft and open-source systems such as Linux remains a hot topic. Deciding which one is better depends on individual preference. Table 2-5 outlines some of the advantages and disadvantages of both proprietary and open-source systems.

Table 2-5 Proprietary Versus Open Standards

	Proprietary	Open
Advantages	A more organized source of funding and development	Free to the public in both price and usage
	Standardization	Faster widespread acceptance and growth
Disadvantages	Copyrighted	Lack of centralized funding and development
	Slower and more limited technology growth	More effort is required by independent sources to ensure standardized progress

The OSI Reference Model

In 1984, the International Organization for Standardization developed the *Open System Interconnection (OSI) reference model* to promote interoperability in networking. This model is an overall description of the functions performed in a computer network and the relationship between them. The model's intent was to provide a framework within which more-detailed standards would be developed for each function. The OSI reference model has served that purpose well, and its terminology is widely used as a common language among networking personnel.

The OSI reference model divides network functions into seven layers. Viewing the layers from top to bottom, it presents a service model. At each layer, the function provided depends on the services of the layer below it. The layers are separated by well-defined boundaries, or interfaces. After a given layer has performed its function, it passes information across the boundary to the layer below. It then expects that layer to deliver its service. This works like the postal service. After a letter is properly addressed and dropped in a mailbox (the interface), it is expected that the postal service will deliver it. The details of the delivery system (the layer below) are not important to the sender. In fact, the method of delivery can change as long as the expected service is still performed. Likewise, in the OSI reference model, each layer expects a service to be performed by the layer below it, and each layer provides a service to the one above it. Between two networked systems, each layer of the OSI reference model communicates with its peer layer in the other system. As a tool, the OSI reference model offers a framework, or architecture, for the development of protocols that implement the functions of each layer.

The following list outlines the major functions of each layer. Figure 2-18 illustrates some of the functions that are specific to these layers.

Figure 2-18 OSI Reference Model

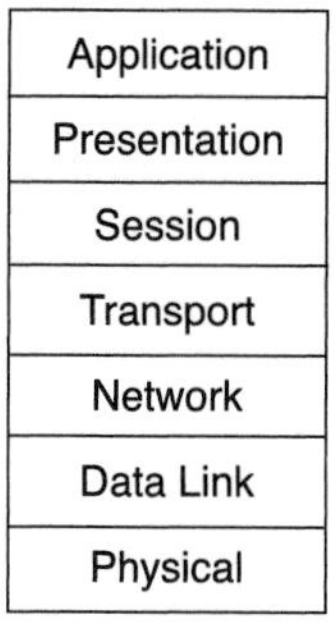

Application
Presentation
Session
Transport
Network
Data Link
Physical

- **Layer 7: Application**—The *application layer*, which is further defined in Figure 2-19, provides the connection point for applications. It specifies the details of how an application makes requests and how the application on another machine responds. A request for network services originates at this layer. FTP, Telnet, ping, and e-mail are typical protocols at the application layer.

Figure 2-19 OSI Reference Model: Application Layer

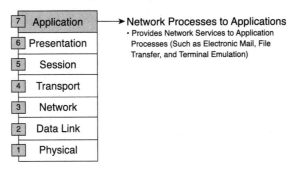

- **Layer 6: Presentation**—The *presentation layer*, which is further defined in Figure 2-20, specifies the arrangement, or syntax, of the data that the application expects. Because applications on different systems may represent or format their data in different ways, the presentation layer may include translations from one format to another. The presentation layer also includes security and efficiency functions (encryption and compression). This defines what application is used independently of what operating system is used to view the data. .gif, .jpeg, .mpeg, and .avi are some examples of what the presentation layer recognizes to make data available to the user at the application layer.

Figure 2-20 OSI Reference Model: Presentation Layer

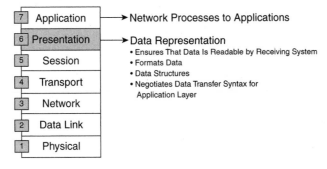

- **Layer 5: Session**—The *session layer*, which is further defined in Figure 2-21, establishes the rules of the conversation between two applications. Will they take turns speaking, or can they send and receive at the same time? The session layer also allows a number of copies of an application to communicate with other applications at the same time by identifying each instance of the application as a separate session.

Figure 2-21 OSI Reference Model: Session Layer

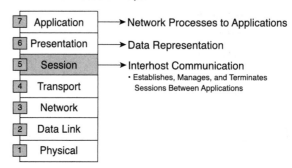

- **Layer 4: Transport**—The *transport layer,* which is further defined in Figure 2-22, provides delivery services for each session. It segments the data into more-manageable parts. It can provide a reliable delivery service that guarantees that data arrives at its destination, or it can provide an "unreliable" best-effort delivery service that transports the data without checking for errors.

Figure 2-22 OSI Reference Model: Transport Layer

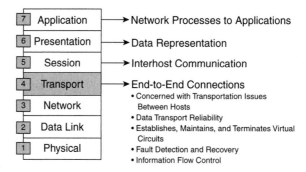

- **Layer 3: Network**—The *network layer,* which is further defined in Figure 2-23, specifies how addresses are assigned and how packets of data are forwarded from one network to another toward the destination. Routers operate at this level because they direct information to the correct location based on the type of routing protocol that is being used. Routing protocols are discussed further in the next section.

Figure 2-23 OSI Reference Model: Network Layer

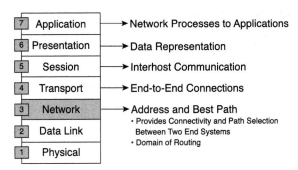

■ **Layer 2: Data Link**—The *data link layer,* which is further defined in Figure 2-24, specifies how packets of data are organized into frames on a particular type of network and the rules for inserting frames onto the network media. The data link layer is where hardware such as switches and bridges operates. Switches and bridges do not perform routing functions. Instead, they send network data based on information such as MAC addresses.

Figure 2-24 OSI Reference Model: Data Link Layer

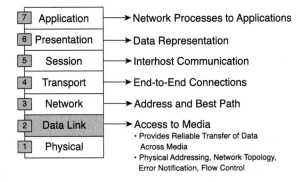

■ **Layer 1: Physical**—The *physical layer,* which is further defined in Figure 2-25, corresponds to the network hardware (cabling, media). This layer determines how binary data is translated into electrical, optical, or other types of physical signals transmitted between systems.

Figure 2-25 OSI Reference Model: Physical Layer

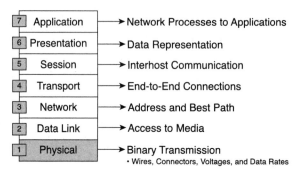

Each layer of the OSI reference model provides specific functions. Layering simplifies protocol design and allows one layer's implementations to change without affecting the other layers. By dividing a complex problem into modular units, the layering approach has accelerated the evolution of networking technology.

Encapsulation

The main functions of these OSI reference model layers are to efficiently and effectively transmit data from one computer to another computer via network media. Each of these layers performs specific functions that allow and prepare the data for transmission. The process of this data being passed down the OSI reference model layers and these layers preparing the data for transmission is called *encapsulation*. Figure 2-26 shows the encapsulation process.

Encapsulation occurs with every process of the OSI reference model. Data is created by the user's application system and is passed through the application, presentation, and session layers. Then the data is passed to the transport layer, where it is broken into more-manageable pieces. A header is added to the data units (pieces) for sequencing and error checking. The data unit is then called a *segment*. A *header* is information that gets added to the data. It provides the control information that is added to the data. The transport layer then passes the segment to the network layer, where a protocol header is added, and the segment becomes a *packet*. The packet is then passed to the data link layer, where it gets packaged into a Layer 2 header and trailer, and it becomes a *frame*.

Figure 2-26 Data Encapsulation

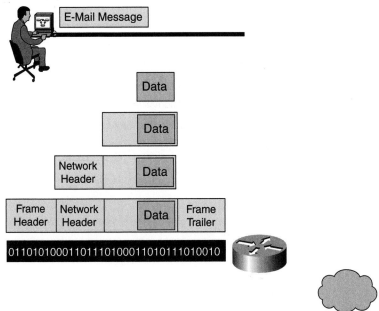

 Worksheet 2.3.2   The OSI Reference Model

Covers some of the important topics regarding the OSI reference model.

The DoD Model

Before the publication of the OSI reference model, the U.S. Department of Defense (DoD) sponsored a research network called ARPANET. This DoD network was a predecessor to the Internet. Figure 2-27 outlines a timeline of events leading up to what we know as the Internet today. ARPANET connected hundreds of universities and government agencies over leased telephone lines. However, the DoD network protocols couldn't keep up with the rapid growth. An architecture that allowed networks to connect to each other in a seamless manner was required. The TCP/IP model evolved to meet this demand. Figure 2-28 shows how the DoD model is broken down and how the layers compare to the layers of the OSI reference model, which eventually replaced the DoD model.

Figure 2-27   Birth of the Internet

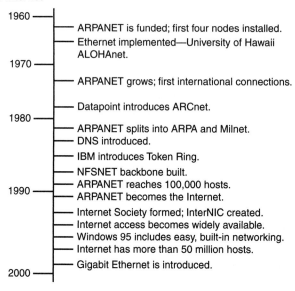

Figure 2-28   DoD Model

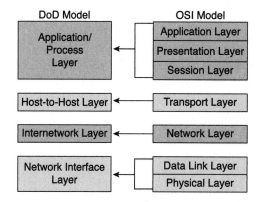

The IEEE

Among the many organizations that develop standards for computer networks, the *Institute of Electrical and Electronic Engineers (IEEE)* has been the most active in defining LAN standards. Through its "802" working groups, which began meeting in February (month 2) of 1980 (the "80" in 802), the IEEE has published standards for the most widely implemented LANs. These include Ethernet (802.3), Token Ring (802.5), fiber-optic networks (802.8), and wireless LANs (802.11). The IEEE has also defined a standard for providing error and flow control over different LAN types in its specification for *Logical Link Control (LLC)*, 802.2.

The IEEE LAN standards are now central for LANs used today. Devices such as Network Interface Cards (NICs) that conform to the IEEE standards permit equipment built and sold by different manufacturers to interoperate on the same LAN.

The ITU

The International Telecommunications Union (ITU) has defined standards for modems (the V.*nn* series), packet-switching networks (X.25), directory services (X.500), electronic messaging (X.400), dialup devices (ISDN), and many other technologies for WANs. Under the auspices of the United Nations, the ITU has developed and maintained these WAN standards through its subcommittee called the Consultative Committee for International Telegraph and Telephone (CCITT).

Other Standards

Other standards and trade organizations have been instrumental in developing the successful networking technologies in use today. The Electronic Industries Association (EIA) supports a large library of technical standards, including the definition for serial connections for dialup modems (originally known as RS-232). This is one of a number of standards that define the interfaces between computers and communications equipment. The EIA also develops recommendations for cabling that are used by manufacturers of network media and recommendations for networking wiring that are used by network installers.

The American National Standards Institute (ANSI) also contributes standards for a range of LAN technologies, including Ethernet and Token Ring. The scope of ANSI standards includes character encoding (ASCII), programming languages (C, COBOL, FORTRAN), and internal computer interfaces such as the widely used Small Computer Systems Interface (SCSI). Table 2-6 lists some of the other organizations and the standards they have developed.

Table 2-6 Other Standards Organizations

Name	Acronym	Technologies
Electronic Industries Association	EIA	Communications interfaces, such as serial connections for modems Network cables and wiring
American National Standards Institute	ANSI	LAN technologies, such as Ethernet and Token Ring Character encoding Programming languages Internal computer interfaces, such as SCSI

Sometimes, these standards overlap and duplicate each other. Overall, the definition and coordination of standards for networking have been essential to its success.

Networking Protocols

This section covers the following topics:

- Protocol suite
- TCP/IP
- IPX/SPX
- AppleTalk

Protocol Suite

Protocols are the engines of networks. The function of the OSI network model is carried out by the protocols that are active at each layer. When a set of protocols operates in a coordinated way to deliver a number of functions, it is grouped into a *protocol suite*. TCP/IP represents one such suite of protocols, Novell IPX/SPX is another, and Apple AppleTalk is another. A *protocol* is a controlled sequence of messages exchanged between two or more systems to accomplish a given task. Protocol specifications define this sequence, together with the format or layout of the messages that are exchanged. In coordinating the work between systems, protocols use control structures in each system that operate like a set of interlocking gears. Computers can then track the state of their protocols precisely as they move through the sequence of exchanges. Timing is crucial to network operations. Protocols require messages to arrive within certain time intervals, so systems maintain one or more timers during protocol execution and take alternative actions if the network does not meet the timing rules. To do their work, many protocols depend on the operation of other protocols in the suite. Table 2-7 briefly describes some of these protocols.

Table 2-7 Three Popular Protocol Suites

Protocol Suite	Description
TCP/IP	The most popular Internet protocol today
IPX/SPX	The proprietary protocol suite created by Novell
AppleTalk	Apple Computer's proprietary protocol suite for Macintosh computers

TCP/IP

The TCP/IP suite of protocols has become the dominant standard for internetworking. Originally defined by researchers in the U.S. Department of Defense, *TCP/IP* represents a set of public standards that specifies how packets of information are exchanged between computers over one or more networks.

Application Protocols

The following protocols function at the application layer of the OSI reference model:

- *Telnet*—Enables terminal access to local or remote systems. The Telnet application is used to access remote devices for configuration, control, and troubleshooting.

- *File Transfer Protocol (FTP)*—An application that provides services for file transfer and manipulation. FTP uses the session layer to allow multiple simultaneous connections to remote file systems.

- *Simple Mail Transport Protocol (SMTP)*—Provides messaging services over TCP/IP and supports most Internet e-mail programs.

- *Domain Name System (DNS)*—Provides access to name servers, where network names are translated to the addresses used by Layer 3 network protocols. DNS greatly simplifies network usage by end users.

Transport Protocols

The following protocols are seen at the transport layer of the OSI reference model:

- *Transmission Control Protocol (TCP)*—The primary Internet protocol for reliable delivery of data. TCP includes facilities for end-to-end connection establishment, error detection and recovery, and metering the rate at which data flows into the network. Many standard applications, such as e-mail, web browsing, file transfer, and Telnet, depend on TCP's services. TCP identifies the application using it by a *port* number.

- *User Datagram Protocol (UDP)*—Offers a connectionless service to applications that do not want the overhead of TCP and that can tolerate a level of data loss. Applications in network management, network file systems, and simple file transport use UDP. Like TCP, UDP identifies applications by port number.

Internet Protocols

The following protocols are seen at the network layer of the OSI reference model:

- *Internet Protocol (IP)*—Provides source and destination addressing and, in conjunction with routing protocols, packet forwarding from one network to another toward a destination.

- *Internet Control Message Protocol (ICMP)*—Used for network testing and troubleshooting. It enables diagnostic and error messages. The ping application uses ICMP echo messages to test remote devices.

- *Routing Information Protocol (RIP)*—Operates between router devices to discover paths between networks. In the Internet, routers depend on a routing protocol to build and maintain information about how to forward packets toward their destinations. RIP chooses routes based on their distance or *hop count.*

- *Open Shortest Path First (OSPF)*—Like RIP, OSPF lets routers build forwarding tables. Unlike RIP, OSPF selects routes based on other characteristics of the links between networks, such as bandwidth and delay. OSPF is more suitable than RIP for routing in large internetworks.

- *Address Resolution Protocol (ARP)*—Used to discover a station's local (MAC) address on the network when its Internet address is known. End stations as well as routers use ARP to discover local addresses.

IPX/SPX

This protocol suite, originally employed by Novell Corporation's NOS, NetWare, delivers functions similar to the ones included in TCP/IP. To allow desktop client systems to access NetWare services, Novell deployed a set of application, transport, and network protocols. Although NetWare client/server systems are not tied to a particular hardware platform, the native, or original, NetWare protocols remained proprietary. Unlike TCP/IP, the Novell IPX/SPX protocol suite remained the property of one company. As a result of market pressure to move to the industry-standard way of building networks, IPX/SPX has fallen into disfavor among customers. In current releases, Novell supports the TCP/IP suite. However, many NetWare networks continue to use IPX/SPX.

Native NetWare client/server systems include the following key protocols:

- *Service Advertisement Protocol (SAP)* and *Get Nearest Server (GNS)*—These protocols work in tandem to make services known to NetWare clients and to help clients locate the services they require, such as print or file services.

- *Sequenced Packet Exchange (SPX)*—Functions much like TCP to provide a reliable, connection-oriented transport between client and server systems.

- *Internet Packet Exchange (IPX)*—Like IP, IPX controls network addressing and forwards packets from one network to another toward a destination. The Microsoft implementation of IPX is called NWLink. Also like IP, IPX depends on the forwarding tables built by a routing protocol. NetWare provided the two routing protocols RIP and NLSP.

- *Novell Routing Information Protocol (RIP)*—The Novell version of RIP. It operates much like RIP in a TCP/IP environment, but with variations that make it unique to NetWare networks.

- *Novell Link-State Protocol (NLSP)*—Functions like OSPF in a TCP/IP environment to build and maintain routing tables. Also like OSPF, NLSP supports larger networks than RIP.

AppleTalk

Like Novell, Apple Computer developed its own proprietary protocol suite to network Macintosh computers. A sizeable number of customers still use AppleTalk to interconnect their systems. However, just as other companies have transitioned to the use of TCP/IP, Apple now fully supports the public networking standards.

AppleTalk is comprised of a comprehensive suite of protocols that span the seven layers of the OSI reference model. AppleTalk protocols were designed to run over the major LAN types, notably Ethernet and Token Ring, and also the Apple LAN physical topology called LocalTalk. There are several key AppleTalk protocols:

- *AppleTalk Filing Protocol (AFP)*—Allows desktop workstations to share files. Typically, files are stored on file servers, and clients use AFP to locate and transfer files by name.

- *AppleTalk Data Stream Protocol (ADSP)*, *Zone Information Protocol (ZIP)*, *AppleTalk Session Protocol (ASP)*, and *Printer Access Protocol (PAP)*—All these protocols function at Layer 5 to establish sessions. Depending on the task, the sessions are used to do different kinds of work. ADSP supports the flow of unstructured data between systems. ZIP maintains a correspondence between networks and partitions, called *zones*. ASP establishes connections between clients and server so that sequences of messages can be associated with each other. PAP, as its name implies, helps clients locate printers and controls the execution of print jobs on the network.

The AppleTalk suite includes the *AppleTalk Transaction Protocol (ATP)* at Layer 4, which provides a reliable, connection-oriented transport, and the *Name Binding Protocol (NBP)*, which associates network names for services with their addresses. For building and maintaining routing tables, AppleTalk uses the Routing Table Maintenance Protocol (RTMP). Finally, for diagnostic and troubleshooting purposes, the Echo Protocol (AEP) is used.

AppleTalk moves packets of data, called *datagrams*, from one endpoint to another across a series of networks. All the higher-layer protocols rely on the Datagram Delivery Protocol (DDP) at Layer 3 to forward or route their datagrams between endpoints. DDP functions like IP in a TCP/IP Internet.

Like carrier sense multiple access collision detect (CSMA/CD), *carrier sense multiple access collision avoidance (CSMA/CA)* is used to reduce network collisions by listening to the network before broadcasting. The collision avoidance broadcasts to the network that is about to transmit and warns others that it is about to use the network.

CSMA/CA is a good method of avoiding collisions on a network. However, CSMA/CA has additional overhead that CSMA/CD does not. CSMA/CA actually increases network traffic, because it must broadcast before any real data is put onto the cable.

The AppleTalk protocol might disrupt network bandwidth or cause it to be extremely slow. For this reason, the AppleTalk protocol is not recommended for networks that run other protocols, such as TCP/IP, IPX, RIP, or IGRP. If the network has MAC systems that use AppleTalk, use a router to isolate the AppleTalk protocol. An access list will prevent the AppleTalk protocol from going anywhere but to and from the specific Macintosh systems that require it.

Worksheet 2.4.4   Network Protocols

Covers some of the important topics regarding the various network protocols used on most networks.

LAN Architectures

This section covers the following topics:

- Ethernet
- Token Ring
- Fiber Distributed Data Interface (FDDI)

Ethernet

The Ethernet architecture is the most popular type of LAN link used today. It is based on the 802.3 standard. This specifies that a network that implements the CSMA-CD access control method must use a baseband transmission over coaxial or twisted-pair cable that is laid out in a bus topology (that is, a linear or star bus). CSMA/CD means that multiple stations have access to the medium, and before a station can access that medium, it must listen (carrier sense) to detect if another system is using the same medium. If another system is using the medium, that system must wait before it can transmit. If both systems attempt to send data at the same time, a collision results. Standard transfer rates are 10 Mbps and 100 Mbps. The new standards provide for Gigabit Ethernet, which can attain speeds of up to 1 Gbps over fiber-optic cable or other high-speed media. Table 2-8 shows the main Ethernet specifications.

Table 2-8 Ethernet Specifications Summary

	10BASE2	10BASE5	10BASE-T	100BASE-X
Cable Type	Thin coaxial RG-58 A/U	Thick coaxial RG-8 or RG-11	UTP Category 3, 4, 5, and 5e	UTP Category 3, 4, 5, and 5e
Connector Type	BNC connector	AUI/DIX receiver (to transceiver)	RJ-45 modular	RJ-45 modular
Maximum Segment Length	185 meters (607 feet)	500 meters (1640 feet)	100 meters (328 feet)	100 meters (328 feet)
Maximum Network Length	925 meters (3035 feet)	2500 meters (8200 feet)	Star-bus topology	Star-bus topology
Nodes Per Segment	30	100	2 (1024 per network)[*]	2 (1024 per network)[*]
Transfer Rate	10 Mbps	10 Mbps	10 Mbps	100 Mbps

[*]Because a hub is used as a central connection point with UTP-based networks, each segment of cable has only the computer or network device at one end and the hub at the other as nodes on that segment.

10BASE-T

Currently, 10BASE-T is one of the most popular Ethernet implementations. It uses a star bus topology.

The term *Ethernet cable* can be used to describe the unshielded twisted-pair (UTP) cabling generally used in this architecture. Shielded twisted-pair (STP) also can be used. 10BASE-T and 100BASE-X create networks that are easy to set up and expand.

One advantage of 10BASE-T is that it is relatively inexpensive. Although a hub is required when you connect more than two computers, small hubs are available at a low cost, and 10BASE-T network cards are inexpensive and widely available.

UTP, which is the most commonly used twisted-pair cabling, is thin, flexible, and easier to work with than coaxial. It uses modular RJ-45 plugs and jacks, so it is easy to connect the cable to the NIC or hub.

Another big advantage of 10BASE-T is the ability to upgrade. By definition, a 10BASE-T network runs at 10 Mbps. If you use a Category 5 or above cable and 10/100-Mbps dual-speed NICs, you can upgrade to 100 Mbps by simply replacing the hubs.

NOTE

Inside the Ethernet hub, the signaling system is a bus, as with coaxial Ethernet networks.

NOTE

10BASE-T specifications require a hub. However, if you're connecting only two computers (for example, for a home network), and UTP is preferred over Thinnet, you can use a crossover cable. This type of cable has wire pairs that are cross-connected. Crossover cables are also used to connect two hubs to each other if the hubs do not have uplink ports.

The disadvantages of 10BASE-T are that the maximum length of a 10BASE-T segment (without repeaters) is only 100 meters (about 328 feet). Also, the UTP used is more vulnerable to electromagnetic interference (EMI) and attenuation than other cable types. Attenuation is the decreasing of the signal as it gets farther away from the source. For example, in a 10BASE-T segment, the signal strength would be good for a distance of up to 100 meters. From that point on, it would lose reliability without the use of a repeater.

The high-bandwidth demands of many modern applications, such as live videoconferencing and streaming audio, have created a need for speed. Many networks require more throughput than is possible with 10-Mbps Ethernet. The next evolution is 100BASE-X, also called Fast Ethernet.

100BASE-X

100BASE-X comes in several flavors. It can be implemented over Category 5 UTP (100BASE-T), over two-pair Category 5 UTP or STP (100BASE-TX), or as Ethernet over two-strand fiber-optic cable (100BASE-FX).

- **Advantages of 100BASE-X**—Regardless of the implementation, the big advantage of 100BASE-X is high-speed performance. At 100 Mbps, transfer rates are ten times that of 10BASE-T.

  Because it uses twisted-pair cabling, 100BASE-X shares the advantages of 10BASE-T. These include low cost, flexibility, and ease of implementation and expansion.

- **Disadvantages of 100BASE-X**—100BASE-X shares the disadvantages of 10BASE-T, which are inherent to twisted-pair cabling, such as susceptibility to EMI and attenuation. 100-Mbps NICs and hubs are generally somewhat more expensive than those designed for 10-Mbps networks, but prices have dropped as 100BASE-X has gained popularity. Fiber-optic cable remains an expensive cabling option, not so much because of the cost of the cable itself, but because of the training and expertise required to install it.

1000BASE-T

The new addition to the Ethernet family, 1000BASE-T, is called Gigabit Ethernet. Although it isn't yet in widespread implementation in production networks, this architecture supports data transfer rates of 1 Gbps, which is many times faster than a T-1 line.

- **Advantages of 1000BASE-T**—The greatest advantage of 1000BASE-T is, of course, performance. At 1 Gbps, it is ten times as fast as Fast Ethernet and 100 times as fast as standard Ethernet. This makes it possible to implement bandwidth-intensive applications, such as live video, throughout an intranet.
- **Disadvantages of 1000BASE-T**—The only disadvantages associated with 1000BASE-T are those common to all UTP networks, as detailed in the sections "10BASE-T" and "100BASE-X."

Half Duplex Versus Full Duplex

When data is transmitted over all these different media, it is sent in either half duplex or full duplex. *Half duplex* allows only one direction to be used at a time when data is being transmitted over the lines. This means that data can be sent and received only at separate times. Figure 2-29 illustrates this concept by showing a transmission in which signals can be transmitted in only one direction at a time. *Full duplex* allows for two simultaneous directions of data flow. As you can see from Figure 2-30, a telephone conversation between two people is a good example of how full-duplex transmission occurs. In this case, both people can talk at the same time, sending signals in both directions simultaneously. With full duplex, data can be sent and received at the same time. The data flows in either direction simultaneously, allowing for faster data transfer rates through the network.

Figure 2-29 Half-Duplex Transmission

Figure 2-30 Full-Duplex Transmission

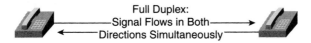

Bus and star structures with bus hubs (CSMA-CD) cannot support full duplex. The only way full duplex can be supported is if only two nodes are connected. Replacing the hub with a switch and using only one host on each switch port permits full duplex to be used.

Token Ring

Token Ring was originally developed by IBM. It was designed to be a reliable network architecture based on the token-passing access control method. It is often integrated with IBM mainframe systems such as the AS/400, which is used with PCs, minicomputers, and mainframes. It works well with Systems Network Architecture (SNA), the IBM architecture used for connecting to mainframe networks.

The Token Ring standards are provided in IEEE 802.5. The Token Ring topology can be confusing. It is a prime example of an architecture whose physical topology is different from its logical topology. The Token Ring topology is called a star-wired ring. This is because the outer appearance of the network design is a star, with computers connecting to a central hub called a *Multistation Access Unit (MSAU)*. Inside the device, the wiring forms a circular data path, creating a logical ring. Figures 2-31 and 2-32 demonstrate the Token Ring process. You can see from Figure 2-31 that a computer must wait its turn. The token is passed around the ring until it comes to that computer, which then can transmit. Figure 2-32 shows how a Token Ring network is connected.

Figure 2-31 Token Passing

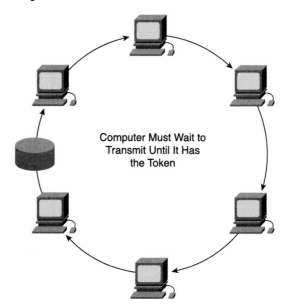

Computer Must Wait to
Transmit Until It Has
the Token

Figure 2-32 Token Ring Hardware Components

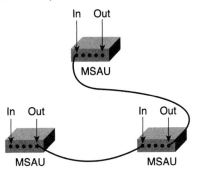

Token Ring is named for its logical topology and its method of token passing. Its transfer rate can be either 4 Mbps or 16 Mbps. Token Ring is a baseband architecture that uses digital signaling. In this way, it resembles Ethernet, but the communication process is quite different in many respects. Token Ring is an active topology. As the signal travels around the circle to each network card, it is regenerated before being sent on its way.

The Ring Monitor

In a Token Ring network, the first computer that comes online becomes the "hall monitor" that must keep track of how many times each frame circles the ring. It has the responsibility of ensuring that only one token is on the network at a time.

The monitor computer periodically sends a signal called a beacon, which circulates around the ring as does any other signal. Each computer on the network looks for the beacon. If a computer does not receive the beacon from its Nearest Active Upstream Neighbor (NAUN) when expected, it puts a message on the network that notifies the monitoring computer that the beacon was not received, along with its own address and that of the NAUN that failed to send when expected. In many cases, this causes an automatic reconfiguration that restores the communications.

Fiber Distributed Data Interface

Fiber Distributed Data Interface (FDDI) is a type of Token Ring network. Its implementation and topology differ from the IBM Token Ring LAN architecture, which is governed by IEEE 802.5. FDDI is often used for larger LANs, such as those connecting several buildings in an office complex or campus.

FDDI runs on fiber-optic cable and combines high-speed performance with the advantages of the token-passing ring topology. FDDI runs at 100 Mbps, and its topology is a dual ring. There are two rings with data traveling in opposite directions; one is the primary ring, and the other is the secondary ring. Figure 2-33 demonstrates how a FDDI network works. You can see how the two rings enable a fault-tolerant design while delivering fast data speeds.

Figure 2-33 How FDDI Works

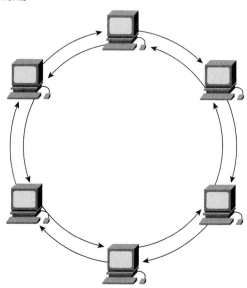

Normally, traffic flows only on the primary ring, but if it fails, the data automatically flows onto the secondary ring, in the opposite direction. The network is said to be in a wrapped state when this occurs. This provides fault tolerance for the link.

Computers on a FDDI network are divided into two classes:

- **Class A**—Computers connected to the cables of both rings
- **Class B**—Computers connected to only one ring

Another difference between FDDI and 802.5 Token Ring is the allowed number of frames on the network. A FDDI network lets multiple frames circulate on the ring simultaneously. As opposed to a basic Token Ring network, in which at any instant a single active ring monitor supplies the ring's master clock, on FDDI networks, each interface that is connected to the ring has its own local clock. Because each interface has its own local clock, each interface permits outgoing transmission. The main reason that a FDDI network has this capability that a basic Token Ring does not is because of the much-faster transmission speeds of fiber cabling. And because FDDI uses two rings, the second ring can be used for data transfer as well. This is called shared network technology. Like 802.5 Token Ring, FDDI uses beaconing to detect and isolate problems within the ring. Another advantage that FDDI has over basic Token Ring is that FDDI rings can also support the transmission of synchronous data. An example of synchronous data transfer is digitized voice.

A FDDI dual ring supports a maximum of 500 nodes per ring. The total distance of each length of the cable ring is 100 kilometers (62 miles). A repeater is needed every 2 kilometers, which is why FDDI is not considered a WAN link.

FDDI ring topology can be implemented as a physical ring or as a star-wired logical ring by using a hub.

- **Advantages of FDDI**—FDDI combines the advantages of token passing on the ring topology with the high speed of fiber-optic transmission. Its dual-ring topology provides redundancy and fault tolerance. The fiber-optic cable is not susceptible to EMI and noise, and it is more secure than copper wiring. It can send data for greater distances between repeaters than Ethernet and the traditional Token Ring.
- **Disadvantages of FDDI**—As always, high speed and reliability generally are more expensive to implement. The distance limitations, although less restrictive than those of other LAN links, make it unsuitable for true WAN communications.

Table 2-9 compares the cabling types, transfer speed, access speed, and topology used in different networking architectures.

NOTE

These specifications refer to FDDI implemented over fiber-optic cable. It is also possible to use FDDI technology with copper cabling. This is called Copper Distributed Data Interface (CDDI). The maximum distances for CDDI are considerably lower than those for FDDI.

Table 2-9 Networking Architectures Compared

Network Architecture	Cabling Type(s)	Transfer Speed	Access Speed	Topology
Ethernet 10BASE2	Thin coaxial	10 Mbps	CSMA/CD	Linear bus
Ethernet 10BASE5	Thick coaxial	10 Mbps	CSMA/CD	Linear bus
Ethernet 10BASE-T	UTP Categories 3 to 5	10 Mbps	CSMA/CD	Star
Ethernet 100BASE-T	UTP Category 5	100 Mbps	CSMA/CD	Star
Ethernet 100BASE-FX	Fiber-optic	100 Mbps	CSMA/CD	Star
Ethernet 1000BASE-T	UTP Category 7	1 Gbps	CSMA/CD	Star
Token Ring	STP or UTP	4 Mbps or 16 Mbps	Token passing	Physical star, logical ring
FDDI	Fiber-optic	100 Mbps	Token passing	Dual ring

Summary

This chapter introduced networking. Some of the important concepts to retain from this chapter include the following:

- The benefits of networking including e-mail, the Internet, and the ability to share applications, devices, and files.
- Local-area networks (LANs) are used to connect many computers in a relatively small geographic area. A direct connection from one computer to another is called a point-to-point link.
- The three types of LAN topology are star, bus, and ring.
- A wide-area network (WAN) can provide the means for connecting single computers and many LANs over large distances to allow networks to span whole countries and even the entire globe. Wide-area connections between computers use point-to-point serial communications lines.
- The OSI reference model is made up of seven layers. It is important to know what each layer is and the function that each provides in the network.
- Although TCP/IP is becoming the standard for protocols, other companies such as Novell and Apple have protocol suites for their systems. A protocol is a controlled sequence of messages exchanged between two or more systems to accomplish a given task.

The next chapter details a network's physical components. This includes NICs, topology, networking media, devices, and connecting to the Internet.

Check Your Understanding

The following review questions help you assess what you learned in this chapter. Answers can be found in Appendix A, "Answers to Check Your Understanding Questions."

1. Match the definitions to the following networking terms.

Term	Definition
Star	A network's general shape or layout
Topology	Many interconnected users and systems in close proximity
WAN	Computers attached to a single long cable
LAN	All computers are connected to a central point
Bus	A network separated by a large geographic area

2. Which type of communication lines are used by point-to-point WAN connections? (Select two.)

   A. Serial

   B. Ethernet

   C. Leased

   D. Parallel

   E. Ring

   F. Coaxial

3. Correctly order the layers of the OSI reference model by name.

Layer 7	
Layer 6	
Layer 5	
Layer 4	
Layer 3	
Layer 2	
Layer 1	

4. Select the five items that are part of the TCP/IP protocol suite.

   A. FTP

   B. SMTP

   C. IPX

   D. SPX

   E. SAP

   F. Telnet

   G. DNS

   H. RIP

   I. UDP

5. Fill in the blank with the maximum allowable cable distance between the switches for this type of network.

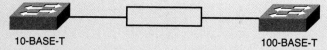

   10-BASE-T   100-BASE-T

   Options

100 meters
1000 meters
100 feet
1000 feet

6. Which of the following are not advantages of using FDDI Token Ring over basic Token Ring?

   A. Faster transmission speeds

   B. Fault tolerance

   C. Transmission of synchronous data

   D. Transmission of asynchronous data

   E. Costs

7. Describe the difference between half-duplex and full-duplex transmission modes.

8. Which of the following Ethernet standards are used in linear bus topologies?

    A. 100BASE-T

    B. 1000BASE-TX

    C. 10BASE-T

    D. 10BASE2

    E. 1000BASE-T

    F. 10BASE5

9. Fill in the following chart.

Network Architecture	Cabling Type(s)	Transfer Speed
	Thin coaxial	
	Thick coaxial	
	UTP Categories 3 to 5	
	UTP Category 5	
	Fiber-optic	
	UTP Category 7	
	STP or UTP	
	Fiber-optic	

10. Which of the following are not characteristics of UTP cabling?

    A. Flexible and easy to work with

    B. Not susceptible to EMI

    C. RJ-45 connector

    D. Operates at only 10 Mbps

    E. Maximum cable length without repeaters is 100 meters

    F. Fast Ethernet-compatible

Key Terms

Address Resolution Protocol (ARP)   Used to discover a station's local (MAC) address on the network when its Internet address is known.

AppleTalk Data Stream Protocol (ADSP)   Supports the flow of unstructured data between Macintosh systems.

AppleTalk Filing Protocol (AFP)   Allows Macintosh desktop workstations to share files.

AppleTalk Session Protocol (ASP)   Establishes connections between clients and the server so that sequences of messages can be associated with each other in Macintosh systems.

AppleTalk Transaction Protocol (ATP)   Provides reliable, connection-oriented transport in Macintosh systems.

application layer   Specifies the details of how an application makes requests and how the application on another machine responds.

bus topology   Each computer is attached to a single long cable.

Channel Service Unit/Data Service Unit (CSU/DSU)   The connection point where the user's data coming from the computer or network interfaces with the WAN connection.

client/server   Network services are located on a dedicated computer called a server, which responds to the requests of clients. The server is a central computer that is continuously available to respond to a client's requests for file, print, application, and other services.

CSMA/CA   Reduces network collisions by listening to the network before broadcasting.

datagram   Another name for a packet of data.

data link layer   Specifies how packets of data are organized into frames on a particular type of network and the rules for inserting frames onto the network media.

de facto   Something has become the industry standard just because the majority has chosen to implement it.

Domain Name System (DNS)   Provides access to name servers where network names are translated to the addresses used by Layer 3 network protocols.

encapsulation   Data is passed down the OSI reference model layers, and these layers prepare the data for transmission.

Ethernet cable   The unshielded twisted-pair (UTP) cabling generally used in the 10BASE-X architecture.

Fiber Distributed Data Interface (FDDI)   A network that runs on fiber-optic cable and combines high-speed performance with the advantages of the token-passing ring topology.

File Transfer Protocol (FTP)   An application that provides services for file transfer and manipulation.

frame   A packet is passed to the data link layer, where it gets packaged into a Layer 2 header and trailer.

full duplex   Allows for two simultaneous directions of data flow.

Get Nearest Server (GNS)   Makes services known to NetWare clients and lets clients locate the services they require, such as print or file services.

half duplex   Allows for only one direction that can be used at a time when data is transmitted over the lines.

Institute of Electrical and Electronic Engineers (IEEE)   The group that has been the most active in defining LAN standards. Through its "802" working groups, which began meeting in February 1980, the IEEE has published standards for the most widely implemented LANs.

Internet   A worldwide public network, interconnecting thousands of other networks to form one large "web" for communication.

Internet Control Message Protocol (ICMP)   Used for network testing and trouble-shooting. It enables diagnostic and error messages. The ping application uses ICMP echo messages to test remote devices.

Internet Package Exchange (IPX)   Controls network addressing and forwards packets from one network to another toward a destination in Novell networks.

Internet Protocol (IP)   Provides source and destination addressing and, in conjunction with routing protocols, packet forwarding from one network to another toward a destination.

local-area network (LAN)   Connects many computers in a relatively small geographic area, such as a home, an office, a building, or a campus.

Logical Link Control (LLC)   An IEEE-defined standard for providing error and flow control over different LAN types. Defined in the IEEE's 802.2 specification.

medium   The communications channel that all the computers on a LAN share.

Media Access Control (MAC)   Rules for coordinating the use of the medium.

Multistation Access Unit (MSAU)   The central device to which systems are connected in a Token Ring network.

Name Binding Protocol (NBP)   Associates network names for services with their addresses in Macintosh systems.

network layer   Specifies how addresses are assigned and how packets of data are forwarded from one network to another toward the destination.

Novell Link-State Protocol (NLSP)   Functions like OSPF in a TCP/IP environment to build and maintain routing tables.

Novell Routing Information Protocol (NRIP)   The Novell version of RIP operates much like RIP in a TCP/IP environment, but with variations that make it unique to NetWare networks.

Open Shortest Path First (OSPF)   Lets routers build forwarding tables. Unlike RIP, OSPF selects routes based on other characteristics of the links between networks, such as bandwidth and delay.

Open System Interconnection (OSI) reference model   Designed to promote interoperability in networking. This model is an overall description of the functions performed in a computer network and the relationships between them. The intent of the model is to provide a framework within which more-detailed standards can be developed for each function.

packet   A segment becomes a packet when the transport layer passes the segment to the network layer, where a protocol header is added.

peer-to-peer network   Networked computers act as equal partners, or peers, to each other. As a peer, a computer can take on the client function or the server function.

physical layer   Corresponds to the network hardware (cabling, media). This layer determines how binary data is translated into electrical, optical, or other types of physical signals transmitted between systems.

point-to-point link   A direct connection from one computer to another.

post-office box   The place on the e-mail server that is created to store incoming e-mail messages until the user downloads them from the server. Each user with an e-mail account has his or her own post-office box.

presentation layer   Specifies the arrangement, or syntax, of the data that the application expects. The presentation layer may include translations from one format to another and also includes security and efficiency functions (encryption and compression).

Printer Access Protocol (PAP)   Lets clients locate printers and controls the execution of print jobs on the network in Macintosh systems.

proprietary technology   Hardware and software that are owned by one company and are generally incompatible with equipment sold by other vendors.

protocol   A controlled sequence of messages exchanged between two or more systems to accomplish a given task.

ring topology   Connects computers in a closed loop, in which a cable is run from one computer to the next until the last one is connected to the first.

Routing Information Protocol (RIP)   Operates between router devices to discover paths between networks to build and maintain information about how to forward packets toward their destination.

segment   Results when a header is added to a data unit for sequencing and error checking.

Sequenced Packet Exchange (SPX)   Functions much like TCP to provide a reliable, connection-oriented transport between client and server systems.

serial line   A line that transmits bits of information one after another in a series, like cars traveling on a single-lane highway.

Service Advertisement Protocol (SAP)   Makes services known to NetWare clients and helps clients locate the services they require, such as print or file services.

session layer   Allows a number of copies of an application to communicate with other applications at the same time. Also establishes the rules of the conversation between two applications.

Simple Mail Transport Protocol (SMTP)   Provides messaging services over TCP/IP and supports most Internet e-mail programs.

star topology   When all the computers connect to a central point, or hub.

TCP/IP   A set of public standards that specifies how packets of information are exchanged between computers over one or more networks.

Telnet   Enables terminal access to local or remote systems. The Telnet application is used to access remote devices for configuration, control, and troubleshooting.

time stamp   The information that is marked on an e-mail message to indicate the time at which the e-mail was sent by an individual and received by the e-mail server.

Transmission Control Protocol (TCP)   The primary Internet protocol for reliable delivery of data. TCP includes facilities for end-to-end connection establishment, error detection and recovery, and metering the rate of data flow into the network.

transport layer   Provides delivery services for each session. Provides a reliable delivery service that guarantees that data arrives at its destination, or an "unreliable" best-effort delivery service that transports the data without checking for errors.

User Datagram Protocol (UDP)   A connectionless service to applications that do not want the overhead of TCP and can tolerate a level of data loss.

wide-area network (WAN)   Usually segmented into multiple LANs. A WAN uses dedicated point-to-point or serial communications lines to connect the various LANs to make up the WAN.

Zone Information Protocol (ZIP)   Maintains a correspondence between networks and the names of partitions, called zones, between Macintosh systems.

Objectives

After completing this chapter, you will be able to complete tasks related to

- Configuring a network interface card
- Topologies
- Media types
- Devices
- Connecting to the Internet (WANs)

## Chapter 3

Physical Components of a Network

This chapter covers network fundamentals. The choices you make when designing a computer network determine how well the system works. This chapter discusses how the physical and logical topology, combined with the network media and devices, allow all the computers connected to the system to communicate with each other and the Internet.

Configuring a Network Interface Card

This section covers the following topics:

- What is a NIC?
- Setting the IP address
- DHCP servers
- Domain Name System
- Default gateway

What Is a NIC?

A *network interface card (NIC)*, shown in Figures 3-1, 3-2, and 3-3, is a device that plugs into a motherboard and provides ports for the network media connections. It is the component of the computer that interfaces with the local-area network (LAN). The NIC communicates with the network through serial connections and with the computer through parallel connections. When network interface cards are installed in a computer, the IRQ, I/O address, and memory space for the operating system drivers are set automatically to perform their function. With older NICs, however, these settings would need to be set manually.

Figure 3-1 Network Interface Card

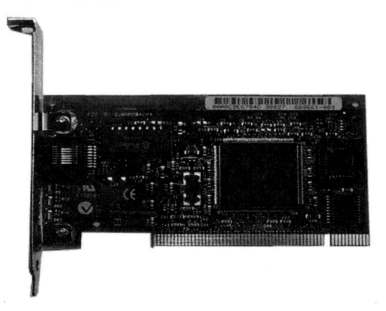

Figure 3-2 Network Interface Card: Top View

Figure 3-3 Network Interface Card: Front View

The following things are important to consider when selecting a NIC to use on a network:

- **The type of network**—NICs are designed for Ethernet LANs, Token Ring, Fiber Distributed Data Interface (FDDI), and others. A NIC designed for Ethernet LANs does not work for Token Ring networks, and vice versa.

- **The type of medium**—The type of port or connector on a NIC that provides network connection is medium-specific. Media types include twisted pair, coaxial, fiber optic, and wireless.

- **The type of system bus**—Protocol Control Information (PCI) slots are faster than Industry-Standard Architecture (ISA). It is recommended that PCI be used with FDDI cards because an ISA bus cannot handle the speed required.

Setting the IP Address

In a TCP/IP-based LAN, PCs use Internet Protocol (IP) addresses to identify each other. These addresses give computers that are attached to the network the ability to locate each other. An *IP address* is a 32-bit binary number. This binary number is divided into four groups of 8 bits known as *octets*, each of which is represented by a decimal number in the range of 0 to 255. The octets are separated by periods. An example of an IP address is 190.100.5.54. This type of address is called a *dotted-decimal* representation. Each device on the network that has an IP address is called a *host* or *node*.

A secondary dotted-decimal number, known as the *subnet mask*, always accompanies an IP address. A subnet mask is a tool used by a system administrator to segment the network address that has been assigned to the network. The technique of subnetting allows the entire network to be represented to the Internet by one address. An example of a subnet mask is 255.255.0.0. The subnet mask is also used to determine whether a particular host IP address is local (on the same network segment) or remote (on another segment).

There are several options for assigning IP addresses for hosts on a LAN:

- **Static**—Assigned by the network administrator manually.
- **Dynamic**—Assigned by a Dynamic Host Configuration Protocol (DHCP) server (DHCP servers are discussed in the next section).
- **Automatic**—Private IP addressing.

If there are more than a few computers, manually configuring TCP/IP addresses for every host on the network can be a time-consuming process. The network administrator assigning the addresses must understand IP addressing and know how to choose a valid address for the particular network. An IP address is unique for each host and is stored in the Network Settings of the operating system's software. Alternatively, the MAC address resides on the NIC card hardware. TCP/IP addressing is covered in later courses.

In the Windows operating system, the IP address is manually entered into the Internet Protocol (TCP/IP) Properties dialog box. Figure 3-4 shows the TCP/IP configuration dialog box that is used to set the address settings or configurations, which include the following:

- IP address
- Subnet mask
- Default gateway address
- Optional values, including a Domain Name System (DNS) server address and Windows Internet Naming Service (WINS)

The default gateway address and the Domain Name System are discussed later.

DHCP Servers

Another way for computers on a network to obtain an IP address is through a *Dynamic Host Configuration Protocol (DHCP)* server. DHCP is a software utility that automatically assigns IP addresses to PCs. The computer running the software is called a DHCP server. DHCP servers assign the IP addresses and TCP/IP configuration information to computers configured as DHCP clients. This dynamic process eliminates the need for manual IP address assignments. However, any device requiring a static or permanent IP address must still have its IP address manually assigned. Figure 3-5 shows an example of the tool you would use to configure a server to run DHCP services to client systems on the network.

Figure 3-4 Specifying the IP Address in Windows 2000

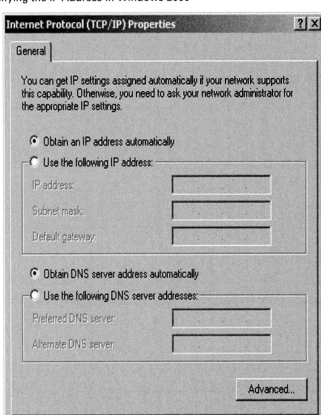

When the DHCP server receives a request from a host, it selects IP address information from a set of predefined addresses that are stored in its database. After it has selected the IP information, it offers these values to the requesting device on the network. If the device accepts the offer, the DHCP server then leases the IP information to the device for a specific period of time.

Figure 3-5 Configuring DHCP Service in Windows 2000

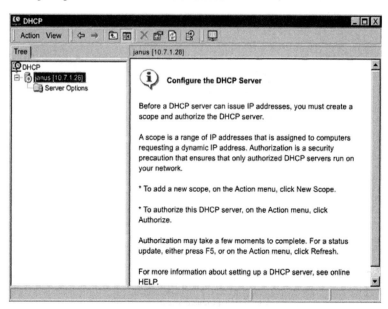

The IP address information that a DHCP server can assign to hosts that are starting up on the network includes the following:

- IP address
- Subnet mask
- Default gateway
- Optional values, including a DNS server address and WINS

The use of this system simplifies network administration because the software keeps track of IP addresses. Automatically configuring TCP/IP also reduces the possibility of assigning duplicate or invalid IP addresses. For any computer on the network to take advantage of the services provided by the DHCP server, it must first be able to identify the server on the local network. The option to obtain an IP address automatically is selected in the Internet Protocol (TCP/IP) Properties dialog box. Figure 3-6 shows an example of Windows client's IP address configuration dialog box when it is configured with an IP address via DHCP. In other cases, an operating system feature called Automatic Private IP Addressing (APIPA) lets a computer assign itself an address if it is unable to contact a DHCP server.

Figure 3-6 Using DHCP in Windows 2000

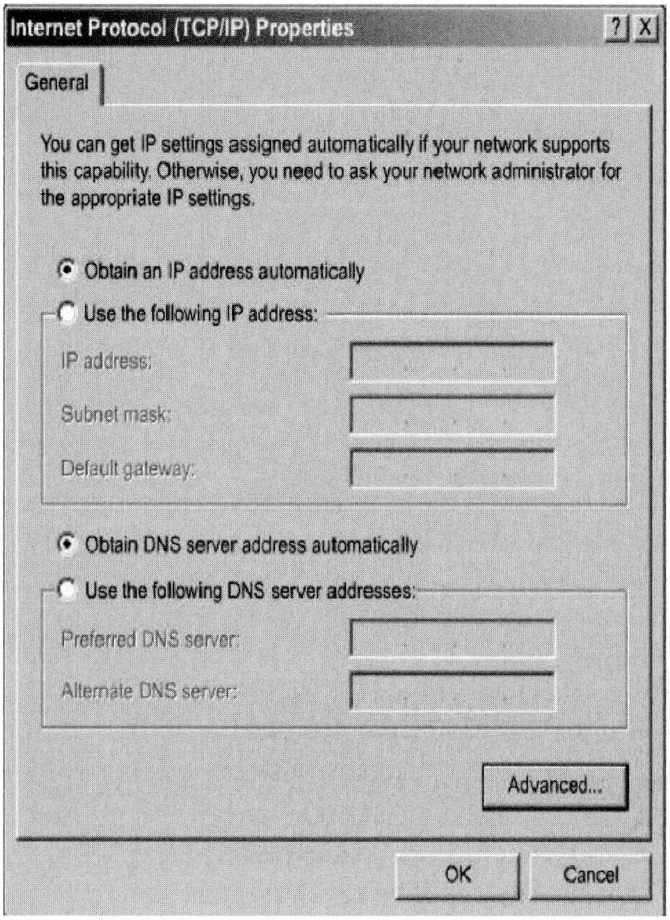

Domain Name System

If a LAN is large or is connected to the Internet, it is often challenging to remember hosts' numeric addresses (IP addresses). Most hosts are identified on the Internet by friendly computer names known as *host names*. The Domain Name System (DNS) is used to translate computer names such as www.cisco.com to the corresponding unique IP address. Figure 3-7 shows how this translation process is assigned. The DNS software runs on a computer acting as a network server and translates the addresses. DNS software can be hosted on the network itself or by an *Internet service provider (ISP)*. Address translations are used each time the Internet is accessed. The process of translating names to addresses is called *name resolution.*

Figure 3-7 Domain Name System Functions

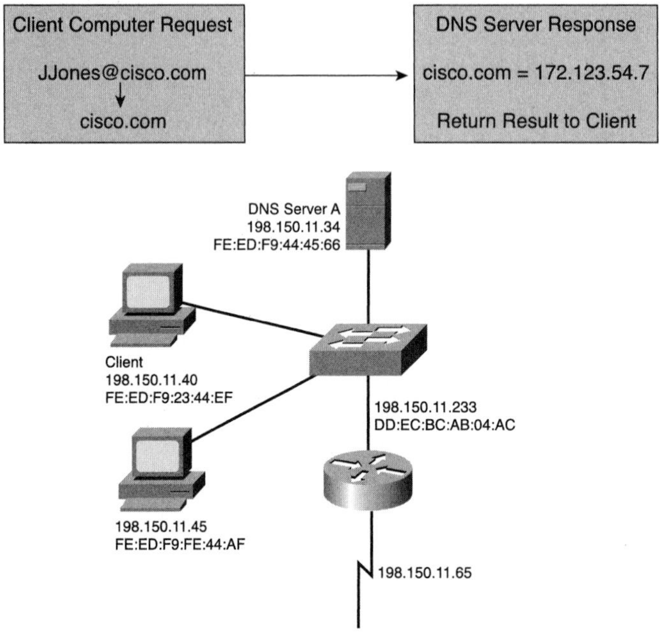

The DNS server keeps records that map computer (host) names and their corresponding IP addresses. These record types are combined in the DNS table. When a host name needs to be translated to its IP address, the client contacts the DNS server. A hierarchy of DNS servers exists on the Internet, with different servers maintaining DNS information for their own areas of authority, called *zones*. If the DNS server that is consulted by a computer does not have an IP mapping for the host name that is being sought, it passes the query to another DNS server until the information is obtained. If the name cannot be resolved to an IP address at the highest-level DNS server, an error is returned. Figure 3-8 shows an example of the tool you would use to configure a server to run DHCP services to client systems on the network.

DNS is not an absolute requirement to communicate on the Internet, but without it, all communications must use IP addresses instead of host names. It is much easier to remember www.cisco.com than 198.133.219.25.

For the computers on the LAN to access and use the DNS services, the DNS server IP address must be entered into the Internet Protocol (TCP/IP) Properties dialog box, as shown in Figure 3-9, as well as the IP address/subnet mask.

Figure 3-8 Configuring DNS Service in Windows 2000

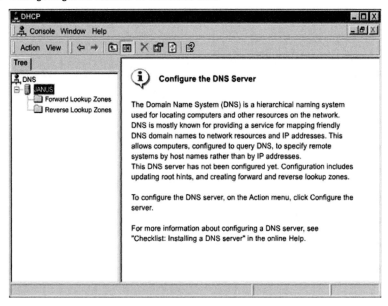

Figure 3-9 Specifying DNS in Windows 2000

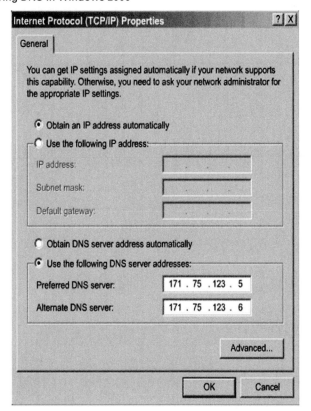

Default Gateway

A computer located on one network segment that is trying to talk to another computer on a different segment (across the router, for example) sends the data through a *default gateway*. The default gateway is the router's *near-side* interface. It is the interface on the router to which the local computer network segment or wire is attached. For each computer to recognize its default gateway, the corresponding near-side router interface IP address has to be entered into the host's Internet Protocol (TCP/IP) Properties dialog box. Figure 3-10 demonstrates how the default gateway is set up and its relationship to the other router interfaces on the network.

Figure 3-10   Setting Up a Default Gateway in Windows 2000

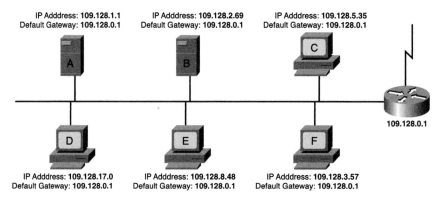

Topologies

This section covers the following topics:

- The network topology
- Physical versus logical topology
- Bus topology
- Star topology
- Ring topology
- Mesh topology
- Hybrid topology

The Network Topology

The network topology defines the network's layout. It shows how devices on the network are interconnected. Devices on the network are called *nodes*. Examples of nodes include computers, printers, routers, bridges, and other components attached to the network. The topology influences how the network operates.

The following sections discuss the different types of topologies. These types include the bus, star, extended star, ring, mesh, and hybrid topologies. A network has both a physical and a logical topology. Figure 3-11 shows a network topology that might exist on a typical network. Notice how several of the various types of network topologies exist in this example.

Figure 3-11   Network Topology

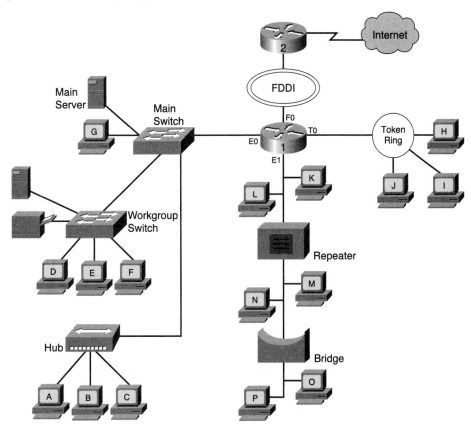

Physical Versus Logical Topology

Networks can have both a physical and logical topology:

- **Physical topology**—As you can see from Figure 3-12, a network's *physical topology* refers to the layout of the devices and media.
- **Logical topology**—As you can see from Figure 3-13, a network's *logical topology* refers to the paths that signals travel from one point in the network to another (that is, the way in which data accesses the medium and transmits packets across it).

Figure 3-12 Physical Topology

- - - - - Water Pipes
- - - - - Flourescent Lighting
- - - - - High Voltage Power Lines
- - - - - Air Conditioning and Heating Ducts

Figure 3-13 Logical Topology

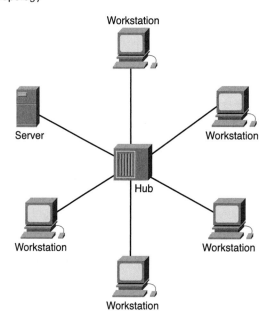

These two terminologies can be a little confusing, partly because the word "logical" in this instance has nothing to do with how the network appears to be functioning.

A network's physical and logical topologies can be the same. For instance, in a network physically shaped as a linear bus, the data travels in a straight line from one computer to the next (as discussed in the next section). Hence, it has both a bus physical topology and a bus logical topology.

A network can also have physical and logical topologies that are quite different. For example, a physical topology in the shape of a star, where cable segments can connect all computers to a central hub, can have a logical ring topology. Remember that in a ring, the data travels from one computer to the next. That is because inside the hub, the wiring connections are such that the signal travels in a circle from one port to the next, which creates a logical ring. Therefore, you cannot always predict how data travels in a network by simply observing its physical layout.

Token Ring uses a logical ring topology in either a physical ring or physical star. Ethernet uses a logical bus topology in either a physical bus or physical star.

Bus Topology

Commonly called a linear bus, all the devices on a *bus topology* are connected by a single cable, which proceeds from one computer to the next like a bus line going through a city. The main cable segment ends with a terminator that absorbs the signal when it reaches the end of the line or wire. If there is no terminator, the electrical signal representing the data bounces back at the end of the wire, causing errors in the network. Only one packet of data can be transmitted at a time. If more than one packet is transmitted, they collide and have to be resent. A bus topology with many hosts can be very slow due to the collisions. This topology is rarely used and is suitable only for a home office or small business with only a few hosts. Figure 3-14 shows an example of a typical bus topology layout. Table 3-1 outlines some of the advantages and disadvantages of using a bus topology in a network.

Figure 3-14 *Bus Topology*

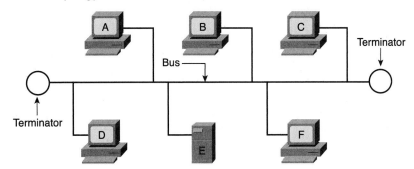

Table 3-1 Advantages and Disadvantages of a Bus Topology

Advantages	Disadvantages
The Thinnet cabling it uses is quite inexpensive.	It results in slower access to the network and less bandwidth because the same cable is shared by all devices.
It uses less cable compared to other physical topologies such as star and extended star.	It can be quite challenging to identify and isolate problems.
It works well for small networks—those with fewer than ten computers or devices.	A break at any point in the bus cable can disable the entire bus network.
It does not need a central device, such as a hub, switch, or router.	It needs terminators.

Star Topology

The *star topology* is the most commonly used architecture in Ethernet LANs. It resembles spokes in a bicycle wheel. It is made up of a central connection point that is a device such as a hub, switch, or router where all the cabling segments meet. Figure 3-15 shows how each host in the network is connected to the central device with its own cable.

Figure 3-15 Star Topology

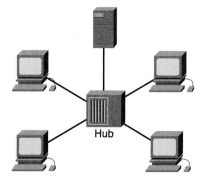

Hub

A star topology generally costs more to implement than a bus topology because more cable is used and a central device is needed, such as a hub, switch, or router. However, the advantages of a star topology are worth the additional costs. Because each host is connected to the central device with its own wire, only that host is affected when there is a problem with that cable. The rest of the network remains operational. This benefit is extremely important; it is the reason why virtually every newly designed network has this topology.

When a star network is expanded to include an additional networking device, such as a hub or switch connected to the main networking device, it is called an *extended star topology*. Figure 3-16 shows an example of a typical extended star topology. Most larger networks, such as those for corporations or schools, use the extended star topology. This topology, when used with network devices that filter data packets, such as switches and routers, significantly reduces the traffic on the wires. Packets are sent to only the wires of the destination host.

Figure 3-16 Extended Star Topology

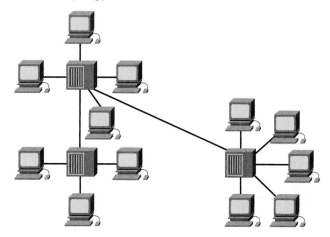

Table 3-2 lists the advantages and disadvantages of a star topology.

Table 3-2 Advantages and Disadvantages of a Star Topology

Advantages	Disadvantages
It is upgradeable. Adding a new computer is as easy as plugging the cable that is connected to the new workstation into the hub.	It requires a lot of cable to connect the computers, because a cable is required between each device and the central location.
It is flexible. The layout is easy to modify, and new hosts or devices can be added quickly.	It is more expensive to build because of the additional cost of cables and devices such as the hubs and switches that are needed to run between the central device and each computer.
It is reliable. If one line of the networking medium is broken or shorted out, only the device attached at that point is out of commission. The rest of the LAN remains functional.	
It is easy to design and install. The networking medium runs directly out from a central device such as a hub to each workstation or device.	
It makes diagnosing problems relatively easy, because the problem is localized to one computer or device.	
It allows for more throughput than any other topology.	

Ring Topology

The ring topology is another important topology in LAN connectivity. As the name implies, hosts are connected in the form of a ring or circle. Unlike the bus topology, it has no beginning or end that needs to be terminated. Data is transmitted in a way that is unlike either the bus or star topology. A frame called a *token* travels around the ring and stops at each node. If a node wants to transmit data, it adds that data and the addressing information to the frame. The frame then continues around the ring until it finds the destination node, which takes the data out of the frame. The advantage of using this method is that there are no collisions of data packets.

There are two types of rings:

- With *single ring*, shown in Figure 3-17, all the devices on the network share a single cable, and the data travels in one direction only. This means that each device waits its turn to send data over the network.

Figure 3-17 Single-Ring Topology

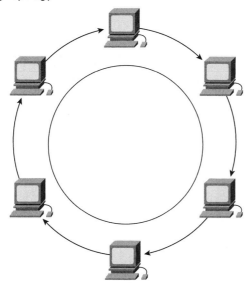

- With *dual ring*, shown in Figure 3-18, two rings allow data to be sent in both directions. This creates redundancy (fault tolerance), meaning that if one ring fails, data still is transmitted on the other ring.

Figure 3-18 Dual-Ring Topology

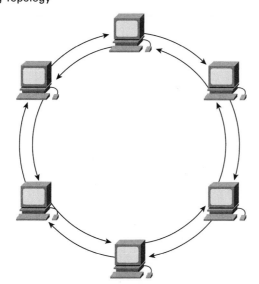

The most common implementation of the ring topology is in Token Ring networks. The 802.5 standard is the Token Ring access method that is used. FDDI is a technology similar to Token Ring. It uses light instead of electricity to transmit data over a dual ring. It is important to know the advantages and disadvantages of choosing a ring topology. They are listed in Table 3-3.

Table 3-3 Advantages and Disadvantages of a Ring Topology

Advantages	Disadvantages
It is much easier to locate problems with the cable on a ring topology than on a bus topology.	A break at any point in most types of ring networks disables the network.
Separate terminators are not needed, because there are no open cable ends.	The addition of a new computer to the network requires an interruption in the network.
Collisions cannot occur on a ring topology, because only one frame can carry data.	Because ring topology is not a very common LAN implementation, equipment for ring networks is not readily available.
	It has limited bandwidth and access.

Mesh Topology

The *mesh topology*, shown in Figure 3-19, connects all devices (nodes) to each other for redundancy and fault tolerance. It is used in wide-area networks (WANs) to interconnect LANs and in critical networks such as those used by governments. The mesh topology is expensive and difficult to implement.

Figure 3-19 Mesh Topology

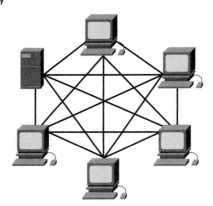

Hybrid Topology

The *hybrid topology* combines more than one type of topology. For example, when a bus line joins two hubs of different topologies, the configuration is called a *star bus*. Businesses or schools that have several buildings, known as campuses, sometimes use this topology. The bus line is used to transfer the data between the star topologies, as shown in Figure 3-20.

Figure 3-20 Hybrid Topology

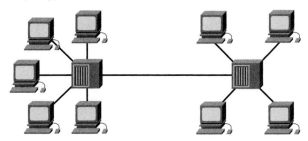

 Worksheet 3.2.7   Network Topologies

Covers the design and implementation of various network architectures.

Media Types

This section covers the following topics:

- Networking media
- Coaxial cable
- Twisted-pair cable
- Fiber-optic cable
- Wireless

Networking Media

Networking media is simply the means by which signals (data) are sent from one computer to another. This includes cable and wireless means. There are a wide variety of networking media in the marketplace, such as the following:

- **Copper**—Includes coaxial and twisted pair
- **Glass**—Fiber optic
- **Waves**—Wireless

Each type of cable (such as coaxial, twisted pair, and fiber optic) has two grades:

- **Plenum**—Refers to the space between a false ceiling and the floor above it in a building. Network cabling that is laid in this space must be fire-retardant. Plenum-grade cable, commonly called plenum cable, refers to cable with an outer jacket made of Teflon or another material that complies with fire and building codes.

- **PVC**—The outer jacket of non-plenum-grade cables is made with Polyvinyl Chloride (PVC). PVC is a less-expensive protective material than plenum-grade materials. It does not meet most safety codes for installation in the area above the ceiling, because it gives off a poisonous gas when burned. Check your local building and fire codes for the locations where PVC-grade cable can be used.

Coaxial Cable

Coaxial cable uses copper shielding to resist interference from outside electrical sources. A braided copper shield surrounds the center conductor and constitutes one half of the electrical circuit. In some other types of shielded wire, the outer shield is not part of the circuit. Coaxial cable consists of four parts:

- Center conductor
- Insulation
- Shield
- Jacket

Coaxial cable is a copper-cored cable surrounded by heavy shielding that is used to connect computers in a network. Figure 3-21 shows the various components of coaxial cable. There are several types of coaxial cable, including Thicknet (shown in Figure 3-22), Thinnet (shown in Figure 3-23), RG-59 (the standard cable for cable TV), and RG-6 (used in video distribution). *Thicknet* has a very large diameter, is rigid, and is difficult to install. In addition, the maximum transmission rate is only 10 Mbps. This is significantly less than twisted pair or fiber optic. The maximum length the cable can be run without the signal's being boosted is 500 meters. A thinner version, known as *Thinnet* or Cheapernet, is occasionally used in Ethernet networks. Thinnet has the same transmission rate as Thicknet.

Figure 3-21 Coaxial Cable

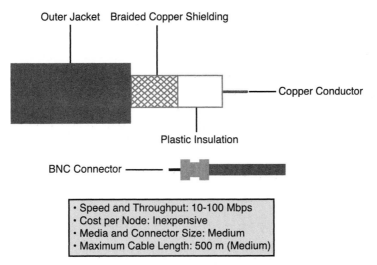

Outer Jacket   Braided Copper Shielding

Copper Conductor

Plastic Insulation

BNC Connector

- Speed and Throughput: 10-100 Mbps
- Cost per Node: Inexpensive
- Media and Connector Size: Medium
- Maximum Cable Length: 500 m (Medium)

Figure 3-22 10BASE5 Thicknet Cable

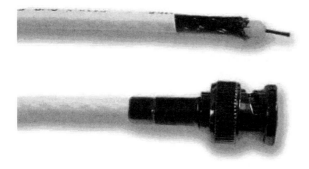

Figure 3-23 10BASE2 Thinnet Cable

Table 3-4 lists the advantages and disadvantages of using coaxial cable.

Table 3-4 Advantages and Disadvantages of Coaxial

Advantages	Disadvantages
It can be run for longer distances between nodes than twisted-pair cable.	Thicknet's large diameter makes installation difficult.
It is less expensive than fiber-optic cable.	Coaxial needs to be grounded; otherwise, noise problems will cause data errors.
	Bandwidth is limited.

Twisted-Pair Cable

Twisted pair is a type of cabling that is used for telephone communications and most modern Ethernet networks. A pair of wires forms a circuit that can transmit data. The pairs are twisted to prevent crosstalk, the noise generated by adjacent pairs. Pairs of copper wires that are encased in color-coded plastic insulation are twisted together. All the twisted pairs are then protected inside an outer jacket. Figures 3-24 and 3-25 show two examples of twisted-pair cables.

Figure 3-24 Twisted-Pair Cable

There are two basic types of twisted-pair cabling:

- Shielded twisted-pair (STP)
- Unshielded twisted-pair (UTP)

Worksheet 3.3.3   Twisted-Pair Cabling

Covers the principles and standards for twisted-pair cabling.

Figure 3-25 Twisted-Pair Cable with an RJ-45 Connector

STP

Shielded twisted-pair (STP) cable, shown in Figure 3-26, combines the techniques of cancellation and twisting of wires with shielding. Each pair of wires is wrapped in metallic foil to further shield the wires from noise. The four pairs of wires are then wrapped in an overall metallic braid or foil. STP reduces electrical noise from the cable (crosstalk) and from outside the cable (EMI and RFI).

Figure 3-26 Shielded Twisted-Pair

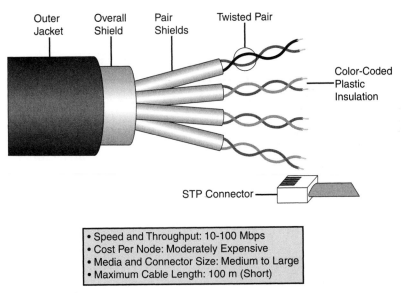

Although STP prevents more interference than UTP, it is more expensive and difficult to install. In addition, the metallic shielding must be grounded at both ends. If it is improperly grounded, the shield acts like an antenna, picking up unwanted signals. STP is primarily used in Europe.

UTP

Unshielded twisted-pair (UTP) cable, shown in Figure 3-27, is used in a variety of networks. It has two or four pairs of wires. This type of cable relies solely on the cancellation effect produced by the twisted wire pairs to limit signal degradation caused by Electromagnetic Interference (EMI) and Radio Frequency Interference (RFI). UTP is the most commonly used cabling in Ethernet networks.

Figure 3-27 Unshielded Twisted-Pair

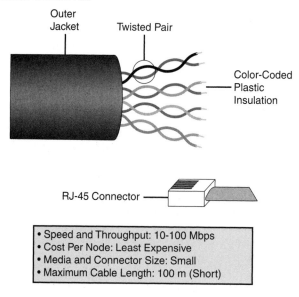

Most networks today are built using UTP cable. The connector on the end of the cable is called an RJ-45 connector. After you have arranged the wires in the correct color-coded order, you can terminate them with an RJ-45 connector. A crimping tool, shown in Figure 3-28, is used to terminate a UTP cable and secure the connectors.

Figure 3-28 Crimping Tool

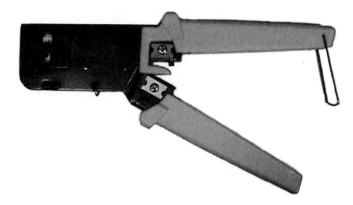

UTP comes in several categories based on the number of wires and the number of twists in those wires, as shown in Table 3-5.

Table 3-5 Categories of UTP Cable

Category	Maximum Transmission Speed	Characteristics and Uses
1	Voice only	Used in old telephone installations
2	4 Mbps	Not recommended for data transmission
3	16 Mbps	Lowest recognized data grade; used for most telephone wiring
4	20 Mbps	Suitable for networking 10-Mbps Ethernet networks
5	100 Mbps	Most popular grade for LAN networking; used for Fast Ethernet/100

Category 3 is the wiring used for telephone connections. It has four pairs of wires and a maximum data rate of 16 Mbps.

Categories 5 and 5e are currently the most common Ethernet cables used. They have four pairs of wires with a maximum data rate of 100 Mbps. Category 5e has more twists per foot than Category 5 wiring. These extra twists further prevent interference from outside sources and the other wires within the cable.

Category 6 is a newer category that has been ratified by cabling industry organizations. Category 6 is similar to Category 5/5e, except that the pairs of wires are separated by a plastic divider to prevent crosstalk. Also, the pairs have more twists than Category 5e cable.

Fiber-Optic Cable

Fiber-optic cable is a networking medium that can conduct modulated light transmissions. To modulate light is to manipulate it so that it travels in the way it transmits data. Fiber-optic refers to cabling that has a core made of strands of glass or plastic (instead of copper) through which light pulses carry signals. Figure 3-29 shows the various components that make up a fiber-optic cable. Fiber-optic cable does not carry electrical impulses, as do other forms of networking media that use copper wire. Instead, signals that represent data are converted into beams of light. Fiber has many advantages over copper in terms of transmission bandwidth and signal integrity over distance. However, it is more difficult to work with and more expensive than copper cabling. The connectors are expensive, as is the labor to terminate the ends of the cables. Figure 3-30 shows a fiber-optic cable with the ends terminated.

Figure 3-29 Fiber-Optic Cable

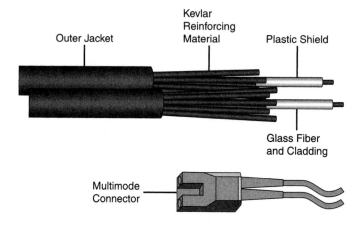

- Speed and Throughput: 100+ Mbps
- Cost Per Node: Most Expensive
- Media and Connector Size: Small
- Single Mode, Maximum Cable Length: Up to 3000 m
- Multimode, Maximum Cable Length: Up to 2000 m
- Single Mode: One Stream of Laser-Generated Light
- Multimode: Multiple Streams of LED-Generated Light

Figure 3-30 Fiber-Optic Cable with Terminated Ends

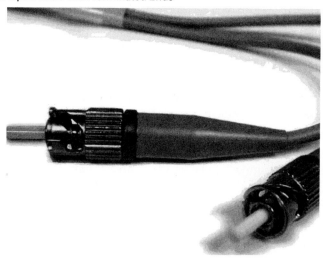

Table 3-6 discusses fiber optic's advantages and disadvantages.

Table 3-6 Advantages and Disadvantages of Fiber Optic

Advantages	Disadvantages
Not susceptible to EFI or RFI	Expensive labor and material costs
Longer distances can be spanned	
No need to ground the cable when used between buildings	
Capable of higher data rates than copper media	

Wireless

A *wireless network* is an alternative method of connecting a LAN. There are no cables to run, and computers can be easily moved. Wireless networks use Radio Frequency (RF), laser, infrared (IR), and satellite/microwaves to carry signals from one computer to another without a permanent cable connection. Wireless signals are electromagnetic waves that travel through the air. No physical medium is necessary for wireless signals, making them a very versatile way to build a network.

A common application of wireless data communication is for mobile use. Some examples of mobile use include commuters, airplanes, satellites, remote space probes, space shuttles, and space stations.

At the core of wireless communication are devices called transmitters and receivers. The source interacts with the transmitter that converts data to electromagnetic (EM) waves that are received by the receiver. The receiver converts these electromagnetic waves back into data for the destination. For two-way communication, each device requires a transmitter and a receiver. Many networking device manufacturers build the transmitter and receiver into a single unit called a transceiver or wireless network card. All devices in wireless LANs (WLANs) must have the appropriate wireless network card installed.

The two most common wireless technologies used for networking are IR and RF. *IR technology* has its weaknesses. Workstations and digital devices must be in the transmitter's line of sight to operate. An infrared-based network suits environments in which all the digital devices that require network connectivity are in one room. IR networking technology can be installed quickly, but the data signals can be weakened or obstructed by people walking across the room or moisture in the air. However, new IR technologies are being developed that can work out of sight.

RF technology allows devices to be in different rooms or even buildings. The limited range of the radio signals still restricts the use of this kind of network. RF technology can be on single or multiple frequencies. A single radio frequency is subject to outside interference and geographic obstructions. Furthermore, a single frequency is easily monitored by others, which makes the transmission of data insecure. Spread spectrum avoids the problem of insecure data transmission by using multiple frequencies to increase the immunity to noise and to make it difficult for outsiders to intercept data transmissions.

Two approaches are currently being used to implement spread spectrum for WLAN transmissions:

- Frequency-Hopping Spread Spectrum (FHSS)
- Direct Sequence Spread Spectrum (DSSS)

The technical details of how these technologies work are beyond the scope of this book. Figure 3-31 illustrates how wireless networking technologies work.

Figure 3-31 Wireless Media

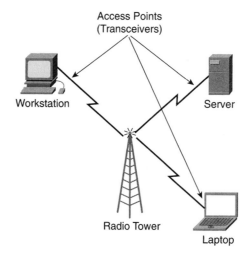

 Worksheet 3.3.5 Physical Media Types

Covers the standards and principles regarding different types of network cabling.

Devices

This section covers the following topics:

- Hubs and repeaters
- Bridges and switches
- Routers

Hubs and Repeaters

Many types of devices are connected to make up a LAN. These are called the LAN hardware components. This section discusses some of the common hardware components that are used in a LAN environment. Typical LAN devices include repeaters, hubs, bridges, switches, and routers. Figures 3-32 and 3-33 show examples of hubs and repeaters.

Figure 3-32 Hub and Repeater

Hub   Repeater

Figure 3-33 Hub

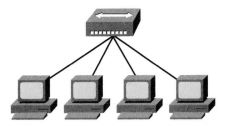

A *repeater* receives the signal, regenerates it, and passes it on. Repeaters are used mainly at the edges of networks to extend the wire so that more workstations can be added.

Hubs are actually multiport repeaters. Figure 3-34 shows what typical Cisco hubs look like. In many cases, the difference between a hub and a repeater is the number of ports that each provides. Although a typical repeater has just two ports, a hub generally has from four to 20 ports. Figure 3-35 shows an example of where a repeater might be placed between two objects to extend the cable's signal strength. Hubs are most commonly used in Ethernet 10BASE-T and 100BASE-T networks, although other network architectures use them as well.

Figure 3-34 Cisco Hubs

Figure 3-35 Repeater

Using a hub changes the network topology from a linear bus, in which each device plugs directly into the wire, to a star. With hubs, data arriving over the cables at a hub port is electrically repeated on all the other ports connected to the same Ethernet LAN, except for the port on which the data was received.

Hubs come in three basic types:

- **Passive**—A *passive hub* serves as a physical connection point only. It does not manipulate or view the traffic that crosses it. It does not boost or clean up the signal. A passive hub is used only to share the physical medium. As such, the passive hub does not need electrical power.

- **Active**—An *active hub* must be plugged into an electrical outlet, because it needs power to amplify the incoming signal before passing it back out to the other ports.

- **Intelligent**—*Intelligent hubs* are sometimes called "smart hubs." These devices basically function as active hubs but also include a microprocessor chip and diagnostic capabilities. They are more expensive than active hubs but are useful in troubleshooting situations.

Finally, it is important to remember these points about hubs:

- All devices that are attached to a hub hear all traffic. Therefore, hubs maintain a single *collision domain*. A collision is described as a situation where two end stations send data over the network wire at the same time.

- Sometimes hubs are called concentrators. This is because they serve as a central connection point for an Ethernet LAN.

- Hubs operate at the Physical Layer of the OSI reference model.

Bridges and Switches

There are times when it is necessary to break a large LAN into smaller, more easily managed segments. This decreases the amount of traffic on a single LAN and can extend the geographic area past what a single LAN can support. The devices that are used to connect network segments include bridges, switches, routers, and gateways. Switches and bridges operate at the data link layer of the OSI reference model. Figure 3-36 shows the graphics that are used in this course to represent a bridge and a switch. The function of the *bridge* is to make intelligent decisions about whether to pass signals on to the network's next segment. Figure 3-37 shows how bridges and switches can be used to divide a network into separate segments. Figure 3-38 shows what a Cisco wireless bridge looks like.

Figure 3-36 Bridge and Switch

Bridge   Switch

Figure 3-37 Bridges

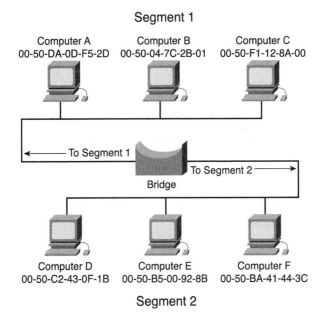

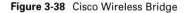

Figure 3-38 Cisco Wireless Bridge

When a bridge sees a frame on the network, it looks at the destination MAC address and compares it to the forwarding table to determine whether to filter, flood, or copy the frame to another segment. This decision process occurs as follows:

- If the destination device is on the same segment as the frame, the bridge blocks the frame from going on to other segments. This process is known as *filtering*.
- If the destination device is on a different segment, the bridge forwards the frame to the appropriate segment.
- If the destination address is unknown to the bridge, the bridge forwards the frame to all segments except the one on which it was received. This process is known as *flooding*.

If placed strategically, a bridge can greatly improve network performance.

A *switch* is sometimes described as a multiport bridge. Although a typical bridge might have just two ports (linking two network segments), the switch can have multiple ports, depending on how many network segments are to be linked. Figure 3-39 shows how a switch can be used to segment a network and how it can be used as a central device for the system to attach to the network. Figure 3-40 shows what a typical Cisco switch looks like. Like bridges, switches learn certain information about the data packets that they receive from various computers on the network. They use this information to build forwarding tables to determine the destination of data being sent from one computer to another computer on the network.

Figure 3-39 Switches

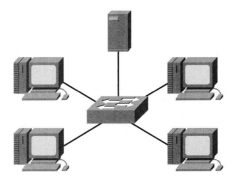

Figure 3-40 Cisco Switch

Although there are some similarities between the two, a switch is a more sophisticated device than a bridge. A bridge determines whether the frame should be forwarded to the other network segment based on the destination MAC address. A switch has many ports with many network segments connected to them. A switch chooses the port to which the destination device or workstation is connected. Ethernet switches are becoming popular connectivity solutions because, like bridges, they improve network performance (speed and bandwidth). Switches further help segment a network and reduce network traffic congestion by limiting each port to its own collision domain.

A collision on networks occurs when packets are sent over the network. This usually occurs when more than one device attempts to send one packet at a time. These collisions result in corrupt messages and excess bandwidth's being used. For this reason, it is important that all networks implement devices to reduce these collisions. Switches help reduce these collisions by segmenting the network into multiple collision domains.

A *collision domain* is defined as an area of the network that includes all the Ethernet segments that exist between any pair of switches or other Layer 2 devices. It is considered a domain because only the devices that are in the domain that are transmitting packets can have collisions. They do not interfere with any other device that is transmitting on another segment of the network. You see how a switch that can make each port its own collision domain can conserve resources on the network by limiting the device connected to that port to its own collision domain. This significantly reduces interference for that device as well as interference from other devices transmitting packets in other segments on the network. Keep in mind that although a switch can segment a network into multiple collision domains to reduce packet collision, it cannot segment the network into separate broadcast domains that can segment a network into multiple parts that no broadcast traffic can enter.

Routers

A *router* must make smart decisions on how to send data from one segment to another, such as from a computer on network segment 1 to a computer on network segment 3. Figure 3-41 shows the graphic that is used throughout this course to represent a router. Figure 3-42 demonstrates how routers can be implemented to further segment a network.

Figure 3-41 Router

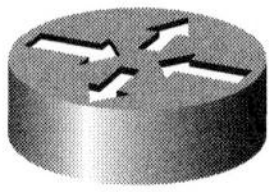

Figure 3-42 Segmentation with Routers

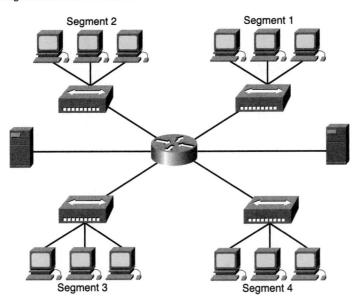

Routers are the most sophisticated internetworking devices discussed so far. They operate at the network layer of the OSI reference model. They are slower than bridges and switches but make "smart" decisions on how to route packets received on one port to a network on another port. Like switches, routers can segment the network. Routers can segment a network into multiple collision domains as well as into multiple broadcast domains. A *broadcast domain* is a logical area in a computer network where any computer connected to the computer network can directly transmit to any other in the domain without having to go through a routing device. More specifically, it is an area of the computer network made up of all the computers and networking devices that can be reached by sending a frame to the data link layer. Each port to which a network segment is attached is called a router interface. Routers can be computers with special network software installed on them, or they can be other devices built by network equipment manufacturers. Routers contain tables of network addresses along with optimal destination routes to other networks. Figure 3-43 shows Cisco routers.

Figure 3-43 Cisco Routers

 Worksheet 3.4.3 Networking Devices

Defines the uses of and differences between the various devices used to inter-connect a network and share data.

Connecting to the Internet (WANs)

This section covers the following topics:

- Synchronous and asynchronous serial lines
- Modems
- Dialup networking, modem standards, and AT commands
- ISPs and Internet backbone providers
- DSL
- Cable modems
- Cable modems versus DSL Internet technologies

Synchronous and Asynchronous Serial Lines

Serial lines that are established over serial cabling connect to one of the computer standard RS-232 communication (COM) ports. Serial transmission sends data 1 bit at a time. Analog or digital signals depend on changes in state (modulations) to represent the binary data. To correctly interpret the signals, the receiving network device must know precisely when to measure the signal. Therefore, timing becomes very important in networking. In fact, the biggest problem with sending data over serial lines is keeping the transmitted data bit timing coordinated. Two techniques are used to provide proper timing for serial transfers:

- *Synchronous serial transmission*—Data bits are sent together with a synchronizing clock pulse. In this transmission method, a built-in timing mechanism coordinates the clocks of the sending and receiving devices. This is known as guaranteed state change synchronization. Guaranteed state change synchronization is the most commonly used type of synchronous method.

- *Asynchronous serial transmission*—Data bits are sent without a synchronizing clock pulse. This transmission method uses a start bit at the beginning of each message. When the receiving device gets the start bit, it can synchronize its internal clock with the sender clock.

PC serial ports and most analog modems use asynchronous communication methods, whereas digital modems (also called terminal adapters) and LAN adapters use synchronous methods. The industry standard for the serial line interface is the Electronic Industries Association (EIA) RS-232C.

PC and modem makers have developed single-chip devices that perform all the functions necessary for serial transfers to occur. These devices are called Universal Asynchronous Receiver/Transmitters (UARTs). The synchronous devices are known as Universal Synchronous/Asynchronous Receiver/Transmitters (USARTs) and can handle both synchronous and asynchronous transmissions.

Modems

A *modem* is an electronic device that is used for computer communications through telephone lines. It allows data transfer between one computer and another. UARTs convert byte-oriented data to serial bit streams. Blocks of data are handled by software (internal modems combine a UART and a modem on board). Modems convert digital data to analog signals and analog signals back to digital data. Figure 3-44 shows an internal modem and its identifying features. The term *modem* derives from this device's function. The process of converting analog signals to digital and back again is called modulation/demodulation. Modem-based transmission is remarkably accurate, despite the fact that telephone lines can be quite noisy due to clicks, static, and other problems.

Figure 3-44 Internal Modem

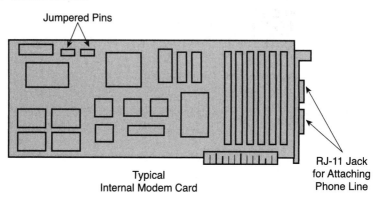

Jumpered Pins

Typical
Internal Modem Card

RJ-11 Jack
for Attaching
Phone Line

There are four main types of modems:

- Expansion cards are the most common. They plug into the motherboard expansion slots (ISA or PCI) and are called internal modems.

- PCMCIA modems are a variation of modems designed for easy installation in notebook computers. Also called PC cards, they look like credit cards and are small and very portable.

- External modems can be used with any computer by simply being plugged into a serial port (COM1 or COM2) on the back of the computer.

- Built-in modems are used in some notebook or laptop computers.

Internal modems simply plug into one of the expansion slots on the motherboard. They usually cost less than the ones that are plugged externally into the computer and do not take up extra space on the desktop. To configure them, you might have to set jumpers to select the IRQ and I/O addresses. No configuration is needed for a Plug-and-Play (PnP) modem, which is installed on a motherboard that supports PnP. A modem using a serial (COM) port that is not yet in use must be configured. Additionally, the software drivers that come with the modem must be installed for the modem to work. Figure 3-45 shows the main features you see on any typical external modem.

Figure 3-45 External Modem

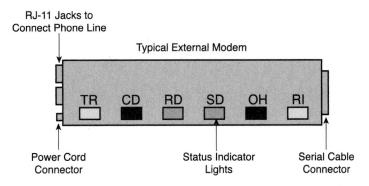

External modems are typically a bit more expensive than the internal varieties. However, they connect to the computer simply by plugging into one of the serial ports. The computer case does not have to be opened. Newer USB modems are plugged into a USB port or hub. An external modem uses the IRQ and I/O address assigned to the serial port. A status light on the modem indicates whether the modem is online. Software must be installed for the external modem to work properly. Figure 3-46 illustrates the modulation/demodulation process.

Figure 3-46 Modems

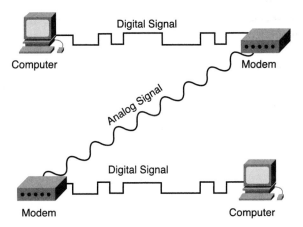

In most current modem types, a phone line is plugged into a standard RJ-11 telephone jack. Other modem types and devices, such as cable modem and DSL, are discussed later.

Dialup Networking, Modem Standards, and AT Commands

When computers use the public telephone system or network to communicate, it is called dialup networking (DUN). Computers can connect to the phone network using modems. Modems communicate with each other using audio tone signals, which means that they can duplicate a telephone's dialing characteristics. For example, if a computer is running Windows 95 or a later version, and a modem is being used to connect to a network (LAN or WAN), DUN establishes the connection. DUN creates a Point-to-Point Protocol (PPP) connection between the two computers over a phone line. In this process, PPP causes the modem to act like a network interface card. PPP is the WAN protocol that transports the networking protocol (TCP/IP, IPX/SPX, or NetBEUI) over the telephone line to allow network activity between the connected PCs.

The modem must operate in the following two states to enable DUN:

- **Local command state**—The modem is offline and is receiving commands and providing status information to the host computer to which the modem is installed.

- **Online state**—In this state, the modem transfers data between the host machine and a remote computer via the telephone system.

Three activities occur during the local command and online states. These states include dialing, data exchange, and answering. The modem normally shifts between the two states if, for example, the system tells it to go online and dial out to another unit or if the modem receives an incoming call.

After the line connection has been established, a *handshaking sequence* takes place between the two modems and their computers. This is nothing more than a flurry of short events that take place between the two systems. It establishes the readiness of the two modems and their computers to engage in data exchange. Dialup modems send data over the serial telephone line in the form of an analog signal. Analog signals can be drawn as waves because they change gradually and continuously. Recall that digital communications are based on binary. In this system, the digital signals represent 1s and 0s. These signals must be converted to a waveform to travel across telephone (analog) lines. They are converted back to digital form (1s and 0s) by the receiving modem so that the receiving computer can understand the data.

The outcome of the handshake and negotiation between the sending and receiving devices is the establishment of a common modulation that is supported by both computers. This completes the process of session negotiation so that effective data exchange can occur.

Other devices might determine the actual speed of data transfer. As previously mentioned, small single-chip devices (UARTs) run the COM port to which an external modem is attached. The type of UART chip determines the top speed at which devices can communicate using the port. Current UART 16450 and 16550 chips enable speeds of up to 115,200 bps, and the 16650 chip supports a transmission rate of 230,400 bps.

AT Commands

All modems require software to control the communication session. The set of commands that most modem software uses is known as the Hayes-compatible command set (named after the Hayes Microcomputer Products Company, which first defined them). The Hayes command set is based on a group of instructions that always begins with a set of attention characters, AT, followed by the command characters. Because these attention characters are always an important part of any Hayes command, the command set is usually called the AT command set. It is described in Table 3-7.

Table 3-7 AT Commands

AT Command	Function
AT	The attention code that precedes all modem action commands.
ATDP *xxxxxxx*	Dials the phone number *xxxxxxx* using pulse dialing.
ATDT *xxxxxxx*	Dials the phone number *xxxxxxx* using tone dialing.
ATA	Answers the phone immediately.
ATHO	Hangs up the phone immediately.
ATZ	Resets the modem to its power-up settings.
ATF	Resets modem parameters and settings to the factory default.
AT+++	Breaks the signal and changes from data mode to command mode.

Simply put, the AT commands are modem-control commands. The AT command set is used to issue dial, hang up, reset, and other instructions to the modem. Most user manuals that come with modems contain a complete list of the AT command set. This is just a summary of the most commonly used AT commands. The standard Hayes-compatible code to dial is ATD*xxxxx*. Sometimes a T is added to signify tone dialing.

ISPs and Internet Backbone Providers

The services of an Internet service provider (ISP) are usually needed to surf the Internet. An ISP is a company that connects computers to the Internet and World Wide Web. The connection to the Internet is tiered. This means that the ISP might link to a larger regional ISP, which in turn connects to one of a number of nationwide computer centers. Therefore, by just sitting in front of a computer and browsing the Internet, a user can benefit from hundreds or even thousands of computers that are networked. This can enable access to all kinds of documents, music downloads, and videos from all over the world.

When connecting to an ISP, the computer becomes a remote client on the ISP's local network. It is amazing how far the Internet has gone toward turning the entire world into a "global village." At the onset of the Internet era, a local computer or LAN had to have a direct connection to the Internet backbone, which was not affordable for individuals and smaller companies. Now, new technologies have led to easier and cheaper ways of building networks. ISPs today play a critical role in providing Internet access to most homes and businesses in this country. ISPs use more expensive and complex equipment to establish a point of presence, or access point, on the Internet. They either lease the dedicated high-speed lines from a telephone company or, in the case of large ISPs, install their own lines. Note that a very small, local ISP might not link directly to the Internet backbone. Instead, the small ISP might actually go through a larger regional ISP that is directly connected. Not all ISPs are created equal.

The current U.S. Internet infrastructure consists of a commercial backbone and a high-speed service known as the Very High-Speed Backbone Network Service (vBNS). The vBNS connects five supercomputer networks across the United States and is used for scientific purposes (see Table 3-8). The commercial backbone is basically an internetwork of commercially operated networks. Companies that provide the commercial backbone include the following:

- UUNET (a division of WorldCom)
- Cable & Wireless USA
- Sprint
- AT&T
- BBN Planet

Table 3-8 vBNS

Supercomputer Center	National Location
National Partnership for an Advanced Computational Infrastructure (NPACI)	San Diego, California
National Center for Atmospheric Research	Boulder, Colorado
National Center for Supercomputing Applications (NSCA)	Urbana, Illinois
Pittsburgh Supercomputing Center	Pittsburgh, Pennsylvania
Cornell Theory Center	Ithaca, New York

The vBNS connects five supercomputer networks across the country for scientific research.

ISPs connect to commercial networks. Usually the backbone providers and ISPs enter into agreements (called peering agreements) that allow them to carry one another's network traffic. In the United States, much of the physical cabling is still owned by the Regional Bell Operating Companies (RBOCs). They then lease it to the providers. The provider networks connect with T1, T3, or OC-3 lines.

An ISP that cannot connect directly to the national backbone is charged a fee to connect to a regional provider (see Table 3-9) that, in turn, links to the national backbone through a Network Access Point (NAP). A NAP, which provides data switching, is the point at which access providers are interconnected (see Table 3-10). However, not all Internet traffic goes through NAPs. Some ISPs that are in the same geographic area make their own interconnections and peering agreements. A Metropolitan Area Exchange (MAE) is the point where ISPs connect to each other and traffic is switched between them. MAE EAST (located in the Washington DC area) and MAE WEST (located in Silicon Valley, California) are the first-tier MAEs in the U.S.

Table 3-9 Regional Providers

Regional Provider	Region Covered
NEARNET and NYSERnet	Northeastern part of the U.S.
BARRNet	North-central California
MIDnet	Central part of the U.S.
SURAnet	Southeastern part of the U.S.
Westnet	Western part of the U.S.

These are the regional providers in the United States and the regions they cover. Regional providers are instrumental in allowing small ISPs to connect to the National Internet backbone.

Table 3-10 NAPs

NAP Location	Operating Company
Washington, DC	WorldCom
New York, New York	Sprint
San Francisco, California	Pacific Bell
Chicago, Illinois	Ameritech
Jacksonville, Florida	—

These are the NAP locations and the companies that operate them. The NAP is the point at which access providers are interconnected, and it provides data switching.

Figure 3-47 shows how Internet components work.

Figure 3-47 Internet Components

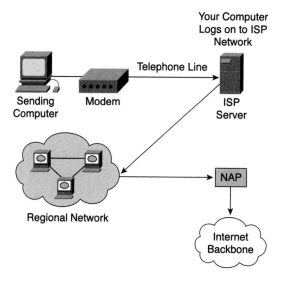

DSL

Digital Subscriber Line (DSL) is an always-on technology. This means that there is no need to dial up each time when connecting to the Internet. It is a relatively new technology currently being offered by phone companies as an add-on service over existing copper wire or phone lines.

DSL comes in several varieties:

- *Asymmetric DSL (ADSL)* currently is the most common implementation. It has speeds that vary from 384 kbps to more than 6 Mbps downstream. The upstream speed is typically lower.

- *High Data Rate DSL (HDSL)* provides bandwidth of 768 kbps in both directions.

- *Symmetric DSL (SDSL)* provides the same speed, up to 3 Mbps, for uploads and downloads.

- *Very High Data Rate DSL (VDSL)* is capable of bandwidths from 13 Mbps to 52 Mbps.

- *ISDN DSL (IDSL)* has a top speed of 144 kbps but is available in areas that do not qualify for other DSL implementations. IDSL is actually DSL over ISDN lines.

Table 3-11 summarizes useful information on the different varieties of DSL. The generic term for DSL, including all its implementations, is xDSL.

Table 3-11 DSL Types

DSL Variety	Average Speeds	Pros	Cons
ADSL	Downstream speeds of 384 Kbps to 6 Mbps. Upstream speeds are slower.	Most widely implemented of all the current DSL varieties. Relatively inexpensive.	Much slower upstream speed. Installed only within 17,500 feet of a telco central office (CO).
SDSL	Up to 3 Mbps for both upstream and downstream.	Same upstream and downstream data speeds.	Generally more expensive and also less widely available than ADSL.
IDSL	144 Kbps for both upstream and downstream.	Can be installed in many locations where other DSL varieties are unavailable due to distance.	Considerably slower speed, but more expensive than ADSL.

Transfer rates are often broken into upstream and downstream rates. Upstream is the process of transferring data from the end user to the server. Downstream is the process of transferring data from the server to the end user. For instance, when a username and password are submitted to gain access to an e-mail account, that data is uploaded, or transferred upstream, to the e-mail server. When the content of that mailbox is displayed on the web browser, that data is downloaded, or transferred downstream, to that computer.

ADSL is currently the most commonly used DSL technology. Its fast downstream speed, typically 1.5 Mbps, appears to work in its favor, because most Internet users spend the majority of their time doing tasks that require a lot of downloading, such as checking e-mail and surfing the web. The slower upload rate does not work that well when you're hosting a web server or FTP server, both of which involve upload-intensive Internet activities.

ADSL uses a technology called *frequency-division multiplexing (FDM)* to split bandwidth to create multiple channels. Other DSL implementations use another technique known as echo cancellation, which is more efficient but also more expensive. This ability to create multiple channels is why a user with DSL can surf the Internet while using the telephone to call a friend.

Cable Modems

A cable modem acts like a LAN interface by connecting a computer to the Internet. The cable modem connects a computer to the cable company network through the same coaxial cabling that feeds cable TV (CATV) signals to a television set. Generally, cable modems are designed to provide Internet access only, whereas analog modems and ISDN adapters allow dial-in to any service provider or service in a remote-access server. With a cable modem, the cable company must be used.

The cable modem service, similar to DSL, is also an always-on technology. A standard cable modem has two connections. One port is connected to the TV outlet, and the other is connected to the subscriber's PC. The cable modem then communicates over the cable network to the Cable Modem Termination System (CMTS). The cable modem's speed depends on traffic levels and how the overall network is set up. Although the server being contacted is at a remote location, the cable modem access is more like a direct LAN connection than remote access.

Cable modems can receive and process multimedia content at 30 Mbps, literally hundreds of times faster than a normal telephone connection to the Internet. In reality, subscribers can expect to download information at speeds of between 0.5 and 1.5 Mbps, because the bandwidth is shared by a number of other users. The modem receives digitally altered signals. A demodulator is built into the modem and, if it is a two-way modem, a burst modulator is used for transmitting data upstream.

Cable modems are available as internal and external units. Most internal cable modems are in the form of PCI cards. An external cable modem is a small box with a coaxial CATV cable connection. A splitter is used to divide the signal between the TV and the cable modem. The box is connected to an Ethernet card in the computer through UTP Ethernet. External USB devices might also be available, connecting the modem to the computer USB port without requiring an Ethernet card.

Currently, no standard exists for cable modems in the cable access industry. As a result, there are many competing proprietary products. Cable service, speed, reliability, setup, and configurations can vary significantly from one cable company to another. Currently, the most common cable modem brands are from Cisco Systems, 3Com, Com21, Bay Networks, Motorola, RCA, Toshiba, and Terayon. Figure 3-48 shows a typical Cisco cable modem.

Figure 3-48 Cisco Cable Modem

Cable Modems Versus DSL Internet Technologies

When it comes to comparing cable modem and DSL Internet technologies, both have their pros and cons. DSL service can be added incrementally in an area. This means that the service provider can upgrade the bandwidth as the subscriber base grows. DSL is also backward-compatible with analog voice and makes use of the existing local loop. This means that DSL service works simultaneously with normal phone service. However, DSL suffers from distance limitations, because most DSL services currently require the customer to be within 18,000 feet of the provider's central office location. Additionally, the longer and older loops present problems, and the best form of voice support is still being debated. Also, the upstream (upload) speed is usually considerably slower than the downstream (download) speed.

Conversely, cable modem technology presents plenty of relatively inexpensive bandwidth. The downstream and upstream Internet channels are seen as just another premium TV channel by the system. This is a major advantage, especially when you're hosting a web server or FTP server, which involves upload-intensive Internet tasks. The use of fiber (hybrid fiber-coaxial, or HFC) solves some of the service shortcomings initially encountered with this technology. Unfortunately, the cabling infrastructure needed to support cable modem technology has been slow to be upgraded, so most homes in the U.S. cannot use this technology. Upgrading is a big investment, particularly for small providers. The advantages and disadvantages of these two Internet technologies are summarized in Table 3-12.

Table 3-12 Advantages and Disadvantages of DSL and Cable Modem Connections

	Advantages	**Disadvantages**
DSL	DSL offers speeds up to and exceeding those of T1 at a fraction of the cost.	DSL's availability is presently still limited, with service for most "flavors" or varieties possible only in ISP areas that fall within a specified number of feet from the telephone company central office.
	DSL service can be added incrementally as more users subscribe.	The best form of voice support is still being debated.
	Both voice and data can be transmitted over the same line at the same time.	The telephone company central office that is servicing the location must have DSL equipment installed.
	DSL is an always-on technology. This means that users do not need to dial up each time they want to connect to the Internet.	
	DSL is backward-compatible with conventional analog phones.	
Cable	Existing cable TV systems offer plenty of available bandwidth for both upstream and downstream traffic.	Cable almost always requires an overhaul of the existing cable infrastructure.
	Cable TV infrastructure upgrade with HFC has addressed many of the existing service bottlenecks.	Being a shared media structure.

Summary

This chapter discussed a network's physical components. Some of the important concepts to retain from this chapter include the following:

- Important considerations when selecting a Network Interface Card (NIC) are the type of network, the type of medium to be used, and the type of system bus.
- In a TCP/IP-based LAN, PCs use Internet Protocol (IP) addresses to identify each other. These addresses can be assigned manually or with a Dynamic Host Configuration Protocol (DHCP) server.
- Physical topology refers to the layout of devices and media on a network. Logical topology refers to the path that signals travel on the physical topology.
- Networking media is defined as the means by which signals (data) are sent from one computer to another. It is important to understand the advantages and disadvantages of copper (including coaxial and twisted-pair cables), fiber-optic, and wireless connections.
- Timing is important in networking. PC serial ports and most analog modems use asynchronous communication methods, whereas digital modems (also called terminal adapters) and LAN adapters use synchronous methods.

The next chapter details the TCP/IP networking model. TCP/IP is the predominant protocol suite used in networking today.

Check Your Understanding

The following review questions help you assess what you learned in this chapter. Answers can be found in Appendix A, "Answers to Check Your Understanding Questions."

1. Which three of the following are advantages of a star topology?

    A. It's easy to add more nodes

    B. It requires less cable to connect computers

    C. It has a flexible topology

    D. It's less expensive to build than a bus topology

    E. It's easier to diagnose problems

2. Which topology provides connections for each node to every other node?

3. When selecting a NIC, which three of the following features must you consider?

    A. Network type

    B. Serial connection

    C. Medium

    D. Parallel connection

    E. System bus

    F. IRQ

4. Which component allows a computer to connect directly with the physical medium to connect to the LAN?

    A. Hub

    B. Active hub

    C. Network Interface Card (NIC)

    D. Modem

    E. Ethernet cable

5. You must consider three things when selecting an appropriate NIC to install. Which of the following choices do you *not* need to consider?

    A. Type of network

    B. Type of medium

    C. Type of protocol used

    D. Type of system bus

    E. Type of operating system

6. Select the options that are available to assign IP addresses for hosts on a LAN.

    A. Manual

    B. Static

    C. DNS

    D. Automatic

    E. Dynamic

7. Explain the difference between physical and logical topology.

8. The following definition is an example of what type of hub?

    It must be plugged into an electrical outlet, because it needs power to amplify the incoming signal before passing it back out to the other ports. It can manipulate and view the traffic that crosses it.

    A. Passive

    B. Intelligent

    C. Active

9. All the following choices are advantages of a star topology except which one?

    A. The star topology is flexible. The layout is easy to modify, and new hosts or devices can be added quickly.

    B. It is upgradeable. Adding a new computer is as easy as plugging the cable that is connected to the new workstation into the hub.

    C. It requires additional costly devices, such as hubs and switches, which are needed to run between the central device and each computer.

    D. It makes diagnosing problems relatively easy, because the problem is localized to one computer or device.

10. Fill in the following chart.

UTP Category	Maximum Transmission Speed	Characteristics and Uses
	Voice only	Used in old telephone installations
	4 Mbps	Not recommended for data transmission
	16 Mbps	Lowest recognized data grade; used for most telephone wiring
	20 Mbps	Suitable for networking 10 Mbps Ethernet networks
	100 Mbps	Most popular grade for LAN networking; used for Fast Ethernet/100

11. All the following choices are advantages of a cable Internet service over DSL service except which one?

    A. Existing cable TV systems offer plenty of available bandwidth for both upstream and downstream traffic.

    B. Much faster upstream data rates.

    C. Cable TV infrastructure upgrade with HFC has addressed many of the existing service bottlenecks.

    D. Backward-compatible with conventional analog phones.

Key Terms

active hub   A hub that must be plugged into an electrical outlet because it needs power to amplify the incoming signal before passing it back out to the other ports.

Asymmetric DSL (ADSL)   The most common DSL implementation. It has speeds that vary from 384 kbps to more than 6 Mbps downstream.

asynchronous serial transmission   Data bits are sent without a synchronizing clock pulse. This transmission method uses a start bit at the beginning of each message.

bridge   Makes intelligent decisions about whether to pass signals on to the next segment of a network.

broadcast domain   A logical area in a computer network where any computer connected to the computer network can directly transmit to any other computer in the domain without having to go through a routing device.

bus topology   All the devices are connected by a single cable, which proceeds from one computer to the next like a bus line going through a city.

coaxial cable   A copper-cored cable, surrounded by a heavy shielding, that is used to connect computers in a network.

collision domain   An area of the network that includes all the Ethernet segments that exist between any pair of switches or other Layer 2 devices.

default gateway   The router's near-side interface. It is the interface on the router to which the local computer network segment or wire is attached.

Digital Subscriber Line (DSL)   An always-on technology that provides Internet access over regular telephone lines.

dual ring   Two rings allow data to be sent in both directions, which creates redundancy.

Dynamic Host Configuration Protocol (DHCP)   A software utility that automatically assigns IP addresses to PCs.

extended star topology   A topology in which a star network is expanded to include an additional networking device, such as a hub or switch connected to the main networking device.

fiber-optic cable   A networking medium that can conduct modulated light transmissions. Fiber-optic cable is cabling that has a core made of strands of glass or plastic (instead of copper), through which light pulses carry signals.

frequency-division multiplexing (FDM)   The process of splitting bandwidth to create multiple channels. This ability is why a user with DSL can surf the Internet while using the telephone to call a friend.

High Data Rate DSL (HDSL)   Provides bandwidth of 768 kbps in both directions.

hub   A multiport repeater. In many cases, the difference between hubs and repeaters is the number of ports that each provides.

hybrid topology   Combines more than one type of topology. When a bus joins two hubs of different topologies, the configuration is called a star bus.

intelligent hub   Basically functions as an active hub but also includes a microprocessor chip and diagnostic capabilities.

Internet service provider (ISP)   A company that provides Internet access to homes and businesses.

IP address   A 32-bit binary number that is divided into four groups of 8 bits known as octets, each of which is represented by a decimal number in the range of 0 to 255. These addresses give computers that are attached to the network the ability to locate each other.

IR (infrared) technology   A common wireless technology in which workstations and digital devices must be in the transmitter's line of sight to operate.

ISDN DSL (IDSL)   Has a top speed of 144 kbps but is available in areas that do not qualify for other DSL implementations.

logical topology   The paths that signals travel from one point in the network to another.

mesh topology   Connects all devices (nodes) to each other for redundancy and fault tolerance.

modem   An electronic device that is used for computer communications through telephone lines by converting digital data to analog signals and analog signals back to digital data.

name resolution   The process of translating names to addresses that is done by the DNS server.

network interface card (NIC)   A device that plugs into a motherboard and provides ports for the network media connections. It is the component of the computer that interfaces with the LAN.

networking medium   The means by which signals (data) are sent from one computer to another.

passive hub   Serves as a physical connection point only. It does not manipulate or view the traffic that crosses it.

physical topology   The layout of the devices and media.

repeater   Receives the signal, regenerates it, and passes it on.

RF (radio frequency) technology   Allows devices to be in different rooms or even buildings. The limited range of the radio signals still restricts the use of this kind of network.

router   The most sophisticated internetworking device. It operates at the network layer of the OSI reference model. It is slower than a bridge or switch but makes "smart" decisions on how to route packets received on one port to a network on another port.

shielded twisted-pair   Combines the techniques of cancellation and twisting of wires with shielding. Each pair of wires is wrapped in metallic foil to further shield the wires from noise.

single ring   All the devices on the network share a single cable, and the data travels in one direction only.

star topology   Resembles spokes in a bicycle wheel. It is made up of a central connection point that is a device (such as a hub, switch, or router) where all the cabling segments meet.

subnet mask   Used to determine whether a particular host IP address is local (on the same network segment) or remote (on another segment).

switch   Also called a multiport bridge. Although a typical bridge might have just two ports (linking two network segments), a switch can have multiple ports, depending on how many network segments are to be linked.

Symmetric DSL (SDSL)   Provides the same speed, up to 3 Mbps, for uploads and downloads.

synchronous serial transmissions Data bits are sent together with a synchronizing clock pulse. In this transmission method, a built-in timing mechanism coordinates the clocks of the sending and receiving devices.

Thicknet A very large version of coaxial cable in which the diameter is rigid and difficult to install. In addition, the maximum transmission rate is only 100 Mbps.

Thinnet A thinner and more flexible version of coaxial cable that is occasionally used in Ethernet networks. Thinnet has the same transmission rate as Thicknet.

unshielded twisted-pair Used in a variety of networks. It has two or four pairs of wires and is the most commonly used cabling in Ethernet networks.

Very High Data Rate DSL (VDSL) DSL that is capable of bandwidths from 13 Mbps to 52 Mbps.

wireless network An alternative method of connecting a LAN in which there are no cables to run and computers can be easily moved. Radio frequency (RF), laser, infrared (IR), and satellite/microwaves are used to carry signals from one computer to another without a permanent cable connection.

Objectives

After completing this chapter, you will be able to complete tasks related to

- History of TCP/IP
- IP addressing
- Name resolution
- TCP/IP protocols

## Chapter 4

TCP/IP Networking

The U.S. Defense Advanced Research Projects Agency (DARPA) produced the designs and experimental networks that evolved into the public Internet. The Transmission Control Protocol/Internet Protocol (TCP/IP) network model that was developed is based on the OSI reference model. It is now the predominant protocol suite used in networking.

This chapter shows you how the layers of TCP/IP work together to communicate on a network, how addresses are assigned, and how a computer name is translated into an IP address and back again. Additionally, the functions performed by each of the major protocols that compose the TCP/IP protocol suite are discussed.

History of TCP/IP

This section covers the following topics:

- Origins and growth of TCP/IP
- The TCP/IP network model
- TCP/IP and network operating systems

Origins and Growth of TCP/IP

Inventions that begin in a government or military context often turn out to have great value in civilian life. For example, World War II stimulated the development of large computer systems. Similarly, military research sponsored by DARPA produced the designs and experimental networks that evolved into the public Internet. DARPA also accelerated the spread of TCP/IP by including it in distributions of the UNIX operating system.

In the competitive business world, private companies protect the technologies they develop by using patents and trade secrets to gain an advantage in the marketplace. A network system is called *closed* when one company owns and controls it. In contrast, the TCP/IP protocol suite is an *open* system. This means that the specifications for the Internet protocols were made publicly available so that any company could build computer hardware or software that implements them. This strategy allows customers to buy network products from different companies with the assurance that the products will work together (interoperate).

Based on TCP/IP open standards, the Internet has been enormously successful. In the early 1980s, the Internet connected only a few hundred computers. By the year 1997, it connected more than 16 million computers, and it had doubled in size approximately every ten months. Mathematicians call such growth *exponential*. Although the Internet cannot continue to grow indefinitely at this rate, no one can predict how large it can and will become. Today, corporations and individuals are increasingly dependent on the Internet to conduct business and the activities of daily life. Figure 4-1 describes the evolution and growth of the Internet.

Figure 4-1 Birth of the Internet

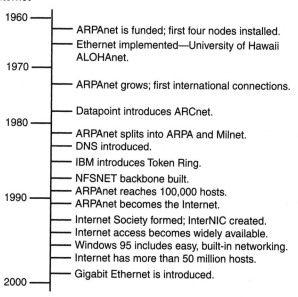

A look at the history of the telephone and the television can provide some insight into the speed at which TCP/IP technology has grown. Figure 4-2 compares how fast the Internet has grown in relation to other forms of technology. It took more than 38 years for radio to achieve *universal service*. Universal service means that almost all households in the technologically advanced world use and depend on access to radio. Television is now taken for granted as a source of news and entertainment. The first TVs appeared in living rooms in the late 1940s. However, it took 50 years to achieve universal service, in which most homes have one or more TVs. By comparison, the Internet has achieved most of its explosive growth within the past ten years and is now beginning to absorb elements of telephone and television systems. No other technology can match this achievement. Figure 4-3 shows how rapidly users, e-commerce, and web content have grown. It also shows the dramatic cost savings that the Internet has provided for various companies.

Figure 4-2 Internet Versus Other Technologies

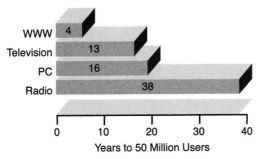

Figure 4-3 Internet Revolution

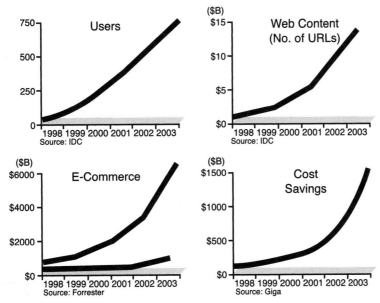

The TCP/IP Network Model

The TCP/IP network model closely resembles the OSI reference model. It is the predominant protocol suite used in networking today. The TCP/IP network model contains four layers, unlike the OSI reference model, which contains seven layers. The application layer is at the top, followed by the transport layer, the Internet layer, and the network interface layer. Figure 4-4 illustrates how the four layers of the TCP/IP network model map to the OSI reference model.

Figure 4-4 TCP/IP Network Model Compared to the OSI Reference Model

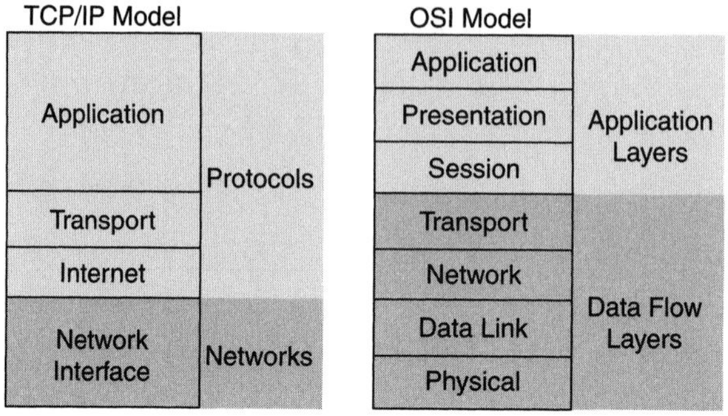

Application Layer

The application layer of the TCP/IP network model defines many of the applications that are used in networks throughout the world. The application layer is *not* the application itself that does the communicating. It is a service layer that provides these services. The application layer is responsible for performing many tasks. One of them includes determining protocol and data syntax rules at the application level. File Transfer Protocol (FTP) and Trivial File Transfer Protocol (TFTP) are TCP/IP-based applications used for file transfer. Common TCP/IP-based e-mail applications are Simple Mail Transfer Protocol (SMTP), Internet Message Access Protocol (IMAP), and Post Office Protocol version 3 (POP3). *Telnet*, which is used for remote administration, uses the TCP/IP protocol stack as well. The Simple Network Management Protocol (SNMP) is also defined in the TCP/IP protocol stack. Another task performed is ensuring agreement at both ends about error-recovery procedures, data integrity, and privacy. Session control is another major function that the application layer is responsible for. Session control includes features such as making sure that the other party is identified and can be reached, and making sure that necessary communication resources exist (for example, seeing if the sender's computer has a modem).

Transport Layer

The transport layer of the TCP/IP network model defines many of the same functions as the transport layer of the OSI reference model. However, unlike the transport layer of the OSI reference model, which defines protocols such as Novell SPX, the TCP/IP transport layer defines only Transmission Control Protocol (TCP) and User Datagram Protocol (UDP). (TCP and UDP functions are covered in greater detail later in this chapter.) Briefly, the purpose of transport layer protocols is to provide reliability and flow control. Reliability is achieved through a sequence of acknowledgments that guarantee the delivery of each packet. Flow control is achieved through the use of a technique called windowing, which allows communicating hosts to negotiate how much data will be transmitted during a given period.

Either TCP or UDP is used at the transport layer in TCP/IP networking, depending on the particular network environment and what type of data is being transmitted.

Port Numbers

Both TCP and UDP use port numbers to pass data to the upper layers. Port numbers help define and keep track of all the different types of conversations that take place throughout the network. Each application layer protocol, including FTP, Telnet, SMTP, DNS, TFTP, SNMP, and Routing Information Protocol (RIP), has a specific port number that identifies it and separates it from other protocols. These *well-known* port numbers are defined by the Internet Assigned Numbers Authority (IANA). Some of the most commonly used well-known port numbers are FTP (21), Telnet (23), SMTP (25), DNS (53), TFTP (69), SNMP (161), and RIP (520). Table 4-1 lists some of the major preassigned ports, protocols used, and applications that are designed to use the specific port numbers.

Table 4-1 TCP/UDP Well-Known Ports

Preassigned Port	Protocol	Application
80	TCP	HTTP
21	TCP/UDP	FTP
23	TCP/UDP	Telnet
25	TCP/UDP	SMTP
110	TCP/UDP	POP3
119	TCP/UDP	NNTP
137	TCP/UDP	NetBIOS name service
161	TCP/UDP	SNMP
194	TCP/UDP	IRC
389	TCP/UDP	LDAP
396	TCP/UDP	NetWare over IP
458	TCP/UDP	Apple QuickTime
500	TCP/UDP	ISAKMP

A system administrator should become familiar with the port number system and should closely monitor the types of traffic flow into and out of the network. The system administrator can specify which types of traffic are allowed into a network by permitting or denying Internet traffic based on these port numbers. This process of filtering based on port numbers is usually accomplished with routers or firewall devices. There are risks associated with allowing traffic into a network based on port number. Many hackers use port scanners to find open ports in networks to gain unauthorized access.

Internet Layer

The Internet layer of the TCP/IP network model (also called the network layer) defines addressing and path selection. This is the same function as performed by the network layer in the OSI reference model. Routers use Internet layer protocols to identify an appropriate path for data packets as they travel from network to network. Some of the protocols defined at this layer are IP, Internet Control Message Protocol (ICMP), Address Resolution Protocol (ARP), and Reverse Address Resolution Protocol (RARP). The IP provides addressing that routers use to move data to the desired destination. The ICMP provides control and messaging capabilities, which are used when there is a problem somewhere in the network. ICMP is used to send a message back to the host, informing it that the destination host was unreachable. Figure 4-5 shows some of the Internet layer's responsibilities. ICMP is also the basis for the PING and TRACEROUTE commands. *Address Resolution Protocol (ARP)* is used to find the MAC address of a host, switch, or router when given its IP address. RARP is very similar to ARP. RARP is used when a host's MAC address is known but its IP address is unknown. Table 4-2 outlines some of the major TCP/IP utilities that are available.

Figure 4-5 Internet Comtrol Message Protocol

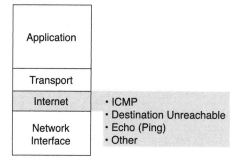

Table 4-2 Internet Control Message Protocol

Utility	Use
ARP/RARP	To view IP address-to-MAC address entries that have been resolved by ARP, to delete entries from the ARP cache, and to add permanent IP-to-MAC mappings.
Netstat (Windows/UNIX), tpcon (NetWare)	To view network connections and protocol statistics.
Nbtstat (Windows)	To view connections and statistics for NetBIOS over TCP/IP (NetBT).
Ipconfig (Windows NT/2000), Winipcfg (Windows 95/98), Config (NetWare), Ipconfig (UNIX)	To view TCP/IP configuration information such as IP address, subnet mask, default gateway, MAC address, services enabled, and more.
Tracert (Windows), Iptrace (NetWare), Traceroute(UNIX)	To discover the route taken by a packet on its journey from the source to the destination computer and to identify the routers through which it passes.
Ping	To determine IP connectivity between two systems.

Network Interface Layer

The network interface layer of the TCP/IP network model maps to the data link and physical layers of the OSI reference model. This layer defines TCP/IP-specific functions related to the preparation of data for transmission over the physical medium, including addressing. The network interface layer also specifies what types of media can be used for data transmission.

 Worksheet 4.1.2 The TCP/IP Network Model

Covers the principles and standards for the TCP/IP network model.

TCP/IP and Network Operating Systems

In the 1980s, a number of companies designed and sold network operating systems (NOSs) that allowed LAN users to share expensive devices and information. Generally, these products employed a client/server model in which client computers made requests for information or for the use of devices, and server computers responded to these client requests. Companies such as Novell, Banyan, Apple, IBM, and Microsoft competed for network customers.

To carry the requests and responses between clients and servers, NOS vendors designed their own special rules or protocols. Novell called its protocols IPX/SPX, Banyan called its protocols VINES, Apple produced AppleTalk, and IBM and Microsoft used NetBIOS. Each of these solutions was closed, or *proprietary,* meaning that it was owned and controlled by one company. Customers could not combine systems from different companies in their networks, because they used different languages (or protocols) that were incompatible with each other.

Today, all NOS vendors have adopted the TCP/IP protocol suite for carrying data between client and server systems. Figure 4-6 represents how the TCP/IP protocol is used to manage the communication exchange between two computer systems. Although the older proprietary protocols remain in use, TCP/IP is the standard that is implemented by all the NOS vendors. Understanding the components of the TCP/IP protocol is necessary to understand communication in a NOS environment.

Figure 4-6 TCP/IP

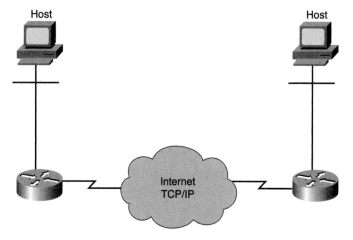

IP Addressing

This section covers the following topics:

- IPv4 addressing
- IPv4 addressing overview
- Class A addresses
- Class B addresses
- Class C addresses
- Class D and E addresses
- The IPv4 address crisis
- Subnetting

IPv4 Addressing

For any two systems to communicate, they must be able to identify and locate each other. Figure 4-7 illustrates how IP addresses can be used to locate other computer systems when data must travel and be forwarded by other network hardware such as switches and routers. In everyday life, names or numbers (such as telephone numbers) are often used as unique identifiers. Similarly, each computer in a TCP/IP network must be given at least one unique identifier, or address. This address allows one computer to locate another on a network. Figure 4-8 shows how specific numbers are assigned to computers so that they can locate and distinguish between one another.

Figure 4-7   TCP/IP Addresses

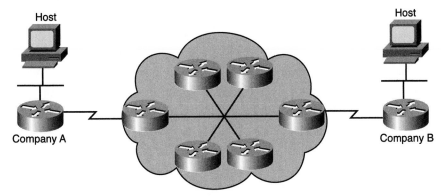

Figure 4-8 Host Addresses

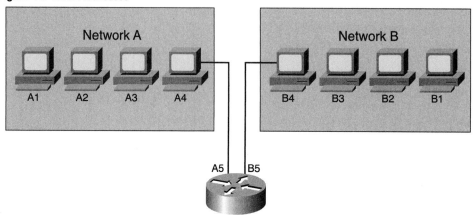

A computer can be connected to more than one network. If this is the case, the system must be given more than one address, each address identifying its connection to a different network. Strictly speaking, a device cannot be said to have an address. Each of its connection points (or interfaces) to a network has an address that allows other computers to locate it on that particular network.

IPv4 Addressing Overview

TCP/IP is designed as an internetworking set of protocols. IP forwards packets from the network on which they originate to the destination network. This addressing scheme, therefore, must include an identifier for both the source and destination networks.

By using the network identifier, IP can deliver a packet to the destination network. As soon as the packet arrives at a router connected to the destination network, IP must locate the particular point where the destination computer is connected to that network. Figure 4-9 shows how the addresses represent the path to travel through the various media connections. This works in much the same way as the postal system. When mail is routed, it first is delivered to the post office at the destination city using the zip code, and then that post office must locate the final destination in that city using the street address. This is a two-step process.

Figure 4-9 Network Layer: Communication Path

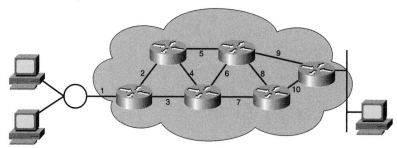

Accordingly, every *IP address* has two parts. One part identifies the network to which the system is connected, and the second part identifies that particular system on the network. This kind of address is called a *hierarchical address*, because it contains different levels and because the address can be broken into two parts, with each part being used as an identifier. Another example of a hierarchical address is a telephone number. Each part of a telephone number identifies the phone's location. The country code identifies which country the phone is in. The area code represents the city or area within the country in which the phone is located. The other parts of the number even further define where the phone is located. An IP address combines these two identifiers into one number. This number must be a unique number, because duplicate addresses are not allowed. The first part tells you which network the system is located on. The second part, the host part, tells you which particular machine it is on that network. Figure 4-10 illustrates this hierarchical addressing system and how it is used to identify computer systems across the network.

Figure 4-10 Addressing: Network and Host

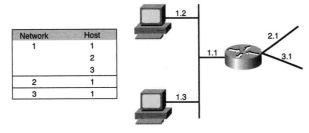

Inside a computer, an IP address is stored as a 32-bit sequence of 1s and 0s. Figure 4-11 shows one of these 32-bit numbers. To make the IP address easier to use, it is usually written as four decimal numbers separated by periods. For instance, an IP address of one computer is 192.168.1.2. Another computer might have the address 128.10.2.1. This way of writing the address is called *dotted-decimal* format. Each part of the address is called an *octet* because it is made up of eight binary characters. For example, the IP address 192.168.1.8 in binary notation is 11000000.10101000.00000001.00001000.

Figure 4-11 IP Addressing Format

How does a user determine which portion of the address identifies the network and which portion identifies the host? The answer begins with the designers of the Internet, who thought that networks would be built in different sizes, depending on the number of computers (hosts) they contained. It was thought that there would be a relatively small number of large networks, possibly with millions of computers each. The designers envisioned a larger number of medium-sized networks, with perhaps thousands of computers each. Finally, they saw a great number of networks having several hundred or fewer machines. Thus, the designers divided the available IP addresses into classes to define the large (Class A), medium (Class B), and small (Class C) networks, as shown in Table 4-3. Knowing the class of an IP address is the first step in determining which part of the address identifies the network and which part identifies the host. Tables 4-4 and 4-5 illustrate how the IP address ranges are classified.

Table 4-3 IP Address Classes

IP Address Class	Number of Networks	Number of Hosts Per Network
A	126[*]	16,777,216
B	16,384	65,535
C	2,097,152	254
D (multicast)	—	—

[*]The 127.x.x.x address range is reserved as a loopback address, used for testing and diagnostic purposes.

Table 4-4 Identifying Address Classes

IP Address Class	High-Order Bits	First Octet Address Range	Number of Bits in the Network Address
A	0	0–126[*]	8
B	10	128–191	16
C	110	192–223	24
D	1110	224–239	28

[*]The 127.x.x.x address range is reserved as a loopback address, used for testing and diagnostic purposes.

Table 4-5 IP Address Classes

	1 Byte 8 Bits	1 Byte 8 Bits	1 Byte 8 Bits	1 Byte 8 Bits
Class A	N	H	H	H
Class B	N	N	H	H
Class C	N	N	N	H

N = network number assigned by ARIN
H = host number assigned by the administrator

 Worksheet 4.2.2   IPv4 Addressing Overview

Covers the principles involved in converting and creating IPv4 Internet addresses.

Class A Addresses

In a Class A address, the first number (octet) is the network portion, and the last three numbers are the host portion. The format is network.host.host.host, or N.H.H.H. For example, in the address 56.1.2.3, the first octet (56) identifies the network, and the last three octets (1.2.3) identify the host on that network. Address 56.1.2.4 identifies a different host (1.2.4) on the same network (56). The address 57.1.2.3 identifies host 1.2.3 on network 57.

Because of the way the address is stored in binary in the computer, the first octet always falls between 1 and 127. If the first octet in an IP address falls in the range 1 to 127, it is a Class A address. Figure 4-12 illustrates a Class A address, showing the host and network portions of the address. Only 1 to 126 is valid for Class A networks, because 127.0.0.1 is reserved. This address, known as the *local loopback* address, is used to test the local system's NIC.

Figure 4-12 Class A Address

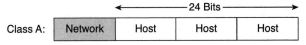

Class B Addresses

A Class B IP address divides the network portion and the host portion between the second and third octet. The format is N.N.H.H. For example, the address 165.5.6.7 represents network 165.5 and host 6.7.

Because of the way Class B addresses are stored in binary, the first octet always falls in the range 128 to 191. If the first octet in an IP address is greater than 127 but less than 192, it is a Class B address. Figure 4-13 illustrates a Class B address, showing the host and network portions of the address.

Figure 4-13   Class B Address

Class C Addresses

A Class C IP address divides the network portion and the host portion between the third and fourth octet. The format is N.N.N.H. For example, the address 192.8.9.10 represents network 192.8.9 and host 10.

Because of the way Class C addresses are stored in binary, the first octet always falls in the range 192 to 223. If the first octet of the IP address is greater than 191 but less than 224, it is a Class C address. Figure 4-14 illustrates a Class C address, showing the host and network portions of the address.

Figure 4-14   Class C Address

Class D and E Addresses

Class D and Class E addresses are used for special purposes. Class D is reserved for a technique called *multicast,* and Class E addresses are used for experimental purposes. Commercial organizations use Class A, B, or C addresses to identify networks and hosts. Figure 4-15 shows an example of the Class D address architecture.

Figure 4-15 Class D Address

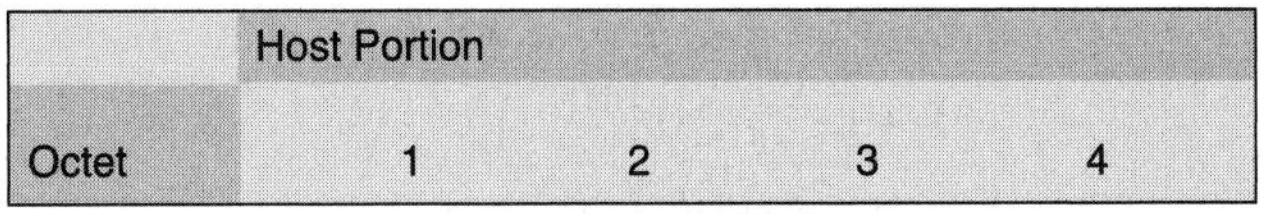

Octet	Host Portion			
	1	2	3	4

The IPv4 Address Crisis

The designers of the early Internet could not have foreseen the explosive growth that the Internet has experienced. They naturally believed that the number of addresses required to identify interconnected networks and host systems would be sufficient for many years to come. They assigned addresses to companies and organizations as requests were made. By the mid-1980s, however, it became clear that unless some action were taken, the number of unused addresses would diminish rapidly, and the Internet would face a crisis that would be the result of its own success.

The total number of addresses that are available for use is called the *address space.* Think about what might happen if the telephone companies used up all the available phone numbers (that is, their address space) for telephones, fax machines, and other devices that allow communication over the phone system. No new phones could be connected to the system, and that would stop its expansion. The Internet was faced with this situation when it appeared that growth would be limited or even stopped because the Internet address space could become exhausted.

In response to this problem, Internet engineers developed a set of techniques to make more efficient use of the Internet address space. Among these techniques was the subnetting of networks. *Subnetting* is the process of splitting a network portion of an IP address. This allows an administrator to partition or divide a network without having to use a new address for each network partition. By using subnetting techniques, the designers of networks could divide them using the same network number, but each partition would be given its own subnet number. Remote systems could still reach the network by sending packets to the destination network address. As soon as the packets arrived at the boundary of the destination network, they could be forwarded to the appropriate subnet within the network. This technique has been very successful in conserving the number of major network addresses and allowing for continued growth of the Internet. Figure 4-16 shows a network address that has been subnetted.

Figure 4-16 Subnets and Subnet Mask

SOLUTION: Create another section in the IP
address called the **Subnet**.

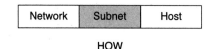

HOW

By Using a **Subnet Mask**

The basic idea is to take the IP address, which is divided into a network portion and a host portion, and then divide it further by adding a third part, the subnet number. The result is an address that has the form network number, subnet number, host number. As discussed earlier, the address is divided into the network portion and the host portion by knowing its class. When a subnet number is added between the network and host portions, how is the part that identifies the subnet identified?

To answer this question, you must understand the function of another number that was invented to go along with subnetting—the *subnet mask*. Like the IP address itself, this new number is written in dotted-decimal notation as four octets that represent 32 bits. In the mask number, 1 values are placed if the corresponding bit in the IP address belongs to the network or subnet part of the address. 0 values are placed in the mask where the corresponding bit in the IP address is part of the host portion. So, if the class of the IP address is known, and the subnet mask is known, the IP address can be divided into network-subnet-host. It takes some practice to thoroughly understand this process.

Whereas the class of an IP address determines the size of the network part, the size of the subnet part can vary. The information needed to determine the size of the subnet part is contained in the mask. Write the mask in binary as 1s and 0s. This takes practice in converting decimal numbers to binary. Next, proceed as follows:

- Identify the address's class.
- Eliminate any 1 bits from the mask that correspond to the network part of the address.
- The remaining 1 bits in the mask indicate the bits in the address that are the subnet part of the address.

Private IP Addresses

When dealing with IP addresses, corporate networks, and home networks, it is important that you know the difference between private IP addressing and public IP addressing. IPv4 refers to version 4 of the IP, and the number of these available public IP addresses is quickly diminishing. The reason is that there is a limit to the number of IP addresses that IPv4 can provide. To help reserve the number of public IP addresses that are available, the concept of private IP addressing is used. The address ranges of the reserved private IP addresses are shown in Table 4-6. This means that, for example, a corporation might have only a few IP addresses that are public or "known." All the IP addresses that the company uses within its network are contained within its network and therefore are considered private. They are considered private because they are "known" only to the company administrator and are not "known" to the public. Figure 4-17 illustrates this process, showing how private IP network address are used within the WAN.

Table 4-6 Private IP Network Addresses

Class	RFC 1916 Internal Address Range	CIDR Prefix
A	10.0.0.0 to 10.255.255.255	10.0.0.0/8
B	172.16.0.0 to 172.31.255.255	176.16.0.0/12
C	192.168.0.0 to 192.168.255.255	192.168.0.0/16

Figure 4-17 Using Private Addresses in the WAN

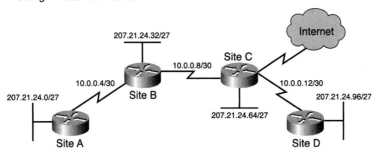

Network Address Translation (NAT)

The concept of public and private IP addressing can be further explained through the use of *Network Address Translation (NAT)*. NAT lets companies keep their private addresses secure and not known to the public. NAT is enabled on a router or gateway device that translates all the incoming and outgoing traffic through the known or public IP addresses. Figure 4-18 illustrates how the IP address structure might appear when you're using NAT. As you can see, the internal IP address is different and is kept private from the external public address, which is exposed to others through the Internet. The public IP addresses are what allow people with the company to access information and networks outside the LAN by connecting to other public IP addresses. NAT also provides security by hiding the IP addresses of clients and servers within the company network. This is done by assigning the public IP address to the NAT device. If someone attempts to gain access to the network, he is directed to the NAT device and then usually is stopped by a firewall in place on the same system or device that NAT is configured on.

Figure 4-18 NAT Router

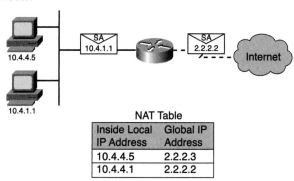

IP6

IPv6 stands for Internet Protocol Version 6. IPv6 is the next-generation protocol designed to replace the current version of the Internet Protocol, IPv4. The following examples show how IPv6 addresses are numbered.

IPv6 addresses are written in hexadecimal:

> 1080:0000:0000:0000:0008:0800:200C:417A

Leading 0s in each 16-bit value can be omitted. So the same address can be expressed as the following:

> 1080:0:0:0:8:800:200C:417A

Because IPv6 addresses, especially in the early implementation phase, may contain consecutive 16-bit values of 0, one such string of 0s per address can be omitted and replaced by a double colon. As a result, this address can be shortened as follows:

> 1080::8:800:200C:417A

Most of the Internet now uses IPv4, which is nearly 20 years old. IPv4 has been remarkably resilient in spite of its age, but it is beginning to have problems. Most importantly, there is a growing shortage of IPv4 addresses, which are needed when new systems are added to the Internet.

IPv6 fixes a number of problems in IPv4, such as the limited number of available IPv4 addresses. It will also add many improvements to IPv4 in routing and in various network-configuration tasks. IPv6 is expected to gradually replace IPv4, with the two coexisting for a number of years during a transition period.

Software is available that supports IPv6. This software is available only in the latest releases, such as Windows XP, and some of the latest versions of Linux. Many common Internet applications already work with IPv6, and more are being adapted.

Subnetting

It is impossible to cover TCP/IP without mentioning subnetting. As a system administrator, you must understand subnetting as a means of dividing and identifying separate networks throughout the LAN. Figure 4-19 shows how a network can be subnetted. It shows how internally networks can be divided into smaller networks called subnetworks, or simply subnets. By providing this third level of addressing, subnets offer a network administrator extra flexibility. For example, a Class B network address provided by the American Registry for Internet Numbers (ARIN) can be broken into many smaller and more manageable subnets. In Figure 4-19, the three networks 131.108.1.0, 131.108.2.0, and 131.108.3.0 are all subnets of the network 131.108.0.0. It is not always necessary to subnet a small network, but subnetting is required for large or extremely large networks. Figure 4-20 shows why it is important to subnet a large network. Subnets are similar to the American telephone numbering system. This numbering system is divided into area codes, which are divided into exchanges, which are divided into individual connections. Subnet addresses specify a network number, a subnet number within the network, and a host number within the subnet. Simply stated, subnetting is a means to use the subnet mask to divide the network and break a large or extremely large network into smaller, more efficient and manageable segments (subnets). Figure 4-21 shows a 32-bit binary address that is subnetted.

Figure 4-19 Addressing with Subnets

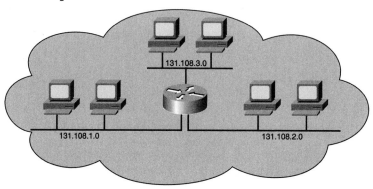

Figure 4-20 Subnet Addresses

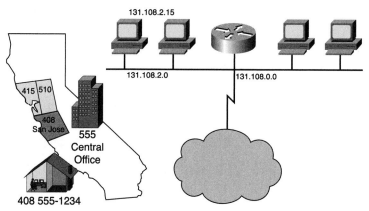

Figure 4-21 32-Bit Binary IP Address

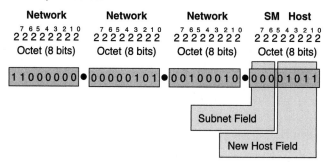

Subnet Masks

An understanding of subnetting requires an understanding of subnet masks. The IP address 210.168.1.8, for example, is a Class C IP address (remember, Class C addresses fall in the 192 to 223 range). The corresponding default subnet mask is 255.255.255.0, which is a Class C subnet mask. The method of distinguishing the network portion of the address from the host part of the address was discussed previously. The first three octets represent the network portion of the address. The last octet is reserved for the host address.

Class A default subnet masks are 255.0.0.0. A Class B default subnet mask is 255.255.0.0, and a Class C address range has a default subnet mask of 255.255.255.0. Table 4-7 lists the Class A, B, and C network masks.

Table 4-7 Default Network Masks

Address Class	Binary Network Mask	Decimal Network Mask
A	11111111.00000000.00000000.00000000	255.0.0.0
B	11111111.11111111.00000000.00000000	255.255.0.0
C	11111111.11111111.11111111.00000000	255.255.255.0

The subnet mask helps identify all computers on the 255.255.255.0 network. Therefore, all the hosts on this network have an IP address of 210.168.1.x. They all contain the same values in the first three octets of their IP address, but the x that represents the host portion of the address is unique for every computer on the network. This is the value that identifies the host on network 210.168.1.0. The IP address 210.168.1.8 identifies a specific host on network 201.168.1.0.

The available maximum number of hosts that are allowed on a Class C network is 254. The range of IP addresses that can be given to these hosts is 210.168.1.1 to 210.168.1.254 for a total of 254 hosts. You can determine the number of hosts on a particular subnet or network by using the formula $2^N - 2$. Here, N equals the number of available octets for host addresses.

There cannot be 255 hosts because that value is reserved for a broadcast address. For example, the IP address 210.168.1.255 cannot be used as a host address on the 210.168.1.0 network because it is reserved as the broadcast address for that network.

Examples:

In a Class C subnet mask (255.255.255.0), only one octet is available for hosts. Convert these octets to decimal notation and get 8 bits (one octet) left for a host address. Apply this formula:

$2^8 - 2 = 254$ hosts on a Class C network

For a Class B (255.255.0.0) network, 16 bits are available for a host address. Apply this formula:

$2^{16} - 2 = 65,534$ hosts on a Class B network

For a Class A (255.0.0.0) network, 24 bits are available for a host address. Apply this formula:

$2^{24} - 2 = 16,777,124$ hosts on a Class A network

The system administrator must resolve these issues when adding and expanding the network. It is important to know how many subnets/networks are needed and how many hosts will be allowed to be on that network. With subnetting, the network is not limited to the standard Class A, B, or C subnet masks, and you have more flexibility in the network design. Table 4-8 is a quick reference chart.

Table 4-6 Quick Reference Subnetting Chart

Decimal Notation for First Octet	Number of Subnets	Number of Class A Hosts Per Subnet	Number of Class B Hosts Per Subnet	Number of Class C Hosts Per Subnet
.192	2	4,194,302	16,382	62
.224	6	2,097,150	8,190	30
.240	14	1,048,574	4,094	14
.248	30	524,286	2,046	6
.252	62	262,142	1,022	2
.254	126	131,070	510	—
.255	254	65,534	254	—

The following example describes how to create a subnet for 1500 hosts. A Class B subnet mask provides 65,534 hosts. A Class C subnet mask provides only 254. However, only 1500 hosts are needed. Creating a subnet that provides 65,534 hosts would be a huge waste of space. It is possible to create a subnet mask that gives the required 1500 hosts but doesn't use all 65,534. This is done by "borrowing" bits from an octet to create a subnet mask.

A subnet is required that provides 1500 hosts. A Class C subnet mask cannot be used, so a Class B subnet is used instead:

255.255.0.0

This provides 65,534 hosts, but all the other host addresses should not be wasted. Use the $2^N - 2$ formula to determine the subnet mask. (Converting to the binary form was discussed in the section "IPv4 Addressing Overview.") For example, the subnet mask 255.255.0.0 is equal to the following:

11111111.11111111.00000000.00000000

To create the subnet mask you need to conserve these IP addresses, you must borrow 5 bits from the third octet. By doing this, you create a subnet mask that limits the number of subnets you can use to 30. However, instead of having 65,534 available hosts, you have only 2046 hosts. This creates a subnet mask that provides the 1500 hosts you need, and then you don't have to waste the rest of the IP addresses. The new subnet mask is as follows:

11111111.11111111.**11111000**.00000000 = 255.255.248.0

Now, instead of 16 bits, 11 bits are available for a host address. Remember that 16 bits are used for host addresses with a standard Class B subnet mask, and 8 are used with a standard Class C address. This allows more than 254 but fewer than 65,534 hosts. The $2^N - 2$ formula helps you calculate how many hosts this subnet mask provides:

$2^{11} - 2 = 2046$ hosts

2046 hosts provide the 1500 hosts you need, with 546 host addresses left over. If the leftover hosts do not get used, only 546 hosts are wasted, not 65,534. From this example, you can see that in a large network where the number of IP addresses is limited, subnetting can help conserve IP addresses.

Worksheet 4.2.8   Subnetting

Covers the main concepts involved in subnetting IP addresses.

Name Resolution

This section covers the following topics:

- Overview of name resolution
- Host names and host tables
- The domain name system
- Name services and the NOS
- WINS

Overview of Name Resolution

IP address numbers are necessary to identify points of connection to a network, and they are designed to make possible the efficient operation of networked devices. But in their numeric form, addresses are difficult to remember and manage. This is especially true when there is a need to change addresses to adapt to changing network conditions. Although network devices use numeric addresses, names are easy to work with. The technique that allows names to represent network addresses is *name resolution*.

For example, you can access the website Cisco.com without knowing the IP address that the device at Cisco is configured to use. A name-resolution service translates, or *maps*, the name Cisco.com to an IP address to reach the destination device. A device can be named for its function or purpose, or even to attract attention. Networking names, such as Yahoo.com and Amazon.com, have become well known among users of the World Wide Web. Names are also used to identify the location or function of network devices. For example, a router named San Jose indicates its location, and the host name Eng-Server indicates its function in the engineering department.

Using names to represent addresses provides another advantage. Because users now can identify network devices by name, the address that corresponds to a given name can be changed without any disruption. Users of the network can continue to use the same name to refer to the device and leave it up to the name-resolution service to find the new address that equates to that name. This makes the network much easier to use and administer. Networks use host tables and the Domain Name Service (DNS) to associate names with addresses.

Host Names and Host Tables

On the network, each computer is given a unique name to identify it. This name is used to communicate with a particular computer. Figure 4-22 shows an example of the host-name settings for a particular computer system. To reach another computer, the network needs to use that computer's IP address. *Host tables* are lists that can be configured in each computer, associating the names of the computers in the network with the IP address host table. Table 4-9 is a sample host table. You can see that it includes the IP address and name that are mapped to that address.

Figure 4-22 Host Names and Host Tables

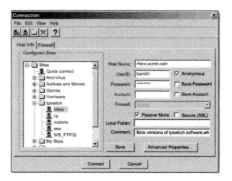

Table 4-9 Sample Host Table

IP Address	Mapping Name	Unique Name
102.54.94.7	rhino.acme.com	# source server
38.25.63.10	x.acme.com	# x client host
127.0.0.1	localhost	—

On a computer using a host table, a user can refer to another computer by name, and the computer looks up the name in the host table and finds its IP address. The IP address can even be changed, and that system can still be referred to by the same name. When a computer must reach the other system, it finds the new address in the host table.

Although a host table allows communication with other computers by name, it has some disadvantages. For one, a host table must be configured in each separate computer to tell it the names and corresponding IP addresses of each of the other computers. In a large network with many computers, this requires much configuration. Second, when there is a change in the network (the addition of a new computer, for example), the tables must be updated in every computer to reflect the change. The task of maintaining accurate host tables in a large network can be time-consuming and error-prone.

The Domain Name System

Using host tables requires a lot of maintenance. In contrast, the *Domain Name System (DNS)* assigns this task to servers in the network. The work of translating names into addresses is accomplished by specialized servers within the network. Host computers are then relieved of keeping a list of name-to-address mappings. This simplifies network maintenance and allows greater flexibility.

The DNS works like directory assistance in the phone system. A person's name and address might be known, but not his phone number. A call to the directory assistance operator produces the phone number that matches the name and address. If the phone number of a person in another country is needed, the operator might need to contact the directory assistance service in another country. DNS works in a similar way. The service is distributed across a number of systems. Each one knows the addresses for a set of names and knows how to reach other servers to find addresses for names outside its scope. For example, when an application on a computer in California needs to know the IP address of a computer in South Africa, the application sends its request to a DNS in California. The server in California might not know the answer, but it does know how to connect to the appropriate server in South Africa.

To guarantee that the full names of any two computers are different, the Internet has adopted a naming system that uses additional strings of letters, or suffixes, after the names. The parts of a name are separated by periods. This is similar to IP addresses, but there is no relationship between the parts of a name for a system and its IP address. The *Internet name* marx.ps.uofr.edu, for example, might have the IP address 128.11.3.2. The string marx is unrelated to the 128. Neither are any other parts of the name related to parts of the address. The whole name corresponds to the whole address.

In the name marx.ps.uofr.edu, the final suffix, .edu, identifies the type of organization (an institution of higher education). The .uofr suffix identifies a particular university (the University of Rochester). The .ps identifies a department (political science), and the name marx identifies a particular computer. Other common final suffixes include .com for commercial organizations, .gov for governmental agencies, and .net for network enterprises.

The task of setting up and maintaining domain name servers falls to network administrators. To make use of the DNS, each host or client system must be configured with the address of at least one DNS server to contact for translating names into addresses.

A program becomes a client of the DNS when it sends a computer name to the local DNS server. The program asks for the IP address of the system with that name. The local server might contact other servers to translate the name into an address, but the client receives the answer from the local server. Figure 4-23 illustrates the process of a client system's requesting DNS information from the server.

Figure 4-23   DNS

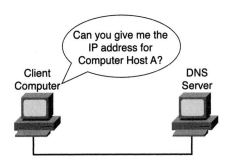

Name Services and the NOS

In NOSs, user programs can access network devices and services by name. Today, all NOSs use DNS to translate computer names into IP addresses. But before the general adoption of TCP/IP and the Internet domain naming system by the makers of different NOSs, other naming techniques were used to identify systems and services. To accommodate earlier naming schemes and the applications that use them, NOS vendors have developed extensions to DNS that allow their own types of names to be associated with IP addresses. In this way, applications that use the older naming conventions can find the IP addresses of devices and services.

One older but widely used service for communicating between client applications and network services is the *Network Basic Input/Output System (NetBIOS)*. This service was developed by IBM in 1985 and is still used on Microsoft Windows computers. To translate the names used by NetBIOS applications into IP addresses, Microsoft developed an addition to DNS called the *Windows Internet Naming Service (WINS)*. Figure 4-24 shows the DNS configuration page on a Windows 2000 system.

Figure 4-24   Name Services and the NOS

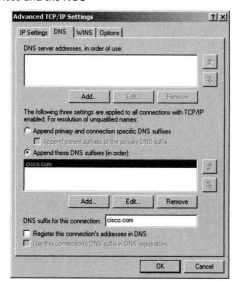

WINS

WINS is not a built-in part of the Internet DNS name-to-address service. To *resolve* or map the NetBIOS names used by applications into IP addresses, Microsoft added WINS as an extension to DNS. WINS automates the process of translating NetBIOS names into IP addresses so that packets can be properly delivered to devices or services. A WINS server dynamically associates NetBIOS names with IP addresses and automatically updates its database of name-to-address associations as systems enter and leave the network, so it does not require ongoing maintenance. Client systems, however, must be configured with the address of a WINS server that performs this translation. Figure 4-25 shows the WINS configuration page on a Windows 2000 system. Microsoft is making efforts to phase out the WINS service because NetBIOS is largely not used in many networks today.

Figure 4-25 WINS

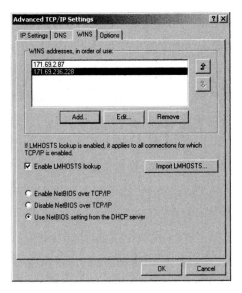

TCP/IP Protocols

This section covers the following topics:

- Overview of TCP/IP protocols
- Address Resolution Protocol (ARP)
- Internet Control Message Protocol (ICMP)
- Transmission Control Protocol (TCP)
- User Datagram Protocol (UDP)
- DHCP services
- Hypertext Transport Protocol (HTTP)
- File Transfer Protocol (FTP)
- Telnet
- SMTP
- POP3
- IMAP

Overview of TCP/IP Protocols

A *protocol* is a set of messages that is exchanged between systems in a defined sequence to accomplish a specific networking task. The layout, or format, of the messages is strictly defined, and the rules for the exchange of messages between systems are strictly specified in standards documents. TCP/IP is a *suite* or collection of different protocols, each one performing a specialized task. In a well-functioning network, the individual protocols are coordinated so that, taken together, they deliver network services to application programs. Figures 4-26, 4-27, and 4-28 show which protocols function at the specific layers of the TCP/IP network model. Like a specialist on a construction team, each protocol performs its particular function at a particular time. Each one depends on the work of the others. The following section outlines the functions performed by each of the major protocols that compose the TCP/IP protocol suite.

Figure 4-26 Application Layer

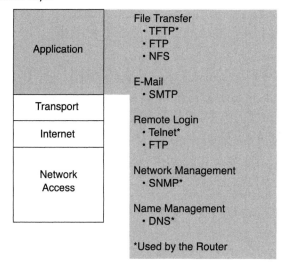

Figure 4-27 Transport Layer

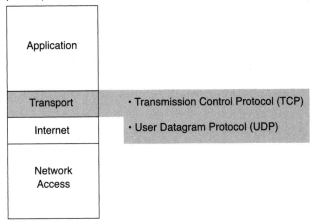

Figure 4-28 Internet Layer

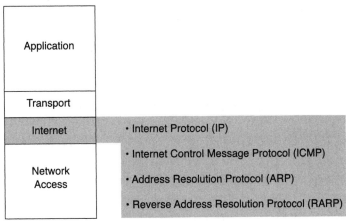

Address Resolution Protocol

The Address Resolution Protocol (ARP) comes into play when a system begins a conversation with another host on a local-area network (LAN). Figure 4-29 illustrates the communication process that occurs between systems using ARP.

Figure 4-29 Address Resolution Protocol

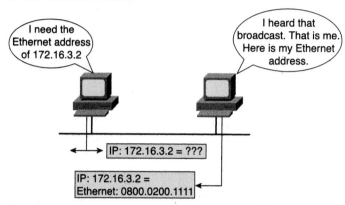

The first system knows that the second is located somewhere on the network (its IP address), but it does not know its exact location on the network (its Ethernet address). This problem is similar to knowing that someone named Mary is in a classroom, but not knowing in which seat she is sitting. To discover Mary's seat number, the whole class could be asked, "If your name is Mary, please tell me where you are." Assuming that only one person named Mary is in the room, Mary raises her hand to identify her seat number. ARP consists of mapping network addresses with Media Access Control (MAC) addresses. When the source (system A) and destination (system B) systems are both attached to the same LAN, the source (system A) broadcasts an ARP request to find the MAC address of the intended destination (system B). Because the signal sent is a broadcast message, it is heard by all the devices in LAN broadcast domain, including the destination (system B) device. However, only the destination (system B) device responds to the ARP request. System B sends an ARP reply message that contains its MAC address to the source (system A) device. System A then saves the MAC address in its ARP cache. When system A needs to communicate with system B again, it only needs to check its ARP cache to find the MAC address of system B, and then it can send data directly without having to send an ARP request first.

Internet Control Message Protocol (ICMP)

A network requires tools for reporting errors that might arise, and network administrators need tools for discovering the reasons for errors. The *Internet Control Message Protocol (ICMP)* provides a set of error and control messages to help track and resolve network problems. Figure 4-30 shows at which layer of the TCP/IP network model ICMP operates. Suppose, for example, that a physical path in the network fails, and some hosts become unreachable. Figure 4-31 illustrates the scenario in which ICMP is used to send a "Destination Unreachable" message when an error somewhere in the network prevents the frame or packet from being forwarded to the destination system or device. ICMP includes a type of message called an echo request that can be sent from one host to another to see if it can be reached on the network. Figure 4-32 illustrates the scenario in which ICMP is used to send an echo reply message to see if the destination system or device is available and can be reached. If it can be reached, the destination host replies with an ICMP echo reply message. The Ping program uses ICMP to send echo request messages and receive echo reply messages.

Figure 4-30 Internet Control Message Protocol

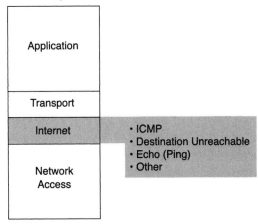

Figure 4-31 ICMP Testing: Destination Unreachable

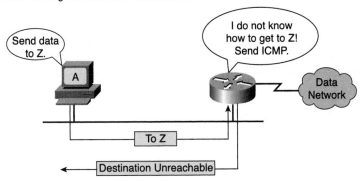

Figure 4-32 ICMP Testing: Echo Reply

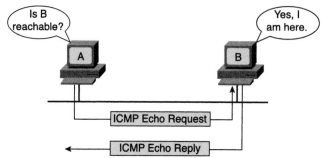

As another example, suppose a remote host can be reached from a local computer, but the path that messages take to reach that host is unknown. ICMP allows the path, or route, from the local computer to the remote host to be traced using the Traceroute routine. The ICMP troubleshooting tools are part of almost every TCP/IP protocol stack. ICMP is also used in instances where an undeliverable packet might arrive at a server or router. If a router or server is unable to deliver a packet to its destination, the router sends an ICMP "Destination Unreachable" message back to the source to inform it of the problem. The router then discards the original packet. Destinations might be unreachable because the sending host specified a nonexistent address or, although less frequent, the router might not know the route to the destination. If a router cannot deliver an ICMP message for whatever reason, it does not send an ICMP message to report the failure. Doing so could flood the network with an endless saturation of ICMP messages. For this reason, an undeliverable ICMP message is discarded. Another important issue to know about ICMP messages is reachability. ICMP messages are also sent by systems and devices to test the reachability of another system or device across the network. Any TCP/IP host can send an ICMP echo request. An ICMP echo request is generated by the Ping command.

Transmission Control Protocol (TCP)

Two programs might communicate with each other across a series of many interconnected networks. An e-mail application, for example, might send a message to a mail server in another city or country for the recipient to read. The IP forwards the message from one network to the next, but it might not be able to deliver the message to the destination because of network problems. IP makes its best effort, but it does not guarantee delivery of the message. The *Transmission Control Protocol (TCP)* has the job of guaranteeing that messages arrive at their destination or, if they cannot be delivered, informing the application programs of the failure. Applications such as e-mail must have the guarantee that TCP provides. This is also true of other applications, such as web browsers, that require the reliable delivery service provided by TCP. As soon as a TCP connection is made between two applications, all the messages flow from the origin to the destination over that logical connection. Figure 4-33 shows how TCP establishes a logical connection.

Figure 4-33 TCP Establishing a Logical Connection

User Datagram Protocol (UDP)

Whereas some applications require a reliable, guaranteed delivery service (TCP), others do not. They need a service that makes its best effort to deliver messages but does not guarantee delivery. Just as the post office makes its best effort to deliver the mail, but does not guarantee that letters will arrive at their destination, *User Datagram Protocol (UDP)* provides an "unreliable" service to applications that can tolerate a loss of some messages but still function. Applications that send streams of video or audio data fall into this category. They can experience a certain amount of data loss and still function in a way that is acceptable to network users. Other applications that use UDP include the DNS and some forms of file transfer, including TFTP. Each UDP message is sent independently of the others without first establishing a logical connection between the origin and destination. The characteristics that identify the UDP protocol are as follows:

- Unreliable
- Fast
- Assumes that the application will retransmit on error
- Often used in diskless workstations

DHCP Services

The purpose of the *Dynamic Host Configuration Protocol (DHCP)* is to allow individual computers on an IP network to extract their configurations from a DHCP server. When a computer on the network needs an IP address, it sends a request to a DHCP server. The DHCP server can then provide the host computer with all the configuration information it needs, including IP address, subnet mask, gateway, DNS and WINS server, and domain. DHCP also allows for recovery and the ability to automatically renew network IP addresses through a leasing mechanism, which allocates an IP address for a specific time period and then releases it and assigns a new IP address. DHCP is a widely used method of reducing the work necessary to administer a large IP network. Figure 4-34 shows the process that takes place when a client requests a DHCP IP address from the DHCP server.

Figure 4-34   DHCP Request

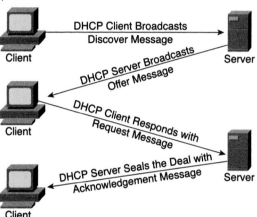

Hypertext Transport Protocol

The *Hypertext Transport Protocol (HTTP)* specializes in the transfer of World Wide Web pages between web browser client programs such as Netscape Communicator and Internet Explorer and web servers, where web pages are stored. Figures 4-35 and 4-36 show two popular web browsers, Internet Explorer and Netscape Navigator. HTTP defines the exact format of the requests that the browser sends, as well as the format of the replies that the server returns. The content of web pages is organized using Hypertext Markup Language (HTML). The rules for transporting these pages make up the HTTP protocol.

Figure 4-35 Internet Explorer

Figure 4-36 Netscape Navigator

File Transfer Protocol (FTP)

Whereas HTTP specializes in the transfer of web page files, the *File Transfer Protocol (FTP)* is used to transfer any type of file from one system to another. This includes text documents, graphics, sounds, videos, and program files. FTP is a general-purpose protocol that can be used to copy all types of files from one computer to another. FTP makes use of the TCP reliable transport services to establish a logical connection between the systems. FTP is one of the most heavily used protocols on the Internet. Figure 4-37 shows an FTP client that is connected to an FTP server. On the left side are the local system files, and on the right are the folders and files that are located on the FTP server that are available for download.

Figure 4-37   FTP

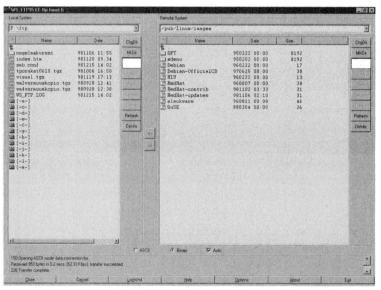

Telnet

To interact with and control a particular local computer or network device, users normally connect a monitor or terminal to the system and log on to it. The Telnet protocol allows users to connect and log on to a remote system from their computers. Telnet enables interactive terminal communications with remote systems as if they were directly connected to the terminal, even though many networks might separate the terminal from the remote system. Using Telnet, users can type commands to the system as if they were directly connected to it. Telnet uses the services of TCP to establish a logical connection between the terminal and the remote computer. This connection is called a Telnet session. Figure 4-38 shows an established Telnet session from a Windows 2000 workstation to a Red Hat Linux 7.2 server.

Figure 4-38 Telnet

SMTP

Simple Mail Transfer Protocol (SMTP) is a protocol for sending e-mail messages between servers. Figure 4-39 illustrates the relationship that an SMTP server has with a client system. This figure illustrates how a client system that sends e-mail must do so through the SMTP e-mail server. Most e-mail systems that send mail over the Internet use SMTP to send messages from one server to another. The messages can then be retrieved with an e-mail client using either Post Office Protocol (POP) or Internet Message Access Protocol (IMAP). In addition, SMTP is generally used to send messages from a mail client to a mail server. Figure 4-40 shows how you might configure a client system to use the SMTP server. This is why both the POP or IMAP server and the SMTP server must be configured in an e-mail application.

Figure 4-39 SMTP

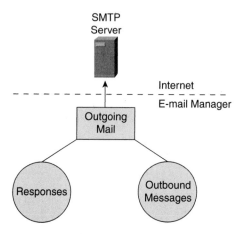

Figure 4-40 SMTP Mail Server Preferences

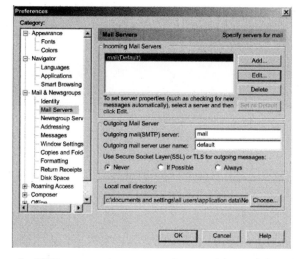

After establishing the TCP connection to port 25 (used by SMTP), the sending machine, operating as the client, waits for the receiving machine, operating as the server, to talk first. The server starts by sending a line of text giving its identity and saying whether it is prepared to receive mail. If it is not, the client releases the connection and tries again later.

If the server is willing to accept e-mail, the client announces from whom the e-mail is coming and to whom it is going. If a recipient exists at the destination, the server gives the client the go-ahead message. Then the client sends the message, and the server acknowledges it. If there is more e-mail, it is now sent. When all the e-mail has been exchanged in both directions, the connection is released.

POP3

Post Office Protocol version 3 (POP3) is a common mail service protocol that is used by ISPs that provide Internet and e-mail service to home customers. POP3 permits a workstation to retrieve mail that the server is holding. Figure 4-41 illustrates the relationship that an e-mail server has with client systems. It shows how a client system that receives e-mail must do so through the SMTP e-mail server. After the mail is retrieved, it can be deleted from the server. Figure 4-42 shows a typical client interface that is used to configure the system to use a POP3 e-mail server to retrieve e-mail.

Figure 4-41   POP3

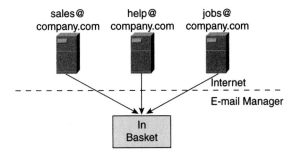

Figure 4-42   POP3 Mail Server Properties

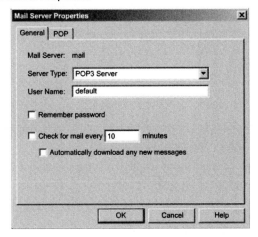

IMAP

Internet Message Access Protocol (IMAP) is a newer e-mail protocol that is more robust than POP3. IMAP is offered by many ISPs. Some of them are even discontinuing their POP3 support. IMAP is a method of accessing e-mail or bulletin board messages that are kept on a mail server. IMAP is fully compatible with Multipurpose

Internet Mail Extension (MIME) Internet messaging standards, and it allows message access and management from more than one computer. Also, the client software needs no knowledge of the server file store format. Figure 4-43 shows a typical client interface that is used to configure the system to use a POP3 e-mail server to retrieve e-mail.

Figure 4-43   IMAP

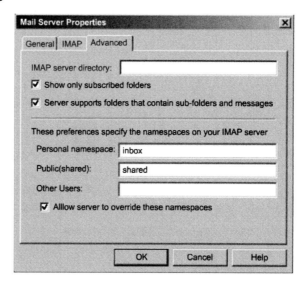

Summary

This chapter discussed TCP/IP. Some of the important concepts to retain from this chapter include the following:

- A network system is called closed when one company owns and controls it. In contrast, the TCP/IP protocol suite is an open system.
- The four layers that make up the TCP/IP network model are the application layer at the top, followed by the transport layer, the Internet layer, and the network interface layer.
- Every IP address has two parts. One part identifies the network to which the system is connected, and the second part identifies that particular system on the network.

- Available IP addresses are placed into classes to define large (Class A), medium (Class B), and small (Class C) networks.

- Subnetting a network means to use the subnet mask to divide the network and break a large or extremely large network into smaller, more efficient, more manageable segments, or subnets.

- Networks use two basic techniques to associate names with addresses: host tables and the Domain Name Service (DNS).

- The major protocols that comprise the TCP/IP protocol suite include Address Resolution Protocol (ARP), Internet Control Message Protocol (ICMP), Transmission Control Protocol (TCP), User Datagram Protocol (UDP), Dynamic Host Configuration Protocol (DHCP), Hypertext Transport Protocol (HTTP), File Transfer Protocol (FTP), Telnet, Simple Mail Transfer Protocol (SMTP), Post Office Protocol version 3 (POP3), and Internet Message Access Protocol (IMAP).

An important network service is remote administration. Information to accomplish this and other network services is provided in the next chapter on Network Operating Systems (NOSs).

Check Your Understanding

The following review questions help you assess what you learned in this chapter. Answers can be found in Appendix A, "Answers to Check Your Understanding Questions."

1. Enter the layers of the OSI reference model and map them to the corresponding layers of the TCP/IP network model. Layer names may be used more than once.

OSI Reference Model	TCP/IP Network Model

2. Enter the *well-known* port number for each protocol.

Protocol	Port Number
DNS	
FTP	
RIP	
SMTP	
SNMP	
Telnet	
TFTP	

3. Convert the decimal number 206 to binary.

4. ARP is used to find a host's _____ given its _____.

5. Match the dotted-decimal number with the appropriate term.

Term	Number
Host address	192.168.140.255
Subnet mask	192.168.140.11
Broadcast address	192.168.140.0
Network address	255.255.255.0

6. Which layer of the TCP/IP network model determines protocol and data syntax rules; ensures agreement at both ends on error-recovery procedures, data integrity, and privacy; and maintains session control?

   A. Network interface

   B. Internet

   C. Application

   D. Transport

7. Which layer of the TCP/IP network model defines addressing and path selection? Routers use the protocols that function at this layer to identify an appropriate path for data packets as they travel from network to network.

   A. Network interface

   B. Internet

   C. Application

   D. Transport

8. What formula helps you determine the number of available host addresses?

9. Determine the address class and calculate the subnet of the given network address in the following IP address and subnet mask:

15.5.6.18

255.255.255.240

10. Determine the address class and calculate the subnet of the given network address in the following IP address and subnet mask:

108.163.211.115

255.255.128.0

Key Terms

Address Resolution Protocol (ARP)   A discovery protocol that helps a server or other network device such as a router locate where other systems are on the network.

Domain Name System (DNS)   The process of assigning and associating a name with an IP address to help identify and locate other client and server systems throughout the network.

Dynamic Host Configuration Protocol (DHCP)   Allows individual computers on an IP network to extract their IP address configurations from a DHCP server automatically when they start up without having to manually configure them.

File Transfer Protocol (FTP)   A general-purpose protocol that can be used to copy all types of files from one computer to another.

hierarchical address   A naming system in which the name consists of multiple parts, with each part of the address being an identifier.

host table   A list that can be configured in each computer, associating the names of the computers in the network with the IP address host table.

Hypertext Transport Protocol (HTTP)   The protocol that is used to transfer World Wide Web pages between web browser client programs such as Netscape Communicator and Internet Explorer and web servers, where web pages are stored.

Internet Control Message Protocol (ICMP)   An error correction and control protocol that provides a set of error and control messages to help track and resolve network problems.

Internet Message Access Protocol (IMAP)   A newer e-mail protocol that is more robust than POP3. IMAP is a method of accessing e-mail or bulletin board messages that are kept on a mail server.

Internet name   A naming system that uses additional strings of letters, or suffixes, after the names to guarantee that the full names of any two computers will be different.

IP address   A two-part number used to identify a system on the network. One part identifies the network to which the system is connected, and the second part identifies that particular system on the network.

Network Address Translation (NAT)   A technique that lets companies keep their private addresses secure and unknown to the public by translating all the incoming and outgoing traffic through "known" or public IP addresses.

Network Basic Input/Output System (NetBIOS)   A widely used service for communicating between client applications and network services in older, small, native Windows networks.

Post Office Protocol version 3 (POP3)   A common mail service protocol that is used by ISPs that provide Internet and e-mail service to home customers. POP3 permits a workstation to retrieve mail that the server is holding.

protocol   A set of messages and rules that is exchanged between systems in a defined sequence to accomplish a specific networking task.

Simple Mail Transfer Protocol (SMTP)   A protocol for sending e-mail messages between servers.

subnet mask   A 32-bit dotted-decimal number that is assigned to networks and used to differentiate between networks that are subnetted.

subnetting   Using the subnet mask to divide the network and break a large or extremely large network into smaller, more efficient, more manageable segments, or subnets.

Telnet   Allows users to connect and log on to a system that is remote from their computers as if they were directly connected to the terminal, even though many networks might separate the terminal from the remote system.

Transmission Control Protocol (TCP)   A connection-oriented protocol that guarantees that messages arrive at their destination or, if they cannot be delivered, informs the application programs of the failure.

universal service   How long it takes almost all households in the technologically advanced world to use and depend on access to a certain technology.

User Datagram Protocol (UDP)   Provides an "unreliable" service to applications that can tolerate a loss of some messages but still function.

Windows Internet Naming Service (WINS)   An addition to DNS that native Windows systems use to translate the names used by NetBIOS applications into IP addresses.

Objectives

After completing this chapter, you will be able to complete tasks related to

- Network services
- Remote administration and access services
- Directory services
- Other NOS services

Chapter 5

Overview of Network Services

This chapter introduces network operating systems. The ability to access a remote system is also discussed. This allows a system administrator to efficiently maintain a network. A directory service provides system administrators with centralized control of all users and resources across the entire network. You will learn about other network operating system services that allow users to communicate, share files, and print. You will also learn how to access the Internet, an intranet, and an extranet.

Network Services

Network operating systems (NOSs) are designed to provide network processes to clients and peers. Network services include the World Wide Web (WWW), file sharing, mail exchange, directory services, remote management, and print services. Remote management is a powerful service that allows administrators to configure networked systems that are miles away. It is important to understand that these network processes are called *services* in Windows 2000, *daemons* in Linux, and *Netware Loadable Modules (NLMs)* in Novell. Essentially they all provide the same functions, but how they are loaded and interact with the NOS is different in each operating system. Services, daemons, and NLMs are covered in more detail in later chapters.

Depending on the NOS, some of these key network processes might be enabled during a default installation. Most popular network processes rely on the TCP/IP suite of protocols. Table 5-1 lists some of the most popular TCP/IP-based services. Because TCP/IP is an open, well-known set of protocols, TCP/IP-based services are especially vulnerable to unauthorized scans and malicious attacks. Denial of service (DoS) attacks, computer viruses, and fast-spreading Internet "worms" have forced NOS designers to reconsider which network services are started automatically.

Table 5-1 TCP/IP-Based Services

Service	TCP/IP Protocol
World Wide Web server	HTTP
File transfer	FTP, TFTP
File sharing	Network File System (NFS)
Internet mail	SMTP, POP3, IMAP
Remote administration	Telnet
Directory services (Internet)	DNS, LDAP
Automatic network address configuration	DHCP
Network administration	SNMP

Recent versions of popular NOSs, such as Windows 2000 and Red Hat Linux 7, restrict the number of network services that are "on" by default. When deploying a NOS, you need to enable some key network services manually.

 Worksheet 5.1.1   Network/NOS Services

Covers identifying the various network/NOS services and matching these services with the proper terminology.

Remote Administration and Access Services

This section covers the following topics:

- What is remote access?
- Telecommuting
- Mobile users
- Terminal emulation services
- Telnet services
- Configuring remote access for a client
- Controlling remote-access rights
- Remote administration on a Linux system

What Is Remote Access?

Remote access is becoming more important as network users become more mobile and as companies expand their business to multiple locations or open their resources to selected outsiders without putting those resources on the Internet.

Some popular uses of remote access include the following:

- Connecting branch offices to one another
- Providing a means for employees to connect to the network after business hours
- Allowing employees to telecommute by working at home on a part-time or full-time basis
- Allowing employees who are on the road, such as traveling salespeople or executives on business trips, to connect to the corporate network
- Giving company clients or partners access to network resources

In an expanding global economy, even small businesses frequently need to open offices at multiple sites. If these locations can connect to the network at headquarters, up-to-date information can easily be shared, and resources can easily be pooled.

When the need for access is infrequent, or when it applies to only a few computers, a dialup connection might suffice. Then, at the headquarters office, a networked computer can be set up as the dialup server. Users at the branch office can dial and connect to the network when necessary. For many corporate employees, the workday spills over into off-duty time. Executives and others often take work home. They might need to connect to the corporate network after business hours, especially if they have to work across time zones.

With a remote-access connection, employees can access the corporate remote-access server and log in to the network with their regular user accounts. Then they can use all the resources that would be available from the office desktop computer. Figure 5-1 illustrates how this process is accomplished via a service provider.

Figure 5-1 Remote Access

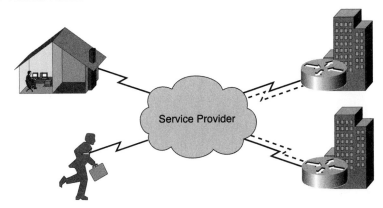

Telecommuting

A large number of employees, including creative personnel, technical writers, software programmers, salespeople, and clerical staff, work from home all or part of the time. These workers telecommute to the office and stay in touch throughout the day through e-mail, live chat, and even audio and videoconferencing.

Telecommuting is attractive to employees because it saves travel time and other costs associated with working in an office, such as business attire, lunches out, and transportation costs. It saves the company money as well, because office space for telecommuting employees is not required.

Dialup access is the most common way for telecommuting employees to connect to the company LAN, although in some cases a dedicated connection might make more sense. If a company has many telecommuting employees, the remote-access server requires multiple modems (a modem bank) so that numerous connections can be made simultaneously. Of course, each modem requires its own telephone line, as shown in Figure 5-2.

Figure 5-2 Telecommuting

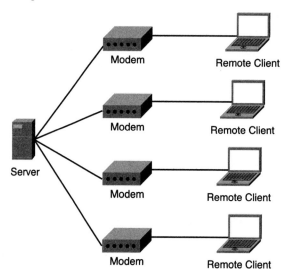

Mobile Users

Business travel is becoming more prevalent as companies market their products on a national or international scale. Salespeople, recruiters, trainers, top-level management personnel, and others can spend a great deal of time on the road. The needs of mobile users are similar to those of after-hours users.

It can be difficult or impossible to store all the files needed on a laptop or notebook computer. It is a security threat as well, because the laptop and its contents could be stolen. A better solution might be for mobile users to dial in to the company LAN. As shown in Figure 5-3, their user accounts are authenticated, and they can access the data here instead of copying it to their own hard disk.

Figure 5-3 Mobile Users

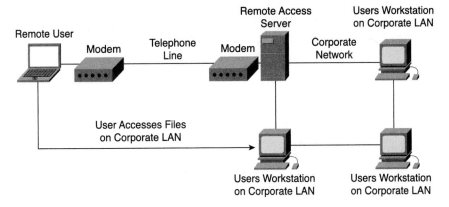

Terminal Emulation Services

Terminal emulation is the process of accessing a remote system via a local computer terminal, as shown in Figure 5-4. The local terminal runs software that emulates, or mimics, the look of the remote system terminal. Using terminal emulation, the local user can type commands and execute programs on the remote system. The terminal emulation program runs on the local system like any other program. On a Windows system, users can run a terminal emulation program in one window while running separate applications in other windows.

Figure 5-4 Using Terminal Emulation

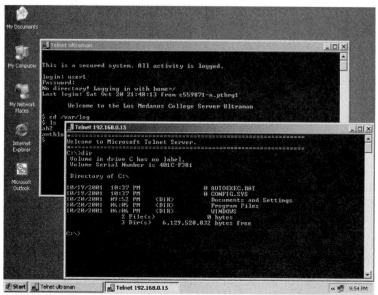

Different types of terminal emulation are required for specific types of terminals. Here are some of the terminal types common in computer networking:

- IBM 3270
- DEC VT100
- AS/400 5250
- TTY

The most common terminal emulation application is Telnet, which is part of the TCP/IP protocol suite. Telnet provides a command-line interface (CLI) that allows clients to access a remote server. Windows, UNIX, and Linux NOSs support Telnet services.

In addition to remote management, terminal emulation can be used to deliver applications and services to clients. For example, an organization can install a high-end application on the server and then allow underpowered clients to access the application via terminal emulation. From the end user's point of view, the high-end application appears to run locally on the client machine. In reality, the application is run on the server, which probably has significantly more processing horsepower and RAM.

Telnet Services

Telnet is the main Internet protocol for creating a connection with a remote machine. It gives the user the opportunity to be on one computer system and do work on another, which might be across the street or thousands of miles away. Telnet provides an error-free connection. It has the following security considerations:

- Hacking
- Password guessing
- DoS attacks
- Packet sniffing (viewable text data)

Telnet is covered further in Chapters 8 and 9 as it relates specifically to Windows 2000 and Linux. Figures 5-5 and 5-6 illustrate a remote user accessing a Windows 2000 server using Telnet services.

Figure 5-5 Remote User Accessing a Server Via Telnet

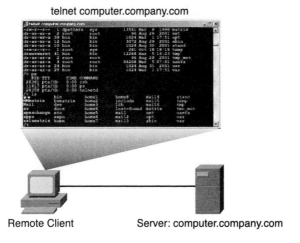

Figure 5-6 Windows 2000 Telnet Server Administration

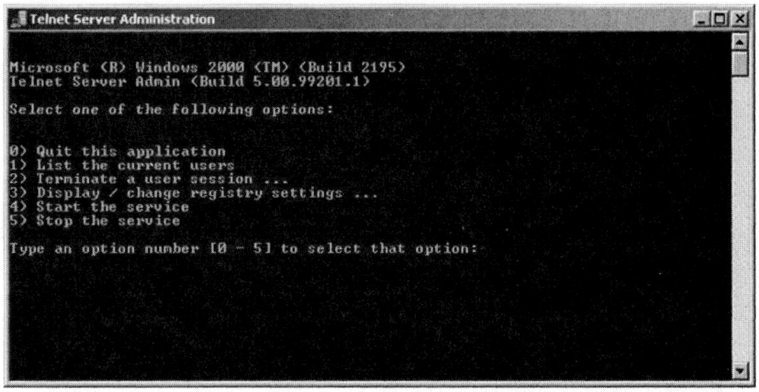

Configuring Remote Access for a Client

Today most computers are connected to the network on a permanent basis through the system's network card. These types of connections are done by assigning IP addresses to the system (this was covered in Chapter 4, "TCP/IP Networking"). Sometimes establishing a remote connection to a computer must be done in other ways when the computer is located somewhere that is not connected to the network with an IP address. In that case, a dialup telephone connection, ISDP, or broadband connection must be used to connect to the computer.

Point-to-Point Protocol

Point-to-Point Protocol (PPP) can be used to establish a TCP/IP link between two computers using a modem. A PPP connection is designed to be used for only short periods of time, because it is not considered an "always-up" Internet connection. Some ISPs offer full-time PPP links, but this is not the recommended means of running a connection to a server. Some configuration is necessary to initiate and establish a PPP connection on a Linux system. The first step is making sure that the PPP daemon, pppd, is installed. The PPP daemon can both initiate and respond to attempts to initiate a connection.

Text-Based PPP Configuration

There are two ways to create a PPP connection—by using the text-based PPP utilities or by using the GUI Dialer. If you're using a text-based version, you must first make an entry in the /etc/ppp/pap-secrets or /etc/ppp/chap-secrets file. Figures 5-7 and 5-8 show examples of the entries you see in these files. You edit these two files the same way. They provide authentication information between the two computers. The /etc/ppp/pap-secrets file uses *Password Authentication Protocol (PAP)*, and the /etc/ppp/chap-secrets file uses *Challenge Handshake Authentication Protocol (CHAP)*. The PAP and CHAP protocols present the user's username and password information. When editing these files, you have to put in the username and password information that is provided by the ISP. You also need to enter the name of the server or computer that you are connecting to. This value can be an asterisk (*), which means that you can connect to any server or computer. The last piece of information you need for the secrets file is the IP address of the system that pppd is supposed to get when it connects. If you leave this value blank, you can connect to any IP address.

Figure 5-7 /etc/ppp/chap-secrets File

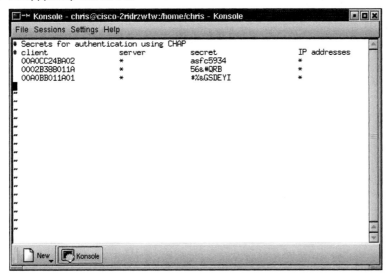

Figure 5-8 /etc/ppp/pap-secrets File

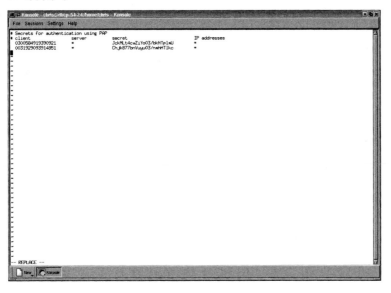

Making a connection through the command line also requires modifying a few scripts—pop-up, ppp-on-dialer, and ppp-down. The pop-up and ppp-on-dialer scripts handle the start connections, and the ppp-down script ends them. The first step in modifying these scripts is to copy them from the default directory,

/usr/share/doc/ppp-2.3.11/scripts, to a directory that is in your path, such as /usr/local/
bin. After copying these files to the new location, you need to edit them with the information relevant to your ISP. Do the following:

Step 1   In the ppp-on script, shown in Figure 5-9, find the lines that start with
TELEPHONE=, ACCOUNT=, and **PASSWORD=,** and enter the information that is relevant to your ISP.

Figure 5-9 ppp-on script File

Step 2   Located in the ppp-on script is a variable that points to the location of
the ppp-on-dialer. The default location is /etc/ppp. If it is not pointing to
the correct location, change this location accordingly.

Step 3   Located at the very bottom of the ppp-on script, you see the "call to
pppd" values. These values are difficult to interpret, but the only information you need to check is that this script is using the correct modem
device filename and speed. Typically, serial modems use /dev/ttyS0 or
/dev/ttyS1. The modem speed in most cases should be 115200, but 38400
is the default value.

Step 4   Check the ppp-on-dialer script, as shown in Figure 5-10. This script handles the "chat" sequence. You need to modify the last two lines of this script with the information from your ISP. This information is the dialog between the modem and your ISP about your username and account when you sign on to the Internet. Alternatively, if your ISP uses PAP or CHAP, these last two lines need to be commented out. Precede them with a pound sign (#) so that they are not read when the script is executed. Also, remove the backslash (\) from the **CONNECT** line.

Figure 5-10 ppp-on-dialer Script

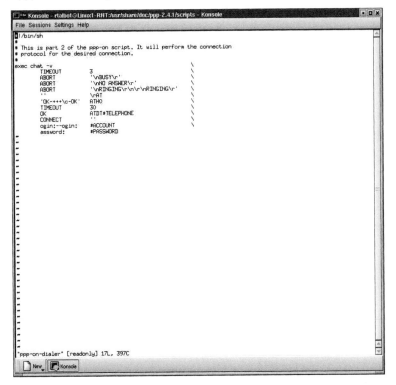

After making all these changes, log on as root, and enter **ppp-on** from the shell. (You might have to precede this command with the full path.) If the scripts were edited successfully, the system should dial the modem and establish a connection.

GUI Dialer PPP Configuration

PPP configuration can also be done from the GUI using the GUI dialing utilities. The GUI PPP dialer that comes with KDE is the KPPP dialer, shown in Figure 5-11. To start the KPPP window, enter **kppp** at the shell or select it from the KDE menu. The first time the KPPP dialer is started, it needs to be configured.

Figure 5-11 KPPP Dialer

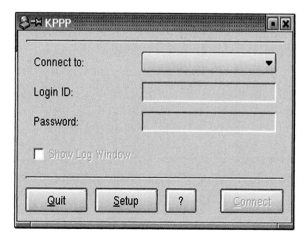

Follow these steps to configure the KPPP dialer:

Step 1 Type **kppp** at the shell. This starts the KPPP dialer.

Step 2 When the dialer starts, click Setup. This starts the KPPP configuration window, as shown in Figure 5-12.

Figure 5-12 KPPP Configuration Window

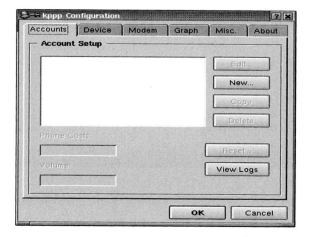

Step 3 Click New. This creates a new account. Note that if you are in the U.S., you have to select the dialog box option and not the wizard because the wizard does not support U.S. ISPs. After you select the dialog box option, the New Account dialog box opens, as shown in Figure 5-13.

Figure 5-13 New Account Dialog Box

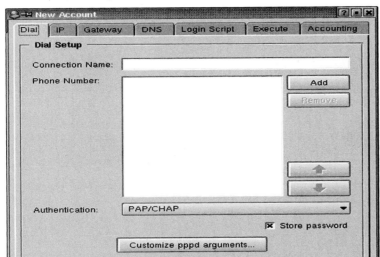

Step 4 In the Connection Name box, enter the name you want this account to be called.

Step 5 Click Add, enter your ISP's phone number, and click OK. Sometimes an ISP provides more than one number to dial. In this case, you can repeat this step for additional numbers to dial.

Step 6 On the Authentication tab, select the type of authentication your ISP uses—PAP or CHAP. Then click OK to close the New Account dialog box.

Step 7 Check the Modem and Device tabs to confirm that the correct modem device and connection speed are selected.

After you configure all the settings, enter the **kppp** command. Then select the ISP from the Connect To list and enter the username and password.

Connecting Using ISDN

ISDN is an alternative to using analog telephones lines to establish a connection. Figure 5-14 shows an ISDN connection. ISDN has many advantages over using telephone lines. One of these advantages is speed. ISDN uses a pair of 64 Kbps digital lines to connect, which provides a total of 128 Kbps throughput. This is much better than using a telephone line that connects at a maximum speed of 56 Kbps (and that often doesn't even reach that rate in some areas). Although ISDN is better than using telephones lines, an even better alternative to ISDN is DSL or cable modem services, which are discussed in the next section.

Figure 5-14 ISDN Connection

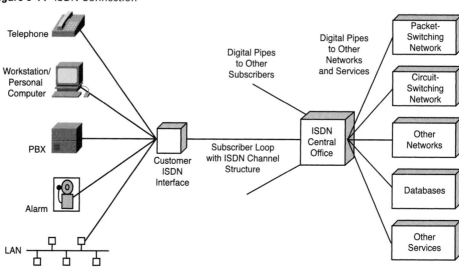

Instead of using a modem to connect to a remote computer, ISDN uses a terminal adapter. The terminal adapter essentially performs the same role that a modem plays in a PPP connection. You establish a connection with the terminal adapter the same way as with a modem and a PPP connection. Therefore, just follow the same instructions outlined in the preceding section on PPP connections to configure an ISDN connection.

A terminal adapter is an external device that acts much like an external modem. However, you can use an internal device that plugs into one of the PCI slots in the computer. These internal ISDN devices are called ISDN modems. Keep in mind that you need to have the proper drivers installed for the ISDN modem to function properly in Linux. Another important thing to remember about using ISDN modems is that, unlike regular modems that dial to a telephone line, ISDN modem cannot use the /dev/ttyS0 filename. Instead, an ISDN modem must use the /dev/ttyI0 filename and the subsequently numbered device filenames.

Connecting Via DSL and Cable Modem Service

A popular means of establishing a remote connection to a computer is via DSL or cable modem service, sometimes called *high-speed remote access* or *broadband remote access*. Figure 5-15 shows how a DSL or cable Internet connection is made. This service is provided by an ISP, but it offers some advantages over PPP and ISDN connections. First, DSL and cable have much higher speeds than PPP and ISDN. Whereas PPP connects at a maximum of 56 Kbps and ISDN at 128 Kbps, DSL and cable connect at a range from 1000 to 3000 Kbps. The speed varies, depending on several factors such as the amount of Internet traffic. These higher connection speeds also allow for video, voice, and digital data transmissions rather than just data. PPP and ISDN connections are simply too slow to allow for anything other than regular data transmissions. Another advantage of high-speed remote access is that a permanent connection is established. This means that the connection can be used 24 hours a day. You don't need to go through a dialer configuration or even enter a command to initiate the connection. The two exceptions to this rule are discussed next.

Figure 5-15 DSL and Cable Internet Connections

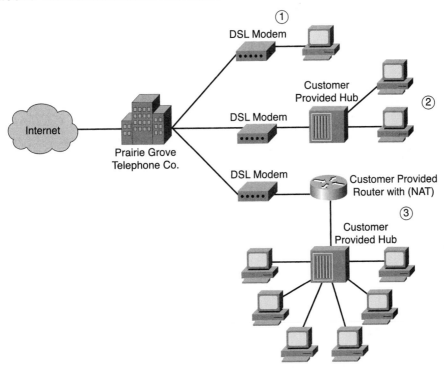

When you use Linux, compatibility issues regarding hardware and the IP address assignment method arise when you use a DSL or cable modem service. Hardware compatibility issues arise when you choose the proper modem to use with Linux. Most DSL and cable modems are external and interface with the computer via an Ethernet port. This is the preferred method of connection and the one that a Linux system is the most compatible with. However, some external DSL or cable modems use a USB interface or are not external but internal. Using these two types of DSL and cable modems requires the use of special drivers in a Linux system that are rare and hard to find. A broadband ISP assigns IP addresses in four ways—with a static IP address, with DHCP, with PPP over Ethernet (PPPoE), or with PPP over ATM (PPPoA). If the ISP gives you an incompatible modem, the best idea is to replace it with one that is compatible. If your ISP uses a PPPoE or PPPoA, you must enter some configuration information to set up the connection. You also have to enter commands at the shell to initiate the connection and to end it. The **asdl-start** command initiates the connection, and the **asdl-stop** command ends it.

Lab 5.2.5   Configuring Linux as a NIS Client

Covers how to configure a Linux system so that it can retrieve NIS services from the server.

Controlling Remote-Access Rights

When you set up a server for remote access, it is important to maintain a strict access rights policy. This can be a major network administration operation. The Linux operating system provides many options to choose from when controlling remote-access rights. When setting up remote-access controls, it's best not to use just one of these options. A good practice is to use a combination of at least two of these options. The reason is that if one fails or goes down, you always have a backup.

Firewalls

A *firewall* acts a barrier between one network, such as the Internet, and another network. This other network could be the network you are in charge of controlling security for. The firewall is placed between where these two networks interface, thus blocking unwanted traffic. You can set up a firewall in a variety of ways. One of the traditional ways is to install a router that can block and control undesired traffic into and out of a network. Other types of firewalls include dedicated external firewalls such as Cisco's PIX firewall, or having just a regular computer act as a firewall. Linux provides a distribution called the Linux Router Project (www.linuxrouter.org) that can be installed on a regular computer to provide firewall capabilities.

All network traffic flowing into and out of the network does so by using ports. A *packet filter* firewall restricts traffic based on these port assignments. This type of firewall examines the source and destination port numbers and the source and destination IP addresses. For example, if you have a Samba server running on your internal network, you would configure the firewall to block the port used by Samba on the firewall. This would prevent any unwanted access to the server from a malicious hacker outside the network.

As mentioned, the Linux operating system alone can be configured to provide firewall services. Linux uses the ipfwadm, ipchains, and iptables tools to configure firewall functions. You can configure firewall functions manually, by using a GUI configuration tool, or via a website:

- **Manually**—If you decide to configure your Linux system as a firewall, it is recommended that you first read up on this subject. Some books are dedicated to this difficult subject. This task involves writing your own scripts, which can be complicated and can result in the firewall's not functioning properly.

- **GUI configuration tool**—Some of the GUI configuration tools you can use for firewall configuration are Firestarter (http://firestarter.sourceforge.net) and Guarddog (http://www.simonzone.com). The latest distributions of Linux are being shipped with these programs. These tools give you a much easier way to control network ports as well as the client and server protocols of your choice. These tools also generate scripts that can run automatically when the system starts up.

- **Website configuration**—This tool is available at http://linux-firewall-tools.com/linux. It functions like the GUI configuration tools. You enter the necessary information, and the website generates the firewall scripts for you.

TCP Wrappers

TCP Wrappers are used in conjunction with inetd. Keep in mind that inetd is no longer used with Mandrake and Red Hat Linux. These two distributions use xinetd. TCP Wrappers use a program called tcpd. Without tcpd running, a server would call another server directly with inetd. When you use the tcpd program, the inetd program calls tcpd first. The tcpd program checks to see if the client is authorized to access the server. If it is, the tcpd program allows the client to access the server.

Two files are used to configure TCP Wrappers—/etc/hosts.allow and /etc/hosts.deny, shown in Figures 5-16 and 5-17. By editing these files and adding host names to them, you can either allow or deny access to the system. Host names entered in the hosts.allow file specify what systems are allowed to gain access to the system. If an attempt is made to access the system, and the host name is not entered in the hosts.allow file, it is denied access. Host names entered into the hosts.deny file also are denied access to the system.

Figure 5-16 /etc/hosts.allow File

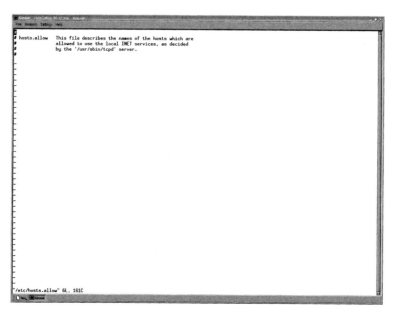

Figure 5-17 /etc/hosts.deny File

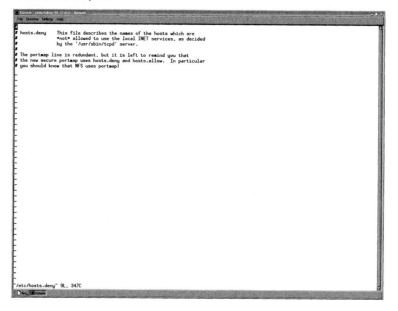

Entries in these files consist of lines like the following:

- **daemon-list: client-list**—The *daemon list* specifies the names of servers that appear in /etc/services. These are the servers to which access is either granted or denied. The *client list* specifies which clients are granted or denied access to the server in the corresponding daemon list. Entries in the client list can be by host name or IP address.

- **xinetd**—As mentioned, the Mandrake and Red Hat distributions of Linux no longer use inetd or TCP Wrappers. Instead, they use xinetd. Mandrake and Red Hat control access by editing the /etc/xinetd.conf file, shown in Figure 5-18. The edits that are made in xinetd.conf make calls to other files located in the /etc/xinetd.d directory. Figure 5-19 shows some of the daemons that are in the /etc/xinetd.d directory. The files in the /etc/xinetd.d directory are what control the access to the different daemons running on the system. Configuration is done on a server-by-server basis using the **bind, only_from,** and **no_access** parameters:

  — **bind**—This tells xinetd to listen to only one network interface for the service. For example, adding the entry **bind = 10.2.5.1** to the file causes a router to listen to only that specific Ethernet card address on the network.

  — **only_from**—This works similar to the hosts.allow file in that you can specify IP addresses, network addresses, or host names on this line to allow connections only from the entries listed in the file.

  — **no_access**—This works similar to the hosts.deny file in that entries listed on this line are denied access to the server.

Figure 5-18 /etc/xinetd.conf File

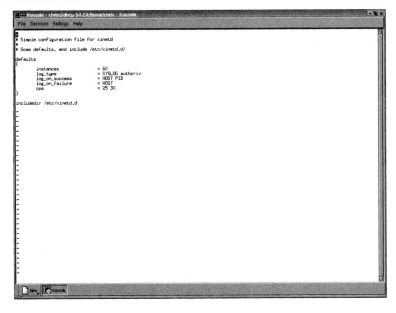

Figure 5-19 /etc/xinetd.d Directory

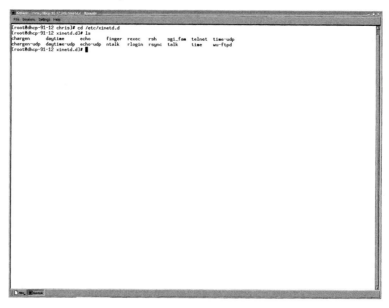

Passwords

Passwords are a convenient way to control remote access to a server. Passwords are very useful when you're specifying who has access to servers such as e-mail servers, FTP servers, and Telnet servers. Enforcing a password forces users to authenticate themselves in some way to the servers to gain access to the servers' resources.

Although passwords can be an effective means of preventing access to a server, they also have some security issues you should be aware of. Unless passwords are sent in an encrypted form, you run the risk of an experienced user's being able to read them. The FTP, POP, IMAP, and Telnet protocols send password information in an encrypted form by default; others do not. There are ways, however, to securely encrypt passwords and even data. One such method is by using the *SSH* protocol. It is designed to be secure and prevents a password from being used even if it is intercepted.

SSH provides another means of secure authentication to a server. SSH can store a special key on the server and one on the client. The client uses this key, and not a password, to authenticate to the server. Although this configuration provides a secure means of authentication, some security risks are involved. For example, if for some reason an intruder were to gain access to a user's client computer, he or she would be able to gain access to the server.

It is also important to mention the "r commands" when discussing password authentication. The r commands include **rlogin, rsh,** and **rcp.** They allow a user on a UNIX or Linux system to log into, run programs on, and copy files to and from another UNIX or Linux system without having to be authenticated. This is accomplished by creating an .rhosts file in the user's home directory. This file contains lists of other trusted hosts. These trusted hosts can gain access to a server without having to be authenticated. Again, there can be some security issues with this form of authentication, so be careful when determining which hosts will be trusted.

File Permissions

File permissions can be useful to give general access to files or certain directories without having to specify a particular user. Basically, anyone can log in and gain access to the server. However, the file permissions can limit what files or directories that person has access to. For example, if there were an FTP, Telnet, or SSH server that people needed access to, you could specify a directory or a group of directories that these users have access to after they log in. An even better example is allowing anonymous access to an FTP server. The anonymous access control specifies that anyone can gain access to the server, but they can access only the particular directories and files that have the appropriate file permissions to do so.

Remote Administration on a Linux System

One benefit of using the Linux operating system on a server is that it provides many ways to remotely administer the system. This is why it is so important to control access rights. As with any type of remote access to a system, some security risks need to be addressed. Many of these were discussed in the preceding section. However, remote administration can be very convenient and is necessary in some cases. Linux provides several tools for remote administration, including text-mode logins, GUI logins, file transfers, and dedicated remote administration protocols.

Text-Mode Logins

A text-mode login consists of logging in to a system via Telnet or SSH. You can use Telnet or SSH to remotely administer the Linux server from any system running any operating system, such as Macintosh or Windows. It does not have to be a Linux operating system. This is typically done by logging in with a regular user account and then using the **su** command with the root password to gain superuser privileges. At this point, you can do anything you can do from the shell prompt at the main console.

The command syntax for using Telnet in Linux is **telnet** *hostname,* where *hostname* is the DNS name of the system you are attempting to gain access to. Figure 5-20 shows the **telnet** command being used.

Figure 5-20 telnet Command

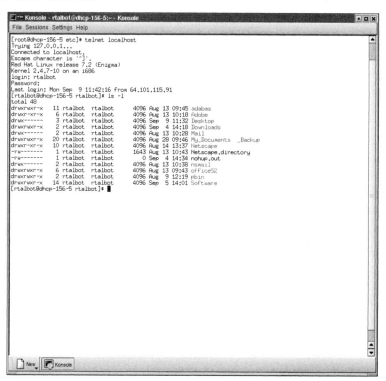

SSH works the same way, but it does not use the **login:** prompt. If you recall the previous section on how SSH uses authentication, you know that you do not need to specify a username or password. Instead, SSH passes the current username to the system you are attempting to access remotely to authenticate you. However, you can log in to an SSH server with a different username and password by using the -l *username* parameter. The output is as follows (note that *hostname* represents the remote system's DNS name):

$ **ssh** *hostname* -l **jsmith**
jsmith@*hostname* password:
Last login: Wed Feb 18 08:34:23 2002 from *hostname*
[jsmith@*hostname* jsmith]$

After you have successfully gained access to the system, you can do just about anything you can do from a shell prompt on the main console.

GUI Logins

To remotely administer a Linux server via a GUI login, you first need to install some software on the system that you are making the remote administration attempt from. The software that you have to install is X server. If you are making the attempt from a

Linux system, X server should already be installed. You can also use a Windows system with X server installed on it to remotely administer a Linux server via a GUI. As with Telnet and SSH, after you have logged on, you can use the **su** command with the root password to acquire root privileges.

File Transfers

Generally this is not what you could call remote administration, but it is in fact a way to edit and configure files remotely. You can use a file transfer tool such as FTP to transfer files from one system to another, edit them, and then send them back. For example, you could have a Linux server that is configured as a print server. Because this server is a print server, it might not have the proper editing and configuration tools needed to edit files on the print server, which would make Telnetting to the server pointless. If FTP, NFS, or Samba were installed on the print server, you could log in to the print server remotely and transfer the file to a system that has the proper editing and configuration tools, edit the file, and transfer it back to the print server.

Keep in mind, however, that it is not recommended that you grant direct access to the configuration files' target directory, such as the /etc directory, using NFS or Samba. This makes it easier to transfer the file to the correct location but can leave the server vulnerable to attacks. Instead, the best practice is to transfer the file using a general user account that places the file in that user account's home directory. Then use a remote login protocol such as SSH to copy the file to the appropriate directory.

Remote Administration Protocols

Linux provides several tools to help an administrator remotely manage a computer. You need to install the server version of these tools onto the client computer, which is the computer you are planning to manage remotely. You need to install the client version of the tool you are using on the computer you plan to use for the administration. Most of these tools use web browsers to do the remote administration, which is helpful if you are in an environment that has multiple operating systems such as Macintosh or Windows. The system does not need to be a Linux system. Here are a few of these tools:

- **SNMP**—This protocol is discussed in detail in later chapters. It is important to note that SNMP has never been the remote management tool of choice for Linux systems, as it has for the Windows environment. The reason is that SNMP requires a lot of complicated configuration on the systems that are to be administered.
- **SWAT**—This is a web-based tool that is used to administer a Samba server. SWAT, shown in Figure 5-21, stands for Samba Web Administration Tool. After configuring SWAT, you can access the server remotely using a web browser.

SWAT uses port 901. To access the SWAT administration page, you enter the URL of the server you want to access remotely, followed by port 901. For example, you would enter **http://cisco-flerb.cisco.com:901**. Keep in mind that SWAT allows you to administer only the server's Samba functions. You cannot perform any other administration tasks with SWAT. However, you have complete control of Samba on the remote server.

■ **Webmin**—As its name implies, Webmin is another web-based remote administration tool. Webmin was designed to be used on all Linux distributions and UNIX systems. When Webmin is installed, configuration files specific to that particular distribution of Linux or UNIX are installed. Webmin uses port 10000. To access the Webmin administration page, you enter the URL of the server you want to access remotely, followed by port 10000. For example, you would enter **http://cisco-flerb.cisco.com:10000**.

Figure 5-21 SWAT Administration Page

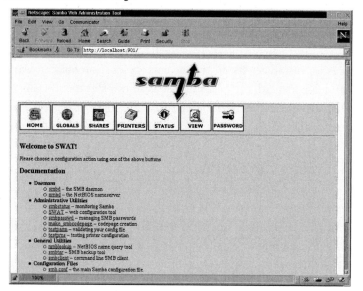

Directory Services

This section covers the following topics:

■ What is a directory service?

■ Directory service standards

■ Windows 2000 Active Directory

■ The Novell Network Directory Service

■ Network Information Service

What Is a Directory Service?

As intranets continue to grow, the complexities of these networks are also growing. Today's modern intranets can feature thousands of users, each needing different services and various levels of security on the network. The task of managing this logistical challenge has grown beyond the capacity of the NOS alone. Many system administrators now use *directory services* to supplement the NOS's management tools. Figure 5-22 shows the basic concepts of how a directory service is built. The top object in a directory, which holds all the other objects, is called the *root* object.

Figure 5-22 What Is a Directory?

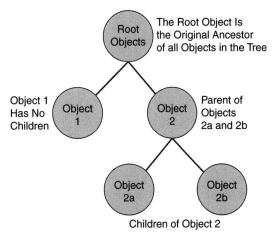

A directory service gives system administrators centralized control of all users and resources across the entire network. They help an administrator organize information. They help simplify network management by providing a standard interface for common system administration tasks. This feature is important when a large network is running multiple operating systems and various network protocols. With a single directory service in place, the network administrator can centrally manage all such resources with a defined set of tools instead of manually attending to each device separately. These directory services can be local, which means that they are restricted to one machine, or the directory information can be spread across multiple machines. This is called a distributed directory database.

In the computing world, a directory can be different things. You're probably familiar with the term *directory* as it relates to computer file systems, in which a directory is a collection of files grouped under an identifying name. Directory services used by a NOS are a different but related concept. In this context, a directory is a special type of database. It can contain varying types of information.

Benefits of Using a Directory Structure

The benefits of using directory services on a network include the following:

- The data can be easily organized.
- The data can be easily secured.
- The data can be easily located and accessed.

There are advantages to using directory services to access network resources. Traditionally, shared files and folders were stored on the hard drives of individual workstations or file servers. To connect to the shared files, the user needed to know where they were located.

A directory service eliminates this requirement. Shared resources are published to the directory. Users can locate and access them without ever knowing on which machine the resources physically reside. Figure 5-23 illustrates how this process is intended to work.

Figure 5-23 Distributed Directory Services

LDAP Client

Directory Server   Distributed Directory
Service

The files, directories, and shares that users access from a single point can be distributed across multiple servers and locations using distributed directory and replication services. The following two methods can be used to browse the entire distributed directory from a single location:

- **Browse the Microsoft Windows network in the traditional way**—You browse each machine to locate shared files.
- **Browse the directory**—This option displays all resources published to the active directory. Figure 5-24 illustrates how to use Microsoft Windows Explorer to browse the directory.

Figure 5-24 Using Directory Services

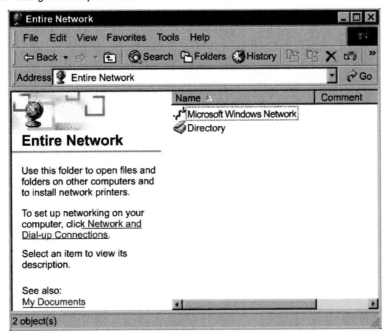

Directory Service Standards

It is necessary to conform to a standard when creating distributed directories. To operate within a NOS, different directory services need to have a common method of naming and referencing objects. Without these standards, each application would have to use its own directory, which would require more disk space. Additionally, the products of one vendor cannot use the databases compiled by the products of another vendor. Without these standards, it would be impossible to have a functioning directory structure. Standards-compliance directory service vendors design their services so that they are compatible over a broad range of platforms and with other directory services.

X.500

X.500 defines Electronic Directory Service (EDS) standards. The directory services described in X.500 are designed to work in conjunction with X.400 messaging services.

An X.500-compliant directory has three primary components:

- *Directory System Agent (DSA)*—Manages the directory data.
- *Directory User Agent (DUA)*—Gives users access to directory services.
- *Directory Information Base (DIB)*—Acts as the central data store, or database, in which directory information is kept.

The X.500 standards address how information is stored in the directory and how users and computer systems access that information. Data security, the naming model, and the replication of directory data between servers are all defined by X.500.

X.500 specifications define the directory structure as an inverted tree, and the database is hierarchical. An X.500-compliant directory service uses Directory Access Protocol (DAP), which is discussed next.

DAP and LDAP

Directory Access Protocol (DAP) enables the DUA to communicate with the DSA. DAP defines the means by which the user can search the directory to read, add, delete, and modify directory entries.

DAP is a powerful protocol, but the associated overhead is high. *Lightweight Directory Access Protocol (LDAP)* was developed as a subset of DAP to simplify access to X.500-type directories. LDAP has become a popular standard because it integrates directories from different vendors. LDAP is designed to use fewer system resources than DAP, and it is easier to implement. The current version of LDAP is LDAPv3.

LDAPv3 offers several major improvements over earlier LDAP versions. Enhanced security is a primary focus of the new version. LDAPv3 supports Secure Sockets Layer (SSL) encryption between client and server and enables X.509 certificate authentication.

LDAPv3 also lets the server refer the LDAP client to another server if it cannot answer the client's query.

Figure 5-25 shows a typical DAP and LDAP directory service.

Figure 5-25 Typical Directory Service Structure

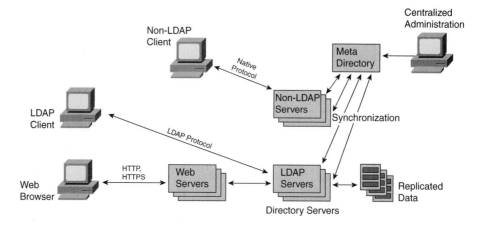

Windows 2000 Active Directory

With the release of Windows 2000 Server, Microsoft made fundamental changes to its networking components that are even more drastic than those made by Novell in the transition from NetWare 3 to 4. The *Active Directory* is central to these changes. Where the Novell NDS functions as a service that works with the NOS, the Microsoft Active Directory functions as an application that is deeply integrated with the operating system.

The following sections discuss the structure of the Active Directory database, Active Directory integration, and Active Directory information.

Active Directory Database Structure

Active Directory information is stored in three files:

- Active Directory database
- Active Directory log files
- Shared System Volume

The database is the directory. The log files record changes made to the database. The Shared System Volume (called Sysvol) contains scripts and group policy objects on Windows 2000 domain controllers. Group policy is the means by which Windows 2000 administrators control user desktops, automatically deploy applications, and set user rights.

Windows 2000 Domains

Active Directory's logical structure is based on units called domains. Although the same terminology is used, domains in Windows 2000 function differently from those in Windows NT. In both Windows NT and Windows 2000, a domain represents a security and administrative boundary, as well as a replication unit. However, Windows NT uses a flat domain structure, and Windows 2000 arranges domains in hierarchical domain trees.

The hierarchical tree concept works differently in Active Directory than in NDS. NDS does not divide the network into domains. Windows 2000 networks can have multiple domains, organized into domain trees. Additionally, these trees can be joined to other trees to form *forests*. Figure 5-26 shows a Windows 2000 domain structure with two domain trees (with root domains shinder.net and tacteam.net) joined in a forest.

Figure 5-26 Windows 2000 Domains

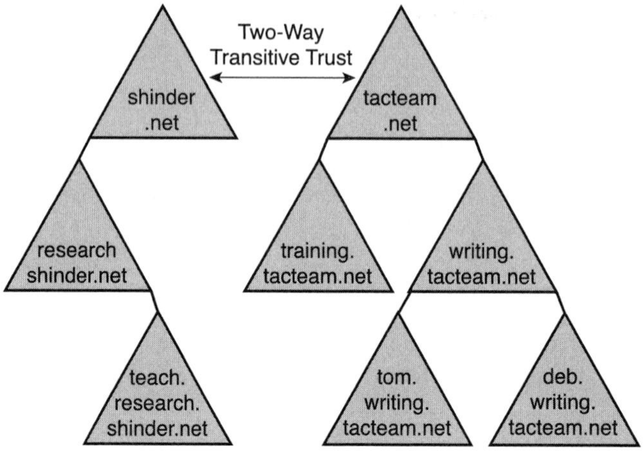

Windows 2000 Organizational Units

Active Directory, like NDS, uses *organizational units (OUs)* to organize resources within domains. Administrative authority can be delegated to individual OUs. In contrast, NT networking lets administrative privileges be assigned only at the domain level.

Active Directory and DNS

Active Directory uses Domain Name System (DNS) naming conventions. It depends on DNS to operate. There must be a DNS server on every Windows 2000 network. In addition, DNS zone information updates can be integrated with Active Directory replication, which is more efficient than traditional DNS update methods.

Windows 2000 supports Dynamic DNS (DDNS), which enables the automatic updating of the DNS database.

Active Directory Servers

To use Active Directory, at least one server must be configured as a domain controller (DC). It is recommended that there be at least two DCs in each domain, for fault tolerance. Configuring the first domain controller on the network creates the directory for that domain.

Unlike Windows NT servers, Windows 2000 Servers that are running Active Directory have no primary domain controller (PDC) or backup domain controller (BDC). In the former Windows NT domains, only the PDC would contain a full read/write copy of the directory of user accounts and security information. The PDC would authenticate usernames and passwords when members logged in to the network. The BDC would maintain a read-only backup of the PDC's master directory, so any changes needed to be made on the PDC. Windows 2000 Servers that are running Active Directory approach the domain controller concept a little differently. Unlike Windows NT Server, in which a PDC must be accessible to make changes to the directory, Windows 2000 Server relies on Active Directory's multimaster replication model to update all the domain controllers within the forest when a change is made to any other domain controller. There is no PDC or BDC. All domain controllers are equal. All domain controllers contain a read/write copy of the Active Directory partition. This information is kept up to date and is synchronized through the process of replication, which is discussed in the next section.

Active Directory Replication

Replication is the process of copying data from one computer to one or more other computers and synchronizing that data so that it is identical on all systems.

Active Directory uses multimaster replication to copy directory information between the domain controllers in a domain. Changes can be made on any domain controller, and those changes are then replicated to the others, except during the performance of a single-master operation.

Windows 2000 administrators can establish replication policies that determine when and how often directory replication takes place. This enables optimum use of network bandwidth. Controlling the replication schedule is especially important when domain controllers are located on opposite sides of a slow link, such as a 56 KB WAN link.

Active Directory Security

Each object in Active Directory has an access control list (ACL) that contains all access permissions associated with that object. Permissions can be either explicitly allowed or denied on a granular basis.

There are two different types of permissions:

- *Assigned permissions*—Permissions explicitly granted by an authorized user.
- *Inherited permissions*—Permissions that apply to child objects because they were inherited from a parent object.

Permissions can be assigned to an individual user or a group of users. Windows 2000 lets administrators control this process. Note the checkbox at the bottom of the object security properties sheet, shown in Figure 5-27.

Figure 5-27 Active Directory Security

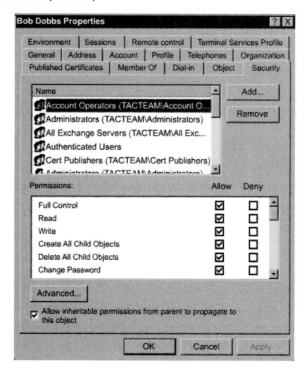

Active Directory Compatibility

Active Directory is dependent on the operating system and runs only on Windows 2000 servers. Because Active Directory is LDAP-compatible, services and information can be accessed or exchanged with other LDAP directory services. Microsoft also provides tools for migrating information from other directories, such as NDS, into Active Directory.

Worksheet 5.3.3 Windows 2000 Active Directory

Identify and understand the components and terminology associated with Windows 2000 Active Directory.

The Novell Network Directory Service

Versions of NetWare up through 3.*x* use a directory database called the *bindery*. The biggest drawback of this directory service is its local nature. Each NetWare server on a network has to maintain an individual database, and a user has to have an account on each server to access those server resources.

The following sections discuss the structure of the Novell *Network Directory Service (NDS)* database, NDS security issues, and NDS compatibility within various operating systems and hardware platforms. Figure 5-28 shows the Novell login box that is used to log in to Novell's NDS.

Figure 5-28 Logging on to Novell's NDS

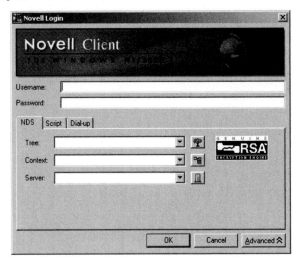

The NDS Database Structure

NetWare introduced NDS in version 4. NDS is a global database that is replicated between servers on the network. With it, users can log on to any server and access resources. Figure 5-29 illustrates how the NDS database structure is organized into a hierarchical database.

Figure 5-29 NDS Database Structure

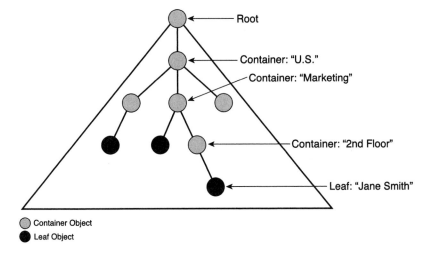

The NDS database is hierarchical and uses the inverted-tree arrangement. It includes two basic types of objects—container and leaf. As the names imply, a container object can contain other objects, and a leaf object is the endpoint of a branch or the resource. Shared files and printers are examples of leaf objects. OUs are examples of container objects.

NDS Security

NDS permissions to access objects are assigned to OUs, and users and groups are placed in OUs. User permissions can be changed by moving the account from one OU to another. For example, if the johndoe user account is moved from the Training OU to the Sales OU, that user will no longer have the access permissions assigned to Training. However, the user will acquire all permissions granted to Sales. This is different from the way in which permissions work in Microsoft Windows NT and Windows 2000 networks. Assigning permissions is discussed in Chapter 11, "Advanced NOS Administration."

NDS Platform Compatibility

NDS can run on a variety of platforms, although it is generally associated with the NetWare NOS. Novell provides NDS for the following platforms:

- NetWare 4 and 5
- Microsoft Windows NT and Windows 2000
- IBM AIX and OS/390
- Caldera OpenLinux
- SCO UNIX
- Sun Solaris

The NDS directory is the Novell cross-platform solution for integrated enterprise computing with directory-enabled applications.

NDS enables the use of a variety of protocols to access directory information, including the following:

- Novell Directory Access Protocol (NDAP)
- LDAP
- HTTP (when using a web server)
- Open Database Connectivity (ODBC) API
- Active Directory Services Interface (ADSI)

Worksheet 5.3.4   The Novell NDS

Identify and understand the components and terminology associated with Novell's NDS.

Network Information Service

Linux uses its own version of directory services called the Network Information Service (NIS). NIS provides a simple network lookup service consisting of databases and processes. NIS provides the information required on all machines on the network. Linux's standard libc library supports NIS, which is called "traditional NIS." NIS, unlike Active Directory in Windows, can be installed by default when you install the operating system. However, this option is available on only certain distributions. On other distributions you have to install it after the installation. Configuring NIS on your system lets the Linux server obtain information about user accounts, group accounts, file systems, and other databases located on other servers throughout the network.

NIS functions for Linux much the same way as NDS does with Novell and Active Directory does with Windows. A system using NIS can access files and information from any system on the network. To correctly establish this relationship, NIS often works in conjunction with NFS. NFS running on Linux allows a user to mount to a user's local directory file systems that can be located on any server in the network.

The NIS Structure

In a NIS configuration, the network consists of the NIS server, slaves, and clients. The NIS servers are where the NIS database is created and maintained. The NIS slaves act the same way that NDS servers act in Novell. The NIS databases are copied to all the NIS slave servers. The slaves then can provide NIS directory information to clients, but any changes made to the database must be performed in the NIS server. The NIS clients are the systems that request database information from the servers and slaves. The NIS slaves perform load balancing for the NIS servers. Figure 5-30 shows the logical layout of a Linux NIS topology.

Figure 5-30 Linux NIS Topology

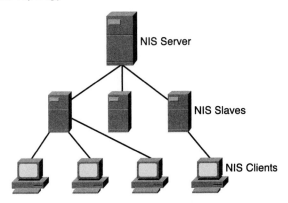

Configuring NIS on a Client

If you are configuring NIS during the installation of Linux, all you need to do is select the option when it is presented. Then you have to select the NIS domain name and the IP address of the NIS server. It is important to note here that the NIS domain name is not necessarily the same as the DNS domain name. To configure NIS after installing Linux, you use the linuxconf utility, shown in Figure 5-31. At this point you enter the NIS domain name and the NIS server's IP address.

Figure 5-31   linuxconf Utility

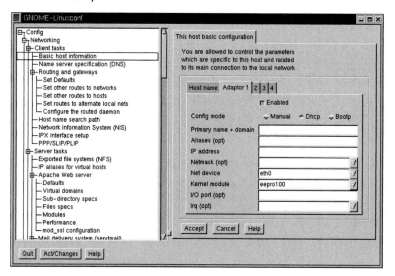

Other NOS Services

This section covers the following topics:

- Mail
- Printing
- File sharing
- FTP (file transfer)
- Web services
- Intranets
- Extranets
- Automating tasks with script services
- Domain Name Service
- DHCP
- Domains

Mail

Mail might be the most important network process. Mail provides users with a mechanism to send and receive e-mail. Mail services come in various forms. Over the years, many companies have developed proprietary methods of exchanging e-mail. Today, virtually all mail services rely on TCP/IP or can at least act as a gateway between proprietary and TCP/IP mail services. Figure 5-32 shows how one client can send mail to another client through the Internet using TCP/IP services.

Figure 5-32   Client Mail

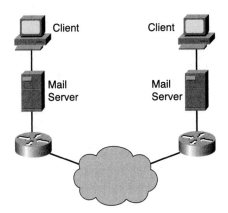

It is a misconception to think that mail is sent from one user's computer directly to another. Although this scenario is possible, it can occur only if both PCs are acting as mail servers. Most of time, the sender's mail is sent to a mail server that belongs to his or her ISP or employer, not directly to a destination. The mail server then forwards the mail (if necessary) to a server used by the recipient.

For example, suppose that Maria types an e-mail to john@foo.com. Maria's mail program forwards the mail to a mail server she uses. This is typically a mail server run by Maria's ISP or her company. Maria's mail server then attempts to forward the message to a mail server used by John. Maria's mail server uses the information after the @ symbol in John's address to determine where to send the message. In this case, Maria's server looks for mail servers that handle mail for foo.com. After the message arrives at the foo.com mail server, it waits there until John's e-mail program retrieves it.

Mail services are comprised of a combination of the following components:

- Mail Transfer Agent (MTA)
- Mail User Agent (MUA)
- Mail Delivery Agent (MDA)

Sendmail is the most popular MTA used on UNIX and Linux servers. Sendmail relies on Simple Mail Transfer Protocol (SMTP) to receive mail from clients and forward mail to other mail servers. SMTP is part of the TCP/IP suite of protocols.

Popular mail clients (MUAs) include Microsoft Outlook, Eudora, and Pine. MUAs can compose and send mail to MTAs, such as Sendmail. Mail clients send mail to servers using SMTP.

An MDA is a program that is responsible for routing received mail to the appropriate mailboxes on the mail server. Some MDAs include security features and filters that can prevent the spread of e-mail viruses.

E-mail is not usually read while a user is logged on to a shell account on the mail server. Instead, software is used to retrieve mail from a mailbox, which resides on the server. To retrieve mail from a mail server, remote mail clients use two common protocols:

- **Post Office Protocol version 3 (POP3)**—A simple protocol that is used by mail clients to authenticate mail servers and retrieve mail. POP3 does not encrypt usernames and passwords, so it can be a security risk on some LANs.
- **Internet Message Access Protocol (IMAP)**—A complex protocol that typically results in higher server overhead than POP3. IMAP can encrypt passwords and has other features. IMAP implementations are typically designed to store e-mail on the mail server and allow users to access from multiple clients.

When implementing mail services, remember that clients send mail to servers using SMTP and retrieve mail from servers using POP3 or IMAP.

Additionally, many mail servers include other features, including support for other activities:

- Lightweight Directory Access Protocol (LDAP) provides corporate address book sharing.
- Web interface programs allow clients to read and compose mail using a web browser.

It is not necessary for every NOS on a network to run the mail service. Typically, only one server on a network is needed to perform e-mail-related duties for all users. This server runs the mail service at all times, and users connect to the server when sending and reading e-mail.

Printing

Although the world is quickly headed into an electronic era, a need still exists for physical printouts of data. In large networks and some small networks, it is impractical to provide every workstation computer with a printer. The solution is to provide networked printers to support all users within a physical location. For this reason, network administrators use print services to help manage these network printers and their respective print queues.

When a user decides to print in a networked printing environment, the job is sent to the appropriate queue for the selected printer. Print queues stack the incoming print jobs and service them using a "First In, First Out" (FIFO) order. That is, when a job is added to the queue, it is placed at the end of the list of waiting jobs and is printed after all the jobs before it. The wait for a print job can sometimes be long, depending on the size of the print jobs that entered the queue before it. Thus, a network print service provides system administrators with the necessary tools to manage the large number of print jobs being routed throughout the network. This includes the ability to prioritize, pause, and even delete print jobs that are waiting to be printed. Print services are usually confined to a local intranet environment for the sake of maintenance and manageability. Figure 5-33 shows an example of the print job manager for Windows 2000.

Figure 5-33 Managing Print Jobs in Windows 2000

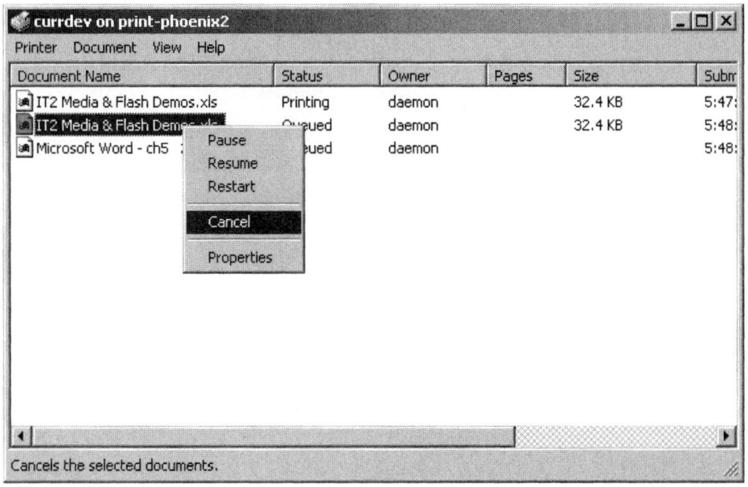

File Sharing

The capability to share files over a network is an important network service. Many file-sharing protocols and applications are in use today. Within a corporate or home network, files are typically shared using Windows File Sharing or the NFS protocol. In such environments, an end user might not even know if a given file is on a local hard disk or a remote server. Windows File Sharing and NFS allow users to easily move, create, and delete files in remote directories.

In contrast to file sharing within a home or office network, file sharing on the Internet is often done using File Transfer Protocol (FTP). FTP is a client/server protocol that requires clients to log in before transferring files. Files are always available with Windows File Sharing and NFS, but FTP sessions are made only for the duration of the file transfer. Most TCP/IP-capable NOSs include FTP services, although the commands supported by each NOS might vary slightly.

Today, many end users share files using peer-to-peer protocols over the Internet. Gnutella is an example of a peer-to-peer networking protocol. Peer-to-peer protocols work without a central server. Each host that participates in the peer-to-peer network is considered equal to every other host. Peer-to-peer networking is popular among home users, but the technology has yet to be deployed as a widespread business solution. Peer-to-peer networks often rely on common TCP/IP protocols to share files. For example, Gnutella peers use HTTP to download files from one peer to another. Figure 5-34 shows a domain with shared directories and files that can be accessed via a peer-to-peer connection.

Figure 5-34 File Sharing in Windows 2000

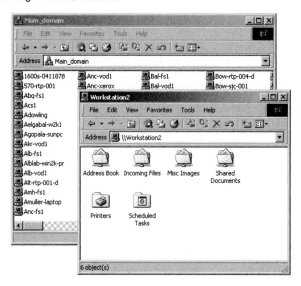

FTP (File Transfer) Web Services

Many organizations make files available to remote employees, customers, and the general public via FTP. FTP services are made available to the public in conjunction with web services. For example, a user might browse a website, read about a software update on a web page, and then download the update using FTP. Smaller companies might use a single server to provide FTP and HTTP services, whereas larger companies might choose to use dedicated FTP servers. Figure 5-35 shows a typical FTP program that can be used to download files from a remote server.

Figure 5-35 FTP

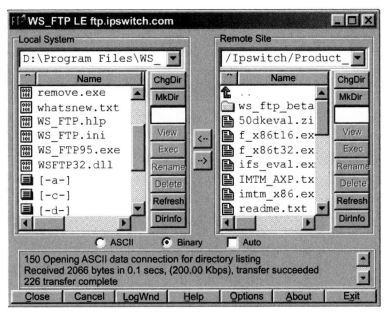

Although FTP clients must log on, many FTP servers are configured to allow anonymous access. When users access a server anonymously, they do not need to have a user account on the system. The FTP protocol also allows users to upload, rename, and delete files, so administrators must be careful to configure an FTP server to control levels of access.

FTP is a "session-oriented" protocol. Clients must open a session with the server, authenticate, and then perform an action such as downloading or uploading. If the client's session is inactive for a certain length of time, the server disconnects the client. This inactive length of time is called an idle timeout. The length of an FTP idle timeout varies depending on the software.

FTP connections are established through GUI programs or using the following standard CLI command:

ftp *hostname or IP_address*

Examples include the following situations:

ftp computer.company.com

or

ftp 123.45.67.90

FTP services are typically not enabled by default on a NOS. This prevents administrators from unknowingly making restricted files available for download. Also, FTP server programs have historically been a target of DoS and other malicious attacks. A DoS attack is characterized by attackers attempting to prevent legitimate users from gaining access to a service, such as an FTP service. Examples include the following:

- Attempts to "flood" a network, preventing legitimate network traffic
- Attempts to disrupt connections between two machines, preventing access to a service
- Attempts to prevent a particular individual from accessing a service
- Attempts to disrupt service to a specific system or user

A network administrator should be prepared to monitor this type of activity before deploying a high-profile FTP service. Table 5-2 lists common FTP commands.

Table 5-2 Common FTP Commands

Command	Description
binary	Enables binary transfer mode
ascii	Enables ASCII transfer mode
hash	Enables hash mark progress indicators
lcd *local-directory*	Changes the local directory
cd *remote-directory*	Changes the remote directory
get *remote-file*	Downloads a file
put *local-file*	Uploads a file
bye	Exits the FTP service

Chapters 9 and 10 describe how to configure FTP services on Red Hat Linux 7 and Windows 2000.

Web Services

The World Wide Web is now the most visible network service. In less than a decade, it has become a global network of information, commerce, education, and entertainment. Figure 5-36 shows the exponential growth of the Internet. Millions of companies, organizations, and individuals maintain websites on the Internet. Websites are collections of web pages stored on a server or group of servers.

Figure 5-36 Exponential Growth of the Internet

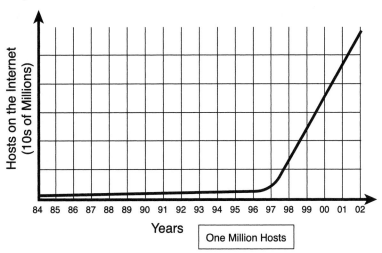

The World Wide Web is based on a client/server model. Clients attempt to establish TCP sessions with web servers. After a session is established, a client can request data from the server. Client requests and server transfers are typically governed by HTTP. Web client software includes GUI web browsers such as Netscape Navigator, shown in Figure 5-37, and Internet Explorer, shown in Figure 5-38. Web clients can also be text browsers. A text browser can display a web page using typographical characters, but not graphics. Examples of text browsers include Lynx (used on UNIX/Linux systems) and wireless web (cell phone) browsers.

Figure 5-37 Netscape Navigator

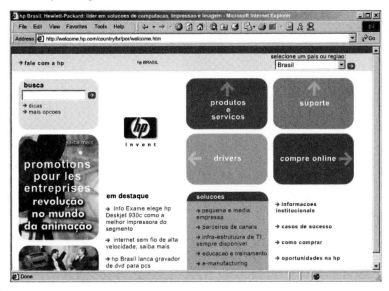

Figure 5-38   Internet Explorer

In the early 1990s, HTTP was used to transfer static pages composed of text and simple images. These early web pages were written almost exclusively using HTML. As the World Wide Web has developed, the role of HTTP has expanded. Websites now use HTTP to deliver dynamic content and transfer files. HTTP Secure (HTTPS) is an extension to the HTTP protocol that is used to support data sent securely over the Internet. HTTPS is designed to send individual messages securely. An example of a web application that might use HTTPS is a bank that has websites for its customers where they can perform financial transactions.

Web pages are hosted on computers running web services software. The two most common web server software packages are Microsoft Internet Information Services (IIS) and Apache Web Server. Microsoft IIS can be run only on a Windows platform, whereas Apache Web Server is typically used on UNIX and Linux platforms. There are dozens of other web server programs. Web services are available for virtually all operating systems currently in production.

The most obvious use of web services is to communicate using the Internet. Companies advertise and sell their products using websites, organizations make information available, and families post pictures and online journals to share with friends. However, web services are also used on public or private networks to deploy computer applications, collaborate on projects, and manage remote systems. The following sections discuss private World Wide Web networks, called *intranets*, as well as web-based remote management.

Intranets

Web services play a significant role in private and corporate networks. An organization can deploy a private World Wide Web network for a variety of purposes:

- Internal information, memoranda, and reports
- Staff and employee directories
- Calendars and appointment schedules
- Application and software deployment
- Payroll information
- Employee services
- Collaborative tools

Organizations typically do not want such information and services to be made public on the Internet. Instead, organizations build web servers to create a private intranet. The Latin prefix "intra" means "within," so an intranet is a network within some boundary or limitation. In contrast, the Latin prefix "inter" means "between," so the word "Internet" can be thought to literally mean "between networks." This literal meaning makes sense, because the Internet provides a way to interconnect different networks of computers around the world. Figure 5-39 shows a logical representation of an intranet. You can see that several networks located throughout the world are connected. They use their own intranet to exchange information and display web pages, which is a much more secure alternative than displaying this information on the external Internet.

Figure 5-39 Intranets

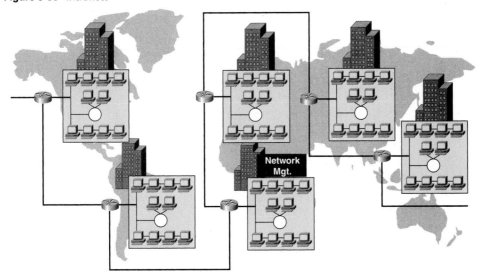

Intranets use the same technology used by the Internet, including HTTP over TCP/IP, web servers, and web clients. The difference between an intranet and the Internet is that intranets do not allow public access to private servers.

One approach to building intranets is to configure them so that only on-site users can access the intranet servers. This is typically accomplished by using an Internet firewall.

However, because many employees work at home or on the road, organizations have found ways to extend intranets beyond the geographic boundaries of the office building or campus. This type of intranet, which allows outside users to connect to the private web servers, is sometimes called an *extranet*.

Extranets are configured to allow employees and customers to access the private network over the Internet. To prevent unauthorized access to the private network, extranet designers must use a technology such as virtual private networking. Figure 5-40 shows how a virtual tunnel is established via the Internet to provide a secure remote connection to a company's internal network. A *virtual private network (VPN)* makes it possible for employees to use a web client connected to the Internet to access the private network securely. VPNs rely on encryption software, usernames, and passwords to ensure that communication occurs privately and only among authorized users. Figure 5-41 illustrates how a VPN can also be used as a way to securely transfer data to another remote branch office using the Internet as a means of transport.

Figure 5-40 Virtual Networking

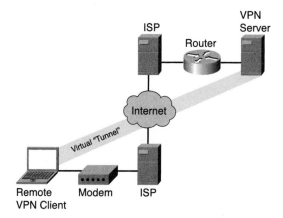

Figure 5-41 Remote-Access VPNs

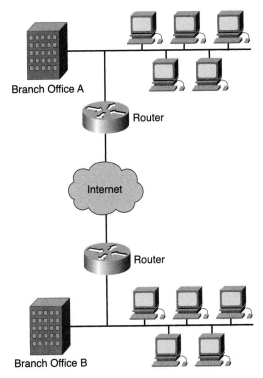

Extranets

Extranets are an emerging technology that many of the largest corporations in the world are beginning to build. They provide a means of including the outside world, such as customers and suppliers, and conducting valuable market research. For example, a company's intranet can be linked to its external website (or extranet). This can allow the company to gather information about a customer who is surfing its website. The information would include where the customer is looking on the site, which products he samples, what processes produce requests for technical support, or what parts he is buying. Extranets are intranets taken to the next step. An intranet is company-wide, and an extranet can be worldwide. Extranets can partition off and separate company data contained in the company intranet from the web services offered to the world via the Internet. A few advantages of an extranet for a company could be e-mail and program sharing. It can extend the company's capabilities to provide customer support, as well as e-commerce and online sales. One of the obvious dangers of extranets is security, but it is possible to provide security with firewalls and encrypted passwords. This does not guarantee that an extranet is safe, however.

Table 5-3 outlines the various types of networks that have been discussed.

Table 5-3 Different Types of Networks

Network Type	Characteristics
Internet	Spans the entire globe. Unrestricted public access.
Intranet	Network hardware is used to create boundaries and restrict access. Access is granted only to members of that intranet, typically within a single organization.
Extranet	Network hardware is used to create boundaries and restrict access. Access is granted only to members of that extranet, including both internal members and external members.

Automating Tasks with Script Services

Modern NOS software provides system administrators and users with many built-in tools and automated features to increase productivity. Sometimes these features and commands are not enough to perform certain tasks efficiently. For this reason, most NOSs include support for scripts. A *script* is a simple text program that allows the user to perform many automated tasks at once. Depending on their design, scripts can range from single lines of code to lengthy amounts of programming logic.

Scripts are considered much simpler than the standard programs and applications found in a NOS. The operating system sequentially processes the lines of code in a script file whenever the file is run. Most scripts are designed to execute from the top of the file to the bottom without requiring any input from the user. This process is somewhat different from regular programs, where lines of code are compiled into executable files, and user interaction typically plays a key role. However, the average user or system administrator does not have time to develop such complex applications and often has no need for the additional programming power they provide. Scripts provide a nice middle ground, offering the ability to use standard programming logic to execute simple, noninteractive tasks.

Many different scripting languages exist. Each offers its own advantages to the user:

- *VBScript (Visual Basic Script)*—A very popular Microsoft scripting language based on the Visual Basic programming language. VBScript is considered easy to learn and is widely used in Windows 2000.

- *JavaScript*—Another popular scripting language that is based on the Java programming language. JavaScript is most often used in web pages, allowing a web browser to execute the script and providing web users with added functionality.

- *Linux shell scripting*—Specific to the Linux NOS, these shell scripts consist of many Linux commands and programming logic to perform a series of commands at once.

- **Perl, PHP, TCL, REXX, and Python**—Many other scripting languages exist. They have varying degrees of difficulty and intended purposes. Most users are not experts in all such languages and instead focus on learning only those that best accommodate their needs.

Although they differ in functionality and syntax, these scripting languages provide users with the tools necessary to customize the NOS. NOSs now typically support several of these scripting languages and provide users with flexibility in determining which scripting language to implement.

Script Solutions

Most average NOS users do not create and execute their own scripts. The majority of scripting is performed by system administrators and experienced users who are comfortable with programming concepts. They tend to build such scripts for the purpose of automating specific tasks through the execution of a single script file. These script files can then be scheduled to run at set times, to run when an event occurs, or to be executed manually by the user. The following examples demonstrate common scenarios in which scripts are an appropriate solution:

- **Logging on to the NOS**—A system administrator can use scripts to perform additional tasks when users log on to the network. These tasks include configuring default settings, initializing services, and connecting to other network drives, devices, and printers.

- **Printing messages to the screen**—Customized scripts are often created that display messages to the users of a network. These messages typically notify users of events such as the arrival of new mail, the status of a print job, or the shutting down of a network server.

- **Installing software**—A typical software installation process requires system administrators to select and confirm many options. Scripts can be created to automate this process and reduce the amount of time necessary to install the software on countless PCs across a network.

- **Automating complicated commands**—Some tasks often involve a series of complicated commands that must be repeated quite often. To simplify this process, scripts are created that contain all of these commands, thus allowing the user to execute only the script file and perform all the tasks automatically.

Writing a script in Windows 2000 and Linux is covered in Chapter 10, "Linux." Table 5-4 outlines some of the major programming languages that are used in some of the major operating systems discussed in this course.

Table 5-4 Scripting Environments and Languages

Environment(s)	Language(s)
MS-DOS	Batch scripts (*.bat)
Microsoft Windows Scripting Host (WSH)	VBScript, JScript
Linux, UNIX	Shell scripting
Server-side web scripting	PHP, Perl, ASP (VBScript)
Client-side web scripting	JavaScript, VBScript

Domain Name System

The Domain Name System (DNS) protocol translates an Internet name (such as www.cisco.com) into an IP address. Many applications rely on the directory services provided by DNS to do this work. Web browsers, e-mail programs, and file transfer programs all use the names of remote systems. The DNS protocol allows these clients to send requests to DNS servers in the network for the translation of names to IP addresses, as shown in Figure 5-42. Applications can then use the addresses to send their messages. Without this directory lookup service, the Internet would be almost impossible to use.

Figure 5-42 Domain Name Service

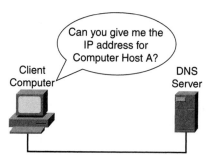

Host Names

Host names and the DNS services that computer systems run are all linked. The Internet name that the DNS resolves to the IP address is also called the *host name*. Computer systems find it easier to work with numbers, so computers can very easily and quickly distinguish between and locate different computers by using a binary IP address. It is far more difficult for humans to do this. This is why host names are resolved to IP addresses via DNS services. For example, if you were given two IP addresses for two computers, such as 192.168.1.5 and 168.5.59.7, it would be hard to distinguish which computer system these IP addresses represented—especially if DHCP services were enabled, which means that the IP address might change at times. It would be impossible for a system administrator or end users to keep track. On the other hand, if the system administrator or end users could find this computer by using a host name such as fileserver_A or fileserver_B, you could very easily and quickly distinguish between computer systems. Host names also make it easy to locate specific systems such as web servers and FTP servers on the Internet, because it is much easier to remember a name rather than an IP address.

It's important to know a few rules about host names. Host names have two parts, similar to how an IP address has two parts. The first part of the host name is the machine name, and the second part is the domain name. The *machine name* refers to the actual computer, and the domain name refers to the collection of computers to which the specific computer belongs. The domain names are unique and are registered for use by individuals, small businesses, and corporations, which can assign the machine names to systems within the domain and link those machine names to IP addresses.

To understand how this process of machine names and domain names works, you must understand the hierarchical structure of Internet domains. This structure is made up of *top-level domains (TLDs)*, which are considered the top of the domain tree. Examples of TLDs are .com, .edu, .gov, and .mil. You are probably familiar with these names if you have ever been on the Internet. Within each TLD are various registered domain names that represent specific individuals, small businesses, corporations, and organizations, such as cisco.com and linux.com. These domains even break into smaller *subdomains* within the domain, such as SanJose.Cisco.com and Phoenix.Cisco.com. The domain/subdomain structure represents logical groupings of computers within companies or organizations. Even subdomains can be divided into smaller subdomains.

Host names are usually assigned by system administrators, or they have a specified naming convention that is used to identify computers by who uses them, what they are used for, or what department they are in. The system administrator usually creates this naming convention so that every computer in the domain can be easily identified. For this reason, it is very rare for any computer on a network that is part of the domain to have its host names configured by the user. There are also some instances if DHCP is being used in which host names can be assigned automatically. However, this is not usually done, because host names are usually controlled by the system administrator and must be manually configured.

DHCP

The purpose of Dynamic Host Configuration Protocol (DHCP) is to allow individual computers on an IP network to extract their configurations from the DHCP server or servers. These DHCP servers have no exact information about the individual computers until information is requested. The overall purpose of this is to reduce the work necessary to administer a large IP network. The most significant piece of information distributed in this manner is the IP address that identifies the host on the network. DHCP also allows for recovery and the ability to automatically renew network IP addresses through a leasing mechanism. This mechanism allocates an IP address for a specific time period, releases it, and then assigns a new IP address. DHCP allows all this to be done by a DHCP server, which saves the system administrator considerable amounts of time.

Linux can use three different DHCP clients—pump, dhclient, and dhcpd. Not all distributions of Linux contain all three of these. Some have all three, some have just two, and others have only one. However, all distributions have a default DHCP client that is used when you choose to use DHCP during the installation process. The distributions that come with multiple DHCP clients allow them to be swapped out by removing the old package and installing the new one.

The Linux DHCP client starts when the system is booted. The configuration information is stored in a startup file called network or networking. This file has a line of text that indicates whether to run the DHCP client:

BOOTPROTO="dhcp"

The Red Hat distribution of Linux stores this information in the /etc/sysconfig/network-scripts/ifcfg-eth0 file. Deleting the **"dhcp"** in this line stops the DHCP services.

Domains

A *domain* is a logical grouping of networked computers that share a central directory or database. The directory or database is installed on computers called *servers*. A server usually manages all security-related and user-related domain interactions. It also provides a centralized place from which to administer these services.

The concept of a domain does not just include computers that are next to each other, or in a specific location, or even on the same LAN (although it can). It can also include computers and servers located in different locations throughout the world that can communicate with each other with various types of connections to maintain a synchronized database. The idea of a domain is not physical, but rather a logical grouping of company computers and servers (see Figure 5-43). Domains have several advantages:

- Centralized administration, because all user information is stored centrally.

- A single logon process that lets users access network resources, such as file, print, and application resources, as well as specify permissions that control who can and cannot access these services.

- A domain lets you expand a network to extremely large sizes throughout every corner of the world.

Figure 5-43 Specifying the Domain in Windows 2000

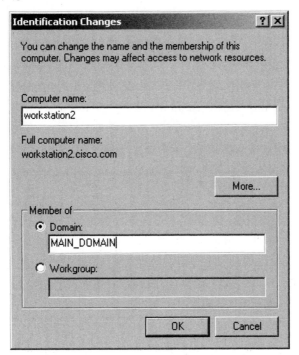

Summary

This chapter discussed network services. Some of the important concepts to retain from this chapter include the following:

- Remote administration allows an administrator to access a system's file database, run various programs, or even download information or files from another room, another city, or another country.

- Several applications and protocols can be used to remotely administer a network server. The most common method of remote administration is terminal emulation.

- Novell Network Directory Service (NDS) uses a directory database called the bindery. The biggest drawback of this directory service is its local nature. Each NetWare server on a network has to maintain an individual database, and a user has to have an account on each server to access that server's resources.

- Whereas Novell NDS functions as a service that works with the NOS, Microsoft Active Directory functions as an application that is deeply integrated with the operating system.

- Linux uses another version of directory services called Network Information Service (NIS). NIS provides a simple network lookup service consisting of databases and processes.

- The World Wide Web is now the most visible network service. An intranet does not allow public access to private servers. It is specific to an individual company. An extranet is an emerging technology that combines the best of the Internet and intranets.

NOS computers take on specialized roles to accomplish concurrent access to shared resources. The next chapter discusses the characteristics of the network operating system.

Check Your Understanding

The following review questions help you assess what you learned in this chapter. Answers can be found in Appendix A, "Answers to Check Your Understanding Questions."

1. Match the protocols with the function they represent.

Service	TCP/IP Protocol
World Wide Web server	SMTP
File transfer	DHCP
File sharing	NFS
Internet mail	Telnet
Remote administration	FTP
Automatic network address configuration	SNMP
Network administration	DNS
Directory services (Internet)	HTTP

2. Which two of the following are standard CLI commands to open a Telnet connection to a remote computer?

   telnet candy.company.com

   connect candy.company.com

   telnet 204.45.55.90

   connect 204.45.55.90

3. Many companies, both large and small, have deployed private networks called intranets. Select the five best reasons for a company to create an intranet.

   Internal information, memoranda, and reports

   Staff and employee directories

   Store backup files

   Calendars and appointment schedules

   Purchase items securely

   Application and software deployment

   Conduct research on competitors

   Employee services

4. DNS translates _____ into _____, and DHCP assigns _____ to computers.

Options are as follows (they may be used more than once):

Internet names

NetBIOS names

IP addresses

MAC addresses

Key Terms

Active Directory   Microsoft's distributed directory implementation that is used to manage all objects, computers, and user accounts.

assigned permission   A permission explicitly granted by an authorized user.

broadband remote access   The name that is given to high-speed DSL and cable Internet connections.

Challenge-Handshake Authentication Protocol (CHAP)   A protocol that presents the user's username and password in an encrypted form when used for authentication.

client list   Specifies which clients are granted or denied access to the server in the corresponding daemon list.

daemon list   Specifies the names of servers that appear in /etc/services. These are the servers to which access is either granted or denied.

Directory Access Protocol (DAP)   Lets the Directory User Agent (DUA) communicate with the Directory System Agent (DSA). DAP defines the means by which the user can search the directory to read, add, delete, and modify directory entries.

Directory Information Base   Acts as the central data store, or database, in which directory information is kept.

directory service   Provides system administrators with centralized control of all users and resources across the entire network to simplify network management by providing a standard interface for common system administration tasks.

Directory System Agent   An X.500 Electronic Directory Service (EDS) standard that manages directory data.

Directory User Agent   An X.500 Electronic Directory Service (EDS) standard that gives users access to directory services.

extranet   A technology that allows employees and customers to access the private network or intranet via the Internet.

firewall   A barrier between one network, such as the Internet, and another network. It controls security and traffic that is allowed into and out of the network.

forest   A Microsoft term for the collection of all the different domain trees in the Active Directory hierarchical structure.

inherited permission   A permission that applies to child objects because they were inherited from a parent object.

intranet   Organizations build web servers to create a private network to prevent information and services from being made public on the Internet.

JavaScript   A popular scripting language that is based on the Java programming language most often used in web pages.

Lightweight Directory Access Protocol (LDAP)   Developed as a subset of DAP to simplify access to X.500-type directories. LDAP is designed to use fewer system resources than DAP, and it is easier to implement.

Linux shell scripting   Specific to the Linux NOS, these shell scripts consist of many Linux commands and programming logic to perform a series of commands at once.

Network Directory Service (NDS)   Novell's distributed directory implementation that is used to manage all objects, computers, and user accounts. It is a global database that is replicated between servers on the network.

network operating system (NOS)   Software that is designed to provide network processes to clients and peers. Network services include the World Wide Web (WWW), file sharing, mail exchange, directory services, remote management, and print services.

organizational unit (OU)   Combining groups of the same user accounts or computers for easier administration to organize resources within domains.

packet filter   A type of firewall that restricts traffic based on port assignments.

Password Authentication Protocol (PAP)   A protocol that presents the user's username and password in an unencrypted form when used for authentication.

remote access   Lets employees access the corporate remote-access server and log in to the network with their regular user account. Employees can then use all the resources that would be available from the office desktop computer.

replication   The process of copying data from one computer to one or more other computers and synchronizing that data so that it is identical on all systems.

script   A simple text program, written in a specific programming language, that allows the user to perform many automated tasks at once.

SSH   A secure means of authenticating users to a server by storing a special key on the server and another one on the client. The client uses this key, and not a password, to authenticate to the server.

terminal emulation   The process of accessing a remote system via a local computer terminal. The local terminal runs software that emulates, or mimics, the look of the remote system terminal.

VBScript (Visual Basic Script)   A very popular Microsoft scripting language based on the Visual Basic programming language.

virtual private network (VPN)   A technology developed by extranet designers that allows employees and customers to access the private network over the Internet in a secure manner.

Objectives

After completing this chapter, you will be able to complete tasks related to

- Characteristics of a network operating system
- Windows NT/2000
- Linux
- Determining software requirements for a Linux NOS

Chapter 6

Introduction to Network Operating Systems

A computer *operating system (OS)* is the software foundation on which the computer applications and services run. Similarly, a *network operating system (NOS)* enables communication between multiple devices and the sharing of resources across a network.

A NOS is, generally, an operating system that runs on a network server, such as Novell NetWare or Microsoft Windows NT Server. This chapter covers the following network operating systems:

- Microsoft Windows NT 4.0
- Microsoft Windows 2000
- Windows XP
- Novell NetWare
- Linux
- UNIX
- Macintosh OS X (10)

Characteristics of a Network Operating System

This section covers the following topics:

- Overview of NOS characteristics
- Differences between a PC and a NOS
- Multiuser, multitasking, and multiprocessor systems
- NOS server hardware
- Choosing a NOS
- Types of NOSs

Worksheet 6.1.6 Characteristics of a Network Operating System

Identify the main concepts and characteristics that define a network operating system as opposed to a standalone operating system.

Overview of NOS Characteristics

The function of an OS is to control the computer hardware, program execution environment, and user interface. The OS performs these functions for a single user or a number of users who share the machine serially rather than concurrently. An administrator may set up accounts for more than one user, but users cannot log on to the system at the same time.

In contrast, NOSs distribute their functions over a number of networked computers. A NOS depends on the native OS in each computer. It then adds functions that allow access to shared resources by a number of users concurrently. Figure 6-1 shows how a client/server relationship is designed compared to other typical environments.

Figure 6-1 Client/Server Environment Compared to Other Typical Environments

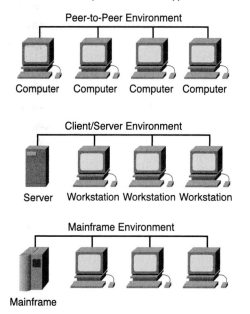

NOS computers take on specialized roles to accomplish concurrent access to shared resources. *Client* systems contain specialized software that allows them to request shared resources that are controlled by server systems responding to a client request. Figure 6-2 illustrates how data that is stored in servers is made available to clients' requests.

Figure 6-2 Data Stored in Servers Is Made Available to Clients

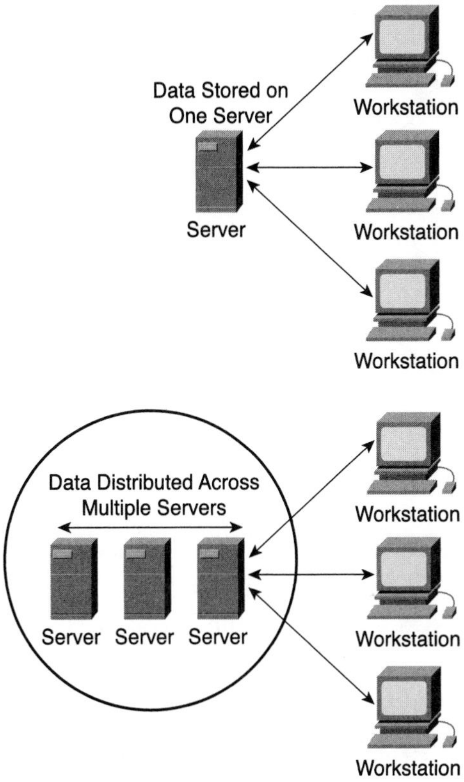

Differences Between a PC and a NOS

PCs function as clients in a NOS environment. By using the functions of the PC native operating system, the user can access resources that are local to the PC. These include applications, files, and devices that are directly attached, such as printers. When a PC becomes a client in a NOS environment, additional specialized software lets the local user access nonlocal or remote resources as if these resources were a part of the local system. The NOS enhances the client PC's reach by making remote services available as extensions of the local native operating system.

Although a number of users may have accounts on a PC, only a single account is active on the system at any given time. In contrast, a NOS supports multiple user accounts at the same time and enables concurrent access to shared resources by multiple clients. Servers must support multiple users and act as repositories of resources that are shared by many clients. Servers require specialized software and additional hardware. Figure 6-3 further illustrates this concept. You can see that the server must contain several user accounts and be capable of giving more than one user access to network resources at a time.

Figure 6-3 PCs Accessing a NOS Server

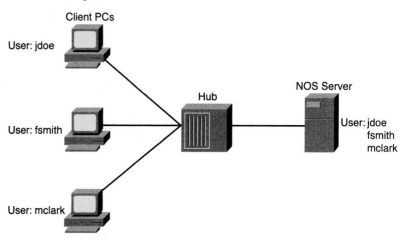

Multiuser, Multitasking, and Multiprocessor Systems

To support multiple concurrent users and to provide shared access to network services, resources, and devices, NOS servers must run operating systems with characteristics that extend beyond those of client PCs. A number of operating systems, such as Linux, Windows NT/2000/XP, and Novell NetWare, can integrate the features that are required to function as a NOS server.

A system that can operate as a NOS server must be able to support multiple users concurrently. The network administrator creates an account for each user, allowing the user to connect to and log on to the server system. The user account on the server lets the server authenticate that user and allocate what resources the user is allowed to access. Systems that provide this capability are called *multiuser systems*. UNIX, Linux, and Windows NT/2000/XP all support this multiuser capability.

A NOS server is a *multitasking system*. Internally, the OS must be capable of executing multiple tasks or processes at the same time. Server operating systems accomplish this with scheduling software that is built into the execution environment. The scheduling software allocates internal processor time, memory, and other elements of the system to different tasks in a way that allows them to share the system's resources. Each user on the multiuser system is supported by a separate task or process internally on the server. These internal tasks are created dynamically as users connect to the system and are deleted when users disconnect.

Another feature of systems that can act as NOS servers is their processing power. Ordinarily, computers have a single Central Processing Unit (CPU), which executes the instructions that make up a given task or process. To work efficiently and deliver fast responses to client requests, an OS that functions as a NOS server requires a powerful CPU to execute its tasks or programs. Single-processor systems with one CPU can meet the needs of most NOS servers if they have the necessary speed. To achieve higher execution speeds, some systems are equipped with more than one processor. Such systems are called *multiprocessing systems*. They can execute multiple tasks in parallel by assigning each task to a different processor. The aggregate amount of work that the server can perform in a given time is greatly enhanced in multiprocessor systems.

Figure 6-4 illustrates a typical multitasking server that is running multiple instances of network services and that is being accessed by multiple client systems. Servers of this nature are sometimes called *enterprise servers* because of their capacity to handle large and multiple services. Enterprise servers also can run concurrent copies of a particular command, which allows them to execute multiple instances of the same service or program, called threads. A *thread* is a program that can execute independently of other parts. Operating systems that support *multithreading* allow programmers to design programs whose threaded parts can execute concurrently.

Figure 6-4 Multitasking

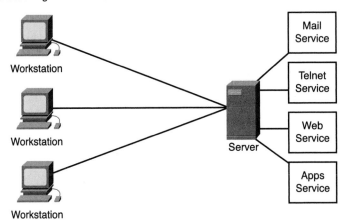

NOS Server Hardware

In a NOS environment, many client systems access and share the resources of one or more servers. Desktop client systems are equipped with their own memory and peripheral devices, such as a keyboard, monitor, and disk drive. To support local processing, the server systems must be equipped to support multiple concurrent users and multiple tasks as clients make demands on the server for remote resources.

NOS servers, therefore, are typically larger systems with additional memory to support multiple tasks that are all active, or resident, in memory at the same time. Additional disk space is also required on servers to hold shared files and to function as an extension to the system's internal memory. Also, servers typically require extra expansion slots on their system boards to connect shared devices, such as printers and multiple network interfaces. On multiprocessor servers, additional CPUs enhance processing power.

Because NOS servers function as central repositories of resources that are vital to the operation of client systems, the servers must be not only efficient but also robust. The term "robust" indicates that the server systems can function effectively under heavy loads. It also means the systems can survive the failure of one or more processes or components without experiencing a general system failure. This objective is met by building redundancy into server systems. *Redundancy* is the inclusion of additional hardware components that can take over if other components fail. Redundancy is a feature of *fault-tolerant* systems, which are designed to survive failures and even be repaired without interruption while they are up and running. Because a NOS depends on the continuous operation of its servers, the extra hardware components justify the additional expense.

Choosing a NOS

The main features to consider when selecting a NOS include performance, management and monitoring tools, security, scalability, and robustness/fault tolerance. The following sections briefly define each of these features.

Performance

A NOS must perform well at reading/writing files across the network between clients and servers. It must be able to sustain fast performance under heavy loads when many (perhaps hundreds) of clients are making requests.

A NOS must respond to client requests for access to server databases. An example is a transaction request to extract records from a database housed in the NOS server. Consistent performance under heavy demand is an important benchmark for a NOS.

Management and Monitoring

The *management interface* on the NOS server provides the tools for server monitoring, client administration, file and print management, and disk storage management. The management interface provides tools for the installation of new services and the configuration of those services. Additionally, servers require regular monitoring and adjustment.

Security

A NOS must protect the shared resources under its control. *Security* includes authenticating user access to services to prevent unauthorized access to the network resources. Security also performs encryption for the protection of information as it travels between clients and servers.

Scalability

Scalability is the NOS's ability to grow without performance degradation. The NOS must be capable of sustaining its performance as new users join the network and new servers are added to support them.

Robustness/Fault Tolerance

A measure of robustness is the ability to deliver NOS services consistently under heavy load and to sustain its services if components or processes fail. Using redundant disk devices and balancing the workload across multiple servers can improve NOS robustness.

Types of NOSs

Choosing a NOS can be a complex and difficult decision. Each popular NOS has strengths and weaknesses. A NOS might cost thousands of dollars more than a desktop operating system, depending on how many clients will connect to the server.

It is important to know the basics of popular NOS families. Many networks now include more than one server type, and knowing how to get these diverse systems to interoperate is an important skill for a network administrator.

Operating systems on the network have their own "language." Different NOS vendors use the same terms in different ways. For example, in a UNIX environment, *root* refers to the master administrative account, but in NetWare networks, it identifies an NDS object. In Windows, *root* can mean the domain at the top of a Windows 2000 or XP domain tree, or it can refer to the basic component of a Distributed File System (DFS).

The following sections discuss these popular NOS-based networks:

- Windows NT and Windows 2000
- Linux

Figure 6-5 shows some of them.

Figure 6-5 Types of NOSs

Windows NT/2000

This section covers the following topics:

- Windows terminology
- Windows NT 4.0
- Windows 2000 operating systems
- Windows 2000's family of operating systems

Windows Terminology

Windows server-based networks that run Windows NT Server or Windows 2000 Server are based on the concept of the domain. A *domain* is a group of computers and users that serves as a boundary of administrative authority. Windows NT domains and Windows 2000 domains, although similar in function, interact with one another differently.

Microsoft uses the term *domain* to describe groups of computers, users, and resources that form an administrative boundary. Microsoft uses the term *domain controller* to describe the logon authentication servers that hold a copy of the security accounts database. Also specific to Microsoft networks is the distinction between the printer, used to describe a logical software construct, and the print device, which refers to the piece of hardware that prints the document.

Windows 2000 networking terminology is familiar to those who have worked with Windows NT 4.0. However, some terms and concepts, such as *domain tree* and *forest*, might be new to NT administrators. In addition, administrators who come to Windows networking from a NetWare environment might find that some familiar terms, such as *tree*, now have different meanings.

The following sections examine specific characteristics of Windows NT 4.0 and Windows 2000. Figure 6-6 shows the various ways in which computers can be arranged in a network, either standalone, as a member of a single-group domain, or as a member of a multiple-group domain.

Figure 6-6 Networked Computer Systems

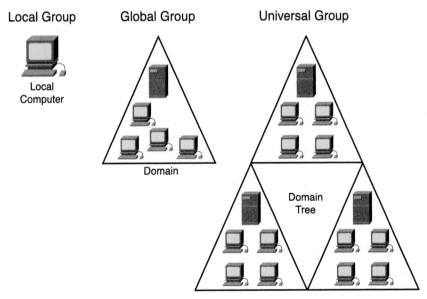

Windows NT 4.0

Windows NT Workstation was the first Microsoft desktop operating system that was aimed at the corporate market. The latest version of the NT operating system is NT 4.0, which has a user interface similar to the one in Windows 95. Before the release of

NT 4.0, Microsoft released NT 3.*x*, which has the Windows 3.*x* interface. Windows NT was designed to provide an environment for mission-critical business that would be more stable than the Microsoft consumer operating systems.

When the first version of Windows NT was released, Microsoft said the acronym stood for "New Technology." More recently, the company has stated that "NT" stands alone and is not an acronym.

Here are some advantages of Windows NT Workstation as a desktop operating system and network client:

- It is a true 32-bit operating system, and it supports preemptive multitasking and greater system stability.
- It includes file-level security and data compression on a file-by-file basis.
- It is backward-compatible with many 16-bit programs without sacrificing reliability. NT runs DOS and older Windows programs in virtual machines (VMs). Using this method, if one application crashes, it does not affect other applications or require a reboot of the operating system.

Network integration is a primary focus in the design of Microsoft Windows NT. NT includes support for common NICs as well as software needed to connect to Microsoft and NetWare networks. Also built in is the capability to function as a remote-access client or server.

Windows NT Domain Structure

The domain structure of Windows NT is entirely different from the domain structure of Windows 2000. Instead of Active Directory, Windows NT provides an administrative tool called the User Manager for Domains. Figure 6-7 shows the Windows NT User Manager for Domains account management screen. It is accessed from the domain controller and is used to create, manage, and remove domain user accounts. The User Manager for Domains allows the administrator to create new user and group accounts; rename, modify, and delete accounts; assign passwords; set account policies; and set restrictions on users. Restrictions on users include specifying when they can log on and from which workstations.

Figure 6-7 User Accounts in Windows NT 4.0

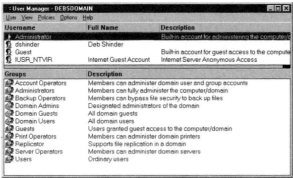

Each NT domain requires one (and only one) Primary Domain Controller (PDC). This is a "master" server that contains the Security Accounts Management Database (often called the *SAM*). A domain can also have one or more Backup Domain Controllers (BDCs), each of which contains a read-only copy of the SAM. The SAM is what controls the authentication process when a user logs on to the domain. When a user attempts to log on, the account information is sent to the SAM database. If the information for that account is stored in the SAM database, the user is authenticated to the domain and has access to the workstation and network resources.

Users can log on and receive authentication from either the PDC or a BDC. However, changes to the SAM can be made only on the PDC. These changes are then replicated to the BDCs on a regular basis. BDCs balance the load of authentication traffic and serve as backups in case the PDC goes down. If the PDC goes down permanently, a BDC can be "promoted" to become the PDC.

Windows 2000 Operating Systems

Windows 2000 is one of Microsoft's operating systems for the corporate desktop. Like the Windows 2000 server products, it is based on the NT kernel and includes many enhanced features. For example, Windows 2000 Professional provides a high level of security and stability for mission-critical tasks.

Windows 2000 Professional supports Plug and Play technology. It can be installed on hard disks that can use either the FAT32 file system or NTFS. It includes file encryption for securing data on the hard disk. Plug and Play technology is a very useful tool that allows an administrator to quickly and easily add components to the system. The OS automatically recognizes and installs the drivers for the device. Essentially, as soon as the component is "plugged" into the system, it "plays" automatically without additional configuration from the administrator. Previously, when a new component was added, drivers had to be installed, and the device needed to be configured manually. Windows 2000 comes with a huge database of drivers for common Plug and Play devices.

Other advantages of Windows 2000 Professional as a desktop operating system and network client include the following:

- It offers better support for mobile users through Advanced Power Management (APM) and ACPI. Windows NT does not support ACPI.

- It provides for more secure virtual private networking with the Layer 2 Tunneling Protocol (L2TP) and IP Security (IPSec). Earlier versions of Windows supported only the Point-to-Point Tunneling Protocol (PPTP) for virtual private networks (VPNs). *L2TP* is an extension to the PPP protocol that lets ISPs operate VPNs. *IPSec* is a set of protocols developed to support secure exchange of packets at the IP layer, which is also used in VPN connections.

- The offline folders feature lets users copy and synchronize documents from the network to the local system so that they can be accessed when the computer is not connected to the network.

- *The Internet Printing Protocol (IPP)* lets users print to a URL and manage printers through a web browser interface.

- Built-in disk defragmenters and other tools and utilities help users maintain and manage the operating system. These have to be purchased separately from third parties for Windows NT.

- Windows 2000 Professional supports Kerberos security (a developing standard for authenticating network users) and the features of a Windows 2000 domain as an Active Directory client.

Account Administration in Windows 2000

Administrative tasks in Windows 2000 use a common framework, the *Microsoft Management Console (MMC)*. This tool uses snap-ins, which are modules that contain the tools for specific administrative functions. Users and groups are created and managed with the Active Directory Users (ADUs) and Computers MMC snap-in. You access the MMC by choosing Start > Programs > Administrative Tools > Active Directory Users and Computers. Windows 2000, unlike Windows NT 4.0, allows objects such as users and resources to be placed in container objects called organizational units (OUs). Administrative authority over each OU can be delegated to a user or group. This feature allows more specific control than was possible with Windows NT 4.0. Figure 6-8 shows the Active Directory Users and Computers Management Console. Notice all the different types of objects that are managed using this console.

Figure 6-8 Account Administration in Windows 2000

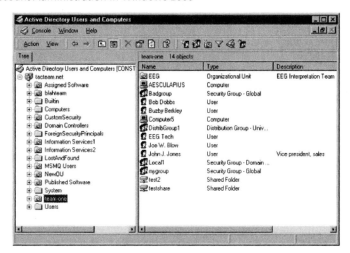

Windows 2000's Family of Operating Systems

The Windows 2000 family of operating systems includes Windows 2000 Professional, Windows 2000 Server, and Windows 2000 Advanced Server. The network's specific needs determine the best version of Windows 2000 for the installation.

Windows 2000 Professional

The design of Windows 2000 Professional is based on the technology that Microsoft developed with its previous client-based network operating system, Windows NT. Windows 2000 takes the technologies from Windows NT and adds many new features and enhancements. Windows 2000 Professional is not designed to be a true NOS. It does not provide a domain controller, DNS server, or DHCP server. Nor does it render any of the services that can be deployed with the Windows 2000 server family. Its main purpose is to be part of a domain as a client-side operating system. The type of hardware that can be installed on the system is limited. For example, many servers require multiple processors and NICs. Windows 2000 Professional can support up to two processors. If the system needs to do a lot of "data crunching," a system that supports more than two processes would be required. Windows 2000 Professional can provide some server capabilities for small networks and peer-to-peer networks. For example, Windows 2000 Professional can serve as a file server, a print server, an FTP server, and a web server. However, an FTP site or website that will receive a lot of simultaneous traffic needs to be upgraded to Windows 2000 Server or Windows 2000 Advanced Server. Windows 2000 Professional supports only up to ten simultaneous connections at a time.

Windows 2000 Server

Windows 2000 Server includes all the Windows 2000 Professional features just discussed, as well as many new server-specific functions. Windows 2000 Server can also operate as a file, print, web, and application server. What separates Windows 2000 Server from Windows 2000 Professional is a complete set of infrastructure services based on Active Directory services. Active Directory, similar to Novell NDS, serves as a centralized point of management for users, groups, security services, and network resources.

Windows 2000 Server also supports four-way *symmetric multiprocessing (SMP)* systems and allows up to 4 GB of physical memory. Symmetric multiprocessing is a computer architecture that provides high performance by making multiple CPUs available to individual processes. Symmetric multiprocessing allows multiple processors to work in parallel while using a single operating system image, common memory, and disk I/O resources. Simply stated, symmetric multiprocessing is when multiple processors work together to share a computer's workload. It includes the multipurpose capabilities required for workgroups and branch offices as well as for departmental deployments of file and print servers, application servers, web servers, and communication servers. Windows 2000 Server is intended for use in small-to-medium-sized enterprise environments.

Some other enhancements that come with Windows 2000 Server are built-in support for the major network protocols that are in use throughout networks today, such as TCP/IP and IPX/SPX. Windows 2000 Server provides integrated connectivity with Novell NetWare, UNIX, and AppleTalk systems. A Windows 2000 Server configured as a communications server can provide dialup networking services for mobile users. Windows 2000 Server can support up to 256 simultaneous inbound dialup sessions, as opposed to Windows 2000 Professional, which can provide support for only one dialup session at a time.

Windows 2000 Advanced Server

Windows 2000 Server and Windows 2000 Advanced Server are the same, except that Advanced Server provides hardware and software support that a system administrator needs in an enterprise that has an extremely large network that might include several WAN links to offices all over the world. Advanced Server is a more powerful departmental and application server operating system that includes all the functions of Windows 2000 Server and adds the advanced high availability and improved scalability required for larger networks. Windows 2000 Advanced Server supports eight-way SMP, which is ideal for database-intensive work. Advanced Server also provides support for higher-end hardware supporting an enterprise network. For example, Advanced Server provides support for more than 4 GB of physical memory.

Windows .NET Server

Microsoft developed Windows .NET Server with the ability to provide a secure and reliable system to run enterprise-level web and FTP sites to compete with Linux and UNIX server operating systems. With the growing emergence of e-commerce, web-based companies, and companies that are expanding their services to the Internet, there is a need for a server that can provide secure and reliable web and FTP services. Windows .NET Server, which is built on the Windows 2000 server kernel, is tailored to provide these types of services. The Windows .NET Server provides XML web services to companies that run medium-to-high-volume web traffic. .NET server provides support for companies just getting started in this new generation of business, as well as businesses that have provided Internet-based business solutions for some time. Table 6-1 compares the Windows 2000 family of operating systems.

Worksheet 6.2.4   Windows NT/2000

Identify the main concepts and principles of the Windows family of network operating systems.

Table 6-1 Comparing the Windows 2000 Family

NOS	Features	Usage	Price
Windows 2000 Professional	Dual-processor support, limited server capabilities	Client workstations, small web servers	Least expensive
Windows 2000 Server	Expanded server capabilities, Active Directory, SMP	Small-to-medium-sized organizations	↓
Windows 2000 Advanced Server	Full server capabilities, including applications server, increased hardware support	Large organizations	↓
Windows 2000 .NET Server	Robust Internet server	Enterprise Internet	Most expensive

Linux

This section covers the following topics:

- History of Linux
- What is UNIX?
- Linux operating systems
- Linux clients

History of Linux

Linux is an operating system similar to UNIX. It runs on many different computers. Linux was first released in 1991 by its creator, Linus Torvalds, at the University of Helsinki. Since then, it has grown in popularity as programmers around the world embraced the idea of building a free operating system, adding features, and fixing problems. Linux is popular with the current generation of computer users for the same reasons that early versions of the UNIX operating system enticed fans more than 20 years ago. Linux is portable, which means that versions can be found running on name-brand or clone PCs, Apple Macintoshes, Sun workstations, or Digital Equipment Corporation Alpha-based computers. Linux also comes with source code, so the user can change or customize the software to his or her needs. Finally, Linux offers many features adopted from other versions of UNIX. Figure 6-9 shows a timeline of UNIX/Linux development.

Figure 6-9   Linux Development Timeline

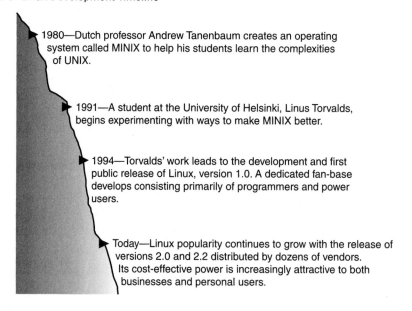

1980—Dutch professor Andrew Tanenbaum creates an operating system called MINIX to help his students learn the complexities of UNIX.

1991—A student at the University of Helsinki, Linus Torvalds, begins experimenting with ways to make MINIX better.

1994—Torvalds' work leads to the development and first public release of Linux, version 1.0. A dedicated fan-base develops consisting primarily of programmers and power users.

Today—Linux popularity continues to grow with the release of versions 2.0 and 2.2 distributed by dozens of vendors. Its cost-effective power is increasingly attractive to both businesses and personal users.

The Open Source Initiative

The Open Source Initiative provides a trademark for software developers who want to share, modify, and redistribute their code. To use the trademark, the software must meet certain criteria. It must be freely distributed without restriction, and the source code must be available. Examples of compliant software include Linux, the BSD version of UNIX, the X Window System, and applications developed under the GNU project.

What Is UNIX?

It is important to mention the features and uses of UNIX when discussing Linux. The UNIX NOS was developed in 1969, and it has evolved into many varieties. The source code is open; that is, it is available at no cost to anyone who wants to modify it. Additionally, it is written in the C programming language, so businesses, academic institutions, and even individuals can develop their own versions.

UNIX operating systems are used on high-end workstations such as Silicon Graphics and Sun machines. UNIX can run as a command-line operating system or with a graphical user interface (GUI) such as the X Window System. Figure 6-10 shows the UNIX X Window System GUI.

Figure 6-10 The UNIX X Window System GUI

UNIX Operating Systems

There are hundreds of different versions of UNIX. Some of the most popular are the following:

- Berkeley Software Design, Inc. (BSD UNIX, which has spawned variations such as FreeBSD)
- Santa Cruz Operation (SCO) UNIX
- Sun Solaris
- AIX (IBM UNIX)
- HP-UX (Hewlett-Packard UNIX)

Open-source code is both the strength and the weakness of the UNIX operating system. Developers are free to improve and customize the operating system. Although this results in a lack of standardization that can be frustrating to users, administrators, and application developers, a large body of application software can be used across multiple UNIX and Linux platforms.

Despite the popularity of Windows and NetWare in corporate LANs, much of the Internet still runs on powerful UNIX systems. UNIX is usually associated with expensive hardware and is considered "user-unfriendly," but recent developments have changed that image. In particular, the emergence of Linux in the 1990s brought UNIX computing to the PC world.

Linux Operating Systems

Linux is sometimes called "UNIX Lite." It is designed to run on Intel-compatible PCs, but it runs on other machines as well. Linux brings the advantages of UNIX to home and small-business computers.

As with UNIX, there are numerous distributions of Linux. A distribution includes elements such as an installation program, a kernel, startup scripts, configuration files, and critical support software. The different distributions might use completely different versions of any or all of these features, which produces a clearly different look and feel. In all, from 24 to 36 different major distributions are available. In addition to that, several other less-popular and specialized editions of Linux exist. Some of these distributions are free downloads from the web, and others are commercially distributed. The following sections describe a few of the most popular.

Red Hat Linux (www.redhat.com)

Red Hat Linux, shown in Figure 6-11, is one of the older versions of Linux. It has been one of the most influential distributions as well. Red Hat Linux is famous for creating the RPM format that is now used by other distributions that are not even based on Red Hat. Red Hat contains a GUI installation process as well as GUI configuration tools. Red Hat is compatible with various CPUs, including x86, IA-64, and Alpha.

Figure 6-11   Red Hat Linux

Linux Mandrake (www.linux-mandrake.com/en)

Mandrake is a French-based version of Linux. It probably is the most similar to Red Hat Linux. Mandrake was originally developed as a version of Red Hat with the KDE desktop environment. Since then, Mandrake has developed an identity of its own. It has a GUI installation process but also has different features for its server configuration. For example, Mandrake uses Postfix rather than Sendmail as its mail server. Mandrake is compatible with various types of CPUs, including x86, IA-64, SPARC, Alpha, and PowerPC. Mandrake Linux is shown in Figure 6-12. It doesn't look all that different from Red Hat.

Figure 6-12 Mandrake Linux

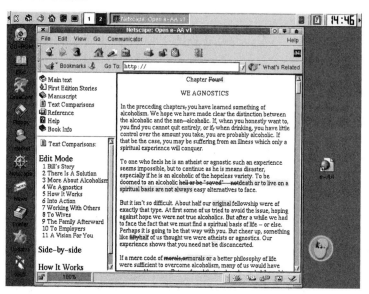

Caldera eDesktop and eServer (www.caldera.com)

As noted by its name, this version of Linux is released by Caldera, much like Red Hat releases Red Hat. Caldera Linux, shown in Figure 6-13, has two releases. One is targeted at workstations alone, and the other is targeted at servers alone. Like Red Hat, Caldera Linux is RPM-based and has very sophisticated GUI configuration tools. However, the Caldera distribution of Linux is not derived from Red Hat. Caldera Linux is available only on an x86 CPU.

Figure 6-13 Caldera Linux

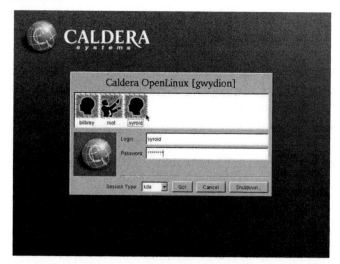

Debian GNU/Linux (www.debian.org)

This distribution of Linux, shown in Figure 6-14, is different from the other distributions in that it is built solely for nonprofit use. The other distributions are built mainly for for-profit companies. This makes Debian Linux a very popular choice for users who like the open-source initiative, because it lets them customize these files to their own liking—a fact that Linux likes to promote. Debian uses many of the GUI configuration tools used by the other versions of Linux. Debian Linux can be used on x86, PowerPC, Alpha, SPARC, and 680x0 processors.

Figure 6-14 Debian Linux

Corel Linux (http://linux.corel.com)

The Corel Linux distribution is based on Debian GNU/Linux, but it has some additional user-friendly features, such as a new installation process and new GUI configuration tools. Executing traditional Linux commands from the command line does not always work. Instead, Corel Linux is designed mainly for desktop/workstation use and is targeted at Linux beginners who are familiar with Microsoft Windows. Corel Linux is available only on an x86 CPU. Corel Linux is shown in Figure 6-15.

Figure 6-15 Corel Linux

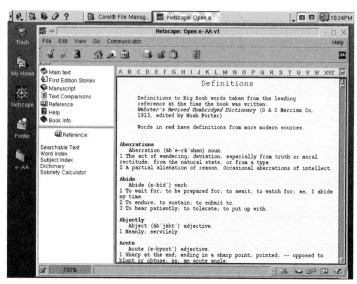

LinuxPPC (www.linuxppc.com)

This distribution of Linux, shown in Figure 6-16, is specifically designed for use on systems that have a PowerPC CPU. The PowerPC CPU is used with every modern Macintosh system, so LinuxPPC is designed for the Macintosh market. This distribution is a derivative of Red Hat.

Figure 6-16 LinuxPPC

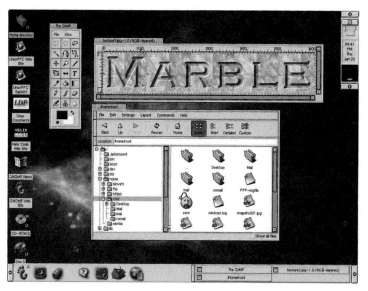

Slackware (www.slackware.com)

Slackware is a distribution of Linux that is very similar to Debian Linux in that it is intended for advanced users who prefer the standard UNIX environment in Linux. Slackware uses all text-based configuration tools. It does not use a GUI for these configuration purposes. It is also the oldest Linux distribution available and the only one that relies on tarballs for package management. Slackware can run on x86, Alpha, and SPARC CPUs.

Storm Linux (www.stormix.com)

Storm Linux, a variation of Debian Linux, is distributed by Stormix. Storm Linux is also similar to Corel Linux in that it adds GUI configuration tools to the Debian core. However, Storm Linux differs from Corel Linux in that it is not as dependent on these tools as Corel Linux is. Storm Linux can run only on x86 processors.

SuSE Linux (www.suse.com)

This distribution of Linux is popular in Europe and is produced by a German company. Like Red Hat Linux, SuSE Linux can use RPMs, but other than that, it is not based on Red Hat. SuSE uses DVD-ROM software to open packages if the system has a DVD-ROM drive. Unlike the other distributions, SuSE Linux ships with about a half-dozen CDs, which contain just about every package you could ever want for your Linux system. It can be difficult at times to search through these CDs to find the package you are looking for. SuSE Linux also comes with the essential GUI configuration and installation tools. SuSE Linux can be installed on systems using x86, IA-64, PowerPC, and Alpha processors.

Turbo Linux (www.turbolinux.com)

Turbo Linux is strictly targeted toward the server market. It is derived from Red Hat Linux. Turbo Linux contains strong support for Asian languages. It can be installed on x86, IA-64, and Alpha processors.

Yellow Dog Linux (www.yellowdoglinux.com)

Yellow Dog Linux is similar to LinuxPPC in a couple of ways. First, it is derived from Red Hat Linux, and second, it is mainly designed to run on PowerPC processors, which make it mainly for Mac systems.

A recent trend has been to create versions of Linux that fit on one or two floppy disks. One such trimmed version is called Linux on a Floppy (LOAF), which fits on one disk. DOS Linux is another small Linux NOS. It can be installed on an existing DOS system. A third, Coyote Linux, is a small, specialized distribution designed for Internet connection sharing.

With all the different distributions of Linux available on the market, it might be difficult to choose which one you want to use. But some of the obvious factors, such as the processor your system is using, help when you're deciding which distributions you should choose from. Other factors, such as whether you are using a Mac or a PC, help you narrow down your choices even more. Another factor that can help narrow down the decision is what type of system you are building. If the system is a server, you might want to think about Caldera eServer or Turbo Linux, which are specifically targeted toward the server market. However, keep in mind that many of the other Linux distributions can be used to run servers as well. Another factor that might determine which version to use is if you are interested in using a GUI or not. Last, you might want to think about the experience level of the user who will use the system. If he or she is new to Linux, Caldera eDesktop, Corel, or Mandrake Linux might be a good option.

 Worksheet 6.3.4   Linux

Identify the main concepts and principles of the Linux/UNIX family of network operating systems.

Linux Clients

Windows clients can access resources and Linux servers. The client/server file system used by most varieties of Linux file servers is a Network File System (NFS), which was developed by Sun Microsystems. It can be installed on Windows clients using software such as Solstice Network Client by Sun. NFS requires TCP/IP, or other NFS client software, for file transfer. Windows operating systems do not include an NFS client.

Windows clients can access Linux servers without client software if the UNIX servers run *Samba*, which is a program that uses the Server Message Block (SMB) application layer protocol. Windows computers use SMB for file access across the network. Samba permits them to see the Linux file system. Figure 6-17 illustrates how a Samba server allows different types of systems to access the Samba file server.

Figure 6-17 Benefits of Samba

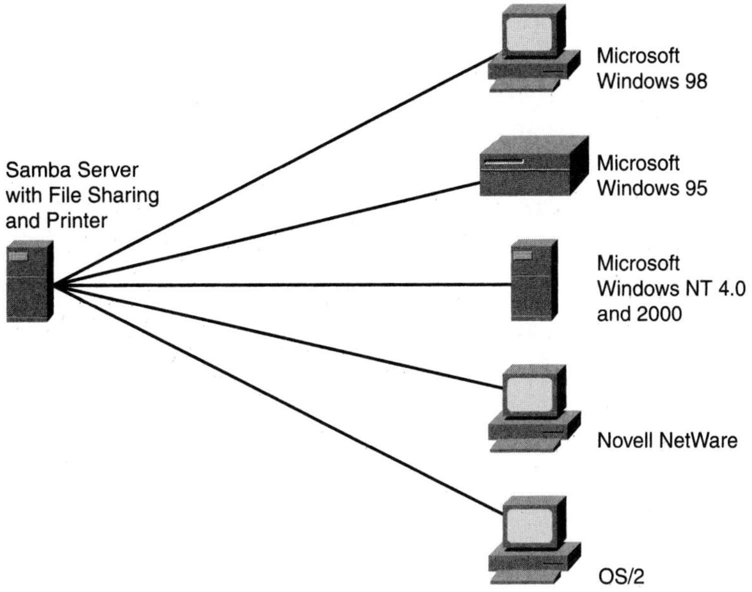

Determining Software Requirements for a Linux NOS

This section covers the following topics:

- Workstation software and programs
- Server software and programs
- Additional software and programs
- Verifying software compatibility

Workstation Software and Programs

Most of the software and programs you find on a Linux workstation are designed to help you get work done. A Linux workstation does not need any of the programs or software you typically find on a Linux system configured as a server. If any server software or programs are installed on a Linux workstation, it would be a *mail server*, which provides local services for sending and receiving e-mail.

The X Window System

The *X Window System* (or just X for short) is what comprises the Linux GUI environment. Linux can run without a GUI. However, if you are configuring Linux as a workstation, you most likely want to make sure that the X Window System is installed. The X Window System is usually installed through the Xfree86 package. Installing and configuring the X Window System and the Xfree86 package are covered in detail in Chapters 9 and 10. There are several reasons why the X Window System must be installed on a Linux workstation, but most importantly, just about every workstation program requires the X Window System to run.

Several additional tools that are also part of the X Window System help the GUI operate and run smoothly. These include *window managers*, which provide borders and control around the windows, and desktop environments, which help a user customize and control his or her working environment. Two of the most popular desktop environments that come with Linux are the K Desktop Environment (KDE, www.kde.org) and the GNU Network Object Model Environment (GNOME, www.gnome.org).

Office Tools

Having efficient office suite software is a must for any workstation, especially if this workstation is part of a network and is in a company of some kind. If Linux has any shortcomings, they are in its lack of providing office suite software that runs on Linux but is as good as Microsoft Office. However, Linux can run Office suite software. Corel's WordPerfect and Sun's StarOffice are the top two Office suite software packages that can run on Linux. StarOffice is a popular choice in Linux, because it can also be used in Windows. This can help prevent any compatibility issues in an environment that has both Linux and Windows computers. Another Office suite alternative is Applix's ApplixWare (www.applix.com), shown in Figure 6-18. There also are single packages rather than full Office suites that ship with Linux and some that are installed by default during the installation process. Two examples are LyX (www.lyx.org) and AbiWord (www.abisource.com). Figure 6-19 shows the LyX word processing tool, and Figure 6-20 shows the AbiWord word processing tool. These two popular word processors can be installed without your having to install a full Office suite.

Figure 6-18   ApplixWare Office Suite

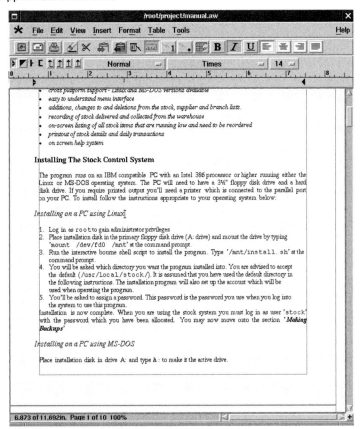

Figure 6-19   LyX Word Processing Tool

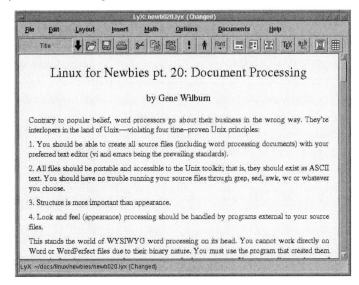

Figure 6-20 AbiWord Word Processing Tool

Network Clients

A workstation running on an enterprise network or even a small network needs to be able to access networking resources. Workstations use a variety of network client software to accomplish this. Examples include web browsers such as Netscape and Opera, mail readers such as KMail, and FTP clients such as gFTP. A wide variety of network clients ship with every distribution of Linux. However, if you need a network client that doesn't ship with the installation CDs, you can download it from the Internet.

Audiovisual Programs and Software

With the number of multimedia functions that today's computers are capable of performing, a workstation is not complete unless it provides programs and software to view, play, and edit video, graphic, and music files. These features are important not only to the home user but can also be important in a business. Graphic artists, web designers, and architects all need these features on their systems. Some of the popular audiovisual programs available for Linux include tools for viewing and editing graphics such as XV (www.trilion.com) and Gimp (www.gimp.org), multimedia players such as Xanim (http://xanim.va.pubnix.com), and audiovideo editors such as Broadcast (http://heroines.sourceforge.net/bcast2000.php3) and Linux Video Studio (http://ronald.bitfreak.net). Figure 6-21 shows some of the editing tools that are available with Gimp. Audiovisual programs are another area in which Linux has not been able to compete in the past, just like with the Office suites. However, better software has begun to emerge that can provide these multimedia features to a Linux user.

Figure 6-21 Gimp Editing Tool

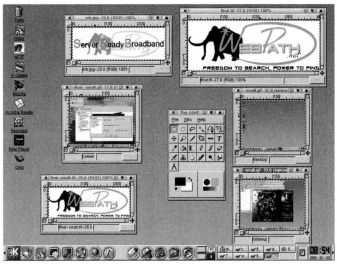

Server Software and Programs

Software and programs that are installed on a server supply some sort of service to other computer systems that are attached to it through a network. The software and programs that are running on a server are used differently than software and programs that are installed in a workstation. Users do not directly use the software and programs that are on the server. Typically, the server administrator is the only user who uses this software, and even then, it isn't used much. Instead, software and programs that are installed on servers run constantly in the background. When a client computer makes a request, the server responds to that request.

Web Servers

One of the most popular uses of a Linux system is as a *web server*. Web server software uses Hypertext Transfer Protocol (HTTP) to deliver files to users who request them, using a web browser from their workstation. The most popular web server software available for Linux is Apache (www.apache.org), an open-source program that comes with the installation CD. Other web server software available for Linux includes Roxen and thttp. Roxen is designed as a high-powered commercial web server, and thttp is more for small, low-traffic websites.

Mail Servers

A mail server is a system that is configured with programs and services that enable the exchange of e-mail that is sent from one client to another. You will learn more about this exchange in later chapters. Every distribution of Linux ships with a mail server. One version that is popular and that comes with Red Hat is Sendmail (www.sendmail.org). Other popular mail servers available for Linux include Exim (www.exim.org) and Postfix (www.postfix.org). These mail servers use a variety of protocols to receive incoming mail and distribute outgoing mail to the proper locations. For example, the Simple Mail Transfer Protocol (SMTP) is used to deliver mail between mail servers over the Internet. SMTP is also used on local-area networks (LANs) to transfer mail. Every Linux distribution ships with the Post Office Protocol (POP) and Internet Control Message Protocol (ICMP) servers. These protocols are used to send mail to the end users or the destination computer within the LAN.

Many Linux servers rely on the SMTP protocol for other services as well. For example, SMTP is used to deliver important system status reports to the system administrator. For this reason, it is recommended that the SMTP server on a Linux system never be disabled, even if it is not a mail server.

Remote Login Servers

Chapter 5, "Overview of Network Services," discussed accessing a server remotely, as well as the many different programs you can use to do so. The most widely know remote login server is Telnet. In Linux, the telnetd or in.telnetd server runs the Telnet protocol.

The Telnet server is included with every distribution of Linux, but it is not enabled by default. It is a good practice, however, not to use the Telnet protocol on a Linux system. You should keep it disabled because of the security issues involved with using Telnet. Telnet is an insecure protocol. It is susceptible to being intercepted while being transferred between two systems and thus compromising sensitive data. Other, more-secure remote login servers are available, but a better alternative to Telnet altogether is the Secure Shell Protocol (SSH). SSH encrypts all data being sent between two systems, thus making intercepted data useless.

File Access Servers

The Linux operating system provides an excellent file server, either in a Linux environment or in a cross-platform environment consisting of a Windows, Mac, UNIX, or OS/2 workstation. The reason for this is that Linux supports many file-sharing protocols that can be configured to allow access via all these operating systems.

A Linux file server allows users to read and write files and directories from a remote location. You can use several protocols to accomplish this. The File Transfer Protocol (FTP) is more of a traditional means of transferring files to a file server. Other protocols, software, and programs can be installed on a Linux server that lets one computer treat files and directories located on the file server as if they were local. Sun's NFS is an example of this type of program, which can be used for file sharing between UNIX and Linux systems. SMB works almost the same as NFS but allows other OSs such as DOS, Windows, NetWare, Mac, and OS/2 systems to access a Linux file server. DOS and Windows systems use the SMB protocol, NetWare uses the mars_new and lwared packages, and Macs use Appleshare through Netatalk.

Other Linux Servers

The different types of installed Linux servers and programs that were just covered are the ones you mostly find on any number of servers in any medium-to-large-sized company. However, this list is far from complete. Many of the other types of servers that are used might not be as widely used or simply cannot be classified into any specific category. One example is Squid (www.squid-cache.org), which is a Linux proxy server. Proxy servers control things such as network security by restricting access to the Internet. DHCP and DNS servers fall into this category as well.

It is also important to mention the *ipchains* and *iptables* tools here, even though they might not be considered actual servers. These tools are used when you configure a Linux system as a firewall (which was covered in previous chapters). These tools are security tools that can block access to the server based on IP addresses or port numbers. The difference between the two is that ipchains is used on Linux systems running the 2.2.*x* kernel series, and iptables works with the newer 2.4.*x* kernels.

Additional Software and Programs

The preceding two sections discussed many of the essential programs and software that must be installed on either a workstation or a server. However, some programs and software are essential to add to a Linux system regardless of whether it is configured as a workstation or a server. These programs help users perform common tasks on their workstations and allow administrators to properly administer a system.

Text Editors

Text editors are a valuable tool that receives a lot of use in any Linux system, whether it is a workstation or a server. Some examples of text editors available in Linux are vi, jed, pico, and Emacs. Using these text editors is discussed in detail in later chapters. These text editors are essential for performing any type of maintenance tasks that a user or administrator might need to do.

vi, jed, pico, and Emacs are all text-based editors. A couple of them have some X extensions, which allows them to be run in a GUI environment. An example of these X extensions is XEmacs (www.xemacs.org), which is an enhanced version of Emacs. Figure 6-22 shows the XEmacs text editor. Other text editors are designed as strictly GUI text editors—Nedit (www.nedit.org), shown in Figure 6-23; gEdit (which runs with GNOME), shown in Figure 6-24; and KEdit (which runs with KDE), shown in Figure 6-25. These GUI text editors might be easier to use. However, there are some instances in which these cannot be used, and you must use a text editor instead. Therefore, it is a good idea to get comfortable with using one of the non-GUI text editors as well. One example of when this might occur is when you Telnet to a remote server. When you Telnet to the server, you are restricted to text mode, so you are forced to use one of the text editors. Another reason is that not all Linux systems have the X Window System installed. If the GUI is not installed, you do not have the option of using a GUI text editor.

Figure 6-22 XEmacs Text Editor

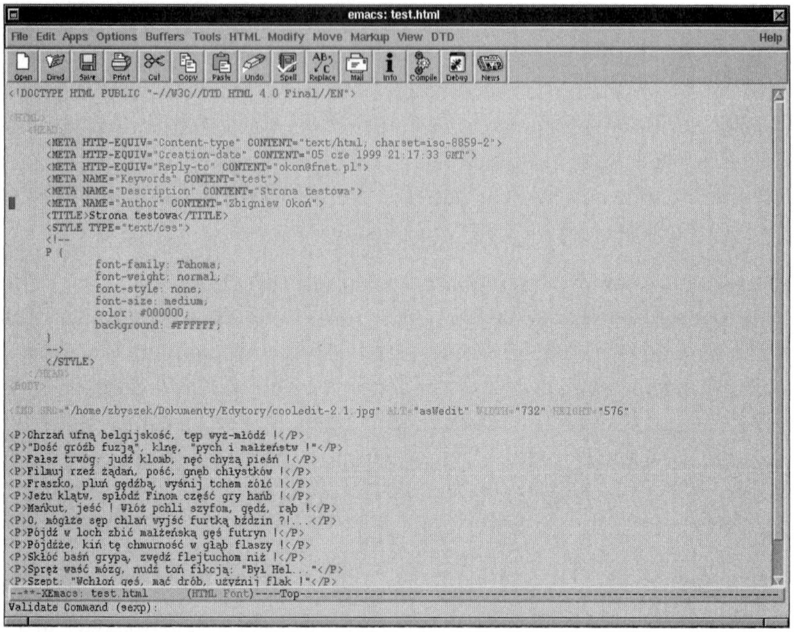

Figure 6-23 Nedit Text Editor

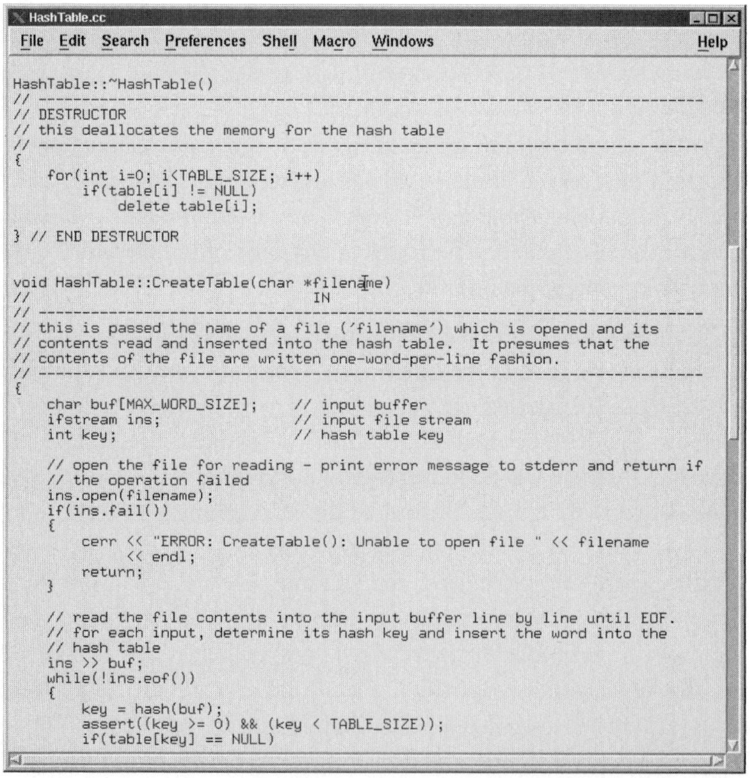

Figure 6-24 gEdit Text Editor

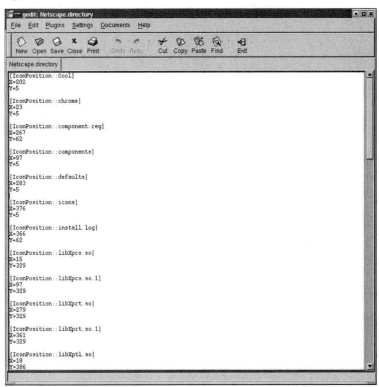

Programming Tools

Programming tools are very helpful to any administrator who runs Linux servers. They are also useful to specific users at workstations if they are programmers. These programming tools are also called *compilers* or *interpreters*. A complier converts the program's source code, which the programmer writes, into binary form, which the computer can read. If the programming language is interpreted, it isn't converted; it just gets translated into machine code right away. Linux ships with a variety of compliers. Probably the best-known and most important of these is the GNU C Compiler (GCC). However, as an administrator, if you are installing these compliers on a workstation for a user, it is a good idea to ask him what specific programming tools he needs.

Figure 6-25 KEdit Text Editor

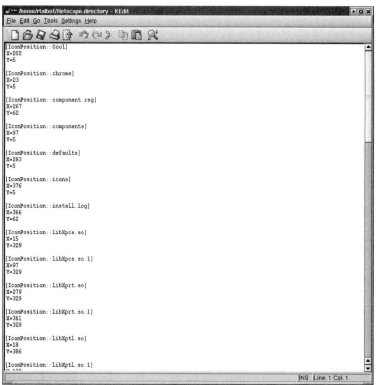

Some other types of programming tools are worth mentioning because, depending on the users that you are supporting or the type of server you might be administering, it might be necessary to install these other programming tools. Some of these programming tools are called *scripting languages*. Common scripting languages include Java, Python, and Perl. These programming tools can be used by programmers using a workstation to create scripts for software they are developing or by administrators using a server to run scripts.

Libraries

Libraries are not typically thought of as software, but they are sets of routines that are used by the software. Linux code is primarily written in C programming code. Every Linux system relies on a library called the C library (libc). Linux systems rely on the C library for the routines that are necessary for C programs to run in Linux. If you are attempting to install a package, you must also have the appropriate library installed for the program to run. If you do not have the proper library installed, an error message warns you about the problem.

Verifying Software Compatibility

For the most part, when you install software on a Linux system from packages that are included on the CD, it works. Some packages have a dependency, which means that they require other packages to be installed as well for it to run correctly. All the major distributions have package managers (discussed in previous chapters) that track this. When the package manager notices a package being installed that has dependencies, a message appears, telling you which additional packages need to be installed. You might need to take extra measures when installing packages that are not shipped with the distribution CDs. It is always good practice to check the manufacturer's website or the package's documentation to see what needs to be installed. Some of these requirements include supported operating systems, supported distributions, CPU requirements, library requirements, and development tools and libraries.

Supported Operating Systems

When installing a package, you should first always check to make sure that the operating system you are installing it on supports it. Generally, any Linux software and packages can be installed on any UNIX-like operating system, but this is not always the case. It is always a good idea to check first. UNIX software and packages should generally run on most Linux systems, because it can compile the source code. However, be careful, because this is not always the case. Sometimes, if a package is too large, the installation might run into some problems if it is not explicitly designed to run with Linux.

Supported Distributions

The same rules that apply to checking for operating system compatibility apply to distribution compatibility. Generally, it is possible to install packages that were designed to be installed on one distribution to run in another distribution. Often this process is simple, but other times you have to install a series of dependencies just to get a package to work when it is not explicitly designed to run in that particular distribution.

CPU Requirements

It is important to verify CPU compatibility when installing software that comes in source code and must be compiled by the CPU. The main reason for this is that not all CPUs can compile software correctly. An example of this is binary-only programs that run only on x86 or PowerPC CPUs.

Library Requirements

Libraries were discussed previously. It was mentioned that certain packages require certain libraries to be installed so that they can run. It's good practice to check which library the particular package you are installing requires.

Development Tools and Libraries

Development tools and development libraries are not something that everyday users need to worry about. These are tools for programmers who want to compile programs by themselves. The main concern to be aware of here is that the correct development tools and libraries are installed. For example, if a program is written in C++, you need a C++ compiler.

Summary

This chapter discussed network operating systems. Some of the important concepts to retain from this chapter include the following:

- Network operating systems (NOSs) distribute their functions over a number of networked computers. They depend on the native OS in each individual computer and then add functions so that resources can be shared concurrently.

- NOS servers must run operating systems with characteristics that extend beyond those of client PCs. To support multiple concurrent users and to provide shared access to network services, resources, and devices, NOS services must be multiuser and multitasking and must support multiple processors.

- Windows server-based networks, running Windows NT Server or Windows 2000 Server, are based on the concept of the domain. A domain is a group of computers and users that serves as a boundary of administrative authority.

- Linux is a UNIX-like operating system that comes with source code so that the user can change or customize the software to adapt to specific needs. The Open Source Initiative provides a trademark for software developers who want to share, modify, and redistribute their code.

- Various distributions of Linux are available. Which one you use can depend on a lot of things. Some of the basic considerations when you're deciding which version of Linux to use are factors such as who will use the system and what type of work he or she will do with it. Other factors can include what type of hardware is installed if the system will be used as a workstation or server.

- Even after a successful Linux installation, you need to address several other types of software compatibility issues. Several criteria, such as hardware and what the system will be used for, determine which type of software to install.

Check Your Understanding

The following review questions help you assess what you learned in this chapter. Answers can be found in Appendix A, "Answers to Check Your Understanding Questions."

1. Of the following, which three are the main functions that the operating system performs?

   A. Store security information

   B. Control the computer hardware

   C. Make changes to the database

   D. Program the execution environment

   E. Provide a user interface

   F. Establish network control

2. There are a number of differences between a standalone client operating system and a network operating system. Decide whether each of the following statements refers to a standalone client, a NOS client, or both.

   Access resources that are local to the PC: _____

   Access devices that are directly attached: _____

   Access nonlocal or remote resources: _____

   A single account is active on the system: _____

   Multiple user accounts at the same time: _____

   Concurrent access to shared resources: _____

   Specialized software and additional hardware: _____

3. Provide an example of a multiuser system, and state why it is a multiuser system.

4. There are many different areas of concern when choosing a specific NOS to install. Which of the following are points to consider?

   A. Management and monitoring

   B. E-mail settings

   C. Security

   D. Robustness/fault tolerance

   E. Bandwidth

   F. Scalability

5. Windows server-based networks that run Windows NT Server or Windows 2000 Server are based on the concept of a group of computers and users that serves as a boundary of administrative authority called _____.

   A. NDS

   B. Workgroups

   C. Domains

   D. NIS

6. Microsoft's Windows 2000 is an upgrade from the previous Windows NT operating system. It includes many new features and advantages. Which of the following are advantages of using Windows 2000 as opposed to Windows NT?

   A. Support for mobile users through APM and ACPI

   B. Secure virtual private networking with L2TP and IPSec

   C. Directory replication using PDCs and BDCs

   D. IPP lets users print to a URL and manage printers through a web browser interface.

7. Several different distributions of Linux are available. Of the following, which are key elements that are included in these distributions to make them different?

   A. Startup scripts

   B. Kernel

   C. Configuration files

   D. NIS structure

   E. Support software

8. Which client systems can connect to a Linux file server running Samba?

   A. Windows

   B. Novell

   C. UNIX

   D. Macintosh

   E. OS/2

   F. All of the above

Key Terms

client   A system that a user interfaces with. Using the functions of the PC native operating system, the user can access resources that are on the network to which the client is connected and has access permissions to.

compiler   A tool that converts the program's source code, which is written by the programmer, into binary form, which the computer can read.

Internet Printing Protocol (IPP)   Allows users to print to a URL and manage printers through a web browser interface.

ipchains and iptables   Tools you use when configuring a Linux system as a firewall. These tools are security tools that can block access to the server based on IP addresses or port numbers.

IPSec   A set of protocols developed to support secure exchange of packets at the IP layer.

Layer 2 Tunneling Protocol (L2TP)   An extension to the PPP protocol that lets ISPs operate virtual private networks (VPNs).

library   A set of routines that are used by software. Every Linux system relies on a library called the C library (libc). Linux systems rely on the C library for the routines that are necessary for C programs to run in Linux.

mail server   A system that is configured with programs and services that let it handle the exchange of e-mail from one client to another.

management interface   The part of the NOS that provides the tools for server monitoring, client administration, file and print management, and disk-storage management.

Microsoft Management Console (MMC)   This tool uses snap-ins, which are modules that contain the tools for specific administrative functions.

multitasking system   A system that can execute multiple tasks or processes at the same time.

multiuser system   A system that can support multiple users concurrently.

network operating system (NOS)   The software foundation on which the computer's applications and services run. A NOS has extra features that enable communication between multiple devices and the sharing of resources across a network.

operating system (OS)   The software foundation on which the computer's applications and services run.

Samba   A program that uses the Server Message Block (SMB) application layer protocol, which gives Windows computers access to the Linux file system over the network.

security   When referring to a NOS, this includes authenticating user access to services to prevent unauthorized access to the network resources.

Security Accounts Management Database (SAM)   Controls the authentication process when a user logs on to the domain.

symmetric multiprocessing (SMP)   A computer architecture that provides high performance by making multiple CPUs available to individual processes.

thread   A program that can execute independently of other parts. This lets programmers design programs whose threaded parts can execute concurrently.

web server   A system that uses Hypertext Transfer Protocol (HTTP) to deliver files to users who request them using a web browser from their workstation.

window manager   Provides borders and control around windows and desktop environments, which include several additional utilities that help users customize and control their working environment.

X Window System   The set of programs that comprise the Linux GUI environment.

Objectives

After completing this chapter, you will be able to complete tasks related to

- Preparing for the installation
- Verifying the network
- The installation process
- The boot process
- Troubleshooting NOS installation

Chapter 7

Installation and Boot Process Overview

An IT professional is typically asked to perform software installations, including application software and operating systems. Installing an operating system, especially a network operating system, can be one of the most complex installation tasks. This chapter is an overview of the NOS installation process, including how to plan for the installation and how to troubleshoot installation problems.

Preparing for the Installation

This section covers the following topics:

- Background: installing a NOS
- Planning the system
- Planning hardware installation
- Server hardware components
- Hardware requirements
- Creating a hardware inventory
- Identifying hardware using Device Manager
- Checking hardware compatibility lists

Background: Installing a NOS

Network operating system (NOS) installation refers to the process of creating and copying NOS system files to a hard disk. *System files* are the files that allow the operating system to function. Many vendors ship computers with the operating system already installed. This is especially true of desktop computers.

Preinstalled operating systems (OSs) or NOS software has several advantages. By purchasing a PC or server with a preinstalled OS, you avoid the complex process of installation and configuration. Also, an OS that is preloaded on a system is typically optimized for that system's particular hardware configuration.

The drawback of preinstallation is that you might not be able to control the exact features, packages, and configuration of the OS or NOS. Although you can make changes to an OS after the installation process, some configurations cannot be undone or can be modified only with extreme difficulty.

Despite these drawbacks, some customers might want the server vendor to install a NOS before shipping the system. However, most organizations install the NOS themselves. Doing the installation in-house ensures that the server is optimized for the organization's specific functions. Also, NOS administrators usually prefer to have direct control of software versions, updates, and patches installed on the system. Figure 7-1 shows specific settings that an administrator might need to set. If a system comes with a preinstalled operating system, certain settings, such as the LILO boot loader configurations, might not be set properly.

Figure 7-1 LILO Boot Loader Options

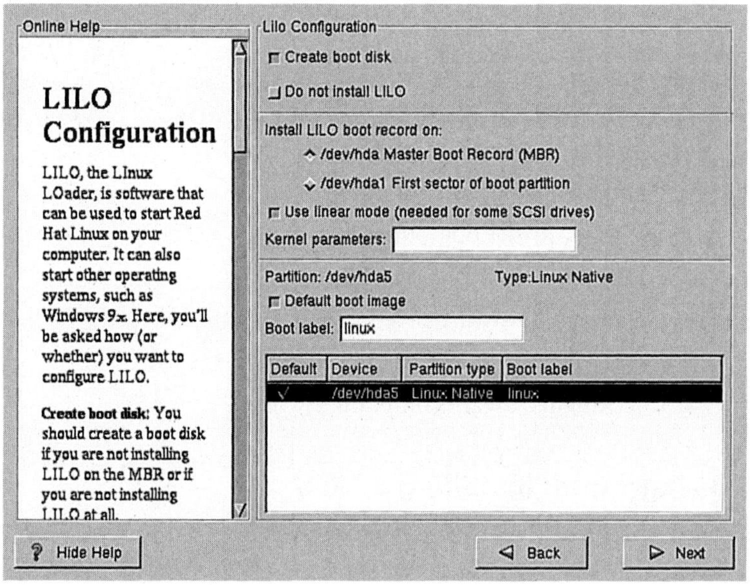

Planning the System

The NOS installation should be carefully prepared. First, inventory the system hardware. No one NOS works with all computer hardware, so determine whether the currently available hardware will work with the NOS. Second, determine whether the

NOS supports all application software that will be loaded on the system. Third, become familiar with the NOS itself. As part of the installation process, you have to make important (and sometimes irreversible) configuration decisions.

Each NOS manufacturer sets what are called *minimum hardware requirements* for its software. Minimum hardware requirements typically focus on the central processing unit (CPU) type and speed, the amount of RAM, and the amount of available hard disk space. The next section reviews these key components.

It is relatively easy to determine whether a system meets NOS minimum requirements. Also determine if the NOS can support the system hardware peripherals. This is especially important for expensive or mission-critical peripherals such as high-end video equipment and high-capacity storage hardware.

When planning to install a NOS, perform a complete hardware inventory. In production environments, a formal, written inventory should be compiled. When you are done, check with vendor websites, support staff, and even news groups to determine whether the inventory hardware is supported. You might need to download and install software drivers or firmware updates before hardware will work properly with the NOS.

Inventory any applications that will run on the server itself. If the organization relies on custom software or legacy software, check with vendors to ensure compatibility. Software is considered legacy software if it is old and cannot be upgraded but is still in use because some network components need the services this software provides. Most administrators choose to load and test applications on the NOS before introducing a NOS to a network.

Finally, know the basics about a particular NOS before installing it. For example, know how a particular NOS handles drive partitioning, disk formatting, and administrative accounts. Here is a system planning checklist:

- Inventory the system's hardware, and determine compatibility with the NOS.
- Verify that the NOS supports all desired software applications.
- Research the NOS, and become familiar with the installation procedure before you begin.

These topics are covered later in this chapter.

Planning Hardware Installation

The first step that the server hardware specialist should attempt is to verify that everything specified in the installation plan is ready and available before beginning the installation. Verification activities include the following:

- Verify that the location where the server is to be installed is ready for the installation.
- Verify that the power outlet for the network server is available and active. (Test it with a volt/ohm meter.)
- Verify that the network connection is available and active.
- Verify that all the hardware for the network server has arrived and that the hardware is as specified in the installation plan.

Verifying the Installation Site

After reading and verifying the installation plan, the server hardware specialist should visit the installation site and verify the location's readiness. One of the first things to look at is the room itself. The room needs to be modified to ensure that the server's life will not be limited. The two things that have the largest impact on the server are the temperature and humidity. Power availability, floor space, and flood and fire suppression are a few other elements you need to look at before getting started.

Verifying the Power Source

The server hardware specialist should verify that the power needed for the network server is available and live. Be sure to check that the voltage for the power source is correct by using a *volt/ohm meter* or a digital *multimeter*. The correct voltage for North America and Latin America is a nominal 120 volts. The correct voltage for Europe, the Middle East, and Africa is a nominal 230 volts. The power source also should be on a power circuit unto itself. Also check that the power source has the correct amperage rating and that the power plug is of the correct configuration. Because the *uninterruptible power supply (UPS)* is the component that is to be plugged into the power source, this information can be found in the UPS documentation. The UPS might require a 20-amp or 30-amp circuit instead of the more common 15-amp circuit. The UPS also might have a special locking power plug, which of course would require a special power socket.

Verifying the Uninterruptible Power Supply Size

The UPS should be of adequate size to keep the network server running long enough for it to perform a normal shutdown. This time period is usually 5 to 10 minutes. An undersized UPS keeps the server running only a very short time. An oversized UPS not only keeps the network server operational for a longer period of time during a power backup but also allows for growth of the network server (adding components to the network server over time). The UPS should be large enough to support all the components of the network server that are connected to (plugged into) the UPS. The size of a

UPS is specified with a *volt-amp (VA) rating*. The larger the UPS's VA rating, the longer the UPS can keep the network server running in the event of a power failure. A larger VA rating also allows additional network server components to be added.

Adequate Temperature in the Server Room

The site should have adequate air-conditioning capacity to handle the addition of the network server to be installed. The installation plan should state the heat output of the devices that will be part of the network server installation (chassis, monitor, UPS, and so on). It might be difficult to ascertain the current heat load (measured in British Thermal Units [BTUs]) of the room where the network server is to be installed. An adequate indicator of the available cooling capacity of the room where the network server will be installed is the room temperature. If the room temperature is more than 72 degrees Fahrenheit without the new network server's being installed, it is doubtful that there is adequate cooling for the new network server. This is why it is a good idea to have a dedicated air-conditioning unit just for the server room.

Most network servers use internal fans for cooling. For these fans to work properly and provide adequate cooling, there has to be adequate clearance around the server for proper air flow. According to most specifications, a three-foot area in front of and behind the server provides adequate cooling. Figure 7-2 shows a server with the proper space around it. This allows proper air flow and temperature to pass through the server.

Figure 7-2 Server Specifications

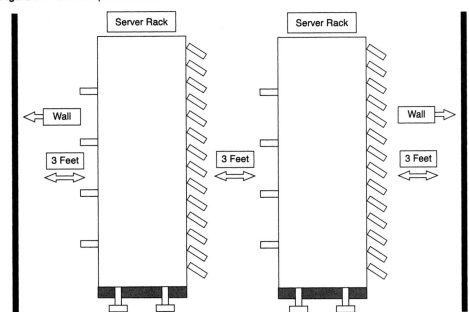

Verifying the Network Connection

You should determine the correct type and speed of the connection to the server before the server is installed. You can test this by using another computer system with the proper network adapter installed to see whether the network connection that the network server will use is working and correct.

Worksheet 7.1.3   Planning the Installation

Identify the necessary procedures and steps to take to plan a successful installation.

Server Hardware Components

First you need to check the components that will be used to assemble the network server. Some network server vendors do not assemble all the hardware for a network server when they are ordered. You must be able to take all the components and assemble them into a working network server.

Server Chassis

Verify that the *server chassis* is the correct model that was ordered and the correct form factor. Most server chassis are either a tower configuration, a wide or "fat" tower configuration, or a rack-mount configuration. Make sure that, if you ordered model X in a tower configuration, Model X in a tower configuration is indeed delivered, not Model X in a rack-mount configuration. Figures 7-3, 7-4, and 7-5 show the different styles of servers. Which one is best depends on various things, including how much space you have available for the server.

Figure 7-3 Rack-Mount Server

Figure 7-4 Tower Server

Figure 7-5 Wide-Body Server

Server Rack

A rack-mount server chassis must be mounted in an equipment rack designed for rack-mounted hardware. Most server vendors that sell servers in a rack-mount chassis also sell the server rack. Server racks generally come in several sizes (heights). Server rack size is measured in rack units (U). A standard rack unit is 1.75 inches. Either a new network server is installed in an existing server rack, or a new server rack is purchased for the new network server. Server racks generally have both front and rear doors and side panels to form a completely enclosed unit. The doors and side panels help form a secure environment and are designed to help cool the equipment in the rack by controlling air flow patterns. In most cases, multiple server racks can be joined to form an installation space for a large number of servers. Figure 7-6 shows a server rack without doors. Figure 7-7 shows a server rack with doors.

Figure 7-6 Server Rack Without Doors

Figure 7-7 Server Rack with Doors

A rack-mounted server installation conserves space in the room where the servers reside. However, if you go with a rack-mounted configuration, generally all equipment must be designed to fit into the server rack. This includes the server's UPS, keyboard/ mouse, and monitor (either LCD or CRT). The equipment installation in the server rack should be done to the server vendor's specifications. Several server vendors offer software to aid in the proper placement of the equipment into the server rack. For example, all server vendors recommend that the UPS be installed on the bottom of the rack. This is done for several reasons, including the weight of the rack-mount UPS and the need to avoid possible damage to a network server caused by a leaking UPS battery.

Processor(s)

Network servers commonly have more than one processor. Verify that the correct number and type of processors are available for the network server. Some server vendors install all the processors that were ordered; other server vendors supply the server with zero or one processor installed, and you must install any additional processors. Verify that the processors are of the same type, speed, and stepping (version). Also verify that each processor has the same size of L2 cache. Follow the network server vendor's instructions for installing additional processors.

Memory

Network servers generally require a considerable amount of memory to adequately perform their functions. Some server vendors install all the memory that was ordered; however, other server vendors supply the server with a "standard" amount of memory, and you must install the memory above the standard amount. Verify that the server has the amount of memory that was ordered. If some of the memory must be installed, verify that the memory is the correct type for the server, and follow the server hardware vendor's instructions for installing the additional memory. This is a critical step. Some servers require that memory be installed in groups of two or four memory modules. (Check the server vendor's documentation to see whether memory modules must be installed in groups of two or four instead of singly.) Failure to install the memory correctly will cause the server not to recognize all the memory installed or not to start at all.

Disk Drives

Many network server configurations require that a large amount of disk storage be available in the server. Verify that the disk drives are the correct size, speed, and type (IDE/ATA, EIDE/ATA-2, SCSI, SCSI-2, SCSI-3). The disk drives might come installed in the server chassis, or they might be shipped in separate cushioned boxes to avoid damage. The installation plan will specify which disk drives (size, speed, and type) should be installed in the network server.

Monitor, Keyboard, and Mouse

Verify that the monitor for the network server is what was ordered. In general, the monitor should support a VGA resolution of at least 1024 × 768 dots per inch. The monitor can be the traditional CRT type or one of the newer LCD flat-panel monitors. If the monitor is to be rack-mounted, you need to purchase a special monitor shelf. Special rack-mounted LCD flat-panel monitors are available; these often include a keyboard/trackball or touch pad (a mouse substitute) combination in a single rack drawer.

Uninterruptible Power Supply

Verify that a UPS is available for the network server. The UPS should be of adequate size to support the network server for a short period of time, which allows a graceful shutdown of the server. Rack-mounted UPSs are available for rack-mounted network server installations. All UPSs should be capable of being monitored by the network server through a USB or serial communications cable. If the UPS is to be monitored via the serial connection, make sure that a serial connection is available on the network server. Through the purchase of additional hardware for the UPS, you can usually monitor a UPS through the network. Top-of-the-line UPSs often let you monitor them via an SNMP management console or a built-in Web interface. This lets you track the UPS from any Internet connection—a handy feature for an administrator.

Backup System

Verify that the backup system is as specified in the installation plan and that it is adequate to support the backup of the network server. The backup system is generally a magnetic tape drive of one form or another. The tape drive should be capable of backing up the contents of the disk drives on the network server in a timely manner. The capacity of the tape drive and the speed at which data can be transferred to the tape drive are both of critical importance. For example, if you determine that, given the tape drive's specifications, a full backup of the network server would take 10 hours, and you have only 4 hours to perform the backup, the tape drive is inadequate for the job. You also can back up other devices, such as hard disk drives, CD-R devices, and CD-RW devices. The backup devices should be installed on a controller separate from the network server's disk drives to provide peak performance during the backup process.

SCSI Cables

Verify that the correct cables have been delivered to connect the SCSI channel controller to the SCSI devices (disk drives). SCSI cables differ significantly (for example, SCSI-1, SCSI-2, and SCSI-3). The wide versions of SCSI-2 and SCSI-3 use different cables. Internal SCSI cables are generally ribbon cables, with pin 1 identified by a colored (usually red) strip on the edge of the ribbon cable. External SCSI cables are generally in a round bundle. Verify that the SCSI cables have the correct number of connectors for the network server configuration. Make sure that they do not exceed the SCSI channel length maximums. Also make sure that the SCSI cables have enough connectors to allow all the SCSI devices to be attached. If you need to attach four SCSI disk drives to a SCSI channel, for example, the SCSI cable needs at least four connectors for the disk drives, plus one where it can be attached to the SCSI adapter.

SCSI Adapter(s)

Verify that the correct SCSI adapter is available. Many network servers have one or more SCSI adapters built in. Additional SCSI adapters might be required to support the number of SCSI devices that will be used with the network server. Make sure that the SCSI adapter and SCSI devices are of the same type of SCSI (SCSI-1, SCSI-2, SCSI-3, and so forth). Make sure that the SCSI adapter's interface matches the bus that is in the network server—for example, EISA, PCI, or PCI-64.

RAID Controller(s)

If the network server will use the hardware version of RAID, verify that the RAID controller is available. The RAID controller should be delivered with configuration software. The RAID controller must be configured before the network operating system can be installed. Most RAID controllers are designed to support some version of SCSI disk drive. Make sure that the RAID controller matches the bus that is in the network server—for example, EISA, PCI, or PCI-64.

Fibre Channel-Arbitrated Loop Host Bus Adapter

If the network server will use *Fibre Channel-Arbitrated Loop (FC-AL)* disk systems, verify that the correct Fibre Channel host bus adapter (HBA) has been delivered. Fibre Channel can use either fiber-optic cable or copper wire for the connection media. Make sure that the HBA has the correct connection (fiber-optic or copper) and that the correct cables are included. The vast majority of FC-AL installations have the disk system external to the network server chassis.

Network Interface Card(s)

Verify that the network interface card (NIC) for the network server is available. Some network servers have the NIC built in to the network server. If redundant NICs are required for the network server, verify that all NICs are available. Make sure that the NIC supports the type of network where the network server will be installed (Ethernet, Token Ring, and so on). Multiple NICs might also be installed in a single network server if it is to be attached to multiple networks.

Miscellaneous Hardware

Other hardware might be required for the network server. The network server requires a video adapter to support the network server monitor. There is no reason to spend lots of money getting a fancy video adapter that has a large amount of video memory to support extremely high video resolution and billions of colors. The video monitor on a network server is generally used only to perform administrative functions on the network server. A video adapter that can support VGA resolutions of up to 1024, 768, and 65,536 colors should be adequate for most network servers.

Many server hardware vendors have a specialized server management adapter that can be purchased and installed in their network servers. These devices generally monitor the health of the server hardware and can be used by server management software running on a designated management computer. Some of these devices have a built-in modem, which allows monitoring of the server hardware via a dial-in connection.

A rack-mounted network server might include a keyboard/video/mouse (KVM) switch to allow one keyboard, one video display, and one mouse to be used by multiple network servers that are in a single rack. The KVM switch allows the keyboard, mouse, and video display to switch (usually from the keyboard) among the network servers in the rack. This saves space in the rack, because each network server does not require its own keyboard, mouse, and monitor. Some cost savings also are associated with sharing the keyboard, mouse, and monitor, because you don't have to buy them for each server.

A network server also should have some devices commonly found on most desktop computer systems, such as a 3 1/2-inch floppy disk drive and a CD-ROM drive or a DVD-ROM drive. These devices are required to install operating system software, hardware drivers, and other software onto the network server.

 Worksheet 7.1.4   Server Components

Understand and identify the various components that should be installed in a server.

Hardware Requirements

The most current versions of popular NOSs, such as Windows XP and Red Hat 7, can run on only certain hardware configurations. Tables 7-1, 7-2, and 7-3 outline the minimum system requirements for Windows and Linux operating systems. When choosing a NOS version to install, verify that the key elements of the system hardware meet the NOS's minimum requirements. These key areas are CPU type (architecture), CPU speed (measured in megahertz or gigahertz), amount of RAM, and amount of available hard disk space.

Table 7-1 Minimum System Requirements for Windows 2.0 Advanced Server

Component	Description
Computer/processor	133 MHz or higher Pentium-compatible CPU. Windows 2000 Advanced Server supports up to eight CPUs on one machine.
Memory	256 MB of RAM recommended minimum (128 MB minimum supported; 8 GB maximum)
Hard disk	1.0 GB recommended minimum free hard disk space
Drive	CD-ROM or DVD drive
Display	VGA or higher-resolution monitor
Peripheral	Keyboard and Microsoft mouse or a compatible pointing device (optional)

Table 7-2 Minimum System Requirements for Windows XP Professional

Component	Description
Computer/processor	PC with 300 MHz or higher processor clock speed recommended; 233 MHz minimum required (single- or dual-processor system); Intel Pentium/Celeron family, or AMD K6/Athlon/Duron family, or compatible processor recommended
Memory	128 MB of RAM or higher recommended (64 MB minimum supported; might limit performance and some features)
Hard disk	Minimum: 1.5 GB of available hard disk space Actual requirements vary based on system configuration and the applications and features installed. Additional available hard disk space might be required if you're installing over a network. For more information, see www.microsoft.com/windowsxp.

Table 7-3 Minimum System Requirements for Red Hat Linux 7.x

Component	Description
Computer/processor	x86 processor or higher CPU. Recommended minimum is a Pentium-class or better CPU.
Memory	32 MB of RAM recommended minimum
Hard disk	300 MB minimum free hard disk space; 1.2 GB disk space for a full workstation
Drive	CD-ROM drive or a 3 1/2-inch floppy drive
Display	VGA or higher-resolution monitor
Peripheral	Keyboard and mouse or a compatible pointing device (optional)

NOTE

Microsoft has made its Upgrade Advisor tool available to the public on its website:

www.microsoft.com/ windowsxp/pro/ howtobuy/upgrading/ advisor.asp

This tool, shown in Figure 7-8, checks system hardware and software to see if it is ready and has sufficient resources for an upgrade to Windows XP. The Windows XP CD-ROM also includes this utility.

NOS vendors publicize these minimum requirements so that administrators can plan their systems. Some NOS installation programs do not complete if they detect a system that does not meet the minimum hardware requirements.

In addition to these key areas, create an inventory of peripherals and expansion cards used with the system, as described in the next section.

Figure 7-8 Windows XP Upgrade Advisor

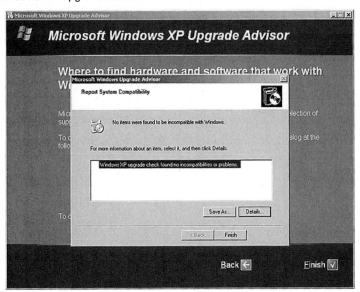

Creating a Hardware Inventory

The hardware inventory should be created before any installation programs are run and before any attempt to prepare the hard disk for installation. If necessary, open the system case and examine the expansion cards to determine the manufacturer and chipset that are being used. If manuals came with the system, consult these as well. Finally, if another operating system is already installed on the system, use the system utilities, such as Windows Device Manager, shown in Figure 7-9, to get information on the installed hardware.

Figure 7-9 Windows 2000 Device Manager

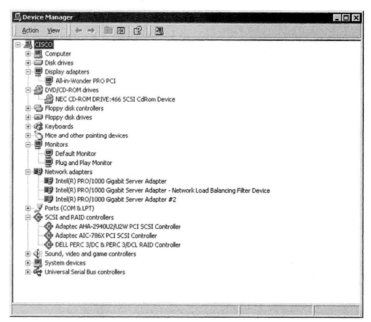

The hardware inventory should include the following information for each device:

- Device type
- Manufacturer
- Model number
- Device driver version
- BIOS revision number

A hardware inventory also lists all expansion cards and peripheral devices attached to the system.

Some installations might require more details about the hardware, such as the slot where an expansion card is located, or even the jumper settings on a particular card. Most of this information can be obtained using a utility such as Device Manager. Figures 7-10, 7-11, and 7-12 show the different screens that are used to view the properties, extra details, and resources that the device is using.

Figure 7-10 Windows 2000 Device Manager Properties

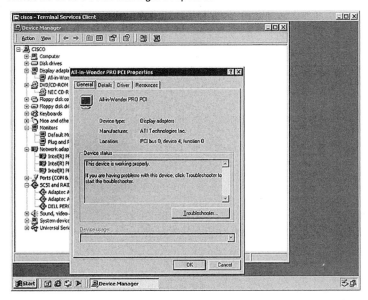

Figure 7-11 Windows 2000 Device Manager Details

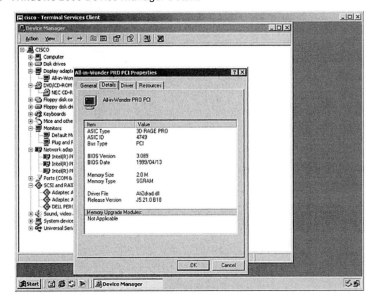

Figure 7-12 Windows 2000 Device Manager Resources

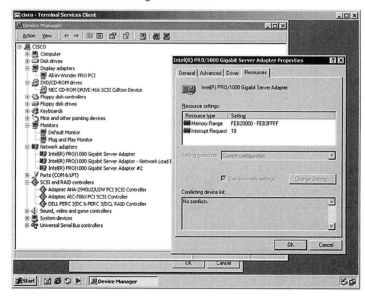

The latest versions of most hardware and NOSs use various methods to automatically detect and configure the hardware. However, older expansion cards and software might be incompatible with these automatic detection methods, such as Plug and Play. In some cases, it is necessary to physically inspect the expansion card to record its jumper settings and slot number. Table 7-4 displays a sample hardware inventory.

Table 7-4 Completed Hardware Inventory

Device Type	Manufacturer	Model Number	Driver Version
Display adapter	ATI Technologies, Inc.	Rage 128	
CD-ROM	Matshita	CR-588	
Network Interface Card	Intel	8255x-based PCI 10/100	

Identifying Hardware Using Device Manager

It used to be simple. If you installed a device, its drivers were installed too. Today, PCI-based Plug and Play is the new method. It is still easy to see which devices have not had drivers installed. In the Windows 2000 OS, such a device has a yellow question mark next to its name in Device Manager. Figure 7-13 shows what you see if a device does not have an installed driver.

Figure 7-13 Resource or Driver Conflict

In Windows 2000, the easiest way to find out if the hardware driver has not been installed is to look at the device name in Device Manager. If it has a question mark in a yellow circle next to it, Windows 2000 recognized the device but could not find a suitable driver for it. Device Manager gives you the option of updating the driver. You can tell Windows 2000 to search the CD or the Internet for the most suitable driver. You can also delete the driver and reboot the PC. Windows prompts you again to search for a suitable driver.

Checking Hardware Compatibility Lists

After completing the hardware inventory, check with the NOS and hardware manufacturers to verify that the hardware is compatible with the NOS. Software and hardware manuals might contain compatibility information, but the most up-to-date source of this information is the World Wide Web. The hardware manufacturer website provides the latest information about a particular expansion card or peripheral. These websites typically include software drivers, firmware updates, and, if applicable, information about jumper settings. You can use the Microsoft support page to find compatibility information on specific third-party hardware. The Red Hat website offers a *hardware compatibility list*, as shown in Figure 7-14.

Figure 7-14 Red Hat Hardware Compatibility List

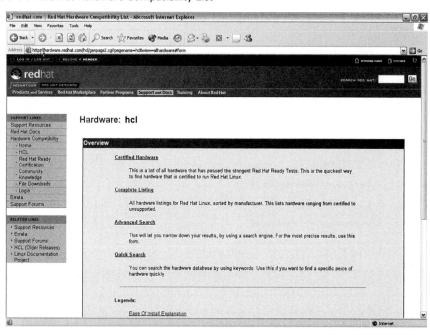

The latest hardware compatibility lists for popular network operating systems can be found on the following websites:

- **Microsoft Windows NT and Windows 2000**—www.microsoft.com/hcl/default.asp.
- **Linux (Red Hat)**—www.redhat.com/support/hardware/
- **Linux (SuSE)**—http://cdb.suse.de/cdb_english.html
- **Caldera OpenLinux**—www.calderasystems.com/support/hardware/
- **IBM OS/2**—http://service.software.ibm.com/os2ddpak/html/index.htm

Verifying the Network

The network configuration consists of selecting the network protocol and configuring it to operate correctly on your network. Most network servers use either the TCP/IP protocol or the IPX/SPX protocol or both.

To configure TCP/IP, you need the following information:

- IP address
- Subnet mask
- Default gateway
- IP address of DNS server(s)

You can use the following commands to view or change the network configuration for various network operating systems:

- Windows NT/Windows 2000 Server—ipconfig
- UNIX/Linux—ifconfig

Verifying Network Connectivity

To test network connectivity when using the TCP/IP protocol, all network operating systems use the **ping** command. (It is covered more in Chapter 13, "Troubleshooting the Operating System.")

A successful **ping** command using a TCP/IP address in a Windows system looks like Figure 7-15. A successful **ping** in Linux resembles Figure 7-16. An unsuccessful **ping** command in Windows is shown in Figure 7-17. An unsuccessful **ping** command in Linux is shown in Figure 7-18.

Figure 7-15 Successful **ping** Command for Windows

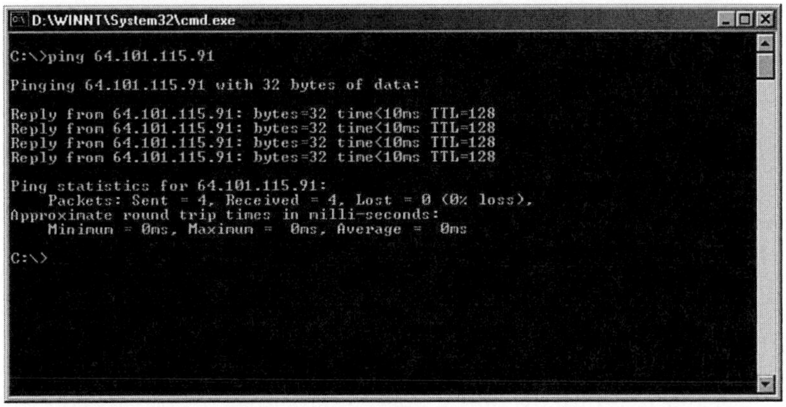

Figure 7-16 Successful **ping** Command for Linux

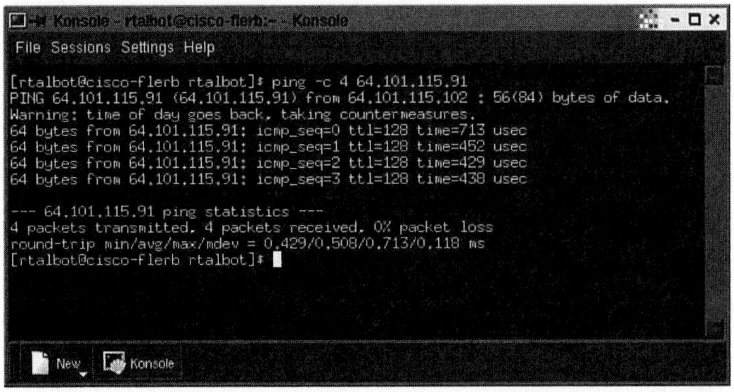

Figure 7-17 Unsuccessful **ping** Command for Windows

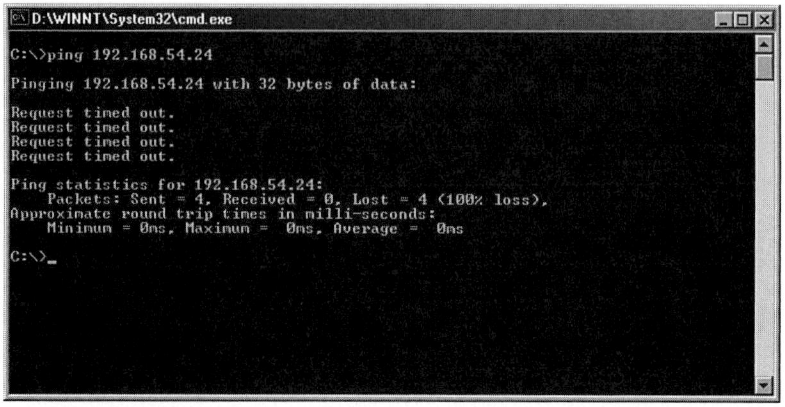

Figure 7-18 Unsuccessful **ping** Command for Linux

The best IP address to ping is the IP address of the default gateway, because it should always be available to return the ping request if the system is properly configured to access the network or the Internet. This is a common troubleshooting technique that is used when a system is not connecting to the network. It determines if the problem lies within the system itself or elsewhere on the network.

The Installation Process

This section covers the following topics:

- Installation media
- BIOS settings
- The installation program
- Disk partitions

- Partitioning a disk
- Swap files
- Formatting the disk
- Creating the initial administrative account
- Completing the installation

Installation Media

After you select the NOS that meets your network and hardware requirements, you must choose the installation medium, such as a CD-ROM, the network, or floppy disks. Typically, a NOS is installed using a CD-ROM that contains the system files and an installation program. In some cases, a NOS is installed via floppy disks. Installation using floppy disks has become increasingly uncommon as operating systems have grown in size and CD-ROM drives have become standard on virtually all PC models.

If a high-speed Internet connection is available, it might be possible to install a version of Windows, UNIX, or Linux over a network. With a LAN connection, it is possible to install most NOSs using the local network.

The following list summarizes the most common installation methods:

- **Bootable CD ROMs**—If the system has a CD-ROM drive and can boot from the CD, a local CD-ROM installation can be performed. This method is relatively fast and is the simplest installation method. You might need to download patches and other updates from the manufacturer's website before placing the computer in production.

- **Floppy boot and CD-ROM**—If the system has a CD-ROM drive but cannot boot from the CD, you can still perform a local CD-ROM installation after booting from a floppy disk (or, in some cases, a hard disk). When booting from a floppy, make sure that the CD-ROM software drivers are loaded either from the boot disk or from some other source. Without the software drivers, the CD-ROM cannot be accessed. Booting from a floppy and then installing from a CD-ROM has the same advantages and disadvantages as booting directly from the CD, with the added complication of the need to create the boot disk first. Most NOS manufacturers provide programs that create the appropriate installation floppy disks.

- **Floppy only**—Some older or very small NOSs can be loaded entirely from a series of floppy disks. One advantage of this method is that no CD-ROM is required. The obvious disadvantage is that copying files from multiple floppy disks is incredibly slow.

■ **Floppy disk/hard drive/CD boot and network installation**—In this case, the system is booted via a floppy, and the NOS is then installed from a local network server. You can also use this method when booting from a hard drive or CD. Network installations can be fast and convenient, but they do require a complex setup and testing. For this method to work, an administrator must load a copy or image of the NOS on a server and configure the server to allow client access. Typically, network installations rely on either the Network File System (NFS) or File Transfer Protocol (FTP). A few NOSs give you the option of booting via a floppy disk (or even a CD-ROM) and installing the latest version of the NOS from the Internet. The advantage of this method is that the latest version of the NOS is installed. A minor advantage is that you can perform the installation even if the system does not have a CD-ROM drive. However, this method does require a relatively high-speed Internet connection. Also, installing via the Internet is typically complex and unreliable.

BIOS Settings

Particularly with older motherboards and older operating systems, the *Basic Input/ Output System (BIOS)* settings play a large part in the installation process. The system BIOS typically resides in ROM on the motherboard and is the first program run when a system is powered on. It is responsible for testing hardware devices using a process called the *Power-On Self Test (POST)*. The BIOS also loads the operating system from various media, including hard disks, floppy disks, and (usually) CD-ROMs.

When configuring older systems, you might have to manually enter information about each connected disk drive in the BIOS setup utility. With hardware and operating systems that are new or only a few years old, the system BIOS can automatically detect disk drives and other hardware.

For CD-based installations on these newer systems, the only BIOS setting that is important is the setting that allows the system to boot from the CD-ROM. Figure 7-19 shows the BIOS setup utility for an Award BIOS. For this BIOS, the Boot Sequence option determines whether the system boots first from the CD-ROM, the hard disk, or the floppy disk.

The Installation Program

An installation program controls and simplifies the installation process. Depending on the NOS, the installation program prompts the user for configuration information. Most installation programs allow you to partition and format the hard disk before copying system files. Partitioning and formatting are discussed in the next few sections.

Figure 7-19 BIOS Setup Utility

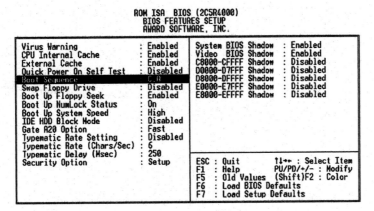

In Windows, the installation program is called setup.exe. On a Red Hat Linux system, the installation program is currently called Anaconda. These programs guide you through the NOS installation process.

The installation program asks you a series of questions. Figures 7-20 and 7-21 show how the Red Hat 7.*x* installation program asks what language and keyboard layout you want to use. These questions are typical of installation programs.

Figure 7-20 Red Hat Installation Program

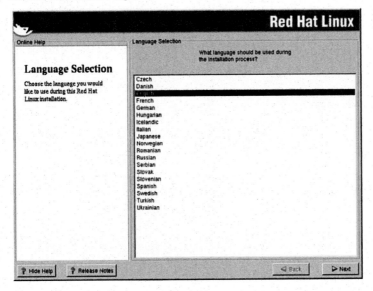

Figure 7-21 Red Hat Keyboard Configuration

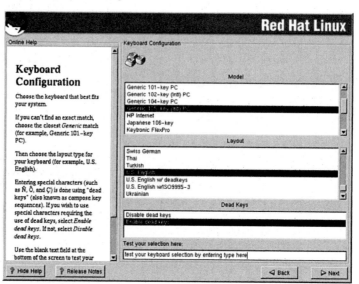

Installation programs also give you the option of installing a default set of components or choosing each component manually. Figure 7-22 shows the Linux installation screen, where you choose whether you want to customize your installation options. If you're installing a NOS for the first time or you're installing a NOS on a nonproduction server, consider using one of these defaults. Using a default setting simplifies the installation process and ensures that a crippled or nonfunctioning system will not be created.

Figure 7-22 Default Versus Custom Installations

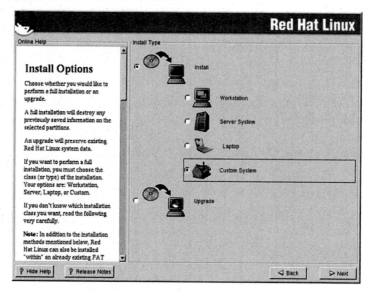

If the server will be put into production, strongly consider a custom installation. Manually choosing the components and features guarantees that the system is built for the specific tasks required in a specific environment.

Disk Partitions

To efficiently use the storage space on a hard disk, the disk is divided into sections called *partitions* or *slices*. Each partition or slice is a logical division of the hard disk. A disk can have one or more partitions. Typically, a network server is configured with multiple partitions before the NOS is installed. A system with multiple disk partitions has the following advantages:

- Multiple operating systems can be installed on the same disk.
- Data can be physically separated from the system files to provide security, file management, and/or fault tolerance.
- A specific partition, called a swap partition, can be created to supplement the system RAM and enhance performance.

After a disk is divided into partitions, each partition must be formatted so that data can be stored there. On a Windows system, formatted partitions on a hard drive are labeled using a letter of the alphabet. The first partition is labeled with a C, the second partition (if present) is labeled with a D, and so on. Three types of partitions can exist on a hard drive. A *primary partition* is the same as an original partition. An *extended partition* is a variations of a primary partition that acts as a placeholder for a logical partition. *Logical partitions* (also called *volumes* or *logical drives*) are partitions that are created within the extended partitions. Any operating system can have up to four primary partitions or three primary partitions and one extended partition.

The layout of the partitions is stored in the *partition table*. Figure 7-23 shows how a sample partition table is laid out. You can see from this example how the two logical partitions (hda5 and hda6) are contained in the extended partition hda2. The partition table is located in the first sector of the hard disk on which the operating system is installed. This sector of the hard disk is called the Master Boot Record (MBR). Figure 7-24 illustrates how the MBR contains information on all the other partitions that are created. This section also contains certain parameters and code, which the computer needs to run after the BIOS initializes. Even though the logical partitions are stored within the extended partition, which is outside the MBR, they are still considered part of the partition table, because they do define partition locations.

Figure 7-23 Partition Table

```
[root@localhost /root]# fdisk -l

Disk /dev/hda: 240 heads, 63 sectors, 776 cylinders
Units = cylinders of 15120 * 512 bytes

   Device Boot   Start    End     Blocks    Id     System
/dev/hda1   *       1      7       52888+    83      Linux
/dev/hda2           8    776     5813640     5     Extended
/dev/hda5           8    678    5072728+    83      Linux
/dev/hda6         679    722     332608+    82    Linux swap
```

Figure 7-24 Master Boot Record

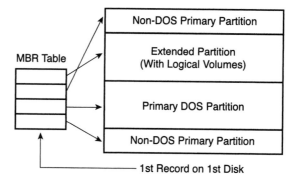

Requirements for Linux Partitions

Linux handles the primary, extended, and logical partition schemes a little differently than other operating systems. Linux numbers its primary and extended partitions 1 to 4, and the logical partitions are numbered from 5 up. For example, if you create two primary partitions and one extended partition, the primary partitions are numbered 1 and 2, and the extended partition is numbered 4. The extended partition is numbered 4 and not 3 because slots 1 through 3 are reserved for primary partitions even if they are not all used up. In this case, only two primary partitions are created, so slot 3 is omitted. Logical partitions are always numbered consecutively, starting at 5, regardless of the number of partitions.

Linux has a root partition, which is the partition on which the OS is installed and boots from. The root partition is also identified as /. It's called the root partition because the entire file structure is identified by its location relative to /. Figure 7-25 shows an example of the root files being installed on the root partition. At a minimum, Linux needs at least one partition for the operating system to be installed and boot up.

Figure 7-25 Linux Root Partition

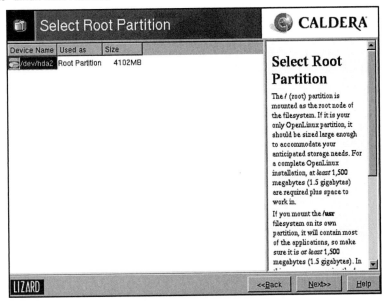

Partition Options and Advantages

When you partition a disk in Linux as well as in other operating systems, you have several options and choices. Several advantages come with partitioning a hard drive instead of having just one giant root partition.

Multiple Disks

When installing multiple disks, you must by default create more than one partition. You must create at least one partition for every disk that is installed. The advantage of doing this is that the root partition can be installed on one disk, and another directory, such as the /home directory, can be installed on the other disk. The /home directory disk would contain all the user's data that is saved in his or her home directory, and that data would be saved in the event that the drive with the root directory fails.

Better Security Options

Partitioning a hard disk can improve security on the drive as well. The security access for one partition can be greater or less than the security access for another. For example, if the /home directory is located on its own partition, the administrator can have stricter security for access to that partition.

Data Overrun Protection

Anyone who uses any operating system knows that errors or attacks will occur. Sometimes one of these errors can cause a file to continuously grow to huge sizes, thereby taking up all the space in a partition and causing the file system to seize up or crash because it can no longer create files or directories in that partition. Partitioning a hard drive can help reduce the amount of damage done and sometimes allow an administrator to catch the problem before it causes too much damage. Partitioning reduces the amount of hard drive space that this runaway process can consume.

Disk Error Protection

Partitioning a disk can also help if a sector on the hard drive goes bad or if a virus corrupts a portion of the hard drive. You lose only the data in the hard drive that has not been backed up elsewhere. If you do not partition the hard drive, all the data on the drive could be lost.

Ideal File Systems

Partitioning a disk can be useful when you need to use multiple file systems. You can have one file system that the operating system is installed on and boots from, and you can have another file system in another partition that certain files or programs might need to operate.

Depending on the OS, partitioning is done either before you run the installation program or from the installation program itself. Partitioning can be done manually or automatically. Many installation programs allow automatic partitioning. Although this option is helpful for novice administrators, automatic partitioning might not result in a system optimized for specific needs.

To manually partition a disk effectively, you must understand what types of partitions the NOS requires. How the server will be used also dictates how it is partitioned. For example, if you're configuring a Linux server to be a mail server, ensure that the appropriate partition is large enough to contain every user's unread mail.

Partitioning a Disk

Information about the number of partitions, their size, and their location on the disk is kept in the first sector of the disk. This information is called the partition table. Partition tables can have one of several formats, including DOS and BSD/Sun.

On systems that use a DOS-type partition table, such as Windows and Linux, the first sector of the disk is sometimes called the Master Boot Record (MBR) or the Master Boot Sector. DOS-type partition tables can describe up to four primary partitions. On BSD and Sun UNIX, the first sector of the hard drive is called the *disk label* or the *Volume Table of Contents (VTOC)*. The Sun-type partition table can describe up to eight primary partitions, as shown in Figure 7-26.

Figure 7-26 Sun-Type Partition Table

```
partition> print

Current partition table (original):

Total disk cylinders available: 6919 + 2 (reserved cylinders)

Part      Tag   Flag   Cylinders      Size           Blocks
0        root    wm     0 -   845    1.04GB     (846/0/0)    2172528
1        swap    wu    846 -  964    149.21MB   (119/0/0)     305592
2       backup   wm     0 - 6918     8.47GB     (6919/0/0) 17767992
3     unassigned wm     0              0         (0/0/0)           0
4     unassigned wm     0              0         (0/0/0)           0
5     unassigned wm     0              0         (0/0/0)           0
6     unassigned wm     0              0         (0/0/0)           0
7        home    wm    965 - 6918     7.29GB     (5954/0/0) 15289872

partition>
```

The partition table includes information that tells the OS which partitions are bootable. A bootable partition is one that contains an operating system. When you manually define partitions, you must configure a partition to be bootable if you want to boot from it. The MBR or disk label contains a program that locates the first sector of a bootable operating system and then turns control of the system over to that OS.

If the MBR or disk label is corrupted or otherwise lost, the system will no longer boot properly. For this reason, you should keep a copy of the MBR/disk label as a backup on a floppy disk.

Partitioning Tools

Before an operating system can be installed on a hard drive, it must be properly partitioned. Several tools help you partition a hard drive, but only a few should be used if you are installing Linux on the hard drive.

FDISK

Most NOS installation software includes a program called *FDISK*, which stands for fixed disk. FDISK programs are designed to manipulate a hard disk's partition table. The FDISK program can be used to create partitions, delete partitions, and set partitions as "active." Figure 7-27 shows the options that are available for disk management using the fdisk tool on a Linux system (using the -l switch).

Figure 7-27 Linux fdisk Program

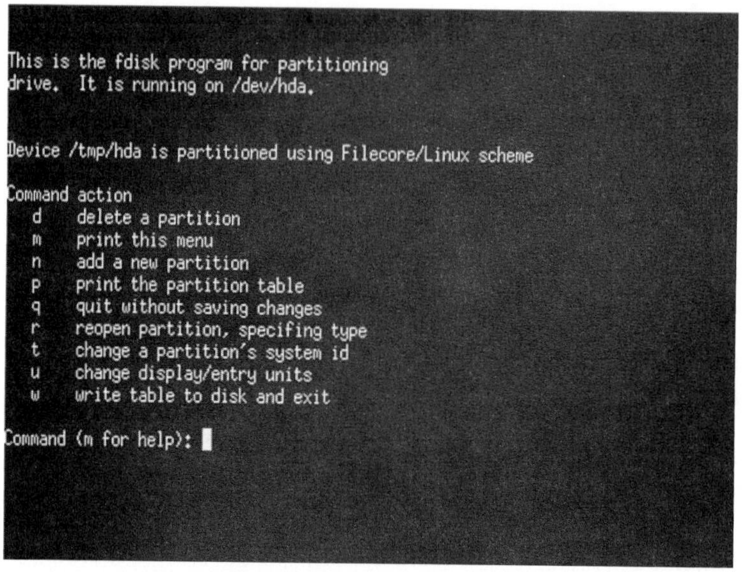

```
This is the fdisk program for partitioning
drive. It is running on /dev/hda.

Device /tmp/hda is partitioned using Filecore/Linux scheme

Command action
   d   delete a partition
   m   print this menu
   n   add a new partition
   p   print the partition table
   q   quit without saving changes
   r   reopen partition, specifing type
   t   change a partition's system id
   u   change display/entry units
   w   write table to disk and exit

Command (m for help): █
```

Microsoft provides a version of the FDISK program that is readily available. It gives you a text-based means of creating partitions on a hard drive that Linux can use.

Linux provides a version of FDISK as well, although the version that Linux uses is fdisk, with all lowercase letters. The Linux version of fdisk is text-based as well but provides a more flexible means of partitioning a hard disk than does Microsoft's version.

Linux Installation Tools

Linux provides its own tools that you can use when installing a Linux-only system. These are GUI tools that are much easier to use than fdisk. This is probably the best way and easiest way to partition a Linux system.

Third-Party Partitioning Tools

You can use third-party tools to partition a Linux system. The best-known tool for doing this is PowerQuest's PartitionMagic (www.powerquest.com). PartitionMagic is a GUI-based tool that can partition a hard drive formatted with a variety of file systems, including FAT, NTFS, HPFS, ext2, and ext3. PartitionMagic is DOS-based, but it comes with a floppy disk that can be used on operating systems other than Windows. It provides an excellent means of partitioning a disk that has more than one type of operating system or file system. PartitionMagic is also helpful for doing other things. It can be used to change a partition's size without damaging the files within the existing partition.

FIPS

This partitioning tool is included in the installation CDs that come with most of the Linux distributions. First Nondestructive Interactive Partitioning Splitting (FIPS) is a large partitioning tool that splits a FAT partition into two partitions. FIPS is most commonly used on Windows systems that need a separate partition to install Linux on. FIPS does this by first splitting the existing FAT partition. Then you can delete that partition and install Linux on that new partition. Figure 7-28 shows the FIPS partitioning tool.

Figure 7-28 FIPS Partitioning Tool

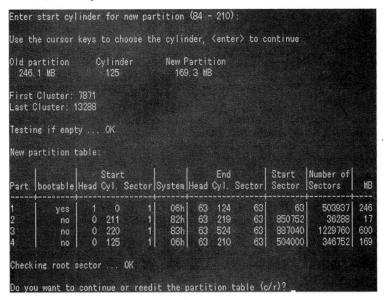

General Guidelines for Partitioning

You need to know some general rules when partitioning a hard drive. Following these rules will save you lots of time spent troubleshooting or repairing a file system down the road. Generally, any OS can be installed on any partition that is created by any partitioning tool, provided that the tool uses the standard x86 partition table. However, this does not always work. You should follow two rules when partitioning a hard drive:

- It's a good idea to use a cross-platform partitioning tool such as PartitionMagic. It can partition a hard drive for just about any operating system.
- If using a third-party partitioning tool is not an option, the next-best idea is to use the partitioning tool that comes with the OS. Both Linux and Windows 2000 and XP come with their own partitioning tools that can be used during the OS installation.

Swap Files

A *swap file* is an area of the hard disk that is used for virtual memory. *Virtual memory* is hard disk space that is used to supplement RAM. Figure 7-29 shows the Windows virtual memory settings. Data is written to the swap file (also called a paging file) when not enough RAM is available. Data is then swapped between RAM and the swap file as needed. If the system has sufficient RAM, the swap file might be small and used infrequently. If RAM usage increases, the swap file might grow larger, and swaps might occur more frequently. This allows programs to be run that the system would otherwise be unable to support.

Figure 7-29 Windows 2000 Virtual Memory Settings

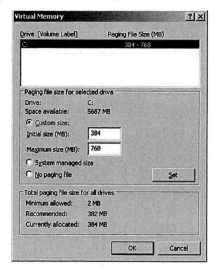

Although Windows uses a swap file, it does not have to be configured. The swap file is created as a file in the NOS partition.

UNIX systems typically dedicate an entire partition to swap space. This partition, or slice, is called the swap partition. The minimum size of the swap partition should be equal to twice the computer's RAM, or 32 MB, whichever is larger, but no more than 128 MB on a Red Hat Linux system. It is important to manage swap space usage, because if the system begins running out of swap space, the OS might start to seize up.

Configuring a Swap File

Network operating systems that use virtual memory (Windows NT, Windows 2000, UNIX, Linux) have a swap file on the network server disk drive. For optimum performance, the swap file should be installed on or moved to a different physical disk drive than the disk drive that contains the operating system files or frequently accessed application files (such as databases). The following sections describe the swap files and default sizes for various network operating systems.

Windows 2000 Server

Microsoft Windows 2000 Server defaults include the following:

- Swap filename: C:\PAGEFILE.SYS
- Default size: The amount of RAM in the server times 1.5
- One swap file is allowed per volume.

To change the number of paging files or to change the size of a paging file, select Start > Settings > Control Panel > System. On the Advanced tab, click the Performance Options button, and then click the Virtual Memory Change button.

Linux

You can use the **free** command in Linux to check the system's memory. It displays the system's total memory use, as shown in Figure 7-30. The **free** command has the following options:

- **-b | -k | -m**—By default, the **free** command displays the memory usage in kilobytes. However, these options let you display the output in bytes, kilobytes, or megabytes, respectively.
- **-o**—The **free** command displays a correction for memory used by disk caches and buffers. The **-o** option omits this information.
- **-s: delay**—This option sets the report to be displayed for a specific period of time before it goes away.
- **-t**—Adding this option to the command displays the RAM plus swap space totals.
- **-v**—This option displays the version number.

Figure 7-30 **free** Command

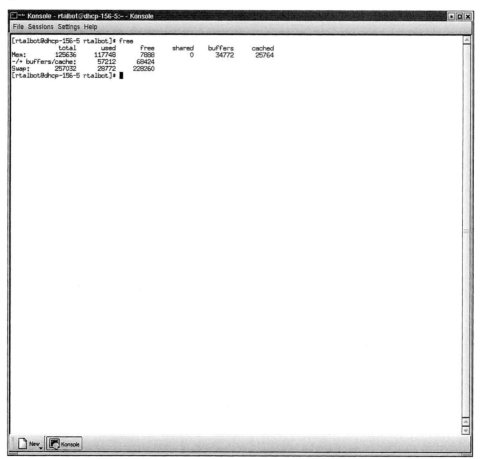

This command can be very useful for determining a system's overall performance and also when RAM might need to be added. By checking the total, used, and free columns, you can see how much RAM the system has, how much is being used, and how much is free. If the used column begins to approach the same value as the total column, it might be a good idea to add more RAM.

The last row of the output displays swap file space and usage. You can decide whether to add more swap space the same way you decide whether to add more RAM. The only difference is that it is hard to estimate swap file usage just by looking at this output. A better evaluation needs to be made over a period of time when the system is being used regularly. You can do this by capturing the output and saving it to a text file that you can read and evaluate later. To do this, you use the -s option along with the > command, which redirects the output to a text file. The command would look like this:

```
free -s 900 > swapeval.txt
```

This causes the swap file usage output to be displayed for 900 seconds. Then the output is directed to a text file that you can read later.

Adding a Swap File

One way to add swap space is to add a swap file:

Step 1   Create a file that takes up the space equal to the size of the swap file that you will create. To do this you use the **dd** command. The output is as follows:

```
# dd if=/dev/zero of=swap.swp bs=1024 count=131072
```

This command states that bytes will be copied from /dev/zero, and then a swap.swp file that is 128 MB in size will be created.

Step 2   You need to initialize the swap.swp file that was created so that the Linux system can use it to swap memory to disk. By using the **mkswap** command, you can allow Linux to use the new swap file, but it will be inactive. The output for this command is as follows:

```
# mkswap /swap.swp
```

Step 3   To make this swap file active, use the **swapon** command. The output is as follows:

```
# swapon /swap.swp
```

To make this swap file inactive, use the **swapoff** command.

The swap file you just created will not be used the next time the system is rebooted unless that entry is made in /etc/fstab, as shown in Figure 7-31. You need to list the complete path of where the swap file is located in this file.

Adding swap space using this method is definitely the quickest and easiest way. However, it does have some drawbacks. If you create this swap file on a partition that is already being used, the file can become fragmented as the partition gets used more and more. This fragmentation degrades performance. The only other option is to create an entirely new swap partition. However, this is much more complex and is not recommended unless it is absolutely necessary.

Figure 7-31 /etc/fstab File

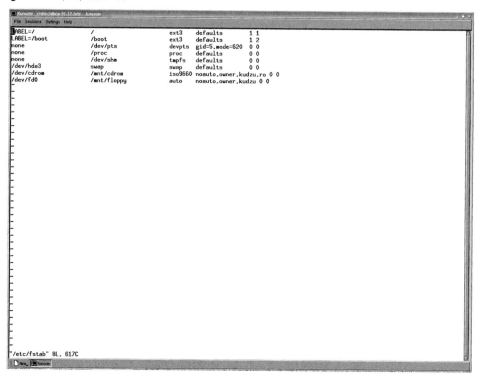

Formatting the Disk

After the partitions have been created, they need to be formatted. Typically, the installation program prompts you with the available format options. Partitions can be formatted with various utilities, such as Windows FORMAT.EXE.

The *formatting* process defines the partition's file system. Figure 7-32 shows the GUI for selecting partitions in Red Hat. The operating system keeps track of all the files that are stored in each partition. Each file is stored on the hard disk in one or more clusters or disk spaces of a predefined uniform size.

Figure 7-32 Red Hat Disk Formatting

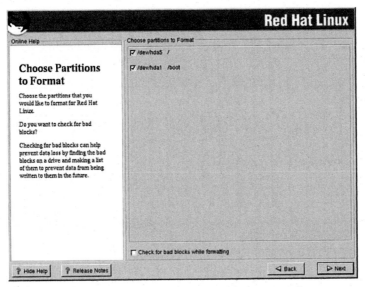

When formatting a partition on a Windows NOS, you must choose between the following file systems:

- NTFS (New Technology File System)—Recommended for network servers
- FAT32
- FAT

When formatting a UNIX or Linux partition, you must choose between the following file systems:

- UFS (UNIX File System)
- EXT3

Another notable file system is HFS (H File System), which is used with OS/2.

Creating the Initial Administrative Account

One of the most important parts of any NOS installation is the creation of the administrative user account. As discussed in earlier chapters, a NOS is a multiuser system. The administrative account has unrestricted access to create and delete users and files. For this reason, the administrative account is called the *superuser account* on some systems. Table 7-5 is a partial list of the names given to the administrative user account in common NOSs. Table 7-6 describes the capabilities of an administrator in Windows XP.

Table 7-5 Administrative Account Names

NOS	Name of Superuser Account
Windows NT 4.0/2000/XP	Administrator. Also user-defined during installation.
UNIX/Linux	root
Novell NetWare	Admin
MacOS X	User-defined during installation

Table 7-6 Windows XP Account Privileges

	Computer Administrator	Limited
Install programs and hardware	➡	
Make system-wide changes	➡	
Access and read all nonprivate files	➡	
Create and delete user accounts	➡	
Change other people's accounts	➡	
Change your own account name or type	➡	
Change your own picture	➡	➡
Create, change, or remove your own password	➡	➡

When installing the NOS, the installation program asks the user to create an administrative account. Because this account is very powerful, it is critical that a strong password be assigned. A password is considered strong when it contains eight characters or more and does not use recognizable names or words found in a dictionary. Strong passwords also use a combination of uppercase and lowercase letters, numbers, and other characters.

Completing the Installation

After you provide the installation program with the necessary information, the program creates the NOS system files on the hard disk. Other basic applications and components also are copied to the hard disk, as determined by the installation program. Depending on the NOS's size, the number of selected components, and the server's speed, it can take from a few minutes to more than an hour to complete the copying process.

After the copying process is complete, the installation program might ask you some final configuration questions before it reboots the system. After the system reboots, the administrator should be able to log in to the newly installed NOS using the administrative account created during the installation process.

The Boot Process

This section covers the following topics:

- Steps of the boot process
- Basic files required
- BIOS interaction
- Detailed steps of the boot process
- Linux boot process

Steps of the Boot Process

The boot process of the Windows 2000 operating system is very different from Windows 9*x*. The Windows 9*x* boot process is much simpler and more straightforward. Windows 9*x* and Windows 2000 use completely different files to start the operating system. Windows 9*x* has a few files that load the startup programs and check for device drivers, but the Windows 2000 boot process is much more involved and requires the use of many more files. Windows 2000 requires a few extra steps and files because of its added security and logon features. In addition, many of the features that are supported in Windows 98, such as specific device drivers, are not supported by the Windows NT/2000 operating system.

Windows 2000 goes through a series of steps as it boots the computer. If everything is working, the user will not care much about the details of the process. However, when troubleshooting boot problems, it is helpful to understand how the boot process works. As shown in Figure 7-33, the Windows 2000 boot process occurs in five stages:

Step 1   The preboot sequence

Step 2   The boot sequence

Step 3   The kernel load

Step 4   The kernel initialization

Step 5   The logon process

NOTE

This section covers the boot process as it relates to the Windows 2000 operating system. Keep in mind that although the Windows 2000 boot process is discussed here, the same steps take place in Linux, although the files names are different. The Linux boot process is discussed later.

Figure 7-33 Five Steps of the Boot Process

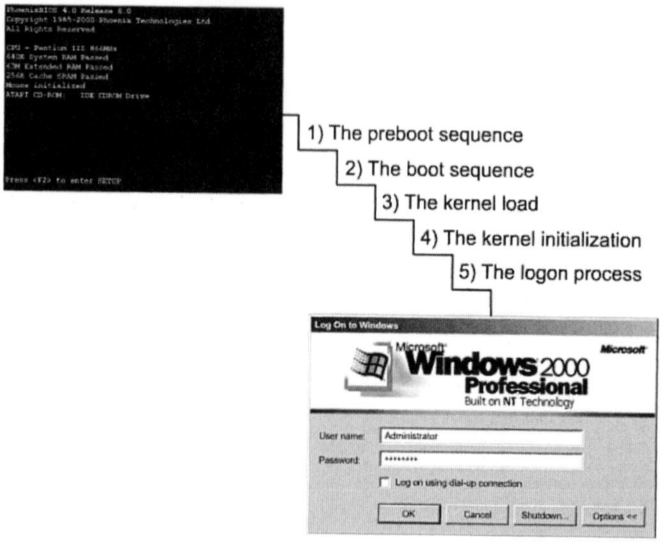

1) The preboot sequence

2) The boot sequence

3) The kernel load

4) The kernel initialization

5) The logon process

Learning about the boot process and the files that are used in the stages of this process will help you effectively troubleshoot problems with the operating system.

Basic Files Required

Before looking at the details of the boot process, it might be a good idea to look at the files that are required to complete a successful boot and to see where these files must be located. Table 7-7 lists some of the major files that a Windows 2000 system needs to boot properly.

Table 7-7 Necessary Boot Files

Filename	Default Location
NTLDR	Root of the active partition (C:\)
boot.ini	Root of the active partition (C:\)
bootsect.dos (only if dual-booting)	Root of the active partition (C:\)
Ntdetect.com	Root of the active partition (C:\)
Ntbootdd.sys	Root of the active partition (C:\)
Ntoskrnl.exe	C:\Winnt\System32
hal.dll	C:\Winnt\System32
SYSTEM Registry key	C:\Winnt\System32\Config
Device drivers	C:\Winnt\System32\Drivers

It is important to note that this chapter describes an Intel-based boot process. The boot process is slightly different on non-Intel-based systems, because NTLDR is not needed. These systems have a file called OSLOADER.EXE that performs this function. The NTDETECT.COM file also is not needed on non-Intel-based systems, because that function is performed during the POST, and the information gathered from the POST is given to NTOSKRNL.EXE through OSLOADER.EXE. From that point on, Intel-based and non-Intel-based systems boot the same way.

BIOS Interaction

The boot process cannot function without the BIOS, because the BIOS controls all aspects of the boot process. The BIOS includes the instructions and data in the ROM chip that control the boot process and the computer hardware. During the boot process, the BIOS performs a series of interactions with the system hardware. These include checking the necessary hardware to make sure that it is present and operational. This occurs during the POST. During the POST, the computer tests its memory and verifies that it has all the necessary hardware, such as a keyboard and a mouse. The BIOS uses this information to control all aspects of the boot process. When there is a problem during the POST, the BIOS produces audio and video error codes. The BIOS provides the computer with basic instructions to control devices in the system during the boot process. The BIOS also locates any BIOS codes on expansion cards and executes them during the boot process. Finally, the BIOS locates a volume or boot sector on the drives to start the operating system. Figure 7-34 shows the screen that appears during the boot process when the POST has completed and verified that all the necessary hardware is present.

Figure 7-34 BIOS POST

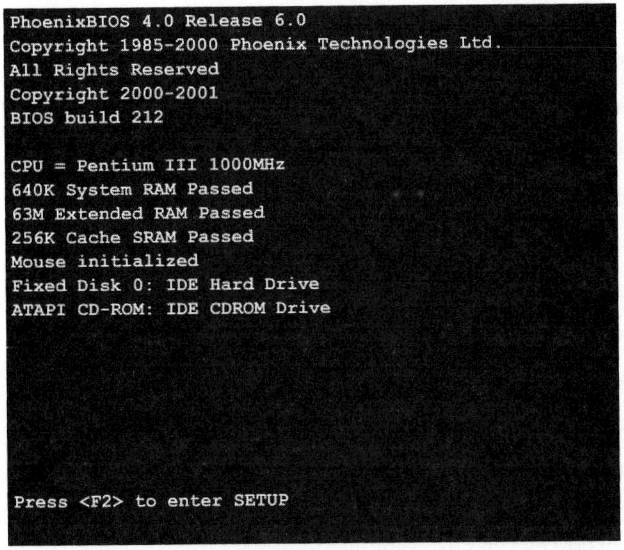

```
PhoenixBIOS 4.0 Release 6.0
Copyright 1985-2000 Phoenix Technologies Ltd.
All Rights Reserved
Copyright 2000-2001
BIOS build 212

CPU = Pentium III 1000MHz
640K System RAM Passed
63M Extended RAM Passed
256K Cache SRAM Passed
Mouse initialized
Fixed Disk 0: IDE Hard Drive
ATAPI CD-ROM: IDE CDROM Drive




Press <F2> to enter SETUP
```

Detailed Steps of the Boot Process

Step 1   Preboot sequence

After the power is turned on, the first step of the boot process is the POST. Every computer does this, regardless of its operating system. After the computer completes the POST, it lets other adapter cards run their own POSTs, such as a SCSI card that is equipped with its own BIOS. After the POST routine is complete, the computer locates a boot device and loads the Master Boot Record (MBR) into memory, which in turn locates the active partition and loads it into memory. The MBR allows the operating system to load into RAM. Up to this point, the computer hardware has played an important role. Without properly functioning hardware, the operating system will not load. At this point the computer loads and initializes the NTLDR file, which is the operating system loader, and begins loading the operating system.

Step 2   Boot sequence

After the computer loads NTLDR, the boot sequence begins gathering information about hardware and drivers. NTLDR uses the Ntdetect.com, boot.ini, and bootsect.dos files. The bootsect.dos file is used only if the computer is set up to dual-boot. A major function provided by NTLDR is switching the processor into 32-bit flat memory mode. Until this point, the computer was running in real mode, just like the old 8086/8088 CPUs. Next, NTLDR starts the file system, either FAT or NTFS, so that it can read the files from the disk. NTLDR reads the boot.ini file to enable the display of the boot menu onscreen. Here the user can select which operating system to load if the computer is set to dual-boot. If an operating system other than Windows 2000 is selected, NTLDR loads the bootsect.dos file and passes control to it. bootsect.dos then boots the other OS. If Windows 2000 is selected, or if the computer is not dual-booting, NTLDR runs Ntdetect.com, which gathers information about the computer hardware. It is also in this step that you can press F8 for troubleshooting and advanced startup options. Ntdetect.com detects the following hardware components:

- Computer ID
- Bus/adapter type
- Keyboard
- Com ports
- Parallel ports
- Floppy disks
- SCSI adapters
- Mouse/pointing devices
- Floating-point coprocessor
- Video adapters

After Ntdetect.com has collected the hardware information, NTLDR loads Ntoskrnl.exe and passes it that information.

Step 3   Kernel load

The kernel load phase begins with Ntoskrnl.exe loading along with the file. At this point, NTLDR still plays a role in the boot process. NTLDR reads the system Registry key into memory and selects the hardware configuration that is stored in the Registry. It loads the configuration needed for the computer to boot. At this point of the boot process, you can select which hardware profile is to be loaded, provided that you can choose from more than one hardware profile. Next, NTLDR loads from the Registry any device drivers that have a start value of 0x0. At the end of this step, all the kernel files have been loaded into memory.

Step 4   Kernel initialization

The initial kernel load phase is complete, and the kernel begins to initialize. This simply means that it recognizes everything that was loaded previously so that NTLDR can give control to the operating system kernel. The operating system begins the final stages of loading. The GUI appears. It shows a status bar indicating that the GUI is loading. Four additional steps take place:

a. The hardware key is created. After the kernel has completed the initialization process, it uses the information collected during the hardware detection phase to create the Registry key HKEY_LOCAL_MACHINE\HARDWARE. This Registry key contains all the information about the hardware that is located on the computer motherboard, as well as the interrupts used by the hardware devices.

b. The clone control set is created. The kernel references the Registry subkey HKEY_LOCAL_MACHINE\SYSTEM\Select and then creates a clone (copy) of the Current Control Set value in the Registry. The computer uses this clone to maintain an identical copy of the data used to configure the computer, so this Registry value does not reflect changes made during the startup process.

c. Device drivers are loaded and initialized. During this step, the kernel first initializes the low-level device drivers that were loaded in the kernel load phase of the boot process. Now the kernel must scan the Registry subkey HKEY_LOCAL_MACHINE\SYSTEM\CurrentControlSet\Services for device drivers that have a value of 0x1. This device driver value indicates at what point in the process the driver will load. This is the same for the device driver value in the kernel load phase as well.

d. Services are started. The final step is starting the Session Manager. The Session Manager is started when the SMSS.EXE file is loaded. The Session Manager is responsible for loading the programs in its BootExecute Registry entry. The Session Manager also loads the required subsystems, which start the Winlogon.exe file. This file starts the Local Security Administration (Lsass.exe) file, and the Ctrl-Alt-Delete window appears. The Service Controller (Screg.exe) checks the Registry for services that have a start value of 0x2 and loads them. Services that have a start value of 0x3 are started manually, and services that have a start value of 0x4 are disabled.

Step 5   Logon

The Logon screen begins the final step in the bootup process. Although this is the final step, the boot is not considered complete or successful until a user logs on. After the user has logged on, the clone of the Current Control Set value from Step 4 is copied to the last known good control set value in the Registry. This is a safety measure that the OS performs so that a user can reboot the computer if the boot process becomes corrupt. An example is if a bad device driver gets loaded and does not allow the user to log on. Selecting this value during startup loads the last successful boot configuration that was saved without this bad device driver, allowing the user to log on.

Worksheet 7.3.5.1   The Windows 2000 Boot Process

Identify the steps and files that are used to boot Windows 2000.

Linux Boot Process

The boot processes of Windows 2000 and Linux are very similar. Obviously one main difference is the file types that are used. The names of the file types that are used to boot the two systems might be different, but they essentially perform the same functions. For example, Windows 2000 uses the NTLDR file as the main file that gets the system stated until the operating system takes over the process. In Linux, the LILO file performs this function. Figure 7-35 shows the LILO screen that is used to boot the operating system. This screen is also where you decide which operating system you want LILO to begin booting if you are dual-booting. Both systems start the boot process by locating the master boot record and loading it. Next, in Windows 2000, NTLDR loads the kernel files (NTDETECT, NTOSKRNL, and HAL). In Linux, the same process occurs, using the Linux kernel. At this point in both systems, the root files are loaded to prepare the operating system to take over. The next step of the Windows boot process is loading the services, which is done by the SMSS.EXE file. In Linux, this process is done by INIT. At this point, the boot processes take separate paths as Linux begins loading its operating system and Windows does the same. In the end, both systems come to a logon prompt that asks for a username and password to authenticate into the system.

Figure 7-35 LILO Boot Menu

Worksheet 7.3.5.2 The Linux Boot Process

Identify the steps and files that are used to boot Linux.

Troubleshooting NOS Installation

This section covers the following topics:

- Unable to boot from the installation medium
- Problems during the installation process
- Post-installation problems

Unable to Boot from the Installation Medium

If the system will not boot from the installation medium (such as a CD or floppy disk), the installation program will not run.

You can follow several steps if the system will not boot from a CD-ROM:

- Consult the system BIOS setup menu, as shown in Figure 7-36. A hotkey sequence is generally required to enter the BIOS monitor. The key sequence varies from manufacturer to manufacturer. The BIOS is built-in software that contains all the code required to control the system's hardware devices. These can include the keyboard, monitor, hard drives, parallel and serial ports, and a number of other functions. The PC BIOS on computers today is standardized, so aside from differences in manufacturers, they all work in much the same way.
- Make sure that the BIOS can support and boot from a CD-ROM and that the correct boot sequence is configured. If the system BIOS cannot support or boot from a CD-ROM, the system must be booted using a bootable floppy.
- Consult the documentation that came with the CD. Make sure that the CD contains system files and is designed to be bootable. Some CDs contain the installation files but are not bootable. If this is the case, try booting from a floppy disk.
- Check that the CD is recognized by the operating system and that proper device drivers are available.
- Check to see if another system can boot from the CD or read the CD. If another system cannot read the disc, the problem is most likely with the disc itself. If another system can read the disc, the problem is most likely a faulty CD drive.
- Inspect the data side of the CD for scratches, fingerprints, or dust if you think the problem is with the disc itself. Clean the CD using a dry cotton cloth, gently wiping from the center of the disc to its edge. Repeat this process until the entire surface of the CD appears clean. Replace the CD in the drive, and try booting again. If the boot fails, obtain another copy of the installation disc.

- Determine if the problem is with the CD-ROM drive. Do this by turning off the power, opening the case, and inspecting the cable connection between the CD-ROM drive and the motherboard. Make sure that the cable is plugged in firmly at both ends. After checking the cable, verify the CD-ROM configuration settings such as master/slave, cable select, SCSI ID, and SCSI termination, depending on the type of drive. If the CD-ROM still fails, replace the drive or the cable. If booting still fails, consult the hardware documentation before proceeding.

Figure 7-36 BIOS

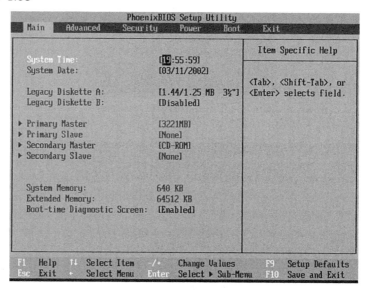

Problems During the Installation Process

Occasionally, something goes wrong during the installation process. If you make an incorrect choice while using the installation program, look for a Back button or key so that you can reverse the configuration. Here are some other common problems:

- Partitioning or formatting the hard disk fails. Check the BIOS settings and hard disk documentation to troubleshoot this problem. The hard disk might be faulty. Checking the page in the BIOS that contains the information about the hard drives installed in the system lets you perform a test to see if the system recognizes the disk.
- The system hangs during the installation process. A *hang* is defined as a period of several minutes during which there is no discernable activity on the system. The installation screen appears frozen or black, and the hard disk drive activity LED is not blinking. Wait at least 5 minutes under these conditions before declaring a hang. If the system hangs, turn the power off and then back on again. After you turn the power back on, the installation program might give you the option of

resuming or repairing the previous installation. If it does not, start the installation process over. If the hang occurs again at the same point during the installation process, there is most likely a hardware compatibility problem. Check the hardware inventory against the vendor's compatibility list.

- The installation medium cannot be read at some point during the installation process. This problem occurs when you install with a CD that is dirty or scratched. In some cases, the problem is a "bad burn," which is a CD-RW that has had the installation files copied onto it incorrectly. If cleaning the CD does not correct this problem, obtain another copy of the installation files.

Post-Installation Problems

After you install the NOS, the system might not load the NOS properly or might not allow a logon. If the system fails to load the NOS, consult the manufacturer website and documentation. First-time load failures are difficult to troubleshoot. You must gather very specific information about the system and the NOS. If the system reports specific errors, write them down and search for information about them on the web or in the documentation. If necessary, call a technical support line and ask for help.

If you're unable to log on, the problem is usually forgotten administrator account information that you configured during the installation process. In many systems, usernames and passwords are case-sensitive, so check to make sure that the Caps Lock key on the keyboard is not on. Figure 7-37 illustrates a sample error message you receive when you leave the Caps Lock key on during the login process.

Figure 7-37 Post-Installation Problems

Summary

This chapter discussed how to plan, install, and troubleshoot a NOS installation. Some of the important concepts to retain from this chapter include the following:

- The planning process includes gathering information about the minimum system requirements and known hardware compatibility issues. In some cases, you can use a utility program that can verify if the system will work with the NOS.

- The hardware inventory should include device type, manufacturer, model number, and device driver version information for each device.

- The two types of partitions are primary and extended. Every system requires at least one primary partition. The first primary partition is always labeled with a C on a Windows system. A system can have only one extended partition, but an extended partition can be subdivided into multiple logical partitions. The logical partitions that make up an extended partition are called volumes or logical drives.

- The formatting process defines the partition's file system. When formatting a partition on a Windows NOS, you choose between NTFS, FAT32, and FAT. NTFS is recommended for network servers. When formatting a UNIX or Linux partition, you choose between UFS and EXT3.

- The Windows 2000 boot process is similar to Linux. Its five stages are the preboot sequence, boot sequence, kernel load, kernel initialization, and logon process.

- Occasionally you might have problems with the installation. When this happens, reverse the process to ensure that you followed all the steps correctly. Gather all the information about the system, and search for resolution on the web or in the documentation. If necessary, call a technical support line for help.

The next chapter details the Windows 2000 operating system. You will learn the steps to complete the installation through the administrative logon.

Check Your Understanding

The following review questions help you assess what you learned in this chapter. Answers can be found in Appendix A, "Answers to Check Your Understanding Questions."

1. When formatting a partition on a Windows NOS, which three file systems can you select?

   A. NTFS

   B. UFS

   C. FAT32

   D. EXT3

   E. FAT

   F. HFS

2. List the steps in the Windows 2000 boot process.

Step 1	
Step 2	
Step 3	
Step 4	
Step 5	

3. Match each file with its default location on a Windows 2000 client.

File	Default Location
NTLDR	C:\Winnt\System32
Ntoskrnl.exe	C:\Winnt\System32\Drivers
SYSTEM Registry key	Root of the active partition (C:\)
Device drivers	C:\Winnt\System32\Config

4. Which two of the following are types of physical partitions?

   A. A.Secondary

   B. B.Primary

   C. C.Logical

   D. D.Extended

   E. E.Volume

5. It is recommended that you perform some verification activities before installing any hardware in a server. Which of the following would you *not* do?

   A. Verify that the power outlet for the network server is available and active. (Test with a volt/ohm meter.)

   B. Verify that the network connection is available and active.

   C. Verify the release version of the operating system that the hardware will be installed in.

   D. Verify that the location where the server is to be installed is ready for the installation.

   E. Verify that all the hardware for the network server has arrived and that the hardware is as specified in the installation plan.

6. What approximate server room temperature tells you that you need to install a secondary cooling device for the room?

   A. 65 degrees

   B. 68 degrees

   C. 70 degrees

   D. 72 degrees

   E. 75 degrees

7. Complete the following table by filling in the minimum system requirements for installing Linux.

Component	Description
Computer/processor	
Memory	
Hard disk	
Drive	
Display	
Peripheral	

8. Fill in the blanks in the following sentences.

   To view or change the network configuration for a Windows system, use the _____ command.

   To view or change the network configuration for a Linux system, use the _____ command.

9. Which of the following are advantages of partitioning a disk before installing an operating system?

   A. You can create a swap partition to supplement the system RAM and enhance performance.

   B. You can install multiple operating systems on the same disk.

   C. You can physically separate data from the system files to provide security, file management, and fault tolerance.

   D. You can exchange files between operating systems that are installed on the separate partitions.

10. When you partition a hard drive that has Linux installed on it, numbers are assigned to each partition. The partition numbers 1, 2, and 3 are reserved for what kind of partition?

    A. Extended

    B. Logical

    C. Primary

    D. DOS

Key Terms

Basic Input/Output System (BIOS)   Typically resides in ROM on the motherboard and is the first program run when a system is powered on. It is responsible for testing hardware devices using a POST.

extended partition   A variation of a primary partition that acts as a placeholder for a logical partition.

FDISK   A program that manipulates a hard disk's partition table by creating partitions, deleting partitions, and setting partitions as active.

Fibre Channel-Arbitrated Loop (FC-AL)   Fibre Channel can use either fiber-optic cable or copper wire as the connection medium.

formatting   The process that defines the partition's file system.

hardware compatibility list   A support page that you can view or download from an operating system vendor's website. You use it to find compatibility information on specific third-party hardware that you will install.

logical partition   A partition that is created in an extended partition.

multimeter   A device for checking the voltage of a power source.

partition table   The section on the hard drive that contains the partition information and the MBR.

Power-On Self Test (POST)   The point during the boot process when the computer tests its memory and verifies that it has all the necessary hardware, such as a keyboard and a mouse.

primary partition   The same as an original partition. It is usually the partition that contains the MBR and the default operating system files.

server chassis   The casing that houses the server hardware.

swap file   An area of the hard disk that is used for virtual memory.

system files   The files that allow the operating system to function. NOS installation involves creating and copying NOS system files to a hard disk.

uninterruptible power supply (UPS)   A backup power supply system that is commonly found on servers. It provides power for a short period of time if a power loss occurs in the building where the server is located.

virtual memory   Hard disk space that is used to supplement RAM.

volt-amp (VA) rating   A unit of measure for a UPS that specifies how long the UPS can keep the network server running in the event of a power failure.

volt/ohm meter   A device that verifies that a power outlet is available and active.

Volume Table of Contents (VTOC)   The first sector of the hard drive on BSD and Sun UNIX systems. Also called a disk label.

Objectives

After completing this chapter, you will be able to complete tasks related to

- Installation
- Administrator/user interface
- User accounts
- Managing the file system
- Services

Chapter 8

Windows 2000 Professional

This chapter details the Windows 2000 operating system. The installation has four steps. After it is verified that the system is compatible, Windows 2000 guides the administrator to the final step of logging on. This chapter also covers managing user accounts and the file system to provide the administrator with the necessary information to share folders and files and assign permissions. You also learn about Windows 2000 services that are configured to provide access to the web, e-mail, and other computers.

Installation

This section covers the following topics:

- Installing the OS
- Installing OS add-on options

Installing the OS

You must consider a few things before installing Windows 2000. First, check to make sure that the hardware can run Windows 2000. Microsoft recommends that users observe the following requirements before installing the operating system:

- Pentium 133 MHz or higher microprocessor
- 64 MB RAM
- 2 GB hard drive or a partition with a minimum of 1 GB of free space
- VGA monitor
- 12X CD-ROM minimum
- Network card

Microsoft has a tool called the *Hardware Compatibility List (HCL)* that you can use to verify that the hardware will actually work with Windows 2000. Microsoft provides tested drivers for only those devices that are included on this list. Using hardware that is not listed on the HCL might cause problems during and after installation. You can view this HCL by opening the hcl.txt file in the Support folder on the Windows 2000 Professional CD-ROM, or by visiting http://www.microsoft.com/hwdq/hcl/. Figure 8-1 shows the HCL text file that you can view on any Windows 2000 system.

Figure 8-1 Windows 2000 Hardware Compatibility List

Understanding the Steps in the Windows 2000 Installation

The Windows 2000 installation process has four main steps:

- The Setup program
- The Setup wizard
- Installing Windows 2000 networking
- Completing the Setup program

The installation begins when the Setup program runs. This prepares the hard disk and copies files. Setup then runs a wizard that provides informational pages that are used to complete the installation.

NOTE

Microsoft uses *wizards,* which are made up of a systematic series of dialog boxes, to guide users through many administrative tasks.

The Setup Program

The first step of the installation process is preparing the hard drive for the other stages of the installation. Files that are needed to run the setup wizard are copied, and the text portion of the setup is displayed. You can start the Windows 2000 installation by either using the Setup boot disks or booting from the CD-ROM.

If you choose the Setup boot disks, insert the first disk into the computer and turn it on. Follow the steps to insert the other three disks to begin copying the files.

Using the Windows 2000 Professional CD-ROM can be much easier. After you boot from the CD-ROM, a minimal version of Windows 2000 is copied into memory, which is used to start the Setup program.

This is where the text-based portion of Setup starts. The administrator does the following:

- Reads and accepts the licensing agreement
- Reconfigures the hard disk partitions or deletes a partition if necessary
- Creates and formats a new partition to install Windows 2000 or reformats an existing partition
- Selects either FAT or NTFS as the type of file system

Setup then formats the partition with the file system selected. You can select either FAT or NTFS. Figure 8-2 shows the options available during the installation process. Remember that FAT can be converted to NTFS, but NTFS cannot be converted to FAT unless you reinstall the OS. This is one of the security features that NTFS provides. When installing the OS on a network, NTFS is preferred because of the file system security for the user and system administrator.

Figure 8-2 Windows 2000 Setup Program

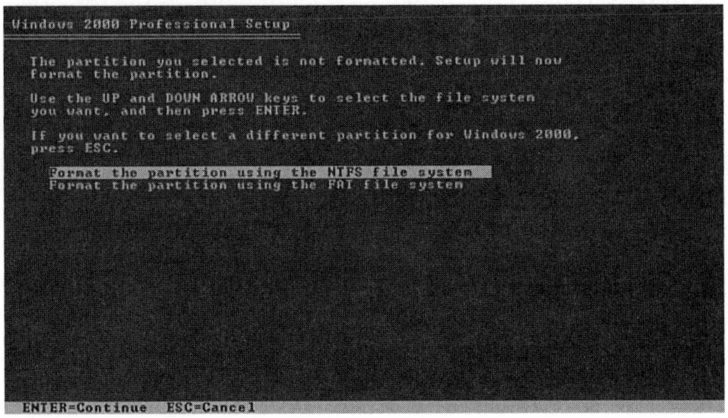

After the partition has been formatted, the Setup program begins copying the necessary files to the hard disk and saves configuration information. Setup then automatically restarts the computer and starts the Windows 2000 Setup wizard. By default, the Windows 2000 operating system files are installed in the C:\Winnt folder.

The Setup Wizard

The Setup Wizard begins the graphical user interface (GUI) portion of the installation process and prompts the administrator through the next stage of the installation. Figure 8-3 shows the Windows 2000 GUI Setup screen. It gathers information about the administrator, the organization, and the computer. This step installs the security features and configures the system devices. The administrator then is prompted through a series of setup screens in which the Windows 2000 Setup wizard asks for some information:

- **Regional settings**—Windows 2000 was designed to be a global operating system. This is where the information designed to customize language, locale, and keyboard settings is entered. Windows 2000 can be configured to use multiple languages and regional settings.

- **Name and organization**—Enter the name of the person who will be the user of the computer and the organization to which this copy of Windows 2000 Professional is licensed.

- **Product key**—Microsoft ships every copy of Windows 2000 with a specific 25-character product key that is usually located on the back of the CD case.

- **Computer name**—When you connect the computer to a network, each computer on the network needs a unique name so that it can be identified on the network. A computer name must be entered. It can be no longer than 15 characters. The Windows 2000 Setup wizard displays a default name, using the organization name that was entered earlier in the setup process, but it is recommended that this be changed.

- **Password for the Administrator account**—Windows 2000 can have many different profiles for the users of the computer. It also has a built-in Administrator account that includes privileges to make any changes to the computer. At this point, the administrator must supply the password for the Administrator account. This password can be changed later, but only by the user who has local administrative privileges to the system.

- **Modem dialing information**—Because modern networks use high-speed LANs and network cards, this option first depends on whether a modem is being used. Most laptops still use them, so it could be necessary to enter information here. First, select the country or region where the computer is located. Often this is already completed, based on the selected regional setting. The area (or city) of the computer location must also be entered, as well as the number for obtaining an outside line. Finally, select whether the phone system uses tone dialing or pulse dialing.

■ **Date and time settings**—The correct date, time, and time zone must be specified. Whether Windows 2000 automatically adjusts the computer clock setting for daylight saving time changes can also be selected.

Figure 8-3 Windows 2000 Setup Wizard

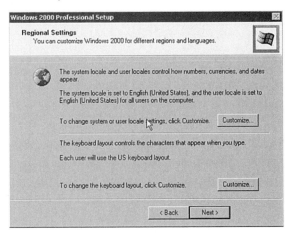

Installing Windows 2000 Networking

Because Windows 2000 was designed to be a network operating system (NOS), specifying the network settings is a major step in the installation process. After gathering information about the computer, the Windows 2000 Setup program automatically installs the network software. Figure 8-4 shows the network settings screen that is used to configure the system for network access during the installation process.

Figure 8-4 Installing Windows 2000 Networking

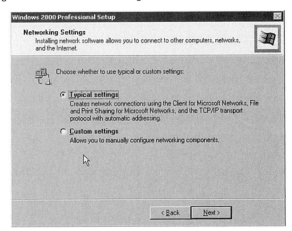

Lab 8.1.1   Installing Windows 2000

Learn how to properly and successfully install Windows 2000.

Worksheet 8.1.1   Installing Windows 2000

Identify some of the concepts involved in and what processes are occurring as the Windows 2000 operating system is installed.

Windows 2000 Professional installs networking components in a series of steps:

- **Detect network adapter cards**—The operating system first needs to detect the network cards. If no cards are installed, this step is skipped.

- **Install networking components**—Necessary files must be installed to allow the computer to connect to other computers, networks, and the Internet. The Setup program prompts the administrator to choose whether to use typical settings or customized settings to configure the following networking components. If Typical is chosen, the system installs the default settings. By choosing the Customized option, the administrator can enter the information that is specific to the company network. For example, Client for Microsoft Networks allows the computer to gain access to network resources. File and Printer Sharing for Microsoft Networks allows other computers to gain access to file and print resources on the computer and allows the local computer to gain access to shared files and printers on the network. TCP/IP is the default networking protocol that allows a computer to communicate over LANs and wide-area networks (WANs). At this stage, other clients, services, and network protocols can be installed if the network requires them. These can include NetBIOS Enhanced User Interface (NetBEUI), AppleTalk, and NWLink IPX/SPX/NetBIOS-compatible transport.

- **Join a workgroup or domain**—The administrator needs to decide whether the computer will be part of a domain or workgroup. This information should be known before this step. If a computer account is created in the domain for the computer during the installation, the Windows 2000 Setup wizard prompts the administrator for the name and password to join the domain.

- **Install components**—The last step is to install and configure the networking components that have just been selected.

Completing the Setup Program

After the networking components have been installed, the Setup wizard copies additional files to configure Windows 2000 Professional. The Setup program automatically starts the fourth step in the installation process. There are four basic steps to the final stage of the installation process, which is shown in Figure 8-5:

1. **Install Start menu items**—This is where all the shortcut items that appear on the Start menu are installed.

2. **Register components**—Windows 2000 begins to apply the configuration settings that were specified in the Windows 2000 Setup wizard.

3. **Save the configuration**—After the configuration settings are applied, they need to be saved in the Registry so that they are used every time the computer is started.

4. **Remove temporary files**—While the operating system is being installed, many files need to be copied to run these installation steps. After installation, the files are no longer used. The Setup wizard automatically deletes these files. After this step is complete, the computer automatically restarts, and the administrator can then log on to finish the installation procedure.

Figure 8-5 Completing the Windows 2000 Setup Program

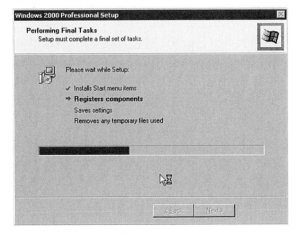

Lab 8.1.2   Configuring an IP Address

Configure a Windows 2000 Professional IP address.

Windows 2000 Setup Options

The installation steps that were just described are the typical or default installation procedures. Other setup options can be selected when installing Windows 2000:

- A *Typical installation* is the basic type of installation that was described in the preceding section.

- A *Portable installation* installs the options that might be needed with a portable computer, such as a laptop.

- A *Compact installation* should be used when installing Windows 2000 on a computer with a limited amount of hard drive space.

- A *Custom installation* should be chosen if customized selections for the device configurations are needed, such as if non-Plug and Play adapter cards or hardware devices are being used.

Installing OS Add-On Options

After the Windows 2000 operating system has been successfully installed, the user might need some features that are considered add-on options. For example, Internet Information Services (IIS) should be installed if the user will set up an FTP or web server. Most of these add-ons can be installed from the installation CD from which the operating system was initially installed. When starting these services, the user is prompted to insert the CD so that the necessary files can be copied to the hard drive. The process is automated. All the user needs to do is insert the CD.

Other post-installation add-ons include service packs or updates to the operating system that have been made since the installation CD was purchased. These can be downloaded and installed from the manufacturer website at any time. Updates and service-pack installations are usually installed immediately following the operating system installation to prevent errors from occurring later. Figure 8-6 shows the Adding or Removing Windows Components screen.

Figure 8-6 Adding or Removing Windows Components

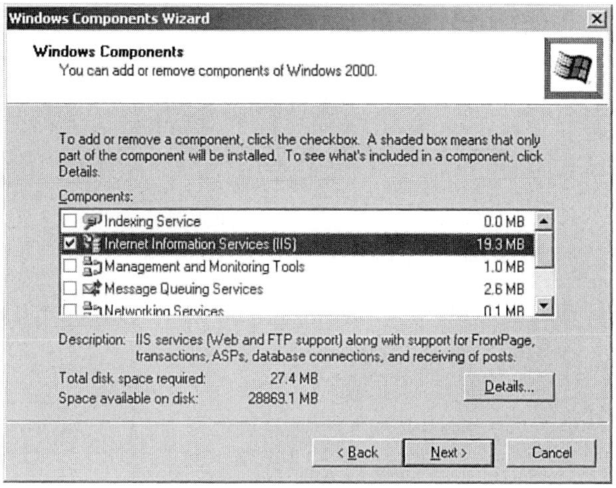

Administrator/User Interface

This section covers the following topics:

- Login procedures
- Graphical user interface
- Command-line interface
- Windows Explorer navigation

Login Procedures

The first step in using any NOS is to log on to the system. Windows 2000 implements a GUI and allows a user to log on to the system using the Log On to Windows screen, shown in Figure 8-7. After first booting the computer into Windows 2000, users might be prompted to press Ctrl-Alt-Delete to display this window. The required username and password can be entered on this screen, as well as more detailed information, such as the network domain assigned to the user. For security reasons, password characters are masked with asterisks (*) as they are typed. Note that the password is case-sensitive and should be entered exactly as created. If the password is entered incorrectly, the system prompts the user to reenter the account information until it is correct.

Figure 8-7 Logging on to Windows 2000

Lab 8.2.1 Log on to Windows 2000

In this exercise, you learn how to log on to Windows 2000.

Graphical User Interface

At this point, the user should be familiar with basic GUI navigation, such as how to operate a mouse. From here, the user is ready to explore the Windows 2000 NOS by pointing the mouse and clicking the interface's various elements. There are several basic elements:

- *Icons*—The most basic feature of Windows 2000, icons are small images with text names that are used to represent larger functionality. Figure 8-8 shows a few common icons of Windows 2000. By double-clicking an icon, the user invokes the functionality represented by that icon. For example, double-clicking the My Computer icon opens a system window, whereas double-clicking the Internet Explorer icon runs the Microsoft Internet Explorer program. Other icons may represent files or documents stored on the computer, and double-clicking them both runs the appropriate program and displays the file's contents. In this case, double-clicking the icon for British History.doc both launches Microsoft Word and opens the document within the program.

- *Buttons*—Buttons in Windows 2000 are similar to icons, with a few important differences. First, buttons come in a wider variety of shapes and sizes than standard icons. They can have text only, images only, or both text and images. They are usually designed into an application's interface as a control for the user to perform a specific task. For example, the user can confirm a choice with an OK button or save a document with a Save button.

Figure 8-8 Icons and Buttons

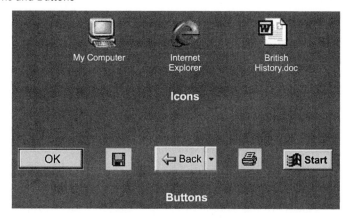

- *Windows*—In most popular GUI systems, users interact with the system through displays called windows. Figure 8-9 shows a window that is displaying the contents of directory C:\WINNT. The importance of this concept (first conceived by Xerox and used by Apple during the early 1980s) is reflected by the name given to the Microsoft line of operating systems. A window functions very much like its real-world counterpart as a portal for viewing other areas. In the case of GUIs, windows give the user access to the data and programmed functionality of the operating system and its applications. If a program calls for user interaction, as do most Windows 2000 applications, it is typically displayed in a window with controls for user input. The user can view multiple windows simultaneously by arranging and sizing them as needed, thereby allowing him or her to multitask more efficiently. In the case of Windows 2000, the OS itself has the responsibility of creating, managing, and closing these windows.

Figure 8-9 Windows

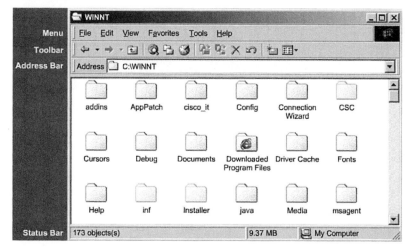

- *Menus*—A very common feature of all programs that use windows is the menu. These groups of text buttons are usually found lined at the top of windows. They offer specific functionalities related to that particular window. For example, a word processing program might have a menu named Tools, under which there is a menu option named Word Count. The menu choices available change from window to window as well as between different sections of the same window. The most common menus are File and Edit, where the user can issue commands to open, close, and save documents as well as copy and paste data. Other important Windows 2000 menus include the Start menu (click the Start button located on the taskbar) and the right-click menu (found by right-clicking almost anywhere).

- *Taskbar*—Usually found at the bottom of the screen, the Windows 2000 taskbar performs many important functions. The Start menu (for launching applications) and the system tray (showing background programs and the clock) are located on the taskbar. Most importantly, the taskbar keeps track of all open windows. Figure 8-10 shows a menu and the Windows 2000 taskbar. A horizontal button displaying the application icon and title represents each open window. Users can click these buttons to navigate between the various windows and restore any that have been minimized. This tool is particularly useful to users who work with many windows at once.

Figure 8-10 Menus and the Taskbar

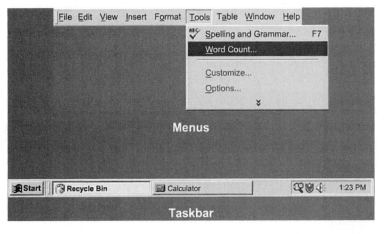

The last basic Windows 2000 skill is the ability to power down the PC. This option is available on the Start menu as the Shut Down command, where users can also choose to Log Off and Restart the computer. Figure 8-11 shows the window used to properly shut down a computer running Windows 2000.

Figure 8-11 Shutting Down a PC Using Windows 2000

Shut Down Windows
Microsoft Windows 2000 Professional
Microsoft
What do you want the computer to do?
Shut down
Ends your session and shuts down Windows so that you can safely turn off power.
OK
Cancel
Help

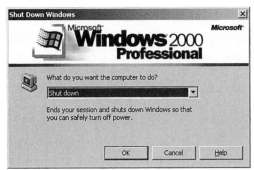

Lab 8.2.2 Exploring Windows GUI

In this lab, you explore the basic features of the Windows GUI.

Command-Line Interface

The Windows 2000 *command-line interface (CLI)* is based on the previously popular MS-DOS operating system of the 1980s. It is now called the Windows 2000 command interpreter, although many users probably still think of it as classic MS-DOS. Regardless, its basic functionality is nearly identical to that of MS-DOS, with the exception of a few new commands added and a large number of outdated commands removed. The command interpreter runs on top of Windows 2000 to provide users with all the benefits of a CLI within the Windows 2000 GUI. Figure 8-12 shows the Windows 2000 command interpreter.

Figure 8-12 Windows 2000 CLI: cmd.exe

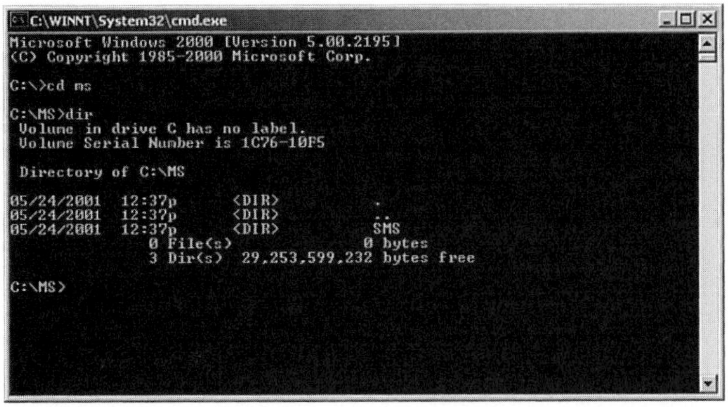

C:\WINNT\System32\cmd.exe
Microsoft Windows 2000 [Version 5.00.2195]
(C) Copyright 1985-2000 Microsoft Corp.
C:\>cd ms
C:\MS>dir
Volume in drive C has no label.
Volume Serial Number is 1C76-10F5
Directory of C:\MS
05/24/2001 12:37p <DIR> .
05/24/2001 12:37p <DIR> ..
05/24/2001 12:37p <DIR> SMS
0 File(s) 0 bytes
3 Dir(s) 29,253,599,232 bytes free
C:\MS>

As shown in Figure 8-13, the command interpreter in Windows 2000 can be launched in several ways:

- On the taskbar, select Start > Programs > Accessories > Command Prompt.
- On the taskbar, select Start > Run. In the Open box, enter **cmd**.

Figure 8-13 Launching the Windows 2000 Command Interpreter

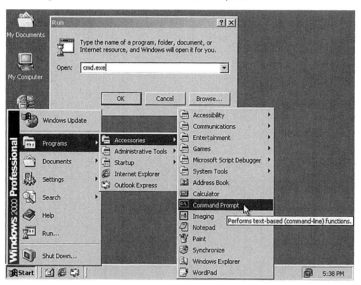

After opening a command interpreter window, the user is given a prompt for entering commands. The default command prompt can vary depending on how the command interpreter is launched, but typically it looks something like this: C:\>. The appearance of the command prompt might change, but its functionality stays the same. It is simply a place for the user to type commands on the screen.

The basic process of entering commands is very simple. Type the command at the prompt, press the Enter key, and view any output on the screen. This process is the standard flow of user activity for nearly all CLI systems. One helpful command to remember is the **doskey** command. It has no output, but when it is executed, the user can press the up arrow on the keyboard to scroll through previously entered commands.

If a user is spending a great deal of time with the command interpreter, another helpful tool is running the window in full-screen mode. When the user presses Alt-Enter, the display switches to fill the entire screen with the Windows 2000 CLI. This greatly improves the interface's readability and is reminiscent of the MS-DOS days. To close either the full screen or the windowed command interpreter, enter the **exit** command.

This command immediately closes the command interpreter and returns the user to the Windows 2000 GUI. Closing this window manually using the mouse is considered improper by Windows 2000.

Lab 8.2.3   Windows CLI

In this lab, you learn how to use the Windows 2000 CLI by running and executing several commands.

Windows Explorer Navigation

Windows Explorer, shown in Figure 8-14, is an important component of Windows 2000 and of every other Windows operating system since and including Windows 95. This is not to be confused with Internet Explorer, which is used for browsing the Internet. Windows Explorer is used to navigate the entire file system. Windows Explorer gives system administrators an easy way to view all the files on the network or that are located on a server. Collapsing and expanding folders displays all the contents in the right-side window. All folders and directories are located in the left-side window, which makes it easy to navigate through any drive that is installed on the system that might contain directories or files.

Figure 8-14   Windows Explorer

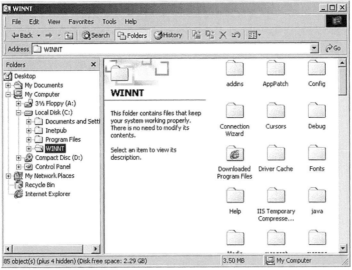

There are a variety of ways to open Windows Explorer. Users can always find it by selecting Start > Programs > Accessories > Windows Explorer. Windows Explorer can also be opened by right-clicking the Start menu button and choosing Explore. Another way to open Windows Explorer regardless of what window the user is currently in is to press the Windows key and the E key on the keyboard at the same time. The Windows key is located between the Ctrl and Alt keys on the keyboard.

Lab 8.2.4   Windows Explorer

In this lab, you learn how to navigate the Windows 2000 file system with Windows Explorer. Also, you learn how to use the navigation tools provided by Windows 2000 to locate files and folders.

User Accounts

This section covers the following topics:

- Adding users
- Managing user accounts

Adding Users

Before a user can log on to any Windows 2000 client, the administrator must create a user account on the appropriate network server. This account allows the user to log on to a specific network domain using the account information specified by the system administrator. The task of creating this account in Windows 2000 is performed with the Computer Management tool. Select Start > Programs > Administrative Tools > Computer Management to display the Computer Management tool, as shown in Figure 8-15.

Figure 8-15   Windows 2000 Computer Management Tool

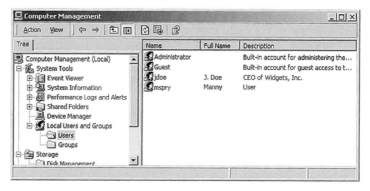

The *Computer Management* tool allows a system administrator to manage all aspects of a particular computer, including authorized users and, in the case of a network server, the authorized users of a network domain. To create a new user for a local machine, expand the directory tree on the left to reveal System Tools, Local Users and Groups. Click the Users icon to display all the existing user accounts in the right half of the window. From either the Action or right-click menu, select New User to display a screen that prompts you for all the necessary account information. Figure 8-16 shows the window for adding new users.

Figure 8-16 Adding a New Windows 2000 User

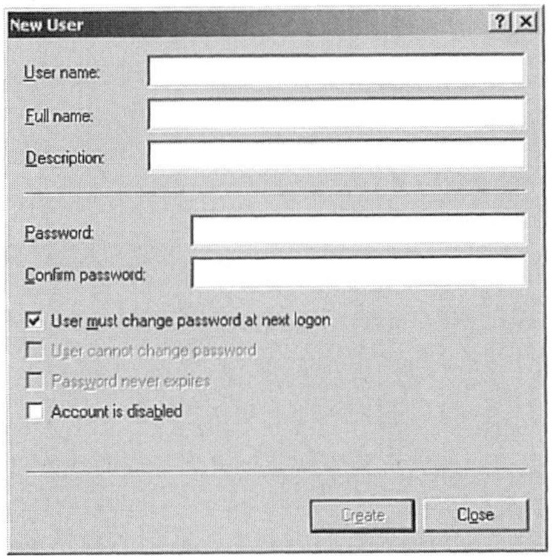

User name is a required field. It cannot be longer than 20 characters, and it cannot contain the following symbols:

$$/ \setminus [\ ] : | < > + = ; , ? * .$$

Both Full name and Description are for informational purposes only and are not required. After you enter all the account information and click the Create button, the new user is created and can immediately log on to the computer with the username and password specified.

Managing User Accounts

As previously discussed, the Computer Management tool is the primary means for a system administrator to add and manage users in Windows 2000. These tasks should be much more intuitive in this GUI environment than in a CLI such as Linux. Instead of memorizing command names, Windows 2000 users can carry out these operations in a number of ways, ranging from using simple menu selections to using keyboard commands.

The simplest user management technique is to right-click the username listed in the right half of the Computer Management window and select the appropriate task from the menu. Figure 8-17 displays the options available after a user is right-clicked. From here, the system administrator can choose to set a password, delete the user, or rename the user. The administrator can also disable the account by selecting Properties and checking the Account is disabled check box. Figure 8-18 shows the options available in the account's Properties window. These and other user management options can be found by navigating the window's remaining menus. Great care should be taken when using the Delete option, because there is no way to undo such a change.

Figure 8-17 Managing User Accounts in Windows 2000

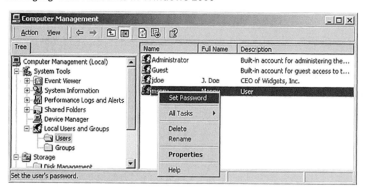

Figure 8-18 Disabling a Windows 2000 Managing User Account

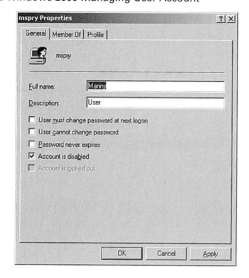

Worksheet 8.3.2 User Accounts

Identify and understand some underlying concepts of Windows 2000 user accounts.

Managing the File System

This section covers the following topics:

- Creating and sharing folders
- Creating groups and adding users
- Passwords and permissions

Creating and Sharing Folders

One important system administration task is creating folders and directories that users throughout the network will share and use to back up files. To accomplish this in Windows 2000, the administrator must first navigate to the directory where the shared folder will be created. When in that directory, the administrator right-clicks the desktop and chooses New > Folder. The administrator names the folder. To share this folder, the administrator right-clicks it and selects Sharing. The Program Properties dialog box appears, and the administrator clicks the Sharing radio button. The administrator chooses a name for this directory. This is the name it will be known as on the network. The administrator selects the Permissions tab to assign which users or groups will have permission to access this directory. The folder displays a hand under it. This indicates that the folder has been shared. Figure 8-19 shows the Sharing tab for the My Documents folder.

Figure 8-19 Sharing Tab in Windows 2000

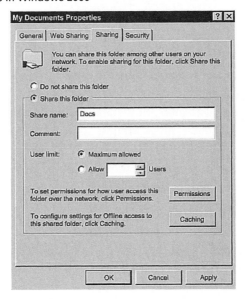

Another way to share a folder on a network is to create a drive on the server. Clients can map to a network drive, which provides access to that drive on the server to save and back up their files. This is a more advanced way of accomplishing the task, but it is the recommended way for a system administrator to create shared folders on the network. Typically in this arrangement, the drive is shared, and a password is set on the drive. Then folders are added to that drive, and permissions can be set on those folders. Certain users or groups may be given access to the directories. Figure 8-20 shows a shared network drive with various shared folders available to network users.

Figure 8-20 Sharing Folders in Windows 2000

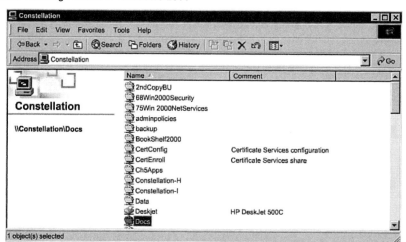

Creating Groups and Adding Users

Windows 2000 allows system administrators to create groups of many different types and uses. One such type is a local group. A *local group* exists on only a single computer and is composed of various users of that computer. Other more network-oriented groups found in Windows 2000 include global groups, domain local groups, and universal groups. The different types of groups vary in both scope and functionality and are used by Windows 2000 system administrators to manage large numbers of users on a network. In contrast, local groups are not used across a network but do provide a sufficient example of how to use groups in Windows 2000.

During the installation process, Windows 2000 creates default local groups such as Administrators and Users. Each of these groups has differing levels of control over the local system. In addition, users can create new local groups using the Computer Management tool (found by selecting Start > Programs > Administrative Tools). Expanding the directory tree on the left reveals the Local Users and Groups tool, where the Groups folder displays all existing groups on the system. Using this window's right-click or Action menu allows the user to select the New Group menu choice. The New Group window, shown in Figure 8-21, appears. After a name, description, and members are specified, the group is added to the local system. Any users listed as members are given the same access and restrictions of that group. To add more users, rename, or delete the group, simply right-click the group name in the window and select the appropriate menu choice.

Figure 8-21   Windows 2000 New Group Dialog Box

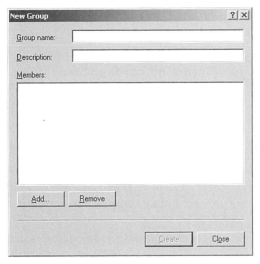

Lab 8.3.1   User Account Planning

Describe the role and purpose of user accounts. Plan and create local and domain user accounts.

Lab 8.3.2   Managing User Accounts

In this lab, you learn how to manage user accounts using the Windows 2000 Professional operating system. Also discussed are the features and tools that manage user accounts.

Passwords and Permissions

Maintaining a network of countless users can pose serious security issues for a system administrator. As previously mentioned, security is one of the primary considerations for all system administrators, and steps must be taken to ensure that users do not abuse or accidentally interfere with network operations. The most basic user-related security tools available to an administrator are passwords and permissions.

In today's Internet-based society, most users readily understand the concept of pass-words. A *password* is a secret collection of characters that only one user knows. All users have their own passwords. A password is often chosen by the individual user so that he or she can remember it easily (as opposed to a randomly generated system password that might be difficult to remember). Passwords are used in conjunction with a username when logging on to a NOS to verify the user's identity. A good password has at least five characters and is alphanumeric (it includes both letters and numbers or special characters). Table 8-1 shows examples of good and bad passwords.

Table 8-1   Good and Bad Passwords

Password	Good or Bad?	Reason
fsh	Bad	Too short. At least five characters is recommended.
fishing	Bad	At least one numeric or special character is recommended. Using complete English words is not a good idea.
F!shngco94	Good	Longer than five characters. Uses an exclamation point and numerals. Not an English word, so is not easily guessed.

Passwords do not necessarily need to be unique among users, but they should be kept secret to ensure network security. System administrators often require network pass-words to be changed frequently, much to the annoyance of some users. However, if a user's password were made public, anyone could use it to log on to the network and operate under that user's identity and access level. This threat is a big concern for system administrators, who attempt to control such access through the use of permissions.

Types of Permissions

Permissions are restrictions created by the system administrator that enable and disable the actions a user can perform on the network. For example, a system administrator usually has full permissions (that is, no restrictions) and retains full access to all parts of the network. A financial executive might have full control over certain financial directories on a server but no control over human resources data. This division of access enforces tight network security, because each user is granted access to only specific, necessary areas.

Permissions are assigned to users during the account-creation process and are typically broken down into the following categories:

- *Read permission*—The ability to read the contents of a file or directory.
- *Write permission*—Also referred to as "change" or "modify" permission. This allows the user to edit and save changes to a file or add and delete files from a directory.
- *Execute permission*—Allows the user to run a file or enter a directory.

These permissions can typically be assigned to individual users or groups of users in any combination. For example, a financial executive may be allowed to enter and view the contents of a human resources directory (execute and read permissions) but cannot modify the directory or save changes to any of its files (write permission). Permissions provide an effective tool for system administrators to enforce security on the network. They are discussed in more detail later.

Lab 8.4.1   Creating Files and Directories

In this lab, you learn how to create files and directories in Windows 2000.

Lab 8.4.2   Creating Groups in Windows 2000

Create groups in Windows 2000, add members to these groups, and organize user accounts.

Lab 8.4.3   Assigning NTFS Permissions Directories

In this lab, you learn how to assign NTFS permissions to the folders based on the scenario that is described in the next section, "Services."

Services

This section covers the following topics:

- Hypertext Transfer Protocol
- File Transfer Protocol
- Telnet
- E-mail server/client relationship
- Printing in Windows 2000
- Scripts

Hypertext Transfer Protocol

Configuring *Hypertext Transfer Protocol (HTTP)* services on Windows XP is the same as configuring HTTP services on Windows 2000. When the HTTP service on a NOS is enabled, the computer becomes a web server capable of sending out information over the World Wide Web (WWW). In prior versions of the Windows NOS, separate programs were necessary to allow the system to handle such operations. However, with the release of Windows 2000, the tools to perform Internet services are included and built into the software. As previously discussed, these services are activated and configured through the use of the *Internet Information Services (IIS)* tool, found under Start > Programs > Administrative Tools.

Launching this tool displays the current computer and a list of available Internet services. The HTTP web service is found here under the name Default Web Site. Figure 8-22 shows the IIS window with Default Web Site selected. Selecting this icon or clicking the plus sign to expand the navigation tree reveals the many default directories and files included with this service. Right-clicking the Default Web Site icon displays a menu that lets the administrator start, pause, or stop the service in addition to configuring its various properties. Figure 8-23 shows the Default Web Site Properties window. Some of these properties are fairly self-explanatory based on their descriptions, but the majority require an experienced system administrator to properly and securely configure the HTTP service.

Figure 8-22 IIS Tool and the Default Web Site

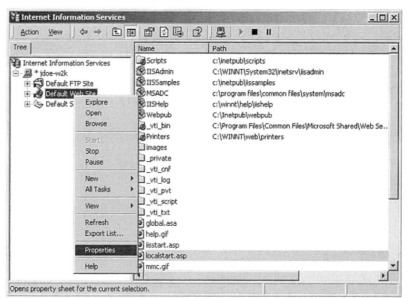

Figure 8-23 Default Web Site Properties

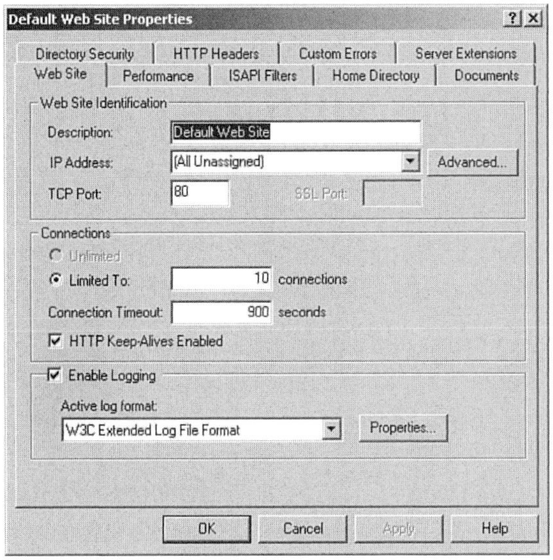

As soon as this web service has been started, users can view the system default web page by entering the following address in their web browser:

http://127.0.0.1

This IP address is called the *loopback address*. It is a networking standard address that always points to the local computer. Unless a Domain Name System (DNS) entry exists for the IP address of the NOS system, either this loopback address or the system's true IP address is necessary to access these pages via the World Wide Web. By default, Windows 2000 displays the file named localstart.asp when receiving an incoming information request from a web browser. If the NOS's HTTP service is enabled for the purpose of web page hosting, the system administrator will likely update the majority of these files and settings.

Lab 8.5.1 Configuring HTTP Services

In this lab, you configure a Windows 2000 system with HTTP services and create a HTTP server.

File Transfer Protocol

In earlier versions of the Microsoft Windows NOS, providing users with *File Transfer Protocol (FTP)* service was only possible through the installation of a separate program. With the release of the current Windows 2000 NOS, this service has been included as a standard feature that can be easily configured. Before the service is initiated, it must be determined if the appropriate tools were loaded during the Windows 2000 installation. Specifically, the IIS tools are necessary to run both the FTP and HTTP services (among others) for Windows 2000 computers.

To determine if the IIS package needs to be installed, select Start > Settings > Control Panel > Add/Remove Programs. Click the Add/Remove Windows Components button, and make sure that the IIS box is checked, indicating that it is ready for use. If the box is not checked, a system administrator must check the box and provide the necessary Windows 2000 software to upgrade the NOS to include the component.

As soon as the IIS component of Windows 2000 is added, the FTP service is ready to be configured. This is done by launching the IIS tool. Select Start > Programs > Administrative Tools > Internet Services Manager to display the window. Clicking the plus sign next to the computer name reveals the various Internet-related services this tool maintains, including the FTP service for Windows 2000. By right-clicking the Default FTP Site icon, the system administrator can start, stop, and pause the service in addition to configuring its various properties. Figure 8-24 shows the options available for the default FTP site, and Figure 8-25 shows the Default FTP Site Properties window. After the FTP service is started, authorized users can remotely connect and transfer files.

Figure 8-24 Default FTP Site Options

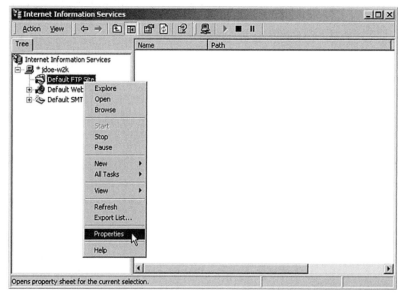

Figure 8-25   Default FTP Site Properties

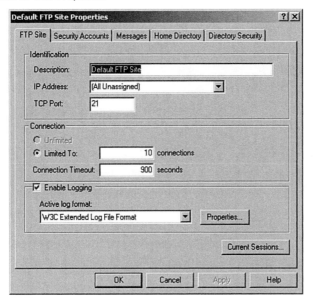

  Lab 8.5.2   Configuring FTP Services

In this lab, you configure a Windows 2000 system with FTP services and create a FTP server.

Telnet

Before a *Telnet* connection can be established with a remote Windows 2000 computer, the system must be configured to accept incoming Telnet sessions via the Telnet Server Administration tool. Select Start > Programs > Administrative Tools > Telnet Server Administration. Here, a system administrator can start, stop, and configure the Telnet service. Figure 8-26 shows the options available to administer the Telnet Server. For security reasons, only a user with administrator privileges can manage the Telnet server on a Windows 2000 machine. Enabling these Telnet sessions presents a potentially serious security issue that system administrators must always consider. Without the appropriate users, groups, and permissions in place, the Telnet server can become a back door for unauthorized access to the system.

Figure 8-26 Telnet Server Administration Tool

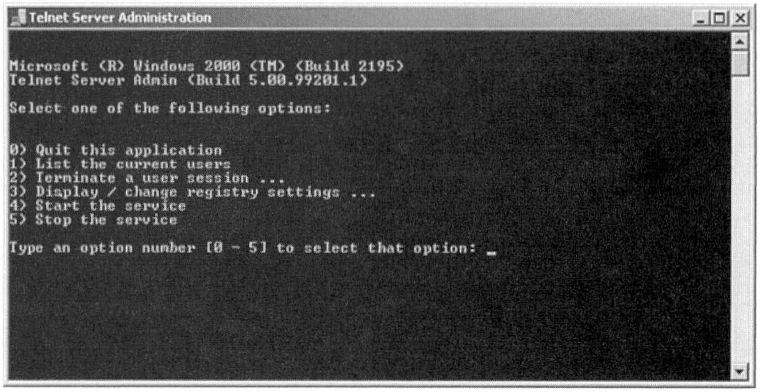

As soon as the Telnet server is activated, access is controlled using the local user accounts created on that machine. For a user to Telnet to a Windows 2000 machine, he or she must also be able to log on to that machine locally. By default, the Windows 2000 Telnet server is configured to use Windows NT LAN Manager (NTLM) for user authentication. This means that users are not prompted to manually enter their usernames and passwords but are instead verified through the logon information previously submitted when the current Windows 2000 session was started. With NTLM, the logon process takes place automatically, and authorized users are instantly given a command prompt. This feature can be turned on or off through the Telnet Server Administration tool by selecting menu option 3 to change Registry settings and then menu option 7 to specify a new NTLM value. Table 8-2 shows valid NTLM values.

Table 8-2 Valid NTLM Values

Value	Description
0	Disables NTLM authentication. All users are verified by the entering of a username and password.
1	Tries NTLM first. If unsuccessful, prompts the user for a username and password.
2	NTLM authentication only.

If the system administrator wants to restrict Telnet access to specific local users, a local Telnet Client group can be created. Windows 2000 automatically recognizes this group and allows only its members (and system administrators) to log on remotely via Telnet. As soon as a local user is successfully logged on, he or she is granted file and directory permissions through the command interpreter based on NTFS file system security. Figure 8-27 shows an active Telnet session. Note that only two incoming Telnet connections are permitted per Windows 2000 Telnet server.

Figure 8-27 Telnet Session

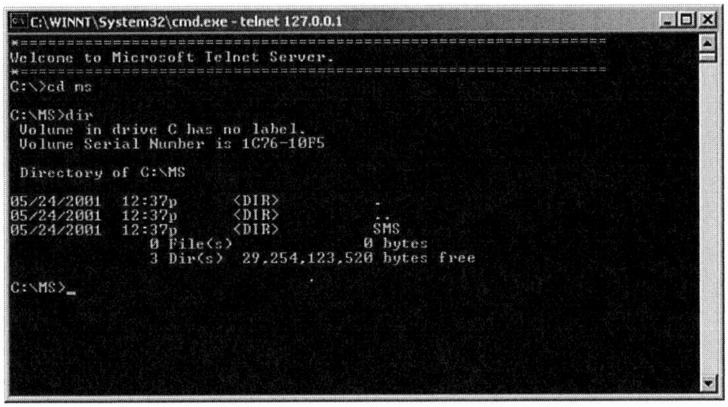

Lab 8.5.3 Configuring Telnet Services

Configure telnet services on Windows 2000.

E-Mail Server/Client Relationship

A typical network environment has an e-mail server. Microsoft uses Exchange as the e-mail server. The client side of e-mail can be a variety of Office suite products. The most widely used client software is Outlook, which is distributed by Microsoft and works with Exchange. Other examples of a server and client e-mail system are Novell Groupwise, which can also be accessed by Microsoft Outlook, and Lotus Notes.

The e-mail server controls all the e-mail that is sent and received. When a user sends an e-mail to another user, it is sent first to the server, where it is placed in the recipient's mailbox. The user who is receiving the e-mail opens the e-mail program and reads the e-mail from his or her mailbox. When the user deletes the e-mail, it is removed from the server. E-mail services work like the postal system, with some computers taking on the function of the post office. Figure 8-28 shows the process of sending an e-mail. The user's e-mail account operates like a post office box, where mail is held for the user until it is picked up over the network by an e-mail *client* program running on the user's system. E-mail continues to be the most widely used function of computer networks in many parts of the world.

Figure 8-28   Mail Services

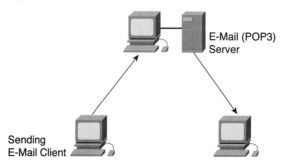

E-mail works as a *store-and-forward* application. Mail messages (and their identifying information, such as the sender, receiver, and time stamp) are stored on an e-mail server (post office box) until the recipient retrieves the mail. Typically, e-mail messages are short communications. Current e-mail systems also allow users to *attach* larger files of many different types (documents, pictures, movies) to their messages. These attachments can be retrieved or *downloaded* along with the e-mail message. In this way, e-mail services blend into file transfer services on the network.

E-mail systems have evolved along with networking technology. The rapid growth of the Internet has allowed more and more people to connect *online*. This allows for immediate communication between users of the network. The store-and-forward nature of e-mail systems does not require that the recipient be connected when the e-mail is sent. The recipient can pick up the e-mail at a later time.

In addition to e-mail, the Internet has spawned a variety of instant messaging systems that let network users "chat" with little delay. This capability is called *real time*. It is used when two or more users are connected to the network at the same time to chat.

Printing in Windows 2000

In addition to sharing important information in directories and setting up an e-mail server/client relationship, networks let users share expensive printing devices. By implementing print services, a network can make an expensive high-speed printer accessible to many users as if it were directly attached to their own computers. The network can carry print requests and copies of documents from many users to a central print service where these requests are processed. Multiple print services, each offering a different quality of output, can be implemented according to users' requirements. Under administrative control, users can select the service they need for a particular job. In this way, networks allow for a more efficient use of expensive printing devices without duplication.

A *print server* is a computer dedicated to handling client print jobs in the most efficient manner. Because it handles requests from multiple clients, a print server is usually one of the most powerful computers on the network. A print server should have the following components:

- **A powerful processor**—Because the print server uses its processor to manage and route printing information, it needs to be fast enough to handle all incoming requests.
- **Adequate hard disk space**—Print servers often capture print jobs from clients, place them in a print queue, and feed them to the printer in a timely fashion. This requires the computer to have enough storage space to hold these jobs until they are completed.
- **Adequate memory**—The server processor and random-access memory (RAM) feed print jobs to a printer. If server memory is not large enough to handle an entire print job, the job must be fed from the hard drive, which is much slower.

The role of a print server is to provide client access to print resources and to provide feedback to the users. When using printers that connect directly to the network, the print server *routes* print jobs to the proper printer. With host-based printing technology, the print server acts as the interpreter between the client and the printer to which it is directly connected. If configured properly, the print server can also send clients the printer driver software needed to access the printer. Because print servers manage print jobs through a print queue, they can also provide feedback about the printers to the users on the network. This feedback can include a confirmation message that a print job has been completed and an estimated time of print job completion. It can also report any errors that were encountered in the printing process, such as printer out of paper, wrong paper type, paper jam, out of toner/ink, and so on.

Sharing a Local Printer

To share a printer that is attached to the local computer, go to the Printers folder, which is accessible through the Control Panel, right-click the printer name, and choose Sharing, as shown in Windows 2000. Click the Shared as option button, and then either enter a share name or accept the default.

Figure 8-29 Sharing a Local Printer

Connecting to a Shared Printer

There are two ways to connect to a shared network printer. A user can use the Add Printer Wizard or enter the **net use** command at the command line. Each method is examined in detail in the following sections.

Using the Add Printer Wizard

The easiest way to use a remote printer in Windows is to add it with the Add Printer Wizard. To do so, double-click the Add Printer icon in the Printers folder and follow the wizard's instructions.

When the wizard is finished, the network printer appears in the Printers folder, and users can print to it from their applications as if it were a local printer.

Print jobs are *spooled* (stored in memory or on the hard disk) to "wait in line" to be printed. The list of pending print jobs is called the print spool.

Using the net use Command to Capture a Printer Port

The **net use** command can be used to capture a printer port and redirect print jobs from the local port (LPT1) to the network printer. The syntax for this command, which is entered at the command prompt, is as follows:

`net use LPT1: \\computername\ printername`

computername is the print server to which the printing device (*printername*) is physically attached.

Scripts

Windows 2000 can accommodate many types of scripting languages using its built-in *Windows Script Host (WSH).* This component of Windows 2000 and XP lets users create scripts using either the VBScript or JavaScript languages. WSH can also recognize any other scripting language the user wants. When a text file is created, the user simply names the file with the appropriate file extension to indicate its scripting language to WSH. For example, a VBScript file has a .vbs file extension, whereas a JavaScript file ends with the .js extension. Figure 8-30 displays a file with a .vbs extension in Windows 2000. When either script file is run, WSH handles the code based on these file extensions.

Figure 8-30 Script Files and Output in Windows 2000

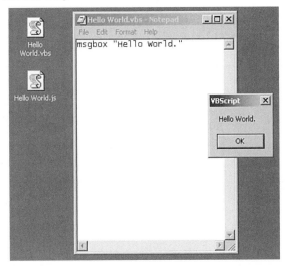

Although scripting languages are considered easier to learn than standard programming languages (such as Microsoft Visual C++), the ability to create functional scripts in Windows 2000 and Windows XP requires specific training and practice. Although VBScript and JavaScript offer similar functionality, each consists of differing syntax and coding structure. Becoming proficient in VBScript does not necessarily increase your ability to create proper JavaScript code, and vice versa. Many users do not have the training to take advantage of scripting in Windows 2000, but system administrators are more likely to spend the necessary time studying these languages. Doing so allows many of the common administrative tasks mentioned earlier to be both simplified and automated.

A Simple Windows 2000 Script

To see how scripts function in Windows 2000 and XP, a simple "hello world" script can be created easily. Users can open the Notepad text editor (select Start > Programs > Accessories > Notepad) to edit this and other scripts. In Notepad, the following line of code is all that is necessary for the script to operate:

```
msgbox "Hello world."
```

Saving this file with the .vbs file extension (Hello World.vbs) indicates to WSH that this is a VBScript file. Double-click the file to execute the script. A single message box appears with the previously coded message, as shown in Figure 8-30. This example is extremely simple and does not illustrate the complexities of the VBScript language, but it does provide a glimpse into the inherent power behind Windows 2000 scripting.

Lab 8.5.6   Writing Scripts

This lab's objective is to learn how to write a script in Windows 2000.

Summary

This chapter discussed the Windows 2000 operating system. Some of the important concepts to retain from this chapter include the following:

- The Windows 2000 installation process has four main steps. The installation begins when the Setup program runs. This prepares the hard disk and copies files. Setup then runs a wizard that provides informational pages, which are used to complete the rest of the installation.

- Windows Explorer gives system administrators an easy way to view all the files that are on the network or that are located on a server. Collapsing and expanding folders displays all the content in the right-side window.

- The Computer Management tool allows a system administrator to manage all aspects of a particular computer, including authorized users and, in the case of a network server, the authorized users of a network domain.

- Many users do not have the training to take advantage of scripting in Windows 2000, but system administrators are more likely to spend the necessary time studying these languages. Doing so allows many common administrative tasks to be simplified and automated.

Although there are similarities in the Windows 2000 and Linux installation processes, there are also many differences. The next chapter details the installation of the Linux operating system.

Check Your Understanding

The following review questions help you assess what you learned in this chapter. Answers can be found in Appendix A, "Answers to Check Your Understanding Questions."

1. Order the four main steps in the Windows 2000 installation process, starting with the first step.

   Options:

   The Setup wizard

   Completing the Setup program

   The Setup program

   Installing Windows networking

2. Complete this table using the following options. Choose whether each password is good or bad, and indicate two reasons that support your choice. You can use some of the options more than once.

Password	Good or Bad?	Reason 1	Reason 2
Sco			
cisco			
C!isco98			

   Options:

   Contains a number or a special character

   Contains no numbers or special characters

   Too short

   Too long

   Uses a complete English word

   Not an English word

3. In the following table, match the permission level to the correct description.

Permission	Description
Execute	Allows the user to edit and save changes to a file and add files to and delete files from a directory
Read	Allows the user to run a file or enter a directory
Write	Allows the user to read the contents of a file or directory

4. The administrator wants to allow a user to only look at and run a program in Windows 2000. Which of the following permissions should be set? (Select two.)

   A. Write

   B. Read

   C. Execute

   D. Full control

   E. Modify

5. What command is used to redirect print jobs from the local port to the network printer?

   A. net send

   B. net use

   C. redirect

   D. port print

6. What protocol is used to transfer files to other network devices?

   A. Telnet

   B. HTTP

   C. HTML

   D. FTP

7. What tool allows the system administrator to manage all areas of a computer?

   A. IIS

   B. Taskbar

   C. Computer Management

   D. Windows Explorer

8. Which of the following is not a type of group in Windows 2000?

   A. Global

   B. Local

   C. Universal

   D. Remote

9. In Windows, what is the name of a graphical pane that displays system or program information?

    A. Window

    B. Button

    C. Icon

    D. Menu

10. What tool is used to verify hardware compatibility with Windows?

    A. Device Manager

    B. HCL

    C. Computer Management

    D. Hardware Profiler

Key Terms

button   A graphical control used to perform specific functionality in a program or application.

command-line interface (CLI)   An interface alternative to a GUI in which a user enters specific commands to perform tasks.

Compact installation   Used when installing Windows 2000 on a computer with a limited amount of hard drive space.

Computer Management   A tool providing administration to the computer.

Custom installation   Chosen if customized selections for the device configurations are needed.

execute permission   A permission that allows a user to run a file or enter a directory.

File Transfer Protocol (FTP)   Part of the TCP/IP stack used to transfer files between network devices.

Hardware Compatibility List (HCL)   A tool that can be used to verify that the hardware will actually work with Windows 2000.

Hypertext Transfer Protocol (HTTP)   The protocol used by web browsers and web servers to transfer files, such as text and graphic files.

icon   A small image used to represent a program, service, file, or application.

Internet Information Services (IIS)   Services that can be activated when using FTP or web server services.

local group   A group comprised of various users on a single computer.

menu   A collection of program-specific functions grouped based on like characteristics.

password   A secret series of characters used by the user to gain access to restricted areas.

permission   A set of restrictions and privileges that disable or enable user actions.

Portable installation   Installs the options that might be needed with a portable computer, such as a laptop.

print server   A computer dedicated to handling client print jobs.

Read permission   A permission allowing a file to be read or the contents of a directory to be displayed.

taskbar   A management tool located at the bottom of the screen on Windows operating systems. It maintains a list of open programs, quick launch icons, and the Start menu.

Telnet   A terminal emulation protocol used for remote terminal connection. It lets users log into remote systems and use resources as if they were connected to a local system.

Typical installation   The basic type of installation that is configured for a standard standalone desktop computer.

window   A graphical pane that displays system or program information.

Windows Script Host (WSH)   A component of Windows 2000 and XP that lets users create scripts using VBScript or JavaScript languages.

Write permission   A permission allowing a user to edit and save changes to a file or add files to and delete files from a directory.

Objectives

After completing this chapter, you will be able to complete tasks related to

- Pre-installation tasks
- Installing and configuring the Linux operating system
- Installing and configuring X server
- Post-installation configuration and tasks

Chapter 9

Linux Installation Procedures

Planning is an important step in a Linux installation because of the more complex nature and incompatibility issues that arise with Linux. A good installation plan makes the installation process run much smoother. After the plan has been set, it is time to move on to the installation procedure. It is impossible to cover every installation detail in every distribution of Linux in just one chapter. This chapter presents a detailed installation of Red Hat Linux, which is the distribution that is used in this course. Other distributions' installation procedures are similar, except that the order of installation steps might be a little different.

The X server system is an important aspect of the installation process, and this chapter covers this topic in detail. This chapter covers the installation and configuration of X server on a Linux system. Some distributions install and configure X automatically. However, this chapter covers how to customize or change any of the X server settings after the installation is complete. After the operating system has been installed, several post-installation tasks and configurations need to be done.

Pre-Installation Tasks

In the previous chapters, you learned how to prepare to install the Linux operating system. This included determining hardware and software needs as well as compatibility. The various Linux distributions and choosing the appropriate distribution for the installation were also covered. After you make these decisions, the next step is to begin installing the operating system.

Boot Method

Using this method to install Linux requires that the system be booted first using bootable floppy disks or a bootable CD-ROM. These disks are sometimes bundled with the Linux distribution that is being installed. Using this method is useful for installing that particular distribution of Linux only, as well as performing maintenance on the system.

Using this method requires that proper configuration be done in the system's BIOS first. As you might know, a configuration setting in the BIOS tells the system which medium to boot from. Figure 9-1 shows the boot device order screen in the BIOS. The choices include a floppy disk, a hard drive, a CD-ROM, a network drive that has the files stored on a server, and a high-capacity removable drive such as a Jaz or Zip drive. Of these choices, typically the only ones that are ever used to boot a system are the floppy disk, the CD-ROM, and the existing OS bootstrap method.

Figure 9-1 Boot Options Screen in the BIOS

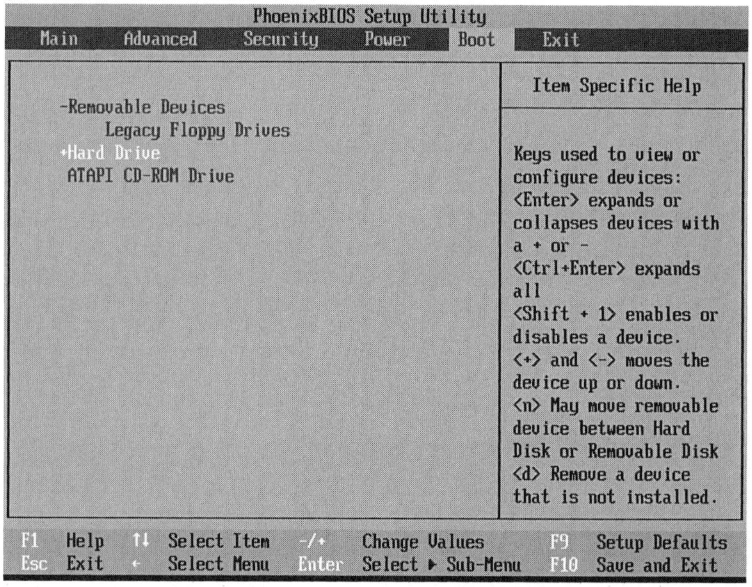

If you choose to boot the system using a floppy drive, the BIOS needs to be set to do so first. Every distribution should ship with bootable floppies. If it doesn't, you can create a bootable floppy. Sometimes, the manufacturer doesn't ship bootable floppy disks because the CDs that contain the OS are bootable, so separate bootable floppies are unneeded. After you have set the proper settings in the BIOS, you insert the floppy into the drive and then restart the system. This starts the installation process.

If the CDs are bootable, you need to configure the proper settings in the BIOS. Then all you need to do is insert the CD into the CD-ROM or DVD-ROM drive and start the system. At this point, the installation begins.

Another means of booting a system to begin the installation process is by using the existing OS bootstrap method. This is an easy way to do an installation if you plan to dual-boot the OS or if you plan to replace the existing OS. Most distributions come with this option on the installation CDs. You insert the CD into the drive, and the program starts automatically. It shuts down the OS that is currently running. Then, when the system starts up, it begins the installation process.

Installation Medium

The first step in the Linux installation process is determining from which medium the installation will be performed. A variety of choices are available, including CD (the method used in this book), network server, floppy disks, and a hard disk that has the CD files copied to it.

The easiest and quickest way to do an installation is with the installation CD. Just about every distribution of Linux comes on CD, making this choice a simple one. Some distributions, such as SuSE Linux, ship some of their installation files on DVD-ROM instead of CD. You'll recall from previous chapters that SuSE Linux ships with just about every package that is available. A DVD-ROM can hold the equivalent of multiple CD-ROMs, which allows SuSE Linux to be able to include all those packages. In this case, you would need a DVD-ROM instead of a CD-ROM.

Another medium you can use to install Linux is a network connection. Keep in mind that this method is recommended only if you have a fast network connection. First, you boot the system from a floppy disk, and then you choose the option to install the OS via the network. You have to know the path to where the installation files are located. You might want to install Linux over the network when you want to install it on a system that does not have a CD or DVD-ROM installed. In this case, you could share the CD-ROM drive of another system on the network. By connecting to that system's CD-ROM drive over the network, you could access the installation files. A drawback of this method is that it can be slow and it is not always reliable. If the network goes down or the computer that you are connected to goes down, the installation must be started all over again.

Linux can be installed from files that are located on a different partition, even if this partition has a different OS running on it. This is known as installing from a hard disk. For example, if the OS is downloaded into a partition that is running Windows, the other partition can access those files and install Linux from that other partition.

Floppy disks were used to install Linux on some old distributions, but this is seldom seen today. One distribution still uses a floppy to install the OS. Although it isn't a real OS, the Linux Router Project (www.linuxrouter.org) is a Linux OS that is installed from a floppy. It can be installed on an old computer, making the computer a network router.

Selecting the Appropriate Parameters for Installation

After you've selected an installation method and booted the system, some of the first screens you see give you choices for selecting certain parameters for the operating system. This includes things such as the language that will be used and the hardware detection phase. All these procedures provide a means of applying certain parameters that the system needs so that it can prepare for the next phase—selecting the proper packages to install.

Language

One of the options you get when you install the Linux OS is what language you want to use. Figure 9-2 shows the language selection screen that is used during installation. This should be a fairly simple step. Obviously, the choice to make here is to select the language of the person who will be using the system or your own language if you are installing the operating system on your own computer.

Figure 9-2 Language Selection Page for Red Hat Linux 7.2

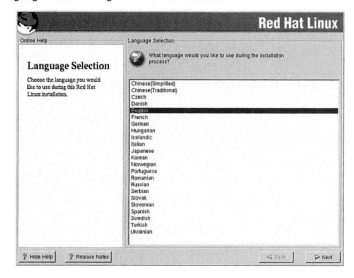

License Terms

Although they aren't as strict with Linux as they might be with other operating systems, such as Microsoft, license terms are important. It is vital that the person who is doing the installation read these terms. Although Linux is open-source, sometimes proprietary software is bundled with the distribution. Therefore, by not following the terms of this license agreement, you could be subject to copyright violations.

Installation Class

After you accept the license terms, the next step is to select the type of installation you want to do. Depending on which distribution you are installing, this phase differs to some extent. Some distributions prompt you to either select a recommended or expert installation at this point. Others, such as Red Hat, give you the option of choosing to do a workstation, server, or custom installation. If you have never installed Linux, choosing the recommended type of installation might be the easiest method. However, by choosing this method, you do not have the chance to make any choices about the type of installation you are doing. The workstation option with Red Hat 7.2 installs the basic features that a workstation might need, including the X Window System. It does not install server features such as FTP, HTTP, and Telnet daemons. If you choose the server installation, these features are installed, but the X Window System is not. This means that you will have only the command line as an option for administering the server. The custom installation option lets you choose what options you want installed. For example, you can choose to have the X Window System installed, as well as some of the daemons you might need for a server, such as FTP, HTTP, and Telnet.

Mouse and Keyboard

After you select which type of installation class is appropriate for you, the system goes through a step in which it detects the system's hard disks. Then it detects the system's mouse and keyboard. Linux can autodetect the mouse and keyboard, so it will most likely accept the correct ones. A window appears from which you can select which type of mouse and keyboard are attached to the computer if they are not autodetected. Figures 9-3 and 9-4 show the keyboard and mouse selection screens. You can select features such as the number of buttons the mouse has and whether it has a wheel. Linux supports many kinds of keyboards as well, and the correct option should be selected. There are not many options here besides choosing whether it is a US keyboard or a US Keyboard (International). Choose US keyboard if the keyboard was sold in the U.S. Choose US Keyboard (International) if it was not.

Figure 9-3 Keyboard Selection Page for Red Hat Linux 7.2

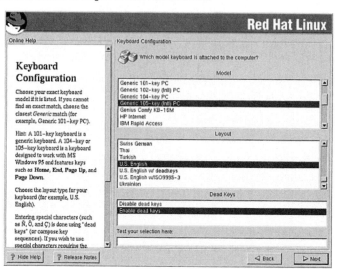

Figure 9-4 Mouse Selection Page for Red Hat Linux 7.2

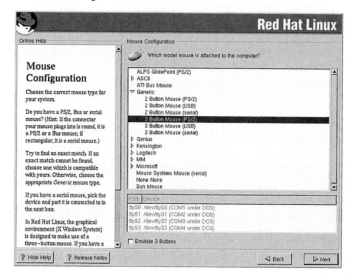

Creating the Linux File System

After specifying the proper parameters for the installation, you have to partition the hard drive and choose which file system you want to be on your Linux system. Figure 9-5 shows the screen on which you select the partitioning method you want to use. Partitioning the hard drive is not covered in this section, because partitioning a hard drive for a Linux operating system is covered in detail in Chapter 7, "Installation and Boot Process Overview." Formatting the hard drive is mentioned in Chapter 7 as well, but it was not covered in detail. Essentially, when Linux creates the file system, it formats the hard drive. This is the process in which the ext2, ext3, or Reiser file system is written to the partition. Keep in mind that, because formatting the hard drive completely erases any data that is currently on the drive or partition that is being formatted, you should make certain that the data on the drive is either backed up or is no longer needed.

Figure 9-5 Partitioning Options During the Installation Process

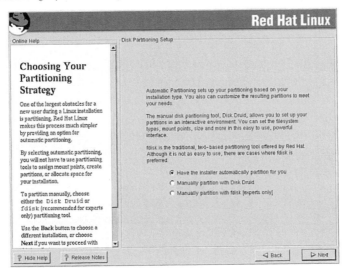

Formatting the hard drive is not always necessary. Sometimes, these file systems might have already been created with another partitioning and formatting tool, such as PartitionMagic. Another instance where you might not need to format the hard drive or partition is if you are just doing an upgrade or if you are dual-booting with another OS already installed. If you are doing a fresh installation of Linux, you certainly want to format the hard drive.

One option that is included with most distributions of Linux when formatting is the option to perform a "bad block check." This is an advanced option that you can select that checks every sector on the disk or partition to make sure that it can hold data before you format it. Performing this check takes more time than just a regular format, but it can save you more time in the long run if a sector is bad and you don't know about it. If bad blocks are found during the check, it is a good idea to replace the disk, because it is a sign that the disk is beginning to fail.

Low-Level and High-Level Formatting

There are two types of formatting. *Low-level formatting* just redefines the physical sectors on the hard drive. *High-level formatting* creates or recreates the file system. Usually, hard drives are shipped with a low-level format, so there is no need to do a low-level format. In Linux, the **fdformat** command performs a low-level format, and the **mkfs** command performs a high-level format. To learn more about these commands, you can view their man pages by typing **man fdformat** or **man mkfs**.

Selecting Packages to Install

After partitioning and formatting the hard drive, you see a list of packages you can install, as shown in Figure 9-6. There are many packages to choose from. Some distributions might have more than others. One thing you should keep in mind is the amount of disk space you have to work with. Installing lots of these packages consumes disk space. For example, many of the packages from the KDE or GNOME workstation can consume hundreds of megabytes of disk space. Some distributions display how much space is needed for that particular package. Others do not show you this until after the package has been selected and the installation process has proceeded to the next step.

Figure 9-6 Selecting Package Groups During the Installation

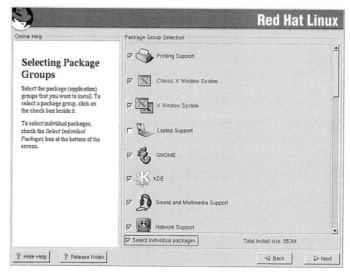

Some distributions, such as Mandrake, give you the option of selecting all or just part of a package to install. This is helpful if you want some of the features of a particular package but not the entire package. If you select this option, you can browse through

the package and select the particular features you need. Some of these individual features of packages have a *dependency*, which means that other programs or features need to be installed for them to work. If you install one of these packages without installing the dependency program or package, the system informs you that you must install other packages as well.

After all the packages you want to install are selected, the installation process proceeds to the next step, which is installing the operating system.

Installing and Configuring Linux

Like the Windows 2000 Professional installation, the Linux installation goes through a number of steps to complete the installation. The Linux boot process is similar to the boot process of Windows 2000. The filenames are different, but these files essentially perform the same operations in both systems. Linux does have a few installation steps that are not found in Windows. For example, because Linux is primarily intended to be a server-based network operating system (NOS), you can do a workstation or server installation.

Linux Hardware Requirements

The next step is to examine the system's hardware to determine if it will run the OS after it is installed. One of the basic hardware requirements for a successful Linux installation is an Intel-compatible processor. Unlike with Windows, you don't need the latest version of the Pentium series processors from Intel. Linux can be installed on Pentium II and Pentium class Intel processors. There are still systems running on 80386 and 80486 processors, but this is not recommended. A floppy disk or a CD-ROM and a hard drive with at least 900 MB of free disk space are required. The minimum requirements for RAM are at least 16 MB, but a minimum of 64 MB of RAM is preferred.

Starting the Installation

In this book and in the accompanying lab, you will install Linux from a CD. The installation starts after you insert the CD and the BIOS is configured to boot from the CD. Select the settings for the system, such as the language to be used. Next, choose what type of mouse and keyboard are being used. You are prompted to choose the type of installation—server or workstation. The X Window System GUI is unavailable if you choose the server installation. The server installation installs the various tools needed for a server, such as file and web server tools. The next step is to partition the hard drive.

NOTE

If the server installation is selected, all data on the system is erased, and the drive must be partitioned and reformatted accordingly. When the workstation installation is selected, another operating system can be installed, but Linux must be on a separate partition.

After the drive is partitioned, you configure the network settings and select the time zone. At this point, the main root account and password are set up, as well as any other accounts that need to be installed on the system. For security purposes, the root account should not be used. It is recommended that you create a second account to administer Linux. (In the accompanying labs, the root account is used, but this should not be done in a working environment.) For a server installation, the next step is to install the operating system. If the workstation installation is selected, you are prompted to configure the X Window System environment before the installation begins. This environment includes things such as selecting the proper monitor and video card settings, as well as the system's resolution and color settings. When the installation process is complete, you see a prompt to create boot disks. After this is done, the installation process is complete.

Configuring Appropriate Security Settings

Some of the most important security settings you choose are the user account and root account settings and passwords. Chapter 10, "Linux," covers in detail how to create user accounts in Linux. This section just focuses on the security aspects important to the installation process. If you're familiar with Windows 2000, you know that to log on to the system you must have a user account either locally stored in the computer itself or in Active Directory to log on to the Windows domain. Linux works much the same way in the sense that user accounts are the main security feature controlling who can and cannot log on to the system. Linux uses the root account, which is similar to the administrator account in Windows 2000. The root account has privileges to perform any task on the system, including adding and deleting other user accounts.

During the installation process, you first are prompted to create the root password. Then you have the option of creating user accounts you want to add to the system at this point. You do not have to add any user accounts now. You can do this later. (This task is covered more in Chapter 10.) Even if you are the administrator and are the only person who will be using this system, it is recommended that you create a separate user account for yourself. Using only the root account can pose some security risks.

Root Account Options

The root account in Linux is also known as the superuser or system administrator account. This account is mandatory. During installation, you are prompted to enter the password twice to protect against typos, as shown in Figure 9-7. Corel Linux is the only major distribution that does not require that the root password be set during installation. Most Linux distributions have rules concerning password length and content. These rules vary depending on the distribution, but generally passwords must be at least four characters long, and they cannot be words found in the English dictionary. Some distributions have other rules, such as mandating that at least one or two characters be something other than letters, such as numbers or a punctuation mark.

Figure 9-7 Root Password Screen

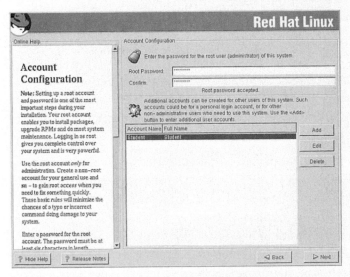

Defining User Accounts During Installation

There are pros and cons to creating user accounts during the installation. Understanding the advantages and disadvantages helps any administrator determine which is best based on the security implementations that have been planned. You've learned that at least one user account should be created during installation for the system administrator to use even if no one else will use or access the system. The major disadvantage of creating user accounts during installation is that you don't have many of the options you would otherwise have, such as setting up nonstandard home directories, account expiration, and defining group policies.

Password Options

Although they can't really be configured during the installation process, it is important to discuss *shadow passwords* at this point, because they are valuable to a Linux system's security. Most Linux distributions use either MD5 or DES password encoding methods. Some distributions have the option of using one or the other, and some use MD5 by default because it is newer and more secure than DES. Some distributions have the option of using shadow passwords as well. Typically, Linux and UNIX systems store account information and passwords in an encrypted form in a file called /etc/passwd. This file needs to be accessible by all users, because various other tools need to access this file for nonpassword information. If you use shadow passwords, the passwords are stored in a different file that is not accessible by all users, which greatly improves security.

Configuring Network Settings

You have the option of configuring the network settings during the installation. This can be done after the installation, but it is much easier and recommended to do so during the installation.

If you select the option to configure network settings during the installation process, the first choice you need to make is to have the system autodetect what type of network connection you have. Options for types of network connections include a normal modem connection and a LAN connection.

Just like the installation process autodetects which type of mouse or keyboard is connected, it detects the type of network card that is installed in the system. Usually, the system detects the proper network card that is installed. Depending on the distribution of Linux that is being installed, the steps to go about this might be slightly different, but at this point, you are prompted to select whether you want to manually configure network settings such as the IP address, subnet mask, host name, DNS server, and default gateway. The other option is to select DHCP if the system is connected to a DHCP server that will provide all this information automatically. The DHCP configuration screen is shown in Figure 9-8.

Figure 9-8 DHCP Option in Red Hat Linux 7.2

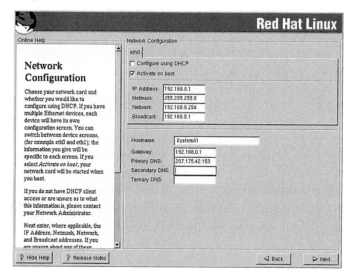

Some distributions have other network configuration settings that might or might not need to be set at this time, depending on what type of network the system is on. For example, if the network uses a proxy server (a server that protects a network by limiting network access into and out of the network), you can enter the IP address to this server as well.

Other Configurations and Settings

At this point, most of the initial installation process should be completed, aside from some of final configurations and settings. These include items such as the time zone configuration, printer configuration, service configuration, and boot options.

Configuring the Time Zone

Again, the specifics of how to configure the time zone setting vary depending on which distribution of Linux you are installing. However, the process is the same. When you reach this point in the installation process, a screen appears from which you select the time zone the system is located in. Figure 9-9 shows the time zone configuration page for Red Hat Linux 7.2. In this screen, you can scroll through the different time zones and select the one that fits your location.

Figure 9-9 Time Zone Configuration for Red Hat Linux 7.2

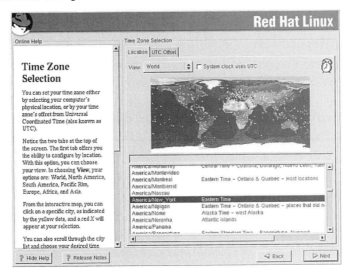

Some distributions let you set the clock to Greenwich Mean Time (GMT), the time in Greenwich, England. In traditional UNIX and Linux systems, this is known as ***Coordinated Universal Time (UTC)***, which is adjusted for daylight saving time. Systems that have this option set their own local time based on the UTC time and store this information in memory or in their hardware clocks. When the system boots up, it reads this information and then sets the local time based on the time zone that was selected on the UTC time that is stored in memory. If Linux is the only operating system on the computer, and the distribution that is being installed has this option, select yes when asked if the clock is set to GMT. This will greatly reduce the chances of the time being off during daylight saving time. However, if the system dual-boots with another OS such as Windows, you don't want to set the system clock to GMT.

Printer Configuration

Configuring a Linux system to connect to a printer is covered in detail in later chapters. This section covers how to do so during the installation process. Keep in mind that not all Linux distributions provide the option of configuring a printer during installation. Linux Mandrake does provide this capability. It lets you choose from two printing systems—Common UNIX Printing System (CUPS) and the lpr printing system. The installation program installs additional packages from the CD after you select the printing system to use. The installation program requires additional information such as the connection type—either a local printer, a remote UNIX or Linux print server, or a remote Windows print server. You also have to specify the details of the connection, such as the printer port to which the printer is connected if it is a local printer. If the printer is located on a remote print server, you have to specify the print server name, queue name, and, in some cases, a username and password. Last, you have to define the printer type. A list is displayed. Depending on what type of printer you will be printing to, you have to select the correct printer from this list.

Service Configuration

Linux systems have a number of different services running on them, depending on what type of system the installation is being configured for. If the system will be a workstation, web server, or mail server, the appropriate services need to be installed on the system. Some of these services can be installed during the installation. When this screen appears during the installation process, check the boxes appropriate for the type of system that is being configured. The services you select are then installed.

Boot Options

Selecting and configuring the system to use the proper boot loader is another part of the Linux installation process in which you have more than one choice. Linux uses either *Linux Loader (LILO)* or *Grand Unified Boot loader (GRUB)*. Figure 9-10 shows the installation screen in which you select which boot loader to use. These two programs boot a Linux system from the hard drive. Most Linux distributions use LILO, and some offer GRUB as an alternative. After selecting which boot loader to use, you have the opportunity to adjust some of the features if you need to do so. Some of these options are as follows:

- Most distributions allow you to select if you want to use a graphical or text-based menu if you pick LILO. If GRUB is selected, graphical is the only option.
- LILO stores its boot-time code in the boot device. If Linux is being installed on an EIDE drive, this file is located in /dev/had. If Linux is installed on a SCSI drive, it is stored in /dev/sda. This is fine if Linux is the only operating system installed on the drive. However, if this system is dual-booting with another OS, LILO or GRUB needs to be placed on the Linux boot partition.

- The delay that LILO uses before booting can be adjusted here as well.

- You can select a compact boot option that speeds up boot times.

- It is possible to configure the video card settings for the boot loader. If this isn't configured, the default resolution is used, but it is possible to change the resolution for the boot loader.

- Linux stores temp files in the /tmp directory. It is possible to configure the boot loader to clean out this directory every time Linux is started.

- In some instances, Linux does not detect the proper amount of RAM automatically as it is supposed to. In other words, it might detect only 64 MB of RAM when 128 MB is installed. A precaution to take against this is to manually enter the amount of RAM installed on this configuration page.

Figure 9-10 Boot Loader Selection

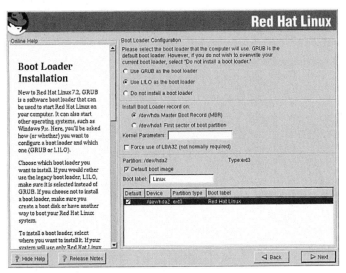

When all the configurations have been entered, the installation program proceeds to the next step. As it is doing so, the system presents a summary of the boot loader options. These options vary depending on the configurations that were entered and if the system is configured to dual-boot with another operating system.

Lab 9.2.1   Installing Linux

Install the Red Hat distribution of Linux, configure the Linux settings as needed, and create a boot disk.

Lab 9.2.3 Configuring Network Settings

Configure a Red Hat 7.2 Linux computer's IP address.

X Server

At this point, Linux should be fully installed and operational. However, to get the full functionality from your Linux system, especially if you plan on using the GUI interface, you need to become familiar with how to install and configure the system's X server. The initial installation is only the first part of installing an operating system. You need to do other configurations after the initial operating system has been installed. The importance of learning how to install and configure X server cannot be underestimated. First, this task will give you the most problems. Other reasons are that users will want to be able to adjust and modify the user environment to suit their own preferences, such as screen size or resolution. If you should decide at some point to upgrade the system's video card, you need to know how to configure the appropriate settings for it to work with the Linux system.

The first step is to select the appropriate X server to install. X is the program that runs the GUI on a Linux system. The *X server* is the engine that drives the X client, which is the GUI that is displayed on the screen. This section assumes that you will be running X programs from the same system that X server is installed on. However, this does not need to be the case. If you recall, it is possible to use X over the network to run programs from remote location.

Video Card Chipset

Finding out what chipset the video card uses is important to being able to properly configure X server on your system. Sometimes, it can be difficult to find what chipset your video card has (unless you are installing a new video card and you can find out the chipset from the box or book that comes with the card). More often than not, the video card is already installed in the system, making it difficult to know what the chipset is.

There are some ways to go about getting this information. The first way is through the installation procedure when the system autodetects the video card. The other way to have the system autodetect the video card is to run the X configuration tool after installation. Another means to find out the video card's chipset is by reading the product documentation. This is not always the best method, because not every video card manufacturer says what its chipset is, and this information can often be hard to find. If the system dual-boots with another operating system, such as Windows, you can go

into Device Manager and open the dialog box for the hardware properties for the
video card. Figure 9-11 shows the Device Manager driver properties for a graphics
card in Windows. Sometimes, the video card's chipset is listed there. The last method,
and probably the least time-consuming aside from autodetecting during installation, is
to take the video card out of the computer and examine it. Some video cards have the
chipset listed on them.

Figure 9-11 Video Card Properties in Windows Device Manager

Other things are important to keep in mind when searching for the chipset version of a
video card. You will not always find consistency because the chipset often has more
than one name. Or, instead of the chipset version, you will find the name of the video
card manufacturer. In the event that this happens, it's a good idea to look for drivers
under both names you find. Also, be careful when you find the name of the manufacturer instead of the chipset name, because one manufacturer might produce the card
while another manufacturer produces the chipset. So if you find the name of the manufacturer on the card, it does not necessarily mean that you have found the name of
the chipset manufacturer.

X Server Options

XFree86 (www.xfree86.org) is the free X server that comes with every major distribution that supports a GUI interface. It is a good idea to visit the XFree86 site, because it
contains useful information regarding video card chipsets.

The most current version of X server available is version 4.0.3. Most Linux distributions shipped after 2001 come with the 4.0.X version of XFree86. This latest version has some compatibility issues with some video card chipsets. Some chipsets are not supported in the latest release. The previous version of XFree86 was version 3.3.X. You have to use this version if you run into any compatibility issues with supported video card chipsets. However, although you have to use the older version of X server, you can still use support programs and libraries from version 4.0.X.

When dealing with unsupported video card issues when installing XFree86, it's a good idea to check the manufacturer's website for the appropriate drivers. Although the appropriate drivers might not have shipped with the video card, sometimes the manufacturer has the drivers available to download from its website. With Linux's growing popularity, many of these manufactures have made drivers available that are supported by XFree86. This is not to say that every manufacturer has the supported drivers, but it is worth checking. Another reason to check the manufacturer's website even if the video card is already supported is that many video cards today have accelerated features that the driver that comes with XFree86 will not support. To be able to use these accelerated features, you might have to get the proper driver from the manufacturer's website. By doing this, you will see a substantial improvement in video card performance.

In some cases, XFree86 does not support the video card at all, even after you follow all the steps mentioned here. In the event that this occurs, there are still a few other measures to take. The first option might be to use the frame buffer XFree86 driver. The Linux kernel has some video card drivers that can be used, but the kernel must include frame buffer support for the video card that is installed. Another approach to take is to not use XFree86 and instead use a third-party commercial X server. Some examples are Xi Graphics (www.xig.com) and Metro Link (www.metrolink.com). One of these commercial X servers might include support for your video card. Finally, if the card is not supported by XFree86, just replace the video card with one that is supported.

Installing X Server

Installing X server is not that difficult. The easiest way to install X server is to do so during the installation of the operating system (which was covered earlier in this chapter). Sometimes, X server is installed after the operating system installation. Installing XFree86 is just a matter of using the system package manager to install the correct package. Keep in mind that X server comes with many packages. Only one of these packages contains the server. The other packages contain the support libraries, fonts, and utilities.

Depending on which distribution you are using, the name of the package might vary a little, but it will have the name XFree86 in it. It should look something like XFree86-server or xserver-xfree86. Again, depending on which distribution of Linux you are using, XFree86 is installed using RPMs or Debian packages. If the distribution uses RPMs, the command to install X server looks like this:

 # rpm -Uvh XFree86-server-4.0.2-11.i386.rpm

If the distribution you are using uses Debian packages, the command you enter on the command line looks like this:

 # dpkg -i xserver-xfree86_4.0.2-7_i386.deb

After the package is installed, the generic X server, XFree86, is installed. The server files are stored in /usr/X11R6/bin. The other files that X server requires, the driver modules, are stored in /usr/X11R6/lib/modules/drivers.

Using the manufacturer's drivers instead of the ones that come with XFree86 has many advantages (which were covered in the previous section). If you decide to use the manufacturer's driver, usually directions are provided for installing it. Most likely, you will have to place the driver in the XFree86 drivers directory. Sometimes, the driver is a package that after installation places the driver in the proper directory for you.

Also mentioned briefly in the previous section about unsupported video cards was the fact that your video card might work with the latest 4.0.X version of X server. It was also stated that you might need to install the previous version of X server, version 3.3.6. However, some special installation procedures need to be covered for installing the 3.3.6 version of XFree86. First, the name of the package will be different than the 4.0.X version. Version 4.0.X of XFree86 comes with all the supported driver files in the package. This means that for any video card installed in the system, only that one package needs to be installed. However, the packages for version 3.3.X work a little differently. For this version, you have to install the package that goes with the video card's specific chipset, which is why is it very important to know the name of the chipset before installing X server. For example, you need to install the package named XFree86-S3-3.3.6-19.i386.rpm for the chipsets that are made by S3. Installing this package installs an X server named XF86_S3. Using this server instead of the 4.0.X version lets you use the video card.

Configuring X Server

Configuring X server is done differently depending on which version of X server is installed, either version 3 or version 4, as well as what type of X server is being used, either XFree86 or one of the commercial versions that were mentioned earlier. To configure X server, you must use the XF86Config configuration file, which is usually located in the /etc or /etc/X11 directory. Figure 9-12 shows the XF86Config file.

Figure 9-12 XF86Config Configuration File

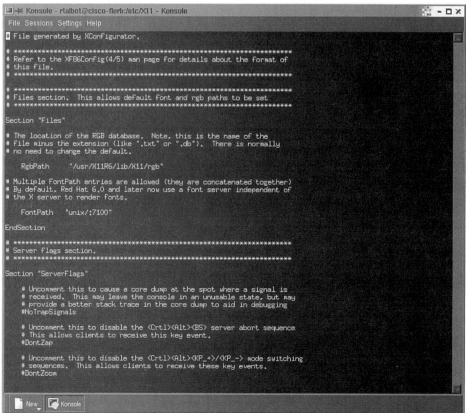

The name of this file for version 4 of XFree86 is XF86Config-4. The names of the configuration files for version 3 are different from version 4 so that an easy distinction can be made between the configuration file for version 3 and version 4. If you are using a third-party commercial X server, it will have a configuration file of its own that you will use. Consult the manufacturer's documentation for instructions on how to use its X server configuration tool.

Covered in more detail in the next section is how to configure the various hardware for X server. Along with configuring the server, you have to provide information for input devices such as the mouse, keyboard, video card, and monitor.

Different Methods of Configuration

As with most Linux configurations, there are two ways to configure X server. One way is to use the graphical configuration tools. You use them to make the necessary changes, and then the operating system automatically writes these changes to the

XF86Config text file. As with the rest of the Linux configuration files, the XF86Config file is a text file that can be manually edited. This requires using a text editor to open the file and make the changes yourself. This is not the recommended method unless you are experienced and you know what you are doing. Any mistakes could render the X server unusable. Usually, this method is used just to tweak a working configuration to get better performance and not to initially configure the X server. Again, don't attempt this unless you have experience doing this. Despite which method you use, the process usually involves making a change and then testing it and repeating the process until you get the correct results.

Testing the Configuration

When doing any type of configuration, you need to test it. As just mentioned, this might be a repetitive process. You might have to test the configuration a few times before it is right. You need to test the X server configuration in a specific way. One way is to restart the system every time and have the X Window System start up. However, this is time-consuming and unnecessary.

The recommended way to test the X server configuration is to switch from run level 5, which is the run level that starts the X server automatically when the system starts up, to run level 3, in which X normally doesn't run. This shuts down the X session that launched during startup. To switch to run level 3, use the **telinit 3** command.

After you change to run level 3, the X Window session ends, and the system enters text mode with a login prompt. From here, you can log on and then configure the X server settings manually. You can also use the **startx** command to start the GUI, change the setting using a configuration tool, and then restart the GUI using the procedure just explained. If the results are fine, you can exit the GUI. Then, from the command line, use the **telinit 5** command to switch back to run level 5, which launches the GUI upon startup. If the results are not what you expected, you can repeat this process until the results are what you want.

XFree86 3.3.X Configuration Tools

Three configuration tools are used with XFree86 3.3.X. Most distributions have at least one of these. Some have more than one:

- *xf86config*—This is probably the hardest configuration tool to work with. It operates entirely in text mode. Its basic process is to ask a series of questions about the hardware in your system and your configuration preferences. This tool provides no means for correcting errors, so if you make a mistake, you have to start over.

- *Xconfigurator*—This tool, shown in Figure 9-13, can be used in either text mode or GUI mode, depending on which mode it is launched from. It goes through a series of menus that allow you to pick the appropriate settings. However, it does so in a fixed order, just like xf86config, so if you make a mistake, you have to run through the menus again.

- *XF86Setup*—This tool can be used only from GUI mode. This means that the X Window System must be running for you to use this tool. XF86Setup can be used to reconfigure the X environment while it is in a nonoperational mode. Unlike the other configuration tools, which step through the process with menus, you can make changes in XF86Setup at any time. You don't have to start over if you make a mistake.

Figure 9-13 Xconfigurator

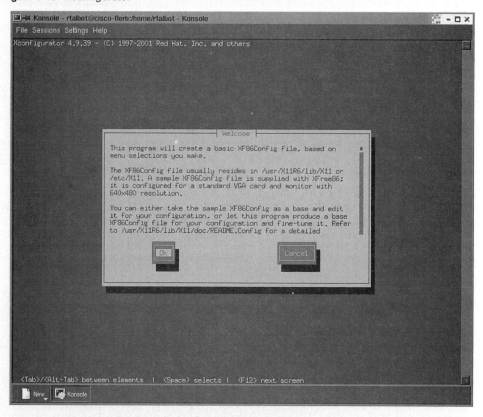

When using these tools, use Xconfigurator when setting up a system for the first time, because the general settings can be set with this tool rather easily. Then, after X is initially set up, use XF86Setup to make adjustments to the GUI.

XFree86 4.0.X Configuration Tools

Three configuration tools are used with XFree86 4.0.X. Most distributions have at least one of these. Some have more than one:

- *XFree86*—The X server by itself can be used to make modifications to the GUI environment. Use the **XFree86 - configure** command to generate a file called /root/XF86config.new. This file is used to make manual modifications to the X server environment.

- **Xconfigurator**—This is the same tool that is used in the 3.3.X version of XFree86.

- *xf86cfg*—This tool is similar to the GUI configuration tool that is used in 3.3.X. This tool can be used only after the GUI is operational. Although this tool works in a similar fashion to XF86Setup, the user interface works a little differently. The xf86cfg tool interface has graphical pictures of the different hardware that is attached to the system. Clicking the specific hardware that needs to be configured displays the menus you can use to make adjustments.

Hardware Configurations

It was mentioned earlier that you need to properly configure the input devices or hardware that is used to interact with the X Window System and the X server. The tools used to do this were discussed as well. Some of the main hardware devices you need to always configure properly with X are the keyboard, mouse, monitor, and video card. If any one of these devices is not configured correctly, the X server will not operate at optimal performance or might not work at all.

Keyboard

Not many settings need to be configured or even changed for the keyboard. The default settings should work fine. However, one setting is recommended to change— the *AutoRepeat* feature. When you hold down a key on the keyboard, the character continuously repeats. This can cause problems and just be really annoying at times, so it is a good idea to disable this feature. You can do this easily using one of the GUI tools, but you can also edit the **AutoRepeat** line in the configuration file, as shown in Figure 9-14. Changing the delay and rate values changes the rate at which keys repeat when they are pressed. The *delay value* is how long (in milliseconds) the system waits until the character is repeated. The *rate* is the interval at which the character is repeated after the system starts repeating it.

Figure 9-14 Keyboard Section of the /etc/X11/XF86Config File

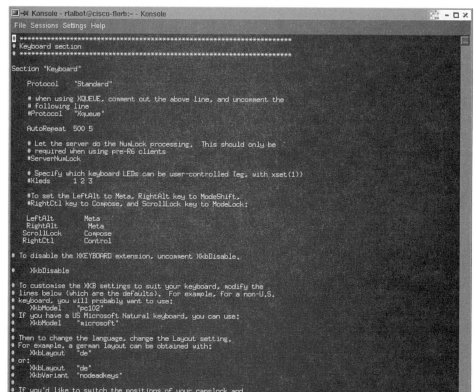

Another important keyboard configuration that might need adjusting is the model and keyboard layout. These values are set during installation and usually don't need to be changed. However, keyboards sometimes break and are replaced. There also might be an instance when you need to change the keyboard's language layout if someone else will be using the system whose native language is not that of the current keyboard configuration.

Mouse

The section of the XF86Config file that controls the mouse settings is the **InputDevice** section in the 4.0.X version. The mouse settings are called the **Pointer** settings in the 3.3.X version, as shown in Figure 9-15. These settings are set during installation and shouldn't need to be configured. An important area to note in the **InputDevice** section is the **Protocol** section. This is the portion of the file that tells what kind of mouse is attached to the system, either USB, PS/2, serial, Microsoft, Logitech, and so on. The **Device** section of this file displays the file that the mouse is associated with. If the mouse is a PS/2, the filename is /dev/psaux, /dev/usbmouse for a USB mouse, or /dev/ttyS0 or /dev/ttyS1 for a serial mouse.

Figure 9-15   Mouse Section of the /etc/X11/XF86Config File

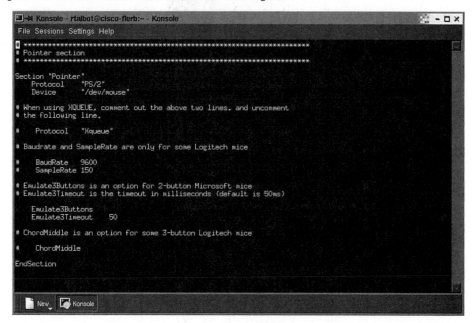

Monitor

The monitor settings can be the most important of these settings that need to be configured. Without these settings being configured exactly, the monitor might not work, and there will be no display. The Monitor section of the XF86Config file, shown in Figure 9-16, contains the settings for the monitor that the system is using. Most of these settings are set during installation. Some of the important lines in this file are the Identifier, HorizSync, VertRefresh, and ModeLine settings.

Figure 9-16 Monitor Section of the /etc/X11/XF86Config File

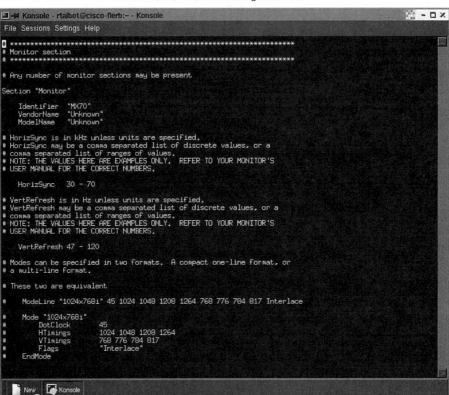

The Identifier line does not contain any crucial settings that affect the monitor. The ModelName also is an identifier that can be edited to say anything. It is just so that the administrator knows what model type the monitor is. Changing this value does not affect the system.

Next, you see the HorizSync and VertRefresh lines. They contain specific configuration information about the monitor. Changing these values affects the monitor's output. These lines control the horizontal and vertical refresh rates that the monitor accepts. Changing these values is not recommended unless you are familiar with how these refresh rates are used in conjunction with resolution values, because all values are used to determine the monitor's maximum refresh rate. Settings these values manually can be difficult. Some distributions have resolution and refresh rate combinations (800 × 600 at 72 Hz, for example), which makes changing these settings manually a little easier.

Window Managers

The foundation of the X Window System environment begins with the X server. You've learned how the X server can run locally on a Linux system, which controls the local X environment. The X server provides driver files for the various input devices that are used to manipulate the GUI interface, such as the monitor, mouse, keyboard, and video card. The window manager is another component of the X server that lets the user control individual windows.

The window manager you choose to use runs separately from the desktop environment. Recall from previous chapters that common desktop environments such as KDE and GNOME control interaction with the shell and run the desktop. Window managers are separate from this and control only the windows that are being used from within KDE or GNOME. The window managers control things such as window borders, which allow users to resize or drag the window to a different area on the desktop. Window managers also control the window's focus. Giving a window focus means that it is the particular window that is being used or is accepting input from the keyboard or mouse. A couple of the types of focus models available are focus follows mouse and click to focus. Figure 9-17 shows a window manager configuration screen.

Figure 9-17 Window Behavior Settings

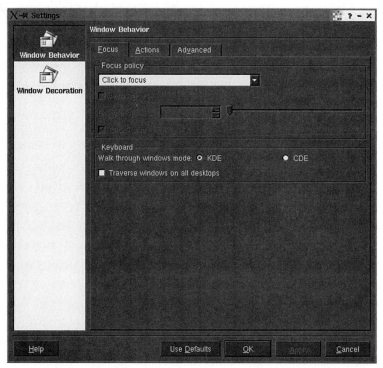

If you select focus follows mouse, all you need to do is drag the mouse over a window to give it focus. You move the cursor to the window and click it to give it focus if you select click to focus. The window manager also controls when a window is moved on top of another window. This usually occurs when that particular window is in focus.

The window manager provides control of the whole screen as well as just individual windows. Users can create menus on the desktop that can be used to run programs and control other aspects of the window manager's operation. These menus can be displayed in several ways. They can be set permanently on the desktop, or they can be displayed when the user right-clicks the desktop.

Another feature of window managers is *paging functions*. This allows a user to have multiple workspaces or desktops open that can be switched back and forth with a mouse click or by selecting the appropriate screen from a menu. This feature is helpful in organizing a user's desktop into specific areas. For example, a user can have one workspace that has a word processor open, another workspace for web browsing, and another workspace for programming tools.

Linux Window Managers

Linux has several different window managers to choose from. You are limited to choosing a window manager that is available for the particular Linux distribution you are using. Generally, all the window managers perform the same functions. They differ in other aspects, such as how elaborately they support the features. Some window managers are very simple and have simple controls. Others have many options for elaborate menus, pagers, and so on. Linux supports many window managers. Here are some of the more popular window managers used today:

- **KWM**—This is the window manager that comes with the K Desktop Environment (KDE). The K Window Manager is popular because it is used with KDE.
- **Sawfish**—Some experienced Linux users might know this window manager as sawmill, which is what it used to be called. This is the default window manager for GNOME. However, it can be used with other desktop environments, such as KDE.
- **Enlightenment**—This was the default window manager in GNOME before sawfish. This window manager is one of the more graphical window managers available.
- **IceWM**—This window manager is one of the smaller and simpler window managers that do not use intensive graphical displays. It does, however, provide basic features such as paging and customizable appearance.

Keep in mind that this is only a short list and that there are several other choices of window managers. A good idea is to check out the website for Linux window managers at www.plig.org/xwinman to find out more about the other window managers

Linux has to offer. Some other popular window managers include FVWM and TWM. These are older window managers that have since been replaced by some of the window managers previously mentioned. No one window manager is best. Choosing a window manager is sort of like choosing which distribution of Linux to use. It depends on what the user's needs are as well as what distribution or desktop environment the user is using. Also, things such as how important graphical features are to the user determine which window manager to use.

Running a Window Manager

When you installed X server on the system, at least one window manager was installed. Actually, the first part of running the window manager is to install it. Again, this should have been done automatically, but if a particular window manager needs to be used, check to see if it was installed. If it was not, it can be installed at this time. When the system boots up and the GUI starts, the window manager should start too. It is good practice to check and see what window managers are currently installed in the system and which one is currently the default. This makes it easier to determine if a new one is needed or if the default window manager will work fine. In most instances, the default window manager is fine.

As an administrator, you usually won't have to install the window managers. In most cases, all you might need to do is change the default window manager that starts when the system boots up. The file that is used to change the default window manager and its location differ, depending on which distribution of Linux is being used. Some of the files that are used in the various distributions are /etc/X11/Xconfig, /etc/X11/xinit/xinitrc/, /etc/X11/xdm/Xsession, and /etc/sysconfig/desktop.

Another way to select which window manager to use is to select it from the login screen. Both KDE and GNOME use this login screen when the X server is running and you are using a GUI login. You can use a session type menu to select which window manager you want to use after logging in.

Desktop Environments

You learned in the previous section how window managers run completely independently of the desktop environment. The window manager helps manage the windows and keep the desktop in working order. Even though the window manager runs independently of the desktop environment, it cannot perform all the tasks that a user needs. If you're familiar with other GUI-based environments, such as Windows or MacOS, you know that they have an abundance of tools that are all integrated into the GUI environment. These include file managers and system configuration tools. Linux has all these tools as well, but in Linux they are not all integrated or designed to be compatible with each other. This has a lot to do with the fact that Linux is an open-source operating system and Windows and MacOS are not. For example, the default fonts that are used in one program in Linux might not be available in another program. The Linux desktop environment solves these incompatibility issues. The Linux desktop environment is built from window managers but is designed to maintain integrated programs, utilities, and tools that solve these incompatibility issues.

Linux Desktop Environments

Just as there are many different window managers to choose from, there are several desktop environments to choose from. The following are some of the more popular ones:

- **KDE**—The *K Desktop Environment (KDE)*, shown in Figure 9-18, is one of the most popular desktop environments used in Linux today. You find it in most of the major Linux distributions. KDE is built on its own window manager, KWM. KDE has been around for a long time and is one of the more advanced and complete desktop environments available for Linux.

Figure 9-18 KDE Desktop

- **GNOME**—This desktop environment, shown in Figure 9-19, is KDE's major competitor. GNOME is newer than KDE and is not quite as complete, but it is quickly growing in popularity. Some distributions such as Red Hat and Debian even have GNOME as their default desktop environment.

Figure 9-19   GNOME Desktop

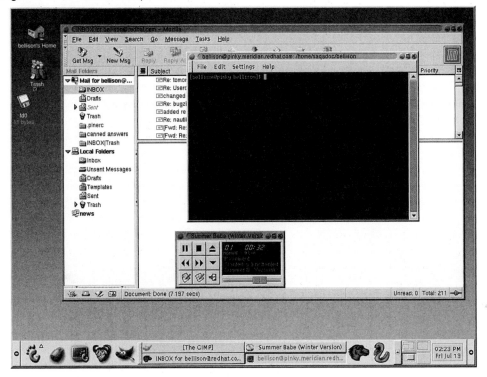

- **CDE**—Although it isn't as common on Linux systems, the *Common Desktop Environment (CDE)*, shown in Figure 9-20, is the GUI of choice on commercial UNIX systems. Many users who have used CDE with UNIX systems use a version available for Linux called DeXtop.

- *Xfce*—This desktop environment, shown in Figure 9-21, is similar to CDE. However, unlike CDE, which is used for commercial UNIX systems, Xfce is entirely open-source. It is not as advanced or complete as KDE or GNOME, but it takes up fewer resources on the system because it does not use as much disk space or memory.

Figure 9-20 CDE Desktop

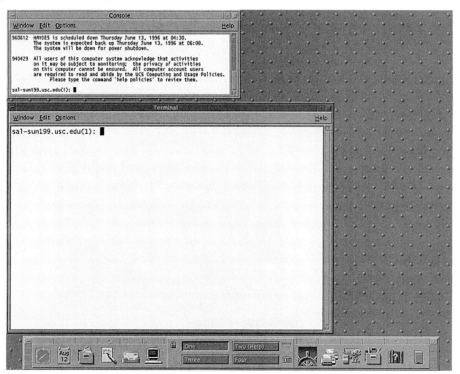

No one desktop environment is best. The decision of which one to use comes down to the user's needs as well as which distribution of Linux is being used. For administrators, the decision might come down to which one is supported. Most distributions come with both KDE and GNOME, so the user can decide which one he wants to use. Keep in mind that installing both desktop environments can consume a lot of disk space, so it is a good idea to make sure that the disk is large enough for both. All the desktop environments mentioned here are open-source except CDE, so getting or distributing them is not a problem. It is a good idea to have both KDE and GNOME installed, because many of the latest applications have dependencies that require both.

Figure 9-21 Xfce Desktop

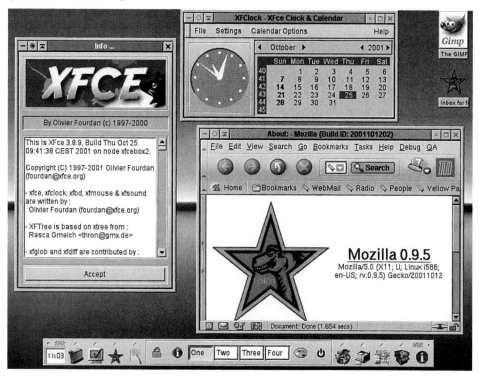

Post-Installation Configuration and Tasks

As in the Windows OS installation, some post-installation add-ons might be needed to run specific services. For example, if you're using Red Hat Linux 7.*x*, the linuxconf file does not get added to the system by default. (The linuxconf tool is shown in Figure 9-22.) You can add this file after the installation is complete by loading it from the installation CD. The latest released sources for e-mail clients like Elm, for example, should also be loaded before you configure the system for e-mail. A Linux administrator needs to be familiar with three main types of package managers. Red Hat Package Manager (RPM), Debian packages, and tarballs (files that are collected using the tar program) are used to install and remove applications and programs in Linux systems after the installation process has completed.

Figure 9-22 linuxconf Page in the X Window System

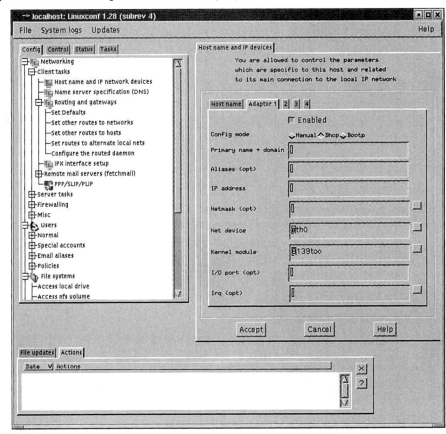

Red Hat Package Manager

Red Hat Package Manager (RPM) is the most popular type of package manager. Although it is created by Red Hat, RPM is supported by just about every major Linux distribution. RPM provides all the tools that are needed to efficiently install and remove programs, such as a package database. However, not all applications and programs use RPM. Some use the Debian packages, and some use tarballs. Both are covered in detail later in this section. The package database is a system that checks for conflicts and ownership of files by keeping track of the entire RPM database of files after they are installed in the system. The package database is stored in the /var/lib/rpm directory. It provides these features:

- *Package information*—Stores all information about a package after it is installed. Information such as build date, description, and version number is copied to the package database directory. Even if the package is removed, the information about that package remains in the database.

- *File information*—Keeps information on all the files that are installed on the system using RPM. This includes things such as being able to keep track of which package a specific file belongs to. This also keeps track of file permissions so that any changes made to files installed via RPM can be tracked and traced back to the person who made the changes.
- **Dependencies**—Covered earlier in this chapter. The database is where the dependency information for a package that is installed is stored.
- *Provision information*—Some packages that are installed provide features for other packages that are installed. A mail client, for example, needs to have a mail server to be able to retrieve and send mail. This is also a type of dependency.

RPM Diversity

Red Hat released the RPM software under the General Public License (GPL). This means that even though it was created by Red Hat, any Linux distribution could include it. For this reason, most of the major Linux distributions support RPM. Some distributions, such as Mandrake, Yellow Dog, TurboLinux, and LinuxPPC, are based on Red Hat and use RPM. SuSE and Caldera Linux are not based on Red Hat but still use RPM. RPM provides compatibility across distributions much as XFree86 does. You learned earlier that XFree86 is supported across multiple distributions.

RPM is also supported on non-Linux and UNIX systems. These systems do not rely on RPM as their primary package distribution system, but it is still supported and can be used. Another aspect of RPM that has made it so popular and diverse is the fact that it is supported by multiple CPUs. You learned in previous chapters that certain distributions of Linux can run on only certain CPUs. This makes it possible for RPM to be compatible with many Linux distributions, and it's why many of those distributions use RPM.

RPM Compatibility

Even though RPM has proven diverse, you need to address some compatibility issues when using RPM packages in multiple distributions:

- It is important to be certain that the version of RPM that is being used is the same in both distributions. If one version of RPM on one distribution is different from the version on another distribution, you can run into compatibility issues.
- Another compatibility issue is dependencies. For example, an RPM package that works fine on one system might not work on another system. The dependency packages might be installed on one system but not on the other.

- Another dependency issue arises when a particular package is installed that relies on another package that has a certain name. If you try to install a package that can't recognize the dependency package name on the Linux distribution it is being installed on, the package will not work. For example, perhaps installing the samba-client package depends on the samba-common package's being installed. If the distribution you are installing the samba-client package on uses a different package name, the package will not work.

- Some packages are meant to be installed only on certain distributions. Certain files in the package might be compatible with only one particular Linux distribution. That distribution might be the only one that package can be installed on.

- One compatibility issue for Linux servers are packages that contain distribution-specific scripts or configuration files that are meant to be installed in certain folders so that they can be run automatically.

Compatibility issues can arise when you're using RPM packages across multiple distributions, but this seldom occurs. For the most part, the packages work fine. If issues arise, try to find a comparable package that comes with the Linux distribution you're using.

Upgrading RPM

Two different distributions of Linux that have two versions of RPM running cannot install the same package on both systems. When Red Hat releases a new version of RPM, only packages associated with that version of RPM can be used on your distribution if you have the upgraded version of RPM. If you have not upgraded to the new version of RPM, you cannot use any of the packages from the new version on your system until you upgrade. For example, Red Hat Linux 7.0 uses version 4 of the RPM utilities, but these version 4 packages cannot be installed on systems that have previous versions of RPM.

One problem arises when you try to upgrade to the new version of RPM. It is impossible to upgrade to the new version 4 without having version 4 installed first. This presents a problem for systems that do not have version 4 currently installed. The only option, it seems, is to upgrade the entire operating system to one that has version 4. However, Red Hat has released an upgrade that allows an upgrade from a previous version of RPM to version 4 without having to upgrade the OS.

RPM Commands

Distributed along with the Linux installation CDs are hundreds of additional RPMs. After the installation of Linux is complete, these RPMs can be installed from the CDs using the **rpm** command. For example, if during the installation of Linux you chose not to install the graphical program Gimp, you can do so after the installation by installing the RPM file from the CD. First, mount the CD that contains the RPM.

Then, navigate to the directory that contains the **rpm** command for Gimp. The commands to accomplish this are as follows:

```
mount /mnt/cdrom
cd /mnt/cdrom/RedHat/RPMS
rpm -UvH gimp-1.0.4-3.i386.rpm
```

The **mount /mnt/cdrom** command mounts the CD. **cd /mnt/cdrom/RedHat/RPMS** is the directory where the RPM is located. **rpm -UvH gimp-1.0.4-3.i386.rpm** is the name of the Gimp RPM package that needs to be installed.

The RPM package might be confusing to someone seeing it for the first time, but it is not all that confusing after the parts are broken down and explained:

- **-UvH**—These are switches that can be placed at the beginning of the command to specify certain functions for the package. For example, the -U switch installs the new package or upgrades an existing one. The -v switch verifies that all the files are present. The -H switch displays a series of pound (#) signs indicating the installation's progress. Other helpful switches include -i, which installs the package only if the system does not contain a package with the same name; -F, which upgrades a package only if a package with the same name already exists; and -e, which uninstalls a package.
- **gimp**—The package's name. The package in this example is named gimp. Another example is **samba** if you are installing the Samba package.
- **1.0.4**—The package's version number. This is not always a three-digit number, but the three-digit version number is the most common type seen.
- **3**—The build number. It represents any changes that might have been made to the package. Any patches, file changes, or configuration changes to the package result in a new build number. In this example, the build is 3. This is not always a number. Sometimes, it is a letter instead.
- **i386**—The extension code that represents the package's architecture. This is the most common type of code you see. In this example, this package is compatible with systems that have x86 CPUs from 80386 up. Other codes you might see are **i586** and **i686**, which are codes for Pentium-class CPUs, and **ppc,** which is for PowerPC CPUs.

Debian Package Manager

Debian packages are similar to RPM packages. Debian contains a package database that has all the features of the RPM database. It is stored in the /var/lib/dpkg directory. Some of the main differences between Debian packages and RPM packages are that they are not interchangeable, and you cannot use Debian packages on a distribution that supports only RPM packages, and vice versa. Another main difference is simply that certain distributions use RPMs and others use Debian packages.

A Debian package looks similar to the RPM package, and it is installed much the same way. A Debian package looks like this:

```
# dpkg -i samba-common_2.0.7-3.deb
```

If you recall from the preceding section what all these parts of the package mean, it will be easy to understand what these parts of the Debian package represent. They mean the same thing with Debian packages as they do with RPM packages. However, Debian packages use **dpkg** instead of **rpm** to identify themselves.

Debian packages also use switches that can be placed at the beginning of the command to give instructions to the package. In this example, -i installs the package. Other switches you can use are -r, which removes the package but leaves its configuration files; -P, which removes the package and its configuration files; and -B, which disables packages that rely on a package's being removed.

Just like the Red Hat Package Manager originated from Red Hat, the Debian Package Manager originated from the Debian distribution of Linux. The evolution of the Debian Package Manager occurred in much the same way as RPM. Other distributions that are based on Debian, such as Storm Linux, Corel Linux, and Libranet, all use Debian packages. Debian packages and distributions have not been as popular because Debian Linux doesn't emphasize any GUI installation or configuration tools. This has made it hard for inexperienced users to feel comfortable using Debian Linux. However, Storm and Corel Linux have added some GUI features that make it more appealing. The Debian Linux approach has traditionally focused more on open-source principles than have distributions that rely on RPM packages.

Also similar to RPM packages, Debian packages can be used across multiple distributions and are compatible with various CPUs. However, it is rare to see a Debian package used on any system other than Linux.

Tarballs

Tarballs are by far the most widely supported type of package available with Linux. Tarballs, just like RPM and Debian packages, are a collection of compressed files that can be uncompressed and installed on a Linux or UNIX system. Tarballs are uncompressed with the compress or qzip utility. Every distribution can use tarballs to install or remove applications and programs. However, tarballs are not as advanced as RPM or Debian packages. First, tarballs do not maintain a package database. This makes it difficult to remove programs that are installed via tarballs, because no database keeps track of where all the files are located. Tarballs also contain no dependency information. This can make it difficult to figure out what other programs might need to be installed for the program you are installing to work. It might even be difficult to know if a dependency issue is causing the problem. RPM and Debian packages let you know right away about any dependency issues.

Tarball packages are identified by the **tar** command. Originally, tarballs were used to archive files to a tape backup device called a tape archiver. Tarballs were and still are an excellent means of backing up and compressing files on a hard drive. Performing a backup with the **tar** command is covered in later chapters. The **tar** command is used in conjunction with a compression utility such as compress, gzip, or bzip2. The most popular of the three is gzip. Files are first compressed with one of these compression utilities and then are archived using the **tar** command. As a result, the file has two extensions, such as .tar.gz. Tarballs are similar to files zipped with the WinZip utility in Windows. An example of a tarball package that is being uncompressed and installed is

```
# tar -xvzf samba-2.0.7.tar.gz
```

Tarballs can be used as a package distribution mechanism on any Linux distribution. However, the Slackware distribution of Linux primarily uses only tarballs. If you recall, Slackware is the oldest of the major Linux distributions, and, like Debian Linux, Slackware does not use fancy GUI configuration or installation tools. Slackware tends to favor a simpler approach rather than using any of the package-management tools that come with the RPM and Debian packages.

Installing and Reconfiguring the Boot Loader

The installation and configuration of the boot loader are initially done during the installation process. However, there are times when the boot loader needs to be reconfigured. For example, after the installation of the operating system, a user might need to adjust how long the boot loader delays until the Linux kernel is loaded. Perhaps the user is adding another operating system to dual boot and needs to make the necessary adjustment to the boot loader. Often the boot loader's configuration files need to be edited to make these changes. Other times you might want to change boot loaders. Linux provides more than one boot loader to choose from. GRUB and LILO are the two main boot loaders that are used in Linux today. It is very easy to install a new boot loader or to switch from GRUB if you are using LILO or vice versa.

The Purpose of the Boot Loader

It is important to understand the role that the boot loader plays in the boot process. Chapter 7 covers the details of the Windows boot process and discusses the Linux boot process as well. As you learned from that chapter, the boot process in Linux is very similar to Windows. You also learned that LILO can be used to boot the Linux operating system. Linux can use boot loaders other than LILO. The Linux boot loader program resides on the Master Boot Record (MBR) on a hard or floppy disk. The MBR is on the first sector of the disk. It is used to boot the operating system. This first sector of a hard disk that controls the boot process is known as the *boot sector*. In Linux systems, LILO is one program that controls the boot process. GRUB, OS

Loader, and System Commander are other boot loaders. LILO is a much more complex boot loader than ones found in other operating systems, such as Windows. You can configure LILO to boot one or more operating systems on a hard drive. LILO can be used to boot operating systems other than Linux. However, LILO must always be installed on the Linux partition, because it will damage most non-Linux file systems. Here are some other Linux boot loaders:

- **GRUB**—The newest boot loader for Linux. It is actually the default boot loader for Red Hat.

- *OS Loader*—The boot loader that is found on Windows and DOS systems. It is also known as NTLDR. This boot loader cannot boot Linux directly, but it can boot a disk that contains LILO and therefore can boot Linux indirectly.

- *System Commander*—A very advanced boot loader with many advanced features and configurations. Like NTLDR, it cannot boot Linux directly, but it can indirectly.

Configuring the LILO Boot Loader

The first thing any system administrator needs to know about configuring the LILO boot loader is the lilo.conf file, which is shown in Figure 9-23. Every line in this file contains information about how the system is booted. It defines which partition to boot from, which is the default OS to boot if there is more than one, and things such as how long the LILO screen delays when booting. To reconfigure LILO, all you need is knowledge about the information contained in this file and how to make the changes necessary to reconfigure LILO. The sections of the lilo.conf file are as follows:

- **boot=/dev/hda**—This section of the file defines where LILO installs itself. In this case, LILO installs itself in the MBR of the first EIDE disk, as indicated by the **hda** portion. To change LILO's location, you simply change this portion of the file to a value that represents another Linux partition.

- **prompt**—Prompts the user to select an OS to boot before booting the OS. You can remove this line if you do not want the user to be prompted.

- **delay=50**—Represents the time in tenths of a second that LILO delays until it boots the default operating system.

- **default=linux**—Defines the default operating system that is loaded.

- **lba32**—Specifies that LILO can boot kernels located past the 1024th cylinder of the hard disk.

Figure 9-23 lilo.conf File Output

A few other things are important to know about the LILO boot loader. The lilo.conf man page is another good place to find out more about the lilo.conf file. After you make changes to the lilo.conf file, you must enter the **lilo** command at the command prompt to activate the changes you have made. It is important not to forget this step, or the system continues to use the old boot loader.

Configuring LILO for Two Operating Systems

You must consider two things when adding or installing another operating system. First, it is a good idea to use LILO, because you can use it to boot the other operating system you are installing. The second consideration occurs if you are adding another Linux OS or another OS, such as Windows. Configuring LILO for a second OS is not that difficult. It just requires making the necessary changes to the lilo.conf file. This topic was covered in the preceding section.

To configure LILO for two Linux operating systems, you just enter the new information in the lilo.conf file for the new OS. This new text looks exactly like the text that is currently there for the existing OS. The only part that needs to change is the **image** line if the new Linux OS has a different kernel version. You also need to specify the correct root partition for the new OS. The correct procedure for doing this can be a little tricky, but it is not as difficult as it sounds. First, you mount the second Linux operating system's root partition within the existing Linux file system, and then you configure the new root partition to point to the second Linux system's kernel. Doing this is quite simple. All you do is add the appropriate line to the lilo.conf file to point to the new Linux system's kernel. First, install the second root partition into a directory on the existing system's partition, such as /linux2. Then, change the **image** line in lilo.conf for the second OS to something like **image=/linux2/boot/bzImage-2.2.17**.

Configuring LILO for an OS other than Linux is a much simpler process. You just add the **other** parameter to the lilo.conf file. For example, you would add the following text to the lilo.conf file if you were configuring LILO to dual-boot with Windows:

```
other=/dev/hda3
label=windows
table=/dev/hda
```

Installing a New Boot Loader

If you are using the LILO boot loader and you want to replace it with another boot loader, such as GRUB, this is a fairly easy process. First, you configure the grub.conf file. This file is similar to the lilo.conf file in that it contains all the information required to boot the operating system. This file should already exist and be configured with the default settings on your system, depending on which distribution you are using. After the grub.conf file has been configured with any changes you want to make, you must decide where you want to install the GRUB boot loader. To install the GRUB boot loader on the MBR of the first hard drive, enter the following command at the prompt:

```
# grub-install /dev/had
```

This lets the MBR boot using GRUB instead of LILO. Now just reboot the computer. You should see the GRUB boot screen.

If you initially used LILO and you want to use the GRUB boot loader instead, you use the same process, but with the lilo.conf file. Then you use the **lilo** command to write the new MBR and have your system boot using LILO.

Kernel Issues

The operating system's kernel has been mentioned a few times, but it has never been fully explained what the kernel is or what it does for the system. The *kernel* is essentially the engine that runs the operating system. An operating system's kernel provides functions such as memory management (swap space), low-level hardware drivers (except X video drivers and printer drivers), scheduling when specific processes get access to the CPU, allowing programs to access the network, and controlling access to a hard drive's file system.

A typical user does not use the kernel directly. Many users do not even know it exists. The programs that are installed on the system interact with the kernel constantly. An administrator has only a few reasons to be concerned with the kernel. As an administrator, you must make sure that the kernel version is up-to-date. If the version is too old, certain hardware devices might not work. Of course, you need to install a new version if the one that is currently installed is not working. You must also be able to configure the system to boot the proper kernel. This was covered in the previous section.

Kernel Numbering

A typical Linux kernel version number might look something like 2.4.3. This doesn't mean all that much to an inexperienced user, but as an administrator, knowing what each of these numbers represents helps you determine when to upgrade the kernel.

The first number is the *major number*. This number does not change often, because it represents a major or significant change in the kernel.

The second number indicates whether the version is a *stable* or *experimental* version. If the number is even, the kernel is stable and available for release and should be safe to install. If the number is odd, it is still in the experimental stage, and it is not recommended for release or to be installed.

The third number represents any small or minor fixes usually done to a stable kernel version. This can be done when bugs have been fixed or maybe drivers have been added.

Recompiling the Kernel

Sometimes, the kernel needs to be upgraded just like any other program. Installing a package, just like with any other program, can do this. Some Linux administrators prefer to compile their own kernel from source code. Compiling the kernel can offer several advantages:

- **Optimizing the kernel**—You can optimize the kernel for maximum performance by compiling the kernel for your system's specific CPU.
- **Individual driver configuration**—By compiling the kernel yourself, you can select what drivers you want to add, and you don't have to install a database of drivers you otherwise wouldn't need.
- **Ability to apply patches**—Compiling your own kernel allows you to apply patches or updates.

Generally, it is not necessary to compile the kernel yourself. However, it can offer some added benefits.

Environment Variables

Environment variables contain information about the computer system that programs use to get a status report on the computer's current state. The environment variables in a Linux system contain information such as the location of a user's home directory, how much disk space is on the system, the system's Internet host name, the name of the shell that is currently being used, and what resources are available on the system. Programs that are installed even contain some of their own environment variables that are used to tell them where their configuration files are located or how to display information.

Common Linux Environment Variables

Many different types of environment variables can be set for a Linux system. To see a list of all the ones that are currently set, enter the **env** command at the prompt. The output of this command is shown in Figure 9-24. Here are some of the variables you might see:

- **PATH**—One of the most important environment variables on a Linux system. This variable contains a list of directories that the system searches for executable programs when they are entered at the command prompt.
- **TERM**—Represents the current terminal type. The TERM variable contains information that tells a Linux system what commands the terminal supports.
- **DISPLAY**—The variable that identifies the display used by the X Window System.
- **PWD**—Displays the current working directory.
- **USER**—A variable that is maintained by the system that allows it to know what user is logged on.
- **HOSTNAME**—Used to display the computer's current TCP/IP host name.
- **LD_LIBRARY_PATH**—The variable that some programs use to indicate the directories in which libraries can be found.
- **PS1**—Represents the default prompt for the bash shell. It is used to distinguish the bash shell from other shells that might be running on the system.

These are only a few of the many environment profiles that can be set on a Linux system. However, these are the most important ones and the ones that are used most often. Sometimes, a program that is installed after the installation of the operating system requires certain environment variables to be set. In this case, you can set them in /etc/profile/ or in any user configuration files that the program can access.

Figure 9-24 Output of the **env** Command

Verifying Proper Application Functioning and Performance

The final stage of the installation process consists of testing and verifying that the programs, applications, and operating system are functioning properly. After the initial operating system has been installed and the post-installation configurations and installations have been done, it is important to test these settings before deploying the system. Proper testing saves an administrator time troubleshooting problems later. Problems are unavoidable. They can happen even after you test for proper functioning and performance. Chapter 13, "Troubleshooting the Operating System," covers how to fix these problems. This section focuses on how to go about testing applications on a test system as well as on a production system.

Verifying in a Test Environment

There are many reasons to test applications and programs before installing them in a production environment. If an entire operating system upgrade is being done, such as if a company wants to upgrade all its Linux systems to Red Hat 7.2, it is a good idea to first install the operating system in a test network. Then, install all the programs and applications on the system and verify that everything works properly. Even if this is just a single application or an upgrade to an application, it is not wise to install it right away on a production system. Doing so can introduce bugs, configuration changes to file formats, incompatibilities with other programs, and so on. Testing and evaluating the new software on a test system helps reduce these problems.

To set up a proper test environment, you should recreate as closely as possible the existing system or systems. This includes having the exact operating system and programs installed on the system, as well as making certain that the test system has all the same configuration files and settings that the production system has. This includes having the exact hardware in the test system that is in the production system. If possible, it is a good idea to copy an image of the production system's hard drive to the test system's hard drive. If an upgrade is being done, it is a good idea to install the old version on the test system and perform the upgrade just as it would be done on the production system.

In some instances, creating an exact replica of the production computer is not an option. This isn't entirely bad, because most software that is installed does not care which hardware is installed. However, you must have the version and distribution of Linux installed on the test system that will be on the production system, because different Linux distributions can contain very different package collections, which contain specific drivers. If this rule isn't followed, when you try to deploy the software on a production system, it could fail miserably.

The extent to which you test the software depends on the program you are installing or upgrading. A single program might simply involve testing a few times and might take very little time. A major installation of software or a package such as a new web server or operating system requires more extensive and formal tests. A good practice when doing the installation or upgrade in the test environment is to take good notes to refer back to when you're doing the real job in the production environment.

Verifying in a Production Environment

After you have performed the proper tests in the test environment and have verified that everything works properly, it is time to install the software in the production system. A good practice is to back up everything on the destination system first in case something goes wrong. Another good practice is to establish performance benchmarks before the upgrade that you can compare after the upgrade is complete to test if the system can effectively handle the new software. Even though this should be covered in the test environment, remember that it is not always possible to establish a complete replica of the production system. With the files backed up, you can restore the system to its original configuration. Even if the tests work, anyone who has done installations and upgrades on computers knows that problems do occur and nothing works 100 percent of the time.

An important issue to keep in mind is that the production system most likely needs to be taken offline to do the upgrade or installation. This is not always the case, but it is sometimes a good idea so that if something goes wrong you don't risk affecting other computers that might be connected to the system. Another important thing to keep in mind is that there might be other computers or users of those computers who rely on the system you are upgrading. This is especially true if the system is a network server. For example, if the system is a file server that holds company files that employees need access to, the best time to schedule the upgrade is during times when the employees use the server the least. Another good idea might be to keep the test system available to temporarily replace the production system while it is being upgraded. Last, it is important to notify users of the work being done so that they can prepare for the server downtime in advance.

After the installation or upgrade is complete and the production system is back online and running just as before, it is a good idea to run through a series of tests to ensure that the system will function properly. A good practice at this point is to establish post-installation or post-upgrade performance benchmarks and compare them with the benchmarks taken before.

Part of the verification in a production environment is ongoing monitoring for days or even a couple weeks if the installation or upgrade was major. In a Linux system, you can use the **ps** command to verify that the process is still running. It is a good idea to check the system log files to monitor the system's performance over a period of time. The log files on Linux systems are usually stored in the /var/log directory tree.

Summary

The Linux installation process involves implementing many of the decisions that were made during the planning stage. Several of the options that need to be considered and implemented during the installation are running the Linux installer, choosing a GUI or text installation, setting various options, and choosing packages that need to be installed. If everything goes well, when the installation is complete, the system should reboot, and the operating system should boot up.

The basic installation is just the first step of the entire installation procedure. One other main task to consider is the X server GUI configuration. The installation process sometimes tries to autoconfigure the X server, but it often does so with suboptimal configuration. You can use many of the configuration utilities to optimize the X configuration after the installation process is complete. Several other post-installation tasks are sometimes needed as well, such as changing the window managers or desktop environments.

Check Your Understanding

The following review questions help you assess what you learned in this chapter. Answers can be found in Appendix A, "Answers to Check Your Understanding Questions."

1. A variety of installation media can be used to install Linux. List all of them.

2. Three main types of file systems that a disk can be formatted with are supported by Linux. What are they?

    A. ext2

    B. Reiser

    C. NTFS

    D. ext3

    E. FAT

3. Two types of formatting can be performed. What are they, and in which situations do you perform them?

4. During the installation process, three main security configurations are made. What are they?

    A. Root account options

    B. Hardware access control

    C. Defining user accounts

    D. Password options

5. Although both LILO and GRUB can be used as the Linux boot loader, there is a specific instance in which LILO must be used instead of GRUB. What is this instance?

6. What are the three main configuration tools used to configure XFree86 3.3.X?

    A. XFree65cfg

    B. Xconfigurator

    C. Xf86config

    D. XF86Setup

7. What are the four main types of window managers used with Linux?

8. What are the four main types of desktop environments used with Linux?

9. What are the three main types of package managers that Linux systems use?

10. RPM uses a database to store information about the packages that are installed. What four types of information are stored in the database?

Key Terms

autorepeat value   A line in the configuration file whose value determines the rate at which keys repeat when they are pressed on the keyboard.

Common Desktop Environment (CDE)   The GUI of choice on commercial UNIX systems. The version of CDE for Linux is called DeXtop.

Coordinated Universal Time (UTC)   The time setting standard that Linux and UNIX distributions use to set their internal clocks by having the option of setting the clock to Greenwich Mean Time (GMT), the time in Greenwich, England.

Debian package   A package system that is similar to RPM packages. One main difference between Debian packages and RPM packages is that they are not interchangeable. Another main difference is that certain distributions use RPMs and others use Debian packages. A Debian package looks similar to an RPM package and is installed in much the same way.

delay value   The time (in milliseconds) that the system waits until the key that was pressed is repeated.

dependency   A package that requires other packages to be installed for them to function.

environment variable   Contains information about the computer system that programs use to get a status report on the computer's current state. These variables contain information such as the location of a user's home directory, how much disk space is on the system, the system's Internet host name, the name of the shell that is currently being used, and what resources are available on the system.

file information   Information on all the files that are installed on the system using RPM.

Grand Unified Boot loader (GRUB)   One of the boot loaders that a Linux system uses to boot the operating system. This boot loader can be used on systems that only have Linux installed.

high-level formatting   Creates or recreates the entire file system, including redefining the physical sectors on the hard drive.

K Desktop Environment (KDE)   One of the most popular desktop environments used in Linux today. KDE is built on its own window manager, KWM.

kernel   The engine that runs the operating system.

Linux Loader (LILO)   One of the boot loaders that a Linux system uses to boot the operating system. This boot loader can be used on systems that only have Linux, or it can be used to dual-boot Linux with another OS, such as Windows.

low-level formatting   Redefines the physical sectors on the hard drive.

OS Loader   The boot loader that is found on Windows and DOS systems. It is also called NTLDR.

package information   Stores all the information about a package after it is installed on the system.

paging function   Allows users to have multiple workspaces or desktops open that can be switched back and forth with one mouse click or by selecting the appropriate screen from a menu.

provision information   Installed packages provide features for other installed packages.

Red Hat Package Manager (RPM)   Provides all the tools that are needed to efficiently install and remove programs, such as a package database.

shadow password   A password that is stored in a file other than /etc/passwd so that it is not accessible by all users. This greatly improves security.

System Commander   A very advanced boot loader with many advanced features and configurations. Like NTLDR, it cannot boot Linux directly, but it can boot it indirectly.

tarball   The most widely supported type of package available with Linux. Tarballs, like RPM and Debian packages, are a collection of compressed files that can be uncompressed and installed on a Linux or UNIX system.

Xconfigurator   A configuration tool used to configure the X Window GUI. Can be used in either text mode or GUI mode.

xf86cfg   Works much like XF86Setup, but the user interface works a little differently. The xf86cfg interface has graphical pictures of the different hardware that is attached to the system.

xf86config   A configuration tool used to configure the X Window System GUI. It operates entirely in text mode. Its basic process is to ask a series of questions about the hardware in your system and your configuration preferences.

XF86Setup   A configuration tool used to configure the X Window System GUI that can be used only from GUI mode. It is used to reconfigure the X environment while it is in a nonoperational mode. You can make changes at any time without having to start over if you make a mistake.

Xfce   A desktop environment that is very similar to CDE. Unlike CDE, which is used for commercial UNIX systems, Xfce is entirely open-source.

XFree86   The free X server that comes with every major distribution of Linux that supports a GUI interface.

X server   The main component that establishes the GUI mode on a Linux system.

Objectives

After completing this chapter, you will be able to complete tasks related to

- User interface administration
- User accounts and group accounts
- File system and services management
- File system configuration files
- Documenting a Linux system configuration
- Daemons

## Chapter 10

Linux

This chapter details the Linux operating system. Linux is primarily intended to be a server-based network operating system (NOS). It includes a few additional installation steps that are not found in Windows 2000. After you verify that the system is compatible, Linux guides you to the final step of logging on. Managing user accounts and the file system is covered in this chapter to provide you with the necessary information you need to share folders and files and assign permissions. You will also learn about e-mail and Linux daemons, which are configured to provide access to the web.

User Interface Administration

This section covers the following topics:

- Login procedures
- Graphical user interface
- Command-line interface
- Linux shells
- vi Editor

Login Procedures

Users can log on to a Linux operating system using the command-line interface (CLI), which is similar to the Windows 2000 interface. Figure 10-1 shows the text-mode login screen for Linux Red Hat. The Linux console is called a CLI and is discussed in further detail later. Instead of displaying text boxes and buttons like the Windows 2000 GUI, the Linux CLI provides the user with successive text-only prompts to enter a username and password. No additional domain information is required. Unlike Windows 2000, Linux passwords are masked as they are typed, making it important to pay close attention while entering them. Users should also be careful not to enter invalid account information continually, because some system administrators implement security functions to lock or reboot the system after a number of failed attempts. After the account information has been successfully submitted, the user is logged on to the system, taken to his or her home directory, and given a command prompt.

Figure 10-1 Linux Console Logon Prompt

When the system is configured to boot into the graphical user interface (GUI), the user needs to enter a username and password to be authenticated to the network.

Lab 10.1.1 Logging Onto Linux

To boot a Linux computer and log in as the root user, navigate using the command-line interface (CLI) and shut down the computer.

Graphical User Interface

It was mentioned that Linux uses a CLI with text-based commands entered at a command prompt. Although this format has its advantages, there are also advantages to the GUI used by Windows. In 1984, a team of software experts from the Massachusetts Institute of Technology (MIT) created a graphical interface called the X Window System that allows Linux to operate similar to the other GUIs.

Because of the robust design of the Linux operating system, the look and feel of the X Window System can be easily customized and programmed in an infinite number of ways. In the Windows 2000 OS, the main elements of the user interface (icons, menus, the taskbar) are identical for all users. Linux users can customize their X Window System interface to meet their specific needs and tastes by installing different programs called window managers and desktop environments. Discussing all these different software packages is beyond the scope of this course, so instead the focus is on the underlying similarities found in all X Window Systems.

Lab 10.1.2 Using the Linux GUI

Explore the basic features of the X Window System and KDE desktop environment.

Similarities to Windows 2000

A typical X Window System interface, shown in Figure 10-2, looks somewhat familiar to a Windows 2000 user. A mouse is used as a pointing device, there is usually a task-bar, icons represent data, and windows display information to the user. Although the sizes, shapes, and colors of these elements can vary, the basic principles are very similar to the Windows 2000 GUI. This familiar design is intended to help users quickly become productive with the X Window System and is typically the standard approach. But Linux's flexibility also allows programmers to create new and innovative X Window System interfaces that can radically differ from anything seen before.

Figure 10-2 X Window System Desktop

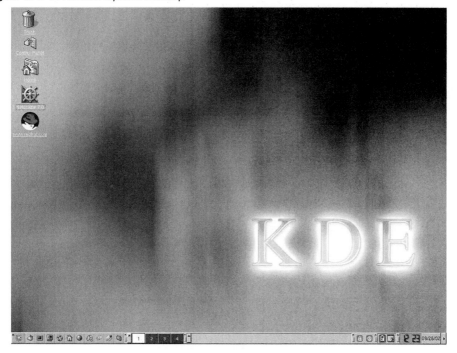

Learning the Basics

First-time users of the X Window System should become comfortable with the system's various elements. Determine whether icons are launched by a single click or a double click. Click the taskbar to investigate the various tools it contains. Practice resizing, minimizing, and closing it. After users feel comfortable navigating the X Window System interface, they are ready to begin learning its basic functions.

No matter what colors, styles, and functionality an X Window System desktop environment might have, one important element is always constant: the command-line console. Remember that Linux is a CLI, and the X Window System is really a graphical representation of this CLI. Therefore, it makes sense that an X Window System user will probably want to interact with a Linux command console at some point. This can typically be done in two ways:

- *Terminal window*—A terminal window displays a standard Linux command prompt in a small window on the screen, as shown in Figure 10-3. The standard X Window System terminal program is called xterm, and running it displays a Linux terminal window for the user to input commands. Look for xterm or any other terminal program on the X Window System taskbar menu.

- *Main console*—In addition to running a windowed Linux CLI within the X Window System, users can switch their displays to the full-screen main console. Remember that when you boot up the computer, Linux is loaded first, followed by the X Window System, the window manager, and then the desktop environment. Because Linux itself is always running in the background, you can switch the system from the X Window System to the Linux CLI using the key combination Ctrl-Alt-*F1 through F6*. The main console and terminal windows function identically; which one you use is a matter of personal preference. It is possible to run two X sessions at one time using virtual terminals. X runs in virtual terminal 7. You can switch to any of the CLI virtual terminals by pressing Ctrl-Alt-*F1 through F6*. You can start a second X session in virtual terminal 8 by using the **startx -- :1 vt8** command.

Figure 10-3 Terminal Emulator Window

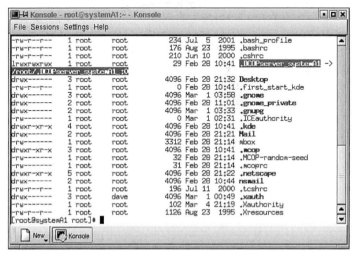

Although many common Linux tasks can be performed using the graphical X Window System applications, many more are only available to users from the command prompt. That's why it's important to know how to reach a Linux command prompt from within the X Window System. Later sections look more closely at the Linux CLI and its basic commands.

The last basic X Window System skill to possess is the ability to exit the system. Depending on which desktop environment is currently running, this is typically done in a very similar manner to Windows 2000. Simply locate the taskbar menu. One of the first menu selections is the option to log off. Selecting this option lets the user shut down or restart Linux.

Command-Line Interface

The Linux CLI allows the user to interact with the system in the same manner as the Windows 2000 command interpreter. After the user logs on to Linux, the system navigates to the user's home directory (you'll read more about this later) and presents the command prompt. Users can enter commands, press the Enter key, and view any output on the screen. Although Linux operation follows the same basic flow as the Windows 2000 command interpreter, the command syntax of the two is usually quite different.

To become better acquainted with using Linux, users should try entering some basic commands at the prompt:

- **date**—Displays the system date and time.
- **cal**—Displays a calendar of the current month.
- **whoami**—Displays the name of the user currently logged into the system, as shown in Figure 10-4.
- **who**—Displays everyone who is currently logged in.
- **cd**—Navigates to the directory above the current directory. Here are some different uses of this command:
    - Using **cd** with an absolute path name:
      ```
      $ cd /home
      ```
    - Using **cd** with a relative path name:
      ```
      $ cd user2/dir1
      ```
    - Using **cd** without a directory name returns you to your home directory:
      ```
      $ cd
      ```
- **Tab completion key**—If the user enters part of a filename or command, the shell fills in the remainder of the name. Some Linux filenames are extremely long and hard to remember. Using the Tab completion key, all the user must do is enter the first letter or two of the filename, directory, or command, and then press Tab. The shell completes the name.

Figure 10-4 whoami Command

```
[root@systemA1 root]# su - student A1
[studentA10systemA1 studentA1]$
[studentA10systemA1 studentA1]$ whoami
studentA1
[studentA1@systemA1 studentA1]$
```

It is recommended that users not attempt to randomly guess commands, because such careless activity could have a serious impact on the system. Most CLI operating systems assume that users know what they are doing and do not verify the intent of their commands. Therefore, users should always be precise and alert when issuing commands to the system to prevent undesired results.

Lab 10.1.3 The CLI Interface

In this lab, you navigate the Linux file system. You learn how to use the navigation tools provided by Linux to locate files and folders.

Man Pages

Users can learn more about any command through the use of *man pages*, which is short for "manual pages." These help files display detailed information about any Linux command available to the user.

The man pages describe what users need to know about system online commands, system calls, file formats, and system maintenance. The online man pages are part of the Linux OS and are installed by default. Man pages are in the form of simple character-based screen displays and are not graphical.

To access the man pages, users need to be at a command prompt. They can log in at the command line or open a terminal window in the KDE interface and start with a command prompt. Man pages are helpful when users want to use a command or utility and they have forgotten its syntax or they just need some information about how to use it. The man pages provide information on the command's syntax, its purpose, and what options or arguments are available. Some commands do not work with all three shells. The man pages tell which commands work with which shells. They refer to the Bourne shell as (sh), the Korn shell as (ksh), and the C shell as (csh). You will learn about these different shells later.

The **man** Command

The **man** command displays online man pages for any of the hundreds of Linux commands that are available. You can get a listing of all the Linux commands with a brief description of what they do by entering **man intro** at the command line. You even can display a man page on the **man** command itself by typing **man man**.

The **man** command can be used in several ways. The basic form is **man** *name*, where *name* is the name of the command for which the user wants information. There are several handy options to use with the **man** command for performing keyword searches and displaying specific sections of the Programmer Manual:

- **$ man** *name*—Provides help on a particular command. *name* is the name of the command that the user wants to get help with, such as **ls**, **cat**, or **mkdir**.
- **$ man -k** *keyword*—Searches the man pages table of contents for the specified keyword and displays a one-line summary for each entry. Figure 10-5 illustrates using the **man** command to get help with the **mkdir** command.
- **$ man -s** *section name*—Displays a particular section of the man pages, which can include multiple commands.

Figure 10-5 man -k mkdir Command

```
[root@systemA1 root]# man -k mkdir
mkdir           (1)  - make directories
mkdirhier       (1x) - makes a directory hierarchy
[root@systemA1 root]#
```

Working with Man Pages

Man pages are a quick and convenient way to check on Linux command syntax while at a command prompt.

A typical man page has a number of different headings or informational areas. Here are the more common ones:

- **NAME**—Contains the name of the command and other commands that might accomplish the same thing.
- **SYNOPSIS**—Shows the command's syntax with any allowable options and arguments.
- **DESCRIPTION**—Gives an overview of what the command does.
- **OPERANDS**—The target of the command or what the command takes effect on, such as a directory or file.
- **OPTIONS**—Switches that can change the command's function or effect. They are normally are preceded by a dash (-).
- **SEE ALSO**—Refers users to other related commands and subjects, such as NAME, SYNOPSIS, DESCRIPTION, OPTIONS, and OPERANDS.

These headings are displayed in the man page output in all capital letters. Depending on the command and its purpose, the man page might not contain all the headings. For example, the **pwd** (print working directory) command does not have an OPTION or OPERANDS information heading because no options or operands can be used with this command. All commands have at least a name, a synopsis, and a description. The results of the man page for the **ls** command are shown in Figure 10-6. Note the different headings. Some of the output has been omitted because the output from the **ls** man page normally takes up several pages.

The **ls** Command

The **ls** command is one of the more important commands you use when navigating around the Linux file system in the CLI. The purpose of the **ls** command is to list the contents of the current directory you are in. The syntax for the **ls** command is as follows:

```
ls [options] [files]
```

Figure 10-6 Man Page for the **ls** Command

```
NAME
     ls - list directory contents

SYNOPSIS
     ls[OPTION]... [FILE]...

DESCRIPTION
     List information about the FILEs (the current
     directory by default). Sort entries
     alphabetically if none of -cftuSUX nor --sort

     -a, --all
          do not hide entries starting with .

     -A, --almost-all
          do not list implied . and .1.

     -b, --escape
          print octal escapes for nongraphic
          characters

     --block-size = SIZE
          use SIZE-byte blocks

     -B, --ignore-backups
          do not list implied entries ending with ~

     -c   with -lt: sort by, and show, ctime (time
          of last modification of file status
          information) with -1: show ctime and sort
          by name otherwise: sort by :
```

If you have already viewed the man page for the **ls** command, you know that numerous options can be used with this command. The following list shows some of the most common options that are used with the **ls** command:

- **-a or -all**—Normally the **ls** command displays only the files in a directory that are not hidden. Hidden files in a Linux system have a leading period, such as .bash_profile. This file would be listed only when the **-a** or **-all** parameter were added to the **ls** command.

- **--color**—When this parameter is added to the **ls** command, the files, directories, symbolic links, and so on are all differentiated by a color code that makes it easier to distinguish between the different types of files.

- **-d or -directory**—When the **ls** command is issued without this parameter and the directory is listed as one of the [*files*], the entire contents of the directory are listed. When this parameter *is* entered, just the directory name is listed.

- **-l**—When the **ls** command is entered without the -l parameter, just the filenames of the files, directories, and so on are displayed. If the -l parameter is used along with the command, much more information appears, such as the file's permission string, owner, group, size, and creation date. That's why this parameter is known as "long listing."

- **-p or -filetype**—This parameter appends an indicator to the output so that you know what type of file it is. For example, **/** is a directory, **@** is a symbolic link, **=** is a socket, and **|** is a pipe.

- **-R or --recursive**—This parameter causes the **ls** command to display the directories recursively. This means that when the **ls** command is issued, it displays the contents of that directory plus all the files in the subdirectories.

The **ls** command can be issued with [*options*] and [*files*] to display the contents of a specific directory. However, these are optional. When the **ls** command is issued without these options, the contents of the current directory are listed. You can also give more than one filename so that the **ls** command lists the contents of multiple directories. Here are some typical navigation tasks performed with the **ls** command:

- Using the basic **ls** command (from /home/user2):

```
$ ls
dante dir1 dir3 file1 file3 practice
dante_1 dir2 dir4 file2 file4
```

- Using ls with a relative path name:

```
$ ls dir1
coffees fruit trees
```

- Using **ls** with an absolute path name:

```
$ ls /var/mail
user1 user2 user3 user4 user5
```

Linux Shells

Linux shells operate as a command interpreter. The "command interpreter" in the MS-DOS environment is similar. The Linux shells function in much the same way as the command.com program functions for MS-DOS. The Linux shells take the input that the administrator enters and use it to launch commands and control the operating system. However, these are the only similar functions of the Linux shells and the MS-DOS command interpreter. For example, in Linux the shell is loaded into the system only when the user requests it or if the user logs on to the shell. In MS-DOS, the command interpreter is integrated into the kernel and is always running. In Linux, the shell runs as any other program does and is not integrated into the operating system kernel. Another main difference with the Linux shells is that the user may choose from many different shells. With Linux, users can choose a shell that suits their preferences or environment:

- *Bourne shell*—This is known as the original UNIX shell. The program name is (sh) and is known as the bash shell in Linux systems. This shell provides all the (sh) functions as well as shell programming using shell script files.

- *C shell*—This shell is not widely used because it is one of the more complicated shells to work with. It uses a much more complex syntax for shell programming than some of the other shells. For this reason, the C shell is not recommended for shell programming or for creating shell programs.

- *Korn shell*—This shell was written by David Korn. It combines the interactive features that make the C shell popular with the easier-to-use shell programming syntax of the Bourne shell. Figure 10-7 shows the syntax used to change to the Korn shell and the resulting Korn shell prompt.

- *Bourne Again shell*—This shell was created as an enhanced extension of the Bourne shell. This shell is called the bash shell and is used for many "UNIX-like" systems, such as Linux. Figure 10-8 shows the bash shell prompt.

Figure 10-7   Korn Shell (ksh)

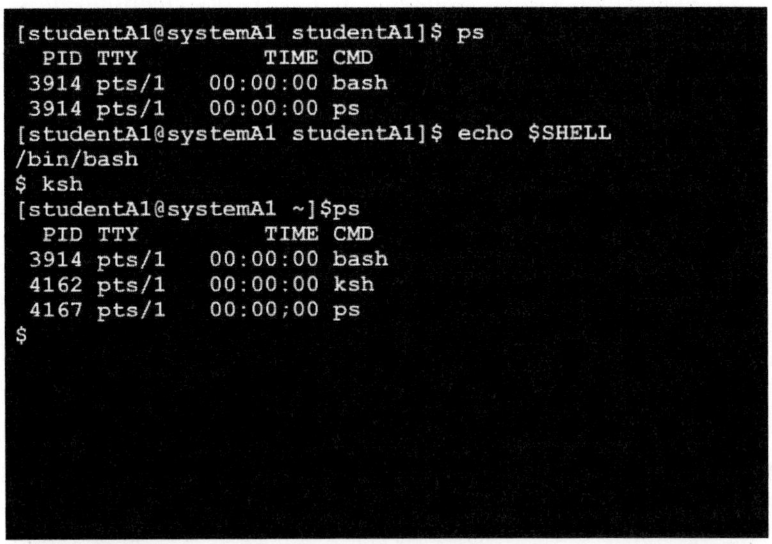

```
[studentA1@systemA1 studentA1]$ ps
   PID TTY          TIME CMD
 3914 pts/1    00:00:00 bash
 3914 pts/1    00:00:00 ps
[studentA1@systemA1 studentA1]$ echo $SHELL
/bin/bash
$ ksh
[studentA1@systemA1 ~]$ps
   PID TTY          TIME CMD
 3914 pts/1    00:00:00 bash
 4162 pts/1    00:00:00 ksh
 4167 pts/1    00:00;00 ps
$
```

Figure 10-8   Linux Bourne Again Shell (bash)

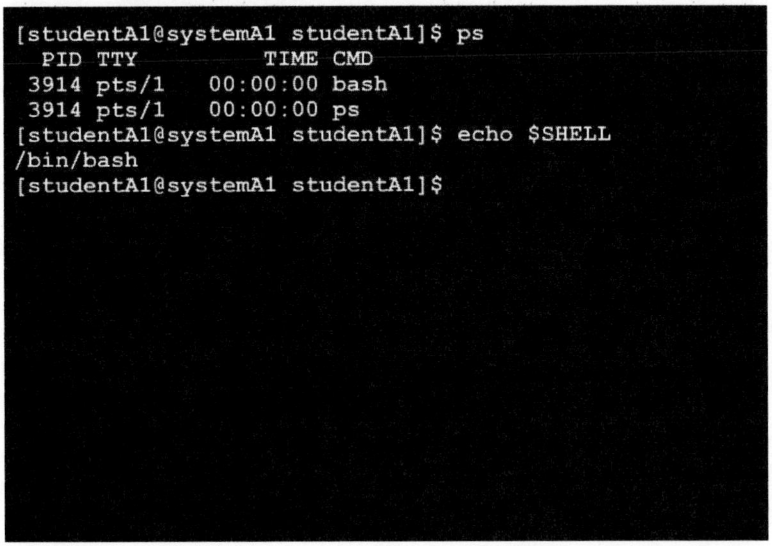

```
[studentA1@systemA1 studentA1]$ ps
   PID TTY          TIME CMD
 3914 pts/1    00:00:00 bash
 3914 pts/1    00:00:00 ps
[studentA1@systemA1 studentA1]$ echo $SHELL
/bin/bash
[studentA1@systemA1 studentA1]$
```

Worksheet 10.1.4 Linux Shells

Identify the basic concepts and uses of the various shells in a Linux system.

vi Editor

The majority of Linux administration is done from the command line using the various commands, configuration files, and script files to perform these functions. Often these commands, configuration files, and script files need to be edited and changed so that they can function in a manner that is suitable to the network environment. Linux includes a powerful editing tool called the *vi Editor*, shown in Figure 10-9, that lets you edit the configuration and script files and create some configuration and script files. Doing any type of system administration with a Linux server requires the administrator to have a working knowledge of the vi Editor. The flexibility of the vi Editor allows for interaction with system applications in a manner that virtually provides an administrator any needed functionality. The vi Editor might seem difficult to understand, because it does not work like Microsoft Word for its Office suite software or other text editors. When vi Editor is opened and typing is attempted, nothing happens. The system just beeps. This is because vi Editor is in command mode when first opened. You must enter the **i** command to enter edit mode (entry mode), where you can begin entering text.

Figure 10-9 vi Editor

```
~
~
~
~
~
~
~                   VIM - Vi IMproved
~
~                      version 5.8.7
~                   by Bram Moolenaar et al.
~
~              Vim is freely distributable
~
~         type :help uganda<Enter>      if you like Vim
~
~         type :q<Enter> or <F1>        to exit
~         type :help<Enter>             for on-line help
~         type :help version5<Enter>    for version help
~
~
~
~
~
~
~
```

The vi Modes

The three modes of operation in vi Editor are command, edit/entry, and last-line, as shown in Table 10-1. Understanding the function of these three modes is the key to working with vi Editor. All commands available with vi Editor can be classified in one of these three modes.

Table 10-1 vi Editor Command Modes

Mode	Functions/Characteristics
Command	The initial default mode for creating and editing files, positioning the cursor, and modifying existing text. All commands are initiated from this mode. Pressing Esc in either of the other modes returns you to command mode.
Entry	Used for the entry of new text. Entering an insert command such as **I** (insert), **a** (append), or **o** (open new line) takes you from command mode to entry mode. Pressing Esc returns you to command mode. You enter entry mode commands without pressing the Enter key.
Last-line	Used for saving your work and quitting vi. Enter a colon (:) to get to this mode. Pressing the Enter key returns you to command mode.

The important thing to know about the vi Editor is that it does not work like a typical text editor. You can enter any kind of text, but vi does not function like a What You See Is What You Get (WYSIWYG) editor such as Microsoft Word. The vi Editor does not contain any formatting features. If the user wants a string of text to be indented, the vi Editor contains no means to do this. The user must type the command that makes the indent.

Worksheet 10.1.5   Using the vi Editor

Identify the uses and different modes of the vi Editor.

Complete coverage of the vi Editor and its capabilities is beyond the scope of this book. Books and classes deal with the vi Editor alone. However, you can't use a Linux server to its full potential without having knowledge of the vi Editor and some of the basic commands that are used to navigate and edit scripts and configuration files. The accompanying labs provide some examples of opening the vi Editor and running some commands to edit text and create a script file.

User Accounts and Group Accounts

This section covers the following topics:

- User and group accounts in a Linux environment
- Adding users
- Managing user accounts
- Creating groups and adding users to groups

User and Group Accounts in a Linux Environment

Before getting into user and group account administration, it is a good idea to learn the concepts and implementation details of user accounts in a multiuser system. Understanding these concepts can help any administrator plan effective user and group account security.

User Accounts in a Multiuser Environment

User accounts in a Linux system allow several people to be logged in to the system at the same time or at different times without interfering with each other. A user can even have multiple logins active at one time. Before you perform administrative tasks with a user or group account, you must understand what user accounts allow you to do on a multiuser Linux system and how different users and groups are identified.

You need to know several important terms to understand the language of user account administration. First, the terms *user* and *account* are sometimes used interchangeably. For example, you might hear the phrase "delete an account" or "delete the user." For this purpose they mean the same thing—to delete the user's account or access to the system. There are several other important terms you need to know:

- *Username*—The name that identifies the person logged on to the system. It is a unique name that is given to each person permitted to log in to the system. It is a good idea to have rules regarding usernames to make it easier to identify a user by his or her username. Common usernames are the first letter of the user's first name and his or her entire last name. For example, John Smith's username would be jsmith.

- *Login privileges*—After a username and password have been given to a user, and he is allowed to log in to the system, he is granted access to only certain directories and is limited as to what he is allowed to do on the system. The login privileges state what kind of rights a user is granted after he accesses the system.

- **Password protection**—Along with a username, the user must supply a password to log on to a Linux system. The password is hidden, unlike the username, which is publicly known. Many Linux systems have rules regarding passwords, such as the length or types of characters used.

- *Permissions*—The file system controls who has permission to access files and run programs. File permissions are covered in detail later in this chapter.
- *Home directory*—In a Linux system, every user account has a home directory associated with it. The user has complete access to this directory. She can add files to it or delete files from it, or she can just use it to store files.
- *User and group IDs*—These are numbers that the Linux operating system uses to identify a user or group. Linux does not use names like we see. The operating system uses numbers, so it uses a user ID (UID) to identify users and a group ID (GID) to identify groups of users.
- *Default shell*—When a user logs in to a Linux system and enters commands at the command line, he or she is doing so from the shell prompt. This is what is used to interpret commands to the Linux kernel. There are several shells to choose from. The default shell is the shell presented to the user when he or she logs in.

All the information for user accounts is stored in two configuration files on a Linux system: /etc/passwd and /etc/shadow.

User Accounts in a Multitasking System

The Linux operating system is both a multiuser and a multitasking system. The nature of Linux user accounts is such that multiple users can be logged in to one Linux system at a time. They can be logged in locally or remotely via a network. For this reason, a multitasking system that is being used by simultaneous users requires network connectivity. These users can use more than one program at a time. They can even use the same program at the same time. For example, one user can be logged in using XEmacs, another user can be logged in using the web browser, and two other users can be logged in using a text editor at the same time. It is possible to configure Linux to be a multiuser OS that multiple users can log in to using a single user account. However, this is not recommended for several reasons. Providing each user with his or her own user account lets an administrator control security on a user-by-user basis.

Keep in mind that although Linux is a multitasking system, it cannot support an unlimited number of simultaneous users. If a large number of users are logged on to the system, and many of these users are all attempting to use the same program, they will experience a performance decrease. How many users a single Linux system can support depends on various factors. It depends on what programs are being used at the time. Some programs take up more of a system's resources, such as RAM, CPU time, or disk I/O, than others. For this reason, other factors include how much of these resources the system has. For example, a system with more RAM, a faster CPU, faster disk speed, and more disk capacity can handle more simultaneous users.

The Superuser Account

The most important user account in a Linux system is the *superuser account*, also called the **root** account. As you might recall from the preceding chapter, this account is created during the installation process by default. The system administrator uses this account to perform administrative tasks on a Linux system. The superuser account can be used in several ways:

- **root login**—The root account can be used to log in to the computer right from the main console. In fact, logging in as root in this manner can be done only from the main console. After you are logged in, any actions that are performed on the system are done as root. This can pose a security threat, so it is recommended that you do this for brief periods of time and then log out from the superuser account.

- **su**—The su account can be used to temporarily acquire superuser privileges on a Linux system to perform administrative tasks or to run any command that requires superuser privileges. Type the command and press Enter. You then are prompted for the superuser password. If you enter it correctly, you are given root privileges. To return to the account with normal user privileges, enter **exit**. You can also use the **su** command to switch to another user's account. For example, by entering **su jsmith**, you can take on the jsmith account role. If you are already logged in as root, you are not prompted for jsmith's password, because as root, you have access to any user account on the system.

- **sudo**—This command allows an administrator to select certain commands that can be entered without having to be root. These commands otherwise would require superuser privileges. This is done by editing the /etc/sudoers file and specifying which users and commands these users can enter at the command line without having to be root.

- **SUID root files**—It is possible to select a file to execute as if it were run by root, but it can be executed by any user on the system.

It is important to be very cautious when using the superuser account because of the security issues and damage it can cause to the computer. For this reason it is not recommended that the root account be used as a regular account, even for the system administrator. A simple typo when executing a command can cause serious and unintentional damage to the system. For example, suppose you wanted to delete /home/jsmith/tempdir. You would enter the command **rm -r /home/jsmith/tempdir** to do so. However, suppose you made a mistake and entered the wrong command. Suppose you entered **rm -r / home/jsmith/tempdir**, by mistake putting a space between **/** and **home**. This would cause the computer to delete all files in the **/** directory as well as in /home/jsmith/tempdir. If this were to happen while you were logged in with a regular user account, you would be prompted to change to the superuser account to do this, and you would catch the error before completing this command.

Group Accounts

Groups on a Linux system are used for the same purposes as in other operating systems. They provide a means for linking similar users for productivity and for making user account administration much easier. Group accounts are similar to user accounts in that they are defined in a single file, /etc/groups, similar to the /etc/passwd file for user accounts. Second, groups have names, similar to usernames for user accounts. Last, as mentioned previously, groups are tied to an ID (GID).

Group accounts, however, are not user accounts. Rather, they are a means of grouping a collection of similar users for security purposes. For example, it is possible to group a company's executives, who might have access to certain files, and group other employees, who might not have access to these files. If you recall, Linux controls access to hardware through files. Groups can be used to limit use of a system's hardware to a specific group of users as well. Creating groups and adding users to groups are covered later in this chapter.

Adding Users

The first user account created during a Linux installation is the root account. The system administrator uses this superuser account to create all other user accounts on the system. By default and for security reasons, no other users have the power to add users except for root. The process of creating a fully customized Linux user can be fairly complex, so only the necessary basic commands, flags, and parameters are discussed here.

The **useradd** Command

The root user creates other Linux users with the **useradd** command. Figure 10-10 shows this process. When this command is entered at the prompt, Linux performs many simultaneous tasks to create the user account, such as creating a home directory and assigning default permissions. The basic syntax of this command is as follows:

useradd *username* *-c real name*

For example:

useradd jdoe -c "John Doe"

You type this entire string at the Linux command prompt and then press Enter. The *username* parameter is the login name for the new user when he logs on to the system. It is case-sensitive and should always be entered in all lowercase characters. The -c flag is used to enter the comment field, which in most systems is used to store the user's real name. The **useradd** command has other flags and parameters. You can see them by viewing the **useradd** man page by entering **man useradd**. The output of this man page is shown in Figure 10-11. System administrators typically use many more of these command options to fully customize their new users, but the example just shown demonstrates the basics of this command with primarily default settings.

Figure 10-10 useradd Command

```
[root@systemA1 root]# useradd studentA2
[root@systemA1 root]# passwd studentA2
Changing password for user studentA2
New password:
BAD PASSWORD: it is based on a dictionary word
Retype new password:
passwd: all authentication tokens updated successfully
[root@systemA1 root]#
```

Figure 10-11 man useradd Command

```
USERADD(8)                                            USERADD(8)

NAME
     useradd - Create a new user of update default
     new user information

SYNOPSIS
     useradd [-c comment] [-d home_dir]
             [-e expire_date] [-f inactive_time]
             [-g initial_group] [-G group[....]]
             [-m [-k skeleton_dir] | -M [passwd]
             [-s shell] [-u uid [ -o]] [-n] [-r]
             login

     useradd -D [-g default_group] [-b default_home]
             [-f        default_inactive]
             [-e default_expire_date]
             [-s default_shell]]

DESCRIPTION
     Creating New Users

        When invoked without the -D option, the
        useradd command creates a new user account
        using the values specified on the command
        line and the default values from the
        system. The new user acount will be entered
        into the system files as needed, the home
        directory will be created, and initial
        files copied, depending on the command line
        options. The version provided with Red Hat
        Linus will create a group for each user
        added to the system, unless -n option is
        given. The options which apply to the
        useradd command:
```

The **passwd** Command

After a new user account has been created, it must be given a password before the user can log on to the system. This is done in Linux with the **passwd** command. Users can enter this command to change their own passwords, but the root user can also use it to modify the passwords of all users. After a new account is created, the root user enters the following command to create the new account password:

```
passwd username
```

For example:

```
passwd jdoe
```

The root user is prompted to enter a new password and confirm it by retyping it. As soon as this process is complete, the new user is ready to log on to the system with the newly created username and password. After the user logs on for the first time, the password should be changed with the **passwd** command (without the *username* parameter) to one that is more private and that is unknown by the system administrator.

Managing User Accounts

With the Linux CLI, user management is performed through various text commands, flags, and parameters. In particular, changing a username, changing a password, and deleting an account can be done with minimal commands, as shown in Table 10-2.

Table 10-2 Common User Management Commands

Task	Command Syntax	Example
Change a username	**usermod -1** *newname oldname*	**usermod -1 johndoe jdoe**
Change a password	**passwd** *username*	**passwd johndoe**
Delete an account	**userdel** *username*	**userdel johndoe**

However, the process of disabling an account requires a bit more effort. The system administrator must edit the file that stores all user information on the system and manually disable the user's password. This procedure is not as difficult as it might sound. In most Linux systems, user passwords are stored in a central file called the *shadow* file, which is located in the /etc directory. This file can be edited with a text editor such as vi Editor. The command to edit the shadow file is as follows:

```
vi /etc/shadow
```

pico (another text editor) lets you use the arrow keys on the keyboard to navigate the list of user accounts until you find the account to be disabled. User information is listed on a single row with a : (colon) separating each field. The first field is the username, and the second is the user's encrypted password. To disable the account, the system administrator can simply place an * (asterisk) at the beginning of the encrypted password. This makes the password impossible to enter correctly when logging on, thus effectively disabling the account until the system administrator manually removes the asterisk. To save the shadow file, press Ctrl-X to quit pico, and press the Y key to save the changes.

Creating Groups and Adding Users to Groups

Every group on a Linux system can have anywhere from no members to as many members as there are user accounts on the system. Recall from the preceding section that group membership is controlled by the /etc/groups file. This is the file that contains a list of all the groups and members of those groups on a Linux system.

Each user, when logging on to a Linux system, logs into his primary group. This is the group that specifies default group membership. It is set in the user's configuration file. When a user is logged into his primary group, he can access files and run programs that are associated with the group of which he is a member. If a user wants to access files or programs that are not in his primary group, he can switch to the group with which the particular file or program is associated. However, the user must be a member of that group to switch to that group. This is an excellent means of controlling security on a Linux system. To change to a different group after logging into the system, use the **newgrp** command. The syntax for this command is as follows:

newgrp *group name*

For example:

newgrp engineering

In a Linux system, only the root account (superuser) has the power to create and manage groups. These tasks are performed using simple commands to create, rename, or delete groups from the system. Most Linux users are assigned to a group during the account creation process. The **groupadd** command is used to create a group on a Linux system:

groupadd *groupname*

For example:

groupadd engineering

This command creates the engineering group. After creating the group, you can begin adding users to it. This can be done with the following commands.

One way to add a user to a group is to do it when creating the user account. The following syntax is used to expand on the **useradd** command:

useradd -g *<group> <username>* **-c** *real name*

For example:

`useradd -g executives jdoe -c "John Doe"`

To add a user to more than one group, the following command is also necessary:

`gpasswd -M username group`

The **gpasswd** command can be used to modify existing groups. Some other options are available with **gpasswd**:

- **-a** *user*—Adds the specified user to the specified group.
- **-d** *user*—Deletes the specified user from the specified group.
- **-R**—Specifies that this group cannot allow new members to be added with the **newgrp** command.
- **-r**—Removes the password from the group.
- **-A** *user* [,...]—Can be issued by the root user to specify group administrators who have privileges to add or remove users to or from groups as well as specify group passwords. Keep in mind that this option overrides any previous administrator lists, so you must enter all the group administrator's usernames in this option. Otherwise, the only group administrator who remains after this command is issued is the one specified in this command.

This command can be entered without any options. In that case, it allows you to change the group password. This is the password that users use to become temporary members of a group should they need access to files or programs associated with that group.

The **groups** command can then be used to display the current groups to which a user belongs (note that the root user is a member of all groups by default). Linux system administrators should be sure to consult the man pages for all these commands to learn more about their other group-related functions.

Lab 10.2.2   Adding Users in Linux

In this lab, you learn how to create user accounts by using the Red Hat Linux 7.*x* operating system.

Lab 10.2.4   Creating Groups in Linux

In this lab, you learn how to create, rename, and delete groups using the Linux operating system and then add members to that group.

File System and Services Management

This section covers the following topics:

- Creating and sharing directories
- Passwords and permissions
- Mounting and managing file systems

Creating and Sharing Directories

Just like navigating the Linux file system, creating files and directories in Linux is simply a matter of knowing the proper commands and how to use them. The commands presented in Table 10-3 allow the user to create, copy, move, rename, and delete files, directories, or both. Notice that some of the commands use the same syntax for both files and directories, and others are different. Like all CLI systems, this requires the user to memorize and understand when to use each command.

Table 10-3 Linux File Management Commands

Function	Command Syntax	Example
Create a directory	**mkdir** *directory*	mkdir docs
Copy a directory	**cp** */path/olddirectory /path/ newdirectory*	cp docs docs2
Copy a file	**cp** */path/oldfile /path/newfile*	cp /save/docs/notes/save/ docs2/notescopy
Move or rename a directory	**mv** */path/olddirectory /path/ newdirectory*	mv /save/docs2/docs2
Move or rename a file	**mv** *path/oldfile /path/newfile*	mv /docs2/notescopy/save/ docs/notescopy
Delete a directory	**rmdir** */path/directory*	rmdir /docs2
Delete a file	**rm** */path/file*	rm /save/docs/notescopy

When using any of these commands for the first time, especially the delete commands, it is a good idea to try them on test files and test directories. Note that users can modify only files and directories for which they have the necessary system permissions. This prevents users from maliciously or accidentally modifying data, such as deleting important Linux system files. Permissions are discussed next.

Lab 10.3.1   Creating Directories in Linux

In this lab, you learn how to create files and directories with the Linux operating system.

Passwords and Permissions

The Linux system of permissions is much more intricate than that of Windows 2000. System administrators are given more control with the use of three distinct permission categories—read, write, and execute. Figure 10-12 shows some Linux files, with detailed explanations of the default file and directory permissions. In Windows 2000, the read permission controls a user's ability to enter and view a directory. This functionality is split into two separate permissions in Linux. Thus, the execute permission controls a user's ability to enter a directory, and the read permission controls its readability. This allows for very detailed control of system permissions. It also makes the need for security even more important, because inexperienced users might not be aware of any security holes they have unintentionally created.

Figure 10-12   Default File and Directory Permissions

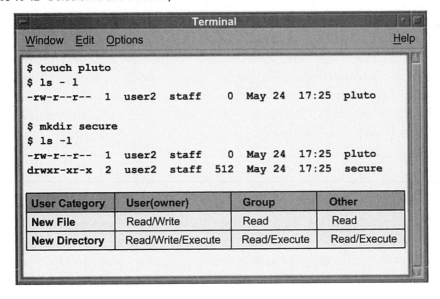

The **chown** Command

File and directory permissions in Linux are controlled through the use of two very important commands—**chown** and **chmod**. The **chown** command is performed by all users to specify the user and group ownership of a file or directory. It has this format:

chown *username.group filename*

For example:

chown jdoe.executives report_01

In this example, the user jdoe and the group executives are now the owners of the file named report_01.

The **chmod** Command

File and directory ownership is an important concept in Linux, because permissions are declared for both users and groups based on this ownership. For example, if the file report_01 allows full user access and denies all group access, jdoe can access the file, but members of the executives group are locked out. These permissions are declared through the use of the **chmod** command:

chmod *mode filename*

For example:

chmod 700 report_01

This sample command grants the user all permissions (read, write, and execute) while giving its group and all other users no permissions. This is specified in *mode,* which in this case is 700. Each digit of the number represents the three different types of users on the system. Starting from the left, the first digit represents the user (or owner), the middle digit represents the group, and the last digit represents all other users on the system (user-group-other). The three permission types (read, write, and execute) are given the following numerical values:

- Read—4
- Write—2
- Execute—1

To give a particular user specific permissions, the appropriate numbers are added together and then listed in the proper order. For example, to give the owner read and execute permission, the group execute permission, and all other users write permission, the appropriate number would be 512. To give no permissions, a 0 is listed for that user category. Assigning permissions in Linux is somewhat more tedious than the menu-driven Windows 2000 interface. However, Linux's flexibility tends to provide greater control to the experienced system administrator.

Mounting and Managing File Systems

The two commands that Linux uses to mount and unmount file systems and partitions are **mount** and **umount**. The two commands that Linux uses to manage file systems and partitions are **df** and **du**.

Using the **mount** Command

The syntax of the **mount** command is as follows:

```
mount [-alrsvw] [-t fstype] [-o options] [device] [mountpoint]
```

A list of the common parameters that can be used with the **mount** command follows.

- **-a**—Mounts all the file systems listed in /etc/fstab. Exceptions are those marked as **noauto**, those that are excluded by the **-t** flag, and those that are already mounted.

- **-d**—Does everything except the actual system call. This option is useful in conjunction with the **-v** flag to determine what the mount is trying to do.

- **-f**—Forces the mount of an unclean file system (dangerous), or forces the revocation of write access when downgrading a file system's mount status from read-write to read-only.

- **-r**—Mounts the file system as read-only. This is identical to using the **rdonly** argument to the **-o** option.

- **-t** *fstype*—Mounts the given file system as the given file system type, or mounts only file systems of the given type. If used with the **-a** option, **ufs** is the default file system type.

- **-w**—Mounts the file system as read-write.

- **-o**—Takes a comma-separated list of the options, including the following:
  - **nodev**—Does not interpret special devices on the file system. This is a useful security option.
  - **noexec**—Does not allow execution of binaries on this file system. This is also a useful security option.
  - **nosuid**—Does not interpret setuid or setgid flags on the file system. This is also a useful security option.
  - **device**—The filename that is associated with a particular disk device, such as /dev/cdrom.
  - **mountpoint**—Specifies the directory to which the device's content should be attached.

As an administrator, more often than not you will just use the default argument with the **mount** command. The syntax looks like this:

```
mount /dev/hda4 /mnt/ITEss2
```

> **NOTE**
>
> Keep in mind that this is not a complete list of all the parameters that can be used with the **mount** command. To see a comprehensive list, consult the **mount** man page.

This command mounts the contents of /dev/hda4 to the /mnt/ITEss2 directory, auto-detecting the file system type and using default options.

Using the **umount** Command

Using the **umount** command is lot simpler than using the **mount** command. Its syntax is as follows:

```
umount [-anrv] [-t fstype] [device | mountpoint]
```

The parameters that are used with the **umount** command are very similar to the ones used with the **mount** command. Some of the major differences are as follows:

- -a—Tells the system to attempt to unmount all the partitions listed in the /etc/mtab directory instead of the /etc/fstab directory.
- -r—Tells **umount** to remount any file system it can't unmount as read-only.
- -t *fstype*—Unmounts only the specified file systems.
- *device* and *mountpoint*—Only the device or mountpoint needs to be specified, not both.

The same rules for **mount** apply to **umount** regarding who is allowed to execute these commands. Only the root user can use the **umount** command unless a specific user or owner listed in the /etc/fstab/ file has permission to use the **umount** command to unmount a partition, file system, or device.

Using the **df** Command

The **df** command helps manage file systems on Linux machines. Figure 10-13 shows sample output from the **df** command. The **df** command displays information about a hard drive or partition, including total, used, and available hard disk space. Many parameters can be used with this command. Here are some of the important ones:

- -h or --human-readable—Tells the command to display the output labeled in units of kilobytes (k), megabytes (M), or gigabytes (G) instead of the standard 1024-byte blocks that are the default output without this option.
- -i or --inodes—Inodes are data structures on Linux file systems that contain file information. Using this option displays information on the consumption of inodes as opposed to displaying disk space used, which is the default.
- -l or --local—Tells the command to ignore network file systems and return information based on local or fixed disks only.
- -T or -print-type—Shows output of the file system type code along with any other information.

Figure 10-13 df Command

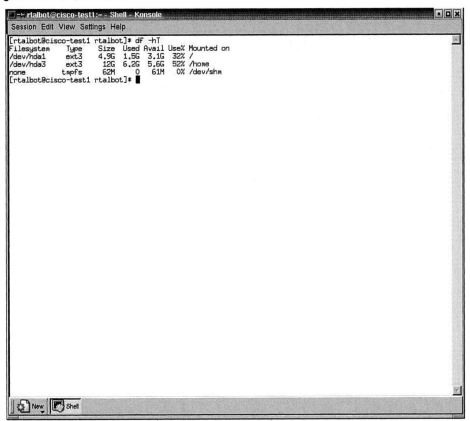

The **df** command can be used alone or in conjunction with these parameters to display information on any file system that is mounted on a Linux system. You can display information on a specific device or partition by adding the device on which the partition resides or any file or directory on the file system, which limits the output to a specific partition.

Using the **du** Command

The **df** command can be used to display information about file systems and partitions that are mounted on a Linux system. However, sometimes it is necessary to find information about individual directories and files that are located on one of these partitions. For example, if you need to free some space on a hard drive, you could use the **du** command to display information about a specific user's home directory to decide which files to either move or delete to make room. An example of the output of the **du** command is shown in Figure 10-14. Using the **df** command can give you information on the entire partition or drive but not on a specific directory.

Figure 10-14 du Command

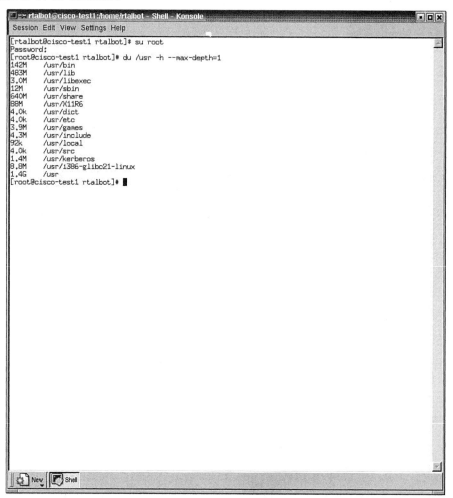

As with the **df** command, several parameters can be used with the **du** command:

- **-c or --total**—Displays a list of the total space used by the file or directory.

- **-h or --human-readable**—Tells the command to display the output labeled in units of kilobytes (k), megabytes (M), or gigabytes (G) instead of the standard 1024-byte blocks that are the default output without this option.

- **-S or --separate-dirs**—Lists the output totals for the individual directories and subdirectories. Without this option, the **du** command lists the total space with subdirectories included.

- **-s or --summarize**—Summarizes the output for each main file or directory instead of each subdirectory.

- **--max-depth=***N*—The **du** command output can sometimes be very long and unmanageable. Using this command limits the output to a maximum of *N* sub-directories. For example, if this command were used where *N* = 1, it would list directories and subdirectories for the directory listed, plus all the subdirectories directly below it, but none below that subdirectory.
- **-x or --one-file-system**—Limits the output of files and directories that are located on one partition. Otherwise, the **du** command scans for all files and subdirectories listed for the specified directory across all partitions.

This is an incomplete list of all the parameters that can be used with the **du** command. To find a comprehensive list, consult the **du** man page. The **du** command can be used alone or in conjunction with these parameters to display information on any file or directory that is mounted on a Linux system.

File System Configuration Files

This section covers the following topics:

- User configuration files
- System configuration files
- Startup configuration files
- System function configuration files
- Configuration files for specific servers
- Editing configuration files
- Managing runlevels

There are two types of configuration files for the Linux file system:

- *User configuration files*—Store information that is specific to an individual user, such as desktop icon placements, window manager preferences, and scripts that are set to run automatically. User configuration files are essential components that make up a multiuser system. These files store information for each user so that when that user logs in to use the system, all of his or her settings remain intact.
- *System configuration files*—Control settings for the entire system. These are files that control services that are set to run for each user who logs into the system.

Knowing where to locate and edit these files helps any administrator solve a variety of problems associated with the Linux operating system.

User Configuration Files

Because these files control settings for each user, the files that store these setting are stored in each user's home directory. The user configuration files are stored as dot (.) files. Figure 10-15 shows a sample home directory with the dot files visible.

Figure 10-15   Dot User Configuration Files

For example, the user settings for the KDE interface are stored in the .kde and .kderc files. These dot files are hidden and are ignored by most Linux tools. If you use the **ls** command to list the contents of a user's home directory, these files won't appear. You can list them by adding the **-A** parameter to the **ls** command. The Linux OS makes these files hidden so that they are less obtrusive and appear to run in the background. Here are some important user configuration files:

- **.kde and .kderc**—The files that set the global desktop settings for the KDE.
- **.gnome**—The equivalent of the .kde directory for the KDE interface.

- **.bashrc**—A script that runs automatically when the bash shell runs. It contains many of the default environment variables that are set when a user logs on.
- **.netscape**—The configuration file that holds information for the Netscape web browser.
- **X configuration files**—Which file is used here depends on what distribution of Linux is being used. This is either the .xinitrc, .xsession, or .xclients file. Like .bashrc, this file runs as a script that runs automatically when the X Window System session is started.
- **Window manager files**—Window managers were covered previously. Each window manager has a configuration file associated with it that stores the settings for these files.

These are only a few of the user configuration files that are stored in a Linux system. As you look through your home directory, you might notice a lot more. As programs are installed and run, even more might show up. Many configuration files are associated with programs that store information specific to an individual user as well.

System Configuration Files

System configuration files control aspects of the operating system that are related to the entire system as opposed to a specific user. These files are usually found in their corresponding subdirectory located in the /etc directory. For example, the configuration files for Samba can be found in the /etc/Samba directory. There are a few different categories of system configuration files. Some run as the system is starting up, others control the system after it has started, and still others control specific servers on a Linux system.

Startup Configuration Files

The main program that is used to run the startup configuration files is the *init program*. This program uses the /etc/inittab configuration file to store the settings of how the system should start up. Red Hat Linux uses the /etc/rc.d/rc.sysinit initialization script, which is specified in the /etc/inittab configuration file, to run a series of startup scripts that indicate how the system should boot. Specifically, these scripts are run according to the system's runlevel. Runlevels are covered later. At this point, just understand that the system is always started at a particular runlevel, 0 through 6. If the system is configured to start at runlevel 5, all the scripts will run that are configured to run in the /etc/rc.d/rc.sysinit initialization script when the system starts in runlevel 5. All the servers and system utilities that are configured to run at a particular runlevel are stored in files according to the particular runlevel at which they start. In Red Hat Linux, the name of this file is /etc/rc.d/rc#.d, where # is the runlevel number. The scripts that are stored in these files are configured to either start or kill a particular server or system utility when the system is started at that particular runlevel.

The result of these startup configuration files is that an administrator can configure a system to control which servers and system utilities are started at any given runlevel automatically as the system is started up.

System Function Configuration Files

System function configuration files control system functions after the system boots. Unlike the startup configuration files, these files are not scripts. Instead, they are files that are used by other programs. Here are some of the more important system function configuration files:

- **fstab**—Specifies what partitions and devices mount automatically.
- **X11**—Contains information about how the X Window System environment should be configured, including XF86Config.
- **modules.conf**—Specifies when and what kernel modules are loaded.
- **passwd, shadow, group, and gshadow**—These files were covered in previous chapters, but they are also system function configuration files.
- **resolv.conf**—Stores information that the OS uses for the locations of name servers such as DNS servers.

These are just a few of the many configuration files that control system functions after the system boots. There are many more, most of which you will never have to configure. Depending on the particular distribution of Linux that is being used, the exact locations or names of these files might be slightly different, but they usually perform the same functions.

Configuration Files for Specific Servers

The server files are located in the /etc directory as well. These files control programs that run in the background, most often unnoticeable to the user. These files are usually configured to start the server or change its behavior in some way if the server has already been started. Here are some of the more important servers you will use as an administrator:

- **xinetd.conf**—Controls servers that run through this program, such as Telnet or FTPD. These files respond to requests made from other servers or workstations and launch the appropriate server when needed. This method saves the system's memory and resources, because the server does not need to run all the time—only when requested.
- **sendmail.cf**—The file that controls the sendmail mail server, a popular e-mail server that is used in many distributions.
- **smb.conf**—The file that controls the Samba server, which allows the sharing of files with Windows systems.

- **exports**—The file that runs an NFS server that is used to share files with other UNIX and Linux systems. This type of server is configured through the /etc/exports file.
- **httpd.conf**—Runs the Apache web server on a Linux system.

Many other servers are placed in /etc or in one of its subdirectories. However, the files just described are the most popular ones you will configure on a Linux system. Server configuration files might also be located in other directories. It is usually easy to match a particular server with the name you find in the directory. For example, it makes sense that the httpd.conf file has something to do with the web server.

Editing Configuration Files

Understanding the difference between user and system configuration files and where these files are located is only the first step in being able to properly administer a Linux system. As a Linux system administrator, you have to be able to properly edit these files for them to properly configure a Linux system. You can't explain to someone how to edit any of these files, because depending on the system itself, the user, and many other factors, how these files are edited can be completely different from one system to the next. A better approach is to explain the format of these files and how all the lines in the configuration files described next change what the system does. By using this approach, any system administrator can configure these files for his or her own needs. Keep in mind that these files can be edited using any text editor, such as vi, and that you can find more information by looking at their man pages.

The /etc/inittab File

This file, shown in Figure 10-16, controls init processes, which run the startup scripts on a Linux system. Two types of lines are found in /etc/inittab files—comment lines and control lines. Comment lines are typical types of lines you find in all scripts in any operating system. They are commented out using a pound sign (#). These lines are ignored and are not processed. Control lines are lines that the program reads. Control lines in the /etc/inittab file have this format:

id:*runlevel*:*action*:*process*

- *id*—Represents the identification string for the runlevel process. If you look at Figure 10-16, you see that that part of the file is displayed in l*n* format, where *n* is the runlevel (0 through 6). This represents the action to be taken when switching to a new runlevel.

- *runlevel*—Specifies at which runlevel the process runs. If you refer to Figure 10-16, you see that this can be displayed using a single runlevel, or multiple runlevels can be used, such as 2345 for runlevels 2 through 5.
- *action*—Tells the init program how to handle the process. The options are as follows:
  - **initdefault**—Specifies the default runlevel.
  - **sysinit**—Indicates that the process will run during system startup.
  - **respawn**—Indicates that the system will start the process whenever it quits.
  - **wait**—Indicates that the system will run the process and wait for it to quit.
  - **ctrlaltdel**—Tells init what process to run when Ctrl-Alt-Delete is pressed.
- *process*—Represents the command to be executed for this process.

Figure 10-16   /etc/inittab File

There are various reasons why an administrator would need to edit /etc/inittab. One of the more common reasons is to change the system's default runlevel. Runlevels are covered in more detail in the section "Managing Runlevels."

The /etc/fstab File

The /etc/fstab file provides access to disk partitions and removable media devices. Linux supports a unified directory structure, which means that every directory is located somewhere in relation to the tree's root, which is /. Any device or partition that is mounted on a Linux system is located in this directory structure as well. For example, files on a mounted CD-ROM can be found in the /mnt/cdrom directory. Directories that are located off of this root (/) can be other partitions, disks, or directories. A Linux system treats them all the same. The /etc directory should be on the same directory as root, but other directories, such as users' home directories, can be stored on another partition or disk that the root is not on. /etc/fstab handles this by allowing a Linux system to know where these files are laid out so that they can be accessible to the operating system.

Figure 10-17 illustrates the structure of the /etc/fstab file.

If you look at this file, you see six columns. The meanings of these columns are as follows:

- **Device**—Specifies the mount device. These are device filenames that represent hard drives, floppy drives, or CD-ROMs.
- **Mount point**—Shows where the drive or partition is mounted in the directory structure relevant to the root directory.
- **File system type**—Represents the type of file system that the drive is formatted with. The type code that is used is the same one used with the **mount** command.
- **Mount options**—This section represents the options available for how the kernel treats the file system. You can specify more than one mount option by separating them with commas. To learn what mount options can be used here, consult **mount**'s man page. Here are some of the values that can be used here:
  - The **defaults** option specifies that the default values will be used.
  - The **users** option allows regular users to mount or unmount the file system.
  - The **noauto** option specifies that the file system will not be mounted during startup.
- **Dump operation**—The value in this field is always either 1 or 0. 1 tells the dump utility to back up the partition, and 0 means that it won't.
- **fsck order**—Recall that the fsck utility checks file system integrity. The value that is placed here represents whether this utility is used on the partition and in what order. A value of 0 indicates that no check will take place. A value of 1 or 2 represents the order in which fsck checks the disk or partition; 1 is the higher priority. The root partition should have a value of 1; any other partition should have a value of 2.

Figure 10-17 /etc/fstab File

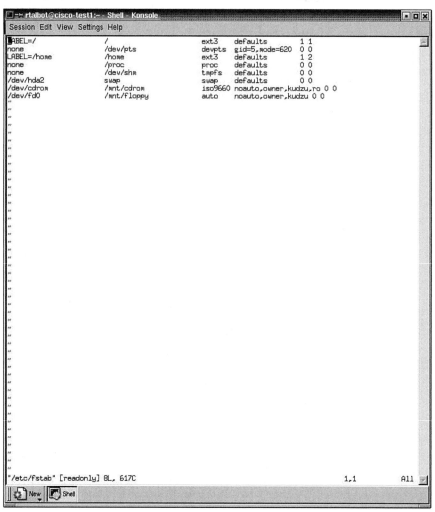

Managing Runlevels

Runlevels have been mentioned in previous sections. Up to this point, all that has been said is that they control what predetermined set of programs run on the computer when the system starts up. In other words, some programs run only at specific runlevels. What runlevel the system boots up in determines what programs are loaded on the system. The same rule applies for runlevels that applies for configuration files. It is not enough for an administrator to simply know what runlevels do. You also need to know how to effectively manage runlevels on a Linux system.

Proper management of runlevels is one method a system administrator can use to change what services are offered on a system. For example, a Linux system can be set to boot with two different configurations. One configuration could be with all the network servers, and the other could be a more limited set of system services in which other tasks such system maintenance need to be done. Instead of manually having to stop all these services, you can boot using a different runlevel, and none of the system's servers would load. Another example in which to use a runlevel is when you use the X Window System. By booting up with different runlevels, you can effectively boot to a text mode interface or to a GUI interface automatically.

Changing the Runlevel

The init program controls runlevels on a Linux system. The settings that control how the system boots and what runlevel to boot into are stored in the /etc/inittab file, and the init program reads the settings in this file and therefore sets the system's initial runlevel.

After the system boots, you can change the runlevel using the init or telinit program. The syntax for these two commands is as follows:

telinit *runlevel*

init *runlevel*

Most of time, for *runlevel*, you enter the runlevel you want to switch to—0 through 6. However, there are also a few codes you can enter here instead of a number. For example, entering **S** or **s** switches the runlevel to single-user mode, and **Q** or **q** reads over the /etc/inittab file and implements any changes that have been made to the file.

To find out what runlevel you are currently in, use the **runlevel** command. It displays the system's previous runlevel as well as the current runlevel.

A useful parameter to use with the telinit or init program is -**t** *time*. This delays the switch until the time specified. This can be useful because when you switch runlevels, many of the system's processes are killed. Initially, the system attempts to do this with the **SIGTERM** command, which allows a program to manage its shutdown process, thereby shutting down safely. However, if the process does not get shut down, the system uses the **SIGKILL** command, which immediately ends the process, which can damage the system. Using the -**t** *time* parameter can delay the process for a period of time to give all the system's processes time to shut themselves down.

Switching to runlevel 0 is a special case, because it requires shutting down the computer and halting it. Depending on which distribution of Linux is being used, changing to runlevel 0 either shuts the system down, as well as all power to the system, or shuts down the system to a point where it is safe to manually turn off the power. You can switch to runlevel 0 to shut down the system with the **telinit** or **init** command, but it is recommended that you use the **shutdown** command instead because of the many options it offers. The syntax for the **shutdown** command is as follows:

```
shutdown [-t sec] [-arkhcfF] time [warning-message]
```

The **shutdown** parameters are as follows:

- **-t** *sec*—The time, in seconds, between the time **shutdown** issues the **SIGTERM** command and the shutdown process begins. If this parameter is not used, the default time of 5 seconds is used.
- **-a**—Forces the system to check the /etc/shutdown.allow file for a list of users who are allowed to issue this command. The system shuts down only if one of the users listed in the /etc/shutdown.allow file is logged in to the system.
- **-r**—Forces the system to reboot after shutdown.
- **-k**—Sends a message to users that the system is being shut down but doesn't actually shut down.
- **-h**—Halts the system after shutdown.
- **-c**—Cancels a previous shutdown command.
- **-f**—Forces the system to skip the file system integrity check with the **fsck** command when the system reboots.
- **-F**—Forces the system to use the **fsck** command when the system reboots.
- *time*—Tells the shutdown to occur at a specific time. If you enter **now**, the system shuts down immediately. You can also specify a time to begin the shutdown process in 24-hour format.
- *warning-message*—A message you can enter that is displayed to all users who are logged in to the system. It is a good idea to let users know that the system will be shut down to give them enough time to save anything they might be working on.

Changing the Default Runlevel

Permanently changing the default runlevel on a Linux system is a very simple process. It just involves editing the /etc/inittab file—specifically, the **id:3:initdefault:** line. This line indicates that the system is set to runlevel 3 by default. To change this runlevel, just change the 3 to the desired runlevel you want the system to start in. After making this change, you can use the **runlevel q** command to scan the /etc/inittab file and implement the change.

Documenting a Linux System Configuration

A very important step to remember for any administrator when changing any type of configuration settings on a Linux system is to document the changes you have made.

Documentation is an extremely important step, especially when you're administering a Linux system. As you have learned, most Linux configurations are achieved when you edit the various configuration files. It can be impossible to keep track of all the changes you have made to a system unless you keep good documentation. Without proper documentation, you likely will forget what changes you've made, which can lead to problems in the future. Proper documentation saves you valuable time in troubleshooting the system later. For example, if you have made configuration changes to a startup script to launch a server upon startup, but then at a later date you upgrade or replace the server without updating the configuration of the startup script, you could run into serious errors that can result in the system's not being able to start. Proper documentation would have saved you a lot of time and trouble, because you could have seen what configuration changes were made and changed them accordingly.

System Maintenance Log

Many administrators keep an administrator's log in which they keep track of any configuration changes they make to their systems. It is generally a good rule to keep an administrator's log in a notebook, not electronically on a computer. This make it easy to reference and also makes it available if the computer goes down that you would have stored it on.

There are several important things to document in an administrator's log. A few of these items are described in the following list, but they might differ depending on the network and system configuration.

- **Initial configuration**—It is important to document how the system was originally configured during the installation process. This can include things such as the hardware installed in the system and any hardware configurations that were done, any hard drive information such as partitioning schemes, the Linux distribution version number, and what installation options were chosen, such as packages.

- **Package installations**—It is important to record what software packages you install on the system. This is especially important if the packages installed are tarballs or if the package is one you compile yourself. No database of these packages is kept, so it is important to keep one yourself.

- **Configuration file edits**—Many files that have been discussed in this chapter require configuration edits. It is a good idea to keep track of these changes in the log book. If the configuration file change is small, writing down the exact change that was made is fine. If it is a big change, it is usually best to write down an overall description of what change was made.

- **File system changes**—Often, many changes must be made to the file system, such as moving files or directories or resizing the file system.

- **Kernel recompilations**—If and when you need to recompile or upgrade the Linux kernel, it is always a good idea to make notes about the changes, including the version number, any features that were added or deleted, and the name of the new kernel.

- **Hardware changes**—Whenever any hardware changes are made, such as adding a new hard drive or video card, it is important to make notes on the changes that will be made to the /etc/fstab file for the hard drive and to the X server configurations for the video card.

The log book should be easily accessible but also stored in a safe place. The time that documenting configuration changes saves an administrator when upgrading or installing any new hardware or software is invaluable and is a good practice for any system administrator.

Backing Up the /etc Directory

Another way to document configuration changes is to back up the entire /etc directory. Using the **tar** command, you can back up the /etc directory to any mounted device. By doing this, you essentially preserve a copy of the system documentation, which you can use as a reference to see what configuration changes have been made. The command syntax to do this is as follows:

```
# mount /dev/xxx /mnt/xxxxx
# tar cvfz /mnt/floppy/etc.tgz /etc
```

xxxxx stands for whatever device you are backing up the directory to. Backing up the entire /etc directory is sometimes a good idea right before you make any extensive configuration changes. That way, if you make a mistake, you can always restore the old directory from the backup.

Keep in mind, however, that this method is not a substitute for keeping a maintenance log. It is just another means to help yourself when making configuration changes. Keeping a log can lead you directly to a configuration change you made. On the other hand, if all you had were a backup, you would have to dig through all those files and find the configuration change you made.

Daemons

This section covers the following topics:

- Introduction to Linux daemons
- Starting, stopping, and restarting daemons
- HTTP
- FTP

- Telnet
- Server Message Block protocol
- NFS
- Mail client
- Printing in a Linux environment
- Scripts

Introduction to Linux Daemons

It might not be entirely correct to call every network process or NOS process a "service." A more generic, operating system-independent term might be more correct. This is because if users call these functions "services," they are using the term that Microsoft uses to refer to network processes. Linux users call these services *daemons*. Novell calls them NetWare Loadable Modules (NLMs). Services, daemons, and NLMs all perform essentially the same tasks. They allow the operating system to provide functions such as the Internet, file sharing, mail exchange, directory services, remote management, and print services. However, they work a bit differently in Windows than they do in Linux or Novell.

Examples of Linux daemons are FTPD and HTTPD. Daemons are not integrated into the operating system as services are in Windows. Daemons run as a background process. They run continuously without producing any visible output. For example, the FTP daemon (FTPD) runs in the background. As it processes incoming requests, it sends out files as needed, but it does not display anything on the screen. The activities of daemons are recorded on a log file. Many daemons can run on a Linux system at any given time. There are several common Linux daemons:

- *HTTPD*—Responsible for web browser requests.
- *inetd*—Waits for an incoming request to be made and then forwards that request to the appropriate daemon.
- *crond*—Runs scripts at a specified time.
- *syslogd*—Records information about currently running programs to the system log file.

Daemons can be loaded or unloaded into memory at any time. They can also be restarted without your having to restart the entire system. Figure 10-18 shows the xinetd.d daemon being started. With Microsoft, the system must be rebooted when an application or service is installed. Both Novell and Linux can load, unload, and restart a daemon (or, in Novell, an NLM) without requiring an administrator to reboot the system.

Figure 10-18   xinetd.d Daemon Being Started

```
[root@systemA1 conf]# /etc/init.d/xinetd stop
Stopping xinetd:                                        [OK]
[root@systemA1 conf]# /etc/init.d/xinetd start
Starting xinetd:                                        [OK]
[root@systemA1 conf]# /etc/init.d/xinetd status
xinetd (pid 1937) is running...
[root@systemA1 conf]#
```

Starting, Stopping, and Restarting Daemons

Before we get into descriptions and examples of specific Linux daemons and how to configure them, you must learn how to start or stop these services. When a Linux system is running, even when there is nothing on the screen but a login prompt, several programs and services are running. Some of these are simple programs that handle things such as text-based login prompts. Other, more complex services that are running make the system available to other, outside systems. In a Linux operating system, many of these services that are started and stopped are daemons. These daemons need to be started in some way. On certain occasions, they even need to be stopped or restarted. Linux provides several different ways to configure a system to start daemons and programs.

Using Sys V Scripts to Start and Stop Linux Services and Daemons

Sys V scripts can be used to start, stop, or restart Linux daemons. These scripts are located in particular directories, most commonly /etc/rc.d/init.d or /etc/init.d. To execute these scripts, you must follow them with options such as **start**, **stop**, and **restart**. The **status** option can be used on some scripts as well to get feedback on the daemon's current state. For example, the following command restarts the Apache web server daemon on a Red Hat Linux 7.2 system:

```
# /etc/rc.d/init.d/httpd restart
```

If for some reason this script is executed and it returns a **FAILED** message, something is wrong with the configuration.

Some things are important to know when manually starting or stopping a daemon this way:

- Depending on which distribution of Linux is being used, the exact name of the script might differ. For example, in some distributions the Samba server uses the smb script, and in others it uses the samba script, to manually start, stop, or restart the Samba daemon. Another instance of when the name of the startup script might not be standardized is when there are scripts that perform complex operations or start several other programs along with the program or daemon that is intended to be started with the script. The Network or Networking script is an example. It is included in some distributions to initialize many network functions.

- The Sys V startup scripts are designed to run on particular distributions of Linux. A Red Hat Sys V startup script does not work on other Linux distributions.

- Sometimes a script executes and appears to be working correctly even though it is not. If the daemon is not functioning properly, check the log file, usually located in the /var/log/messages file. This log file can provide some indication of what errors are being generated.

- It is always a good idea to read the specific daemon's documentation for the different options that the script recognizes, because some scripts support different options than others. For instance, some daemons need to be restarted when a configuration change has been made. To do this, simply run the script with the **restart** option. Some scripts do not need to be restarted but need to be completely stopped and restarted. Some daemons have commands that just reread the configuration without having to restart it.

Permanently Starting or Stopping a Daemon or Service with Sys V Scripts

To be able to effectively start or stop a service or daemon running on a Linux system, you need to first have a good understanding of what runlevels are and how they can be used to control what services, programs, and daemons the system automatically loads when the system starts up.

It was mentioned that the Sys V startup scripts that are used to temporarily start, stop, and restart daemons are located in the /etc/rc.d/init.d or /etc/init.d directory.

Several directories within the Linux directory structure contain symbolic links to these scripts in the /etc/rc.d/init.d and /etc/init.d directories. These symbolic links are associated with the different runlevels. Therefore, when a Linux system is booted into a specific runlevel, these symbolic links that are associated with a specific runlevel reference the Sys V scripts located in the etc/rc.d/init.d and /etc/init.d directories to load services, programs, and daemons permanently. These directories that contain the symbolic links are typically named /etc/rc.d/rc*x*.d or /etc/rc*x*.d, where *x* is the specified runlevel number. The symbolic links in these directories contain files that execute the Sys V scripts when the system boots into the corresponding runlevel. These filenames are in the form of K*xx*daemon or S*xx*daemon, where *xx* is a two-digit number and *daemon* is the name of the daemon. When the system enters a specified runlevel, the K*xx*daemon and S*xx*daemon scripts are executed. The daemons or services that begin with S get the **start** command passed to them, and the scripts that start with K get the **stop** command passed to them. Thus, daemons and services can easily be started or stopped permanently and automatically when the system boots by renaming these scripts in the symbolic link directories with either an S or K. The two-digit number represents the order in which the daemons or services are started or stopped. The system executes lower-numbered scripts first. This can be important, because some services should be started or stopped before others. For example, the Apache web server daemon should be started after the basic networking services have been started.

The xinetd.conf and xinetd.d Files

Sys V scripts are ideal for running daemons and services that need to run all the time. However, running these daemons and services permanently takes up valuable system resources and memory even when they are not being used. The xinetd.d file is called a *superserver.* The main concept behind superservers is to listen for requests for any of the daemons and services on the server and then load the daemon or service into memory only when a request has been made and it is in use. Until the request is made, the daemon does not run or consume any memory. One problem with the superserver arrangement is that it can take a little more time to access the server, because the daemon or service needs to be loaded into memory first. The two types of superservers that are used in Linux are inetd.d and xinetd.d. This course covers only xinetd.d, because this is the superserver used in Red Hat 7.2. Red Hat used inetd.d before switching to xinetd.d. The xinetd.d superserver provides additional security features that are similar to TCP Wrappers. The xinetd.conf file, shown in Figure 10-19, is the configuration file that controls xinetd.d. The xinetd.conf file contains configurations and directives to files that are stored in /etc/xinetd.d. Each daemon and service that has been configured to run installs a file in /etc/xinetd.d with its own configuration options. The following sections describe how to configure individual servers to run using xinetd.d.

Figure 10-19 xinetd.conf File

Using Custom Startup Scripts

There is yet another way to automatically start a daemon or service when the system boots. By placing the proper text in the /etc/rc.d/rc.local script, you can start any daemon or process. This script runs after the Sys V startup scripts run and loads what is specified in this script. This method can be practical to use when performance is an issue or when the daemon or server cannot be run in a Sys V startup script. For example, to start the Apache web server via the /etc/rc.d/rc.local script, which is shown in Figure 10-20, place the following line in the file:

```
/etc/rc.d/init.d/httpd start
```

Figure 10-20 /etc/rc.d/rc.local Script

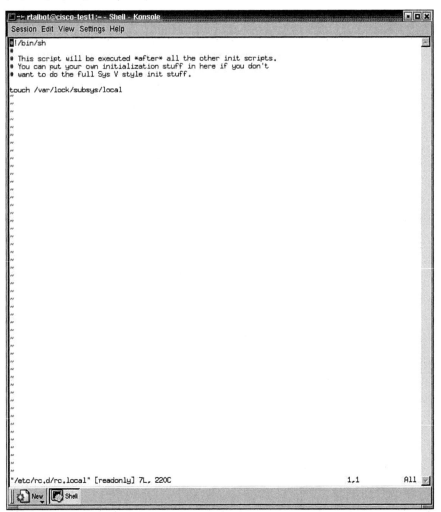

It is important to understand that starting and running a daemon or service this way does not provide any means for stopping the service as you can using the **stop** command. The only way to stop a daemon that has been started by placing an entry in the /etc/rc.d/rc.local script is to use the **kill** or **killall** command after the locating process ID (PID) number using the **ps** command.

HTTP

The Linux NOS cannot provide the HTTP daemon to users. Instead, a separate and extremely popular web-hosting program named Apache is the common solution. Apache provides the same HTTP daemons for Linux that the Internet Information Services (IIS) tool does for Windows 2000. The difference between the two implementations is that the CLI text-based configuration of Apache differs from the menu-driven options found in Windows 2000. In addition, Apache tends to be much more complex, providing a deeper level of customization and power to system administrators. A typical Apache web server setup is shown in Figure 10-21. Notice that any user running any operating system can access the web server. They don't have to be running a Linux system to access the Apache web server daemon, because the Apache web server is accessed via the HTTP protocol, which is operating system-independent.

Figure 10-21 Typical Apache Web Server Setup

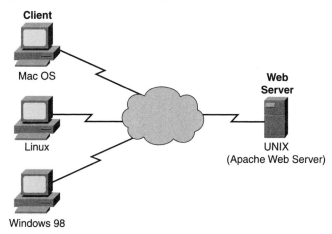

Apache's added complexity often requires a solid understanding of web hosting and security issues before system administrators attempt to configure its HTTP service for Linux. The configuration process takes place through the editing of four setup files— httpd.conf, srm.conf, access.conf, and mimes.types. These are found in the /conf directory of the Apache installation. These files contain all the initialization settings for Apache, such as the types of data to serve and web directory structures. Only experienced system administrators should attempt to edit these files on a web server, because an improper configuration could create security holes in the system.

Apache, like Linux, is available for download at no cost to users (at http:// www.apache.org). Different versions of the program are configured, packaged, and shipped with most of the popular flavors of Linux, such as Red Hat. In such cases,

Linux automatically starts Apache and the HTTP service (HTTPD) in addition to other daemons such as FTP (FTPD) every time the system boots.

Lab 10.4.3   HTTP Apache Web Server

In this lab, you learn to install the Apache web server. You examine the configuration files, check the status of the HTTPD daemon, and test the Apache server using Netscape.

Users of an HTTP-enabled Linux system are typically given a special directory within their home directory where they can put public web files. This directory is often named public_html and automatically becomes the user's root web directory. This page is shown in Figure 10-22. For example, if a user named jdoe exists on a Linux system with an IP address of 123.45.67.90, the user would also have a default web address:

http://123.45.67.90/~jdoe

Figure 10-22 User's Home Page

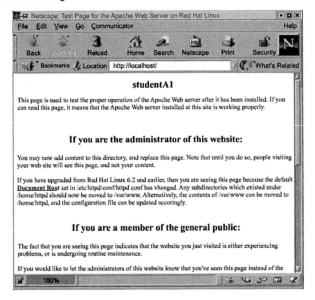

Directories or files placed in the public_html directory and given the proper permissions (the "other" category must have read and/or execute permissions) are also visible via the Internet. For example, a subdirectory named images and a file in it named mom.jpg would be visible at the following web address:

http://123.45.67.90/~jdoe/images/mom.jpg

FTP

The Windows 2000 FTP service might or might not be available by default, but the Linux FTP service (FTPD) needs no configuring. This setting is found in /etc/rc.d/init.d/xinetd. It is the fifth line shown in Figure 10-23.

Figure 10-23 FTP Configuration File

```
# default: on
# description: The wu-ftpd FTP server serves FTP \
    connections. It uses normal, unencrypted \
    usernames and passwords for authentication.
service ftp
{
        socket_type       = stream
        wait              = no
        user              = root
        server            = /usr/sin/in.ftpd
        server_args       = -1 -a
        log_on_success    += DURATION USERID
        log_on_failure    += USERID
        nice              = 10
        disable           = no
}
~
~
~
~
~
~
~
/etc/xinetd.d/wu-ftpd* 15L, 363C
```

If a system administrator wants to disable the service, he or she can place a # (pound sign) at the start of the line. Otherwise, Linux automatically starts the FTP daemon (FTPD) during the boot process, and users can remotely FTP to the machine at any time.

When logging on to a Linux machine via FTP, users are often immediately taken to their home directory. In other cases, system administrators can create a special directory to serve as a system entry point for all users. This virtual root directory appears to the FTP users as the top of the system directory structure and does not allow higher access within the system. Implementing this method gives a system administrator greater control over data and provides tighter system security. It also provides a central location to create public directories where data can be freely shared among FTP users. Remember that the same file and directory ownership and permissions apply in the FTP environment as they do in any other Linux environment. For example, users who want to place a remote file in a specific directory must have "user," "group," or "other" permission for that directory. Otherwise, access to the directory is denied, much as it would be at a standard Linux command prompt.

 Lab 10.4.4 Configuring FTP Services in Linux

In this lab, you configure a Red Hat Linux 7.2 computer with FTP services and create an FTP server.

Telnet

Telnet allows a remote user to log in to a system for the purposes of issuing commands and accessing files via a CLI. Telnet was developed so that end users could access powerful mainframes from dumb terminals. Today, administrators use Telnet to remotely manage network servers, printers, and other devices. Figure 10-24 shows a remote user who is using Telnet to manage remote devices.

Figure 10-24 Telnet

```
Red Hat Linux release 7.2 (Enigma)
Kernel 2.4.7-10 on an i686
login: studentA5
Password:
Last login: Tue Mar 5 02:08:57 from dhcp-171-68-110-
  112.cisco.com
[studentA5@systemA1 studentA5]$ pwd
/home/studentA5
[studentA5@systemA1 studentA5]$ ls -a
    backup          .bash_logout   .bashrc
    .bash_history .bash_profile              mybkup.tar
[studentA5@systemA1 studentA5]$
```

The convenience of remotely managing a system does not come without a price. By configuring a NOS to accept Telnet connections, administrators create a potential security problem. Telnet must be configured so that only authorized users can access the server.

Setting a password is often not enough. When a daemon is configured, such as Telnet, the server is forced to "listen" for requests. Upon discovering that a server is listening for Telnet requests, a hacker can try to use brute force to break into a system. A brute-force attack can involve using a program that guesses the password, using a dictionary as the source of its guesses. Figure 10-25 shows someone trying to hack the remote system by guessing passwords.

Even if a hacker cannot break into the system using brute force, a "listening" server might still be vulnerable to denial of service (DoS) attacks. A DoS attack typically involves flooding a server with bogus requests, preventing the server from replying to legitimate sources.

The Telnet protocol itself is not especially secure. For example, Telnet sends usernames and passwords in clear text, which can be read by other hosts on the network. A more secure alternative to Telnet is SSH (Secure Shell). Many organizations deploy SSH in place of Telnet daemons because SSH encrypts passwords and provides other security features.

Figure 10-25   Telnet Config File

```
# default: on
# description: The telnet server serves telnet sessions; \
      it uses unencrypted username/password pairs for \
      authentication.
service telnet
{
        flags           = REUSE
        socket_type     = stream
        wait            = no
        user            = root
        server          = /user/sbin/in.telnetd
        log_on_failure  += USERID
        disable         = no
}
~
~
~
~
~
~
~
"telnet" 14L, 304C
```

Most UNIX systems run Telnet daemons by default. However, because of the security issues just noted, the administrator must manually enable Telnet on Red Hat Linux 7. Configuring Telnet daemons on Red Hat Linux and Windows 2000 is discussed in the following sections.

Here is the standard CLI command to open a Telnet connection to a remote computer:

`telnet` *hostname* | *IP_address*

For example:

`telnet computer.company.com`

or

`telnet 123.45.67.90`

 Lab 10.4.5 Configuring Telnet in Linux

In this lab, you learn to configure Telnet services on your system so that you can remotely administer your Linux server.

Server Message Block Protocol

The *Server Message Block (SMB)* protocol is designed to be a file-sharing protocol. It has been renamed *Common Internet File Systems (CIFS)* but is still used for file and printer sharing. This protocol is used to allow non-Linux or UNIX systems to mount Linux file systems and printers over the network. The SMB protocol allows a Windows client to do this as if it were connecting to another Windows system. This provides an easy way for client systems running Windows to access a Linux file or print server.

Linux includes a tool to do this called *Samba*. It lets the Linux system interact with the Windows systems that use SMB/CIFS. Samba comes with all major Linux distributions.

Samba uses client programs called *smbclient* and *smbmount*. smbclient allows a non-Linux or UNIX client to access shares on a Linux system via a text-mode login and interface. To use this, you type **smbclient //***server***/***share*, where *server* is the name of the Linux Samba server you are attempting to access and *share* is the drive or directory you want to access. smbclient uses your login name as the username, but you have to supply a password to access the share. After you are authenticated, you can use commands to transfer files and obtain file and directory listings as if you had connected via FTP with the **dir**, **get**, and **put** commands.

The smbclient program is useful if you are restricted to a text-mode interface. However, SMB/CIFS was intended for direct access for file sharing, and using the smbmount utility actually mounts the share in Linux. The syntax is similar to that for smbclient, but you need to add the location of the Linux mount point to the command. You enter **smbmount //server/share /mnt/***xxx*, where *xxx* is the location of the Linux share. Using the smbmount utility has many advantages in that it mounts the share directly on the system so that the user can access it as if it were a local drive. The user can open a document, edit it, and then save it on the server.

Another way to access SMB/CIFS shares is to use the **mount** command to mount the SMB share. You need to specify the smbfs file system type with the **mount** command. The syntax for the command is as follows:

```
# mount -t smbfs //server/share /mnt/xxx
```

The Samba server is configured with the smb.conf file that is located in /etc/samba. The default Samba configuration works, but a couple items might need further configuration before Samba works completely. First, if the client system is part of a workgroup or domain, this workgroup or domain name must be listed in the smb.conf file with the **workgroup** parameter. Second, some newer version of Windows use encrypted passwords, but Samba's default is to use unencrypted passwords. If you're using a version of Windows that uses encrypted passwords, you must set the **encrypt passwords** parameter to **yes** in the smb.conf file. Then, to add a password for the user, use the **smbpasswd** command. The syntax for this command is as follows:

```
# smbpasswd -a jsmith
```

This sets an encrypted password for jsmith. Finally, you need to define what the shares will be on the Linux system. The default configuration allows users to access their home directories. You can find more information at www.samba.org. Entire books are devoted to the Samba server.

NFS

Similar to the SMB/CIFS protocol, *NFS* is used to share files between multiple computer systems connected on a network. However, the main difference with NFS is that it is designed to work on UNIX systems. Because the Linux system architecture closely resembles that of UNIX systems, NFS can be used to exchange files between Linux systems connected over a network. It is the preferred method of sharing files between Linux and UNIX systems.

This is true because the client systems can access NFS shares on an NFS file server with regular Linux file-access utilities. For example, to access an NFS share from a client workstation, all the user needs to do is mount the location of the share using the **mount** command. Using this command, Linux client systems can access NFS shares on the file server and use the share as if it were stored locally on their system. The syntax used from the client workstation to mount the NFS share is as follows:

```
# mount /mnt/xxx
```

To unmount the drive, you enter the following:

```
# umount /mnt/xxx
```

The administrator must follow some steps before the user can mount the NFS share this easily. The shares need to be mounted on the file server and made available first. This is also done using the **mount** command, but the syntax is slightly different:

```
# mount server:/home/jsmith /mnt/xxx
```

server is the server's host name, and *xxx* is the location of the share in the file server. Keep in mind that regular users cannot use the **mount** command by default. Recall that by editing the /etc/fstab file, you can enable a command that normally is available only for the root account to be used by regular user accounts. Specifically, the following line needs to be added to this file:

```
server:/home/jsmith /mnt/xxx nfs user,noauto,exec 0 0
```

When this line is added, any user can mount and unmount the NFS share using the commands mentioned previously. Another option for adding this line to the /etc/fstab file is to leave out the **user,noauto** section, which automatically mounts the share every time the system boots. No password has to be used to access the share. The server relies on client-side security to control access to the share.

Mail Client

When setting up e-mail on the Linux system, the administrator has a variety of choices. The type of e-mail client selected depends on whether a dialup modem is used to access the ISP or if there is a permanent connection to the Internet via a LAN connection. How users send and receive e-mail determines what configuration is chosen to set up e-mail on a Linux system.

To set up the e-mail daemon on Linux, the administrator needs to set up the Mail User Agent (MUA, also called the mailer), the Mail Transfer Agent (MTA), and the transport protocol. The mailer provides the user with an interface for reading and composing messages. The mailer uses the MTA to transfer the mail from the sender to the recipient and back. The MTA uses a transfer protocol to make the transfer.

When setting up mail on a Linux system, the administrator first needs to select which type of MTA to use. The two major MTAs are SMTP and Sendmail. After the MTA is configured and the protocol is determined (IMAP or POP3, for example), a mailer must be configured. There are several popular mailers to choose from, including Elm, Pine, and Netscape Messenger.

Printing in a Linux Environment

Setting up printers in a Linux environment can be a very complicated task, because you must have knowledge of editing and configuring specific print files. It is not a step-by-step process as with a Windows 2000 system. The setup can be very complicated, because you must know what commands and text to enter in the appropriate file. The process works much like Windows 2000 but is not as straightforward. A printer can be set up locally, or a print server can be set up to handle all the printing requests and to forward those requests to the appropriate printer.

Components of Linux Printing

As with other operating systems configured as print servers, the main component of Linux printing is the *print queue*. It resides on a Linux print server that handles all the incoming print jobs directed to network printers. Print queues can be set up on the print server in a variety of ways. Usually there is one print queue for every printer that the print server serves. However, you can configure multiple print queues for one printer. This is helpful when you have one queue that prints one-sided sheets and another queue that prints two-sided sheets.

The Linux utility that is used to print is called lpr. You can enter the **lpr** command at the command line to specify that a print job be sent to the print queue. Other programs may call this command to print files. The *line printer daemon (lpd)* program is what manages print queues on a Linux print server. When lpr or remote computers send a print request to a queue, the lpd program accepts the print job and directs it to the correct printer. The lpd program also monitors print queues and directs print jobs from print queues to multiple printers. To accomplish this, the lpd program uses the /etc/printcap configuration file, which is discussed in the next section.

Another important aspect to know about printing with a Linux system is that it can be difficult to work with sometimes because it is essentially unidirectional. This means that the print jobs originate in an application that blindly sends the information to the printer without knowing what kind of printer it is sending the print job to. Linux sends its print jobs using PostScript printer language, but not all printers can handle PostScript.

The /etc/printcap Configuration File

When setting up the Linux print server, which is most often the case in a working environment, the administrator needs to know about the LPRng print spooling system. The LPRng software lets the server handle multiple printers and queues and provides the security that is needed in a large network. When a print job is sent to the server, lpd processes the request. The main component of the LPRng software is the /etc/printcap file, shown in Figure 10-26. It is edited to define printers on the network. By using the /etc/printcap file entries, Linux knows which printers are online and available for printing. The recommended procedure for editing the printcap file is to use the **printtool** (print system manager) command, which is covered later. These steps are the most complicated tasks when it comes to administering a print server. Editing these files correctly lets the administrator specify things such as permissions and security on a printer.

Figure 10-26 /etc/printcap File

```
lp|hp4000:\
     :lp=/dev/lp0:\
     :br#57600:\
     :rm=:\
     :rp=:\
     :sd=/var/spool/lpd/lp:\
     :mx#0:\
     :sh:\
     :if=/var/spool/lpd/lp/printfilter:
```

As a system administrator, you must know how to edit the /etc/printcap file, because his it is at the core of the LPRng printing software. You can use this file to configure multiple printers in the file, but you must use different printer names. The components of the /etc/printcap file are as follows:

- **Printer name**—This is where you specify the printer's name. As you can see in Figure 10-26, **lp** appears before the printer name. This designates which is the default printer. When there is more than one name, they are entered on the same line and are separated by vertical bars (|).

- **lp**—Specifies the printer's device filename. If the printer were attached to the system locally, this line would be **/dev/lp0**, for example. This means that the printer is connected to the first parallel port. More modern printers support USB connections as well. A printer connected via a USB port would have an entry something like **/dev/usb/lp***n*, where *n* is a number 0 or greater.

- **rm**—Defines the network host name of the system where the print queue is located. This line is present only for a printer that is connected to a print server over the network.

- **rp**—Specifies the name of the print queue on the print server.
- **sd**—Specifies the name and location of the spool directory on the local system. It is always located in the /var/spool/lpd directory and has the same name as the print queue.
- **mx**—This is a very important option for an administrator to consider. This line sets the maximum size of a print job in bytes. The default is 0, which means that no limit has been set.
- **sh**—Specifies if a header page will be printed with each print job the user sends to the print queue. This can be useful in an environment where multiple users are using the same printer.
- **if**—Specifies the input filter name.

After making any changes to this file, you must restart the printer daemon. Keep in mind that it is much easier and more common to configure a printer with the printtool GUI interface utility. However, it is important for an administrator to understand what all the components of the /etc/printcap file do, because then you can make any necessary changes using the GUI tool. Also, because not all Linux distributions use a GUI interface, you need to recognize the features of the /etc/printcap file.

The printtool GUI Utility

Red Hat comes with a GUI tool called *printtool*, shown in Figure 10-27, that you can use to set up printers. To use it, type **printtool** at a shell prompt. This launches the GUI printer configuration tool. It is a much more straightforward way to configure a printer and print queue on a print server or to configure a client workstation to connect to a local printer or to a print server over the network. This tool provides step-by-step menus in which you select the features specific to the printer that is being installed.

To set up a printer on a print server to be used by multiple users, first add the printer locally to the computer that will be the print server. The process to do this is in the accompanying lab. After you have added a printer to the print server, Microsoft, Novell, and UNIX systems can print to it if you configure the Linux print server to allow these systems to do so. Linux users can print automatically if you give them permission. You do this by editing the /etc/lpd.perms file.

Figure 10-27 printtool Utility

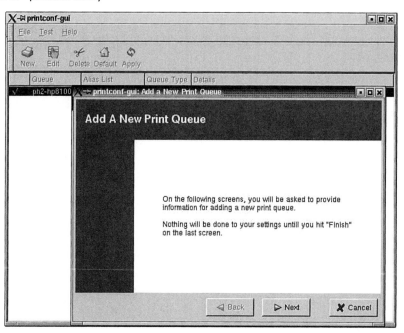

The Ghostscript Translator

As you have noticed, printing administration in a Linux system is very different than it is in other operating systems that might be more commercially well-known or that you might be more familiar with. In other operating systems, such as Windows and Macintosh, the printer interfaces with the operating system via a printer driver. In other words, the printer driver allows the application on the OS to communicate with the print queue. In Linux, the printer driver works in a slightly different manner. The printer driver in a Linux or UNIX system is part of Ghostscript.

Ghostscript is part of the Linux print queue. However, keep in mind that some applications and printers do not need to use Ghostscript. *Ghostscript* is a translator that allows Linux and UNIX systems, which use the PostScript printing language, to print to non-PostScript printers. Just about every printer available today uses PostScript as its main printing language. Therefore, the Ghostscript translator does not need to be used, because the printer can interpret the output from the Linux system. However, some printers do not support PostScript. Therefore, without Ghostscript, Linux and UNIX systems would be unable to print to PostScript printers.

Linux and UNIX systems need to use Ghostscript because they don't have drivers that work the same way that Windows-style drivers do with print queues. Programs written for Windows were developed to interface with the printer driver, unlike Linux programs, which generate PostScript and send this output to the Linux print queue. If the printer is a non-PostScript printer, the information does not print. Also, laser printers have become very popular and are the printer of choice for UNIX and Linux systems. Therefore, programs written for Linux and UNIX systems use PostScript by default.

The problem with UNIX and Linux programs that generate only PostScript is that it is not commonly used in low- and mid-range-priced printers. This is not much of a problem for UNIX systems, which almost always use an expensive laser printer that is compatible with PostScript. However, Linux systems are often used with smaller, less-expensive printers that do not support PostScript. So to allow programs on a Linux system that generate PostScript output to print, you need to use a translator, such as Ghostscript. As mentioned, Ghostscript resides in the Linux print queue and can interpret PostScript language for non-PostScript printers.

Scripts

The Linux operating system can accommodate many different scripting languages, but perhaps the most common and basic of these is its built-in *shell scripting*. Figure 10-28 shows a sample script.

Figure 10-28 Writing a Script in Linux

```
#1/bin/sh
#
ls -R mybkup
tar -cv mybkup > mybkup.tar
ls -1
#
```

Keep in mind that this is a very simple and short script. Often scripts can be very long and complex and contain numerous lines of code that execute various automated tasks. A shell script is a text file that contains a number of Linux commands listed successively. Like the scripting languages of Windows 2000, Linux executes a shell script in a top-down fashion. Each command is executed in turn exactly as if it were typed at the command prompt. Shell scripts can also contain programming logic such as looping and conditional statements, all of which could be entered manually at the command prompt. By creating a script file, users and system administrators can combine a series of commands and parameters into a single, simplified script command.

The best way to understand this process is to create a simple "hello world" script in Linux. Using any text editor, such as vi, enter and save the following line of code:

```
echo "Hello world."
```

Unlike Windows 2000, Linux shell scripts are not required to follow any particular naming conventions. Thus, the user can assign any standard Linux filename to the script, such as hello, helloworld, or hello.world. The file must then be assigned the appropriate execute permissions for the user. You can then run it at the command prompt by entering the relative directory path and the filename:

```
./hello
```

This prints the previously coded message to the screen as expected. This inherent functionality behind shell scripts is attractive to both inexperienced users and system administrators. Because Linux is primarily a command-driven NOS, users can easily create script files by listing multiple commands in such a text file and viewing the scripted output. As soon as these basic concepts are familiar, you can easily learn additional programming logic and syntax.

Lab 10.4.10   Writing a Script File in Linux

After completing this lab, you will be able to create a script file and run it in the Linux environment.

Summary

This chapter discussed the Linux operating system. Some of the important concepts to retain from this chapter include the following:

- Linux has a few installation steps that are not found in Windows. For example, because Linux is primarily intended to be a server-based NOS, you can do a workstation or server installation.

- Linux uses the X Window System as a GUI, but it is important to understand the CLI. You can access the command console using the terminal window or the main console.

- The man pages describe system online commands, system calls, file formats, and system maintenance. The online man pages are part of the Linux OS and are installed by default. Man pages are in the form of simple character-based screen displays and are accessed from the command prompt.

- The Linux shells operate as a command interpreter. The "command interpreter" in the MS-DOS environment is similar. Linux shells are loaded into the system only when the user requests it or logs on to the shell. These shells include the Bourne shell, the C shell, the Korn shell, and the Bourne Again shell.

- Daemons let the OS provide functions such as web service, file sharing, mail exchange, directory services, remote management, and print services. Daemons are not integrated into the operating system as services are in Windows, and they run as a background process.

- The Linux operating system can accommodate many different scripting languages. The most common and basic of these is its built-in shell scripting ability. A shell script is a text file that contains any number of Linux commands listed successively. A system administrator can combine a series of commands and parameters into a single, simplified script command.

One of the most important duties of a system administrator is to protect the information stored on network servers. The next chapter details advanced NOS administration.

Check Your Understanding

The following review questions help you assess what you learned in this chapter. Answers can be found in Appendix A, "Answers to Check Your Understanding Questions."

1. What Linux xterm CLI command would display a calendar for March 2015?

2. Match each task with the Linux command used to perform it.

Task	Command
Add a user	usermod
Change a username	passwd
Change a password	userdel
Delete an account	useradd

3. Which two tasks can be accomplished using the **cp** command?

   A. Change the working directory

   B. Copy a directory

   C. Capture a file

   D. Copy a user account

   E. Copy a file

4. The following two commands have just been executed at the Linux command prompt:

```
chown jose.executives script2
chmod 770 script2
```

Which two of the following have permission to execute script2?

   A. User jose

   B. User executives

   C. User 770

   D. All users in the group executives

   E. All users in the group jose

   F. All users in the group 770

5. What is the web-hosting program used with Linux?

6. What command can you use to start a second X Window System session in a virtual terminal?

    A. **startx** and press Ctrl-Alt-*F1 through F6*

    B. **startx --:1 vt8**

    C. **startx --:F1**

    D. **startx :2 vt8**

7. What command can you issue on a Linux system to view all the files that are in the current directory, including hidden user files and system configuration files?

    A. **dir**

    B. **ls -l**

    C. **ls -a**

    D. **dir -a**

8. Fill in the following chart.

vi Editor Command Mode	Functions/Characteristics
Command mode	
Entry mode	
Last-line mode	

9. Which two Linux commands control file and directory permissions?

10. If you want to change to a different runlevel, what two commands do you enter at the shell prompt?

Key Terms

Bourne Again shell   This shell was created as an enhanced extension of the Bourne shell. It is also called the bash shell and is used for many "UNIX-like" systems, such as Linux.

Bourne shell   Known as the original UNIX shell. Provides all the (sh) functions as well as shell programming using shell script files.

Common Internet File Systems (CIFS)   This protocol is used to allow non-Linux or UNIX systems to mount Linux file systems and printers over the network.

crond   This daemon runs scripts at a specified time.

C shell   This shell uses a much more complex syntax for shell programming than some of the other shells.

daemon   Allows the operating system to provide functions such as the Internet, file sharing, mail exchange, directory services, remote management, and print services.

default shell   The shell presented to the user when he or she logs in.

Ghostscript   Part of the Linux print queue. Acts as a translator that allows Linux and UNIX systems, which use the PostScript printing language, to print to non-PostScript printers.

home directory   The directory that the user has complete access to. The user can add files to and delete files from this directory or just use it to store files.

HTTPD   This daemon is responsible for web browser requests.

inetd   This daemon waits for an incoming request to be made and then forwards that request to the appropriate daemon.

init program   The main program that is used to run the startup configuration files.

Korn shell   Combines the interactive features that make the C shell popular with the easier-to-use shell programming syntax of the Bourne shell.

line printer daemon (lpd)   A program that manages print queues on a Linux print server. The lpd program accepts the print job and directs it to the correct printer. It also monitors print queues and directs print jobs from print queues to multiple printers.

Linux shell   Operates as a command interpreter and takes the input that the administrator enters and uses it to launch commands and control the operating system.

login privilege   A rule that states what kind of rights a user is granted when he accesses the system.

main console   Functions identically to a terminal window, except that it runs in the background, which allows users to switch their displays to the full-screen main console when running X.

man page   A help file that displays detailed information about any Linux command available to the user.

NFS   Used to share files between multiple computer systems connected on a network. However, the main difference with NFS is that it is designed to work on UNIX systems.

permission   The file system controls who has permission to access files and run programs.

printtool   A GUI tool that can be used to set up printers and print queues in Red Hat.

runlevel Controls what predetermined set of programs will run on the computer when the system starts up. Some programs run only at specific runlevels. What runlevel the system is booted up in determines what programs are loaded on the system.

superserver A server that listens for requests for any of the daemons and services on the server. It loads the daemon or service into memory only when a request has been made and it is in use.

superuser account Also called the root account. The account that the system administrator uses to perform administrative tasks on a Linux system.

syslogd This daemon records information about currently running programs to the system log file.

system configuration file Controls settings for the entire system. A file that controls services that are set to run for each user who logs in to the system.

Sys V script A script that is used to automatically start, stop, or restart Linux daemons when the system is booted.

terminal window Also called xterm. Displays a standard Linux command prompt in a small window on the screen so that a command can be entered.

user and group IDs Numbers that the Linux operating system uses to identify a user or group.

user configuration file Stores information that is specific to an individual user, such as desktop icon placements, window manager preferences, and scripts that are set to run automatically.

username The name that identifies the person logged on to the system.

vi Editor A powerful editing tool with which you can edit configuration and script files and create some configuration and script files.

Objectives

After completing this chapter, you will be able to complete tasks related to

- Performing backups to ensure data security
- Sharing resources by mapping drives on the network
- Using Linux utilities to manage partitions and file systems
- Monitoring resources on network servers
- Analyzing and optimizing network performance
- Network monitoring software

Chapter 11

Advanced NOS Administration

A system administrator is required to protect the information that is stored on network servers. This is accomplished by performing a regular procedure called a system backup. This chapter covers the types of backups you can do. In addition, you will learn how to map a drive to provide users with access to information stored on network servers. Monitoring the system is a required task that allows the administrator to keep track of resources, including disk management, CPU usage, and memory usage. This chapter also covers the key concepts of analyzing and optimizing the network. With this information, you can implement problem-solving guidelines in the troubleshooting process.

Backups

This section covers the following topics:

- Overview of backup methods
- Installing backup software
- Backup hardware
- Backup strategies
- Automating backups

Overview of Backup Methods

One of the most important duties of a system administrator is to protect the information that is stored on network servers. This data can be damaged in many ways, including human error, hardware failure, software problems, and even natural disasters. Sometimes users of a network accidentally delete important data stored on a server. It is the system administrator's job to attempt to restore these lost files. Such recovery is made possible through a regular procedure called a system *backup*.

The backup process involves copying data from one computer to another reliable storage medium for safekeeping. After the data has been archived by such a device, the system administrator can restore the data to the system from any previously recorded backup. These alternative storage devices do not need to be extremely fast or easily accessible. Other considerations are more relevant:

- **Cost**—Backups are performed quite often and require cost-effective storage. Fortunately, with the rapid advances in modern technology, storage devices are becoming both faster and cheaper.
- **Size**—Servers typically can store extremely large amounts of data. As a result, it is important to select a backup format that provides comparable storage capacity.
- **Manageability**—Despite their importance, system administrators cannot afford to spend multiple hours each day on system backups. Each device must be efficient and easily managed to help accommodate the process.
- **Reliability**—System backup is beneficial only if the data can be successfully restored at some point in the future. If a storage medium easily wears out or becomes unreadable, the effort taken to back up the system is wasted.

Commonly used backup devices include tape drives, removable disk drives, recordable compact disc (CD-R) drives, and other hard drives. Figure 11-1 shows the most common backup devices that are available. These devices vary. System administrators should select the appropriate tools to meet their particular needs.

Figure 11-1 Common Backup Devices

CD-RW Drive

HP ex2 Hard Drive

HP Superstore Ultrium 215

Large system backups can be very time-consuming and are usually performed only for critical computers, such as network servers. To avoid tying up precious server resources, backups are usually run during off-peak network hours (usually in the middle of the night). They are most effective when performed at regular intervals and are commonly scheduled as often as once a day. Without a regular schedule of system backups, the potential risk of losing data is much greater.

 Worksheet 11.1.1   Overview of Backup Methods

Learn some of the basic concepts and uses of system backups.

Types of Backups

The most common type of backup procedure consists of the administrator's placing a backup tape in a tape drive and copying the data to a *tape backup*. Four types of backup procedures define how the backup will take place. For example, the administrator can specify which data is backed up and at what points that data gets backed up. The backups use a type of backup *marker* that serves as an archive attribute that marks a file when it has changed since the last time the file was backed up. The backup method can use this attribute to determine whether to back up the file. When the file is backed up, the attribute is cleared.

Full

A *full backup*, also called a normal backup, backs up everything on the hard drive at the scheduled point in the day. It does this every day. A full backup does not use the previously mentioned markers or archive attributes to determine which files to back up. When a full backup is performed, every file marker is cleared and marked as being backed up. Normal backups speed up the restoration process because the backup files are the most current.

Partial

A *partial backup* backs up selected files. Partial backup types include copy backup and daily backup. A *copy backup* backs up any files and folders that an administrator selects to be backed up. This type of partial backup is useful for backups that can be done without clearing the markers. A copy backup does not find and clear markers. A *daily backup* is a useful partial backup method that an administrator can perform to select all the files and folders that have changed during the day.

Incremental

In an *incremental backup*, only the files that have changed since the last backup are selected to be backed up. The files are selected based on whether they have changed recently. They aren't selected arbitrarily based on directory names or filenames.

Differential

A *differential backup* backs up files created or changed since the last normal or incremental backup. It does not mark files as having been backed up. A differential backup does not clear the markers. All files, even those that have not changed since the last backup, are backed up.

Installing Backup Software

The following sections discuss how to perform backups in Windows 2000 and Linux.

Installing Backups

Windows 2000 comes with its own backup software produced by Veritas. Veritas' new release with Windows 2000 is much more powerful, useful, and versatile and offers many more backup features than its predecessor, Windows NT. For more information on Veritas and what it has to offer in Windows 2000, visit http://www.veritas.com.

Some NOSs provide a rudimentary backup system that is not feature-rich. This lack of features often requires the purchase of a third-party backup software package. Be sure the backup software is certified with the operating system you are using. For example, if you were using Windows 2000 Server as your operating system, you would check the backup software to see if it is Windows 2000-certified. This ensures that the Registry is properly backed up. When you install the third-party backup software, follow the vendor's installation instructions.

Backups in Windows 2000

With the release of Windows 2000, the backup utility that existed with Windows NT was greatly enhanced. It is now the tool used (rather than RDISK) to back up the Registry. No longer confined to only tapes as output media, it now offers a number of other possibilities. Figure 11-2 shows the backup utility in Windows 2000.

Figure 11-2   Windows 2000 Backup Utility

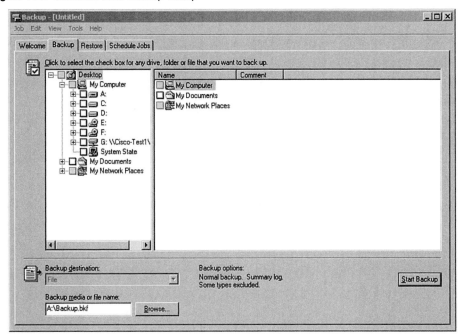

To perform a backup in Windows 2000, follow these steps:

Step 1   Select Start > Programs > Accessories > System Tools > Backup.

Step 2   Choose the Backup tab, and select the files or directories you want to back up.

Step 3   Specify a backup medium (destination) for the backup, and then click Start Backup.

Lab 11.1.5a   Backing Up with Windows 2000

In this exercise, you use the Backup Wizard from Windows 2000 to perform a backup of files to your hard disk.

Backups in Linux

Linux includes two utilities you can use to perform backups: tar and cpio. The *tar* (tape archiver) utility combines multiple files into a single file that can be copied to the medium. The syntax for tar is as follows:

```
tar {options}{target_.le}{source_.les}
```

Both the target file and source file can be paths (such as /dev/tape). This command's options are as follows:

- **c**—Creates a new file.
- **d**—Compares the contents and displays the differences between the target and the source.
- **f**—Specifies a file.
- **p**—Keeps the permissions.
- **r**—Appends to an existing file.
- **t**—Shows the names of the files in the tar file.
- **u**—Adds only files that are new.
- **v**—Runs in verbose mode.
- **x**—Extracts files.
- **z**—Compresses files.

The following command creates a new tar file on the tape in verbose mode:

```
tar cvf /dev/tape {.les}
```

This command extracts and restores the files from the feb.tar backup file:

```
tar  xf  feb.tar
```

The cpio utility is used to copy in and out. It can perform three basic actions, one of which must be specified:

- **-i**—Extracts from an archive.
- **-o**—Makes a new archive.
- **-p**—Prints/passes (through the files).

You can use the following options with the cpio utility:

- **d**—Creates directories, if necessary.
- **f**—Specifies a file.
- **t**—Shows the contents.
- **u**—Overwrites existing files.
- **v**—Runs in verbose mode.

The following command reads files from a tape and displays them as it is operating in verbose mode:

```
cpio -iv </dev/tape
```

This command finds all the files on the system that start with "kad" and copies them to the /home/kad directory, creating all the needed subdirectories in the process:

```
.nd /-name kad* | cpio -pdv /home/kad
```

 Lab 11.1.5b   Backing Up with Linux

Use the backup utilities provided by the Linux operating system to perform a backup of directories and files on your hard disk.

Backup Hardware

When you perform a backup (copying the data and software on a network server), some backup hardware must be available on the network server. The most common backup hardware device (historically and now) is some form of magnetic tape drive. Other backup hardware devices can be used for backup operations, but these are much less common than tape drives.

A backup hardware device is a required part of any network server installation. Backup hardware devices can be expensive. However, the consequences of not having a backup hardware device on a network server, and thus not having a backup copy of its data and software, can be far more expensive.

Tape Drives

Tape drives are most commonly used as the device for backing up the data on a network server's disk drives. Tape devices are known for their long-lasting performance, which is partly due to the tape drive mechanics that some systems include. A variety of tape devices use different tape formats to store data. Many tape drives can also compress the data before it is stored on the tape. In most cases, the compression ratio is 2:1. This has the effect of doubling the tape's storage capacity.

Quarter-Inch Cartridge

In 1972 3M created the *quarter-inch cartridge* (QIC, pronounced "quick") tape standard. As the name implies, the tape used in QIC is one-quarter-inch wide. There have been many versions of QIC tape drives over the years. Table 11-1 summarizes QIC standards. Early QIC tape drives attached to the computer's floppy disk controller. Later versions could be attached to the computer's parallel port. Still-later versions used the IDE hard disk drive interface. The QIC standard has limited storage capacity and is used only in entry-level network servers.

Table 11-1 QIC Tape Standards

QIC Standard	QIC Cartridge	Storage Capacity (Native/Compressed)	Interface
QIC-40	DC-2000	40 MB/80 MB	Floppy
QIC-40	DC-2060	60 MB/120 MB	Floppy
QIC-80	MC-2120	125 MB/250 MB	Floppy, parallel
QIC-80	MC-2120Extra	400 MB/800 MB	Floppy, parallel
QIC-80XL	MC-2120XL	170 MB/340 MB	Floppy, parallel
QIC-3020XL	MC-3020Xl	680 MB/1.36 GB	Floppy, parallel, IDE
QIC-3020XL	MC-3020Extra	1.6 GB/3.2 GB	Floppy, parallel, IDE
QIC-3095	MC-3095	4 GB/8 GB	IDE, SCSI-2
QIC-3220	MC-3220	10 GB/20 GB	SCSI-2
QIC-5010	DC-5010	16 GB/32 GB	SCSI-2
QIC-5210	DC-5210	25 GB/50 GB	SCSI-2

Travan Cartridge Tape

A 3M spin-off company, Imation, introduced the *Travan cartridge tape* standard in 1994. Travan is based on QIC technology. In many cases it is either read-compatible or read/write-compatible with QIC tape cartridges. Travan tape drives have a higher storage capacity than the older QIC tape drives. Travan's most recent standard implemented was hardware compression. It frees up a server's processor, allowing the processor to execute other tasks at the same time. Travan tape drives have the capacity to back up low-end network servers but are relatively slow. Their backup speed is about 1 MBps. Table 11-2 summarizes the Travan tape standards.

Table 11-2 Travan Tape Standards

Travan Standard	Tape Cartridge	Storage Capacity (Native/Compressed)	Interface
Travan-1	TR-1	400 MB/800 MB	Floppy, parallel
Travan-2	TR-2	800 MB/1.6 GB	Floppy, parallel
Travan-3	TR-3	1.6 GB/3.2 GB	Floppy, parallel

Table 11-2 Travan Tape Standards (Continued)

Travan Standard	Tape Cartridge	Storage Capacity (Native/Compressed)	Interface
Travan-4	TR-4	4 GB/8 GB	SCSI-2, EIDE
Travan NS-8	NS-8	4 GB/8 GB	SCSI-2, EIDE
Travan-5	TR-5	10 GB/20 GB	SCSI-2, EIDE
Travan NS-20	NS-20	10 GB/20 GB	SCSI-2, EIDE

8mm Tape

Exabyte Corporation pioneered tape technology that uses 8mm tape. The technology uses a tape similar to 8mm videotape and the same helical scan system used by a VCR. Table 11-3 reviews 8mm tape technologies.

Table 11-3 8mm Tape Technologies

8mm Tape Technology	Storage Capacity (Native/Compressed)	Transfer Speed
8200	2.5 GB/5 GB	246 KBps
8500	5 GB/10 GB	500 KBps

Mammoth 8mm tape technologies are an improvement over the original 8mm tape technologies, with higher storage capacities and faster transfer speeds. Table 11-4 reviews Mammoth 8mm tape technologies.

Table 11-4 Mammoth 8mm Tape Technologies

Mammoth Technology	Storage Capacity (Native/Compressed)	Transfer Speed
Mammoth-1	20 GB/40 GB	3 MBps
Mammoth-2	60 GB/120 GB	12 MBps

Advanced Intelligent Tape

Advanced Intelligent Tape (AIT) technology, developed by Sony, was introduced in 1996. AIT technology uses 8mm tapes that use helical scan recording hardware (much like a VCR). AIT tapes have memory in the tape cartridge, known as *memory in cassette (MIC)*, which stores the tape log to facilitate locating a file during a restore operation. Table 11-5 summarizes AIT tape standards.

Table 11-5 AIT Tape Standards

AIT Standard	Tape Medium	Storage Capacity (Native/Compressed)	Transfer Speed
AIT-1	SDX125C	25 GB/50 GB	3 MBps
AIT-1	SDX135C	35 GB/70 GB	3 MBps
AIT-2	SDX236C	36 GB/72 GB	6 MBps
AIT-2	SDX250C	50 GB/100 GB	6 MBps
AIT-3	Prototype	100 GB/200 GB	12 MBps

NOTE

For more information about AIT technology, see the AIT Forum website at www.aittape.com.

Digital Audio Tape

The *Digital Audio Tape (DAT)* tape standard uses 4mm digital audiotapes to store data in *Digital Data Storage (DDS)* format. There are currently four different DDS standards. Table 11-6 summarizes them.

Table 11-6 DAT Tape Standards

DDS Format	Storage Capacity (Native/Compressed)	Transfer Speed	Also Known As
DDS-1	2 GB/4 GB	1 MBps	—
DDS-2	4 GB/8 GB	1 MBps	DAT8
DDS-3	12 GB/24 GB	2 MBps	DAT24
DDS-4	20 GB/40 GB	6 MBps	DAT40

Digital Linear Tape

Digital Linear Tape (DLT) technology offers high-capacity and relatively high-speed tape backup capabilities. DLT tapes record information on the tape in a linear format, unlike 8mm tape technologies, which use helical scan recording techniques. DLT tape drives support high storage capacity. Depending on the medium used, DLT allows up to 70 GB of compressed data, along with a fast transfer speed. However, DLT tape drives are expensive. Table 11-7 compares DLT tape formats.

Table 11-7 DLT Tape Formats

DLT Standard	Storage Capacity (Native/Compressed)	Transfer Speed
DLT-2000	10 GB/20 GB	1.25 MBps
DLT-2000XT	15 GB/30 GB	1.25 MBps
DLT-4000	20 GB/40 GB	1.5 MBps
DLT-7000	35 GB/70 GB	5 MBps
DLT-8000	40 GB/80 GB	6 MBps
Super DLT	110 GB/220 GB	11 MBps

Linear Tape-Open

Hewlett-Packard, IBM, and Seagate developed the *Linear Tape-Open (LTO)* technology. LTO comes in two distinct forms: one designed for high storage capacity (Ultrium), and one designed for fast access (Accelis). Table 11-8 reviews the LTO tape formats.

Table 11-8 LTO Tape Formats

LTO Format	Storage Capacity (Native/Compressed)	Transfer Speed (Native/Compressed)
Ultrium	100 GB/200 GB	20 MBps/40 MBps
Accelis	25 GB/50 GB	20 MBps/40 MBps

Tape Arrays

Several network server vendors offer an array of tape drives with fault-tolerant characteristics. Most of these technologies use four identical tape drives and implement the tape version of RAID, which is called *redundant array of independent tapes (RAIT)*. RAIT can be used to mirror tape drives, or (with at least three tape drives) it can be implemented as data striping with parity. The result is that if a tape is damaged or lost, data recovery can still occur.

NOTE

For more information about LTO tape technology, see the LTO website at www.lto-technology.com.

Tape Autochangers

A *tape autochanger* (also called a *tape autoloader*) allows the tape drive to load a new tape when the current tape gets full while performing a backup. This relieves the operator from having to remove one tape and insert a new one. This is very handy, because backups are usually performed in the dead of night. Most tape autochangers support unloading and loading a limited number of tapes (ten or fewer).

Tape Libraries

A *tape library* is usually an external system that has multiple tape drives, tens or hundreds of tapes, and an automatic mechanism for locating the tapes, loading them into the tape drives, and returning them to the proper location. With all this intelligence and sophistication, it should be obvious that tape libraries are the high end of backup systems. In other words, they are expensive.

Disk Drives

Disk drives can also be used for backup operations. Performing a backup to a disk drive is faster than performing a backup to a tape drive. However, unless the backup disk drives can be hot-swapped, there is no provision for off-site storage of the backup. Having the backup hard disk drive in the same room as the network server doesn't provide much protection in the event that the network server room is destroyed by fire.

Other Backup Devices

Some sites use other devices for backup, such as CD-Recordable (CD-R) or CD-Rewritable (CD-RW) compact discs. Although these are acceptable backup devices, the writing of compact discs is a relatively slow operation, and the slowness might not be acceptable in all environments.

 Worksheet 11.1.3 Backup Hardware

Identify the basic concepts and uses of backup hardware.

Backup Strategies

Several backup strategies prevent data loss resulting from power outages, disk drive failures, virus infections, and other problems. When you implement careful planning and reliable equipment, file recovery is much less time-consuming. Normal, incremental, or differential backup combinations make up your backup strategy. A backup strategy doesn't just involve developing a plan of when to perform the backup and which type to use. You also need to consider how often you need to test the data and the equipment to verify that it is all working correctly. Also, you need to be sure that you have all the data that is important to the users and that needs to be backed up. You do not want someone to ask if a certain file can be restored if you do not have it archived for backing up.

Grandfather-Father-Son Backup Method

There are several accepted backup strategies, and many of them are based on the popular Grandfather-Father-Son method (also called Child-Parent-Grandparent). With this backup strategy you use three sets of tapes for daily, weekly, and monthly backups. Here is how to implement this method:

- **Son backup**—Label four tapes "Monday" through "Thursday." Son tapes use the incremental backup method. They can be reused weekly on the day they are labeled.

- **Father backup**—Label five tapes "Week 1" through "Week 5." These tapes are used only once a week on Friday; you do not do a Son backup on this day. Depending on your policy, it is recommended that you make a duplicate of a Father tape periodically to store offsite. Some software allows you to have another drive set up so that you can simultaneously make a copy.

- **Grandfather backup**—A good naming scheme is "Month 1" through "Month 3." The tapes are valid for three months and are reused every quarter. The Grandfather backup uses the normal backup method, done the last business day of the month.

For the Grandfather-Father-Son backup method, the number of tapes required in each media set varies depending on how much data you need to back up. Of course, you can modify the method to suit your needs and requirements, but this is a reliable and logical place to start.

Six-Cartridge Weekly Backup Method

A simpler and more cost-effective implementation of Grandfather-Father-Son is the six-cartridge weekly backup. Perfect for small businesses, this backup strategy requires daily backups and a single weekly off-site backup copy to provide a data history of up to two weeks. Friday backups are full backups. Monday-through-Thursday backups are incremental.

Here are the steps to perform a six-cartridge weekly backup:

Step 1   Label six cartridges FRI 1, FRI 2, MON, TUE, WED, and THU.

Step 2   On Friday, start backing up the entire hard disk onto cartridge FRI 1.

Step 3   On Monday, use the MON cartridge and do an incremental backup, which means only the files that have been created or modified since the last backup (FRI 1). This tape should be stored on-site.

Step 4   Repeat Step 3 using the incremental method on Tuesday, Wednesday, and Thursday. Use the corresponding cartridges.

Step 5   On Friday, take data cartridge FRI 2 and perform the second full backup. You have just completed a full rotation. Be sure to store this data cartridge off-site.

Step 6   The weekly process continues by repeating Steps 3 and 4 using the same MON, TUE, WED, and THU data cartridges. Implement Step 5 by alternating cartridges FRI 1 and FRI 2 and taking them to an off-site location.

The Tower of Hanoi

This method uses five sets of media for the rotation. Label them A, B, C, D, and E, and follow these steps:

Step 1   The first day, back up to A. Reuse the A tape every other day.

Step 2   The second day, back up to B. Reuse the B tape every four days.

Step 3   The fourth day, back up to C. Reuse the C tape every eight days.

Step 4   The eighth day, back up to D. Reuse the D tape every 16 days.

Step 5   The sixteenth day, back up to E. Reuse the E tape every 32 days.

The Tower of Hanoi requires only five tapes, assuming that you do not exceed the capacity of one backup. You also might consider making tape E an off-site tape. If you want two months of backup, you can use one more tape. Call it F and use it every 64 days. You can keep adding tapes for as much history as you want to back up.

Documenting the Backup

Having the records of the backup history makes it easier to locate the correct tape(s) to restore the files if the system goes down—especially if your company has a large number of tapes stored. Here are some good backup documentation tips:

- Be sure to label each cartridge with the appropriate criteria, such as backup date, type of backup (whether it was normal, incremental, or differential), and what information it contains. A well-labeled tape is easier to locate when you need to reuse it or restore it.

- The names of all backed-up and restored files and directories are stored as log files. These log files can be very useful when you restore the data. You can read or print the file from any text editor. Keeping the printed logs is a good idea to help you stay organized. This saves you time when you're trying to locate a specific file.

- Most of the software that comes with the backup system includes a mechanism for cataloging the backed-up files. The catalog is typically stored on the tape itself and is temporarily loaded into memory. These catalogs are created for each set or collection of backups.

Verifying the Backup

Before you attempt any upgrade operation, *always* fully back up the entire network server. It cannot be overstated how important a full backup of the entire system is for the successful completion of an upgrade. You also should verify the backup. During verification, you check the tape's contents against the corresponding files on the disk drives. Verifying the backup is usually an option that you can select as part of the backup process. Verification effectively doubles the time it takes to perform a backup, but you get the assurance that the contents of the disk drives and the backup tapes match exactly.

Automating Backups

You should perform system backups at regular intervals to provide consistent data protection. These routine backups can be extremely time-consuming if a system administrator must manually attend to every step of the backup process. Thus, the automation of such regularly scheduled events is an important backup consideration. Automation not only increases backup consistency but also grants system administrators more time to address other pressing network issues.

Depending on the size of the system data, this automation can range from a simple software solution to intricate robotic devices. The type of automation needed also varies, depending on the selected backup device. For example, if data is regularly backed up to another network hard drive, the automation process can be implemented very easily using standard backup software. However, if a server routinely backs up vast quantities of data to a tape drive, a mechanical tape-changing device might also be necessary to fully automate a single backup process. The most common automated backup procedure consists of a system administrator's inserting a tape into the drive at the end of the day. The system performs the regularly scheduled nightly backup of data onto the tape, and then the system administrator ejects that tape the next day and stores it for a predetermined period of time. This pattern can be repeated indefinitely, and the previously used tapes are eventually circulated back into the rotation. Specific methods of performing automated backups in both Windows 2000 and Linux are discussed in the following sections.

Drive Mapping

This section covers the following topics:

- What is drive mapping?
- Mapping drives in Windows networks
- Mapping drives in Linux networks
- Mapping drives in Novell networks

What Is Drive Mapping?

Drive mapping is a useful tool that allows an administrator to share resources that are stored on a server. The client computers that are connected to the network assign a drive letter that acts as a direct path to access those resources stored on a server over the network. Figure 11-3 shows an example of a mapped network drive on a Windows operating system. After a user identifies a network resource to be used locally, the resource can be "mapped" as a drive. Mapping is a two-stage process that requires first defining the path to the network resource and then assigning a drive letter to that resource. Drive letters are locally significant only, which means that the same network resource could be represented by different drive letters on different client computers.

Figure 11-3 Mapped Network Drive

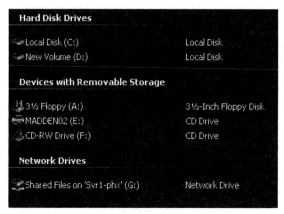

  Worksheet 11.2.4 Drive Mappings

Learn the uses for and benefits of mapping drives in a network operating system.

Mapping Drives in Windows Networks

You can map a network drive in the Windows NOS in one of two ways:

- By using Windows Explorer
- By using the **net use** command

Mapping a Drive with Windows Explorer

To map a drive with Windows Explorer, shown in Figure 11-4, navigate to the folder on the remote system in Explorer by selecting Network > Neighborhood > *Server name* > *Shared folder name*. Another way to do this is to choose Tools > Map Network Drive. You see the dialog box shown in Figure 11-5. Note that if Internet Explorer 4.0 or a later version is installed, another option is to right-click the shared folder name in Explorer and then choose Map Network Drive from the context menu.

Figure 11-4 Windows Explorer

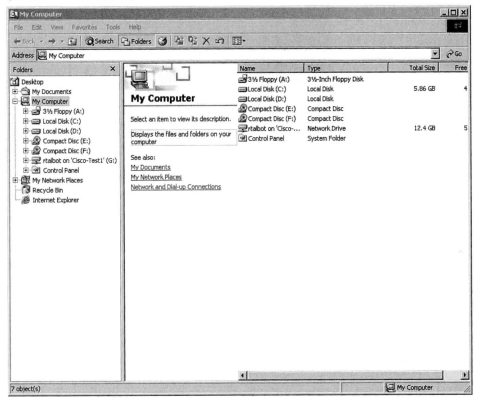

Figure 11-5 Map Network Drive Option

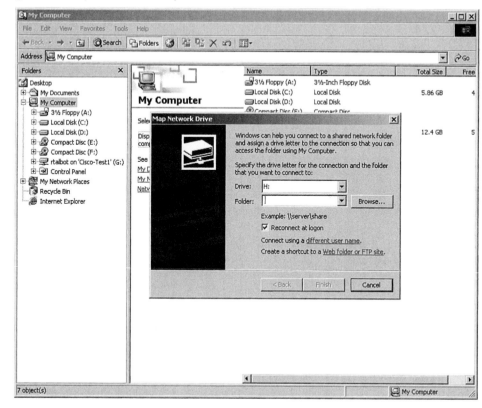

The mapped drive appears as the assigned drive letter in the left pane of Explorer, along with the floppy and CD drives and hard disk partitions. It can be accessed from Windows Explorer, My Computer, or from the desktop if a shortcut has been created.

Mapping a Drive with the **net use** Command

Another way to map a drive in Windows operating systems is to use the Universal Naming Convention (UNC) path. You identify the shared drive by using the following syntax:

`\\computername\ sharename`

To map a network drive to the shared resource, enter the following at the command prompt:

`net use driveletter: \\computername\ sharename`

You can use the **net use** command instead of mapping drives through Windows Explorer. **net use** can also be incorporated into a login script that automatically runs when the user logs in to the network.

Mapping Drives in Linux Networks

You map a drive to a Linux server using one of two methods, depending on the operating system being used by the client machine that is mapping the drive. If the clients are using Windows, the Samba daemon needs to be loaded onto the Linux server. The Samba daemon loads the SMB protocol, which allows communication between Linux and Windows computers. After the Samba daemon has been loaded and has configured the proper directories to be shared, the Windows clients can map a drive to the shared directory on the Linux server, just as if they were connected to a Windows server. The user would follow the steps just outlined to map to the shared directory. In essence, the SMB protocol makes the Windows client believe it is connected to a Windows server.

A client computer running Linux must be mapped in a slightly different way. First, use the **mount** command to establish a connection to the shared directory on the server. Entering the following syntax maps a drive to a Linux/UNIX share:

```
mount servername:/directory/ subdirectory/ localdirectory
```

The local directory designation that points to the remote share denoted by the first part of the command is called the *directory mount point*. The mount point location must exist before a share can be mapped to it. This means that the mount point must first be established on the Linux server that will share the resources.

Mapping Drives in Novell Networks

Just as with Linux, you can map a drive to a share on a NetWare server using Windows Explorer. If the NetWare client machines are running Windows 95, 98, NT, 2000, or XP, follow the process for mapping drives on a Windows network that was described previously.

Also, you can map a drive at the command line by using the **map** command. The syntax is as follows:

```
map driveletter:= server \ volume: directory \ subdirectory
```

This **map** command can also be put in a login script that executes automatically as the user logs in to the network.

The Novell client software also has drive-mapping functionality that allows a drive to be mapped as a root drive or a search drive.

Partition and Process Management

This section covers the following topics:

- Using fdisk, mkfs, and fsck
- Managing system processes with cron jobs
- Core dumps
- Critical and noncritical processes
- Assigning permissions for processes

Using fdisk, mkfs, and fsck

In Chapter 9, "Linux Installation Procedures," you learned about partitioning and using the partitioning tools to create Linux partitions during installation. This section focuses on managing partitions and the file systems that are stored on them. The main tools in a Linux system that are used to manage disk partitions are the fdisk, mkfs, and fsck utilities.

The fdisk Utility

Chapter 7, "Installation and Boot Process Overview," covered the fdisk utility. You learned the basics of what fdisk does, but the details of how to use fdisk and all the options that are available with it were not covered. You might be familiar with the other version of FDISK that is used with Windows or DOS operating systems. Linux's version of fdisk is similar in that it is a partitioning tool native to Linux. However, the version that is included with Linux operates very differently than the version used with Windows and DOS systems.

Like most Linux utilities, fdisk is text-based and has one-letter options. To obtain a list of fdisk's options, enter **m** or **?** at the **fdisk** prompt. Some of the most commonly used options are as follows:

- **d**—Deletes a partition.
- **n**—Creates a new partition.
- **p**—Prints or displays the partition layout.
- **q**—Ends the session without saving any changes.
- **t**—Changes a partition's type code.
- **w**—Saves the changes made and quits.

The command syntax to use fdisk is fairly simple. You must use the **fdisk** command along with the particular device filename associated with the partition. For example, you must issue the following command before you use any of the options:

```
fdisk /dev/hda2
```

After you enter this command, it is a good idea to first use the **p** option to display information about the partition so that you know all the current information before making any changes. From this point, you can use any of the options to make changes to the partition. Keep in mind that is it a good idea to know what information is on the partition and to back it up first, because as soon as the partition is deleted, so is its data. Some of the options require additional information, such as when you are creating new partitions. You need to enter information about the new partition's parameters.

The mkfs Utility

Creating a new partition or changing a partition is only the first step in partition management. After you have made the partition changes, you must create a file system on the partition. This is called *formatting* the partition. To create a file system in Linux, you use the mkfs utility. mkfs was mentioned in Chapter 9. The details of this utility are described in detail in this section.

The syntax for the mkfs utility is as follows:

```
mkfs [-V] [-t fstype] [options] device [blocks]
```

Here are the parameters for this command:

- -V—Displays additional output as the file system is created.
- -t *fstype*—Specifies the file system type that will be created. *fstype* would be something like **ext3** for an ext3 file system or **msdos** for a FAT file system.
- *options*—Specifies options specific to the particular file system.
- *device*—Specifies the device on which you will create the file system. Usually this is the same parameter you use with the **fdisk** command.
- *blocks*—Specifies the size of the file system's blocks (usually 1024 bytes). This value does not always need to be used, because the block size can be determined from the size of the partition.

After you issue this command, the file system or formatting process begins. This process can take a short time or a long time depending on the partition's size and whether a file system check was specified. When this process is complete, the partition is ready to store data.

The fsck Utility

The fdisk and mkfs utilities are important to know, because as an administrator eventually you will have to either install a new hard drive or partition a new hard drive, as well as format the drive or partition. However, you will seldom use these two utilities. You will use the fsck utility much more often. It is used to check file systems for errors, which occur more frequently than the need to add, remove, or format partitions.

Many things can cause a file system to become corrupt. Operating system bugs, viruses, power failures, and hardware failures can all corrupt data on a disk or partition. These file system errors can go unnoticed. If nothing is done about them, they can eventually cause severe data loss. This is why it is a good idea to use fsck often to check for file system integrity. The syntax and parameters that are used with fsck are as follows:

`fsck [-sACVRTNP][-t fstype][--][fsck-options] filesystems`

- -A—Specifies that all file systems marked in /etc/fstab will be checked.
- -C—Displays a text-mode progress indicator while the file system is being checked.
- -V—Displays additional output as the file system is checked.
- -N—Displays the results of what fsck would do without actually doing it.
- -- *fsck-options*—Specifies file system check options that fsck cannot interpret. Examples are **-a** and **-p**, which perform an automatic check; **-r**, which performs an interactive check; and **-f**, which forces a full system check.
- *filesystems*—Specifies which file system is being checked.

Normally fsck is used with the *filesystems* option, and any other parameters can be used as needed. Some other important things to know about file system checks are that in ext2 file systems, a check is performed during startup when the system has not been shut down properly. Also, if they system has gone longer than 6 months without a check, the system performs one automatically. Sometimes an automatic check occurs if the file system has been mounted more than 20 times since the last check.

Newer file systems such as ext3, XFS, and ReiserFS do not perform file system checks during startup even if the system was not shut down properly. These types of file systems use a *journaling system,* which keeps a log of operations that need to be performed if the system crashes or a power failure occurs. These pending operations can be done or undone to keep the file system's integrity intact. This process is done automatically every time the file system is mounted. Keep in mind that these file systems still need to have check programs such as fsck run periodically in case other things should occur, such as an operating system bug, a virus, a power failure, or a hardware failure.

Managing System Processes with cron Jobs

You schedule tasks to run at regular intervals on a Linux system with *cron programs,* also known as cron jobs. Cron programs schedule system maintenance tasks that are performed automatically. For example, the /tmp directory get filled with useless files created by users who log in to the system. It is possible to schedule a task that empties this directory at scheduled times.

cron's Responsibility

Cron is controlled by the entries in the /var/spool/cron and /etc/cron.d directories and the /etc/crontab file. It executes its commands if an entry in these files tells it to do so. Cron is not a command. It is a daemon that runs constantly in the background like an FTP or HTTP server. As it runs, it scans the system for events that might enable it. The cron daemon works slightly differently than other daemons in that it runs once every minute, scans the three configuration files just mentioned, and performs any tasks specified in those files.

The first type of cron job that can be scheduled is the *system cron job*. These jobs consist of essential system maintenance tasks that keep the system running as efficiently as possible. These tasks include cleaning out the /tmp directory on a regular basis. Another example of a system cron job is *log rotation,* which changes the names of the log files and deletes old log files routinely to prevent them from growing too large for the hard drive.

The second type of cron job is a *user cron job*. Regular users can create user cron jobs to perform certain functions that they need to be run for a specific program they use. In contrast, system cron jobs can only be run as root. However, it can be useful to run a user cron job as root to run a task during a time that is specified by the administrator. System cron jobs tend to be fairly rigid in the time in which they are scheduled to run, leaving very little flexibility. User cron jobs can be run in a much more flexible manner.

Creating a System cron Job

System cron jobs are controlled via the /etc/crontab file, which is shown in Figure 11-6. The file begins with a set of environment variables. These set certain parameters for the cron jobs, such as PATH and MAILTO, which specify whose address the job's output is mailed to. The other lines in this file specify things such as the minute, hour, day, month, and day of the week that the system cron job runs. Keep in mind that these time values are entered using the 24-hour clock. These values are indicated by the numbers you see in Figure 11-6. The asterisks (*) indicate that all possible values of the variable will take effect.

Figure 11-6 /etc/crontab File

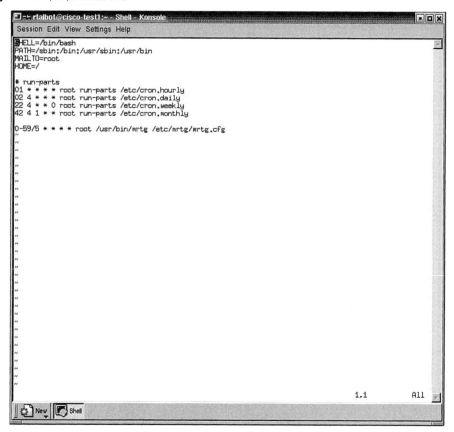

The next variable in this file indicates the account name that is used to run the program. For example, in Figure 11-6, root is indicated, which is usually the case in a system cron job. The last variable indicates which command to run. **run-parts /etc/cron.daily** is one of the commands that is run in this job. According to Figure 11-6, all the scripts in /etc/cron.daily will be run at 4:02 a.m. every day. Using this example, it is easy to understand how to create system cron jobs. You should model other system cron jobs after existing cron jobs. If you need a job to run at a different time than is specified in this file, just edit it or create a user cron job, as explained in the next section.

Creating a User cron Job

User cron jobs are created using the crontab utility. It is not to be confused with the /etc/crontab file; they are two different things. The crontab utility is a command that is entered at the prompt. Its syntax is as follows:

```
crontab [-u user] [-l | -e | -r] [file]
```

The crontab utility can be used with or without the **-u** *user* parameter. If this parameter is used, a user cron job is created for the user specified in the parameter. If no user is specified, the user cron job is created for the current user. It is a good practice on a Linux system to always use the **-u** *user* parameter to specify which user the cron job will be created for. For example, you could use the **su** command to change to the current user and then enter the **crontab** command without the **-u** *user* parameter. However, this sometimes confuses the crontab utility and can produce unpredictable results. Therefore, it is recommended that you use the **-u** *user* parameter, even if you're creating a user cron job for yourself.

The other parameters associated with the crontab utility are used to view, edit, and create user cron jobs. Specifically, the -l, -e, and -r options are used to work on current user cron jobs. The -l option displays the current user cron job. The -e option opens an editor so that you can edit the current user cron job. The -r option removes the current cron job.

To create a new user cron job, enter the **crontab** command using the *file* parameter. For example, the command **crontab -u jsmith js-cronjbs** creates a new user cron job called **js-cronjbs** for jsmith's cron jobs. The syntax for creating a user cron job is the same as for creating a system cron job, which you learned about in the preceding section. Environment variables are still used to indicate where and how the job should be run. The syntax for creating a command to be run at a specific time is the same as well. The only difference is that you do not need to specify the username used to execute the cron job, because this information is already indicated by the cron job's owner.

Core Dumps

Another important aspect of managing processes on a Linux system is dealing with programs and software when they crash. Unfortunately, programs and software do not always run perfectly. Every once in a while they generate errors and cause the system to crash. Sometimes when this happens a *core file* is created. These core files are also called *core dumps*. It is important to understand what these files do and how to manage them, because they can help you find the programs that are generating errors or the users who might be causing them. As soon as the program has been identified, you can replace or repair it. Repairing the software requires advanced programming skills that go beyond the scope of this course. If you as an administrator or the user understands the programming language that the software is written in, you can attempt to repair the program without having to replace it. The core dump files can help identify what the problem is.

Understanding What a Core Dump Is

A core dump is a recording of the memory that a program was using when it crashed. Core dumps are created to allow programmers to study the file and figure out exactly what caused the program to crash. Without a core dump, there would be no way to go back and examine the state that caused the system to crash, because after the program crashes, all its processes are removed from memory. Programmers can study the debugging code to trace through the steps that led to the crash, making it easy to identify what caused the crash.

The size of the core dump depends on the size of the program that produced it. A large program that uses a lot of system resources and memory produces a core dump file much larger than a smaller program that uses less memory and system resources. In either case, however, the file is created in the same directory in which the program that crashed is located. In some cases, a core dump file is not created. For example, a user might not have write permissions to the directory, or there might be a limit to the size of core files that are generated. Limiting the size of a core file can be useful so that the directory's free space does not get used up. The syntax for limiting the size of core files is as follows:

```
ulimit -c [size]
```

The *size* parameter is specified in kilobytes. It ensures that no core file will be created larger than the specified size. If a core file is larger than the size specified, it is decreased to this size. Abbreviated core files are usually not very useful. If you specify 0 as the *size* parameter, no core files are generated. You can use the **unlimited** parameter to place no limits on the size of core files that are generated.

Locating and Deleting Core Files

Unless you have access to the root account on a Linux system, locating and deleting core files is a troublesome task. Without root account access, you can't access all the directories in which these files are located, so you won't have access to all the core files on a system. The command used to locate core files on a Linux system is as follows:

```
# find / -name core
```

It is important to keep in mind that this command returns some files and directories that are not necessarily core dump files. For example, /dev/core is a device file, and /proc/sys/net/core is a directory.

After you issue this command and locate the specific core files you are looking for, what do you do with them? As mentioned, unless you are familiar with the programming language that the program is written in, you won't understand most of the contents of this file. The content *is* useful to programmers who are familiar with the programming code used to create the file. However, an advantage of Linux is that most of the source code for the programs used on a Linux system is readily available to anyone who has the ambition to learn how to read it. Such people can debug the problems outlined in the core file.

A few things in these files might help you figure out what created the core file and whether the file is useful. For example, you might want to become familiar with the core file's **Owner, Creation Date**, and **Creating Program** properties.

The **Owner** of the file tells you who executed the program. Finding out the owner of the core file is useful when you're determining whether to delete the file. For example, if a user is writing programs to the system, and core files exist that have this user as their owner, it might be a good idea to check with that user before deleting the files, because he or she might need them for some reason.

The core file's **Creation Date** is simply the date on which the crash occurred and the core dump was created. Identifying the file's creation date is useful because it can further help you determine which files to delete or keep. Usually the older files are no longer of any use and can be deleted.

The **Creating Program** properties of core files tell you which program crashed and generated the core dump files. However, you find this out indirectly through the use of a different command. To find out which program created the core files, you must enter **gdb -c core**. This command launches the GNU debugger, which displays various output about the core file, including the program that crashed. To exit the GNU debugger, enter **exit**.

Be careful when moving or deleting any core files, because these core files and directories might not be the ones you're looking for. Deleting one of these files can cause other programs not to work. It is possible to include the **find** command in a user cron job. If the MAILTO environment variable is set properly, all the core files on the system will be reported every time the cron job is scheduled to run. It can be useful to generate this report once or twice a month to keep alert to any types of core files you might need to inspect.

Critical and Noncritical Processes

To effectively manage system processes on a Linux system, you must be able to determine what processes are running on a system and which process are critical and noncritical. This concept is important to understand in a Linux system because of the fact that Linux is a multiuser, multitasking system. A *process* on a Linux system is any program that is currently running. Because many users can be logged in to any one Linux system at one time, using the same program, it is possible for a Linux system to have two or more processes of the same program running at the same time. For example, if two users are logged in and both are using the vi Editor to edit a configuration file, the system would show that two processes of vi are currently running. A process is launched in a Linux system from the shell, and the shell in turn launches the process. This is called parent processes and child processes. The original process is the *parent process,* and any subprocess launched from within the parent process is a *child process*. This initial relationship can be traced back to the init program, which spawns the login process, which in turn spawns the shell in which commands are entered.

The **ps** Command

The processes that are currently running on a Linux system can be viewed using the **ps** command. This is one of the most important commands that an administrator needs to know concerning process management on a Linux system. It can be useful in monitoring what is happening on a Linux system. It can be particularly useful when the system is running slowly to kill processes that are consuming too much of the system's resources.

As with most Linux commands that have been covered in this course, the **ps** command has a variety of options that can manipulate its output:

- **-A, -e, -x**—If the **ps** command is issued by itself, it displays only the processes that are currently running in the terminal, which doesn't provide much information. The **-A** and **-e** options display all the processes that are currently running on the system. The **-x** option displays all the processes that are being used by the user who enters the command.

- **-u** *user*—This option lets you display all the processes being used by a specific user. You can enter the user's username or user ID.

- **-H, -f, -forest**—These options group processes in a hierarchy to show the parent-to-child relationship between processes.

- **-w**—By default, the **ps** command shortens its output so that everything can be displayed on the terminal screen. This option tells the **ps** command not to do this. This is helpful when you're redirecting the output to a text file, which accepts wide output and can be read. To redirect the output to a text file, enter **ps -w > ps .txt**. You can view the output using any text editor.

Note that these options can be used together to display the output you want.

ps Command Output

Considerable output can be generated when a command such as **ps -A --forest** is entered, as shown in Figure 11-7.

Figure 11-7 ps -A --forest Command

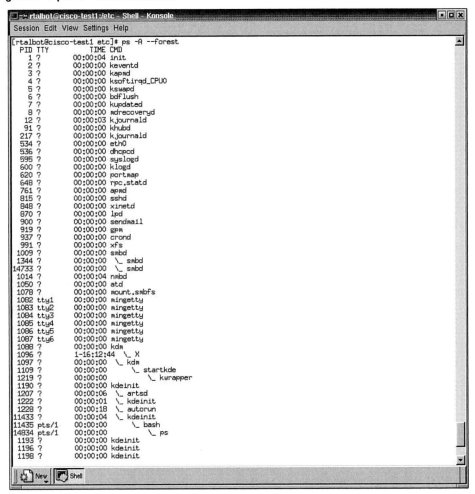

The **ps -A --forest** command displays important information:

- **Username**—This value does not appear in Figure 11-7. However, if the **-u** *user* option had been added, the corresponding username would precede the entries.

- **Process ID (PID)**—This is the process number that is used to identify the process. It is important because it is also used to terminate or kill a process, which is described in a moment.

- **Parent Process ID (PPID)**—This is the same as the PID, but it corresponds to the parent process. The PID refers to the child process.

- **TTY**—Identifies a terminal and is called the teletype. Not all processes have a TTY, such as daemons and X programs. Text-mode programs do have these numbers. They refer to a console or remote login session.

- **CPU time**—Two items are of concern here—the **TIME** and **%CPU** headings. The **TIME** heading indicates the total amount of CPU time consumed, and the **%CPU** heading represents the percentage CPU time that is currently being used when the **ps** command is executed. This heading can help you determine what processes might be consuming too much CPU time and need to be terminated. Terminating (killing) processes is covered shortly.

- **CPU priority**—It is possible to give certain processes priority over others by restricting CPU usage. You can tell a process's priority from its priority code. The default value is 0. A positive number represents decreased priority, and a negative number represents increased priority.

- **Memory use**—A few headings represent the process's memory use. This can help you identify certain processes that might be causing a system's performance to decrease. For example, the **RSS** (Resident Set Size) heading represents the memory used by the program, and **%MEM** shows what percentage of memory the process is using.

- **Command**—If you look at Figure 11-7, you see that the last column, CMD, represents the command that was used to launch the process.

The **top** Command

Another informative command, which is similar to the **ps** command, is the **top** command. It functions much like the Windows 2000 Performance tool by providing detailed information regarding CPU and RAM usage. Figure 11-8 displays the output of the **top** command. Such information includes the number of users currently logged on to the system, the amount of available memory, and the percentage of the CPU being used for various tasks. These tasks are sorted in descending order, allowing the system administrator to quickly see which users are consuming the most CPU cycles. By default, the output is refreshed every 5 seconds to provide continually updated data to the user. System administrators typically run this command quite often to monitor levels of activity on the system and make certain that enough resources are available to its users.

Figure 11-8 top Command

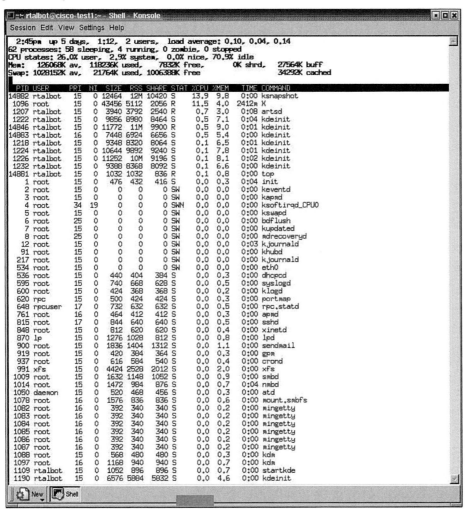

Killing Processes

Sometimes a process causes the system to lock up, or it can begin consuming so many of the system's resources that it begins to run slowly, which makes it impossible for users to run any other programs. In the event that this should happen, the **kill** command can be used to terminate the process. A few different parameters can be used with the **kill** command, which determines how the process is ended. The generic syntax for the command is as follows:

```
# kill -s signal pid
```

The *signal* option represents the specified signal that is sent to the process. Approximately 63 different parameters can be entered for the *signal* that is sent to the process. Each of these terminates the process differently. You can enter either the name of the signal, such as **SIGKILL**, or you can enter the corresponding number for **SIGKILL**, which is 9. Signal 9 kills the process without performing any shutdown tasks. Figure 11-9 shows all the possible *signal* parameters that can be entered. You can see this menu by entering the **kill -l** command. If you don't specify a signal, the default signal 15 is used, which is **SIGTERM**. Signal 15 kills the process but first allows it to close any open files it might be using. A moment ago you learned what a PID is and that you can find out what PID a specific process is using by entering the **ps** command. You must enter the PID for the process you want to terminate.

Figure 11-9 Signal Parameters

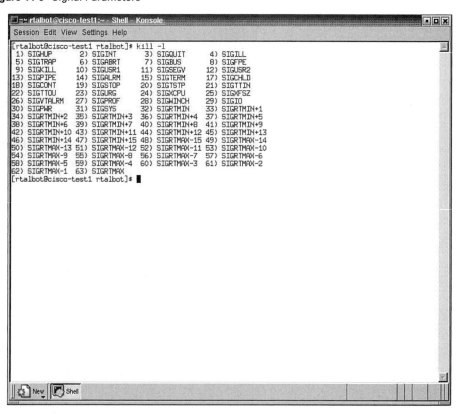

Another option available to kill a process is to use the **killall** command instead of just **kill**. The **killall** command kills every process by name rather than by its PID number. For example, if you wanted to kill all instances of vi that are running, you would enter

killall vi. This would kill all vi processes currently running, regardless of their PID number. There might be times when you need to kill all processes except one. To do this, use the **killall** command with the **-i** option. For example, if you type the command **killall -i vi** at the prompt, you will confirm each instance of vi that is running so that you can terminate them all except the one you still want to run.

Assigning Permissions for Processes

One of the final areas of essential process management on a Linux system is being able to control who can run certain programs by assigning appropriate permissions. Typically, programs have the same permissions and can read the same files as the user who runs that program. However, certain programs require additional permissions to be run by certain users. The **su** command is an example of this. The **su** command allows a user to switch to another user and execute programs with his or her user account. The **su** command cannot be executed by regular users; it requires root account privileges. Programs such as these are run using the SUID (set user ID) or SGID (set group ID) bit, which allows these programs to be run under the permissions of another user. In this example, the **su** command has root's SUID bit to allow regular users to execute it. SUID is used with executable files on a Linux system. It tells the operating system to run the program with the permissions of whoever owns the file, instead of the user who executes the program. In the example with the **su** command, any users could execute this program using the root account permissions. SGID works the same way as the SUID bit, which is set as the root account. However, SGID sets the bit for the group that the program is associated with.

Using these features can be helpful and sometimes necessary to allow users to execute specific programs that require permissions they normally don't have. It is important to limit this ability to as few files as possible because of the security risks it poses. For example, it might not be a good idea to enable this option for the **su** command, as in the preceding example, because you don't want users to be able to assume the identity of other users on the network.

SUID and SGID Security Risks

There are a few security risks involved when using the SUID or SGID bit to allow programs to run with the permissions of other users. The first concern involves allowing users to execute certain programs, such as su, cp, and fdisk. Applying the SUID root permissions for the **fdisk** command could allow a user to completely erase the server's hard drive. Doing this for the **cp** command would allow a user to copy any file from the server. This could cause serious security threats should a user copy a sensitive file such as /etc/shadow, which contains other users' password information.

Another security risk to be aware of is if there are bugs in any of the SUID or SGID programs. If these programs contain problems or bugs and they are executed by users who should not have the permission to do so, they could potentially cause more damage to the system than if they were executed with the normal privileges. For example, suppose a program has an unknown bug that, when the program is run, attempts to delete any files that are in the directory. Not much damage will be done if this program is executed by a user with normal privileges, but if this program had SUID root privileges, the entire directory or more could be damaged.

These two examples are worst-case scenarios that are unlikely to ever happen. This is especially the case with the program that has bugs and wipes out all the files in a directory. It is common for programs to contain bugs, but it is very uncommon for such a bug to begin deleting files. However, files can become corrupted and therefore will no longer work. In any event, it is always a good idea to note which programs are assigned with a SUID or SGID bit permission and minimize the number of programs that have these special permissions.

Monitoring Resources

This section covers the following topics:

- Disk management
- Memory usage
- CPU usage
- Reviewing daily logs
- Checking resource usage in Windows 2000 and Windows XP
- Checking resource usage in Linux

Disk Management

A good system administrator is constantly aware of a NOS's many critical resources. These resources should be monitored on all important network computers, such as an organization's various servers. If a computer runs low on any particular resource, the system administrator must be aware of the issue and immediately correct it before a serious problem occurs. Disk management is one of the most common and important tasks the system administrator performs. By regularly using error-checking and defragmentation programs and continually managing free disk space, the system administrator can maintain a healthy hard drive (or drives). Figure 11-10 shows the Windows 2000 Disk Management screen.

Figure 11-10 Windows 2000 Disk Management

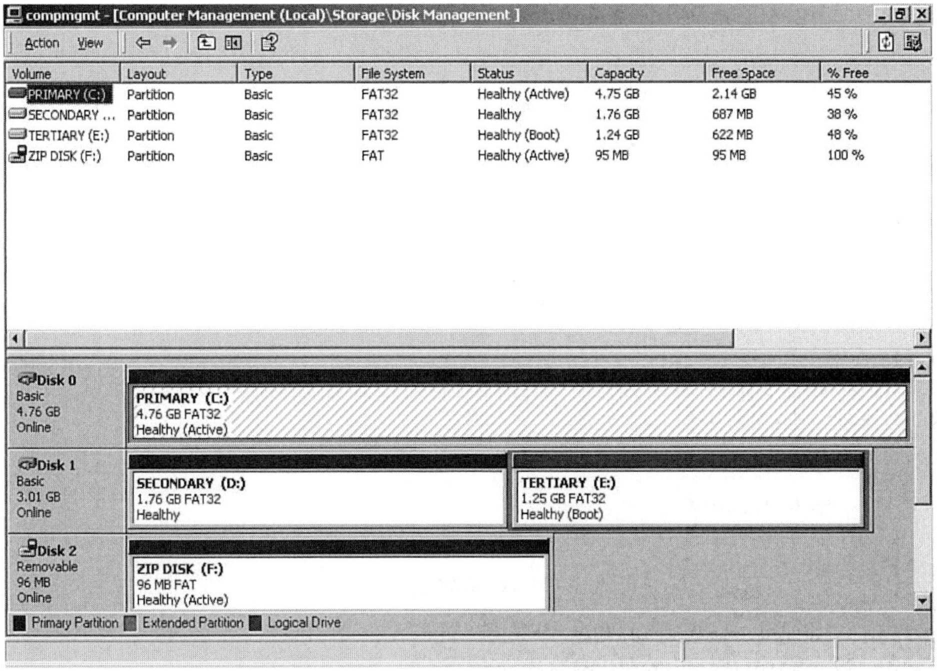

The available disk space on a hard drive is a precious resource that can be quickly devoured on network servers. Each user of a network is typically granted full write permission to either a home directory or some other central network storage. User behavior can be very unpredictable, and when many users store their data on the same hard drive, the disk can become full rather quickly. The consequences of running out of disk space are sometimes unpredictable and can even include unexpected program failures on that server.

Routine disk space management can be performed in several ways. One method includes regularly inspecting the disk's status and making any necessary adjustments manually. Another more practical solution uses automated alert messages to notify the system administrator when the available disk space falls below a predetermined level. Such alerts can be great tools that save time and help you manage not only disk storage, but also all the NOS's resources.

One preventive disk management tool available to system administrators is the use of *quotas* for user accounts. A quota acts as a storage ceiling that limits the amount of data each user can store on the network. Using this tool, a system administrator can better plan and manage the available space on the network hard drive. If a quota is not implemented, users can typically store as much data as desired on the network disk.

Although this method provides greater flexibility to users, it also forces the system administrator to keep a sharp eye on the current level of available disk space. Ultimately, the disk management methods that a system administrator employs are a combination of personal preference and the users' needs.

Memory Usage

Another critical resource that a system administrator must manage is Random Access Memory (RAM). Whenever an application runs on a computer, information is read from the hard drive and placed in the temporary storage of RAM. The computer uses this portion of its RAM to execute the program and eventually frees the space after the program exits. RAM is much faster than a hard drive but is much smaller. As a result, it is possible to use 100 percent of system RAM simply by running several programs at once.

A lack of available RAM can severely affect a computer's performance, especially one functioning as a network server. When memory is low, it severely hinders the system's processing power and can produce negative side effects such as program crashes. In the case of a network server, poor memory performance can even prevent users from logging on to the server. It is the duty of a system administrator to monitor applications' memory usage and to prevent these events from occurring. Memory diagnostic tools that allow RAM-intensive applications to be discovered (and stopped if necessary) are typically built into most NOS platforms. Figure 11-11 shows the Task Manager used to check memory usage.

Figure 11-11 Checking Memory Usage

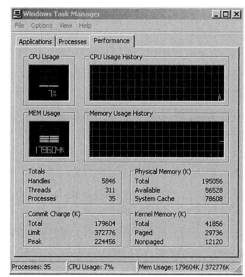

Because RAM is usually a scarce resource, system administrators can compensate for the lack of memory through the use of *virtual memory*. Virtual memory allocates space on the hard drive and treats it as an extension of the system RAM. Although hard drive access is significantly slower than standard RAM, virtual memory helps prevent RAM shortages by greatly increasing the total amount available. Most NOS software lets you manage virtual memory directly with built-in tools. A system administrator can choose to increase the default amount of virtual memory if the NOS continually faces memory shortages.

CPU Usage

The Central Processing Unit (CPU) acts as the brain of a modern computer. All information used by the NOS, including the NOS itself, is processed millions of times per second by the CPU to display this information to the user. Every application that is running, whether visible or in the background, consumes valuable CPU cycles of processing. Most operating systems prioritize these tasks, allowing the CPU to service them according to importance. However, the CPU can occasionally become overloaded with large amounts of processing being performed simultaneously. This is especially common for network servers, where many users attempt to access the computer resources at the same time. As more users request information from the server, the CPU must work harder to meet those demands.

Like all other NOS resources, built-in tools are commonly provided to allow system administrators to monitor the current level of CPU activity. This feedback is often presented in terms of the percentage of the CPU currently being used and is refreshed at frequent intervals. Figure 11-12 shows CPU usage over the period of one week.

Figure 11-12 CPU Usage

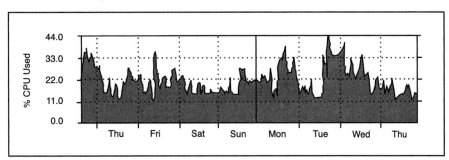

Additionally, applications are usually listed individually with their respective usage statistics. If a particular application or user is causing the system excessive processing strain, the system administrator can choose to terminate the cause of the problem.

Although it might seem unpleasant to force a user to disconnect or halt a program in midstream, the reality is that such actions are often necessary to maintain acceptable processing performance for all users.

Reviewing Daily Logs

An important aspect of monitoring the resources on any computer system is reviewing the system's log files. Most of a computer's programs, servers, login processes, and the system's kernel record summaries of their activities in log files. These files can be used and reviewed for various things, including software that might be malfunctioning or attempts to break into your system.

To help capture a report of these events, logs are automatically generated by the system and its applications. These files typically consist of text statements detailing specific information about the event that occurred. For example, most web servers maintain a log file that details every information request made to the server. Information regarding the time of the request, the remote computer's IP address, and files accessed is stored as unique records in the log. These records provide the system administrator with feedback and statistical data necessary to make improvements to the server's operations.

In Windows 2000, the Computer Management tool allows users to browse the logged events generated by the NOS. Two categories beneath the System Tools heading store logged information—Event Viewer and Performance Logs and Alerts. Several different types of logged events are recorded here, including Information, Warnings, and Errors. Double-clicking any of these entries displays the logged information in further detail.

Using Operating System Log Files

Most operating systems provide a means of automatically writing to a system log file. This file details device failures, failed communications attempts, and other error conditions. The information is a useful starting point for troubleshooting problems. For example, Windows NT and Windows 2000 provide the Event Viewer, which shows a list of system events.

If you select a specific event, such as a TCP/IP error, you can see more details about the event. The information that is displayed indicates that an IP address conflict occurred, which could explain why this computer cannot communicate on the network.

Locating System Log Files on a Linux System

Monitoring and viewing logs on a Linux system is done very differently than on a Windows system. Linux uses log daemons to control the events that are entered in the system's log. The first step to being able to view log files on a Linux system is to be able to locate them. Most of the Linux system's log files are located in the /var/log directory; the log files that are located in this directory are maintained by the system log daemon (syslogd) and the kernel log daemon (klogd). These two daemons are configured using the syslog.conf file, shown in Figure 11-13. As you can see from this example, most of the entries specify a log in the /var/log directory.

Figure 11-13 syslog.conf File

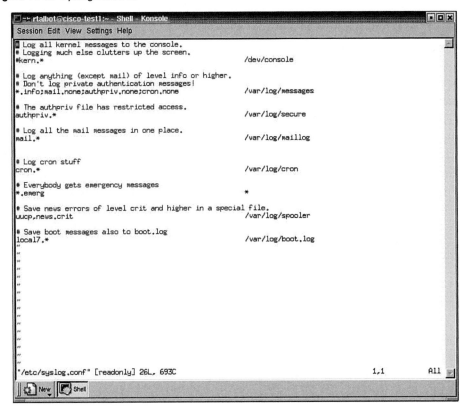

Many of the servers on a Linux system, such as Samba, maintain their own log files. The location where these files are stored can be configured with the server's native configuration file, such as smb.conf with Samba. The **logfile** parameter in the smb.conf file controls where the log file is located, but it is normally found in the /var/log directory or one of its subdirectories by default.

Identifying Important Information in Log Files

A Linux system has several log files. It can be difficult to determine which ones are important or what information you should pay close attention to. Most of the log files you never need to be concerned with or look at. However, some important information is contained in some of these files. For example, the log files in a Linux system keep track of logins made by the root account and attempts to use the **su** command to gain root privileges. Log files also maintain information about attempts to open or access ports that have been closed by the firewall or failed attempts to access servers or xinetd programs. It is rare for a Linux system to need to be shut down, so any unauthorized startup or shutdown could be suspicious. For example, unauthorized restarts of the server could mean a successful intrusion into the system. For this reason, logs are kept of all system startups and shutdowns. Error logs are also kept. An example of an error is when you see a strange error message pop up on the screen. More often than not this is just the result of a misconfiguration in the server, but sometimes it can mean that an attempt was made to break into the system. Other important log files to pay attention to are the kernel log files. Sometimes the kernel gets bugs, or hardware failure can result in *kernel oopses.*

Depending on the distribution of Linux you are using, your log files will be different. For example, you will not find log files for Sendmail in Mandrake or Debian Linux, because these distributions use other mail servers. There are other reasons that you might want to become familiar with the log files in your Linux system and the information in them. This helps you better determine what events are logged as normal events and what are not so that the ones that are not can be easily identified and examined further.

Log File Analysis Tools

The log files on a Linux system can become very large and difficult to manage, which makes doing any productive analysis of them very difficult. Several tools on a Linux system help you manage and analyze the system log files. You learned previously about cron jobs. You can use them to rename old log files so that new ones can be created. You also can delete the old ones on a regular basis to keep the log files from continuously growing to unmanageable sizes and taking up unnecessary hard drive space. This log file rotation can be set to occur daily, weekly, or monthly, depending on the activity on the system and how long you want to keep the files on the system.

Another log file analysis tool you can use is Logcheck (www.psionic.com/abacus/logcheck). Some distributions, such as Mandrake and Debian Linux, include this tool by default. It is easiest to use when it comes preconfigured with the distribution of Linux. If you are using a distribution that does not include Logcheck, you must configure it to run on your system. It's best to check the documentation for specific instructions on how to configure it on a Linux system, but the main file that must be edited is logcheck.sh, which is installed with the package. You must configure this file to check the log files you want to monitor. You can also adjust features such as which user receives reports when a violation is found (usually this is set to root by default). After Logcheck has been configured, you must create a cron job that specifies when Logcheck is run and who the reports are e-mailed to.

Checking Resource Usage in Windows 2000 and Windows XP

You monitor system resources in Windows 2000 and Windows XP with the Performance tool, shown in Figure 11-14. This application is found under Start > Programs > System Administration > Performance. The menu tree on the left shows System Monitor and Performance Logs and Alerts (the same option found in the Computer Management tool). Selecting the System Monitor displays an empty graph by default. Right-click the graph and select Add Counters to specify which system resources to monitor in the graph. Figure 11-15 illustrates the process of adding monitored resources to the Windows 2000 Performance tool.

Figure 11-14 Windows 2000 Performance

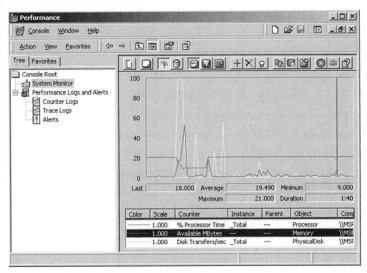

Figure 11-15 Adding Resources to Performance

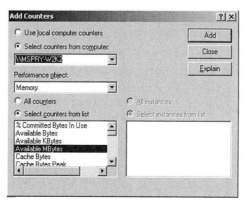

For example, to monitor the system's current RAM usage, in the Performance object section, select Memory. Next, you can decide which aspects of memory usage to view by clicking Select counters from list and clicking Add. From this window you can make multiple additions to the graph. A description of each resource is available if you click the Explain button. Clicking the Close button and returning to the Performance tool displays the statistics of the selected resources using a line graph by default. The line graph provides a visual history of the resources' activity, including information on its current, average, minimum, and maximum values.

To further configure this display, right-click the graph and select Properties. The System Monitor Properties dialog box appears, where you can select alternative views of the data, such as a histogram or a text-only report. Various other customizable options are found here, the most important of which is the Update automatically checkbox. Checking this option tells the Performance tool to refresh the display automatically at the specified interval. A faster refresh rate increases the amount of data provided to the user, but at a significant cost. Ironically, the Performance tool itself uses valuable system resources to monitor and report these very same resources. Specifying a frequent rate of updates could have a slightly negative impact on the resources available to Windows 2000/XP and other applications.

Lab 11.4.5 Checking Resource Usage in Windows 2000

In this lab, you use the System Performance Tool to monitor the resource usage on your computer system.

Checking Resource Usage in Linux

The most common Linux tools used to investigate resource usage consist of several text-based commands entered on the command line. Table 11-9 lists common commands for displaying resource usage. For details on these commands' various parameters, view their respective man pages by entering **man** *command* at the prompt. However, these commands are relatively simple to use and are extremely informative to system administrators with no additional parameters specified. They typically do not generate graphical information such as the charts featured in Windows 2000. Instead, detailed lists of textual information are displayed in an organized fashion to help you interpret the data.

Table 11-9 Displaying System Resource Usage

Command	Description
df	Displays the file system's disk usage
du *name*	Displays a directory's disk usage
top	Displays system resource information

The **df** command is used to display the amount of disk space currently available to the various file systems on the machine. Figure 11-16 displays the output of the **df** command, which is organized into six columns—Filesystem, Size, Used, Avail, Use%, and Mounted on. Each file system is listed on its own line, along with its corresponding usage information. This command provides a high-level look at the system's disk usage. If a particular file system is growing unnecessarily large, you will learn of the problem here first.

Figure 11-16 df Command Output

```
[root@systemA1 boot]# df -h
Filesystem          Size  Used Avail Use% Mounted on
/dev/hda2           1.9G  827M  1.0G  45% /
/dev/hda1            30M  2.7M   26M  10% /boot
none                62M     0   61M   0% /dev/shm
[root@systemA1 boot]#
```

If further tracking of disk resources is necessary, you can use the **du** command to determine the exact location of the problem. When a directory name is specified, the **du** command returns the disk usage for both the contents of the directory and the contents of any subdirectories beneath it. Figure 11-17 displays the output of the **du** command. Running it for high-level directories with many subdirectories can result in a very large set of output. This command is best used within the lower levels of the directory structure to help locate specific areas of the file system that are consuming large amounts of disk space.

Figure 11-17 du Command Output

```
28          ./log.d/conf/logfiles
84          ./log.d/conf/services
120         ./log.d/conf
8           ./log.d/scripts/logfiles/cron
12          ./log.d/scripts/logfiles/samba
12          ./log.d/scripts/logfiles/xferlog
36          ./log.d/scripts/logfiles
144         ./log.d/scripts/services
32          ./log.d/scripts/shared
236         ./log.d/scripts
360         ./log.d
64          ./ssh
20          ./snmp
52          ./isdn
108         ./nmh
40          ./gimp/1.2
44          ./gimp
148         ./sane.d
8           ./httpd/conf/ssl.crl
272         ./httpd/conf/ssl.crt
4           ./httpd/conf/ssl.csr
24          ./httpd/conf/ssl.key
12          ./httpd/conf/ssl.prm
404         ./httpd/conf
408         ./httpd
8           ./mrtg
240         ./squid
6152        .
[root@systemA1 etc]# du -hs
6.1M
[root@systemA1 etc]# du -hs passwd
4.0k    passwd
[root@systemA1 etc]#
```

The third and perhaps most informative command available for basic Linux resource management is the **top** command. It functions much like the Windows 2000 Performance tool by providing detailed information on CPU and RAM usage. The output of the **top** command was displayed previously, in Figure 11-8. Such information includes the number of users currently logged on to the system, the amount of available memory, and the percentage of the CPU being used for various tasks. These tasks are sorted in descending order, allowing the system administrator to quickly see which users are consuming the most CPU cycles. By default, the output is refreshed every 5 seconds to provide continually updated data to the user. System administrators typically run this command quite often to monitor the levels of activity on the system and to ensure that enough resources are available to its users.

Lab 11.4.6   Checking Resource Usage in Linux

In this exercise, you learn how to check the resources on a Linux system.

Analyzing and Optimizing Network Performance

This section covers the following topics:

- Key concepts in analyzing and optimizing network performance
- Determining Internet connection speed
- Network monitoring software
- Network management software
- Management software for small and medium-sized networks
- Management Service Provider
- SNMP concepts and components
- SNMP structure and functions

Key Concepts in Analyzing and Optimizing Network Performance

Administering a computer network is often a busy, high-pressure job. This is true in a large information technology support department with an enterprise-level network or in a small company with a single LAN administrator.

Because they are so busy, many administrators find themselves operating in reactive mode. In other words, they address problems as they occur, which leaves no time to implement measures that would prevent those problems from occurring in the first place.

The network administrator should make time to devise a proactive plan for managing the network. This plan lets you detect small problems before they become large ones. If you anticipate potential trouble spots and take measures to correct them, you can save a great deal of time and money. The two key concepts in analyzing and optimizing network performance are

- Bottlenecks
- Baselines

The following sections take a closer look at each concept and also discuss Internet connection speed, which is another important factor in evaluating and optimizing a network. Many important terms that relate to performance-monitoring issues also are defined.

Bottlenecks

A *bottleneck* is exactly what the name implies. It is the point in the system that limits data *throughput*, which is the amount of data that can flow through the network. A bottleneck in a network limits data just as the neck of a bottle limits the amount of liquid that can flow into or out of the bottle.

A bottleneck can be caused by a problem with a component or by the component's inherent limitations. An example might be a network that has 10/100-Mbps hubs and switches and computers with 10/100-Mbps network cards but only Category 3 twisted pair in the cabling infrastructure. Because Category 3 twisted-pair cable does not support a high data transfer rate, the cable is the bottleneck that slows down the network.

It is doubtful that all network components can be fine-tuned so precisely that they all operate at exactly the same speed. Nonetheless, optimizing performance involves finding the bottlenecks and upgrading, reconfiguring, or replacing the components to bring their performance up to or above the level of the rest of the network's components. This process almost inevitably creates a new bottleneck elsewhere, but with good planning, the new bottleneck should be less restrictive than the old one.

To be able to diagnose which network server component is causing a system bottleneck, you need performance-monitoring software tools specific to the network server operating system. Most network server operating systems have at least a basic performance-monitoring software package included with the operating system. Third-party vendors also have performance-monitoring software tools available for most network server operating systems.

Examples of performance-monitoring software tools for various network server operating systems include the following:

- **Performance**—For Microsoft Windows 2000 Server
- **sar, iostat, vmstat, ps**—For UNIX/Linux

The primary performance-monitoring tool for Microsoft Windows 2000 Server is Performance, shown in Figure 11-18. Performance can monitor nearly all hardware and software components on a Windows 2000 Server. The monitoring can take the form of creating a real-time chart of resource utilization, or it can take the form of a log file for later analysis. You can analyze the log file or export it in a format that can be used by other software, such as a standard statistics software package for analysis or Microsoft Excel to generate charts or statistics. Performance is a snap-in to the Microsoft Management Console. The Windows NT 4.0 Performance Monitor's appearance is slightly different, but the basic functionality is almost identical.

Figure 11-18 Windows 2000 Server Performance Tool

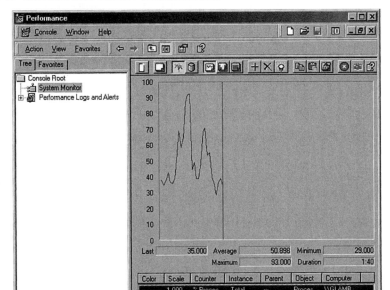

The various versions of UNIX/Linux have command-line utilities that you can use to monitor the performance of the UNIX/Linux network server. The primary tools are sar, vmstat, iostat, and ps. The flags used by these commands can vary among the different versions of UNIX/Linux. Use the UNIX/Linux **man** command to get specifics about the use of these commands. The information displayed by the **man** command also tells you how to interpret the output generated by the particular command.

The UNIX/Linux System Activity Reporter, accessed through the **sar** command, collects and reports system activity (processor utilization, buffer utilization, and so forth) for the UNIX/Linux network server. The UNIX/Linux Virtual Memory Statistics, accessed through the **vmstat** command, provides information about the virtual memory system on the UNIX/Linux network server. The UNIX/Linux Input/Output Statistics, accessed through the **iostat** command, provides information about disk subsystem input/output on the UNIX/Linux network server. The UNIX/Linux Processes, accessed through the **ps** command, lists all the processes that are running on the UNIX/Linux network server.

Worksheet 11.5.2 Bottlenecks

Learn some of the causes of and solutions to network bottlenecks.

Processor Bottlenecks

Using the performance-monitoring tools available for the network server operating system, you can monitor the utilization of the processor(s) in the network server. The two counters to watch most closely are the percent processor utilization and the processor queue length. The *percent processor utilization* is the percentage of time that the processor is busy. If the processor utilization percentage is constantly greater than 70%, the processor is the bottleneck in the network server. The *processor queue length* is the number of processes waiting for the processor. If the processor queue length is constantly greater than 2, the processor is the bottleneck in the network server. You can alleviate the processor bottleneck by doing any of the following:

- Upgrade the existing processor to a faster processor.
- Add a processor to the network server.
- Move applications or services from this network server to another network server.

Memory Bottlenecks

On network servers with operating systems that do not support virtual memory, memory bottlenecks are rather easy to detect. Memory shortages manifest themselves on these systems as an inability to load additional software or as a lack of *buffers* (temporary storage between the system and its disk drives). These problems are easily detected using standard server management software. The solution to a memory shortage is to add more memory.

On network servers with operating systems that do support virtual memory, several indicators or counters should be monitored. The first counter is the amount of available memory (memory that is not being used) after all the network server software has been loaded. To totally prevent paging or swapping of memory pages to disk, just have more actual or physical memory than is needed by all the software running on the network server.

The other counter that should be monitored to check for memory bottlenecks is the number of pages that are read from or written to the paging file on the disk in 1 second. The number of pages per second that is acceptable depends on the processor's speed. Generally, the number should be less than 2000 per second. Heavy paging often manifests itself as high disk utilization, because the memory pages are written to disk when another program needs the memory.

Another indicator of lack of memory is the number of page faults generated per second. A *page fault* is the condition encountered when an attempt is made to access a program page but the page is no longer in memory, so it must be retrieved from disk. A page fault problem is indicated if the number of page faults per second is more than double the number of page faults recorded on the server baseline measurements taken under a normal workload.

To alleviate a memory bottleneck, add more memory to the network server.

Paging performance can often be improved by placing the paging file (or the swap file) on the fastest disk in the network server and on a disk that doesn't contain the network server operating system or the data files used by the major application running on the network server.

Disk Subsystem Bottlenecks

The disk subsystem can cause system bottlenecks, especially when the network server has the role of a network server requiring a fast disk subsystem (for instance, a database server).

The disk subsystem counters that should be monitored are disk subsystem utilization and disk queue length. The disk subsystem utilization percentage should not be constantly greater than 90%. A very high disk subsystem utilization rate indicates that the disk subsystem is the bottleneck.

The disk subsystem queue length indicates how many items are waiting to be written to the disk subsystem. A disk subsystem queue length that is constantly greater than 2 indicates that the disk subsystem is too slow. Several things might improve disk subsystem performance:

- Defragment the disk drive. Having fragmented files on the disk drive can drastically reduce disk performance.
- Move the network server operating system paging file to the fastest disk drive in the network server and off the disk drive where the network server operating system is located.
- Move the application causing high disk utilization to another network server.

If defragmenting the disk subsystem and moving the paging file to another disk drive doesn't improve performance, more drastic (and costly) measures must be taken to improve disk performance:

- Replace the disk controller with a disk controller that has a built-in memory cache.

- Replace the disk drives with disk drives that have a higher rotational speed (and therefore faster access time).

- Replace the entire disk subsystem (controller and disk drives) with a faster disk subsystem.

Network Subsystem Bottlenecks

Network subsystem bottlenecks are perhaps the most difficult to detect and solve. Typical performance-monitoring software can supply counts of packets sent and received and little else. To analyze network performance, you need a network analyzer (hardware or software). A network analyzer can capture packets on the network for later analysis. The percent network utilization, a very valuable indicator of network performance, can be determined easily. A network analyzer can also determine the type of network packets (for instance, broadcasts, multicasts, or unicasts) and the protocols that are consuming the most network bandwidth.

A network utilization percentage that is constantly greater than 65% is generally considered high utilization and can constitute a bottleneck.

Solutions to a network subsystem bottleneck are generally expensive and include the following:

- Replace the network subsystem with a faster network subsystem. Replacing a 10-Mbps Ethernet network with a 100-Mbps Fast Ethernet network will likely eliminate the network subsystem as a bottleneck.

- Replace Ethernet hubs with Ethernet switches. In an Ethernet hub, all the available network bandwidth is shared. Using an Ethernet switch instead provides each port a full amount of bandwidth (no sharing of the bandwidth).

- If the bottleneck appears to be caused by too many clients trying to get to the network server, consider using adapter teaming to increase the network bandwidth available to the network server. This requires the installation of multiple NICs in the network server and the installation of a Fast Ethernet switch that supports bandwidth aggregation.

- Eliminate unnecessary protocols from the network. When multiple protocols are installed on a network server, announcements sent from the network server are sent once for each installed protocol, thus increasing network traffic.

Microsoft Network Monitor and Novell LANalyzer for Windows are a couple of well-known network monitoring and analysis tools.

Baselines

The baseline measurements should include the following statistics:

- Processor
- Memory
- Disk subsystem
- Network queue length

The first step in determining how efficiently a network is performing involves comparing various measurements to the same measurements taken earlier. These measurements may include the number of bytes transferred per second or the number of packets dropped, or a number of other indicators of network performance. When this comparison is made, a number of questions can be answered:

- Has performance improved or degraded?
- What is the effect on performance of implementing a new service or feature?

The only way to know the answers is to have a valid measurement against which to compare the current readings. This point of comparison is called a *baseline*, which is the level of performance that is acceptable when the system is handling a typical workload.

A baseline reading should be made at a time when the network is running normally. The measurement should not be made at the busiest time of the day, nor should it be made when the network is not in use. You should establish a baseline by measuring network performance during typical usage. A good way to do this is to take several separate readings at spaced intervals and then average them.

Using the utilities available for the various NOSs, you can perform baseline measurements. They should include the following statistics:

- Processor: Percent utilization
- Processor: Processor queue length
- Memory: Hard page faults
- Memory: Soft page faults
- Disk subsystem: Percent disk utilization
- Disk subsystem: Disk queue length
- Network: Percent network utilization
- Network: Network queue length

In addition to helping you identify developing bottlenecks, a baseline helps you do the following:

- Identify heavy users
- Map daily, weekly, or monthly network utilization patterns
- Spot traffic patterns related to specific protocols
- Justify the cost of upgrading network components

These items are discussed in the following sections.

 Worksheet 11.5.3   Baselines

Learn how to establish network baselines and the uses and benefits of establishing baselines for a network.

Identifying High Usage

It is not unusual to find that a few network users are using a disproportionate percentage of the bandwidth. When these heavy users are identified, you can do the following:

- Advise heavy users of ways to conserve bandwidth
- Restrict their usage through software controls
- Plan around their heavy usage and find ways to prevent the usage from affecting the network's efficiency

Of course, which option you choose depends on who the heavy users are, their roles in the organization, and the purpose of their heavy use.

Mapping Utilization Patterns

Monitoring also enables the mapping of utilization patterns. Not only is it possible to determine where heavy usage occurs, but also when it occurs. This makes it easier to allocate bandwidth for expected high-usage days or peak hours. It also makes it easier to schedule network maintenance and server downtime at a time when they will have less effect on the network's users.

Pinpointing Protocol-Specific Traffic Patterns

Network monitoring devices and software enable the pinpointing of traffic patterns based on protocol. It is also possible to determine what ports are being used. A network administrator can see if bandwidth is wasted on nonbusiness activities such as gaming and web surfing.

Network monitors are often called *protocol analyzers*. Most analyzers are software-based. They enable the capture of individual packets (also called *frames*) as they travel over the network. A more detailed discussion of protocol analyzers can be found in the

---

NOTE

Some software applications, such as backup programs and server-based antivirus scanners, use a great deal of bandwidth. These should be scheduled to run during low-usage periods.

section, "Network Monitoring Software." Only as many statistics should be captured as are needed to evaluate network performance, and network-monitoring software should be used only during low-usage periods, because the monitoring software itself affects system performance.

Determining Internet Connection Speed

If a network is connected to the Internet, it can be useful to determine its connection speed. The fact that a 56-kbps modem is used to connect does not mean that a 56-kbps connection is established. Depending on line conditions, it is likely that the connection speed will be 50 kbps or less. In addition, some telephone company services such as AT&T's TrueVoice prevent a 56-kbps modem from connecting at its optimum speed.

Data throughput can vary because of factors such as the use of hardware or software compression. This compression makes it possible to get 112-kbps throughput with a 56-kbps modem over an analog phone line.

A connection's speed is limited by its lowest-speed component (that is, the bottleneck). This means that even if the equipment is capable of a 50-kbps connection, if the remote modem supports only 33.6 kbps, the connection will be at the slower speed.

An operating system's dialup networking component might indicate a connection speed, usually in bits per second (bps). For example, a 50-kbps connection is often shown as 50,000 bps. This might not give a true indication of actual throughput, because it measures only the initial connection rate between the local modem and the remote modem. Throughput normally fluctuates during a connection session.

During a file download over the Internet, the download speed is usually shown by the browser or FTP software, often as KBps (kilobytes per second). There are 8 bits per byte, so a 50-Kbps (kilobits per second) connection will probably display a download speed of about 6.25 KBps. Downloading a 5-minute music file and using this connection speed might take a user 15 to 20 minutes. Figure 11-19 shows the time required to download 5 minutes of music in an MP3 file. This information can be used to determine the difference that higher and lower Internet connection speeds make.

NOTE

In the U.S., the Federal Communications Commission (FCC) limits the amount of electrical power that can be transmitted through phone lines. This limits the speed of a 56-kbps modem to about 53 kbps even if all other conditions are optimal.

NOTE

The connection speed can be displayed as either the port speed (the modem-to-computer speed, including compression) or the actual connection speed (the modem-to-modem rate). Windows can display speed in either of these formats, depending on the modem driver that is installed.

Figure 11-19 Internet Connection Speeds

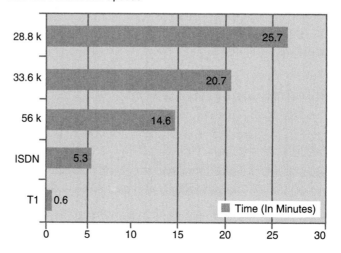

There are many reasons for a slow Internet connection:

- A poor connection to the ISP's remote-access server. This can be caused by noisy lines and modem problems on either end.

- A slow web server, FTP server, or server on the Internet to which requests are being sent.

- Congested conditions on the primary backbone lines, which can occur during events of national or international importance.

- Shared bandwidth on the LAN or within the ISP network.

Occasional temporary slowdowns are to be expected, and little can be done about them. If overall connection speed is unacceptable on a continual basis, it might be necessary to switch to broadband or other high-speed access.

Network Monitoring Software

Many software packages are available to help you monitor and manage a network. Some are included with a NOS, and some can be downloaded from the World Wide Web as freeware or shareware. Many of these packages are both costly and sophisticated.

The following sections examine some popular monitoring and management programs. Network management service providers are also discussed. These are networking professionals who are hired on a contractual basis to manage an organization's network.

Network monitoring software ranges from simple to complex and from free to expensive. Modern operating systems such as Windows NT and Windows 2000 have built-in monitoring tools. These are not as sophisticated or full-featured as third-party products, but they can be useful in establishing performance baselines or troubleshooting network problems.

Sophisticated network monitoring tools are called *protocol analyzers*. They capture the packets (that is, frames) that are transmitted between two or more computers or network devices. The analyzer then decodes (interprets) the packets so that the data may be viewed in English (or another language) as opposed to binary language. A sophisticated protocol analyzer also provides statistics and trend information on the captured traffic.

The term *sniffer* is often used to refer to any program that allows "eavesdropping" on network traffic. Network Associates makes the product trademarked as Sniffer (and its enhanced version, Sniffer Pro). Both products are network analyzers.

Sniffing programs have a bad reputation in some circles because they can be used by hackers and crackers to extract usernames and passwords that are sent across a network in plain text. These credentials are then used to gain unauthorized access to systems. However, sniffers have many legitimate uses for network administrators:

- Connectivity problem analysis
- Performance analysis
- Intrusion detection

Microsoft System Monitor and Microsoft Performance Monitor

System Monitor in Windows 2000 and Performance Monitor in Windows NT 4.0 measure the performance of a large number of system components, including counters for network components.

These monitors can display values in graph format, save data to a log, and compile reports. Measurement can be viewed in real time, updated automatically, or updated on demand.

Performance Monitor and System Monitor can configure alerts and send a notification when a specified value goes above or below a predefined limit.

To identify network bottlenecks, you should monitor network interface counters such as the following:

- Total bytes per second
- Bytes sent per second
- Bytes received per second

You can also monitor these protocol layer object counters:

- Segments received per second
- Segments sent per second
- Frames received per second
- Frames sent per second

Monitoring these counters helps you plan for appropriate bandwidth capacity. For example, if the total number of bytes transferred per second is close to or equal to the maximum capacity of a network medium, either equipment should be upgraded (such as from 10-Mbps Ethernet to 100-Mbps Ethernet) or network usage should be reduced.

Microsoft Network Monitor

System Monitor measures performance-related network values, but to actually capture and analyze packets as they travel across the network, you must use a different tool. Windows NT 4.0 and Windows 2000 include a "lite" version of the Microsoft Network Monitor, which is part of the Microsoft System Management Server (SMS). SMS is discussed in the "Network Management Software" section.

The Network Monitor that comes with Windows NT and Windows 2000 is a functional and useful tool for performing routine protocol analysis. Figure 11-20 shows Network Monitor monitoring network utilization, frames per second, and additional network statistics.

Figure 11-20 Microsoft Network Monitor

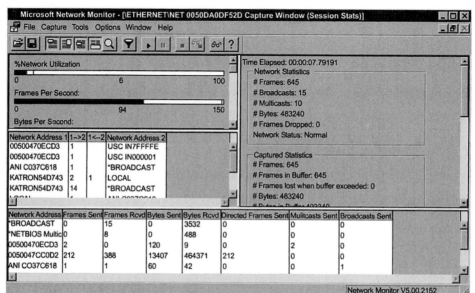

You can use Network Monitor to display individual frames of captured data. Figure 11-20 shows that packets for several different protocols have been captured, including TCP, UDP, and SMB.

Sniffer Technologies

The popular Sniffer network analyzer has evolved into a complex suite of network tools:

- Sniffer Pro LAN and Sniffer Pro WAN
- Sniffer Pro High-Speed
- Gigabit Sniffer Pro
- The Sniffer Distributed Analysis Suite

The Sniffer products enable sophisticated filtering based on pattern matches, IP/IPX addresses, and so on. Sniffer Pro includes a traffic generator to help you test new devices or applications. It can be used to simulate network traffic or to measure response times and hop counts.

Sniffer uses a dashboard-style interface, as shown in Figure 11-21.

Figure 11-21 Sniffer Interface

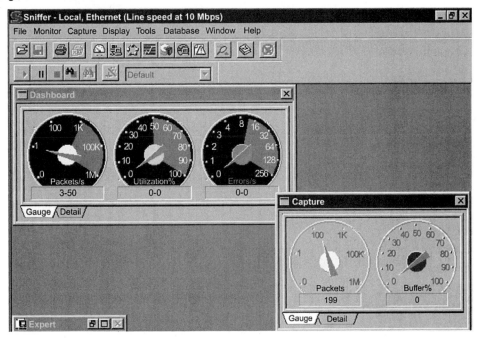

Sniffer includes built-in TCP/IP utilities such as ping, traceroute, DNS lookup, and more. The Sniffer display is highly configurable. Packet information and protocol distribution (displayed in chart form) are shown in Figure 11-22.

Figure 11-22   Sniffer Packet Information and Protocol Distribution

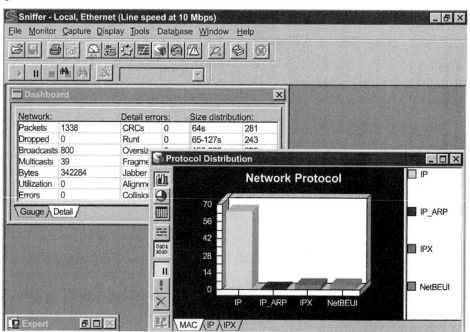

Sniffer includes Expert Analyzer to help you diagnose network problems. Multiple instances of this program or its individual tools can be run simultaneously.

Novell LANalyzer

The Novell LANalyzer network analysis tool runs on Windows, and it includes basic network monitoring and troubleshooting capabilities for Ethernet and Token Ring networks. In addition to capturing packets, the product makes specific recommendations for troubleshooting and optimizing the network's performance.

LANalyzer supports Novell Directory Services (NDS) and works with NetWare, AppleTalk, NFS, SNA, and TCP/IP. The LANalyzer graphical interface uses a dashboard style similar to that of Sniffer Pro, and it identifies network components by name and by MAC address.

Network Management Software

What is the difference between network monitoring software and network management software? The latter is generally more comprehensive. Although it does include monitoring components, it can do much more.

Managing network services is a large part of any network administrator's job, and this is especially true in the enterprise-level environment. A network administrator should be familiar with the tools that can make this task easier, including the management features that are built into modern NOSs, and the software products offered by operating system vendors and third parties.

Managing the network includes a number of tasks:

- Documenting the devices on the network and the status of each.
- Creating an inventory of network software that allows deployment of software and updates over the network.
- Metering software to provide data on what applications are being used and how, when, and by whom they are being used.
- Managing software licensing.
- Remotely controlling client machines and servers over the network and managing remote desktops.
- Notifying administrators of events such as failure of network components or a predefined disk capacity that is reached or exceeded.

There are several network management programs (or, more accurately, suites of programs) on the market. This section examines a few of the most popular:

- Microsoft SMS
- Novell ManageWise
- IBM Tivoli Enterprise
- Hewlett-Packard OpenView

These products are designed with the large, multisite enterprise network in mind.

Network management software that is appropriate for the small-to-medium-sized LAN includes LANExplorer and Lanware Network Monitoring Suite.

Microsoft Systems Management Server

Microsoft SMS is a high-end network management package that provides hardware and software inventory by installing the client agent on target computers. Figure 11-23 shows the Hardware Inventory Client Agent properties dialog box. SMS also allows for remote diagnostic capabilities, remote desktop control, and software deployment.

Figure 11-23 Hardware Inventory Client Agent Properties

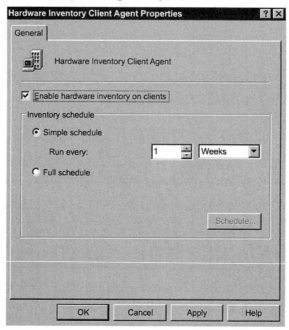

SMS also includes a more robust version of Microsoft Network Monitor than the one built into the Windows NT and Windows 2000 operating systems. For example, the SMS Network Monitor adds the capability to find routers on the network and to resolve addresses from names.

One of the most useful features of SMS is its software distribution feature. With it, a distribution package is created. The package contains the information used by SMS to coordinate the distribution of the software, as shown in Figure 11-24.

SMS uses Microsoft SQL Server to store data, which means that the data can be easily exported to Microsoft Access. SMS includes support for Macintosh clients, and it can be easily integrated into a Novell NDS environment.

Novell ManageWise

Novell ManageWise consists of an integrated group of network management services that can be used to manage NetWare servers or, with the addition of an add-on agent, Windows NT servers. Components include network traffic analysis, control of workstations and servers, and administration of network applications. The ManageWise console also includes the ability to map network drives.

Like SMS, ManageWise can create an inventory of network devices. In addition, it includes an alarm/notification feature. ManageWise includes NetWare LANalyzer agent, the management agent, Intel LANDesk Manager, and LANDesk virus protection. ManageWise includes Desktop Manager, as shown in Figure 11-25.

Figure 11-24   SMS Software Distribution Feature

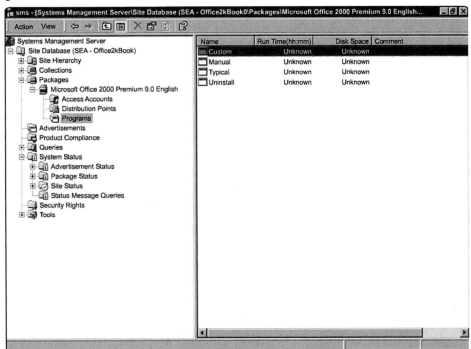

Desktop Manager lets you view the workstation's hardware and software inventories. It also enables file transfer, chat, remote control, and rebooting of the workstation.

IBM Tivoli Enterprise

Tivoli Enterprise, shown in Figure 11-26, is a popular network management package that includes tools designed to provide asset management, availability management, change management, operations management, security management, service management, and storage management. Tivoli Enterprise makes it easy to implement these components in phases.

Tivoli Enterprise provides a complete view of the network topology. Reporting tools let you customize the view in which the data is presented, and you can create "smart sets" that group data logically and that help analyze the network's health.

Tivoli also offers solutions for small businesses (with Tivoli IT Director) and medium-sized organizations (with Tivoli management suites).

Figure 11-25 ManageWise Graphical Interface

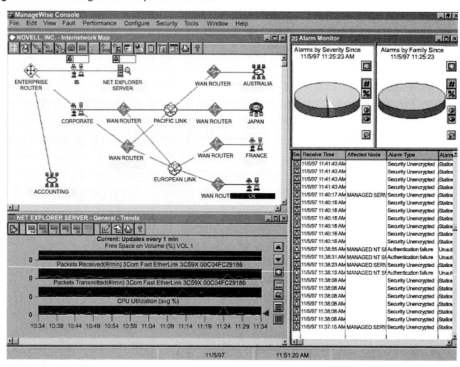

Figure 11-26 IBM Tivoli Enterprise

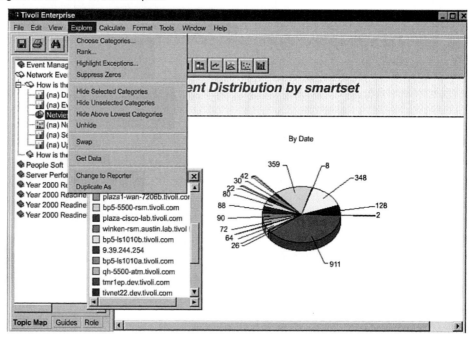

Hewlett-Packard OpenView

Hewlett-Packard OpenView management tools include OpenView Enterprise for large-scale enterprise solutions and OpenView Express for medium-sized companies. OpenView Enterprise is designed for networks that have thousands of servers and more than 5000 workstations and that run Windows NT, Windows 2000, or UNIX NOSs. OpenView Express provides web server management, management of Exchange mail servers, and Windows NT and Windows 2000 mixed-mode networks. The OpenView ManageX component is a server and performance management tool that can be used in NT and NetWare environments.

Management Software for Small and Medium-Sized Networks

In addition to the network management products offered by major software companies such as Microsoft, Novell, IBM, and Hewlett-Packard, numerous smaller companies make products aimed at the small-to-medium-sized network market. These include Lanware Network Monitoring Suite (NMS), which uses *Simple Network Management Protocol (SNMP)*. NMS provides features such as the capability to restart services, schedule events, and reboot servers. NuLink ViewLAN is another relatively simple SNMP-based management and monitoring tool.

The following sections discuss SNMP and Common Management Information Protocol (CMIP). These protocols are the basis of many of these simple software solutions.

SNMP

SNMP is a protocol that is included in most implementations of TCP/IP. It has several advantages as a network management solution:

- Simplicity
- Low cost
- Relatively easy implementation
- Low overhead on the network
- Supported by most network hardware devices

SNMP uses a hierarchical database called a *Management Information Base (MIB)* to organize the information it gathers about the network. Software called the SNMP manager is installed on a host computer that is used to collect the data. SNMP agent software is installed on the computers on the network from which the data is collected. Freeware versions of both SNMP managers and agents are available for various operating systems.

Worksheet 11.5.10   SNMP

Learn some of the basic concepts and uses of SNMP.

CMIP

Common Management Information Protocol (CMIP) was designed to improve on SNMP and expand its functionality. It works in much the same way as SNMP, but it has better security features, and it enables notification when specified events occur.

Because CMIP's overhead is considerably greater than that which is required for SNMP, it is less widely implemented. CMIP is based on the OSI protocol suite, and SNMP is considered part of the TCP/IP suite.

Management Service Provider

A new development in network management is the *Management Service Provider (MSP)*.

A company subscribes to an MSP service, which provides performance monitoring and network management. This saves the organization the cost of buying, installing, and learning to use monitoring and management software.

An example of a company that provides outsourcing of network management tasks is Luminate.Net, which provides a web-based interface for interaction with customers.

SNMP Concepts and Components

SNMP is the Simple Network Management Protocol. Running at port 161 by default, it is the only way to obtain true statistics of network usage under TCP/IP. SNMP lets network administrators remotely troubleshoot and monitor hubs and routers. Much of SNMP is defined within RFCs 1157 and 1212, although many more RFCs discuss SNMP. SNMP can be found, along with other RFCs, on various websites, including http://rs.internic.net. You also can perform a search on SNMP or RFC and find more specific information related to a specific part of SNMP.

Using SNMP, you can find out information about these remote devices without having to physically be at the device itself. This can be a very useful tool if understood and used properly. You can find a wide variety of information about these devices. Some examples include the following:

- A router's IP address
- Number of open files
- Amount of hard drive space available
- Version number of a host (such as Windows NT)

Before you set up SNMP, you need the IP addresses or host names of the systems that will be the initiators or those that will respond to the requests. Microsoft's SNMP Service, for example, uses the regular Windows NT host name resolution, such as

HOSTS, DNS, WINS, and LMHOSTS. Therefore, if you are using one of these resolution methods, add the correct host name-to-IP address resolution for the computers you are setting up with SNMP.

The types of systems on which you can find data include the following:

- Mainframes
- Gateways and routers
- Hubs and bridges
- Windows NT servers
- LAN Manager servers
- SNMP agents

SNMP uses a distributed architecture design to facilitate its properties. This means that various parts of SNMP are spread throughout the network to complete the task of collecting and processing data to provide remote management. Microsoft's SNMP Service lets a machine running Windows NT transfer its current condition to a computer running an SNMP management system. However, this is only the agent side, not the management tools. Various third-party management utilities are available, including the following:

- IBM NetView
- Sun Net Manager
- Hewlett-Packard OpenView

SNMP Agents and Management

SNMP has two main parts:

- The *management system* is the centralized location from which you can manage SNMP.
- The *agent station* is the piece of equipment from which you are trying to extract data.

The following sections discuss each part.

The SNMP Management System

The management system is the key component for obtaining information from the client. You need at least one management system to even be able to use the SNMP Service. The management system is responsible for "asking the questions." As mentioned earlier, it can ask each device a certain number of questions, depending on the type of device. The management system is a computer running one of the various software components mentioned earlier.

In addition, you can issue certain commands specifically at the management system. These are generic commands that are not specific to any type of management system:

- **get**—Requests a specific value. For example, it can query how many active sessions are open.

- **get-next**—Requests the next object's value. For example, you can query a client's Address Resolution Protocol (ARP) cache and then ask for each subsequent value.

- **set**—Changes the value of an object that has read-write properties. This command is not often used due to security and the fact that the majority of objects are read-only.

Usually, only one management system runs the SNMP Service per group of hosts. This group is called a *community*. Sometimes, however, you might want more. Here are some of the reasons why:

- You might want multiple management systems to make different queries to the same agents.

- One community might have different management sites.

- As the network grows and becomes more complex, you might need to differentiate certain aspects of your community.

The SNMP Agent

You have seen so far what the SNMP management side is responsible for and can specifically do. For the most part, the management side is the active component for getting information. The SNMP agent, on the other hand, is responsible for complying with the requests and responding to the SNMP manager accordingly. Generally, the agent is a router, server, or hub. The agent is usually a passive component that only responds to a direct query.

In one particular instance, however, the agent is the initiator, acting on its own without a direct query. This special case is called a *trap*. A trap is set up from the management side on the agent. But the management system does not need to go to the agent to find out whether the trap information has been tripped. The agent sends an alert to the management system, telling it that the event has occurred. Most of the time, the agent is passive, except on this one occasion.

SNMP Structure and Functions

Now that you have learned a little about the management system and agents, you can explore the different types of query databases.

Management Information Base

The data that the management system requests from an agent is contained in a MIB. This is a list of questions that the management system can ask. The list of questions depends on what type of device it is asking about. The MIB is the database of information that can be queried against. What type of system it is determines what specifically can be queried. The MIB defines what type of objects can be queried and what type of information is available about the network device. For example, there are MIBs for routers, hubs, switches, computers, and even some software packages, such as database systems. The MIB contains a list of the items that can be managed by SNMP on the device associated with the MIB.

A variety of MIB databases can be established. The MIB is stored on the SNMP agent. These MIBs are available to both the agent and the management system as a reference from which both can pull information.

The Microsoft SNMP Service, for example, supports the following MIB databases:

- Internet MIB II
- LAN Manager MIB II
- DHCP MIB
- WINS MIB

MIB Structure

The namespace for MIB objects is hierarchical. It is structured in this manner so that each manageable object can be assigned a globally unique name. Certain organizations have the authority to assign the namespace for parts of the tree design. The MIB structure is similar to TCP/IP addresses. You get only one address from the InterNIC and then subnet it according to your needs. You do not have to contact them to inquire about each address assignment. The same applies here. Organizations can assign names without consulting an Internet authority for every specific assignment.

Installing and Configuring SNMP

SNMP allows an SNMP management console to manage devices that have an SNMP agent installed on them. SNMP was designed to make it possible to manage network devices, such as routers. However, the use of SNMP has been expanded to allow it to be able to manage practically any device that is attached to a network, including a computer. You should install the SNMP agent on your NOS by following the instructions that come with the NOS.

After you have installed the SNMP agent, you must configure it with an SNMP community name. The default SNMP community name is Public. You should *always* change this to something other than Public. The community name is a primitive password mechanism. SNMP management console and SNMP agents with the same SNMP community name can exchange information. If the SNMP community names differ, they will not be able to communicate.

The SNMP agent knows what to monitor on the network device by looking at the device's MIB. Each unique network device has a unique MIB defined. For example, there are MIBs for routers, hubs, switches, computers, and even some software packages, such as database systems. The MIB contains a list of the items that can be managed by SNMP on the device associated with the MIB.

Lab 11.5.9   Installing SNMP

Upon completion of this lab, you will be able to set up monitoring agents to run tests and alerts for your system.

What SNMP Does

The following example tracks a sample of SNMP traffic between a manager and an agent. In real life, you would use management software, such as Hewlett-Packard's OpenView, that lets you see the MIBs and query without knowing all the numbers.

Step 1   The SNMP management system makes a request of an agent using the agent's IP address or host name.

    a. The application sends the request to UDP port 161.

    b. The host name is resolved to an IP address if the host name was used using host name resolution methods: localhost, HOSTS file, DNS, WINS, broadcast, LMHOSTS file.

Step 2   The SNMP packet gets set up with the listed information. The packet is routed on the agent's UDP port 161.

    a. The commands for the objects are **get**, **get-next**, and **set**.

    b. The community name and any other specified data

Step 3   An SNMP agent gets the packet and puts it into its buffer.

    a. The community name is checked for validity. If it is incorrect or corrupted, the packet is rejected.

    b. If the community name checks out, the agent checks whether the originating host name or IP address is correct as well. If not, it is thrown out.

    c. The inquiry is passed to the correct dynamic link library (DLL).

      d. The object identifier gets mapped to the specific application programming interface (API), and that call gets made.

      e. The DLL sends the data to the agent.

Step 4   The SNMP packet is given to the SNMP manager with the requested information.

SNMP Communities

A *community* is a group of hosts running the SNMP Service to which they all belong. Communities usually consist of at least one management system and multiple agents. The idea is to logically organize systems into organizational units for better network management.

Communities are called by a *community name,* which is case-sensitive. The default community name is Public, and generally, all hosts belong to it. Also by default, all SNMP agents respond to any request using the community name Public. By using unique community names, however, you can provide limited security and segregation of hosts.

Agents do not accept requests or respond to hosts that are not from their configured community. Agents can be members of multiple communities simultaneously, but they must be explicitly configured as such. This lets them respond to different SNMP managers from various communities.

Security

SNMP really has no established security. The data is not encrypted, and there is no setup to stop someone from accessing the network, discovering the community names and addresses used, and sending fake requests to agents.

A major reason that most MIBs are read-only is so that unauthorized changes cannot be made. The best security you can have is to use unique community names. Choose Send Authentication Trap, specify a Trap Destination, and stipulate Only Accept SNMP Packets from These Hosts.

You also might set up traps that let you know whether the agents receive requests from communities or addresses not specified. This way, you can track down unauthorized SNMP activity.

SNMP Security Parameters

You can set several options that affect the SNMP agent's security. By default, the agent responds to any manager using the community name Public. Because this can be inside or outside your organization, you should at the very least change the community name.

SNMP Agent

In some cases, you will configure other aspects of the SNMP agent. These set the type of devices you will monitor and who is responsible for the system.

The options available on this screen are as follows:

- The contact name of the person you want to be alerted about conditions on this station. Generally, this is the user of the computer.
- The location is a descriptive field for the computer to help keep track of the system sending the alert.

The last part of the screen identifies the types of connections and devices that this agent monitors:

- **Physical**—You are managing physical devices such as repeaters or hubs.
- **Applications**—This is set if the Windows NT computer uses an application that uses TCP/IP. You should check this box every time, because just by using SNMP you should have TCP/IP set up.
- **Datalink/subnetwork**—For managing a bridge.
- **Internet**—Causes the Windows NT computer to act as an IP gateway or router.
- **End-to-end**—Causes the Windows NT computer to act as an IP host. You should check this box every time, because you are most likely an IP host.

Any errors with SNMP are recorded in the system log. The log records any SNMP activity. Use Event Viewer to look at the errors and find the problem and possible solutions.

Lab 11.5.10   Configuring SNMP Security and Traps

Upon completion of this lab, you will be able to configure SNMP monitoring agents to run tests and alerts for your system.

Remote Notification

The single best way to be notified of situations when they arise is through SNMP. SNMP is an application of TCP/IP and is available for any network that uses TCP/IP as its network protocol. This makes it available for Windows 2000, Windows NT, Linux, OS/2, and so on.

Understand that notification is possible using SNMP. It varies on an operating system-by-operating system basis. Within Windows 2000, for instance, you can establish thresholds to notify you when conditions exist (such as when the available memory on a machine drops below a specified level).

Summary

This chapter discussed the advanced administration of a NOS. Some of the important concepts to retain from this chapter include the following:

- There are four types of backups—full, partial, incremental, and differential. Automating the backup process not only increases backup consistency but also grants system administrators more time to address other pressing network issues.

- Drive mapping creates a path or map over the network to the shared drive or folder. It is a useful tool that allows an administrator to share resources that are stored on a server. Resources that are on another end user's computer can be mapped to as well. Assigning permissions allows the system administrator to control the groups and users that can access the drive or folder.

- The system administrator manages hard drive resources using disk management. Automated alert messages notify the system administrator when the available disk space falls below a predetermined level. Other tools that are available are quotas. A quota acts as a storage ceiling to limit the amount of data each user can store on the network.

- Most operating systems provide a means of automatically writing to a system log file. This file details device failures, failed communications attempts, and other error conditions. This information is a useful starting point for troubleshooting problems. For example, Windows NT and Windows 2000 provide the Event Viewer, which shows a list of system events.

- The first rule of troubleshooting is to check for physical connectivity. After that is verified, each troubleshooting scenario has a set of steps you follow to ensure that everything is covered. These include identifying the problem, re-creating it, isolating it, initiating a response, implementing the correction plan, testing the response, documenting the results, and providing feedback to the end user.

Check Your Understanding

The following review questions help you assess what you learned in this chapter. Answers can be found in Appendix A, "Answers to Check Your Understanding Questions."

1. Backup storage devices do not need to be extremely fast or easily accessible. Instead, there are more relevant considerations when you're implementing a backup scenario. What are these four concerns?

2. Only the files that have changed since the last backup are selected to be backed up. These files are selected based on whether they have changed recently, instead of an arbitrary selection based on directory names or filenames. This describes what kind of backup?

   A. Partial

   B. Differential

   C. Incremental

   D. Full

3. Backup files have been created or have changed since the last normal backup. Files are not marked as having been backed up, and the markers are not cleared. All files, even those that have not changed since the last backup, are backed up. This describes what kind of backup?

   A. Partial

   B. Differential

   C. Incremental

   D. Full

4. What two main tools are used in Linux to perform backups?

5. When mapping a drive in a Linux system, you can use two methods. Which method do you use when mapping a network drive to a Linux server from a Windows workstation, and how do you go about doing this?

6. What is the correct command syntax to use when mapping a drive from a Linux workstation to a Linux server?

7. What are the three main tools in a Linux system that are used to manage disk partitions?

   A. disk

   B. mkdir

   C. mkfs

   D. fsck

8. What program do you use to schedule tasks to run at regular intervals on a Linux system?

    A. Core dump

    B. Log rotation

    C. cron

    D. Find

9. The **top** command is one of the most useful commands you can use on a Linux system. You can find much useful information by studying this command's output. Which of the following are facts you can obtain with this command?

    A. The number of users currently logged on to the system

    B. The amount of available memory

    C. The percentage of the CPU being used for various tasks

    D. The amount of available virtual memory the system has left

10. Approximately 63 different parameters can be entered for a signal that is sent to a process. Each of these terminates the process differently. What command can you use to display this entire list of parameter options at the Linux command prompt?

    A. kill -i

    B. ps -i

    C. kill -l

    D. ps -l

Key Terms

advanced intelligent tape (AIT)   Uses 8mm tapes that use helical scan recording hardware (much like a VCR). AIT tapes have memory in the tape cartridge, known as Memory-In-Cassette (MIC), which stores the tape log to facilitate locating a file during a restoration.

agent station   The piece of equipment from which you are trying to extract data.

backup   The process of copying data from one computer to some other reliable storage medium for safekeeping.

baseline   The level of performance that is acceptable when the system is handling a typical workload. This involves comparing various measurements to the same measurements taken earlier.

bottleneck   The point in the system that limits data throughput, which is the amount of data that can flow through the network.

copy backup   Backs up any files and folders that an administrator selects to be backed up.

core dump   A recording of the memory that a program was using when it crashed.

cron program   The way to schedule tasks to run at regular intervals on a Linux system.

daily backup   A useful partial backup method that an administrator can perform to select all the files and folders that have changed during the day.

differential backup   Backs up files created or changed since the last normal or incremental backup. It does not mark files as having been backed up. All files, even those that have not changed since the last backup, are backed up.

Digital Audio Tape (DAT)   Uses 4mm digital audiotapes to store data in the Digital Data Storage (DSS) format.

Digital Linear Tape (DLT)   Offers high-capacity and relatively high-speed tape backup capabilities. DLT tapes record information in a linear format, unlike 8mm tape technologies, which use helical scan recording techniques.

drive mapping   A useful tool that allows an administrator to share resources that are stored on a server. The client computers that are connected to the network assign a drive letter that acts as a direct path to access over the network those resources stored on a server.

full backup   Also called a normal backup. Backs up everything on the hard drive at the scheduled point in the day, every day.

incremental backup   Only the files that have changed since the last backup are backed up.

Linear Tape-Open (LTO)   Comes in two distinct forms: one designed for high storage capacity (Ultrium), and one designed for fast access (Accelis).

Management Information Base (MIB)   The data that the management system requests from an agent. This is a list of questions that the management system can ask.

Management Service Provider (MSP)   A company subscribes to an MSP service, which provides performance monitoring and network management. This saves the organization the cost of buying, installing, and learning to use monitoring and management software.

management system   The centralized location from which you can manage SNMP.

page fault   The condition encountered when an attempt is made to access a program page but the page is no longer in memory, so it must be retrieved from disk.

partial backup   Backs up only selected files. Partial backup types include copy and daily backup.

percent processor utilization   The percentage of time that the processor is busy.

processor queue length   The number of processes waiting for the processor.

quarter-inch cartridge (QIC)   Tapes used in QIC drives are one-quarter inch wide. The QIC standard has limited storage capacity and is used only in entry-level network servers.

RAIT (redundant array of independent tapes)   Can be used for mirroring of tape drives or (with at least three tape drives) implemented as data striping with parity.

sniffer   Any program that "eavesdrops" on network traffic.

SNMP (Simple Network Management Protocol)   Lets network administrators remotely troubleshoot and monitor hubs and routers. Using SNMP, you can find out information about these remote devices without having to physically be at the device itself.

tape backup drive   Most commonly used as the device for backing up the data on a network server's disk drives. Tape devices are known for their long-lasting performance, which is partly due to the tape drive mechanics that some systems include.

tape library   Usually an external system that has multiple tape drives, tens or hundreds of tapes, and an automatic mechanism for locating the tapes, loading them into the tape drives, and returning the tapes to the proper location.

tar   A utility that combines multiple files into a single file that can be copied to the medium.

Travan cartridge tape   Based on QIC technology. In many cases, it is either read/write-compatible with some QIC tape cartridges or read-compatible with QIC cartridges. Travan tape drives have a higher storage capacity than the older QIC tape drives. Travan tape drives have the capacity to back up low-end network servers but are relatively slow.

Objectives

After completing this chapter, you will be able to complete tasks related to

- Hardware terms, concepts, and components
- Hardware installation, configuration, and maintenance in a Linux system
- Checking and confirming hardware configuration in a Linux system
- Diagnosing and troubleshooting devices in a Linux system
- Installing and using Linux with laptop and mobile devices

## Chapter 12

Installing and Maintaining Hardware in a Linux Environment

Most Linux distributions have evolved enough to be able to autodetect and configure themselves to use the software during installation or even after installation. There will always be times when this doesn't happen, or it won't happen exactly the way you want it to. Sometimes, you need to manually configure new hardware or tweak an automatic configuration. This chapter covers how to do this with various hardware that is used on a Linux system. This chapter also covers special installations and tweaks you need to perform when installing Linux on a laptop or mobile device.

Hardware Terms, Concepts, and Components

To properly install, maintain, and troubleshoot hardware, an administrator must first have a firm understanding of all the main hardware that needs to be installed in a Linux system. This chapter and this section in particular focus mainly on how to properly identify, install, maintain, and troubleshoot hardware as it relates specifically to a Linux system. How this is done for a Linux system as opposed to another system, such as a Microsoft Windows system, can be very different. You have already learned about many of these differences.

One of the first things you need to consider when gathering hardware to install in a Linux system is compatibility. Linux has come a long way in providing support for a lot of hardware, but, unlike a Windows system, it is not compatible with every piece of hardware on the shelf at your local computer store. This is especially the case when it comes to video cards, network cards, Small Computer Systems Interface (SCSI) host adapters, and sound cards. These components are known to have various compatibility issues with Linux systems. Doing a little research on the hardware that will work on a Linux system can save you much time and trouble in the future.

Overview of Hardware Components

Most of this course has focused primarily on the administration of Linux software. However, software is only one thing a system administrator is responsible for. As important as knowing how to administer the Linux operating system is, Linux hardware administration is just as important. In fact, at least half a system administrator's time is spent with hardware. Therefore, it is best to compile a list of the various hardware components you will use or find in a Linux system as they relate to Linux systems specifically.

The first piece of hardware that needs to be mentioned is the motherboard, shown in Figure 12-1. This is the central component that allows every other hardware device in the system to run. If the motherboard fails, so does the system. Aside from the CPU, other pieces of hardware can be replaced and do not cause the system to crash if they fail. The motherboard is the component that holds all the other components or what they plug into. Even external devices, which connect through *Universal Serial Bus (USB)*, serial, or parallel ports, do so off the motherboard. The motherboard also determines what type of CPU and RAM you must use in your system. This is particularly important if you are selecting a motherboard to install in a Linux system. As you learned in previous chapters, certain distributions can use only certain processors. This makes choosing the correct motherboard for a Linux system a very important step.

Figure 12-1 Motherboard

The central processing unit (CPU) is considered the "brain" of a computer system because it is what does all the "thinking" or computations. It's important to choose a CPU that is compatible with your Linux system.

Memory is another crucial hardware component in any computer (see Figure 12-2). When memory is discussed, RAM is usually what's referred to. The easy thing about installing RAM is that you really do not have to be concerned with compatibility. You can install RAM from any manufacturer on a Linux system. The only compatibility issues with RAM are that you must install the correct type of RAM that goes with the motherboard you select. For example, if you select a motherboard that supports only SD-RAM, you must purchase and install SD-RAM. Likewise, if your motherboard supports only RD-RAM or DDR-RAM, you must install the correct RAM your motherboard supports.

Figure 12-2 Memory

After you've selected the motherboard, CPU, and memory bundle you want for your Linux system, it is time to start thinking about the other hardware you might need to add to the system. The type of hardware you will add depends a lot on the user this Linux system will be used by or if the system is intended to be a server. If the user just needs a system for basic word processing, e-mail, and Internet access, all he might need is a small-capacity hard drive (see Figure 12-3), CD-ROM drive (see Figure 12-4), and cheap video card (see Figure 12-5). However, if the user needs a system for editing video, CAD (see Figure 12-6), or other architectural drawing software, or if he need a system for doing a lot of mathematical computations, he might need other kinds of more expensive hardware. He needs faster processors, more RAM, much more expensive video cards, faster and larger-capacity hard drives, better monitors, CD-RW and DVD-RW drives, and speakers. If the system is a server, high-end monitors, speakers, and video cards are not needed. However, high-end processors, RAM, hard drives, and RAID controllers might need to be installed on servers.

The main thing to consider with Linux systems is compatibility and driver support. This is most important when you're installing video cards and sound cards. It is also important to keep in mind that if you are installing SCSI hard drives or other SCSI devices, you need to install drivers for the SCSI controllers.

Figure 12-3 Hard Drive

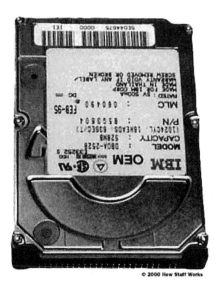

Figure 12-4 CD-ROM Drive

Figure 12-5 Video Card

Figure 12-6 CAD Software

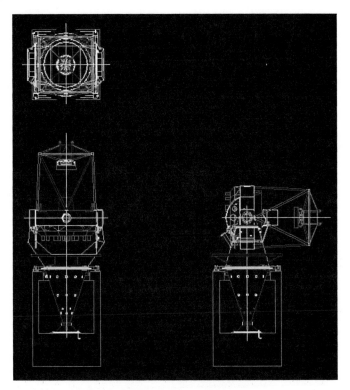

CPU

Previous chapters covered the types of CPUs that the different major distributions of Linux are compatible with. This section deals with the specifics of these processors and how they relate to Linux systems in general. The main processors that a Linux system is installed on are Intel, the AMD K6 series, Athlon, and Duron.

Originally, Linux was developed for Intel's 80x86, also called the x86 processor. The 386 system was the system that Linux was developed on. In fact, Linux can still run on it today. The uses for such a system were mentioned in previous chapters. Linux is also compatible with Intel's subsequent family of processors, such as the 486 and all the Pentium-class processors.

Other x86-compatible chips from other manufacturers, such as the Athlon, Duron, and AMD K6 processors, shown in Figures 12-7, 12-8, and 12-9, are also compatible with Linux. Other manufacturers also produce x86-compatible processors, but they lag substantially in speed and performance, so they are not covered in this course. You learned in previous chapters that other distributions can run on other types of processors as well. It is generally most cost-effective to use x86 processors, and Linux seems to run best on x86 processors, so it is recommended that you use x86 processors on Linux systems whenever possible.

Figure 12-7   Athlon CPU

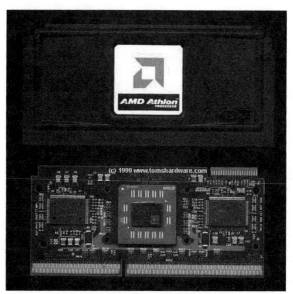

Figure 12-8   Duron CPU

Figure 12-9 AMD K6 CPU

You probably already know that CPU performance is measured in megahertz (MHz) or gigahertz (GHz; 1 GHz is equal 1000 MHz). The first CPUs were measured in megahertz because it was unthinkable that anything above 1000 MHz or 1 GHz was possible. Unless you see a reference to an old processor that has a clock speed of less than 1 GHz, you see processors measured primarily in GHz today because they have more than surpassed the 1 GHz level. The clock speed is what determines how fast a processor runs. The microchip pulses at a particular speed measured in GHz or MHz. The speed at which the microchip produces a pulse is the processor's *clock speed*. This form of measurement is helpful when determining the performance of one processor over another. For example, a 2.4 GHz Pentium 4 processor is faster than a 1.3 GHz Pentium III processor. It is important to note when comparing two processors from different manufacturers that even though they might have the same advertised clock speed, this doesn't mean that they are equal. For example, a 1.5 GHz Pentium processor might be faster than a 1.5 GHz AMD processor. If you're comparing two processors from different manufacturers, look at the *Millions of Instructions Per Second (MIPS)* value or a benchmark test that is relevant to the type of work you will be doing with the processor. The MIPS value is a better way to compare two processors of equal clock speed from different manufacturers.

Video Hardware

Selecting and configuring video hardware for a Linux system is a much more complicated task. Linux systems intended to be just servers do not necessarily need to be concerned with what video card is installed, because there is not always a need to have the X server component installed, which provides the GUI. You can install a cheap, low-level video card that the Linux kernel already supports. However, this task is not so simple when you are designing a system for a user. What tasks this user will perform with the system should determine which video card you select. This makes it difficult to choose a compatible video card or even find documentation about Linux installation.

The drivers that a Linux system uses to operate the video card in the GUI are not located in the kernel; they are part of the X server. Finding a video card/X server combination is where compatibility issues arise. For this reason, it is wise to research the video cards that are compatible with the X server you are using. A good idea of where to start depends on if you are using the default and open-source X server, XFree86, or one of the commercial X servers that were mentioned in previous chapters. You should not plan on using one of the new video cards on the market unless you are using one of the commercial X servers. This will narrow down your selection a little bit. Drivers are generally made available for commercial X server support before XFree86 releases compatible drivers. Depending on the user's needs, you might have to go with a commercial X server if he needs a particular video card.

One more important video card feature that helps determine what kind of video card to install is how much RAM the video card has. Video cards manufactured today have substantial amounts of RAM. This is intended to take the load off the system's RAM, because operating system's GUIs and games have advanced so much that they require a decent amount of RAM just to handle the workload. Without having RAM installed on the video card itself, the system's RAM would be consumed, leaving no memory for applications and processes. This would cause the system to lock up or run at such ridiculously slow speeds that it would render itself useless.

Miscellaneous Hardware and Components

Most hardware that you install on a Linux system (or if you install Linux on an existing system in which the hardware is already installed) works because it is operating system-independent. This simply means that regardless of which operating system you use, there will be little or no configuration and few compatibility issues.

The computer case is an example of hardware that falls into this category. When selecting this piece of hardware, you are more concerned with its compatibility with the other hardware that will be installed in the system. For example, you need to first make sure that the motherboard will fit into the case so that the slots and ports on the back of the motherboard line up with the slots on the back of the case. You also need to make sure that you have enough drive bays for the number of CD, DVD, CD-R, DVD-R, and removable hard drives and fans you might want to install. You also need to make sure that the case provides enough room for the hard drive array. Most cases provide enough space for at least two hard drives. If you have more than two hard drives, or if you are building a server that might have multiple hard drives, obtain a computer case that has the necessary room.

Other hardware that falls into this category includes mice, keyboards, monitors, floppy drives, and tape drives. These pieces of hardware work independently of the operating system that is installed and should not require any configuration or pose any serious compatibility problems.

Some hardware requires special configuration if it is installed in a Linux system. The following devices might require special drivers or configurations before they operate properly with Linux:

- **USB devices**—In a Linux system, you need to install a driver for each USB device you install. Some of the latest Linux kernels provide support for some USB devices, but the support is not universal, which means that you most often still need other drivers. To find out what USB devices are supported, visit www.linux-usb.org. Figure 12-10 shows a USB CD-ROM drive.

- **Sounds cards**—It has already been mentioned that Linux has some compatibility issues with sound cards. The kernel supports several sound cards. You can use an unsupported sound card as long as you obtain the correct driver and can install and configure the card properly. Figure 12-11 shows a typical sound card.

- **Video capture cards**—This type of hardware is a relatively new area that has become increasingly popular. It includes digital video and still cameras as well as internal cards that accept television input signals. Linux support for these devices is spotty at best, but research is being done to provide more support for this type of hardware. The Video4Linux project is currently working to develop tools and support for these devices. To learn more, visit www.exploits.org/v4l. The Linux kernel does support some of these devices, but be sure to check that your hardware is supported before purchasing and installing expensive equipment.

- **Internal modems**—It was mentioned that Linux has some problems with some internal modems. This is because internal modems today are software modems that rely on the CPU to do some of their work. These types of modems require drivers that are not supported in Linux. It is best to just use an older modem or to check to see if the manufacturer has drivers for Linux systems. Figure 12-12 shows a modem.

Figure 12-10   CD-RW Drive

Figure 12-11   Sound Card

Figure 12-12   Modem

The main concept to be aware of when installing hardware on a Linux system is compatibility. Knowing which hardware is fully supported by Linux and which hardware Linux does not have the latest drivers to support will save you lots of time and frustration. It is a good idea to be cautious about adding hardware to a Linux system without first checking compatibility. It is a good idea to be certain you can locate the correct drivers for your hardware device before you purchase or install any hardware on a Linux system.

Hardware Monitoring Devices

Most hardware devices that are used for network monitoring and management are merely dedicated computers (often portable) that run proprietary protocol analysis or network management software. Here are some of the devices that can be useful in troubleshooting network problems:

- *Tone generator/locator* (**also called** *fox and hound*)—The "fox" portion can be attached to one end of the cable, and a tone is generated. A locator (the "hound") at the other end receives the tone, which indicates that the correct cable has been identified. Figure 12-13 shows fox and hound.

- *Crossover cable*—An Ethernet unshielded twisted-pair (UTP) cable in which two of the wire pairs are crossed. Instead of pin 1 connecting to pin 1 on the other end, pin 2 connecting to pin 2, and so on (as in normal UTP), pins 1 and 2 connect to pins 3 and 6 on the opposite end, and pins 3 and 6 connect to pins 1 and 2. The crossover cable is used to connect two computers without going through a hub, or to connect two hubs when there is no uplink port. Figure 12-14 shows the coloring scheme for one end of a crossover cable.

- *Time domain reflectometer (TDR)*—A sonar-type pulse is transmitted through the cable. The pulse is measured to locate shorts or breaks in the cable. Figure 12-15 shows typical TDRs.

- *Hardware loopback*—This device is connected to the serial port to send data, which is then "looped back" to be received by the same computer. This makes a test of the serial port possible without a modem or other device attached to it.

- *Digital volt-ohm meter*—The volt-ohm meter (or voltmeter), shown in Figure 12-16, measures electronic pulses through cable to determine if there are shorts or breaks in the cable.

- *Cable tester*—A cable tester, shown in Figure 12-17, detects breaks and shorts. An advanced cable tester can display additional information about the cable's condition and properties.

- *Oscilloscope*—An oscilloscope, shown in Figure 12-18, is used in electronics calibration and to measure how much signal voltage passes through a cable over a set period of time. The display is output to a small monitor as a waveform. This can indicate attenuation, crimped wires, and shorts and breaks in the cable.

- *LAN meter*—A LAN meter, shown in Figure 12-19, checks for broadcasts, collisions, usage levels, and errors on Ethernet and Token Ring LANs. It also can measure throughput across WANs and can identify devices connected to the network.

Figure 12-13 Tone Generator

Figure 12-14 Crossover Cable

Figure 12-15 TDR

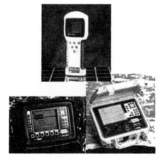

Figure 12-16 Digital Volt-Ohm Meter

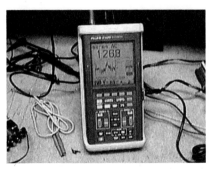

Figure 12-17 Cable Tester

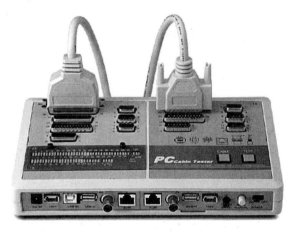

Figure 12-18 Oscilloscope

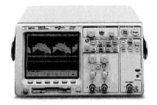

Figure 12-19 LAN Meter

Hardware Installation, Configuration, and Maintenance

Up to this point, you have learned a little about certain pieces of hardware used in computer systems and installing and configuring some hardware in Linux systems, such as printers. By now, you should understand that installing and configuring hardware in Linux is not as easy and straightforward as with a Windows system. For example, printers operate externally, and the drivers are located in Ghostscript.

Installing and configuring hardware on a Windows system is not always easy. Every once in a while, you might run into compatibility issues, but for the most part, you will always find support available. With Windows being such a commercially popular operating system, it makes sense for hardware manufacturers to ensure that their products have drivers that support the Windows family of operating systems. Along with this wide range of hardware support for Windows systems, you will also notice that detailed installation instructions are provided with the hardware. They come with the device or can be located on the manufacturer's website. Unfortunately, hardware support and wide-range compatibility are not as prevalent in Linux systems. In some cases, they are nonexistent. Most users are left to their own trial-and-error efforts when installing and configuring hardware on Linux systems. Often, you will find that some hardware manufacturers do not even have drivers available for Linux. Even when drivers are available, sometimes they do not come with the product, so you must locate them elsewhere, such as from third-party suppliers, to get the device to work in your Linux system. Installation and configuration documentation is also much harder to come by for Linux systems.

Locating Hardware Drivers for Linux

There are several possible sources of hardware drivers for a Linux system. In a Linux system, the kernel serves as the interface between the operating system, which is the software, and the hardware. Most Linux drivers are either located in the Linux kernel initially or are added to it in some way. Some hardware, such as printers, scanners, and video card drivers, is not located in the kernel and resides externally in nonkernel software. An example of this is the printer drivers on a Linux system, which are located in the Ghostscript print queue software. Here are some possible locations of Linux drivers:

- **New kernel drivers**—New drivers are made available for hardware that is downloaded from manufacturers' websites. Sometimes, these updates are made available through a new kernel release.

- **Linux kernel**—As just mentioned, many Linux drivers are located in the main kernel tree. The kernel should be the first place you check for drivers. Most distributions compile these drivers directly into the kernel, so sometimes you need to recompile or upgrade the kernel to get access to the drivers.

- **Hardware/device manufacturers**—It was mentioned that it can be difficult to find drivers for Linux, because some manufacturers do not even make drivers that are supported in Linux operating systems. This is still true, but today more and more manufacturers are beginning to make drivers for Linux systems.

- **USB devices**—The kernels that come with the latest distributions of Linux provide good USB driver support. These distributions support a wide variety of USB devices, including keyboards, mice, external modems, printers, zip drives, printers, and many others. Keep in mind that some USB devices, such as scanners and printers, require secondary packages that include drivers for things such as Ghostscript. For more information on USB-compatible devices with Linux, go to www.linux-usb.org.

- **Ghostscript**—As mentioned, many printer drivers are located in the Ghostscript printing software.

- **Software modems**—There are two types of modems, external and internal. External modems are compatible with Linux standard serial port drivers. Internal modems or software modems have limited driver support in Linux systems. A good website to check when installing any software modem in a Linux system is www.linmodems.org. This site contains more information about software modem drivers for Linux.

- **Sound card drivers**—The Linux kernel that comes with most distributions of Linux supports various sound cards, although some are not supported, which makes Linux's sound card support weak. Two projects are currently under development to improve sound card support for Linux systems. Advanced Linux Sound Architecture (ALSA), located at www.alsa-project.org, is an open-source initiative. Open Sound System (OSS), located at www.4front-tech.com, is a commercially led initiative to develop better sound card support for Linux systems.

- **Scanners**—The drivers for scanners are not located in the Linux kernel. Open-source and commercial project initiatives exist for Linux scanner driver support. Scanner Access Now Easy (SANE), located at www.mostang.com/sane, is an open-source project. The OCR shop (www.vividata.com/ocrshop.html) is a commercially led initiative that works independently of SANE.
- **X servers**—As you know, you can choose from more than one X server. Video card driver support for these X servers can be found at their corresponding websites. XFree86, which is the default X server for Linux, has drivers at its site, www.xfree86.org. Sometimes, you might have a video card installed that the XFree86 drivers do not work with. You can use other commercial X servers that support the video card you are using. Examples of these include Accelerated X (www.xig.com) and Metro-X (www.metrolink.com).

Some hardware requires other types of special drivers or software before it can be used. Examples of hardware that might require this are CD-R, CD-RW, DVD-R, and DVD-RW drives. CD-R and CD-RW drives require software such as X-CD Roast (www.xcdroast.org) to burn CDs. This software should come with the installation CDs. Another example is gPhoto (www.gphoto.org), which is software for digital cameras. These software packages contain low-level drivers such as SCSI or USB drivers that allow the device to interact with the Linux kernel. However, it is the software that allows the user to use the device and that essentially allows the device to work.

Configuring Hardware in a Linux System

Configuring hardware in a Linux system requires special attention because of how complex it can be. Some hardware can be easy to install on a Linux system and does not require going through the steps that are covered in this section. However, to be a proficient Linux administrator, you need to learn how to install any hardware on a Linux system, because eventually you will need to do so. Whether a configuration is easy or extremely complex depends on various factors, such as the type and model of hardware you are installing.

Hardware Replacement

Much of the hardware configuration you do is when a new device is installed, either because you are adding it for a user or replacing it. In either case, you need to follow some specific steps and precautions when doing so in a Linux system. Whichever type of hardware you install—external devices, internal devices, or internal expansion cards—each requires a different procedure.

External devices are available for many devices these days, including hard drives, CD, CD-R, DVD-R drives, digital cameras, scanners, and printers. The list goes on. However, all these devices are attached to the system through either USB, SCSI, serial, or parallel ports. The connectors on these devices are very specific and can only be plugged into those specific ports. For example, an external USB device plug only fits into a USB port, which makes it just about impossible to not hook up the device to the system correctly. An external device has a second plug that you need to plug into a wall outlet that it uses for power. All these devices, with the exception of USB devices, should be plugged into the system when the system is shut down.

Internal devices are also attached to the system with two cables. These devices are typically attached to the motherboard or to an expansion card. However, these devices are installed inside the computer case. One cable is used for data, and the other is used for power. The *power cable* is easy to install. It just plugs into one of the plugs on the power supply. There is only one way the cable will fit. The *data cable* can be a little more confusing. It sometimes fits into many slots or plugs on the motherboard or device. The best idea is to consult the device documentation for the correct placement of the data cable. Internal devices are sometimes attached to the system with screws. Sometimes, these devices are easy to get to, and sometimes they are not. Sometimes, the installation requires that you remove other devices before you remove, replace, or install the new device. It is always a good idea to document how the system was configured or installed before you remove any devices to install a new one. This makes it much easier to reassemble the system.

Internal expansion cards are installed into the system's motherboard. Sound cards, video cards, software modems, SCSI cards, and RAID controllers are all examples of internal expansion cards. These cards are easy to install; they simply plug into their corresponding slot in the motherboard, as shown in Figure 12-20. Again, you can only insert a specific card type into a specific slot, making it almost impossible to not install the device correctly. For example, an ISA card fits only into an ISA slot on the motherboard. Keep in mind that you must first shut down the system before installing any internal expansion card.

Figure 12-20 Motherboard

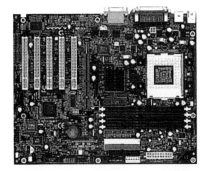

Resource Allocation

One important thing to know about installing hardware in any system, including Linux, is that a limited number of resources are allocated to devices installed on a system. These resources include the *interrupt request (IRQ)*, which signals the CPU when a hardware event occurs; the *direct memory access (DMA) channel*, which allows the transfer of data; and the *input/output (I/O) port*, which is also a means of data transfer. Each device requires one of these. If too many devices are installed, you might encounter resource allocation conflicts. Some devices can share these resources. However, if you are configuring the devices to share resources, make sure that they are not devices that will need to allocate the resources at the same time.

To view the resource allocations on a Linux system, you must view the /proc/interrupt, /proc/dma, and /proc/ioports files. Using the **cat** command, you can see what devices are allocated. Figure 12-21 shows the I/O range assignments. Each IRQ number on the left corresponds to a device on the right. If you are using a GUI interface such as KDE, you can view the resource allocations using the GUI Control Center tool, shown in Figure 12-22. It's important to refer to these files before you install new hardware, because this can help you determine what (if any) resources are still available—unless you are installing a SCSI or USB device. Devices that use these ports do not use typical IRQ, DMA, or I/O ports. These types of devices use ports that are already installed, which means that you do not have to worry about resource allocation. This is why SCSI and USB devices are good alternatives for systems that have a lot of hardware. It makes adding new hardware a much simpler process.

Figure 12-21 Output of /proc/ioports

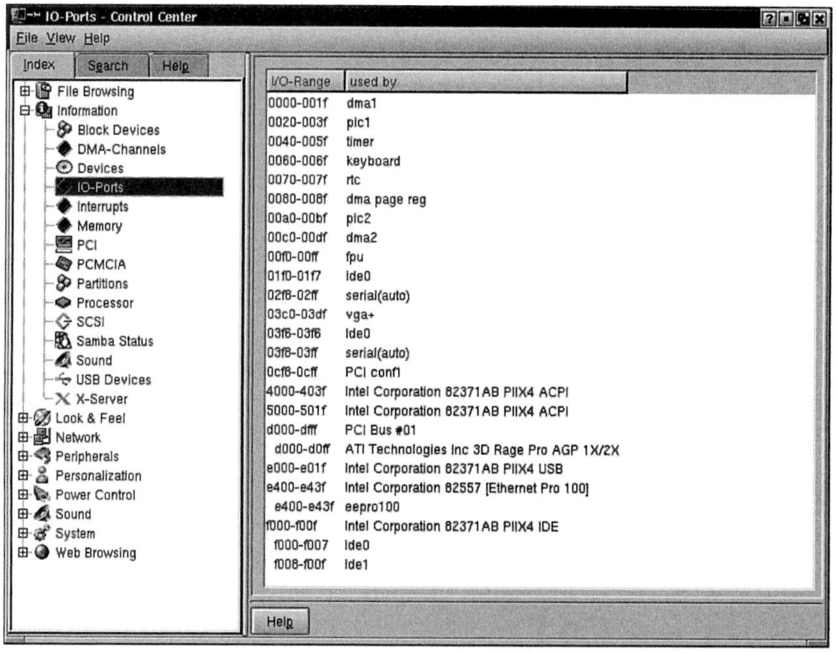

Figure 12-22 KDE Control Center

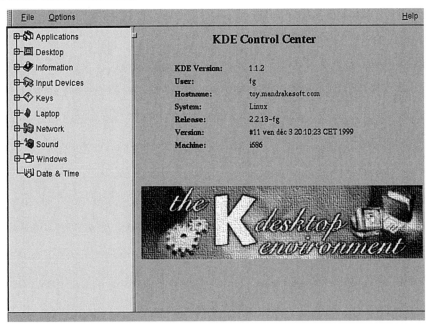

Jumper Configurations

Another aspect of configuring hardware is setting the proper jumpers for the device, as shown in Figure 12-23. A *jumper* is a metal cap covered by plastic that covers the jumper pins and controls how electricity flows through them. This lets the jumper adjust how the hardware operates. Jumpers can be used to enable or disable features if, for example, you are installing multiple hard drives in a system. It is important to select the proper jumper configuration to enable the proper master or slave setting. You do not have to set jumpers for expansion cards, because jumpers are no longer used to make adjustments for them. They are mainly used to adjust settings on hardware such as CD-ROMs, floppy drives, and hard drives, and settings on motherboards such as the CPU speed. Jumpers also can sometimes be used to control things such as IRQ and DMA assignment.

Figure 12-23 Jumper Configurations

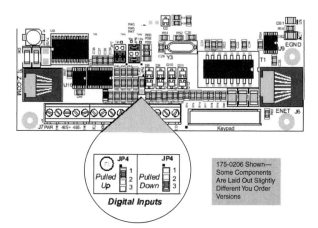

Plug and Play Configurations

Since the mid-to-late 1990s, most hardware devices have been configured through Plug and Play (PnP) technology instead of using jumpers. In fact, when installing any hardware other than hard drives, CD-ROMs, or CPUs, you most likely won't have to configure any jumpers. Plug and Play devices are very simple to install. All you do is plug in the device, and the entire configuration is done automatically by the operating system. As is the case with most Linux configurations, you might need to do a few extra tasks.

PnP is handled in Linux systems in two ways—through the isapnp program or through an ISA configuration option in the Linux kernel. The isapnp program is used to read PnP configuration options from a file to set options for PnP devices when they are installed. Most distributions are configured to automatically start this program when the system starts up. Hence, any new hardware that has been installed should be automatically detected and configured using the PnP technology. Another way this can be done is by an ISA configuration option in the Linux kernel. The 2.4.X Linux kernel includes ISA PnP support that does not require the isapnp program. More than likely, this is the case with the version of Linux you are using. Linux distributions that use the 2.4.X Linux kernel autodetect ISA PnP devices and are configured by the kernel. It is important to keep in mind that there is no PnP support for PCI hardware devices, because the Linux kernel or the BIOS configures these devices automatically.

Loading Drivers and Setting Options

The final step of configuring hardware on a Linux system is being able to load the appropriate drivers and setting the correct options related to the drivers. This can be the most critical step of configuring hardware on a Linux system, because without the correct driver loaded, the hardware will not work. In some systems, loading the incorrect driver causes the system to quit working altogether.

A driver can be loaded in a Linux system in two ways. The driver might be included in the Linux kernel, or drivers might be loaded from modules. Other drivers that are not associated with the kernel, such as Ghostscript and SANE, can have drivers loaded within the application separately. This process is typical with Ghostscript drivers, which you have learned are not located in the kernel and must be loaded from the Ghostscript application. SANE drivers are typically loaded from modules. The second method is the more straightforward of the two. If the driver is located in the Linux kernel, it should automatically be loaded when the hardware that is used with the specific driver is installed. The Linux kernel includes many drivers. It is possible to add drivers to the kernel, but doing so requires recompiling the kernel. It is not recommended that inexperienced users attempt to recompile the kernel—at least not on a production system. Recompiling the Linux kernel was covered in previous chapters. The next section discusses loading Linux kernel modules.

In some cases, the drivers you load need to have some extra options set. The majority don't need any options set, but you might need to define specific hardware settings for the driver. In some cases, you might need to tell the driver that you have installed two identical pieces of hardware, such as network cards. You can set options for drivers through kernel options and module options. To set driver options through the kernel, you must reconfigure specific configuration files that pass these options directly to the kernel. For example, you might need to specify a different IRQ and I/O assignment for a network card other than what the driver defaults to. To do this, you need to edit the /etc/lilo.conf configuration file, shown in Figure 12-24, which passes these options to the kernel. To change the IRQ to 10 and the I/O port 6200 that the Ethernet card uses, you add the line **append="ether=10,0x6200,eth0"** to /etc/lilo.conf. If the driver is loaded through a module, you must enter the driver options in the /etc/modules.conf file. This method is covered in the following section.

Figure 12-24 Output of /etc/lilo.conf

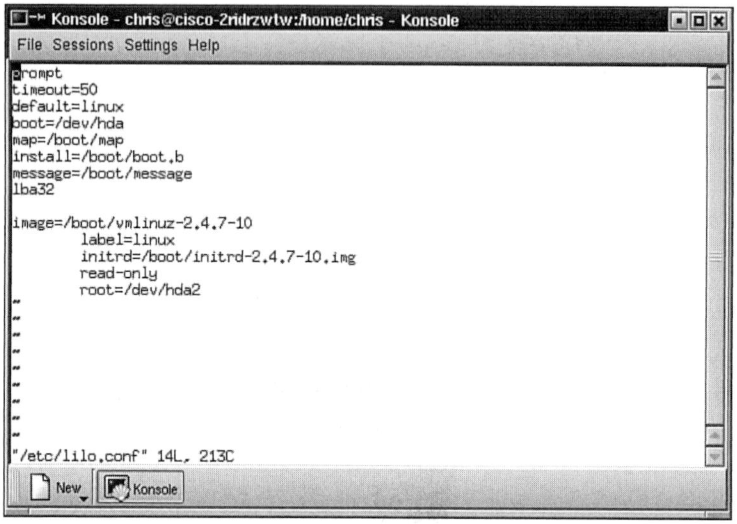

```
█-x Konsole - chris@cisco-2ridrzwtw:/home/chris - Konsole         ■□x
 File  Sessions  Settings  Help
prompt
timeout=50
default=linux
boot=/dev/hda
map=/boot/map
install=/boot/boot.b
message=/boot/message
lba32

image=/boot/vmlinuz-2.4.7-10
        label=linux
        initrd=/boot/initrd-2.4.7-10.img
        read-only
        root=/dev/hda2
~
~
~
~
~
~
~
~
~
"/etc/lilo.conf" 14L, 213C
  New      Konsole
```

Linux Kernel Modules

You just learned that drivers are loaded in a Linux system in two ways. They are either included in the kernel, which is installed and available to the system when the operating system is installed, or they are loaded from applications or modules. Kernel modules are very similar to driver files that you would load in other operating systems, such as Windows.

The first step in understanding how to load and unload kernel modules is to know what the kernel module configuration files are and where they are located. Two files in a Linux system handle module configuration.

The first file, /etc/modules.conf, contains information about modules that are used for specific tasks, as well as information about how the kernel loads and unloads modules.

The second file, /lib/modules/*x.x.x*/modules.dep, contains information about module dependencies that rely on other modules in /etc/modules.conf. *x.x.x* stands for the kernel version that is being used.

Loading and Unloading Kernel Modules

The latest distributions of Linux, including the version of Red Hat Linux that is used in this course, include kernel module loader support. This means that the kernel can load and unload drivers as it needs them. When a device is being used, such as a USB device, the kernel automatically loads the appropriate module and then unloads it when the device is no longer in use. This system works well for devices that have drivers or modules loaded into the kernel or in /etc/modules.conf. Figure 12-25 shows an example of drivers loaded into the modules.conf file. When a device is installed or needs to be used, and the kernel cannot automatically load or unload modules for it, other programs must be used to load and unload the appropriate driver or module. These programs can be included in startup scripts so that they are loaded when the system is booted up, or they can be run from the command line when the device is needed. It is recommended that the startup script method be used to avoid having users load and unload drivers.

Figure 12-25   /etc/modules.conf Screen

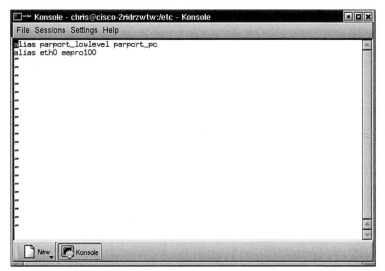

The insmod Program

The *insmod program*, shown in Figure 12-26, is used to insert a single module into the kernel. The syntax for this command includes adding the name of the module that is being loaded, along with any of the following options:

- -s—Sends all output generated by the program to a log file instead of the console.
- -p—Tests the module first to see if the system will load it.
- -f—Instructs the program to load the module even if the module was compiled for a different kernel.
- -k—Automatically unloads the module when it is no longer being used.

For example, the following command loads the parport module. This module provides core functions for sharing a parallel port with multiple devices:

```
# insmod -k parport
```

Module names on the hard drive are characterized by a trailing .o. For example, the filename of the preceding module is parport, but the module name is partport.o. These modules are stored in subdirectories of /lib/modules/*x.x.x*, where *x.x.x* is the kernel version.

Figure 12-26 insmod Screen

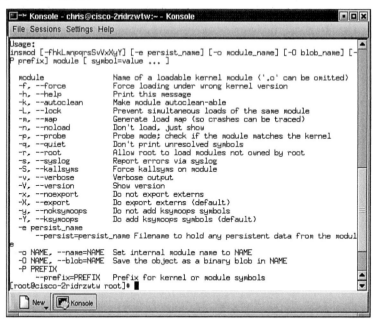

The modprobe Program

The insmod program is a useful tool, but it has some limitations. First, it can be used only to load one driver or module at a time. Also, as you have learned, many drivers and modules have dependencies on other drivers or modules being loaded. Using the insmod program, you must load each of these manually. If you are using a startup script to load them, you must place an entry in the script for each module that is a dependency of the driver or module you need to load. The *modprobe program*, shown in Figure 12-27, reduces this administrative overhead by automatically loading any dependencies a module has so all you must do is load the module you need. The modprobe program uses the contents of modules.dep to determine what modules must be loaded to use the intended modules. Several options can be used with the modprobe program. For example, the -k option used with insmod is also used with modprobe and performs the same function. A few of the other options are as follows:

- **-c or --showconfig**—Displays the module's configuration.
- **-s or --syslog**—Performs the same function as in the insmod program. It sends output generated to a log file rather than to the console.
- **-r or --remove**—Removes stacks of modules.
- **-n or --show**—Performs similar functions as the -p option in insmod. Summarizes the action that would occur if the module were loaded.

Figure 12-27 Modprobe Screen

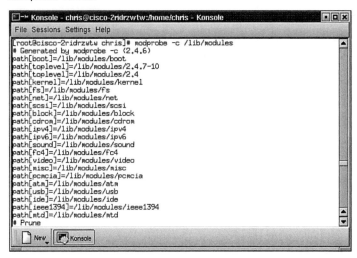

For example, the following command loads the parport module and all the modules on which this module has dependencies. This module provides core functions for sharing a parallel port with multiple devices:

```
# modprobe -k parport
```

The rmmod Program

The *rmmod program*, shown in Figure 12-28, can be used to remove drivers or modules. The modprobe program with the **-r** or **--remove** option also removes modules, but using rmmod instead allows you to enter some other options. It also provides a little more flexibility when you remove modules than if you use the **-r** or **-remove** option with the modprobe command. Here are examples of the options that can be used with this command:

- **-a**—Removes all modules that are not being used and removes all modules that are currently being used after they are no longer being used.
- **-r**—Removes an entire stack of modules, not just the module indicated with the command. A stack of modules would be the indicated module plus any dependency modules that were loaded.
- **-s**—Sends all output to a system log rather than the console.

Figure 12-28 rmmod Screen

You should not need to use this command on a regular basis. Reasons for this are that you should place any commands to load necessary modules in a startup script that will load them when the system is booted up. After that, there should be no reason to use any of these commands other than for troubleshooting purposes. This is more the case with the rmmod program than the others. This program is a good troubleshooting tool that can be used to remove modules if you suspect they are causing problems.

The lsmod Program

The *lsmod program*, shown in Figure 12-29, is used for different purposes than the programs just described. Whereas the other commands are used for loading and unloading modules, lsmod is a useful command because it reveals information other than what modules are currently being used and what device is using them. It also lists the sizes of the modules and dependency modules. Figure 12-29 shows that other important information is revealed with this command as well. You can tell which modules are currently loaded but unused. This means that they have been loaded without the **-k** option, so they remain loaded even when they are not in use.

Figure 12-29 lsmod Command Output

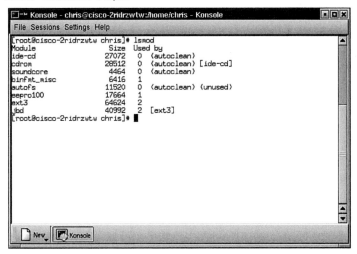

Checking and Confirming Hardware Configuration

One of the first things you need to check is the cabling. Several devices use various cables, which are used to link the device to the motherboard or to a controller card on the motherboard. Depending on which device is being installed, these cable can be entirely internal or external. As you will learn in this section, proper cable installation can be the difference between a device's working or not working, and some types of cables have specific requirements.

Power Cables

You should check or confirm the hardware configuration of two types of power cables. The first and most obvious power cable is the one that plugs into the wall outlet, surge protector, or uninterruptible power supply (UPS) from the back of the computer. This cable is external and is not necessarily the power cable of concern when you're installing a hardware device.

The other type of power cable, shown in Figure 12-30, is internal and connects from the internal power supply to one of the hardware devices. These cables connect to and are used to give power to the motherboard and other disk devices such as hard drives, floppy drives, and CD-ROMs. These power cables have various types of connectors, which are used to connect to different devices. Most power supplies have about six of these power cables that extend from the internal power supply. One cable has a connector that plugs into the motherboard, one that plugs into the CPU, and others that plug into the various disk devices. After a device has been installed that requires a connection from one of these power cables, it's a good idea to confirm that a proper connection has been made to the device. A loose or unstable connection will cause the device to not function.

Figure 12-30 Internal Power Cables

Internal Cables

Other types of internal cables are data cables. These cables allow the transmission of data from one device to another. Usually the cables extend from a controller card or the motherboard to a disk or tape drive that stores the data. The most common form of data cable is ribbon cable, shown in Figure 12-31. Some of these cables have distinct features that distinguish them from other ribbon cables. For example, some have different widths and lengths. Others have a twist in them, which identifies a floppy drive data cable.

Figure 12-31 Ribbon Cable

As with power cables, it is a good idea to make sure that a proper connection has been made. This is probably more important in data cables than in power cables, because you're much more likely to make a mistake connecting data cables than power cables. This is because power cables can be plugged in only one way, and it is easy to identify in which direction the cable should be plugged in. Data cables look the same on both sides, making it more difficult to understand which way they should be connected. Some cables have safeguards (pieces of plastic on the end of the cable) that prevent them from being installed backwards, but others do not. The only way to be certain that the data cable is installed properly is to first locate its red strip. This identifies the pin #1 side of the cable. A corresponding pin #1 in the slot on the motherboard needs to line up with pin #1 in the data cable. After you have located these, you can insert the cable. It is a good idea to be certain that a firm connection has been made, because some of these cables can be tight and difficult to completely attach. Without a proper connection, the device will not work.

If you are installing SCSI devices (see Figure 12-32), some of the data cables might not connect to a device because there are more cables than available devices. For example, if you installed two SCSI drives, you would have a cable with four connectors. One end would connect to the SCSI controller card, and two others would connect to the drives, leaving one extra cable.

Figure 12-32 SCSI Ribbon Cable

Other types of cables besides ribbon cables carry data. When installing CD, CD-R, or CD-RW drives, you have to connect a three-wire cable from the drive's audio output to the sound card, which lets sound be played from CDs in the drive. Other cables link the motherboard to components on the front panel of the computer box, such as the power button, the reset button, and the hard disk activity light.

External Cables

External cables are those that connect the computer to the external devices, such as keyboards, mice, monitor, printers, scanners, and network connections. With any of these devices it is important to install the correct cable into the correct space on the computer box. Some of these cables have mechanisms that snap into place to ensure a tight connection. Others have screws that attach to the computer case. Some cables, such as USB (see Figure 12-33) or keyboard cables, do not have anything to ensure a tight connection, so it is important to make sure that the cable is properly connected when you're using one of these devices.

Figure 12-33 USB Cable

One of the most important concepts to keep in mind when attaching external cables is to be certain that the cable is plugged into the proper port. This is particularly true in the case of serial ports, because most computer cases have more than one. Also, when plugging speakers into the sound card ports, make sure that you are using the proper ports. The one for speakers looks the same as the one for a microphone or audio inputs. Most computer cases have colors indicating which is the keyboard and which is the mouse port, but some do not. These two ports look exactly the same, so it is important to plug the proper cable into the proper port. Otherwise, the device will not work.

IRQs, DMAs, and I/O Settings

Most hardware—specifically, ISA and PCI controller cards that are inserted into the motherboard—use hardware resources located on the motherboard. These are the IRQ, shown in Figure 12-34; the DMA channel; and the I/O port, shown in Figure 12-35. These resources are limited, which means that there are only so many to be given out. There are 15 IRQs. Each one is reserved for a specific device. Figure 12-34 shows all the IRQ numbers and the corresponding devices. There are a limited number of DMA channels as well. There are more I/O ports available than DMA channels or IRQs, but conflicts can still occur with I/O ports. The motherboard uses the IRQ to send a signal to the CPU that a device is about to perform a function and it needs the CPU's attention. The IRQ assignments prevent conflicts from occurring by keeping the CPU requests separate. The DMA channels and I/O ports are used to transfer data from the motherboard to the CPU or to memory.

Figure 12-34 IRQ Numbers and Devices

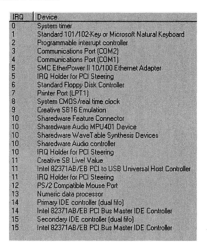

IRQ	Device
0	System timer
1	Standard 101/102-Key or Microsoft Natural Keyboard
2	Programmable interrupt controller
3	Communications Port (COM2)
4	Communications Port (COM1)
5	SMC EtherPower II 10/100 Ethernet Adapter
5	IRQ Holder for PCI Steering
6	Standard Floppy Disk Controller
7	Printer Port (LPT1)
8	System CMOS/real time clock
9	Creative SB16 Emulation
10	Sharedware Feature Connector
10	Sharedware Audio MPU401 Device
10	Sharedware WaveTable Synthesis Devices
10	Sharedware Audio controller
10	IRQ Holder for PCI Steering
11	Creative SB Livel Value
11	Intel 82371AB/EB PCI to USB Universal Host Controller
11	IRQ Holder for PCI Steering
12	PS/2 Compatible Mouse Port
13	Numeric data processor
14	Primary IDE controller (dual fifo)
14	Intel 82371AB/EB PCI Bus Master IDE Controller
15	Secondary IDE controller (dual fifo)
15	Intel 82371AB/EB PCI Bus Master IDE Controller

Figure 12-35 I/O Ports

When installing any device, it is important to check and confirm that there are no IRQ, DMA, or I/O port conflicts. Two ISA boards using the same IRQ can result in one board's not working or can cause the system to crash. PCI boards can sometimes share the same IRQ number, but this is not recommended unless it is absolutely necessary, because sometimes conflicts can still occur. This can cause the system to crash or cause the hardware not to work properly.

Most boards today have their IRQ, DMA, and I/O port numbers configured automatically in the BIOS, or they can be configured using software. Old ISA boards could have their jumpers set manually. The advantage of this was that if there were a conflict, the settings could easily be changed by simply adjusting the jumper accordingly. The new way in which these boards are configured requires the system to be booted up first, which makes it impossible to tell which hardware resource the boards will use until the systems has been started. If a resource conflict occurs, it could prevent the system from booting. Chapter 13, "Troubleshooting the Operating System," discusses the steps to take when this problem occurs.

EIDE Devices

Enhanced Integrated Device Electronics (EIDE) devices are usually hard drives, floppy drives, CD-ROMs, and other types of disk and tape drives. There are several different types of EIDE devices to choose from. These devices usually have to deal with data transfer speeds. Low-end devices usually start at 8 MBps, and high-end devices usually top out at 100 MBps. Some common speeds for data transfer are 33 MBps, 66 MBps, and 100 MBps. The various EIDE devices are referred to by various names, which include the speed. For example, the UltraDMA33 and the ATA66 are common devices available on the market.

Some of the things to check and confirm when installing EIDE devices is that they are set to the proper master or slave setting. It is possible for two devices to both use the same EIDE cable, because the cable provides three connections. One connection connects to the motherboard or controller, and the other two connect to EIDE devices. You do not have to have two connected, but the option is there if you decide to do so. The number of EIDE interfaces on the motherboard is limited, so this is a good way to install two devices and use only one interface on the motherboard. If you decide to use this method, you need to configure one device as the master and the other device as the slave. To do this, you need to set the jumpers on the device accordingly. If you don't check and confirm the proper master and slave jumper settings, the devices will not work.

In Linux, the master drive takes on the lower device letter in its /dev/hd*x* filename, where *x* is the device letter. For example, the master drive would be /dev/hda, and the slave drive would be /dev/hdb. Figure 12-36 shows the allocation of EIDE devices on a computer running Linux.

Most motherboards have two EIDE interfaces, which allows four EIDE devices total in the system. It is possible to install EIDE cards that allow more EIDE devices to be installed. It is also important to know that if both EIDE interfaces are being used, one EIDE interface on the motherboard is the primary EIDE interface, and the other is the secondary EIDE interface. It is recommended that you put the drive that contains the Master Boot Record (MBR) on the primary EIDE interface.

Figure 12-36 /etc/fstab for EDIE Devices

SCSI Devices

Installing SCSI devices can be a little confusing, especially if many devices are being attached to the SCSI chain. You need to confirm several things when doing a SCSI installation.

The first factor to check is the SCSI variant. Many different types of *SCSI interfaces* can be used, ranging from the slower 5 MBps SCSI-1 to the much faster 160 MBps Ultra3 Wide SCSI. This variance in SCSI types can cause problems in the *SCSI configuration.* It is possible to join two different types of SCSI devices, but this is not recommended because it can degrade performance and lead to other problems, causing the configuration to fail.

The second important factor are the *SCSI IDs.* Each SCSI device that is installed needs to be assigned a number or SCSI ID, which the computer uses to identify the device (see Figure 12-37). The number of IDs that SCSI devices are allowed to have depends on which SCSI standard is being used. For example, older SCSI standards that use a bus that is 8 bits wide use SCSI ID numbers that range from 0 to 7. The newer SCSI standards use 16-bit buses, which can use SCSI ID numbers that range from 0 to 15. The SCSI host adapter uses one of these ID numbers to identify itself, leaving the rest of the ID numbers for the devices. Typically, internal SCSI devices' ID numbers are configured by setting jumper pins, and external devices have a switch or dial that is set on the device itself. It is important to check and confirm that two devices do not share the same jumper setting, because this can either cause one device to "mask" the other device or cause both devices not to work. Some new devices can have their IDs set using the *SCSI Configured Automatically (SCAM)* protocol. This allows SCSI devices to acquire their SCSI IDs automatically.

Figure 12-37 SCSI IDs

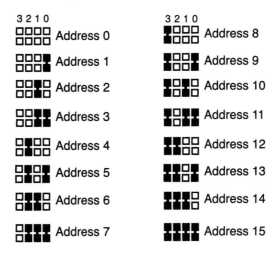

The third factor that you must check and confirm when installing SCSI devices is *termination* (see Figure 12-38). The end of each SCSI chain must have a terminating device so that the signals do not keep bouncing back continuously. A few different types of termination are used, depending on what type of SCSI variation is being used. Some examples of these types of termination are passive, active, and low-voltage differential (LVD). Some SCSI devices can be terminated using a jumper setting. Check the manufacturer's documentation to determine which type of termination is used.

Figure 12-38 SCSI Terminations

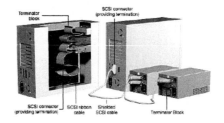

The fourth factor you must check and confirm in a SCSI configuration is cable quality. SCSI devices and installations are much more expensive than other options. The reason for this is that SCSI devices offer much more speed and quality. Some devices that are currently being tested but that have yet to make a big impact on the market will challenge the superiority of SCSI devices. However, because these new devices have not hit the market yet, SCSI devices are still considered the fastest and highest-quality devices. For this reason, it is imperative that you use only quality SCSI cables when installing SCSI devices. This is particularly true when you chain together multiple SCSI devices. A quality SCSI cable can cost about $50. This might seem expensive, but it is not wise to spend a lot of money on an expensive piece of SCSI hardware and then find out it doesn't work because of a cheap cable.

The last factor to check and confirm when doing a SCSI device installation is cable length. Again, depending on the SCSI variant you are using, the maximum cable length for the entire SCSI chain ranges from 1.2 meters to 12 meters. This distance includes the entire cable length. This means both internal and external cables.

BIOS Settings

A computer system's *Basic Input/Output System (BIOS)* is an important component that plays a big role in hardware configuration and installation. The BIOS is software that runs at the lowest level of the computer. When the system is booting up, the CPU runs the BIOS code, which allows the BIOS to configure the basic aspects of the system before the operating system loads. The BIOS also provides tools that help load the Linux kernel into memory.

The BIOS in one system will be different from the BIOS in other systems. It is generally based on the motherboard that is installed. Two systems that have the same motherboard might run the same BIOS software. Another aspect of the BIOS that differs from one system to another is the *Complementary Metal Oxide Semiconductor (CMOS)* setup utility, shown in Figure 12-39. The CMOS is the part of the BIOS where low-level options for certain hardware are set. For example, there are options in the CMOS to control which device the system boots from. There are also options to change the CPU, hard drives and other storage media, and video cards.

Figure 12-39 CMOS Screen

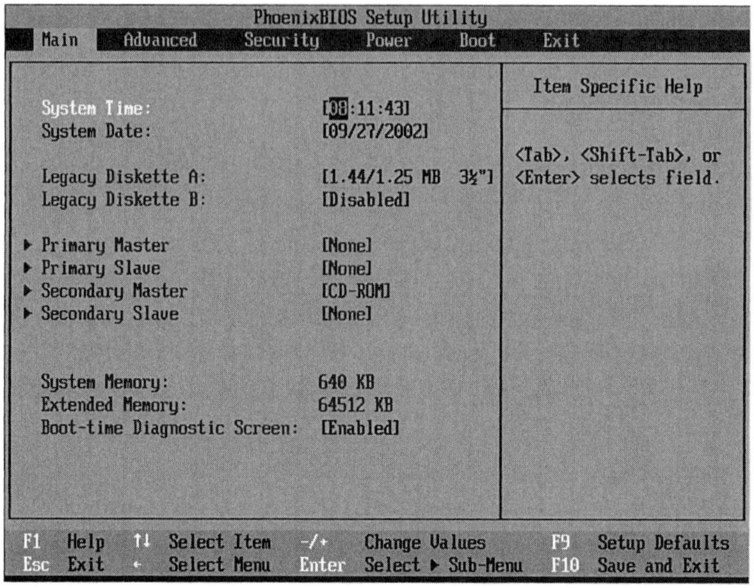

It is important to check and confirm that the BIOS settings are configured correctly using the CMOS setup utility, because if the hardware's BIOS settings are incorrect, it will not work. In some cases, incorrect BIOS setting can cause the system to not even boot up. Most computer systems display a prompt when the system is starting up that tells you what key to press to enter the CMOS setup utility. It is also important to check the BIOS settings of other hardware that might have its own separate BIOS settings. For example, most SCSI adapters have their own BIOS settings that can be used to configure settings specifically related to the SCSI adapter and devices.

Many settings in the BIOS are particularly important or are used often, such as the disk settings. When a new hard disk is installed, erased, or reformatted, you sometimes need to adjust a few disk settings in the BIOS just to remind the system of a few important things about the drive. The system needs to know the disk's capacity. This can be set manually or by using an autodetect feature that most disks have. The other common setting that needs to be made is how the BIOS interprets the disk's cylinder/head/sector addresses. Keep in mind that if you are using SCSI disks, these disk settings have to be configured through the SCSI adapter card's BIOS settings.

Another important BIOS setting are the on-board ports. A motherboard has various ports. For example, there are serial, parallel, USB, EIDE, and other ports. You can configure these ports in the BIOS by changing things such as the IRQ that they use and even enabling or disabling them. Disabling a port in the BIOS settings can free up IRQs if you are experiencing resource conflicts. PCI settings can also be configured in the BIOS settings. These settings are useful to adjust if there are any IRQ conflicts, because you can configure how the system makes IRQ assignments to PCI cards.

It is also possible to set different passwords in the BIOS settings. The BIOS settings allow a password to be set that prevents the system from booting unless the correct password is entered. This is good idea in an environment in which security is a factor. There are ways to bypass the password that prevents the system from booting, but it can stop most unwanted intruders. It is also possible to set a password that prevents someone from entering the CMOS screen and changing the BIOS settings.

Various memory settings can be configured as well. For example, BIOS settings can be configured so that parts of the information or information stored on other devices can be copied to RAM. This process is known as *shadowing*. This process speeds up the system's access to DOS because it can access it straight from RAM. This is helpful in DOS/Windows systems, which use the BIOS for input/output. However, this process does not serve much purpose in a Linux system, because Linux does not rely on DOS to do this as much. Therefore, in a Linux system, this feature can be turned off, which leaves more memory for system processes. A computer has various other memory settings. You can experiment with these to find appropriate settings.

The last important feature that can be configured in the BIOS settings are the boot devices. The system can be booted from many different devices. Using a setting in the BIOS, the system can be configured to boot from the hard drive, a bootable floppy disk, a bootable CD-ROM, or a bootable zip disk. The boot devices settings can be configured so that the system boots from a specific device or set of devices in a specified order. When the system boots, it checks each medium in turn. If that medium is not present or is unbootable, the system moves on and tries the next one. It is a good idea to experiment with these settings to determine the best configuration for your BIOS settings. It depends on what hardware is installed and what CMOS options the BIOS has. Some BIOSs have more CMOS settings than others. It is recommended that you experiment with changes on a system that is not currently in use so that you can test these changes.

Diagnosing and Troubleshooting Devices

Most Linux systems use EIDE hard drives and CD-ROMs that attach to the motherboard's EIDE port. Advanced Technology Attachment (ATA) and ATA Packet Interface (ATAPI) are other names that EIDE devices go by. It is important to be able to properly diagnose and troubleshoot problems with these devices, because problems with these devices can prevent Linux from booting and can destroy valuable data that is stored on the EIDE/ATA hard drives.

Several common types of problems can occur with EIDE/ATA devices. For example, when a sector becomes damaged, Linux can fail to boot or cause data to be damaged. In some instances, these problems can cause the Linux loader (LILO) to fail and not be able to boot Linux. Another common problem related to Linux systems is that sometimes EIDE/ATA controllers have bugs. Many Linux kernels (especially the newer ones) ship with fixes to many of these common bugs, so if the system contains common controllers, there should be no problems. If a new controller is installed that the kernel does not have fixes for yet, some problems might occur. One of these problems is getting weird file system errors. For example, newly created files can become corrupt, and the existing file system might have errors. In other cases, these bugs can cause the system to crash (but this is only in rare and extreme cases). Easy solutions to these problems include upgrading the kernel and recompiling the kernel with the appropriate fix for the controller that is being used. Another suggestion is to use a different controller that has a kernel that contains these fixes.

In some cases, EIDE/ATA devices can produce very slow data transfer speeds in Linux systems. One possible reason for slow performance is the use of incorrect drivers. Linux kernels contain drivers that support just about every EIDE/ATA controller on the market. However, to get optimal results, specialized drivers are needed for the particular EIDE/ATA devices or controller that is being used. In a Linux system, the hdparm utility can be used to test disk speeds and set several options, which can improve performance. It is recommended that you read the hdparm man page to find out more about the complete set of options that can be used with this utility. Here are a few of the more common options:

- **-d [0|1]**—Sets what mode the EIDE/ATA device runs in. Which mode is chosen affects performance. The **-d0** parameter sets the disk to run in Programmed Input/Output (PIO) mode. In this mode, the CPU controls all data transfers, which puts more load on the CPU. The **-d1** parameter enables DMA mode, which takes the load off the CPU by allowing the EIDE/ATA controller to transfer data directly to and from memory.

- **-p** *mode*—Sets the PIO mode to run in. These modes range from 0 to 5. The higher PIO modes correspond to better performance.

- **-S** *timeout*—This energy-saving option specifies how long a disk waits when not being used before going into a low-power state. To disable this feature, set the *timeout* parameter to 0. This option is more popular on laptops, because it saves battery power. Values entered between 1 and 240 represent multiples of 5 seconds. For example, if the *timeout* value is 10, the disk waits 50 seconds with no access attempts before entering the low-power state.

- **-t**—Tests uncached disk reads. This option can be used to test disk performance. Any disk that was made after 2001 should return values well over 10 MBps—even 20 MBps. If the value returned is less than this, and the disk was purchased in the year 2001 or later, the disk is not performing at the optimal level, or something is wrong with it.

Figure 12-40 shows all the available options for the hdparm utility.

Figure 12-40 hdparm Utility Options

Be careful when using these options with the hdparm utility. If they are used wrong, it could seriously damage the system's file system. Also, some of these options can be used in some systems without problems, but the same option used in another system could cause serious problems. In most cases, you won't need to use the hdparm utility, because most systems can autoconfigure themselves for optimal performance.

SCSI Devices

Another option that is available in most systems is SCSI devices. The benefits of using SCSI devices over IDE and EIDE devices were discussed in previous sections. The major complaint that people seem to have with SCSI devices is that they can be difficult to install and troubleshoot. This is not entirely true, however. When done correctly, SCSI is actually simple to configure. However, several problems can arise with SCSI devices, and because SCSI devices are so popular and commonly used, it is important to be able to properly diagnose and troubleshoot these problems. Some of these SCSI issues were briefly discussed earlier. This section specifically deals with how to properly diagnose and troubleshoot SCSI devices.

Termination

SCSI device termination was described earlier, so you already know that in any SCSI chain, each end needs a terminator (see Figure 12-41) to keep the signal from continuously bouncing back. Some SCSI devices can self-terminate by setting the proper jumper or switch. A system administrator must be aware of several different types of termination. The different types of SCSI devices and standards require different types of termination. Improper termination and termination type selection can lead to various data transfer errors. Placing a terminating adapter on a device that is not at the end of the SCSI chain can cause problems as well. Keep in mind that the SCSI adapter is considered a SCSI device too and therefore must be terminated itself, but only if it is an end device in the chain. Most SCSI adapters have BIOS, which allows you to terminate if you need to.

Figure 12-41 SCSI Terminator

Forked Chains

SCSI adapters typically have three adapters—one external and two internal. The two internal adapters (see Figure 12-42) are for wide or narrow internal SCSI adapters. A SCSI chain should be one-dimensional, which means that it should run in a continuous line with one device connecting right to the next one, with the SCSI adapter being one of these devices either in the middle or at the end of the chain. A *forked chain* is a SCSI chain that deviates from this rule by starting another chain off the adapter. This should not be done, because it can cause the configuration to fail.

Figure 12-42 Internal SCSI Adapters

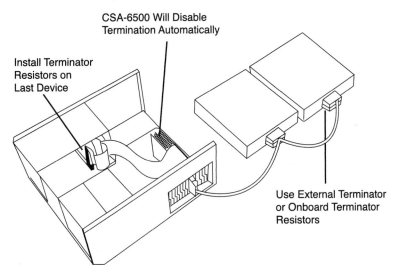

CSA-6500 Will Disable
Termination Automatically

Install Terminator
Resistors on
Last Device

Use External Terminator
or Onboard Terminator
Resistors

Other SCSI Issues

Other SCSI issues include proper SCSI ID selection, proper cable length, and cable quality. These were covered earlier. SCSI device problems can just about always be traced to termination and cable issues. Some good troubleshooting techniques for SCSI devices include ways to simplify the SCSI chain. For example, if you have a SCSI configuration that includes two hard drives, a CD-ROM drive, and a tape drive. Only one of the hard drives needs to be connected for the system to boot. So, first try removing all the devices except the disk that boots the operating system, and then see if the system will boot. If it does, most likely the problem has to do with cable length or a particular device.

It is also important to know that Linux does not support SCSI adapters, as it does EIDE devices and controllers. Therefore, the appropriate drivers need to be installed for the SCSI adapter that is being used. Some distributions ship with SCSI adapter drivers, but it is best to confirm support for the adapter before installation.

Unlike EIDE/ATA drives, SCSI adapters constantly run at optimum performance, so there is no need to use a utility such as hdparm to adjust SCSI drive performance. However, the hdparm utility can be used to check for the presence and performance of a SCSI hard drive.

Peripheral Devices

Peripheral devices connect to the computer through an external or internal port and are controlled by the computer. Examples of external peripheral devices are mice, keyboards, monitors, printers, and scanners. Peripheral devices are generally thought of as external devices only, but some internal devices can be classified as peripheral devices, such as hard drives, CD-ROMs, and tape backup devices. These internal devices are considered peripheral devices as well because they can just as easily be external devices and also can be attached externally.

The range of peripheral devices is a broad one, and the problems that can exist with peripheral devices are broad as well. For this reason, most peripheral problems can be divided into three categories: problems with the device itself, problems with the cables that connect the device to the computer, and problems with the port or interface on the computer.

Peripheral Device Problems

If you are experiencing problems with the peripheral device on a Linux system, the first thing to check is the device itself. Any device that is not working in a Linux system is most often caused by a driver issue because of the lack of driver support for Linux systems. It is important to make sure that the peripheral device that is being installed has drivers that will work in Linux, because not all devices do. This is just an unfortunate fact of using Linux. The reasons for this were discussed in previous sections. A good general rule when diagnosing and troubleshooting problems with peripheral devices on Linux systems is that most common devices, such as monitors, keyboards, mice, external modems, EIDE devices, and SCSI devices, should work fine. Other devices, such as printers, scanners, and digital cameras, will present the most problems.

Another useful approach to take when diagnosing and troubleshooting peripheral device problems is to take the device to a system that is running a Windows operating system and see if the device installs properly. Just about every peripheral device available on the market is compatible with Windows. Therefore, if the device works in the Windows system, but it doesn't work in the Linux system, most likely the problem has to do with a driver or the device itself. This approach also helps you diagnose other problems, because if the device does not work on the Windows system, you know that the problem lies elsewhere, such as with a bad cable or interface on the device.

Peripheral Cable Problems

Any problems associated with cables are usually the easiest to test. All you need to do is replace the cable with a new one. The process can be a little more difficult with SCSI cables, because they are much more expensive, so it is not practical to buy a new SCSI cable just for testing purposes. Some devices, such as keyboards and mice, have cables built in, but these devices are inexpensive, and usually it is easy to just replace the entire device.

Sometimes, cable problems are the result not of bad cables but of improper installation. Most cables can be installed in only one direction, but others can be inserted backwards. Floppy-drive cables are unusual in that they have a twist. This twist plays an important role in how the floppy drive is installed. It is important that the first floppy drive (if the system has more than one) or the only floppy drive (if the system has only one) be installed after the twist in the cable. If it is installed before the twist, the drive identifiers get confused and cause problems.

Peripheral Interface Problems

The ports or interfaces that peripheral devices use to connect to the computer (see Figure 12-43) were discussed earlier. Diagnosing and troubleshooting problems with EIDE and SCSI devices were covered in detail. However, several other peripheral interfaces need to be covered as well for you to be able to fully diagnose and troubleshoot peripheral device problems:

- **Floppy drive**—Most computer systems include controllers to support up to two floppy drives. Seldom are there configuration or compatibility issues with floppy drives in a Linux system, because the kernel almost always has drivers to support any floppy drive that is installed. One thing to check if the floppy drive is not being detected is the BIOS. The port for the floppy drive must be turned on in the BIOS for the floppy drive controller to work. If the port is turned on in the BIOS and the floppy still does not work, the problem is most likely a bad controller or floppy drive. It is easy to replace a floppy drive, but it can be difficult to replace a floppy drive controller on motherboards, because they are a permanent fixture on the board. If the controller goes bad, you can replace the motherboard or search for an expansion card that has a floppy drive controller.

- **Monitor**—The monitor interface resides on the system's video card. Any configuration problem with the monitor usually has to do with the X server that is being used. Hardware problems usually are easy to detect, because the monitor does not turn on or the image is distorted. Unfortunately, monitors are sensitive pieces of hardware that can be damaged easily if they are dropped or turned on near a magnet or light source. They also can get images burned in if they are left on without a screensaver. An easy way to test monitor failure is to replace it with one that works to see if the problem goes away.

- **Keyboard**—Keyboards are fairly standardized pieces of hardware. As with floppy drives, there should be no configuration or compatibility issues with keyboards. Any problems with keyboard interfaces are strictly hardware-related. Either the interface itself could be damaged, or the keyboard could be defective.

- **PS/2 mouse**—A PS/2 mouse connects to the computer via the PS/2 interface, which is typically located next to the keyboard interface. Even though USB mice are typically sold today, many systems still use PS/2 mice. Therefore, it is important that they be covered. PS/2 mouse drivers in Linux are fairly standard, as are keyboards and floppy drives. However, the drivers for the mouse need to be included in the kernel or compiled as modules. If the PS/2 interface is damaged, your options include using a USB or serial mouse instead.

- **Parallel**—Parallel ports are commonly used for printers but are also used for other devices, such as scanners, cameras, and other external media drives. A Linux system requires two types of drivers for a parallel port device to be enabled—one for low-level parallel port hardware and another for hardware that is attached to the parallel interface. As long as the drivers are included in the kernel in some way, you should have no configuration problems with the parallel interface. If the interface itself goes bad, just install an ISA or PCI expansion card that has a parallel interface. Another suggestion is to use another port. Some printers and scanners today can connect through USB ports as well as parallel ports. One configuration item to check with parallel interfaces is to make sure that the port is turned on in the BIOS. If the port is not turned on in the BIOS, the device will not work.

- **RS-232 serial**—Devices that use serial ports are becoming more and more obsolete because they are considerably slower than parallel or USB ports. Driver support for RS-232 serial ports is fairly standard in Linux systems, so there should be no configuration problems with this particular interface type. If the interface is not working, it is a good idea to check the BIOS settings.

- **USB**—The USB interface is becoming the popular choice for connecting external devices to a computer system. The reason is that USB interfaces provide faster speed and more flexibility than RS-232 serial or parallel ports. Many of the problems Linux systems have with USB interfaces depend on which kernel is being used. For example, Linux systems that are using the 2.2.17 or earlier kernel have very limited support for USB interfaces. To have the best USB support for a Linux system, it is a good idea to either upgrade to the 2.2.18 or 2.4.X kernel or upgrade to a distribution of Linux that includes this kernel version. Any Linux distribution that was sold after 2001 includes added support for USB devices. However, some devices still are not supported, so do the appropriate research before purchasing any USB device. It is also important to check the BIOS setting and make sure that the USB interfaces are enabled.

- **IEEE-1394**—Also known as *firewire,* this is the latest standard for high-speed external interfaces (see Figure 12-44). This interface is much faster than USB. In some cases, firewire is considered a successor to SCSI interfaces. Many of these devices are still not widely used, because this is such a new technology. Firewire devices will continue to grow and might eventually become a standard. Support for the IEEE-1394 standard is still very limited in Linux systems, but work is being done to expand Linux support for this technology in the future. Some of the latest motherboards available on the market have a firewire interface built in, but many systems do not. An expansion card can be purchased and installed with a firewire interface.

- **Network**—Network ports are included on network interface cards (NICs), or sometimes the network port is built into the motherboard. Linux supports a wide range of network cards, but it doesn't support all of them. If the network card is new, Linux might not have the drivers to support it.

Figure 12-43   Device Setup

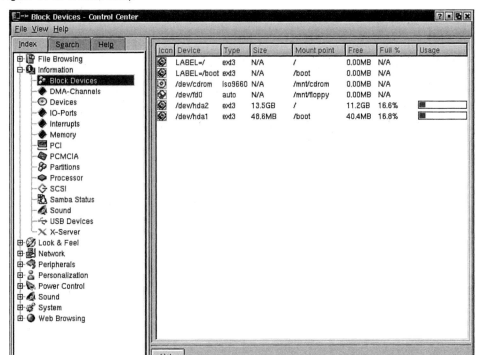

Figure 12-44 IEEE 1394

Most of these interfaces are fairly standard and should present no major problems with Linux systems. However, some network, USB, and firewire interfaces and devices are not as standardized in Linux systems and might cause some problems.

Core System Hardware

Core system hardware is the most critical hardware on a system—the RAM, CPU, and motherboard. If any of these devices are not working properly or are damaged, the entire system might not work. This is typically the case with the CPU and RAM. The motherboard can have sections that fail. This would cause a certain device or interface to not function. For example, if the parallel port were damaged, the system would most likely work except for the particular parallel interface and the device attached to it.

If there is a problem with any of the core system hardware, the system lets you know when it boots up. The system performs a Power On Self Test (POST), which tests the RAM, keyboard, video card, and so on to see if they are present and functioning properly. You might have noticed that when the system boots up, it beeps one or two times. This is how the system indicates to the user whether it passed the POST or if any devices failed the POST. You hear a different beep code for different devices that fail. These beep codes are not standardized, so check the motherboard documentation for your particular system. If the system fails the POST, it's a good idea to make sure that all the hardware is properly installed. The second step is to reconnect all the devices or just the devices that you suspect are not working. On most systems, the POST is accompanied by on-screen indicators that you can monitor to see if any core system hardware devices are not functioning properly. For example, the memory progress indicator shows how much RAM the system recognizes. If the indicator stops halfway through, there is a good chance that the system has found defective RAM.

In a Linux system, some problems associated with core system hardware do not make themselves known until after the system boots up. An on-screen message describing the problem appears when a Linux system detects a problem with the core system hardware. This message is called a *kernel oops*. The summary that is displayed includes the word "oops," which indicates the hardware problem. The oops generally indicates a hardware problem such as defective RAM, an overheating CPU, or a defective hard drive.

Another good indicator that helps you properly diagnose and troubleshoot core system hardware problems is to identify exactly when the error occurs. Does the problem occur right when the system starts up, or does it come up after the system has been running for a period of time? If the hardware fails after the system has been running for a while, it might just be that the system or hardware is getting too hot. It is important to check the heatsinks on the hardware and make sure that the system has proper ventilation so that it does not overheat. This is a problem that most people overlook or think is not a major concern, but more hardware fails as a result of overheating than anything else.

Laptop and Mobile Devices

Installing Linux on laptops is another area that requires special attention because of the fact that Linux was initially not designed to run on a system in which things such as power management and swapping PC cards were needed. The most frustrating part of using Linux on a laptop is the installation, because it can be difficult to get the XFree86 configuration to work properly with the liquid crystal displays (LCDs) that laptops use.

Laptops work essentially the same way as regular desktop computers and include all the same hardware that desktop computers do. The software also works much the way as it would on a desktop computer. Some limitations apply when you install Linux on a laptop computer:

- **Modem**—Most modern laptops have built-in modems. Although having the modem built in is convenient, this poses problems for Linux, because most often these built-in modems are usually software modems for which drivers are rare in Linux systems. To get around this problem, you have to install the proper drivers after Linux has been installed (if drivers are even available). Other options include purchasing an external USB or serial modem. However, be certain that the modem you purchase is supported in Linux.

- **Networking**—Just like modems, network and Ethernet devices are now built-in devices in laptops. It is a good idea to find out what chipset the built-in Ethernet device uses and make sure that it is supported by Linux. If it is not supported by Linux, it is possible to purchase an external Ethernet adapter.

- **Display**—The biggest problem to be concerned with when installing Linux on a laptop is getting the GUI to display properly. Specifically, the LCD screens that are used on laptops use only a narrow range of horizontal and vertical refresh rates. This makes it difficult or even impossible to get the GUI installer to run. When it comes time to configure the X server, it can be hard to find a configuration that works on the laptop. Even if the GUI works, it might not work at the system's optimum resolution. Another important factor to understand is that in laptops, the graphics chipset cannot be removed or replaced, so it is vitally important that the laptop's chipset be supported for the GUI to run on it.

If you need to install Linux on a laptop, visit the Linux on Laptops web page at www.linux-laptop.net. This site contains some good information on installing Linux on laptops. It discusses configuration procedures and gives other useful information that can help you when you install Linux on a laptop.

Power Management

Laptop computers run off battery power when they are not plugged in, so it's important to understand laptop power management and how it relates when Linux is installed. Laptops can run for only a temporary period of time until the battery power runs out. For this reason, laptops are equipped with many extra power-management tools that help reduce battery usage and extend battery life. The two main power-management tools that are included in the Linux kernel are Advanced Power Management (APM) and Advanced Configuration and Power Interface (ACPI). Both of these tools require that the system's BIOS support them. Keep in mind that although these tools were intended for laptops, they are used on desktops as well. Linux uses these tools to power off a system when it shuts down.

The purpose of these power management tools is that they tell the system when to enter power-conserving states. For them to do this, the apmd package needs to be installed and started. This package is included on the distribution's installation disks or is installed automatically. The apmd program runs as a daemon and should be configured to start automatically when the system starts up. To start a daemon such as apmd when the system starts, you need to edit the /etc/rc.d/rc.local file and enter a line of text that references the program in the /etc/rc.d/init.d/ directory. For example, you would place the following line of text in the /etc/rc.d/rc.local/ configuration file:

```
/etc/rc.d/init.d/apmd
```

Figure 12-45 shows the /etc/rc.d/rc.local/ configuration file.

Figure 12-45 /etc/rc.d/rc.local/ Configuration File

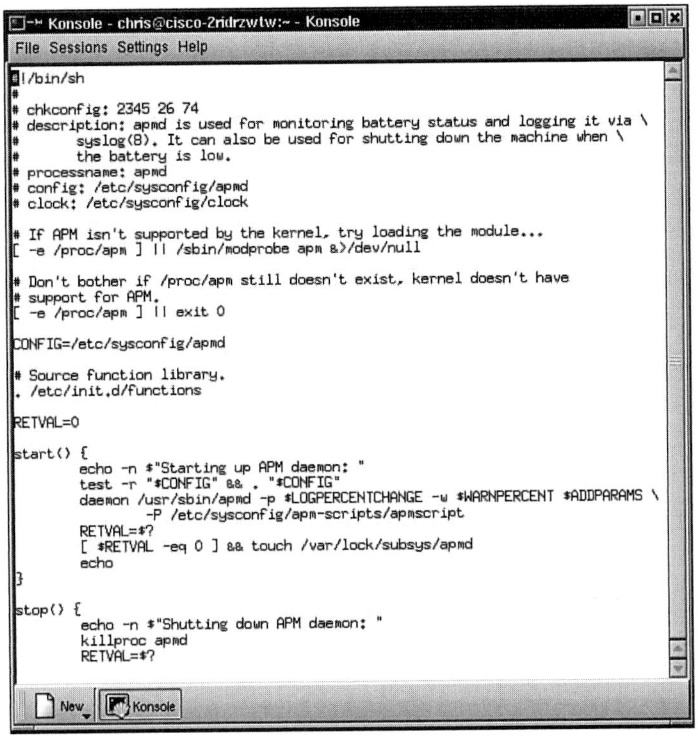


```
#!/bin/sh
#
# chkconfig: 2345 26 74
# description: apmd is used for monitoring battery status and logging it via \
#       syslog(8). It can also be used for shutting down the machine when \
#       the battery is low.
# processname: apmd
# config: /etc/sysconfig/apmd
# clock: /etc/sysconfig/clock

# If APM isn't supported by the kernel, try loading the module...
[ -e /proc/apm ] || /sbin/modprobe apm &>/dev/null

# Don't bother if /proc/apm still doesn't exist, kernel doesn't have
# support for APM.
[ -e /proc/apm ] || exit 0

CONFIG=/etc/sysconfig/apmd

# Source function library.
. /etc/init.d/functions

RETVAL=0

start() {
        echo -n $"Starting up APM daemon: "
        test -r "$CONFIG" && . "$CONFIG"
        daemon /usr/sbin/apmd -p $LOGPERCENTCHANGE -w $WARNPERCENT $ADDPARAMS \
                -P /etc/sysconfig/apm-scripts/apmscript
        RETVAL=$?
        [ $RETVAL -eq 0 ] && touch /var/lock/subsys/apmd
        echo
}

stop() {
        echo -n $"Shutting down APM daemon: "
        killproc apmd
        RETVAL=$?
```

You might not even need to add this line of text to the /etc/rc.d/rc.local/ configuration file, because it might already be there. In some cases, it is put there when the operating system is installed or when the daemon is installed. The apmd program monitors the system to see when the system's battery power is getting low. When it needs to, the apmd program starts and switches the system into suspend mode, in which most of the system's programs and functions are shut down, and only the system's RAM is maintained. The apmd program also suspends the system's hard disk if it goes unused for a specified period of time. You learned earlier how the hdparm program can control hard drive power management more directly.

It is also possible to manually control the APM tool by typing the command **apm** at the shell. Typing this command displays basic power-management information, such as how much battery power is left. The -s parameter, when used with this command, causes the system to go into suspend mode. The -S parameter puts the system in standby mode. The differences between these two modes are subtle. *Suspend mode* shuts down programs and powers off devices except for the CPU and memory, which run at minimal levels. *Standby mode* leaves devices powered up so that the system can recover power more quickly, but it takes more battery power than suspend mode. Depending on what type of battery the laptop has, the system can remain in suspend mode for a day or more without needing to be recharged. The system can remain in standby mode for several hours. It is also recommended that you check the laptop's manual or documentation to see if it has a hotkey sequence that forces the system into suspend or standby mode.

PC Card Devices

Laptops don't let you add and remove devices like regular desktop systems do with ISA or PCI cards. To get around this problem, manufacturers developed a standard for expansion cards that can be easily inserted and removed from the laptop. The industry group that developed this standard is the *Personal Computer Memory Card International Association (PCMCIA)*. These cards, shown in Figure 12-46, are called PCMCIA cards. They are also called PC Cards to avoid having to use the PCMCIA acronym, which can be confusing. Some Linux systems and other manufacturers still use the PCMCIA acronym, though.

Figure 12-46 PCMCIA Card

Three types of PC Cards can be used on laptops—Type I, Type II, and Type III. The difference between them is their size and what they are used for. Type I cards are the thinnest, and Type III cards are the thickest. Type I cards are most often used for things such as memory expansion. Type II cards are the most common type of PC Cards and are used for things such as Ethernet cards and modems. Type III cards are the rarest type of PC Cards and are used for things such as hard drives and other devices that have internal moving components. To find out more about these cards, visit the PC Card website at www.pc-card.com.

Like any other hardware that is installed in a Linux system, you also need to install the proper drivers for the hardware. Some kernels do not come with the PC Card driver package installed, so you must first get the driver package and install it. The PC Card driver package can be downloaded from http://pcmcia-cs.sourceforge.net. Fortunately, most Linux distributions come with these packages included, so you shouldn't need to download them. If you need to find support for a new device, or if you decide to upgrade the kernel by manually recompiling it, you have to download this package and install it.

The main problem that using PC Cards on a Linux system presents is that they are designed to be inserted or removed at will. This forces the driver to be mounted and unmounted whenever the card is inserted into and removed from the laptop. Linux drivers and modules do not work this way. They cannot be mounted and unmounted whenever a PC Card is inserted into or removed from the laptop. However, the PC Card driver package includes a feature called Card Services that helps you smoothly mount and unmount drivers to and from the kernel in a way that is safe for the system and prevents it from crashing. Card Services helps smooth the process of automatically starting and stopping network services each time the Ethernet card is inserted or removed. The /etc/pcmcia directory, shown in Figure 12-47, contains configuration files that the Card Services feature uses. These configuration files allow you to have a variety of PCMCIA cards configured for the laptop. These configuration files are actually scripts that run and tell the system to load certain drivers for different types of services, such as network or IDE, when the PC card is inserted into the laptop. These scripts should work fine. You shouldn't need to edit them to make them work.

Figure 12-47 /etc/pcmcia Screen

Summary

Configuring, installing, and maintaining hardware in a Linux system require a wide range of skills as well as special knowledge of how to accomplish these tasks as they relate specifically to Linux. Most of these configurations are handled much differently in Linux than in any other operating system, so you need to take a different approach when performing these tasks in Linux. For example, driver installation, configuration, and maintenance are major tasks that work much differently than in other operating systems. Physically installing the hardware is done much the same way as with any other operating system, but you must pay particular attention when you're locating and ensuring that Linux drivers are available for the device. As with most hardware and software installations, problems are inevitable. One of the more common problems is overheated or defective motherboards, CPUs, and RAM. Other common problems include misconfigured or defective EIDE and SCSI devices. Laptop installation, power management, and PC card device issues require special attention as well. This might seem like a lot of problems, but in reality it is just typical behavior when you install and configure new hardware with any operating system—including Linux.

Check Your Understanding

The following review questions help you assess what you learned in this chapter. Answers can be found in Appendix A, "Answers to Check Your Understanding Questions."

1. In Linux, what program is used to remove drivers or modules?

    A. lsmod

    B. rmmod

    C. modprobe

    D. insmod

2. What Linux program is used to list all modules that are currently loaded on the system?

    A. rmmod

    B. insmod

    C. modprobe

    D. lsmod

3. What type of PCMCIA card is the smallest and thinnest?

    A. Type I

    B. Type II

    C. Type III

    D. Type IV

4. What IEEE standard is supported by firewire?

    A. 1918

    B. 1386

    C. 1394

    D. 1905

5. As the system loads, what operation produces a series of beeps?

    A. BIOS loading

    B. CMOS loading

    C. POST

    D. OS loading

6. What value is used to compare processors from different manufacturers?

   A. MIPS

   B. Clock rate

   C. Clock speed

   D. TDR

7. What tool displays the output of voltage readings to a monitor as a waveform?

   A. Multimeter

   B. Oscilloscope

   C. Cable tester

   D. LAN meter

8. What component enables a device to send data directly to motherboard memory without the intervention of the processor?

   A. IRQ

   B. I/O

   C. CMOS

   D. DMA

9. What type of port is commonly used with a printer?

   A. Parallel

   B. Serial

   C. RS-232

   D. USB

10. In Linux, what file would you edit to change the assigned IRQ and I/O settings?

   A. /etc/rc.d/rc.local

   B. /etc/lilo.conf

   C. /etc/pcmcia

   D. /etc/fstab

Key Terms

Basic Input/Output System (BIOS)   A software program running at the computer's lowest level. As the computer boots up, the BIOS is loaded to configure basic aspects of the computer before the operating system loads.

cable tester   A device that detects breaks and shorts in a cable.

clock speed   A measurement of CPU speed. Usually measured in gigahertz (GHz) or megahertz (MHz).

Complementary Metal Oxide Semiconductor (CMOS)   An aspect of the BIOS that performs low-level configurations for certain hardware devices.

core system hardware   The most critical hardware on a system (RAM, CPU, and motherboard).

crossover cable   A cable that has reverse pin settings on each end. Used to connect like devices in a network environment.

data cable   A cable that lets devices transmit data.

digital volt-ohm meter   Also called a voltmeter. Used to measure electronic pulses through cable and determine if the cable has any shorts or breaks.

direct memory access (DMA) channel   Allows attached devices to send data directly to the motherboard's memory.

EIDE device   Enhanced Integrated Drive Electronics device. Usually hard drives, floppy drives, CD-ROMs, and other types of disk and tape drives. EIDE technologies enable mass-storage devices to address drive space above 528 MB.

firewire   A faster successor to USB. Firewire devices support IEEE-1394 and speeds up to 400 Mbps.

hardware loopback   A device that is connected to the serial port to send data, which is then looped back to be received by the same computer.

input/output (I/O) port   A port that allows a device to be connected that transfers data to or from a computer.

insmod   A Linux program that inserts a single module into the kernel.

interrupt request (IRQ)   A value of allocated space that signals or interrupts the CPU with a specific operation from a particular device.

LAN meter   Used to test broadcasts, collisions, usage levels, and errors on Ethernet and Token Ring LANs. Can measure throughput across WANs and can identify devices connected to the network.

lsmod   A Linux program that lists all the modules that are currently loaded on the system.

Millions of Instructions Per Second (MIPS)   The MIPS number is a general rating of the CPU's performance. This rating is usually based on a series of benchmark tests.

modprobe   A Linux program that reduces administrative overhead by automatically loading any module dependencies.

oscilloscope   Measures how much voltage passes through a cable over a set period of time. The output is displayed on a monitor and can indicate breaks, attenuation, crimped wire, or shorts in the cable.

peripheral device   A device that connects to the computer through an external or internal port and that is controlled by the computer. Examples of external peripheral devices are mice, keyboards, monitors, printers, and scanners.

Personal Computer Memory Card International Association (PCMCIA)   A standard for credit card-sized memory or I/O devices that fit into computers—mostly laptops. There are three types of PCMCIA cards: Type I, Type II, and Type III. Type I is the smallest and thinnest of the PCMCIA cards. They are also called PC Cards.

power cable   A cable, either internal or external, that provides an electric current for devices or components to use.

rmmod   A Linux program that removes drivers or modules.

SCSI configuration   The process of installing SCSI devices and configuring SCSI parameters.

SCSI Configured Automatically (SCAM) protocol   A protocol that automatically allocates SCSI IDs to SCSI devices.

SCSI ID   An ID used by the computer to identify a SCSI device.

SCSI interface   An ANSI interface that allows communication with peripheral devices at much faster rates than traditional interfaces.

shadowing   A BIOS setting configured so that parts of the information or information stored on other devices can be copied to RAM. This process speeds up the system's access to DOS, because it can access it straight from RAM.

standby mode   A mode in which the system leaves devices powered up so that the system can recover power more quickly.

suspend mode   A mode in which the system shuts down programs and powers off devices except for the CPU and memory.

termination   A device or technique used to properly bring to an end a cable or signal.

Time Domain Reflectometer (TDR)   A tool that tests shorts or breaks in a cable. It works by analyzing a sonar-type pulse that is injected through the cable.

tone generator/locator   A tool that identifies a cable. It consists of two components—the tone generated and the locator.

Universal Serial Bus (USB)   A Plug and Play interface that connects the system to peripheral devices. USB interfaces support data transfer rates up to 12 Mbps.

Objectives

After completing this chapter, you will be able to complete tasks related to

- Identifying and locating symptoms and problems
- Using system utilities and system status tools
- Unresponsive programs and processes
- Examining log files
- Troubleshooting problems based on user feedback
- Troubleshooting LILO boot errors
- Recognizing common errors
- Troubleshooting network problems
- Disaster recovery

## Chapter 13

Troubleshooting the Operating System

Troubleshooting a system that has manifested some level of failure can be one of the most stressful jobs in computing. When the central IT office of a large company telephones a system administrator on call at 3 a.m. to complain about lost network connectivity, or when a corporate vice president is unable to print the report he has been working on for weeks in time for a 7 a.m. breakfast meeting with the CEO, nobody is happy about it. All parties desire nothing more than to resolve the problem efficiently and swiftly.

Experienced system administrators rely on a proven and systematic methodology to solve system problems. They must be able to recognize common error conditions and know their usual causes. They must learn to evaluate symptoms in such a way as to isolate their probable origin and then apply their experience in knowing what sorts of tests to run and avenues to explore to verify hypotheses regarding the problem or to gather more data. They need to know what to do to fix the problem, or where to go to get assistance quickly, and then follow through by doing it. They should document what they learn along the way to make it easier to attack any recurrences of the problem. Finally, when possible, they need to educate users in a way that either prevents the problem from occurring again or at least lets the users provide meaningful feedback if it does.

This chapter provides some strategies for accomplishing these goals.

Identifying and Locating Symptoms and Problems

When a distressed user experiences system problems, it is not enough for him or her to wail, "This computer doesn't work!" The problem might be real, and the emotions expressed about it sincere, but not enough information has been supplied to enable the person charged with fixing it to know where to start.

Although a few problems are due to a combination of factors, most can be isolated to one of these origins:

- **Hardware**—A component of system hardware has malfunctioned or is expected but is not present.
- **Kernel**—A bug or lack of functionality in the system kernel sometimes causes problems of ambiguous origin.
- **Application software**—User-level application software or command utilities might behave strangely or collapse.
- **Configuration**—System services or application software might be misconfigured.
- **User error**—One of the most frequent sources of error conditions is caused by computer users attempting to do something the wrong way.

Every sort of error condition can be categorized as either *consistent* or *inconsistent*:

- A problem that is *consistent* is one that reliably and demonstrably occurs again and again.
- *Inconsistent* problems are those that occur only sporadically or under indeterminate conditions.

The latter type is much more difficult to attack, because unknown factors cause the problem. Before a solution to a problem can be found, you must clearly understand all conditions that might be related. For example, if the user of a piece of office software selects a menu choice and the program crashes every time, leaving a core dump, this is a reproducible problem. On the other hand, if the user selects that choice and sometimes it works and other times the program crashes, it suggests that something unknown about the path the user took to that state might be involved. More information is needed to see what else he or she might have done that bears on the problem.

Hardware Problems

Some hardware errors are obvious. If a disk drive begins rattling or ceases to be heard, if you smell smoke, or if equipment lights that are usually on are off, or lights that are usually off are on, you likely have a physical device problem. If a print job on a printer that has been working well turns out faded or blank, or with strange colors, the printer might need a new cartridge, not different driver software.

Other hardware leaves traces that the kernel detects and records. Assuming that an error is such that it does not crash the system, evidence might be left in the log file /var/log/messages, with the message prefixed by the word oops. An example of this log file is shown in Figure 13-1. The presence of such a message is not necessarily a hardware error, but this is a possibility.

Figure 13-1 Messages Log File

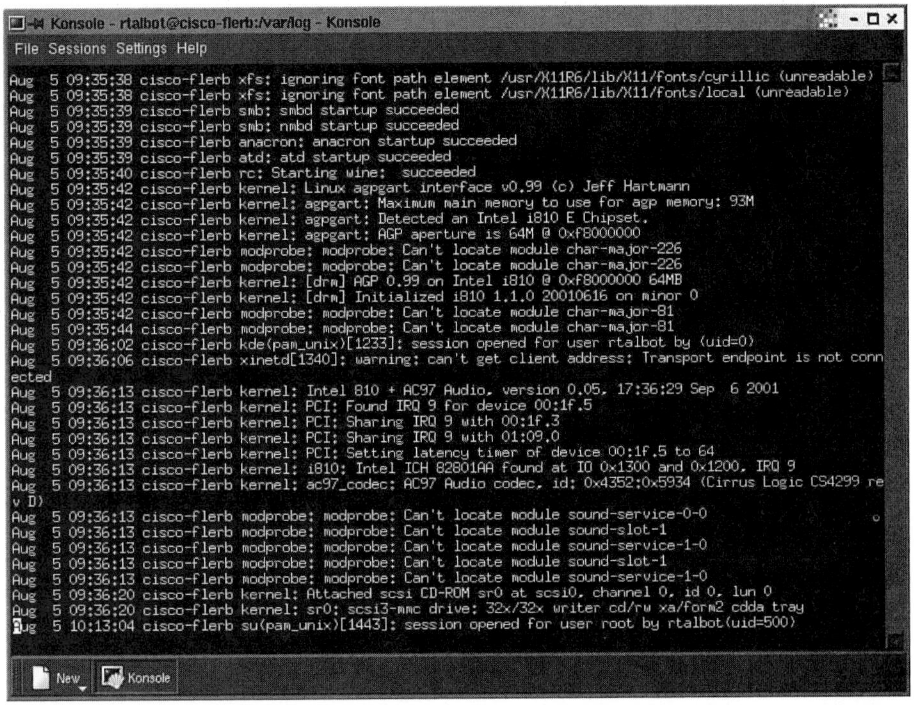

Kernel Problems

Released Linux kernels are remarkably stable unless you work with experimental versions or make your own modifications. Loadable kernel modules are considered part of the kernel as well, at least for the time period they are loaded. Sometimes these can cause difficulties. The good news with modules is that they can be uninstalled and replaced with fixed versions while the system is still running.

Module problems often identify themselves when you're using an application that addresses them. For instance, if a user attempts to play a sound file that requires a special driver that is loaded as a module, but the module has not been loaded, the kernel reports that the driver or a function it calls is not present in memory and needs to be loaded.

Application Software

Errors in application packages are most identifiable in that they occur only when you're running the application, in contrast to hardware and kernel conditions, which affect an entire system. Here are some common signs of application bugs:

- **Failure to execute**—The program doesn't start, suggesting that its main file might not have permission to execute. Or, it seems to start, but it fails to initialize entirely, and it either exits or stalls partway up, sometimes with an error message displayed in a window, on the command line, or in a log file.

- **Program crash**—The bottom drops out of a running program, usually without saving data files a user is working on. Sometimes, error messages are recorded in one of the customary places, and at times a core file is left behind, which is a sure sign that the application itself suffered a catastrophic failure. A core file can be examined with a debugger by someone knowledgeable in the application who happens to have source code available, but in emergency situations, core files are generally of little use.

  A variant of this scenario is when a program locks up, leaving the application running but unable to proceed in any way, and requiring that the process be killed from the command line. Sometimes killing it with signal 3 (SIGQUIT) causes it to terminate, leaving an image of its memory in a core file, which might be sent to the software vendor with a problem description in hopes of getting a response and a long-term fix. The reality is, however, that most software vendors are pitifully unresponsive to the needs of hapless users who have been victimized by their failing software.

  Some applications are designed to display a backtrace upon receipt of certain signals. This can be informative, sometimes even without the availability of source code. Unfortunately, you have to know this before the problem arises.

- **Resource exhaustion**—System resources refers primarily to CPU time, memory, and disk space. An application might consume too much system memory and ultimately begin to swap so badly that the whole system is affected. It might spin in a loop that hogs the CPU. Or, it might begin to write files that grow boundlessly, causing a file system to run out of space. Such misbehavior is generally the fault of the application, not the system.

- **Program-specific misbehavior**—Some errors are caused by things that obviously have to do with the running program itself. For example, if you have a word processor with a function that allows you to jump to a certain page in your document, and you tell it to go to page 999999999999 and it crashes, the application likely lacks code to check for integer overflows.

Configuration

Many packages can and must be tuned up for a local installation before being used. Simply having the software installed on the system is not enough. Configuration problems tend to affect whole subsystems, such as the graphics, printing, or networking subsystems. For example, if an expensive SVGA terminal attached to a high-end graphics adapter card in a desktop system shows only the grainiest low-resolution graphics, it is likely that the X graphics subsystem is misconfigured, and perhaps the Xconfigurator program needs to be run. Programs that depend on networking services are particularly liable to cause problems. If the system is rebooted and a remote file system that once was present is not now present, the first place to look is in the configuration file /etc/fstab (see Figure 13-2) to see if the file system is supposed to be mounted at boot time. Or if e-mail is being sent but mailq shows that outgoing mail just sits in a queue and never leaves the system, it might be necessary to investigate the configuration for the mail transport agent.

Figure 13-2 fstab File

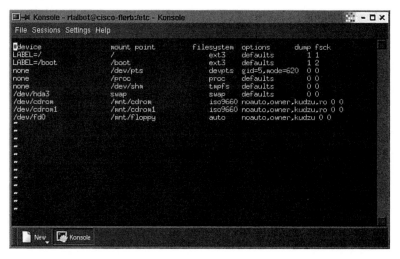

Where a configuration problem occurs in application software, you should ascertain whether it happens system-wide or to only one user. Most configurable software includes system default configuration files and also allows individual users to customize program behavior to their own taste. For example, if a system browser works well for everyone except one user who sees both text and background in the same color, it is likely he has been experimenting with his browser's properties and might need a little assistance restoring reasonable functionality.

User Error

It's no sin to make a mistake when using a computer program. Nor is it a sin to be ignorant of the right way to do something—only to insist on remaining militantly so. There is way more to know about the ins and outs of operating almost any software package than everyday users will ever care to learn or attempt to learn. Unless a user has a particular interest in a program and lots of spare time to explore features he might never have use for, he might have to settle for getting by with what works.

Therefore, it is rarely a great surprise when users paint themselves into corners with software or simply find they are unable to get from point A to point B, so assume "you can't get there from here." Sometimes a little handholding and tutoring are all that is needed to get someone over a hump.

Using System Utilities and System Status Tools

Linux operating systems provide various system utilities and system status tools that are useful in helping identify or diagnose certain problems with the operating system. The utilities described next return information about the system's current configuration and in some cases allow the configuration to be changed if it needs to be fixed. It is important to know that these utilities are useful to the extent that they return information about how the system or a file should be configured, but they do not provide information on what exact file or system configuration is misconfigured.

- *setserial*—This utility provides information and sets options for the system's serial ports. The serial ports on a Linux system are typically /dev/ttyS0 and /dev/ttyS1. If you enter the **setserial -a /dev/ttyS0** command at the shell, the system returns detailed information, including the type of hardware that is attached to the particular serial port, the port's speed, and the hardware resources used by the ports. An example of the output of the **setserial -a /dev/ttyS0** command is shown in Figure 13-3.

Figure 13-3 setserial Command

- *lpq*—This command helps resolve printing problems. It displays all the jobs that are waiting to be printed. This command is helpful because it can be used to determine if there is a problem with the printer queue or if the Linux system cannot find the printer. If the print job that was submitted disappears form the queue, something is wrong with the print queue. However, if the print job remains in the queue, the problem is most likely that the system is having trouble finding the printer. Figure 13-4 shows an example of this command's output.

Figure 13-4 lpq Command

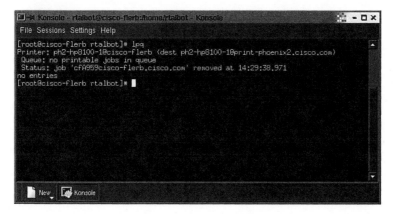

- *ifconfig*—You can enter this command at the shell to return the system's current network interface configuration. This command returns the system's current IP address, subnet mask, default gateway, DNS server, DHCP server, and what IRQ the network card uses. An example of the output of the **ifconfig** command is shown in Figure 13-5.

Figure 13-5 ifconfig Command

■ *route*—This command displays or sets the information on the system's routing, which the system uses to send information to particular IP addresses. This command can be useful to get information that can be very helpful in solving many network connectivity problems. Sample **route** command output is shown in Figure 13-6.

Figure 13-6 route Command

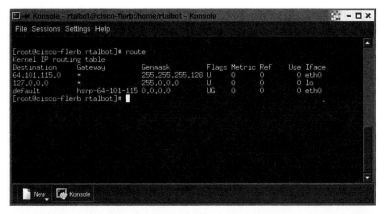

You can use several other types of system utilities and status tools to examine problems with a Linux system. These include the hard disk utilities du and df, the **top** command, and the file system utility fsck.

Unresponsive Programs and Processes

Sometimes, programs and processes become unresponsive or lock up for various reasons. Sometimes, just the program or process itself locks up and becomes unresponsive. Other times, the entire system locks up and becomes unresponsive. One method of identifying and locating the unresponsive program and effectively troubleshooting the problem is to kill or restart the process or program. Some of the issues covered in this section have been discussed in other chapters, but there are some other troubleshooting considerations to take into account with unresponsive programs and processes.

When to Start, Stop, or Restart a Process

Previous chapters covered why it is sometimes necessary to terminate a process when it becomes unresponsive to its normal functions. When a process becomes unresponsive, it can do a lot of harm to a system. Most importantly, these "hung" processes can consume all the system's resources by taking control of CPU time and not letting it go. Eventually these unresponsive processes can cause the entire system to crash if they aren't dealt with properly. It is important to be certain that a process has locked up before you kill it because some processes might appear to be locked up even though they really are not. For example, some processes get hung up for a short time while they are processing data. You also might need to terminate an unresponsive process if, instead of the process's locking up, it begins to run out of control and thus consumes the system's disk space, memory, and RAM.

It is probably easiest to terminate a program by using the **kill** command to end the processes. Other processes need to be terminated by editing the Sys V startup scripts (this is covered in Chapter 10, "Linux"). Some programs and processes need to be stopped by editing the Sys V startup script instead of just using the **kill** command because some programs use other files called *lock files*. Lock files indicate that the program is using a resource it should not be using. If a program is terminated using the **kill** command, the lock file is left behind. When the program is run or started again, it most likely will fail, and an error message is generated. You can view the system's log files to determine the presence of a lock file. If an error message appears, check the program's documentation to determine where the lock file is stored. You can delete it to solve this problem. When restarting a program, service, or daemon, it is best to first consult the documentation, because different programs have to be restarted in different ways. Some support using the **restart** command, others need to be stopped completely and then restarted, and still others can simply reread their configuration files without needing to be stopped and restarted.

Troubleshooting Persistent Problems

Sometimes, you might find yourself getting recurring troubleshooting calls for programs that cause persistent problems and that often need to be restarted. This usually means that the program has some internal problem or bug. One of the first things you can do is check with the manufacturer and see if any updates or patches have been released. Another factor that might cause a program to have recurring problems is a hardware problem. Problems with the CPU, RAM, motherboard, and other hardware components can cause difficulties for some programs. In some instances of such a hardware failure, the entire system or the operating system's file system might crash.

The best way to fix programs that crash repeatedly is to replace them with new software or with a different kind of software that performs the same task. Sometimes replacement software might not be an option or even be available. The solution for this is a much more difficult one. If possible, try using the software in a different way. Or, if a particular keystroke or command causes the program to fail, stop using it. Usually replacement software is available. If it is a daemon that is crashing regularly, try using other methods of starting it and running it. The various methods of starting a daemon on a Linux system are described in Chapter 10.

Examining Log Files

Log files were introduced in Chapter 11, "Advanced NOS Administration." The various activities of a Linux server, the operating system kernel, and system utilities are recorded in log files. Chapter 11 mentioned that most of these log files are located in the /var/log directory or one of its subdirectories. Some of the more important log files on a Linux system are the /var/log/messages, /var/log/secure, and /var/log/syslog log files. Figure 13-7 shows all the various log files that are located in the /var/log directory. Examining these log files can be helpful in identifying several problems with a Linux server. The system's log files can be used to monitor system loads such as how many pages a web server has served, to check for security breaches such as intrusion attempts, to verify that the system is functioning properly, and to note any errors that might be generated by software or programs. These uses can identify several problems. There are several different types of information that it is a good idea to know, which will make using these log files to identify problems a little easier.

Figure 13-7 Linux Log Files

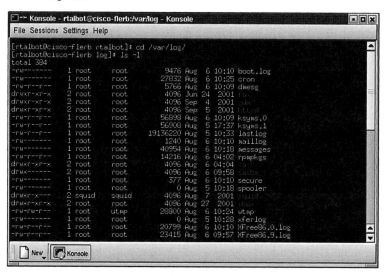

- **Monitoring system loads**—Servers are designed and built to accept incoming requests internally from other users on the local-area network (LAN) or externally from remote users or the Internet. The server needs to be built so that it can handle these requests efficiently. You can use these log files to determine what requests are being made that might be causing the server to run sluggishly. If the server is receiving a large increase in the number of incoming requests or the size of files it is being asked to transfer, you need to take appropriate measures to increase the server's ability to handle the increasing load. Sometimes this might include just adding another server, router, or switch instead of upgrading an existing one. Keep in mind that these log files keep track of increasing loads on the server-specific programs only. This means that they log only the events of the programs and services that are running on the server and not any problems that are caused by increasing workstation demands. However, it can be easy to determine if workstation demands will increase, because as a system administrator, you would know if the users will be using more resource-intensive programs.

- **Intrusion attempts and detection**—It can be difficult to detect an intrusion into a network or server. However, proper examination of system log files can help you find out how and where the intrusion occurred, as well as what changes the attacker made to the system or network. Sometimes when intruders break into a system, they attempt to modify system tools and utilities, which affects the server's performance or reliability. Sometimes intruders just delete important files (often log files) to cover their tracks and make it difficult for you to find out what damage they might have done to the system. For this reason, it is a good idea to continuously monitor the log files so that any changes or unusual entries will be noticed easily.

- **Normal system functioning**—The log files can also be examined to ensure that the system is functioning normally and as intended. If something is wrong with the system, the information in the log files can help identify and eliminate possibilities. For example, a Linux system might be configured as a DHCP server in which it is supposed to distribute IP addresses to client workstations. You can examine the log files to see if the server is receiving requests and distributing IP address leases. Then you can narrow down the problem to a client-side issue and not a problem with the server.

- **Missing entries**—If any of the log files contain missing entries, or if you are examining a log file and a specific entry you are looking for is not present, this can indicate that something on the server is not functioning properly or is misconfigured. Missing entries in log files can also indicate that there might be a problem somewhere other than the server. For example, suppose you have configured a file server to run Samba so that clients using Microsoft Windows can access the Linux server, and you configure Samba to log access attempts to the server. Later you decide to check the log to see who is attempting to access the server, and you see that several entries are missing. These missing entries can indicate that there is a configuration error with the Samba daemon on the server. It can also mean that there is a problem externally on the network with a router or firewall that is preventing access and there isn't necessarily a problem with the server at all.

- **Error messages**—Many of the log files on a Linux system contain various error messages you can use to help locate and identify any problems or misconfigurations with the server. For example, a log file can contain information about an authentication error. This error message is helpful because it can tell a system administrator where he or she should begin troubleshooting. Many programs and server utilities can be configured to log specific information that might help troubleshooting efforts. You should consult the program's documentation to find the available configuration options, because they can differ depending on the program.

Examining log files also can help you identify various kernel, application, configuration, and user problems. The log files can be most helpful when you're trying to identify and locate software problems with the kernel, server, user login tools, and other system utilities.

The dmesg Command

Some of the most important and helpful information recorded in the log files that can be useful in troubleshooting and identifying problems are *kernel startup messages*. They can be particularly helpful in identifying hardware and kernel issues. You can use the **dmesg** command to display recent kernel messages, which are technically known as the *kernel ring buffer*. An example of the output of this command is shown in Figure 13-8. Perhaps you've noticed that when the system boots up and Linux starts loading, a series of messages in the kernel ring buffer scrolls down the screen as the system is initializing the devices and services. These messages contain important information about the drivers and hardware installed in the system. The information in these messages relates to whether the drivers are being loaded successfully and what devices they control, such as EIDE or SCSI controllers.

Figure 13-8 dmesg Command

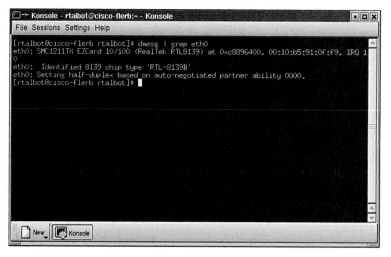

There are various instances in which the **dmesg** command can be very useful. For example, you might be administering a server that contains two Ethernet cards, one of which does not seem to be working. If you enter the command **dmesg | less** after the system starts up, you can view information about the two Ethernet cards that are installed in the system. By looking at the kernel messages in the log file, you can determine whether there is an entry for the nonfunctional card. If there isn't, the issue could be that the driver isn't loading, or it could be the wrong driver for the card. If the card has an entry but it still doesn't work, the issue most likely lies somewhere in the card's network configuration. You can use variables with the **dmesg** command that narrow down the number of messages that are displayed. For example, by using the **grep** command, you can display the lines that pertain to the nonfunctioning Ethernet card only. The command used to perform this operation is **dmesg | grep eth**X, where X is the Ethernet device in question.

The information that is contained in **dmesg** is so valuable to a Linux system that most distributions automatically send the output to the /var/log/boot.messages log file. If the distribution does not do this, you can do so by placing the line **dmesg > /var/log/ boot.messages** in the /etc/rc.d/rc.local script.

Troubleshooting Problems Based on User Feedback

Sometimes, the best source of identifying and locating a problem with a computer system is the person who was using the system when the problem was reported or the person who uses the system on a regular basis. Keep in mind that this depends on the user's ability to convey the correct information to you about the problem or what he was doing when he began experiencing the problem. Users might not always provide exact information. They might give imprecise information or even leave out facts that are critical to your being able to diagnose the problem, such as the exact error message the system displayed. For this reason, you should use any information you elicit from users as a starting point. It's best to investigate and reproduce the problem to be certain of what the problem is. Many problems users report come from their lack of understanding of how computer systems work. Users report several different types of problems. Here are some of the most common ones:

- **Login problems**—One of the more common types of problems you will hear from users is that they can't log on to the system. Most of the time this happens not because of a problem but because the user forgot his password or entered it incorrectly. Remember that passwords in a Linux system are case-sensitive. In some cases, the password might have expired. If so, all you need to do is reenable it so that the user can change his password or you can assign a new one.

- **File permission problems**—File permission problems are not as common as login problems. However, sometimes a user might have problems accessing a shared file. This isn't normally a big problem if the user works with files in his own directories, but it can be a problem when users need access to files in other directories. In some cases, you might need to explain how the Linux file system permissions work to prevent these types of problems.

- **Removable media problems**—Because Linux handles removable media very differently from other operating systems, such as Windows, users often have many complaints. Even though the GUI interface might look like you can access removable media such as floppy drives and CD-ROMs by just inserting the medium and searching for the files, you can't. The media still have to be mounted and unmounted. It is important to point out this fact to users and explain to them how to properly use the **mount** and **umount** commands. Also, because only the superuser account can use the **mount** and **umount** commands, it might be a good idea to modify the /etc/fstab file, shown in Figure 13-9, so that users can mount and unmount removable media themselves. Most devices, such as CD-ROMs, lock up so that they cannot be ejected unless they have been unmounted first. The floppy drive can be ejected without first being unmounted, which can lead to files becoming corrupt. The other types of media that cannot be ejected unless they have been unmounted can lead to many senseless troubleshooting calls unless the users understand how to properly mount and unmount removable media drives.

- **E-mail problems**—E-mail should work for users when it has been configured correctly. This is true especially if all the user has to do is pull his or her mail off the SMTP server locally. However, if you have remote users, it might be a good idea to instruct them on how to configure their mail accounts so that they can read their mail.

- **Program errors**—Users will often report that they have a program crash. The best option here is to approach this on a case-by-case basis, because each program requires a different approach to troubleshoot it. The best idea here is to elicit as much information from the user as possible about any error messages that popped up or what the user was doing when the program crashed. Then you can re-create the events that caused the error.

- **Shutdown problems**—Linux should always be shut down using the **shutdown** command. This was explained in previous chapters. However, this command can be used only by the root user. Users who experience problems shutting down should be shown how to use the GUI shutdown option that lets nonroot users shut down a Linux system. It is important that users know how to properly shut down the Linux system, because improper shutdown can cause various problems, such as lengthy startup processes, serious file system corruption, and data loss. If your users complain of such problems, you might suggest to them properly shutting down their systems.

Figure 13-9   fstab File

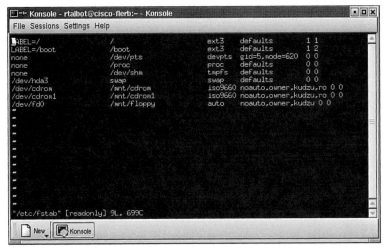

Worksheet 13.4.7   Server Shutdown

Learn how to properly shutdown a server.

LILO Boot Errors

The Linux Loader (LILO) boot loader was first mentioned in Chapter 9, "Linux Installation Procedures," so by now you have a firm understanding of what LILO does in a Linux system. If LILO is the boot loader that is being used, the LILO boot loader is the first piece of code that takes control of the boot process from the BIOS, loads the Linux kernel, and passes control entirely to the Linux kernel. Many things cause LILO boot errors. The BIOS for most x86 processor-driven computers was designed for systems in which maximum hard drive capacity was a mere 40 MB. For these systems, 32-bit or even 64-bit programs and operating systems (which are becoming available) were things of fantasy and science fiction. However, we know today that computer hardware technology evolves with astonishing speed. As a result, the BIOS technology has had to evolve as well. This changing technology combined with LILO's own needs unfortunately leads to LILO's not behaving properly. When LILO doesn't function correctly, it can be very frustrating, because this usually means that your system will not boot. The error messages or codes that LILO produces can be difficult to interpret. Understanding how to fix and work around these problems can help you repair LILO errors and return the system to working order. It is important that you understand how LILO is installed and configured before you proceed with this section, so it might be a good idea to review the section "Installing and Reconfiguring the Boot Loader" in Chapter 9. It is also important to mention that even though you can use other boot loaders to boot Linux, LILO is discussed here because it is the one used on x86 systems. This is the system you will use in this course, and it is the boot loader that is installed in this course. LILO is not used on non-x86 processor systems.

The first step in understanding LILO boot errors is to be able to understand and interpret the various LILO error codes that might be generated. Here are some of the various error codes:

- **None**—If no error code appears, LILO has not loaded. This might be because LILO was not installed, or it might have been installed in the wrong location. Check the /etc/lilo.conf file and make sure that the configuration is correct, and then use the **lilo** command to install LILO. To better understand what the lines in the /etc/lilo.conf file mean, it might be a good idea to look at the man page for lilo.conf, shown in Figure 13-10. LILO might have been installed on a different partition. In that case, you need to make that partition the boot partition. All these topics are covered in Chapter 9.

- **L** *error-code*—This means that LILO has started to boot but it is unable to boot the second-stage boot loader. The *error-code* is a two-digit number that the BIOS generates. The codes that these numbers represent are detailed in the LILO documentation. Most of these types of error codes represent hardware failures such as a bad hard drive or a discrepancy in how LILO and the BIOS agree on how to treat disk addresses. If the hard drive is bad, you should take appropriate measures to confirm that the hard drive has failed. If LILO and BIOS settings are different in how they treat disk addresses, make the necessary changes in the BIOS or in the /etc/lilo.conf file.

- **LI**—This means that LILO has started and the first- and second-stage loaders have been loaded, but the second-stage loader won't run. This type of error code is usually the result of the same symptoms as with the **L** *error-code* condition.

- **LI101010...**—This means that LILO has been loaded and is running properly but cannot locate the kernel image. You usually see this error code when a new kernel has been loaded or upgraded and the **lilo** command was never used to reinstall LILO.

- **LIL**—This means that the first- and second-stage loaders have been successfully loaded and are running properly, but LILO is unable to read the information it needs to work. This error code is usually the result of some hardware failure or disk geometry mismatch between LILO and the BIOS. You can fix this problem by setting or correcting the necessary option in /etc/lilo.conf, shown in Figure 13-11, or by making the necessary changes in the BIOS.

- **LIL?**—This means that the second-stage boot loader has been loaded correctly but is at an incorrect address. This problem can be caused by moving /boot/boot.b, the second-stage boot loader file, without using the **lilo** command to reinstall LILO. The problem also can be caused by a disk geometry mismatch between LILO and the BIOS.

- **LIL-**—This means that the disk descriptor table (/boot/map) is corrupt. This problem can be caused by moving /boot/map, the second-stage boot loader file, without using the **lilo** command to reinstall LILO. The problem also can be caused by a disk geometry mismatch between LILO and the BIOS.

- **LILO**—This means that LILO has successfully been loaded and is running. At this point there should be no problem with LILO that causes the system not to boot. If the system still does not properly boot at this point, the problem lies elsewhere, possibly with the kernel, its drivers, or its system configuration files.

Figure 13-10   Man Page for lilo.conf

```
LILO.CONF(5)                                    LILO.CONF(5)

NAME
        lilo.conf - configuration file for lilo

DESCRIPTION
        This file, by default /etc/lilo.conf, is read by the boot
        loader installer lilo (see lilo(8)).

        It might look as follows:

                boot = /dev/hda
                delay = 40
                compact
                vga = normal
                root = /dev/hda1
                read-only
                image = /zImage-2.5.99
                        label = try
                image = /zImage-1.0.9
                        label = 1.0.9
                image = /tamu/vmlinuz
                        label = tamu
                        root = /dev/hdb2
                        vga = ask
                other = /dev/hda3
                        label = dos
                        table = /dev/hda

        This configuration file specifies that lilo uses the  Mas-
        ter Boot Record on /dev/hda. (For a discussion of the var-
        ious ways to use lilo, and  the  interaction  with  other
        operating  systems,  see user.tex from the lilo documenta-
        tion.)
```

Figure 13-11 /etc/lilo.conf File

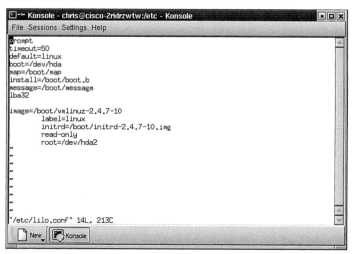

You might have noticed that the majority of these errors are the result of LILO's being unable to read files that have been modified or moved. You also might have noticed that any changes made to LILO, including any files that have moved or changed, must be followed by the **lilo** command to reinstall LILO so that the changes can take effect. Other means to boot Linux without LILO are described next.

Booting a Linux System Without LILO

There might be some instances in which you cannot use LILO to boot the computer because it has failed altogether. When this happens, you need to have some other way to boot the system without LILO. There are a few methods you can use to boot the system without LILO. Using the emergency boot system and using an emergency boot disk to boot a Linux system instead of LILO are covered in the next two sections. However, you might want to try a simpler approach first. Here are some of your options:

- **LOADLIN**—This is a DOS utility that can boot Linux. It usually comes with the installation CDs and is located in the dosutils directory. To use LOADLIN, you need to have either a DOS partition or a DOS boot disk, a copy of LOAD-LIN.EXE, and a copy of the Linux kernel. You must boot DOS and then enter **LOADLIN** *VMLINUZ* **root=/dev/**rootdevice **ro**, where *VMLINUZ* is the name of the kernel and **root=/dev/**rootdevice is the name of the root partition, such as /dev/hda1.

- **Raw kernel on a floppy**—It is possible to boot Linux if the raw Linux kernel is written to a floppy disk. If you choose this method, you must first copy the kernel to the floppy disk by using the **dd if=***vmlinuz* **of=/dev/fd0** command, where *vmlinuz* is the name of the kernel. After you have copied the kernel to the floppy disk, insert the floppy disk into the drive and start the computer. Be sure that the BIOS is configured to boot from the floppy drive. You need to confirm one other step before this will work. You need to first configure the kernel so that it knows the location of the root partition. To do this, you use the **rdev /dev/fd0 /dev/***rootdevice* command, where **/dev/***rootdevice* is the name of the root partition. Keep in mind that these disks appear unformatted in DOS and Windows and can't be mounted in Linux because they don't have any file systems.

- LILO on a floppy—This is probably one of the more preferred methods, because it is the fastest. It is much faster than using LOADLIN or the raw kernel on a floppy method, because the kernel is still on the computer. To install LILO on a floppy disk, you need to edit the lilo.conf file. Change the boot line in the file to **boot=/dev/fd0**. Then enter **lilo** so that LILO will be reinstalled. Keep in mind that you need to edit this line back to what it originally was if you want to install LILO on the hard drive.

Some general rules and extra information are helpful when you use these techniques to boot a Linux system without LILO. The LOADLIN technique is generally thought of as the most flexible, because it allows you to create or modify a boot disk using DOS by using a default kernel from a Linux installation CD. The raw kernel on a floppy method is a very easy technique, because it does not require any configuration to figure out where the boot partition is located. However, if you change the system's configuration—specifically, if you change where the boot partition is located on the system—you need to make the same modifications to the kernel on the floppy. If you fail to do this, you will not be able to boot the system with the configuration on the disk. Using the LILO-on-a-floppy method is considered the least useful, but it can help in some instances. For example, some people prefer to configure the boot partition to boot to a non-Linux operating system. Then, when the system needs to be booted to Linux, all you need to do is insert the floppy disk that has LILO on it. Figure 13-12 shows the LILO configuration page you see during installation. From this screen, you can choose to create a LILO boot floppy disk that you can use to boot Linux.

Figure 13-12 LILO Configuration Screen

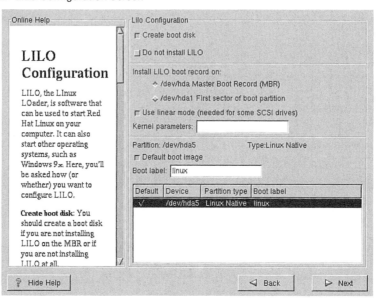

Emergency Boot System

Linux provides an emergency system copy of LILO that you can use to boot Linux if the original LILO boot loader has errors or is not working. It is called the *emergency boot system*. To be able to use this copy of LILO, you must make the appropriate configuration changes in lilo.conf. The steps are as follows:

1. Change where the regular disk's root partition is mounted. It is recommended that you mount it somewhere in the emergency boot system, such as in /mnt/std. Figure 13-13 shows the GUI configuration screen in which this procedure is done.

Figure 13-13 LILO Boot Label

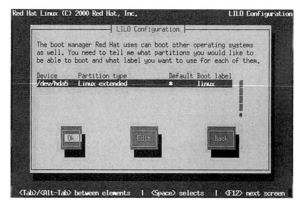

2. Make sure that the /boot directory is in its own partition. You should mount it either instead of or in addition to the root partition.

3. Change any references to /boot or other files so that they point to the regular partition. For example, you would want to change /boot/vmlinuz to /mnt/std/boot/vmlinuz. This changes the reference point back to the regular partition.

4. Change the kernel images and other boot options back to what they would normally be. For example, the **boot** and **root** options should point to the regular hard disk.

After completing these steps, you need to issue the **lilo** command to reload LILO. If everything was configured correctly, the boot loader should install itself normally. It is possible that this might not work. If the version of LILO that the emergency system uses is different from the version that is currently installed on the regular system, the LILO installation might not work. If this happens, just use the LOADLIN method, which was explained in the preceding section, and then reinstall LILO using the regular system tools.

Using an Emergency Boot Disk in Linux

Sometimes, there are reasons that a Linux system does not boot, other than LILO problems. For example, the /etc/fstab file, which is used to map partitions to the file system, might be corrupt. Startup script errors can cause the system to sometimes lock up or shut down. Other reasons include hard disk failure and replacement of the disk from a backup. All these are common errors that show up in a Linux system from time to time, and LILO is not the culprit. To work around these sorts of problems and successfully boot the system, you need to obtain or create an *emergency boot disk*. An emergency boot disk lets you boot the system without using any part of the main partition. The emergency boot disk can be either floppy disks that hold a minimum number of system files with which to boot the system, or complete Linux installations that are stored on high-capacity removable media such as CD-ROMs. A system administrator must know how to properly create an emergency boot disk so that he or she can perform the necessary troubleshooting calls. It is also important to know what tools are on the disk and how to use them to properly troubleshoot a Linux system that can't boot up.

Finding an Emergency Boot Disk

You have several options when it comes to finding a ready-made emergency boot disk for Linux. Most of these are available for download from the Internet. The following popular Linux emergency boot disks are easy to use and often require no configuration:

- **The Linux installation disks**—One of the most obvious places to look is in the installation disks or media that were used to install the operating system. Most distributions include an emergency boot disk system that can be accessed as an option when you load the installation media. For example, when you start the installer program to load Red Hat Linux, you enter **linux rescue** at the **lilo:** prompt. If you are using a different distribution, consult the documentation regarding how to use the emergency disk included with the installation media.

- **Tom's Root/Boot Disk**—The official name of this emergency disk distribution is tomsrtbt, which stands for "Tom's floppy, which has a root file system and is also bootable." This can be downloaded from the Internet and can fit on a single floppy disk. It is a complete bootable Linux system that can be used only from the command line. The GUI is not supported. tomsrtbt comes in packages for DOS as well. To obtain a copy and find out more out Tom's Root/Boot Disk, go to www.toms.net/rb.

- **ZipSlack**—This is available for Slackware Linux. It can be installed on a small partition or on a removable drive such as a zip disk, because its 100 MB size is slightly larger than the capacity of a floppy disk, which is only 1.4 MB. The advantage of having a larger version of Linux than what is available on a single floppy such as Tom's Root/Boot is that it is easier to customize with commercial backup tools and custom kernel drivers.

- **Demo Linux**—This is one of the better emergency boot disk utilities available because it is the most complete. It is even larger than the 100 MB ZipSlack, so it must be burned on a CD-R. The 650 MB file can be downloaded from the web at www.demolinux.org. It offers a complete version of Linux to work with that even allows you to run the X GUI on most video hardware.

- **SuSE evaluation**—This is very similar to Demo Linux in that it is about the same size and must be burned to a CD-R. However, it is an evaluation version of SuSE Linux that can be downloaded from the web at www.suse.com.

Keep in mind that these are only a few of the options available for emergency boot disks on a Linux system. To find out what other ones are available, check out www.linux.org/dist/english/html. This page and the web page for Tom's Root/Boot contain a few other links to help you find small and specialty distributions to use for emergency boot disks.

Creating an Emergency Boot Disk

For the most part, the emergency boot disks just discussed are sufficient for any purpose. However, in some instances you might need to create your own custom emergency boot disk. An example is if the system you are working on contains special hardware that needs special drivers, or if it uses a special file system, special networking features, or any other configurations that normally are not supported in any of the common emergency boot disks.

Creating a custom emergency boot disk can be an easy or difficult task, depending on the requirements of the system that needs to be booted and how you approach creating the disk. The simplest and most recommended method of creating a custom emergency boot disk to suit your computer system's needs is to modify one of the existing boot disks so that you can add the special features your system requires. The ZipSlack boot disk is one of the better options to choose when you need to create a custom emergency boot disk. ZipSlack acts much like a regular Linux distribution, but it lacks some features as well, such as a GUI. ZipSlack also allows you to recompile its kernel, add any necessary tools you might need, or configure many other aspects to suit the Linux system that needs to be booted. Another feature that makes ZipSlack a good choice is that there is some (albeit very little) space to make additions to it on a 100 MB zip disk. It is also possible to strip away any programs you don't need, which can free up a little more space. Another option is to use a 250 MB zip disk to save ZipSlack. This leaves a lot of space for any additional programs or configuration changes you need to make.

It is not recommended that you use any of the other emergency boot disk options to make a custom boot disk. Tom's Root/Boot disk is far too small to do so. With this emergency boot disk fitting on a tiny 1.4 MB floppy disk, there is not much room to add anything or make changes. Another issue is that because these distributions are so tiny, many of the program files have already been changed so that they are optimized for this tiny amount of space. This makes changing or adding anything a very difficult process, because it is almost impossible to do so without exceeding the maximum space on the disk. The distributions that can be burned to a CD are difficult to use to create a custom emergency disk because of the fact that you cannot make any changes to files that are burned to a CD. To make a custom emergency disk with a distribution that is burned to a CD, you must copy the contents to a hard drive of a functioning system, make any changes or additions, and burn it to CD again.

Recovery Tools

Regardless of which emergency boot disk you use, several types of recovery tools should be included that can help in the repair process. The following list includes fairly standard tools that are familiar Linux programs. Keep in mind that the particular system that is being booted up with the emergency boot disk might have some special programs installed or a configuration that might require a special recovery tool besides one that is listed here.

- **Drivers**—It is important to remember that drivers for any hardware and file systems that are supported on the Linux system must be included in the emergency boot disk. It can be difficult to include all of them on a distribution that fits on one floppy, because drivers tend to consume more disk space than what is allowed on a floppy disk. Including drivers for the hardware and supported file systems is important because you need them if you plan on being able to use or troubleshoot any piece of hardware or the file system after you boot the system with the emergency boot disk. This is particularly important if the system has SCSI adapters and hard drives or some other unusual hardware.

- **Text editor**—It is important to include a text editor such as vi so that configuration files can be viewed and edited properly. Every emergency disk distribution should include a text editor. If for some reason it doesn't, vi is a good choice, because it is not very large. Some of the larger emergency boot disk distributions have larger text editors to choose from.

- **Disk utilities**—The emergency boot disk should have the necessary disk utilities, such as FDISK, mkfs, and fsck, which can be used to format a hard drive so that Linux can be installed on it. Figures 13-14, 13-15, and 13-16 show these three utilities. An emergency boot disk with these utilities can be valuable in the event of a file system failure or a problem in which the hard drive or partition needs to be erased and prepared for Linux to be installed. You can use the fsck utility to repair damaged file systems.

- **Backup software**—It is always important to include some sort of backup software utility. If you are about to make a change or repair to configuration files, it might be a good idea to first back them up. Most of the distributions just mentioned come with some sort of backup utility, such as tar, restore, or cpio, and maybe some others. The man pages of these three utilities are shown in Figures 13-17, 13-18, and 13-19. If you are using different commercial or third-party backup software, you need to include it in the emergency boot disk.

- **Network software**—Having network software or utilities included on the emergency boot disk is necessary if you want to establish a network connection. Some networks have network data stored on network servers that can be accessed through a network connection, and you can restore the data by downloading it from the server. You need the drivers for the network hardware that is installed in the system as well as a network client or server package.

Figure 13-14 FDISK

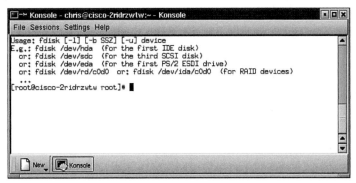

Figure 13-15 mkfs

Figure 13-16 fsck Man Page

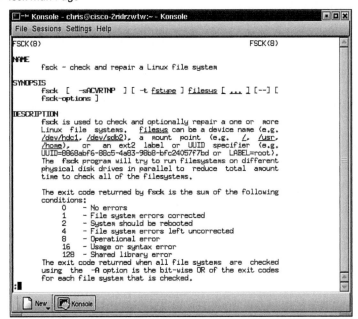

Figure 13-17 cpio Man Page

Figure 13-18 restore Man Page

One last thing that is important to mention about booting a system with an emergency boot disk is that some recovery disk methods require unusual features to access the boot disk itself. For example, if you are using ZipSlack from a zip drive that is attached via a parallel port, you must boot from a kernel stored on a boot floppy. The kernel you boot from must include support for parallel zip drives.

Figure 13-19 tar Man Page

Recognizing Common Errors

Package dependencies were discussed in previous chapters, so by now you probably understand the concept. Basically, when a package is installed in a Linux system, other packages might need to be installed for that package to work properly. The dependency package might have certain files that need to be in place, or the dependency package might run certain services that need to be started before the package you are about to install can work. In any event, this process usually runs rather smoothly. Linux often notifies the user if he or she is installing a package that has dependencies so that they can be installed as well. Sometimes this process does not proceed so smoothly, and problems occur. Usually the problem relates to unsatisfied dependencies or conflicts between packages. This is more likely to happen when you install packages from different vendors. As a system administrator, you must be able to recognize these errors and know how to resolve them.

Various Reasons for Package Dependency Problems

There are various reasons why dependencies and conflicts can arise in a Linux system with RPM, Debian, and tarball packages. If you recall, only RPM and Debian packages can notify the user of dependency issues. Tarballs, unfortunately, do not. Here are a few examples of events that can cause dependency problems and conflicts:

- **Missing libraries or support programs**—This problem is one of the more common causes of dependency problems. *Libraries* are a type of support code that can be used by many different programs on a Linux system. All these different programs can use libraries as if they are part of the program itself. When these libraries are missing, the installed programs do not work. *Support packages* work in much the same way as do libraries. For example, all KDE programs rely on a program called Qt, which is a support program in which all the KDE programs are built. If the Qt support package is not installed, no KDE packages can be installed using RPMs.

- **Incompatible libraries or support programs**—It is important to understand that different versions of libraries and support programs are available. These different versions correspond to the current and past versions of programs that are installed. So if a library or support program is installed, it needs to be the version that corresponds to the programs that are running on the Linux system. It is possible to have multiple versions of libraries and support programs installed, to enable support for programs with competing requirements. For example, if a program requires Qt 2.2, but Qt version 1.4 is installed, you need to install version 2.2. Remember that you want to keep version 1.4 so that other programs that are installed can still run.

- **Duplicate files or features**—Sometimes two different packages include the exact same files. Or, a package that is about to be installed includes files or features that are already installed on the system. When this happens, it can occasionally cause the programs to not function correctly.

Finding the exact cause of a package dependency error can be difficult. Sometimes an error message is produced that can be useful in determining what package is causing the problem and in which category the problem lies. Sometimes these problems do not cause any harm, but some can be very real and serious. For example, having missing libraries and support programs can cause several programs to fail and can cause the system to become unresponsive. When you install RPM or Debian packages, the process of finding the exact cause of the package dependency problem can be a little easier because of the error message that is produced.

Tarballs do not produce an error message when a package dependency error is detected. You see the problem only when the system attempts to run the program. For this reason, the problem might manifest itself right away and produce a message that the program is unable to locate a library or a specific file. Sometimes programs might crash or become unresponsive. For this reason, when installing tarball packages, it is best to use the "keep-old-files" option so that existing files are not overwritten. Using this option lets you uninstall the package and restore the system to its original working condition.

Solutions to Package Dependency Problems

Now that the various problems that cause package dependency problems have been identified, it is time to discuss the steps you take to solve package dependency problems. There are several ways to go about solving a problem. Which one you choose depends on the situation. Before you decide which approach to take, it is wise to review all the possibilities carefully, because some solutions work well in some situations and others do not. Some of the possible solutions that are covered include forcing the installation, modifying the system to meet the dependency, rebuilding the problem package from source code, and finding a different version of the problem package.

Forcing the Installation

One solution for package dependency problems is to simply ignore the error message and forcibly install the package anyway. Although it can be risky to do so, there are instances in which doing so is appropriate. If the error is on a package in which you or the user compiled the source code manually, you might want to force the installation. To force the package installation and ignore failed dependencies with RPM packages, use the **--nodeps** parameter. To force the installation over other errors such as conflicts with existing RPM packages, use the **--force** parameter. Here is the syntax, where *xxxxxxxx*.**rpm** represents any RPM package:

```
# rpm -i xxxxxxxx.rpm --nodeps
```

```
# rpm -i xxxxxxxx.rpm --force
```

These parameter options are slightly different for Debian packages. Recall from previous chapters that Debian packages are identified by dpkg instead of rpm. When using Debian packages, use the following parameters to force the installation, where *package* is the package's name:

```
ignore-depend=package
--force-depends
--force-conflicts
```

Modifying the System

The correct and recommended method of providing solutions to dependency problems is to modify the system so that it has the necessary dependencies to run properly. For example, if the package you are installing requires an updated library or support program, you must install the updated version. If you currently have Qt 1.44 installed, and the package you are installing requires Qt 2.2, you need to install the updated version. Sometimes you can find the updated version on the distribution's installation CDs if that is where you are installing the package from. The installation CD should have updated libraries and support programs that the packages requires for that distribution. All you need to do is install the update libraries and support programs from the CD.

There are a few precautions to take with this approach. You must pay particular attention to what packages and modifications are being made and be certain that any packages and/or updates that are installed are in fact intended for the particular distribution version you are using. For example, programs that use libraries and that support packages for Red Hat 6 will not necessarily work with Red Hat 7's version of libraries and support packages. A package that contains updates for libraries and support packages that you install for a particular distribution has certain requirements that make it compatible only with programs on that specific distribution.

For example, if you are currently running distribution A (Red Hat 6), but you install an update that was built for distribution B (Red Hat 7), the program will produce an error message stating the dependency problems it has in terms of distribution B's files, libraries, and support packages, even though it is running on distribution A. The appropriate version updates might in fact be unavailable for distribution A, but if you install distribution B's version of libraries and support packages, there can be conflicts with the other packages that are already installed in distribution A.

In some cases, if you don't install the appropriate updates for the right distribution version, it will run fine at first. However, there could be problems in the future when other programs are installed or when the distribution of Linux that you are using is upgraded. When you do so, the incorrect libraries and support packages that were upgraded will no longer be recognized. In some cases, you will not be able to upgrade to the new distribution version.

This might seem a little confusing, but it is actually a simple concept. In other words, if you will modify the system in any way, such as upgrading the libraries and support packages, you need to make sure that you are installing the correct updates. This means that if you are using Red Hat 6, you should install the updates for Red Hat 6 and not another version of Red Hat, such as Red Hat 7. If updates are unavailable for the distribution that is being used, it might be a better idea to just upgrade the entire distribution version. Doing so ensures that the updates you need will be installed.

Rebuilding the Problem Package from Source Code
In some instances, it might be necessary to rebuild the package from source code if dependency error messages show up. However, it is important to understand the

dependency conditions that result in needing to do so as opposed to other dependency conditions, in which it is unnecessary to rebuild the package. For instance, some dependencies are the result of the libraries and support packages that are currently installed on the computer, not from requirements of the other packages and software on the system. This often results when the software on a Linux system has been recompiled. When the software is recompiled, dependencies for various programs change. Therefore, it is much easier to rebuild the package from source code to overcome this change than it is to try and forcibly install new packages or modify the system.

Rebuilding an RPM package is fairly simple. To do so, you must call the **rpm** with the **--rebuild** command. The command syntax is as follows:

```
# rpm --rebuild packagename-version.src.rpm
```

packagename-version.src.rpm is the name of the RPM that needs to be rebuilt. This command extracts the source code and executes whatever commands are necessary to build a new package or sometimes several packages. Depending on the computer's speed and the size of the package that is being rebuilt, the process to recompile the package can take from a few seconds to a few hours. After the process is complete, several RPMs in binary form are placed in /usr/src/*distname*/RPMS/*arch,* where *distname* is the code that represents the system's distribution, such as Red Hat or Open-Linux. *arch* represents the system's CPU architecture, such as i386, i586, x86, or ppc. After these files have been placed in /usr/src/*distname*/RPMS/*arch,* they can be moved to any location and then installed like any other RPM package.

It is possible to rebuild tarballs from source code, but this is a much more difficult process. Instead of running one simple command, you have to enter about ten different commands to configure the compilation scripts, recompile the software, and install the software. You also have to edit some configuration files manually. For this reason, it is best not to try to do this with tarball packages unless you have some experience doing this sort of thing. In any event, you should read the package's documentation to find out more information about the package.

One other thing that is good to know if you decide to recompile a package to rebuild it is that you need an appropriate compiler for the software. This is true for whichever package type is being recompiled (RPM or tarball). Usually the GNU C Compiler (GCC) works just fine. Some programs also need to have the appropriate header files installed so that they will recompile properly. This is usually the case for most X-based programs. *Header files* are special files that are needed when you compile a program so that the program uses the correct libraries and support packages. If you recall, in some cases multiple libraries can be installed on a Linux system, and the program needs to know which one it should use. Header file packages can be installed just like any other package, but you need to be certain that the header files that are installed match the library that the program that is being compiled uses. If the header file versions do not match the library versions, the program either will not compile or will not work after it has been compiled.

Rebuilding a program or package from source code is not the easiest method, and it does not always work. There are several reasons why the program might not work after it has been recompiled. The appropriate header files might be missing, or the proper compiler and other development tools are the wrong ones or are missing. Other times the source code relies on features that are not present in the libraries that are installed on the system. If you run into any of these problems, you will most likely see error messages pop up when the system is recompiling the package. If this happens, the best idea is to try some other means of fixing the dependency problem.

Finding a Different Version

The easiest way to fix dependency problems with packages is to locate a different version of the package that is giving you problems. Another option is to look for a newer version of the package. It is also possible to look for an older version. Still another option is to use the same package version but one that is built for the specific Linux distribution you are using rather than another one. To look for other packages, visit RPM Find (www.rpmfind.net) or Debian's package-listing site at www.debian.org/distrib/packages. These two websites can be very helpful in locating alternative versions of packages. Other good locations to check are on the system's installation CDs and on the particular distribution's web or FTP site.

This option usually works well and is much easier than rebuilding a package by recompiling the software. However, the only problem is that sometimes the only acceptable package is the one that doesn't work. The package might contain special features you need, or it might be a patch that is meant to fix important software bugs. In this case, it is almost impossible to find a replacement. Other versions might not be available, so at this point it might be better to just try different software.

Backup and Restore Errors

Another type of common error that is important to be able to recognize and effectively troubleshoot are backup and restore errors. Providing a successful and reliable backup strategy is one of the more important tasks for any system administrator. Without a reliable backup system, the company's data could be at risk of being compromised at any moment. This includes valuable and often irreplaceable data and/or costly server or Internet downtime, hardware theft or failure, and even human error. One thing for certain is that these problems are not completely preventable. However, with a tight and reliable backup and restore program implemented, these problems are not permanent. Another unfortunate and inevitable thing about backups is that they are not immune to errors themselves. It is important to understand how to identify these backup and restore errors as well as their solutions so that the backups are ready to use when needed. It is also important to note that the worst time to discover that the backup and restore plan has errors is when it needs to be used in a critical or emergency situation. For this reason, it is always a good idea to test the backup and restore procedures before they need to be used.

Various methods and types of media are available for backup and restore procedures. The most common type found on Linux systems and other large server environments are tape backups because of how easy they are to use. They can be reused a number of times until they go bad. For this reason, most of the problems and solutions in this section apply to tape backups. There are several other ways to back up and restore data, such as CD-R, CD-RW, DVD-R, and DVD-RW, as well as various RAID technologies that back up data directly to other hard drives. RAID technologies tend to be rather expensive, which is another reason why tape backups are sometimes used. Tape backups provide a reliable and affordable backup solution. The first thing to understand about tape backups that will save you a lot of time and help prevent backup and restore errors is that tape backups should be replaced after they have been used 100 times. Replacing tape backups after 100 uses keeps them from becoming unreliable.

Backup and restore errors can occur at different points. Some errors occur when the system performs the backup. Other times errors occur during the restore process when the system attempts to recover data. Here are some of the most common types of problems:

- **Driver problems**—Like any other piece of hardware on a system, backup devices need to have the proper drivers installed. Be cautious about the various driver issues with Linux systems that have been covered in this course. Usually the EIDE/ATAPI or SCSI tape backup device requires support from a controller or host adapter. If the drivers are installed as modules, the drivers for the controllers or device need to be loaded into memory when the backup is performed. Otherwise, the system will be unable to do any backup.

- **Tape drive access errors**—A tape backup device usually uses the /dev/ht0 or /dev/nst0 files to provide access to the tape drive. As the root user, you should be able to use these files to access the tape backup device for both reading and writing. If for some reason the device cannot be accessed, there most likely is an error with what device files are being used, or the wrong driver files have been loaded.

- **File access errors**—File access permissions can sometimes be a tricky thing. The same is true of doing backups. The type of backup that someone can do on a

Linux system depends on what type of file access he has. For example, any user can back up his own files, because he has both read and write access to them. However, to back up the entire file system on the computer, he needs to have full read access to all the files. This is why most backups are done as root. A nonroot user doing a backup can back up most system files, but not other people's files, and certainly not protected files such as /etc/shadow. Restoring a system works the same way. To restore the entire system, the user needs to be root, because he needs full read and write access to all the directories that are being restored. Only the root account has such file access rights on a Linux system.

- **Media errors**—One of the worst kinds of backup errors is when the medium develops errors. Sometimes the tape backup, CD-R, DVD-R, or secondary hard drive becomes damaged, and any attempt to restore data does not work. Several things can damage a tape backup, CD, or hard drive. Many times the backup medium becomes damaged when it has been in storage for a long time. This is especially true when the storage room's environmental conditions are inappropriate for proper backup media storage. For example, one of the worst things for any type of backup medium is a storage room that does not have proper air circulation or temperature regulation to keep the room at a comfortable temperature. Another fail-safe idea is to make a backup of the backup medium so that if it fails, you have another.

- **File not found errors**—This is another type of error you sometimes see when backing up and restoring data on a Linux system. On Linux systems, when you restore data from backups using the tar command-line utility, tar sometimes can't restore specific files. This is because tar stores files without the leading /. Therefore, when using tar, you should not include the leading / when restoring specific files and directories. (If the -P [--absolute-paths] parameter is used with tar, it backs up files and includes the leading /.) For this reason, it is recommended that you always be at the root (/) directory when restoring any data. If the file that needs to be restored cannot be found, but you know it has been backed up and is on the backup medium, use the -t (--list) parameter with tar. This lists the contents and allows you to manually search for the file. This can be very time-consuming if there are a lot of files on the backup medium. An alternative is to use a more sophisticated compression and backup tool than tar that provides additional searching features when you need to manually locate a file that the system says cannot be found. Some of these added features include things such as an index of files on the backup medium, along with other features that allow you to select the files you want to restore. This prevents things such as mistyping the filename and then having to manually search through an entire backup without finding the file.

Various types of errors can happen when you back up and restore a Linux computer system. These errors can be associated with the backup process itself, the hardware involved in the backup procedure, or the backup media. For this reason, it is important to verify a backup or restoration. On a Linux system, you can do a verification using a backup-time verification option that performs a check right after the data has been backed up. It is possible that during this verification check some files will be returned with errors, but they might just be files that have legitimately changed, so you can disregard the error message. Many backup devices include a verification option that checks the data immediately after it has been rewritten. However, it is still important to run a complete verification check after all the data has been backed up.

Other verification techniques include comparing the information on the drive or backup against any summary information you have. For example, you might want to verify after a restoration that you have the same package installed as before by comparing it to the RPM database. (Recall from previous chapters that some package managers such as Red Hat and Debian have databases that store information about all the packets that are stored or installed on a Linux system.) To do this, use the **rpm -Va** command. Keep in mind that there might also be legitimate variations due to the fact that changes might have been made.

Application Failure on Linux Servers

It can be difficult at times to detect software problems and application failure on a Linux server. This is mainly because these sorts of problems do not present themselves in a way that is obvious. You cannot simply click an option and see the application produce an error message telling you that there is a problem with it and what the problem is. You learned in previous chapters that by using the system's log files, you can learn a lot about any problems the server might be having. Several things can provide some indication of an application failure or software problem on a Linux server:

- **Failure to start**—A first indicator that something is wrong is if the application fails to start. Many things can keep a server or application from starting. Most of the time this is due to a configuration error in /etc/xinetd.d or to an incorrect Sys V startup script. Usually any problems associated with Sys V startup scripts are the result of a script name for a given run level that is causing the server or application to stop rather than start. This process was discussed in previous chapters.

- **Failure to respond**—At other times the program will start or will be running if it is a specific server daemon, such as the Apache web server, but it fails to respond. This might indicate that there is a problem with access through the system's firewall or a hardware firewall on the network, a misconfiguration in /etc/xinetd.d, or any other process that is preventing or blocking access control to the program.

It is also important to check the specific application or server's own configuration files to determine if it has a block. For example, recall that you must change the FTP daemon's configuration file to allow it to work. If you don't make this configuration change, the FTP daemon might run, but it will not respond to requests.

- **Slow responses**—Again, there are several reasons why you or other users might experience slow server response times. If you are receiving complaints from various users that they are getting slow response times from the server, you might want to check external problems first. The problem could be a router or switch issue on the network or some other overloaded Internet backbone. If you check the various external conditions and you and other users are still experiencing slow response times, it might be time to start checking internal reasons. For example, the Linux server's network connection might be slow, or the hardware, such as the CPU, RAM, or hard drive, is inadequate for the job. It is also a good idea to inform users that there are some instances in which the server might be running slowly for a reason. Some applications and servers, such as mail servers, have slight delays before responding. This feature is used to try to slow down spam e-mail from using the mail server as a relay point.

- **Unexpected responses**—Usually a server generates unexpected responses because the application or server is not configured correctly. For example, perhaps you try to access an FTP server anonymously, but you can't. If you are allowing anonymous access to the FTP site, but you are not being granted anonymous access, you should check the configuration to see if you have enabled anonymous access. Another example might be if you access the web server and you see pages that are not supposed to be there, or you expect to see pages that are not there. This might be the result of a configuration error, but it could also mean that you have placed the HTML files in the wrong location.

- **Crashing application or server**—Identifying and providing solutions to an application or server that crashes on a Linux system have been thoroughly covered in this course. Rarely does a Linux server crash, but there are reasons why it can happen. Most of time, if the application or server has been configured properly, it will run without crashing. If an application or server is continuously crashing, it might be the result of a hardware failure, a configuration error, or a bug in the software. Solving the problems that cause a crashed system was covered in previous chapters.

A good general rule when troubleshooting applications and servers on a Linux system is to check the system's logs. The system's log files are usually the place to locate most error messages that are generated, because they are not always displayed on the screen, which makes them easier to see.

Troubleshooting Network Problems

Despite the best preventive efforts, it is inevitable that an administrator will encounter problems with the network. These range from gradual slowdowns that annoy users to a complete loss of connectivity across the entire network that brings the work of thousands of employees to a halt.

All the products that have been discussed can be used to troubleshoot network problems. Because most modern networks run on TCP/IP, several useful troubleshooting utilities are available on every Linux system. They can be used without the need to purchase, install, and learn a complex and expensive network management product.

This section discusses some troubleshooting basics, how to use log files in troubleshooting, and the TCP/IP analysis tools and utilities included in most distributions of Linux. This section covers the use of these tools in troubleshooting network connectivity problems. Finally, detailed network troubleshooting guidelines are provided that you can use to track down and solve network connectivity and performance problems.

Loss of Connectivity

The most basic networking problem is the inability of one computer to communicate with another. Loss of connectivity can be hardware- and/or software-related. The first rule of troubleshooting is to check for physical connectivity. This simple explanation should never be overlooked. More than one networking professional has spent hours reconfiguring protocols, reinstalling software, and perhaps even reinstalling the operating system, only to discover that the reason the computer could not communicate over the network was that someone unplugged the cable from the network interface card (NIC). Therefore, before embarking on a complex troubleshooting mission, ensure that the cables are properly plugged in at both ends, that the network adapter is functioning (check the link light on the NIC), that the hub's status lights are on, and that the communication problem is not a simple hardware malfunction.

Operator Error

Another common cause of network problems is operator error. Perhaps the reason the workstation cannot see the rest of the network is that the user logged in to the local machine and did not connect to the network. Be sure that users are using the correct username and password and that their accounts are not restricted in a way that prevents them from being able to connect to the network. For example, logon times might be limited to business hours on weekdays, or the user might be restricted to logging on only from a specified workstation.

NOTE

One of the most common reasons that a user's password does not work is because of the case-sensitive nature of passwords on most operating systems. Accidentally pressing the Caps Lock key before entering the password causes the password to be rejected.

Hardware problems are relatively simple to deal with after they are discovered. Software problems can be much more difficult to track down and remedy. Software misconfiguration is a common culprit. Software settings might have been changed by the installation routine of a recently installed program, or the user might have been experimenting with settings. Missing or corrupt files can cause problems of many kinds, including network connectivity problems. Users accidentally (or otherwise) delete files, and power surges or shutting down the computer abruptly can damage file data. Viruses can also damage system files or user data.

Whatever the suspected origin of the problem, following a set of steps for each troubleshooting scenario ensures that all bases are covered. The following sequence of troubleshooting steps are recommended for efficient problem solving. Although the first six steps might seem like common sense, many network professionals skip steps 7 and 8. After the problem is "fixed," they believe the job is over. However, the last two steps are critical in a networking environment.

After spending two days troubleshooting a problem and finally solving it, forgetting the details would seem impossible. But a network administrator's life is a busy one, and it is likely that when the same problem occurs again, perhaps a year later, the only things that anyone will be able to remember are that it happened before and somehow the problem was resolved. Documenting the problem-solving steps will not only save time in the future, but will also prevent a great deal of frustration.

NOTE

Feedback should always include instructions for the user if the problem happens again. If it is a simple matter and the user can correct it, step-by-step instructions should be provided, preferably in writing.

Providing feedback to users is also important. Users should be educated whenever possible. This is a key element in problem prevention. The user might not seem to care what was wrong, only that it has been fixed. However, most people appreciate information, especially if that information can help change their habits or allow them to understand what signs of trouble to look for and report before the problem becomes worse. User feedback should always be provided in language that is appropriate for the user's technical knowledge.

Using TCP/IP Utilities

The following sections examine several categories of TCP/IP utilities: those that test connectivity, those used for configuration, and those that provide information that can be useful in troubleshooting network problems.

Connectivity Testing Utilities

The first step in troubleshooting a lost connection is to determine whether it is really lost. Less-experienced network users might be quick to assume that they are unable to connect to a particular website with their browser, when the site server itself might be down.

The most common TCP/IP tool found on Linux, UNIX, and Windows systems that is used to test connectivity to another machine is the command **ping**.

ping and pathping

The *ping* utility stands for packet internetwork groper. This command is a simple utility that sends a message called an *echo request,* using Internet Control Message Protocol (ICMP), to a designated destination computer. The destination computer responds by sending an ICMP *echo reply.*

The first step in checking for a suspected connectivity problem is to ping the host. If the Internet connection could be the problem, a reliable host on the Internet such as www.yahoo.com is a good target for the ping. If you receive a reply, the physical connection between the two computers is intact and working. The successful reply also signifies that the calling system can reach the Internet. Figure 13-20 shows a ping request and response.

Figure 13-20 Ping Request and Response

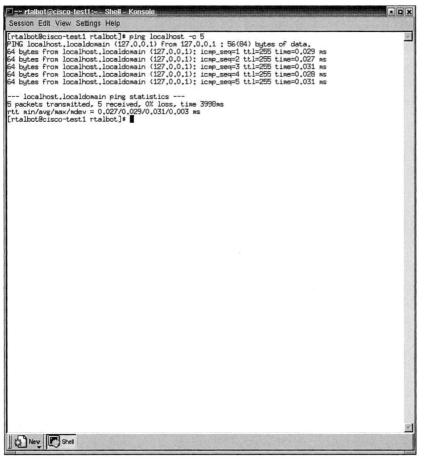

This is the preferred order in which to run the test on TCP/IP:

1. **Host name**—The first step in checking for a suspected connectivity problem is to ping the host. This prints the name of the network server. If you receive a reply, the physical connection between the two computers is intact and working.

2. **ipconfig**—This prints the current TCP/IP configuration. (UNIX/Linux systems use the **ifconfig** command rather than **ipconfig**.) Note the IP address and subnet mask of the network server for future reference. If the IP address of the default gateway is displayed, note it also.

3. **Ping 127.0.0.1**—Ping the loopback address to see whether TCP/IP is installed correctly. If an error message appears, it is time to remove and reinstall the TCP/IP protocol on the network server.

4. **Ping your own IP address**—This tests that TCP/IP can communicate with the network adapter in the network server. The IP address of the network server is displayed in the output of the **ipconfig** command.

5. **Ping the default gateway**—This tests that the network server can communicate from the network to another system on the network—in this case, the router. The IP address of the default gateway (router) is displayed in the output of the **ipconfig** command.

6. **Ping the remote host**—A remote host is a computer on the other side of the default gateway (router). This step tests that the router is doing its job and forwards the TCP/IP packet to a computer system on the other side of the router.

7. **Ping your own IP name**—This tests that the network server can resolve its own IP name.

8. **Ping the remote host's IP name**—This tests that the DNS server is working and resolving the host IP name of a remote computer.

You can issue the **ping** command using either the IP address or the DNS host name of the destination computer. The IP address should be used to test connectivity. If a ping by IP address is successful, but a ping by name is unsuccessful, this indicates a problem with the name resolution (DNS) server or configuration. Such a problem might occur when the user's computer is assigned a static IP address rather than obtaining one through DHCP, but it does not have a DNS server defined in the /etc/resolv.conf file. When the workstation is a DHCP client, the DHCP server usually assigns the DNS server address.

The term *ping time* refers to how much time elapses between the sending of the echo request and receipt of the echo reply. A low ping time indicates a fast connection.

ping can also be used to test whether the computer's TCP/IP stack is properly installed and functioning. To perform the test, ping the 127.0.0.1 loopback address, which is given the host name localhost in the /etc/hosts file. If you receive a response, the stack is working.

A command-line version of ping is included with the TCP/IP stacks of all Windows operating systems and with UNIX and Linux distributions. On a NetWare server, two versions are included. They are loaded as NetWare Loadable Modules (NLMs) at the server console.

pathping is included with Windows 2000, but not with Windows 9x or NT. It combines the features of ping with those of tracert and provides additional information that is not displayed by either utility. With pathping, you can detect which routers are causing problems on the network and measure how many packets are lost at a particular router.

Tracing Packet Routes

Tracing utilities are used to discover the route taken by a packet to reach its destination. The usual way to determine packet routing in UNIX systems is the *traceroute* command. Figure 13-21 shows typical output of traceroute on a UNIX system.

Figure 13-21   Typical traceroute Output on a UNIX System

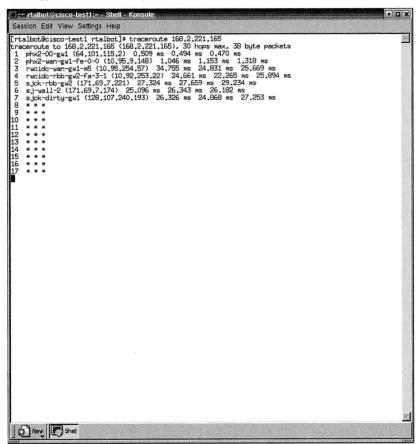

traceroute shows all the routers through which the packet passes as it travels through the network from sending computer to destination computer. This can be useful for determining at what point connectivity is lost or slowed.

Configuration Utilities

Connectivity problems often turn out to be configuration problems. Perhaps the IP address assigned to the computer is not in the correct subnet range, or perhaps the subnet mask, default gateway, DNS address, or other pieces of configuration information were entered incorrectly. If any of these entries is wrong or is accidentally deleted, the computer cannot properly communicate on a TCP/IP network.

ifconfig

/sbin/ifconfig, standard on all newer UNIX systems, lets you view and change the configuration of a network interface, such as IP address, hardware address, broadcast address, and subnet mask associated with a given Ethernet device.

netconfig

Red Hat Linux includes the utility /usr/sbin/netconfig, which allows an administrator to either select DHCP IP configuration or specify a static IP address along with the associated net mask, gateway, and primary name server.

lsof

Although it isn't strictly a networking utility, lsof can identify networking-related resources and what processes might be locking them up. lsof (which stands for list open files) lists information about files that are open by the running processes. An open file may be a regular file, a directory, a block special file, a character special file, an executing text reference, a library, a stream, or a network file (Internet socket, NFS file, or Linux/UNIX domain socket).

Windows NT and Windows 2000: ipconfig

The **ipconfig** command is used in Windows NT and Windows 2000 to display the IP address, subnet mask, and default gateway for which a network adapter is configured. For more-detailed information, the **/all** switch is used.

If the computer is configured as a DHCP client, two additional switches can be used with **ipconfig**. The **/renew** switch causes the lease for the IP address to be renewed. The **/release** switch causes the IP address to be released so that the DHCP server can reassign it.

Other TCP/IP Utilities

Testing connectivity and checking configuration information are the most common uses of the TCP/IP utilities when troubleshooting network problems. However, UNIX systems include additional tools that can be used to gather specific information:

- **netstat**—This informative utility prints information about net connections, routing tables, interfaces, and other useful data.

- **arp**—This is used to display and manipulate the Address Resolution Protocol (ARP) cache, which maps IP addresses of devices your system has communicated with recently to their Ethernet hardware addresses.

- **route**—This is used to view and change routing table entries.

- **nslookup**—With nslookup you may query Internet name servers interactively to convert a domain name to an IP address. Some implementations of Linux display a message saying that the use of nslookup is deprecated and that it might be removed from future releases. It suggests using dig or host instead.

- **dig**—Like nslookup, dig queries name servers to obtain IP address resolutions based on domain names. The output of dig is somewhat verbose and might be hard to understand if you're unfamiliar with it.

- **host**—Like dig and nslookup, host returns IP addresses for domain names. Unlike its predecessors, its default is simply to supply just the answer you are most likely to be looking for. However, with options it can be just as verbosely detailed as dig.

Problem-Solving Guidelines

Troubleshooting a network requires problem-solving skills. The use of a structured method to detect, analyze, and address each problem as it is encountered increases the likelihood of successful troubleshooting. Troubleshooting should always be done in a step-by-step manner. Good problem-solving skills are not specific to computer networking. Consider how a doctor approaches a perplexing medical problem or how an investigator solves a crime. Regardless of the field, the steps are similar:

- **Gather information**—A physician takes a medical history and asks the patient to describe symptoms. A police detective questions victims and witnesses. Both rely on their own observations and might have to turn to books or other experts to research specific facts involved in the case. A network troubleshooter should learn to listen as users describe their experiences. Good questions are an essential part of gathering the information needed to diagnose the problem.

- **Analyze the information**—This is where experience and knowledge come into play. The most obvious possible causes should be eliminated first. If a patient complains of a headache, the doctor doesn't begin by performing brain surgery. He first considers the simpler factors from which the symptoms can originate. As possibilities are eliminated, the search is narrowed.

- **Formulate and implement a "treatment" plan**—Create a plan to rectify the problem. Every plan should include a contingency plan in case the first attempt does not work. Proceed with the plan in an organized fashion. Try only one solution at a time.

- **Test to verify the results of the treatment**—It is essential to confirm the success of the troubleshooting actions. It is also important to verify that the "cure" did not have side effects that caused additional or different problems.

- **Document everything**—The details of the problem and the steps taken to correct it should be recorded, ideally with a filed hard copy. This documentation of the trial-and-error process could save a future administrator a great deal of time.

Realistic goals and priorities are critical during the network troubleshooting and optimization process. A cost-benefit analysis can help determine which problems should take precedence. Costs are not always monetary. Priorities can be dependent on issues including budgets, efficiency, time pressures, and deadlines. Even internal politics can be a cost factor. Troubleshooting is one of the most difficult jobs of the network administrator. It is also the area in which a good administrator proves his or her worth and earns both the salary and the title.

Windows 2000 Diagnostic Tools

The network diagnostic tools for Microsoft Windows 2000 Server include ipconfig, nbtstat, netstat, nslookup, ping, and tracert, which are similar to their Windows NT counterparts. Windows 2000 Server also includes the **netdiag** and **pathping** commands, which are unavailable in Windows NT Server.

 Worksheet 13.4.4   Windows Diagnostic Tools

Learn how to use the various diagnostic tools and interpret output.

netdiag

The Windows 2000 Server **netdiag** command runs a standard set of network tests and generates a report of the results. The Windows 2000 Server **netdiag** command is not part of a standard Windows 2000 Server installation. It must be installed from the Windows 2000 Server CD-ROM from the Support Tools folder. The Windows 2000 **netdiag** command has one very nice feature: It can be used without any flags and it will perform a complete set of network tests. A server hardware specialist just needs to analyze the output from the **netdiag** command, looking for the word "Failed" to find possible network problems. Even though the **netdiag** command can be used without any flags, several are available, as shown in Table 13-1.

Table 13-1 Windows 2000 Server **netdiag** Command Flags

Command Flag	Description
/q	Quiet output (errors only).
/v	Provides verbose output. More-detailed information is provided.
/l	Logs output to Netdiag.log.
/debug	Provides even more verbose output.
/d:*DomainName*	Finds a DC in the specified domain.
/fix	Fixes trivial problems.
/DcAccountEnum	Enumerates DC machine accounts.
/test:*test name*	Tests only this test. Nonskippable tests are still run.

pathping

The Windows 2000 Server **pathping** command is a combination of the **ping** command and the **tracert** command. Table 13-2 describes the flags that can be used with this command.

Table 13-2 Windows 2000 Server **pathping** Command Flags

Command Flag	Description
-n	Specifies to not resolve addresses to host names.
-h *maximum-hops*	Specifies the maximum number of hops to search for.
-g *host-list*	Specifies the loose source route along *host-list*.
-p *period*	Specifies the wait period in milliseconds between pings.
-q *num-queries*	Specifies the number of queries per hop.
-w *timeout*	Specifies the wait timeout in milliseconds for each reply.
-T	Tests connectivity to each hop with Layer 2 priority tags.
-R	Tests whether each hop is RSVP-aware.

Wake-On-LAN

Some network interface cards support a technology known as *Wake-On-LAN* (WOL). The purpose of WOL technology is to enable a network administrator to power up a computer by sending a signal to the NIC with WOL technology. The signal is called a *magic packet*. When the NIC receives the magic packet, it powers up the computer in which it is installed. When fully powered up, the remote computer can be accessed through normal remote diagnostic software. WOL technology also lets you power up a computer so that it can have the data on its hard disk drives backed up to tape over the network.

In the Windows NT Server 4 NT Diagnostics, for example, it is possible to select the computer you want to see information about. If the computer you want to examine using NT Diagnostics is not powered up, however, you cannot perform the examination. If that computer has a NIC with WOL technology, you can power it up remotely by sending the WOL magic packet to that NIC. After the computer is powered up, you can run NT Diagnostics on that computer.

Disaster Recovery

"Why do I need to do a risk analysis?" is a common question asked by technical staff. After all, isn't that what the business people are for? If you're a technical person, probably the last thing you want to do is deal with the processes, procedures, and paperwork involved in doing a risk analysis. And a risk analysis is not usually something a technical person can complete without some input from the business people. As far as why a risk analysis is important, think about driving your car. If you were to do a complete disaster-recovery plan for your car, you would want to stock spare parts for any component that might fail. So in addition to the spare tire, you would have a spare rearview mirror, a spare steering wheel, and a spare windshield. This is an extreme example to illustrate the point. In your car, you know that a tire is the most likely thing to fail that you might have a chance to repair. With your server, not only do you need to know what components are most likely to fail, can be repaired, or can be dealt with using high-availability techniques, but you also need to understand the value of the information.

Your first response is probably something along the lines of "I already know what's important, so why do I have to go through all this analysis? Besides, no one really understands this risk analysis stuff anyway." Let's take a look at what a risk analysis is and why you need one.

A good risk analysis can be broken into the following four parts:

1. **Identify your business processes and their associated infrastructure.** For example, communications is a business process that involves a mail server, a network connection, and the end-user workstation. Remote access is a process that might involve modems, modem lines, a RAS server, and a network connection. It is absolutely critical that you involve someone from the business in this part of the analysis. In a perfect world, the IT department would be fully cognizant of all the processes and procedures used by the business. The reality is frequently that the IT department builds the infrastructure but is not completely sure how the business uses it. And even if you do know what the infrastructure is used for, the value of the business processes is generally not well-understood. In many cases, the risk analysis is the first time anyone thinks to place a value on processes and services.

2. **Identify the threats associated with each of the business processes and the associated infrastructure.** This could be anything from a hard drive in the mail server to a failed modem line on your RAS server to a network cable going bad. Try to be specific and thorough. Be sure to list all the threats, not just the ones you know you can address.

3. **Define the level of risk associated with each threat.** This includes the likelihood of the threat's occurring, as well as the threat's severity. You can do this by ranking the threats on a scale from 1 to 5, where 1 is unlikely and 5 is very likely. The severity scale would also be from 1 to 5, where 1 is minor impact to the business and 5 is major impact to the business. If possible, associate costs with each threat. This makes justifying your disaster-recovery plan much easier.

4. **Rank the risks based on severity and likelihood.** One method that works fairly well is to add the scores of the two levels. The higher the score, the more important it is to avoid that risk. Low scores can generally be placed at the end of the list and are usually the last risks to be planned for.

Now comes the fun part. You have a list of the potential threats. If you have done a thorough job, odds are good that there are things on your list that you would not have thought of if you just started with issues you knew about. You also now have a valuable tool for justifying the costs of your disaster-recovery plan. It is much easier to justify that server cluster for the company's web server when you can show management that a 4-hour outage will cost the company $100,000 in lost business. If you still have any questions about why you should invest your time and effort in a risk analysis, think about this: When the risk that management decided was not worth the cost actually happens (and it inevitably will), and they start looking for someone to blame, it will not be the person who has the risk analysis documentation and management's refusal to make the necessary investment.

Now you need to determine how you can avoid these threats and provide the kind of availability your company needs. Let's start by talking about some of the more basic building blocks of disaster recovery: the use of redundant components, clustering, scalability, and high availability.

Understanding Redundancy, Clustering, Scalability, and High Availability

Because the topic of this course is servers, one of the best places to start discussing some of the mechanisms for ensuring high availability is to look at some server components that can fail from time to time. The most common component to be implemented in a redundant fashion is server hard drives.

Redundancy

Redundancy is the ability to continue providing service when something fails. For example, if a hard disk fails, a redundant hard disk can continue storing and serving files. First, we will focus on RAID types. Following the sections on RAID, the focus will move to some other components that are candidates for redundancy.

- *RAID 0*—Also known as *disk striping*, RAID 0, shown in Figure 13-22, writes data across two or more physical drives. This type of RAID has no redundancy. If one of the drives fails, all the data is lost. For a company to recover, it would have to implement a tape backup procedure or use RAID 0+1.

- *RAID 1*—Also known as *disk mirroring*, RAID 1, shown in Figure 13-23, requires the use of two disk drives and one disk controller to provide redundancy. To further increase performance, you can add a second controller, one for each disk drive. Each drive is completely mirrored, an exact copy of the other. This provides 100% redundancy. If one of the disk drives fails, put in a replacement, and the data is copied over to the new drive.

- *RAID 5*—Also known as *disk striping with parity*. Parity is an encoding scheme that represents where the information is stored on each drive. RAID 5, shown in Figure 13-24, is similar to RAID 0 in that it writes data across disks, but it adds a parity bit for redundancy. Three drives are required to implement this type of RAID. If a drive fails, the data can be recovered using the parity bit and the other two drives.

- *RAID 0+1*—Offers the best of both worlds: the performance of RAID 0 and the redundancy of RAID 1. Four disk drives and a disk controller are required to implement RAID 0+1. This is an expensive solution because of the number of drives it requires. RAID 0+1 is shown in Figure 13-25.

Figure 13-22 RAID 0

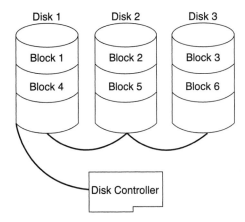

Figure 13-23 RAID 1

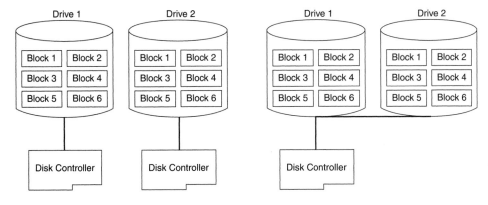

Figure 13-24 RAID 5

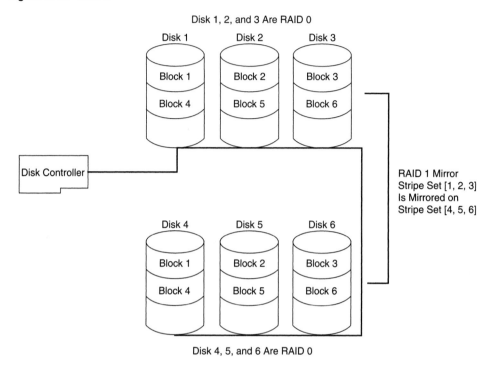

Disk 1, 2, and 3 Are RAID 0

RAID 1 Mirror
Stripe Set [1, 2, 3]
Is Mirrored on
Stripe Set [4, 5, 6]

Disk 4, 5, and 6 Are RAID 0

Figure 13-25 RAID 0+1

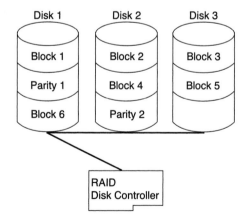

Worksheet 13.5.5   Redundancy

Learn the benefits and needs for building redundant server systems.

Other System Components

A number of other components in your server can be configured in a redundant manner, including the following:

- **Power supplies**—Most high-end servers come with an option to install additional power supplies. This allows the server to shift the power load when a power supply fails.

- **Cooling fans**—Have you ever noticed how hot a server can get after it has been running for a while? If you want to ensure that your server stays cool, you should look for a server that uses redundant cooling fans. Not only does this allow the server to avoid overheating in the event of a fan failure, but your server also benefits from the additional cooling while all the fans are running. Additional cooling fans are usually part of the server configuration and are not usually ordered as an option for the server.

- **Network interface adapters**—NICs are something that are frequently not installed in a redundant manner, in large part due to the challenge of configuring many operating systems in a truly redundant form. Because each NIC (particularly in a TCP/IP environment) has its own address, it is usually difficult to configure a reliable failover method for NICs. If you want truly redundant NICs, you need to buy cards with drivers designed for redundant use. For example, 3Com Corporation makes an EtherLink Server 10/100 PCI dual-port NIC specifically for load balancing and resiliency in a server environment. Be sure you order the correct type of NIC if you want redundant NICs.

- **Processors**—Processors are a relatively easy component to implement in a fault-tolerant way. If you buy a multiprocessor server from most of the major vendors, the server will continue to run with a failed processor—albeit with a degradation in performance.

- **UPS**—Even if you have four power supplies in your server, they are only as good as the available power. To add an additional layer of redundancy to your power supplies, an uninterruptible power supply (UPS) can continue to provide power in the event of a power outage. You need to be sure to calculate the amount of power needed and the duration you need it for and make sure your UPS can accommodate your requirements.

The main point to take away from this section is that with the exception of the system board, any critical components in your server can generally be configured in a redundant manner. If your data is so critical that you think you need an additional motherboard, it's time to think about clustering.

Clustering

A *cluster* is a group of independent computers working together as a single system. This system is used to ensure that mission-critical applications and resources are as highly available as possible. (High availability is discussed in a minute.) These computers are managed as a single system and are specifically configured to tolerate component failures, as well as to support the transparent addition or removal of components. If you have configured your cluster correctly, you can literally drop a bowling ball on one of the servers in the cluster and not see any difference in user performance. Windows 2000, Novell NetWare, and most types of UNIX all support some form of clustering. Figure 13-26 illustrates this clustering concept. You can see how multiple computers are configured to handle the web traffic.

Figure 13-26 Clustering

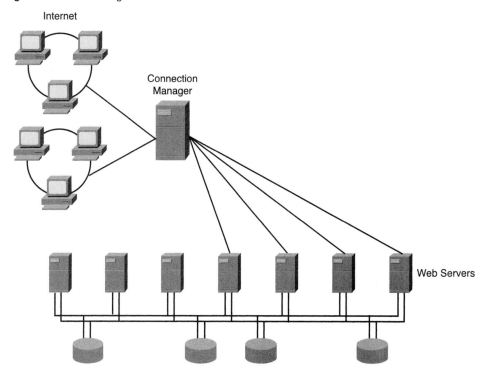

The advantages of running a clustered configuration include the following:

- **Fault tolerance**—A cluster of computers is very fault-tolerant, because it can support the failure of components up to a complete computer without affecting the cluster's capability to support the mission-critical applications.

- **High availability**—One step up from fault tolerance is high availability. High availability indicates not only that the system can remain running in the event of a fault, but also that the cluster will not be unavailable for other reasons, such as maintenance, upgrades, or configuration changes. Although 100% availability is not always possible, a correctly configured cluster comes very close.

- **Scalability**—A cluster is considered scalable because as additional resources become necessary, resources can be added to the cluster transparently to the system users.

- **Easier manageability**—Because the servers can be managed as a group, the number of management tasks is dramatically reduced compared to an equivalent number of standalone servers.

There are a couple of downsides to using clusters. First, clusters can be significantly more expensive than the equivalent standalone servers, due to the additional software costs and the need (in some cases) for specialized hardware. Second, clustering is generally more complex than setting up a server. The latest generation of clustering software has done a lot to reduce this complexity, but it is still very different from setting up a single server. There are two different types of cluster models in the industry: the shared-device model and the nothing-shared model:

- **Shared-device model**—In the shared-device model, applications running within a cluster can access any hardware resource connected to any node/server in the cluster. As a result, access to the data must be carefully coordinated. This function is coordinated by a *distributed lock manager (DLM)*, which handles the arbitration of resources in the event of a conflict. The coordination of the access adds significant overhead to the cluster and makes it much more complex to design, configure, and maintain. This model can also suffer from issues with scalability because of the amount of coordination required between nodes.

- **Nothing-shared model**—In the nothing-shared model, each node has ownership of a resource, so there is no competition for the resources. In this model, two servers share a disk resource, but one of the servers owns the resource, and the other server takes ownership of the resource only if the primary server fails.

Scalability

Scalability refers to how well a hardware or software system can adapt to increased demands. In other words, a scalable e-mail server can start with ten mailboxes but can easily expand to accommodate an additional 1000 mailboxes. In the mid-1990s, when America Online was gaining popularity, its dial-in network was an example of a system that was not scalable. Busy signals, dropped users, and mandatory disconnects became common for AOL users, because the network could not handle the load of users who wanted to get online.

How do you design a system to be scalable? In the case of most clusters, it's relatively easy, because you can add nodes to add capacity. When you are dealing with a standalone server, however, it becomes a little more complex. To ensure that your server is scalable, you need to do two things. First, you need to ensure that you configure the server with excess capacity. If you know you need 5 GB of disk space today, you can plan on needing more in the future. So be sure to put the additional storage in the server at the outset. If you need 5 GB today, put in 10 GB. If your application needs a single Pentium III 850 MHz processor, put in a GHz processor or dual processors. In the long run, spending money at the outset is far cheaper that trying to add components later. That said, the second thing you need to do to ensure that your server is scalable is to make sure that you can add resources if necessary. If you are putting a single Pentium III processor in your server, for example, it is a good idea to purchase a server that can handle multiple processors so that you can add a CPU if you need it. Do not fill every drive bay in the server if you can help it. Leave room to add a couple of 72 GB drives if you need more storage in the future.

The question is how much extra capacity you should build in and how much additional capacity you should be able to add after the server is installed. Although capacity planning is frequently more of an art than a science until you can get some historical numbers to plan from, it is usually a good idea to add 25% to any new server configuration to ensure scalability. You should also try to leave some capacity for each of the components in the system. Do not fill all the card slots, memory slots, drive bays, or CPU slots if you can help it. You never know when you might need to add capacity, and taking out hardware to upgrade it is an order of magnitude more difficult that just adding capacity.

Figure 13-27 illustrates the scalability concept.

Figure 13-27   Scalability

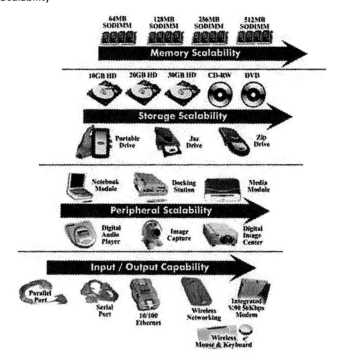

High Availability

The final concept relating to clustering and fault tolerance is the concept of high availability. High availability is by definition the designing and configuring of a server to provide continuous use of critical data and applications. Highly available systems are required to provide access to the enterprise applications that keep businesses up and running, regardless of planned or unplanned interruption. High availability refers to systems that are available nearly 100% of the time. It is not uncommon for mission-critical applications to have an availability requirement of 99.999%. If you do the math for a 24/7/365 installation, you can have no more than 5 minutes of downtime in one year. Some organizations even include scheduled maintenance in those calculations, so that means you would have time for only one maintenance reboot in the course of a year for a system that requires 99.999% availability.

The need for high availability is not limited to 365/24/7 environments. In many companies, the availability requirements might pertain to business hours only. For example, a customer service desk at an electronics firm might need access to its knowledge base during normal business hours but not after hours, when the system can be taken down as needed. However, a system outage during the required hours might be catastrophic.

Now that you understand the concept of high availability, consider some of the components you might use to ensure that high availability.

Hot Swapping, Warm Swapping, and Hot Spares

The types of components you might want to keep on hand in case of a problem fall into the following three basic categories:

- **Hot swap (also known as hot-pluggable)**—A hot-swap component can be added to and removed from a computer while the computer is running, and the operating system automatically recognizes the change. This occurs with no disruption to I/O requests and transactions on the system and no powering down of any part of the system except the failed component. From a user's perspective, the server is never down, and operations (outside of the failed component) are never interrupted. Some examples you might recognize for your PC are PCMCIA adapters and Universal Serial Bus peripherals. Hard drives are frequently capable of hot swap in a server. (This is particularly useful in conjunction with a hardware RAID controller.)

- **Warm swap**—Warm swap is a compromise between hot swap and using a hot spare. Warm swaps are generally done in conjunction with the failure of a hard drive. In this case, you have to shut down the disk array before you can replace the drive. All I/O for that array stops until you replace the drive and restart the drive array. While the drive array is offline, users cannot access the system. This is called a warm swap because the server does not have to be powered down to replace the drive. This eliminates the delays associated with powering up the system after the replacement. It is normally available only in conjunction with a hardware RAID controller. In other words, warm swap falls between hot swap and hot spare. The server is down, but it can be brought back online faster than shutting down the server and using a hot-spare part.

- **Hot spare/redundant components**—A hot-spare component is one that you keep on hand in case of an equipment failure. Examples include disk drives, RAID controllers, NICs, and any other critical component that can be used to replace a failed component. In some mission-critical environments, entire servers are designated hot spares and are used to bring a server back online quickly in the event of a failure.

Now that you know how these components can benefit you, how can you use them as part of your disaster-recovery process? As part of your risk analysis, you should have identified components in your server that are at risk of failure. As part of the mitigation process for providing steps to recover from this potential threat, you need to identify replacement parts. You also need to make sure you understand the underlying technologies involved. Do you need hot-swap hard drives for that server, or can it be down for an hour while you replace the drive from stock? This is where the cost-versus-benefit calculations come into effect. If you determine that your company loses $40,000 for every hour the server is down, you want the best hot-swap drives on the market. If the server is a backup DNS server, you can probably get away with a spare drive.

You want to be sure to have some spare parts on hand for your critical application servers. Hot-plug components are great if you need to keep the server up and running while a fault is corrected, whereas just having parts on hand when a component fails can reduce your downtime by hours.

 Worksheet 13.5.6   Hot Swapping

Learn the various methods for hot swapping server drives.

Creating a Disaster Recovery Plan Based on Fault Tolerance/ Recovery

Here's where it's all put together. You have learned many different ways you can ensure that your system is fault-tolerant, as well as a number of ways to ensure that you can recover from an outage using anything from fault-tolerant technologies to keeping spare parts on hand. This section shows you how you can turn that information into a disaster-recovery plan.

The first thing to recognize is that just using fault-tolerant configurations is not the complete picture from a disaster-recovery plan perspective. You first create the fault-tolerant portion of your plan. Follow these steps:

1. From your risk analysis, identify the hardware failure-related threats. These should include the possibility of the failure of any of the server's components.

2. From your list of components, identify the components that would place your data at the most risk if they were to fail. Remember, if you lose access to data, your users are inconvenienced. If you lose the data itself, you could be out of luck.

3. For each component, list the methods you can use to implement it in a fault-tolerant configuration. List the approximate cost of each solution and the estimated outage time in the event of a failure. Keep in mind that you should consider clustering or other server high-availability solutions.

4. Take any components that can be implemented in a cost-effective manner (this varies from server to server and depends on the cost of an outage) and start documenting the configuration.

5. Take any components that either cannot be implemented in a fault-tolerant configuration or that for which a fault-tolerant configuration would be cost-prohibitive, and determine whether a spare part should be kept on hand in the event of an

outage. If the answer is yes, prepare a list with part numbers and the costs of those components. If the answer is no, try to plan what you would do if that part failed. This could be something such as using a hot-spare server, making sure the server and its components remain under warranty, or making sure you know where to get a new part.

6. Now that you have identified the hardware needed for your disaster-recovery plan, here comes the fun part: documenting the plan. Your disaster-recovery plan should include documented contingencies for any of the threats you identified as part of the risk analysis. The purpose of this is threefold. First, it gives management a warm, fuzzy feeling when they realize that you have your disaster-recovery plan in a folder next to the server and are ready to go in the event of a problem. Second, if you are unavailable in the event of an outage, someone else can get the process started. Third, right now, as you document all this, no alarms are going off, and no VPs are screaming at you to get the server fixed. This is an excellent time to figure out what you need to do in the event of an outage. Then, someday, when you're paged at 2 a.m., you won't have to remember the command to rebuild the RAID array. It will be part of your disaster-recovery plan.

7. After all this information has been documented, you need to place your orders and get ready to start configuring the server. You are now ready to deal with a hardware failure.

Testing the Plan

After the plan is finished, you need to test it. You should not only make sure that your plan is workable, but also ensure that everyone who has a role in the recovery understands what that role is. Because every disaster-recovery plan is different, this section covers some of the areas you should review periodically. Then you'll perform a couple of step-by-step exercises to test specific areas of your plan. Some of the things you should test include the following:

- Have someone check your documentation to ensure that it is understandable and complete.
- Do a "dry run" of each of your plan's components. For example, take the procedure for recovering from a hard drive failure and run through it. Make sure you can locate your spare drives (if applicable) and that you can order replacement parts from your vendor.
- Test your notification processes. A good disaster-recovery plan documents who is to be notified in case of an outage. If the company's e-commerce site crashes, it's a good bet that your boss (and his boss, and possibly her boss) will want to know about it immediately.

- Check the locations of any hot-spare equipment or servers. Are all your spares still in storage? Is the server identified as a hot spare still available, or has it been redeployed as a development server? Do you have numbers for all your vendors, and are they still in business?

- Verify that any support contracts you have on equipment are still in effect and that you have all the contact numbers. Make sure that any other information you need to open a call with them is fully documented.

You should test your tape backups at least once a week. If possible, perform a full restore to a different machine quarterly to ensure that the process works and that your administrators understand it.

You should test your RAID configuration at least twice a year. Any administrators on the system should perform the test at least once to ensure that they are familiar with the process and understand the documentation. Some larger companies conduct yearly full tests of disaster-recovery plans. This can include bringing hot sites (discussed next) online and ensuring that business continuity is maintained, deploying replacement hardware, and basically tying up the IT staff for days of planning and execution to ensure that, in the event of a catastrophic outage, the business systems will remain available.

Hot and Cold Sites

Now that you understand all the facets of recovering from a server outage, you need to consider one final topic: What do you do when your facility is down? This could be due to a natural disaster such as an earthquake or a flood, sabotage such as the bomb, or even just an extended power outage. You need to find a place to resume your critical business activities. This is where disaster-recovery sites come into the picture. Two types of disaster-recovery sites are commonly used in the industry:

- *Hot site*—A hot site is a commercial facility available for system backup. For a fee, these vendors provide a facility with server hardware, telecommunications hardware, and personnel to assist your company with restoring critical business applications and services in the event of an interruption in normal operations. These facilities provide an in-depth disaster-recovery capability, but this level of recovery is very expensive. Be sure to weigh the cost of the service against the risk and cost of a major outage.

- *Cold site*—A cold site (also known as a shell site) is a facility that has been prepared to receive computer equipment in the event that the primary facility is destroyed or becomes unusable. This solution is significantly less expensive than a hot site, but you must supply hardware, software, and personnel in the event of an outage. This location could be an unused office facility, a warehouse (if prepared suitably), or an unoccupied data center.

Summary

Troubleshooting any operating system can sometimes be a very difficult and time-consuming process. It usually involves taking many steps and trying different things to find the problem. The first place to start is by categorizing the cause of the problem into one of three categories: hardware-related, software-related, or user-related. The next logical step is to ask yourself a series of questions to narrow down even more the search for the cause of the problem. Does a specific component seem to be causing problems? After you figure out what the symptoms are, think about what the cause of the problem could be with these symptoms. To be able to answer these questions, you must have extensive knowledge of how all the various components work, how they are installed, and how to properly configure them for a Linux system. Answering these questions also means that you need to know how the various components in the system function when they are working properly as well as improperly.

This chapter covered many common and important problems that can arise in a Linux system. It discussed how to identify, diagnose, and fix these common and important problems. Some of these problems include LILO boot errors, startup and shutdown problems and processes, dependency issues, and various software and application failures. The symptoms of and solutions for all these problems were discussed.

This chapter also described the various tools and resources that are available to help you diagnose problems and provide solutions. For example, the various ways to boot a system without LILO were covered. Also, the various Linux commands that can be helpful in debugging a system were mentioned. Throughout this chapter and this course, you've learned where to find help for troubleshooting these problems. No system administrator has the answer to every problem that arises. Knowing where to find help for problems you can't figure out on your own is important, because even the most knowledgeable system administrator sometimes runs across problems he or she can't fix.

Check Your Understanding

The following review questions help you assess what you learned in this chapter. Answers can be found in Appendix A, "Answers to Check Your Understanding Questions."

1. Many things can cause errors in a computer system. What are the five main areas of concern in which most computer problems occur?

2. If you experience an issue related to a hardware failure, it is a good idea to check some of the log files to find out what piece of hardware is causing the problem. What specific log file do you check, and what specifically are you looking for?

3. There are four specific instances in which common signs of application bugs are apparent. Which of the following is *not* one of them?

   A. Resource exhaustion

   B. Program crash

   C. Failure to execute

   D. Incompatible driver

   E. Program-specific misbehavior

4. Log files are an important and useful component of Linux servers. Which of the following are activities on a server that are recorded in log files?

   A. Monitoring system loads

   B. Intrusion attempts and detection

   C. Normal system functioning

   D. Server bandwidth

   E. Missing entries

5. What three methods can you use to boot a Linux system without using LILO?

6. What are the three key issues to keep in mind when installing a package in a Linux system to avoid package dependency issues?

7. List some of the solutions to package dependency problems.

8. One of the most important tasks for any system administrator is ensuring that employees have network and Internet access at all times. Any network downtime can lead to serious monetary losses for the company. List the steps you follow when testing for TCP/IP errors.

9. Fill in the descriptions for the Windows 2000 Server **netdiag** command flags.

Command Flag	Description
/q	
/v	
/l	
/debug	
/d:*DomainName*	
/fix	
/DcAccountEnum	
/test:*test name*	

10. Fill in the descriptions for the Windows 2000 Server **pathping** command flags.

Command Flag	Description
-n	
-h *maximum-hops*	
-g *host-list*	
-p *period*	
-q *num-queries*	
-w *timeout*	
-T	
-R	

Key Terms

clustering   A group of independent computers working together as a single system. This system ensures that mission-critical applications and resources are as highly available as possible.

cold site   A facility that has been prepared to receive computer equipment if the primary facility is destroyed or becomes unusable.

consistent error   A problem that reliably and demonstrably occurs repeatedly.

distributed lock manager (DLM)   Handles the arbitration of resources in the event of a conflict. The coordination of the access adds significant overhead to the cluster and makes it much more complex to design, configure, and maintain.

emergency boot disk   Lets you boot the system without using any part of the main partition. This is useful when there are errors on the boot partition.

emergency boot system   Linux provides an emergency system copy of LILO that you can use to boot Linux if the original LILO boot loader has errors or is not working.

hot site   A commercial facility available for system backup. For a fee, a vendor provides a facility with server hardware, telecommunications hardware, and personnel to help your company restore critical business applications and services in the event of an interruption in normal operations.

ifconfig   This command can be entered at the shell to return the system's current network interface configuration.

inconsistent error   A problem that occurs only sporadically or under indeterminate conditions.

kernel ring buffer   The process of using the **dmesg** command to display recent kernel messages.

kernel startup message   Contains important information about the drivers and the hardware installed in the system. The information relates to whether the drivers are being loaded successfully and what devices they control, such as EIDE or SCSI controllers.

library   A type of support code that can be used by many different programs on a Linux system.

lpq   This command is useful to help resolve printing problems. It displays all the jobs that are waiting to be printed.

pathping   Combines the features of ping with those of tracert and provides additional information that is not displayed by either utility. With pathping, you can detect which routers are causing problems on the network and measure how many packets are lost at a particular router.

ping   A simple utility that sends a message called an echo request to a designated destination computer using ICMP.

ping time   The amount of time that elapses between the sending of the echo request and the receipt of the echo reply.

RAID 0   Also called disk striping. Writes data across two or more physical drives. This type of RAID has no redundancy. If one of the drives fails, all the data is lost.

RAID 0+1   Has the performance of RAID 0 and the redundancy of RAID 1. Four disk drives and a disk controller are required to implement RAID 0+1.

RAID 1   Also called disk mirroring. Requires the use of two disk drives and one disk controller to provide redundancy. Each drive is completely mirrored, an exact copy of the other. This provides 100% redundancy. If one of the disk drives fails, put in a replacement, and the data is copied to the new drive.

RAID 5   Also called disk striping with parity. Parity is an encoding scheme that represents where the information is stored on each drive. It writes data across disks and adds a parity bit for redundancy. Three drives are required to implement this type of RAID.

route   This command displays or sets the information on the system's routing, which the system uses to send information to a particular IP addresses.

scalability   How well a hardware or software system can adapt to increased demands.

setserial   This utility provides information and sets options for the system's serial ports.

support package   Works in much the same way as a library. For example, all KDE programs rely on a support program called Qt. If the Qt support package is not installed, no KDE packages will be able to be installed using RPMs.

traceroute   Shows all the routers through which the packet passes as it travels through the network from sending computer to destination computer.

Objectives

After completing this chapter, you will be able to complete tasks related to

- Developing a network security policy
- Preventing threats to network security
- Implementing security measures
- Downloading updates, fixes, and patches for a network operating system
- Understanding how to configure and where to place a firewall

Chapter 14

Network Security

Developing a security policy for a network depends on several factors. You must consider the type of business, the type of data, and the management philosophy to determine acceptable use.

This chapter details the importance of developing a security policy to guard against internal and external threats to a network. You will learn the security measures to implement. Patching and upgrading the network operating system (NOS) ensures that the system is current. Additionally, you will gain an understanding of firewalls and proxies.

Developing a Network Security Policy

This section covers the following topics:

- Accessing security needs
- Acceptable-use policy
- Username and password standards
- Rules for network access
- Policy for disposal of materials
- Virus-protection standards
- Online security resources
- Server room security
- Antitheft devices for server hardware
- Securing removable media

Accessing Security Needs

Secure networking is a hot topic in the information technology world. Intrusions into government and business networks, widespread attacks of computer viruses, and high-profile criminal cases involving computer hackers are constantly in the news. From multinational enterprise networks to home computer users with dialup Internet accounts, almost everyone who is "connected" is also concerned, to some degree, about the possibility of unauthorized access.

Security means different things to different people. Although the word (according to the *American Heritage Dictionary*) is synonymous with "guarantee" and "warranty," in the context of networking, security is never absolute. The only completely secure system is the one to which no one has access. This is obviously unworkable. The Microsoft Press *Computer and Internet Dictionary* defines **computer security** as "the steps taken to protect a computer and the information it contains." No guarantees are implied in this definition.

Because the entire purpose of computer networks is to share resources, there must always be a delicate balance between security and accessibility. The more secure a network, the less accessible it is, and the more accessible it is, the less secure it is. Figure 14-1 illustrates how increased accessibility decreases the system's security.

Figure 14-1 Relationship Between Accessibility and Security

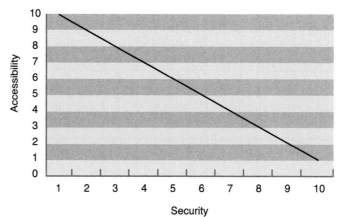

Worksheet 14.1.8   Security Checklist

In this worksheet, you analyze your school computer security policies. Based on you findings, you offer suggestions for improving the existing security policies.

Security issues can make the network administrator's relationship with network users an adversarial one. Users generally prefer more accessibility, and administrators prefer more security. This chapter details the security needs of a particular network, how to assess existing and potential threats to security, and how to implement the appropriate security measures. Also, the workings of security components and advanced identification and authentication technologies are discussed.

When it comes to a computer network, how much security is enough? The answer depends on the organization. The first step in developing a viable plan for protecting network data is to assess its security needs. You must consider several factors:

- The type of business in which the company engages
- The type of data stored on the network
- The organization's management philosophy

Each of these factors is discussed in the following sections.

Type of Business

Some businesses, such as law or medicine, by their very nature generate confidential data. The law protects the privacy of a patient's medical records and attorney-client communications. If sensitive documents are stored on the network, it is imperative that a high level of security be maintained. To do otherwise puts the organization at risk of civil liability and even criminal charges.

Other types of organizations often produce sensitive data:

- Law-enforcement agencies, courts, and other governmental bodies
- Educational institutions that store student records on a network
- Hospitals, mental-health facilities, and substance-abuse facilities
- Companies that contract with the military or that perform other national security-related work
- Any organization that gathers data under a guarantee of confidentiality
- Any organization that produces a product or provides a service in a highly competitive industry or field of research
- Any organization whose network is connected to the Internet

Type of Data

Regardless of the type of business, certain types of data are considered private and should be protected. These types include the following:

- Payroll records and employees' personal information
- Accounting and tax information
- Trade secrets such as original code, plans and diagrams, recipes, and business strategies

If these types of information are stored on a network, a security plan should be implemented to protect them.

Management Philosophy

If the data on the network is not subject to privacy laws, the security level might depend on the personal philosophies of the business owners or managers with regard to how open or closed they want the network to be.

In some organizations, everyone is considered to be part of one big, happy family. Accessibility and ease of use enjoy a higher priority than privacy and security. Other organizations operate on a "need to know" principle. Management prefers that information be accessible only to those whose jobs require it. Neither policy is right or wrong. Network administrators simply need to know and must be willing to implement network security that keeps with the organization's management style.

Acceptable-Use Policy

The first step in creating a security policy for a company network is to define an *acceptable-use policy*. An acceptable-use policy tells the users what is acceptable and allowed on the company network. This can include things such as acceptable websites to visit and what times are acceptable for browsing the Internet. For example, the acceptable-use policy can include information on installing software or hardware. The scope of what to include in an acceptable-use policy can include anything that a system administrator might feel could be harmful to the network if used improperly.

To view some examples of acceptable-use policies, visit the following links:

- www.ja.net/documents/use.html
- www.freeservers.com/policies/acceptable_use.html
- www.rice.edu/armadillo/acceptable.html

Username and Password Standards

Usually, the system administrator defines the naming convention for the usernames on a network. A common convention is to use the first initial of the person's first name and the entire last name, as shown in Table 14-1. It is recommended that you keep the username naming convention simple enough so that people will not have a hard time remembering it. Having a complex username naming convention is not as important as having a complex password standard.

Table 14-1 Username Examples

Person's Name	Username
John Doe	Jdoe
Kevin Smith	Ksmith
Mary Smith	Msmith

When you assign passwords, the level of password control should match the level of protection required. A good security policy should be strictly enforced and should include, but not be limited to, the following:

- The password should expire after a specific period of time.
- Passwords should contain a mixture of letters and numbers so that they cannot easily be broken.
- Password standards should prevent users from writing down passwords and leaving them unprotected from public view.
- Rules about password expiration and lockout should be defined. Lockout rules apply when an unsuccessful attempt has been made to access the system or when a specific change has been detected in the system configuration.

Rules for Network Access

A system administrator who assigns the proper permissions on the share drives and directories defines the rules for network access. By assigning the proper security permissions on the network, the system administrator should know who has access to specific directories. Proper maintenance by the system administrator is required to examine auditing logs of attempts that have been made to access the network shares.

Policy for Disposal of Materials

Hardware, software, and data should never just be thrown away. Strict regulations should be followed to control the disposal of computer components. The system administrator is responsible for developing a policy based on environmental and safety guidelines for hardware that no longer works. It should include the proper procedure for disposing of or destroying the hardware. Recycling used hardware is the best option if it is still in working condition. There are always places willing to accept good hardware. Other options include storing it for replacement parts. The following sites provide examples of disposal-of-materials policies:

- www.bath.ac.uk/bucs/policies/hazardconfiddisposal.htm
- www.virginia.edu/~polproc/pol/xf1.html
- www.ucalgary.ca/UofC/departments/MTRLSMGMT/surplussales/mds.html

A system administrator should keep a room or cabinet to store old software that is no longer being used. It might be needed in the future, and it is often impossible to purchase software that has been discontinued. It is a good idea to maintain an inventory of software that the company might have used in the past in addition to the software that is currently in use.

CAUTION

Back up all data, and completely erase any component that contains data before recycling, disposing of, or destroying it.

Virus-Protection Standards

Proper virus-protection standards require that current virus-protection software be installed on all the systems on the network. Place proper filters and access lists on all the incoming gateways to protect the network from unwanted access. To prevent viruses, you should also develop e-mail policies that state what might be sent and received. These policies might be met with resistance, because people generally like to chat and send non-business-oriented e-mail while they are at work. However, it might be useful to make users aware of the security issues involved and the effect that security violations can have on the network as well as users' data. The following sites provide sample e-mail policy standards:

- www.utexas.edu/policies/email/#policy
- www.ucop.edu/ucophome/policies/email/email.html
- www.onet.on.ca/onetspam.html

In addition, it is important to have a procedure that requires all virus warnings to come from one central administrator. It would be the responsibility of one person to determine if a virus alert is real or if it is a hoax and then to take the appropriate action. A virus hoax might not be as malicious as a virus, but it can be just as frustrating. It takes up resources and valuable time if it isn't identified. An excellent resource to determine if a warning is real or a hoax is http://hoaxbusters.ciac.org.

Online Security Resources

In late 1988, a 23-year-old graduate student at Cornell University released a self-replicating worm on the Internet. In a matter of hours, the rapidly spreading worm resulted in the shutdown of more than 60,000 UNIX computers at universities and military facilities. The worm was eventually eradicated after a group of researchers from across the U.S. worked together to decompile the program. For many network administrators, the November 1988 Internet worm was a wake-up call. The National Computer Security Center facilitated a series of meetings to explore ways to prevent and respond to future Internet attacks.

The heightened awareness of Internet security issues following the 1988 worm led to the formation of the *CERT Coordination Center (CERT/CC)*. The purpose of CERT/CC is to discover and study Internet-related security vulnerabilities. CERT/CC posts security alerts on its website, www.cert.org. CERT/CC also studies long-term trends in Internet security.

Web-based resources offer critical information and powerful tools that can be used to protect a network. Some of the best online security resources are NOS manufacturer websites. Here are some examples of online security resources:

- www.cert.org
- www.microsoft.com
- www.redhat.com
- www.nipc.gov

Also, Internet newsgroups can be an invaluable forum for the exchange of information concerning security-related issues.

Server Room Security

An important consideration in server installation is server security. Removable media are vulnerable and need to be secured. The following sections detail how to physically secure a network server.

To protect your computing resources, keep a locked door and four walls between your server and the rest of the world. There are a variety of ways to permit or deny access to that area after it has been secured. These include lock and key, combination locking devices, card readers and proximity readers, and biometrics.

Lock and Key

Lock and key is a tried-and-true method of physically securing your server environment. It works great if a limited number of people need access, but key management is a real issue in larger environments. This is frequently the most cost-effective solution, although as soon as you've had the lock rekeyed two or three times and new keys issued, the cost savings become a less-compelling reason not to implement a more-expensive solution.

The following guidelines help you manage your keys effectively and securely:

- Keys should be accessible only to people whose official duties require them. Giving a secretary a key to the phone/server room so that you don't have to let the phone technicians in is not effective key control. Her job does not include a requirement for access to the phone/server room.
- If you have key-control responsibilities for a high-security area, you should have a plan for annual replacement of the locking mechanism. This can be a cabinet lock, a padlock, or, in extreme cases, the lock on the door. This is especially important in an area with high employee turnover, unless key tracking and access are closely managed.

- Very few keys to secure areas should be issued. In circumstances where keys are maintained centrally and are issued to access an area or device (this could be a cabinet key, a key to a server rack, or the key to a secure area), you should follow these steps:
  - Secure all keys in a locked, fireproof container when they are not in use. Hanging the keys on the wall, sticking them in a desk drawer where "no one knows they're there," or keeping them in your pocket are not good methods of maintaining key control.
  - Whenever possible, keys should not be issued to people and should not be allowed to leave the building. This prevents unauthorized copying of the keys. The "do not copy" imprint on many keys is ineffective in preventing the key from being copied.
  - You should maintain an access list of users who are authorized to possess keys. Store this list in the key-control container to prevent alteration or misplacement. When the person responsible for key control is asked to give someone a key, he should check the authorization list after opening the key-control container.

- Keep track of your keys. You should know how many keys have been made for each lock, to whom they have been issued, where the spares are stored, and whether the lock is on a building master key. You also need to ensure that you know who has access to that key, as well as ensure that effective key-control measures are in effect for the building master keys. It is also an excellent idea to make users sign for keys.

- Inventory your keys at least once a year.

- Make sure returning keys is on every exit checklist for departing employees, and make sure that the list of keys issued to an employee matches the list of keys returned.

- Only one person should be authorized to create new, duplicate, or replacement keys, to order new keys and locks, and to dispose of keys. This authorization should always be in writing.

Combination Locking Mechanisms

Using a combination locking mechanism is similar to a lock and key. The advantage of this method is that you no longer have to distribute keys or maintain key-control lists. You can also reset the combination when needed. The one drawback of this model is that it is easy to share a combination with someone who isn't on the authorized users list.

If you are using combination locks to secure access to rooms, servers, or media cabinets in your organization, the following five guidelines help you manage your keys effectively and securely:

- Choose good combinations. A good combination should not be made up of repeated numbers (for example, 1111), ascending or descending numbers (for example, 1234 or 8765), be made up of multiples (for example, 2468), or be a known number such as a phone number or birth date. If it is an easy combination for you to remember, it is probably an easy combination for someone to guess.

- Fixed-combination locks should never be used to secure sensitive systems or data. Although the trusty Masterlock was great for a high school locker, your sensitive data should be secured by a configurable-combination lock. If you cannot use a configurable lock, change the lock frequently.

- Combinations of locks should be given only to people whose official duties require access to them. As mentioned, giving a secretary the combination to the phone/server room so that you don't have to let the phone technicians in is not effective security. Her job does not include a requirement for access to the phone/server room.

- Keep track of who has been given combinations. This should be documented, not only so that you know who has access to an area, but also so that you know whom to tell when you change the password. You should also have a written policy concerning disclosure of a combination without authorization. If possible, have the person sign the policy, and have the document stored in his or her HR records.

- Make sure you change the passwords whenever someone leaves, not only if that person has the combination(s) but also even if you suspect that he or she might have learned the combination while working for the company.

Card Readers and Proximity Readers

Card readers are the most common of the access control mechanisms. They work by reading a magnetic signature off an access card or token. The advantage of this system over a key system is that you can authorize and remove access from the central authentication server. So instead of having to rekey a lock and redistribute keys, or reset a combination and redistribute the combination, you just need to turn off the access card or token. This yields a much more secure environment than the previous mechanisms. You also have the added benefit of being able to track access based on access token. You can tell what token was used to access an area.

Biometrics

Biometrics is the most promising access control technology on the horizon for future use. In fact, some of these products are available today, and as the cost comes down, you will see more and more of these systems in place. A biometrics-based access control system uses measurable physical characteristics to authenticate users into an environment. Examples of biometrics that might be used to authenticate a user include fingerprints, retinal patterns, and speech. There have even been some discussions about using DNA or scent as the biometric key for these systems in the future. Although the field is still in its infancy, many people believe that biometrics will play a critical role in future computers—especially in electronic commerce. Privacy advocacy groups are concerned that these types of authentication systems are an invasion of privacy.

You have learned the best ways to keep the general public away from your equipment. The following sections discuss some of the other things you should do to physically secure your server.

Antitheft Devices for Server Hardware

Now that you have secured the perimeter, consider some of the security measures you can take in case an intruder sneaks in through a window:

- **Server security (inherent)**—One of the most common security measures is the locking mechanism included as part of the server itself. Most high-end servers let you lock the case and, in many cases, lock the drives into the server chassis. It is always a good idea to keep your production servers locked with a good key-management program in place so that you can find the key you need when the time comes to get into the server.

- **Server racks**—The logical follow-up to securing the server is securing the rack in which the server is mounted. Almost all rack systems include locking front and back doors. Where people tend to get into trouble is when they decide to save some money and not order the back door for the rack, or they skip the side panels. This is akin to putting a deadbolt on the front door of your new house but forgetting to build the back wall. This is another instance where good key control is critical. You don't want to have a server down and not be able to fix it because the person with the keys took the day off and forgot to take her pager home.

 Worksheet 14.1.9   Antitheft Devices

Learn how to properly install and implement antitheft devices in a server environment.

Add-On Server Security

In addition to the built-in security of the server itself, you might want to use some additional devices to ensure that your server remains secure, including the following:

- **Removable media drive locks**—These are locking devices that fit over the floppy drive, Zip drive, and CD-ROM drive to prevent unauthorized access. A person can't load or copy information without bypassing this additional hardware. As an example, Kensington makes a product for securing floppy drives called FloppyLock, which can be found at www.kensington.com.

- **Additional server case locks**—Some servers ship with holes in the case predrilled for a padlock. In addition, third-party products are available that can be added to secure a server. In an office environment, it is sometimes worth the money to invest in cabling security products that let you tie the server to a desk, similar to how bike locks work.

- **Alarms**—The final add-on is best suited for the shared office environment. It is a paranoid adaptation of a notebook security product. If you are concerned that someone will physically remove your server, you can add a motion-sensitive alarm to it to alert you when the server is moved. This recommendation is only for extremely open environments with a history of thefts. It is not needed in most environments.

Securing Removable Media

The final subject with regard to physical security is the security of your removable media, which includes the following:

- Removable disks (floppy, Zip, Jaz, LS120, CD-RW)
- Removable hard drives
- Backup media (tapes)

As discussed in the preceding section, devices are available to secure the drives for these media. What about the medium itself? Several methods are typically used to ensure the security of your removable media, including the following:

- Lock the media in an office.
- Place the media in a locked cabinet with strict key control.
- Place the media in a safe or, even better, a fire-resistant safe.
- Engage a third-party firm to store the tapes in its secure facility.

Threats to Network Security

This section covers the following topics:

- Overview of internal and external security
- Outside threats
- Denial of service (DoS)
- Distributed denial of service (DDoS)
- Well-known exploits
- Trojan horse programs
- Inside threats

Overview of Internal and External Security

As the networking industry has matured over the last decade, security has become one of the greatest concerns of information technology. Today, networks carry billions of financial transactions, private documents, and personal records. Many sensitive exchanges of such information occur over the public Internet.

From a security standpoint, the Internet presents numerous challenges. First, the Internet relies on the open, well-known protocols that make up the TCP/IP suite. These protocols, including IP itself, were not designed with a worldwide public network in mind. Although the TCP/IP suite has scaled to meet the demands of the global Internet of today, these protocols have a notorious lack of inherent security.

In other words, the Internet essentially works by following rules that are open to the public. If you study the rules enough, you are bound to find loopholes and weaknesses that can be exploited. Unfortunately, there appears to be no shortage of individuals willing to find and exploit these weaknesses, either for profit or just for "fun." A second security concern surrounds the nature of Internet connections. As more individuals, organizations, and institutions connect to the Internet, having an Internet connection has become essential for businesses in many developed parts of the world. But connecting to the Internet opens the door to network intruders. Typically, an Internet connection is a two-way street. If a user connects to the Internet, hosts on the Internet can connect to that user.

Virtually all NOSs have some degree of TCP/IP support. Windows 2000 and Red Hat Linux offer a full complement of IP services. This chapter focuses on TCP/IP-related security issues because TCP/IP is the dominant network protocol today. By running TCP/IP and connecting to the Internet, a company faces significant "outside" threats.

In addition to outside threats from the Internet, corporate networks face numerous "inside" security concerns. Common services such as file sharing and e-mail must be secured on a corporate network so that only authorized users have access to sensitive and personal information. Just as confidential paper files are kept in locked file cabinets in locked offices, electronic records must also be secured.

Inside security lapses can also result in outside attacks. Legitimate users can inadvertently infect the corporate network with a virus just by reading e-mail or browsing the web. Some corporate users might, intentionally or otherwise, install unauthorized software that can open a system or an entire network to attack. And, of course, disgruntled or disloyal employees can pose a security threat from both inside and outside the corporate network. Well-implemented security policies can minimize the risk posed by these scenarios.

Outside Threats

Early forms of NOSs used a variety of network protocols, some proprietary and some not. The explosive growth of the Internet, which began in the late 1980s, fueled demand for TCP/IP-capable software and services. To bring the Internet to users' desktops, network administrators had to deploy TCP/IP. Because TCP/IP also proved capable in the area of corporate networking, network administrators began moving away from using other protocols, such as AppleTalk and IPX/SPX. By the late 1990s, all the major developers of NOSs, including Apple and Novell, built their software around TCP/IP and Internet services.

It has become increasingly uncommon for an organization to deploy a NOS without also having an Internet connection. Remember, an Internet connection can act as an open door. The rules of the Internet are open, well-known, and full of weaknesses. If TCP/IP services are run on a NOS connected to the Internet, there are potential risks:

- **Data theft**—Data theft occurs when an unauthorized party or software program illegally obtains private information that is stored or transmitted on a network. Data theft can come in many forms, including packet sniffing and system break-ins. Typically, data thieves steal information that can be used to generate a monetary profit, such as credit card information, financial account information, and even corporate secrets. However, someone who illegally breaks into a mail server to read employee mail is also "stealing" information. Recently, a high-profile case of stealing a sensitive instant-message chat log resulted in serious financial consequences.

- **Destruction of data**—The destruction of data occurs when an unauthorized person or software program breaks into a system and deletes data. The deletion of data can also involve replacing it with erroneous data. In some cases, the unauthorized entity might be malicious software that is installed on a system. Malicious software can be installed as the result of direct attack, an e-mail attachment, a virus, or a worm.

- **Denial of service (DoS)**—A DoS attack is designed to degrade server performance or knock the server off the network completely. The goal of such an attack is to prevent other hosts from using the server (thus, denial of service). A downed or inaccessible server can cost some companies thousands of dollars an hour.

Several outside sources can be the cause of these attacks:

- **Hackers**—Definitions of the term *hacker* are controversial. The mainstream media and general public typically use *hacker* as a pejorative term that describes any person who performs computer break-ins and tampers with computer data. However, within the so-called hacker community, there is a distinction between those who break in and those who break in with an intent to inflict damage. For some, the term *hacker* refers to someone who is an expert in computer systems. According to this definition, a hacker might break into a system to explore it and expand his or her knowledge. The "true" hacker desires to dissect systems and programs to see how they work. This contrasts with those who are called *crackers* (defined next).

- **Crackers**—Those who break into computer systems to tamper with, steal, or destroy data are called *crackers*. The hacker community refers to a cracker as a "black hat," after the archetypal villain in a melodrama or an American TV western. Benign hackers are sometimes called "white hats."

- **Viruses**—A *virus* is a piece of programming code that is usually disguised as something else. It causes an unexpected and usually undesirable event. A virus is often designed so that it automatically spreads to other computer users. Viruses can be transmitted as attachments to e-mail notes or as downloads, or they can be present on a diskette or CD. The source of the e-mail note, downloaded file, or diskette just received is often unaware of the virus. The effects of some viruses are experienced as soon as their codes are executed. Other viruses lie dormant until circumstances cause the computer to execute their codes. Some viruses are playful in intent and effect, and some can be harmful, erasing data or causing complete system failure.

- **Worms**—A *worm* is a self-replicating virus that does not alter files but resides in active memory and duplicates itself. Worms use parts of an operating system that are automatic and usually invisible to the user. It is common for worms to be noticed only when their uncontrolled replication consumes system resources, slowing or halting other tasks.

Denial of Service

A *denial of service (DoS)* attack occurs when the targeted system cannot service legitimate network requests effectively because the system has become overloaded with illegitimate messages. DoS attacks come in many forms. Common DoS attacks try to take advantage of weaknesses with TCP/IP or weaknesses in NOS software code.

DoS attacks originate from one host or a group of hosts. When the attack comes from a coordinated group of hosts, such attacks are called *distributed denial of service (DDoS)*.

A common DoS attack is to overload a target system by sending more data than it can handle. For example, an attacker sends a large volume of packets to a target. The sheer volume of resulting traffic might overwhelm the target software, causing the software to crash. Moreover, a large-enough volume of DoS traffic might fill up a target link to the Internet. As a result of such an attack, the target is essentially pushed off the Internet.

Several specific types of DoS attacks exist:

- **Buffer overflow (including Ping of Death)**—A *buffer overflow* attack is designed to overwhelm the software running on the target system. Software applications are written so that they can hold incoming (and outgoing) data in a memory buffer. In some cases, it might be possible to send more data than a buffer can hold, or send data that is formatted in such a way as to "confuse" the program or its buffer. If the software code is not written to handle a buffer overflow properly, the program can crash. The so-called Ping of Death is a well-known buffer overflow DoS attack. To execute a Ping of Death attack, the attacker sends ICMP echo requests that are illegally large to the target. Older TCP/IP software could not properly handle such pings and therefore crashed. Buffer overflows typically take advantage of specific weaknesses in NOS software.

- **TCP SYN attack (including land)**—A *TCP SYN attack* exploits the TCP protocol three-way handshake, as shown in Figure 14-2. The attacker sends a large volume of TCP synchronization requests (SYN requests). These requests represent the first part of the three-way handshake. The target system responds with the second part of the handshake and then awaits a reply (the third and final part of the handshake). The target does not wait forever, but it must wait long enough to allow legitimate sessions to be established. The attacking system does not reply, but instead sends additional SYN requests as quickly as possible. The resulting volume of "half-open" connections can be too much for the target to handle, causing its software to crash. Even if the target doesn't crash, it might be so busy with the half-open connections that it cannot effectively service legitimate SYN requests.

Figure 14-2 TCP SYN Attack

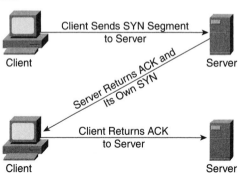

In 1997, a variation of the TCP SYN attack, called a *land attack,* was discovered. The land attack uses a program that alters the SYN request's IP header so that it appears to be sourced from the target itself. Altering the IP header to hide the source is called *spoofing* or *forging.* The target receives the bogus packet and attempts to reply to itself, only to crash or hang almost immediately. When the land attack was first discovered, several TCP/IP-enabled systems were affected, including Windows 95/NT, BSD UNIX, and Solaris.

Today, TCP SYN attacks, including land, are well-known and mostly preventable. Network devices can be configured to block TCP SYN attacks from a single source. Other defenses against TCP SYN attacks include increasing the number of half-open connections allowed by the software and decreasing the amount of time the software waits for a reply.

- *Teardrop*—A program that takes advantage of how IP handles fragmentation. The rules of TCP/IP allow a large IP packet to be broken into smaller, more manageable fragments if needed. Each fragment is sent as an individual packet. Each fragment packet contains the information needed for the destination to reassemble the larger packet. Teardrop sends fragments that have overlapping reassembly information, which confuses the target software, causing a crash. Teardrop is known to affect Windows 3.1, 95, NT, and some versions of Linux. Today, virtually all OSs contain code to protect against this attack.

- **Smurf**—Like the land attack, the *Smurf* attack relies on spoofing the IP packet header. Smurf also relies on ICMP or ping. Many organizations use firewall technology to block ping requests from outside networks. However, ping replies are usually allowed into a network so that inside hosts can use ping to test outside connectivity. If an organization allows ping replies to enter its network, it might be vulnerable to Smurf. In a Smurf attack, the attacker sends a large volume of ping requests to a target network. This might or might not be the same network that the target host resides on. The attacker spoofs the IP headers of these ping requests so that they appear to have originated from the target. As soon as the hosts on the target network receive the ping request, they direct all their replies to the target host. Consequently, the target host and/or its network connections can be overloaded, effectively denying service.

The examples listed here are all well-known vulnerabilities. OS software is now written with these attacks in mind. For example, most systems are now immune to land and Teardrop.

Known vulnerabilities in software represent "holes" in the system. You can be repair, or *patch*, these holes by installing software updates when a vendor makes them available. When installing any OS, check with the manufacturer to determine if any security patches are available for it. Certainly, additional vulnerabilities are waiting to be discovered. It is wise to check with security authorities on the World Wide Web, such as CERT/CC, on a regular basis.

Distributed Denial of Service

Because most DoS attacks work by overloading a target with packets, hardware and software developers have come up with ways to identify suspicious traffic patterns sourced from an individual host address. As soon as suspicious traffic is identified, a filter (firewall) can block traffic sourced from that address.

In the late 1990s, DoS attacks underwent a disturbing evolution. Hackers developed ways to coordinate multiple hosts in an attempt to deny service. *Distributed denial of service (DDoS)* attacks can be difficult to stop because they can originate from hundreds or even thousands of coordinated hosts. How can a target differentiate between legitimate and illegitimate requests? In some cases, the only difference between legitimate packets and bogus packets is their intent. Determining a packet's "intent" can be extremely difficult, if not impossible.

The classic DDoS attack begins with weeks or even months of hacking. Figure 14-3 illustrates the tribal flood network (TFN) DDoS attack. Before the hacker can attack the ultimate target, a *fleet* of systems must be coordinated for the attack. A fleet is made up of *zombie* hosts. A zombie is typically an insecure host with a permanent high-speed Internet connection. The hacker takes advantage of the zombie's lack of security by breaking into the system either directly or via an e-mail virus. The goal of the break-in or virus is to install software on the zombie system that gives the hacker partial control of that system. As soon as that hacker has gained partial control of a large number of zombies, it is triggered to launch a DDoS attack on the ultimate target. A recent trend in DDoS attacks is the use of Internet Relay Chat (IRC) technology to control zombies and trigger attacks.

Figure 14-3   Tribal Flood Network DDoS Attack

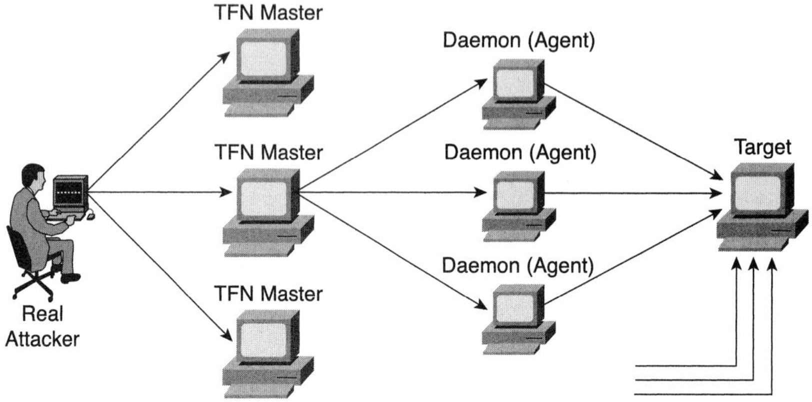

Building a fleet of zombie systems has proven all too easy for some DDoS attackers. The proliferation of residential broadband Internet service has fueled DDoS attacks. Millions of home users now have permanent high-speed Internet connections. Home users are notoriously susceptible to e-mail viruses. By opening an e-mail attachment, the user might unwittingly turn his or her home PC into a zombie. Computers on university and other school networks are also likely zombie candidates. Campus networks are notoriously large and difficult to manage. Many school networks suffer from lax security policies, insecure wireless access, and unregulated student access.

Well-Known Exploits

DoS attacks focus primarily on widespread weaknesses common to many TCP/IP implementations. Outside attacks can also be focused on specific system software, including the NOS itself. Each combination of NOS and application software contains its own unique set of vulnerabilities and weakness.

If a cracker is skilled, knowledgeable, and diligent enough, chances are that some of the attacks against a specific system will eventually succeed. The only 100-percent effective measure to protect against outside attacks is to disconnect from outside networks. Fortunately, there are relatively few highly skilled crackers.

Many network security experts agree that one of the most significant threats to network security comes from individuals with sophisticated tools but relatively weak technical abilities. These people are often called *script kiddies*. *Script kiddy* is a pejorative term used to describe immature individuals who use scripts, software programs, or techniques created by other, more skilled crackers. Script kiddies can be even more dangerous than their more refined counterparts, because they are not likely to understand the consequences of what they are doing. Thus, a script kiddy might randomly attack dozens of systems in attempt to "have fun."

Script kiddies and novice crackers turn to hacker websites and chat rooms to look for tools that can be used to attack targets. These tools can be simple software programs or even just a procedure that can be used against a target. A specific attack is often called an *exploit* because it takes advantage of system weaknesses. Many well-known exploits rely on the following programs:

- **Asmodeus (NetIQ security analyzer)**—A network security analyzer and port scanner for Windows that can scan ranges of hosts for remote security vulnerabilities.

- **SATAN (Security Administrator Tool for Analyzing Networks)**—An outdated network security analyzer for UNIX, similar in function to NetIQ.

- **Saint (Security Administrator's Integrated Network Tool)**—An updated and enhanced version of SATAN.

- **Strobe (strobe-classb)**—A small but fast scanner used to scan for open mail relays over Class B networks.

- **Ogre**—A server and vulnerability scanner for Windows NT, including NetBIOS shares and some Microsoft Internet Information Services (IIS) vulnerabilities.

- **mscan (Multiscan)**—A scanner used to detect vulnerabilities in commonly used UNIX services, such as DNS, NFS, statd, X, and finger.

- **Nmap**—A fast and powerful port scanner for UNIX that can scan ranges of computers via IP address, domain, or randomly for open ports, operating system guesses, and other information.

- **ncat (Network Config Audit Tool)**—A utility for scanning Cisco IOS Config files for user-defined parameters, such as oversights or errors.

- **BackOffice**—A server that runs in the background of the installed computer, waiting for client connections to remotely administer the system, invisible to regular users.

- **NetBus**—The same thing as BackOffice, but made by different people. It isn't as powerful, and it's usually piggybacked onto an unrelated executable.

- **SubSeven**—The same as BackOffice and NetBus, but on par with BackOffice in power.

- **trinoo, Stacheldraht, tribal flood network, mstream, carko, wormkit**—DDoS tools.

- **Ramen**—A collection of tools designed to attack systems by exploiting well-known vulnerabilities in three commonly installed software packages. A successful exploitation of any of the vulnerabilities results in a privileged (root) compromise of the victim host.

Trojan Horse Programs

A *Trojan horse* is a program that presents itself as another program to obtain information. For example, there is a Trojan horse that emulates the system login screen. When users type in their account name and password, the information is stored or transmitted to the originator of the Trojan horse. The username and password can then be used to gain access to the system.

Inside Threats

Security threats that originate from inside a network can be more harmful than outside threats. Inside threats are especially dangerous and can often be overlooked by network administrators. Computers that reside on the inside network typically have a high degree of access to inside resources. Also, employees and trusted users are likely to have critical information about the network, including passwords.

High-profile inside threats include disloyal and disgruntled employees who use their inside access to destroy, steal, or tamper with data. Although these types of attacks cannot be completely protected against, well-defined security policies can minimize the risks from this type of threat. For example, organizations should avoid using just a handful of passwords to protect all computer resources. Also, large companies should establish clear procedures for removing employee accounts and passwords in the event that an employee leaves the company.

The most insidious inside threat is a typical end user of a network. Unwitting end users can bring a network to its knees by carelessly opening e-mail attachments, installing unauthorized software, mounting disks from home, or even browsing the web. The typical cause of inside attacks is an end user who opens an e-mail attachment only to copy a virus to the computer. Many viruses thrive on the corporate network. E-mail viruses typically mail themselves to accounts listed in e-mail address books. Because many corporations keep staff e-mail lists loaded on every computer, such a virus can quickly spread to all a company's employees. Viruses can also seek out and infect shared files and folders, which are common on corporate networks.

A growing problem for corporate networks is the widespread popularity of instant messaging and peer-to-peer file sharing. Employees might download instant-message software, such as MSN Messenger or AOL Instant Messenger, to chat in real time with coworkers or friends and family. Other users might download peer-to-peer file sharing software based on Gnutella or some other technology. Both instant messaging and peer-to-peer file-sharing programs can be used to transfer virus-infected files to the local computer. Moreover, because both of these types of programs listen for connections originating from the Internet, chat and file-sharing applications might be vulnerable to other forms of exploitation.

Again, a well-defined security policy can do much to prevent inside threats. For example, it is possible to configure employee PCs so that they cannot run unauthorized applications. Administrators can also restrict Internet access and even prevent e-mail attachments from entering the network. In some cases, the threat of e-mail viruses can be reduced if users switch to a different e-mail client. Virus-protection software can also be installed on client computers as a supplemental security measure.

Corporate Espionage

Corporate espionage is the most sophisticated type of internal security threat. Theft of trade secrets is big business, and companies can become overnight successes or failures because of it. Employees can be approached by competing companies and offered lucrative rewards for delivering an organization's secret information. In other instances, employees of other companies can procure a job with the user's company to infiltrate and gather data to take back to the competitor. They then get to draw a paycheck from both companies simultaneously.

Finally, there are freelance corporate spies who take assignments on a contract basis. In highly competitive industries, they can steal the data on their own and then auction it to the highest bidder. "Data kidnappers" can even hold confidential data hostage, promising not to release it to another company in exchange for a "ransom" payment.

Corporate spies are often intelligent, highly skilled, technically sophisticated individuals. They are usually well-financed and can evade detection until it is too late. If a business is part of a field in which corporate espionage is common (such as the technology industry, oil and energy, research medicine, engineering, and others in which success hinges on being first to market with innovative products or services), the network can be vulnerable.

Security measures designed to thwart these professional spies must be of the highest level. Businesses might need to call in consultants who specialize in protecting corporate networks from such infiltration.

Rebellious Users

Internal security breaches can also be the result of users who disagree with security policies that they believe are too restrictive. Although these breaches aren't accidental, they aren't designed to cause harm. Instead, they are intended to enable the user to do something that cannot otherwise be done. For example, if security controls do not prevent users from installing application software or hardware drivers, rebellious users who do not like the Internet access policies can connect an external modem, plug in a phone line, install the drivers, and dial in to their own ISPs. Another user can install a remote-control application such as PCAnywhere. This can open that computer and the internal network to outside users who also have PCAnywhere installed on their computers.

> **NOTE**
>
> In addition to a well-planned security policy, organizations should provide training programs for all employees who use the computer network. Because employees are often targeted as a way into the intranet, it is important to instruct them on how to prevent viruses, DoS attacks, data theft, and so on. Damage is more likely to occur from ignorance, not incompetence.

The company's response to rebellious users depends on the policies and the degree of security required on the network. Implementing tighter controls might be appropriate. In other situations, it might be appropriate to evaluate whether the security policies are too stringent and whether users should have more-legitimate access.

 Worksheet 14.2.7   Threats to Network Security

Learn the various events that threaten security on the network and implement measures to prevent them.

Implementing Security Measures

This section covers the following topics:

- File encryption
- IP security
- Secure Sockets Layer (SSL)
- E-mail security
- Public/private key encryption

File Encryption

Protecting network data often requires that a combination of security methods be applied. This section examines how sensitive data can be encrypted, either in files on the disk or in packets that travel across the network.

Technologies available to secure e-mail messages are the focus of this section, because e-mail is one of the most widely used network applications. It is also the form of network communication that is most likely to contain confidential information. This section details how security measures are implemented and how these measures work.

Encryption involves converting data into a form that cannot be easily understood by others. The technical aspects of encryption are discussed in more detail in the section, "Public/Private Key Encryption."

File encryption is a way of encrypting data stored on a computer disk so that it is unreadable to anyone but the creator of the data. Some operating systems, such as Windows 2000, include a file-encryption function. For those that do not supply such a function (such as Windows 9x and Windows NT), third-party encryption programs are available:

- PC Guardian
- Deltacrypt
- Winzap

When documents are encrypted on the disk, only a user who has the correct key can view them. If others attempt to access the file, it either doesn't open or appears as a series of scrambled, meaningless characters.

IP Security

File encryption protects data stored on a disk, but it does not offer security for data as it is sent over a network. The IP Security (IPSec) protocol was developed to remedy this shortcoming. IPSec secures data at the packet level. Because it works at the network layer of the OSI reference model, applications are not aware of it. Cisco Systems includes support for IPSec in its routers, and Windows 2000 includes IPSec in its TCP/IP stack.

IPSec uses two protocols:

- **Authentication Header (AH)**—Enables verification of the sender's identity.
- **Encapsulating Security Payload (ESP)**—Ensures the confidentiality of the data itself.

These two protocols can be used separately or together.

IPSec can operate in either transport mode or tunnel mode, as shown in Figure 14-4, but the packet headers differ. Transport mode provides end-to-end security. This means that the encryption is in place from the source computer to the destination computer. Tunnel mode protects the data from the exit point of one network to the entry point of another.

Figure 14-4 IP Security

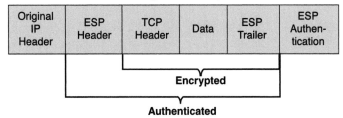

An ESP Datagram in Transport Mode

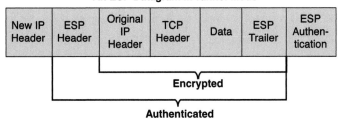

An ESP Datagram in Tunnel Mode

Secure Sockets Layer

Secure Sockets Layer (SSL) is another way of securing communications on the network. The disadvantage of SSL is that because it operates at the application layer, it must be supported by the user application. Figure 14-5 shows how SSL works.

Figure 14-5   Secure Sockets Layer (SSL)

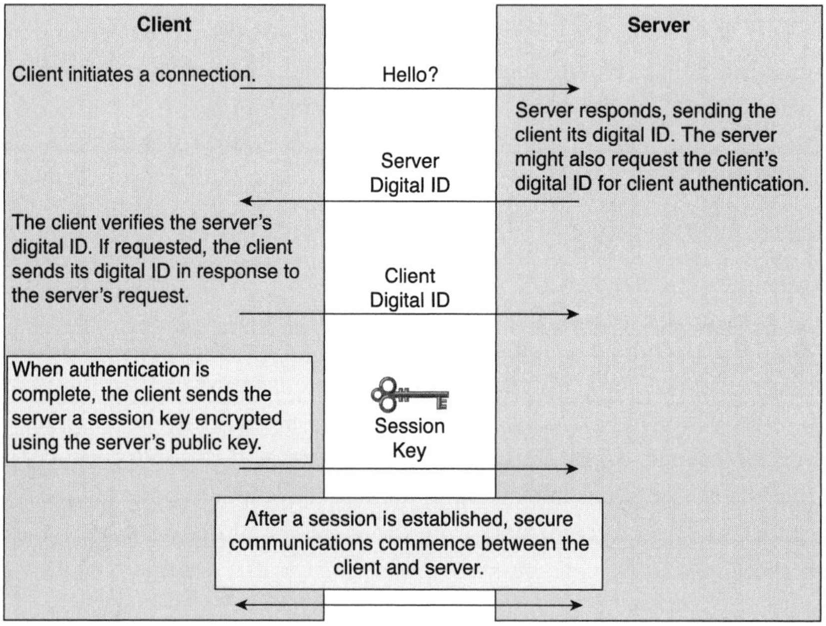

SSL was developed by Netscape to provide security for its web browser. It uses public and private key encryption (which are discussed in a later section).

E-Mail Security

Many computer users enjoy a false sense of security about network communications in general and e-mail messages in particular. Users assume that only the recipient to whom the messages are addressed reads the messages they compose and send over the local network or the Internet. E-mail users behave as if they have the same expectation of privacy when sending e-mail as they do when sending a letter through the postal service. A more accurate expectation would be to assume that the e-mail is like a postcard that can be read by anyone who handles it during its journey from sender to recipient.

E-mail messages are easy to intercept, as shown in Figure 14-6. They often travel through dozens of nodes (servers) on their way from sender to recipient. Even if a message is sent to someone within the local network, a copy of it is stored on at least three machines. These machines include the sender's computer, the recipient's computer, and the internal mail server. E-mail sent over the Internet can pass through several servers as well. Unless it is encrypted or digitally signed, the message can be easily read, copied, or altered at any point along the way.

Figure 14-6 E-Mail Security

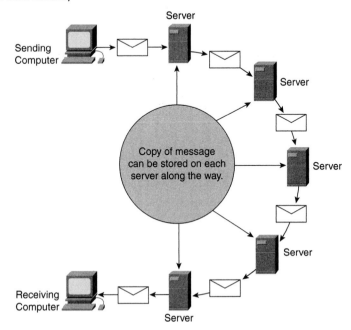

NOTE

Deleting the message on the user's machine does not guarantee that there is not still a copy of it on one or more servers.

Many software products have been developed to address this problem. These products are designed to accomplish several goals:

- Unauthorized parties cannot read the message.
- The message cannot be altered between the time it leaves the sender and the time it is opened by the recipient.
- The person identified as the sender of the message is actually who he says he is.

An important factor in e-mail protection software is ease of use. If users must perform complex or time-consuming tasks to send or read secured e-mail, they are likely to abandon the security software altogether.

Popular e-mail protection programs include the following:

- Pretty Good Privacy (PGP)
- Kerberos
- Baltimore Mail Secure
- MailMarshal from Softek

Most e-mail protection software uses public key encryption (discussed in the next section) and digital signatures to provide data confidentiality and identity authentication.

Public/Private Key Encryption

Although it is often called *public key encryption,* the more accurate term is *public/private key encryption.* This is because this type of encryption uses two keys—one that is published and widely available, and one that is private and known only to the user. Both keys are required to complete the secure communication. This type of encryption, illustrated in Figure 14-7, is also called *asymmetric encryption.*

Figure 14-7 Public/Private Key Encryption

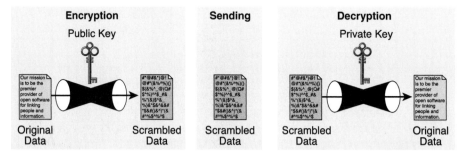

With this type of encryption, each user has both a public and a private key, called a key pair. Public/private encryption works like this:

1. Carol and Ted exchange their public keys. It does not matter that this is done in an insecure manner, because messages cannot be deciphered with just the public key.

2. Carol wants to send a message to Ted, so she encrypts the message using Ted's public key. A public key is associated with only one private key. To decrypt a message that was encrypted using a public key, the associated private key is required. The reverse also applies. To decrypt a message that was encrypted using a private key, the associated public key is required.

3. Ted, using his private key, can decrypt the message, because it was encrypted using his public key. Notice that only Ted's keys, public and private, were used in this encryption process.

If Carol had encrypted the message using her private key, anyone could decrypt the message using her public key, which is available to all.

Both keys of the same key pair must be used for this encryption to work, and there is no need for anyone to know anyone else's private key. A good way to understand this type of encryption is to think of the two pieces of information required to enter a home protected by a digital combination lock. If someone wants to enter the house, he must know both the street address and the number sequence to enter into the locking device. The address is public information that is published in the telephone directory. It is available to anyone, just as the user's public encryption key is available to anyone. The lock combination is analogous to the user's private key. Only the owner of the house knows it. Both keys are unique to that particular home, but one is made known to the public, and the other is kept secret.

Worksheet 14.3.5   Implementing Security Measures

Learn how to properly implement planned security measures.

Patches and Upgrades

This section covers the following topics:

- Finding patches and upgrades
- Selecting patches and upgrades
- Applying patches and upgrades

Finding Patches and Upgrades

Check the manufacturer's website to find the latest security patches and other updates as a part of routine maintenance. *Patches* are fixes to existing software code. A NOS manufacturer typically provides security patches as soon as vulnerabilities or even potential vulnerabilities are discovered and fixed. Depending on the software developer, patches might be called *updates*. Update is a vague term that can be used to describe a security fix or a complete application upgrade.

Microsoft now includes the option to use software called Windows Update with its operating systems, including Windows 2000 Server, as shown in Figure 14-8. Windows Update periodically checks for software patches and upgrades by contacting Microsoft via the Internet. When software updates are found to be available, Windows Update can alert the user. Windows Update can also be configured to automatically download and install the new software. Automatic installation makes sense for most home users. However, system administrators typically prefer to perform all installations manually.

NOS manufacturers also might offer upgrades to portions of the operating system, or a complete upgrade of the OS itself. Unlike security patches, upgrades might significantly change how an OS handles a particular task. For example, an upgrade might include an entirely new web browser.

Figure 14-8   Windows Update Resource Page

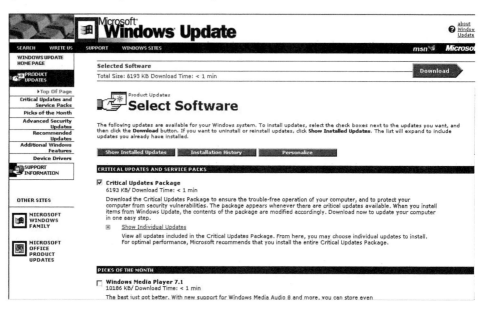

Selecting Patches and Upgrades

Software makers recommend that software security patches be installed immediately to reduce exposure to known vulnerabilities. Software vendors release security updates as soon as they are available. Periodically, software makers collect a group of security updates and package them into a larger update. Microsoft calls these collections of bug fixes and security updates service packs.

As an example, the Security Update for Internet Explorer 5.01 Service Pack 2, dated October 10, 2001, stated the following:

> *This update eliminates three security vulnerabilities affecting Internet Explorer, and is discussed in Microsoft Security Bulletin MS01-051. Download now to prevent a malicious user from taking advantage of the Zone Spoofing vulnerability, the HTTP Request Encoding vulnerability, or a new variant of the Telnet Invocation vulnerability in Internet Explorer.*

Most updates and security patches should be installed, but there might be circumstances where the update is not warranted. Understanding the effect on the system helps you determine whether an update, fix, or patch is necessary. Use caution before installing a software patch on a production server. If the software vendor patch or update is specifically written to fix a security issue, the patch most likely will not adversely affect the production system. However, software makers sometimes post security and bug fixes alongside major software upgrades. You should not install major software upgrades on a production server without testing the results first.

As a rule, you should load new software on a test server and check it for compatibility issues. With small-sized, tight-focused security updates, testing is not essential but is recommended. With major revisions or upgrades of software, you should always do testing to avoid network downtime in the event of a compatibility issue.

Applying Patches and Upgrades

Periodically, NOS vendors issue updates to their NOSs. These updates have various names. Microsoft calls them *service packs,* IBM calls them *fixpacs,* and Novell calls them *patches*. The following websites provide information on updates and patches:

- **Windows 2000 Service Pack 2 (Microsoft)**—www.microsoft.com/windows2000/downloads/servicepacks/sp2/default.asp
- **Fixpacs (IBM)**—www-3.ibm.com/software/webservers/studio/v3fixpacks_entry.html
- **Novell patches**—www.novell.com/coolsolutions/gwmag/qna/patches.html

These updates usually fix bugs or close security holes that have been found in the released version of the operating system. You should download updates that fix or close security holes from the NOS vendor's website and immediately install them on the NOS. Be aware that some network applications (such as Microsoft Exchange Server or an e-mail server) require you to install a specific service pack level before you can install the network application. Such an update is required for the network application to operate correctly.

Download the updates from the NOS vendor's website. To install the update, follow the NOS vendor's instructions.

Before installing the update, do a full backup. This is vital even if the update has been tested on another system.

It is important to keep a record of the patches and upgrades installed on a system. Maintain a logbook for each NOS server, and record any changes to the system configuration, including the installation of security patches and service packs.

Firewalls

This section covers the following topics:

- Introduction to firewalls and proxies
- Packet filtering
- Firewall placement
- Common firewall solutions
- Using a NOS as a firewall

Introduction to Firewalls and Proxies

The key defense against Internet attackers is an *Internet firewall*. A firewall is specialized software, hardware, or a combination of the two. The purpose of an Internet firewall is to prevent unwanted or malicious IP packets from reaching a secure network.

Over the last decade, firewall technology has evolved significantly. Early firewalls, which filtered packets based on addressing information, were built and maintained by large organizations. Today, even desktop operating systems (such as Windows XP) include built-in firewall capabilities geared toward the average home user. The increasing number of hacker exploits and Internet worms make firewall technology one of the most visible and essential aspects of any enterprise network.

The term *firewall* is used loosely to refer to several different approaches to protecting networks, as described in the following sections.

Packet Filters

Typically, an Internet firewall is a host running IP packet-filtering software. Most LANs run IP packet filters on a router or a specialized host, which also performs routing. Home users can run IP packet filtering on an end system, such as a Windows PC.

Access Control Lists

Packet filters are sometimes called access control lists (ACLs). An IP packet filter begins with a list of rules. The rules tell the router or host how to handle packets that match the specified criteria. For example, a packet matching a particular source address can be dropped, forwarded, or processed in some special way. Common matching criteria have several aspects:

- IP address (source and destination)
- TCP/UDP port number (source and destination)
- Upper-layer protocol (HTTP, FTP, and so on)

Simply put, a host configured with an IP packet filter checks packets that come in or go out a specified interface or interfaces. Based on the rules defined, the host can drop the packet or accept it. This approach is also called *rules-based forwarding*. Using this approach, administrators can configure routers to drop unwanted or potentially malicious packets before they reach the secure LAN.

Proxy Services

In networking, a *proxy* is software that interacts with outside networks on behalf of a client host. Figure 14-9 shows the proxy server that responds to workstations, and Figure 14-10 shows a proxy server with internal web servers.

Figure 14-9 Proxy Server for Workstations

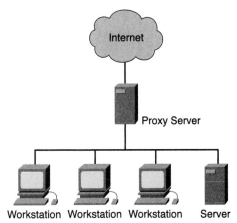

Figure 14-10 Proxy Server for Internal Web Servers

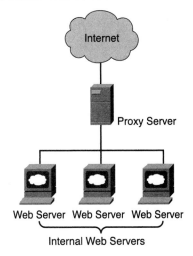

Typically, client hosts on a secure LAN request a web page from a server running
proxy services. The proxy server retrieves the web page from the Internet. The web
page is then copied to the proxy server (a process called *caching*). Finally, the proxy
server transmits the web page to the client. By using the proxy's services, the client
never interacts directly with outside hosts. This protects clients from potential Internet
threats. Administrators can configure proxy servers to reject certain client requests or
outside Internet responses. For example, schools can use proxy servers to control what
websites can be accessed. Because all web requests are directed to the proxy, administrators have tight control over which requests are honored. Microsoft makes a comprehensive proxy service called Microsoft Proxy Server 2.0 available for its NOS.

Proxy servers insulate LANs and protect hosts from the outside. The ability of the proxy server to cache web pages is an important benefit of using a proxy service for HTTP. Because the proxy server caches frequently accessed HTTP content on a local server, multiple clients can access the content with significantly improved response time.

Network Address Translation

Network Address Translation (NAT) is a process that runs on a router (typically a router that acts as a gateway to the Internet). A router running NAT rewrites the addressing information contained in IP packets. Administrators use NAT to alter the source address of packets originating from a secure LAN. This allows secure LANs to be addressed using private IP addresses, as shown in Figure 14-11.

Figure 14-11 Network Address Translation

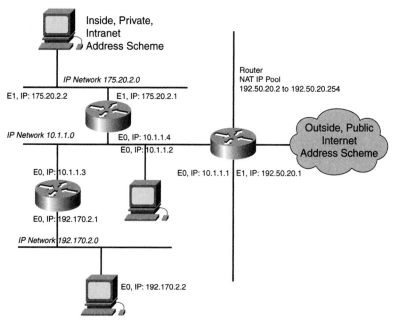

Private IP addresses are not routed on the Internet. An outside hacker cannot directly reach a computer that has a private address. Of course, hosts with private IP addresses cannot directly reach Internet hosts either. But a NAT router can take a packet originating from a host with a private address and replace the packet's source IP address with a public, globally routable address. The NAT router records this address translation in a table. As soon as the addressing information is rewritten, the NAT router forwards the packet toward the destination host. When the outside destination replies, the reply packet is routed back to the NAT router. The NAT router then consults the translation table. Based on the entries in the table, the NAT router rewrites the addressing information so that the packet can be routed back to the original, privately addressed host.

NAT is often deployed in conjunction with proxy services and/or IP packet filters. It is also becoming an important technology in home and small offices, because NAT allows hundreds of computers to "borrow" a single public, globally routable IP address. This process is sometimes called many-to-one NAT, address overloading, or Port Address Translation (PAT). Popular desktop operating systems include built-in NAT services (such as Microsoft Windows Internet Connection Sharing). NAT services are also included in NOSs. Red Hat Linux uses the ipchains program to perform NAT. Other NAT programs include ipmasquerade and natd.

Some experts make a distinction between NAT and a firewall. Others look at NAT as part of a comprehensive firewall solution. Regardless, NAT can have the effect of protecting the network from attack, because outsiders might not be able to send packets directly to inside targets or might use scanning techniques to map the internal network.

Packet Filtering

The most basic firewall solution is an IP packet filter. To configure a packet filter, a network administrator must define the rules that describe how to handle specified packets. Example 14-1 shows one such set of rules, called an access list.

Example 14-1 *UNIX Server Access List*

```
#Clear all rules
/sbin/ipfw-f flush
#Deny Routing Information Protocol on UDP port 520
/sbin/ipfw add deny udp from any 520 to any 520 via x10
#Send all packets to the NAT Daemon for address translation
/sbin/ipfw add divert and all from any to any via x10
#Allow specific hosts access
/sbin/ipfw add allow ip from 172.17.4.5 to any
/sbin/ipfw add allow ip from 172.17.87.52 to any
#Allow Web Requests
/sbin/ipfw add allow tcp from any to 192.168.54.198 80
#Deny everything else to 192.168.54.0/24 network
/sbin/ipfw add deny ip from any to 192.168.54.0/24
#Permit the rest
/sbin/ipfw add permit ip from any to any
```

The first packet filters filtered packets based on the addressing information contained in the packet header—namely, the source and destination IP address. Because the IP packet header operates at Layer 3 of the OSI reference model, early packet filters worked only at Layer 3.

As packet filtering matured, packet filters were designed to base decisions on information contained in the TCP or UDP header at Layer 4. Both TCP and UDP use port numbers to address specific applications running on a host. Layer 4 access lists can be configured to permit or deny packets based on source or destination ports as well as IP address information. For example, a Layer 4 access list can be configured to permit traffic destined for a specific IP address at port 80, which is the well-known port that web servers listen on.

The firewall can also be configured to examine the TCP code bits. The six TCP code bits are used to establish connections between hosts using a three-way handshake. A Layer 4 firewall can identify whether a packet is the first part of a three-way handshake or part of an established connection. That way, an administrator can block TCP traffic from the outside that is trying to establish a connection but permit TCP traffic that is already part of a connection. In other words, the firewall can keep "uninvited" traffic out while allowing "invited" traffic. This technique works only with TCP, because the firewall examines the TCP code bits.

To keep uninvited UDP traffic out while allowing invited UDP traffic in, a firewall has to be "smart." Also, IP can be used without TCP and UDP at Layer 4. For example, ICMP (ping) does not use a Layer 4 header. There is no way to determine if a datagram (an IP packet without a TCP header) is part of an established connection, because IP and UDP are both connectionless. These protocols have no "established" connections.

Firewall software must guess at what connectionless traffic is invited and what connectionless traffic is not. Intelligent firewalls do this by monitoring what kind of connectionless traffic originates from the secure LAN. The UDP source and destination ports and the IP source and destination addresses are noted and are stored in a table. When the firewall detects connectionless traffic that "looks as if" it is invited, the UDP ports and IP addresses match a flow of traffic recently detected from an inside host. The firewall then lets the traffic pass through. This type of packet filtering is called *stateful packet filtering,* because the firewall keeps track of the "state" of conversations, but only for a short period of time (sometimes only a few seconds). Such firewalls are dynamic. The rules that are used to determine which packets are allowed into a network vary based on the traffic flows originating from the inside hosts.

The most comprehensive form of stateful packet filtering examines not just the Layer 3 and Layer 4 headers, but the Layer 7 application data as well. Layer 7 firewalls look for patterns in the packet's payload in an effort to determine what application is being used, such as HTTP, FTP, and so on. Layer 7 stateful packet filtering has many advantages, including the ability to filter a particular application regardless of the TCP or UDP port number used. But this type of packet filtering works only with software that is preprogrammed to "recognize" a given application. Therefore, not all applications are supported. Also, this type of packet filtering adds a significant amount of delay and overhead to the routing process.

Firewall Placement

Knowing where to deploy an Internet firewall is just as important as knowing how to configure packet-filtering rules. Figure 14-12 shows classic firewall placement.

Figure 14-12   Firewall Placement

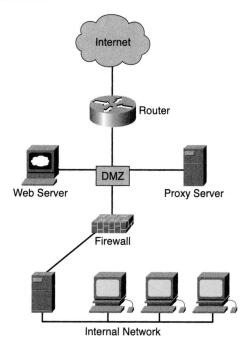

A boundary router connects the enterprise LAN to its ISP (and thus, the Internet). The boundary router LAN interface leads to a network designed for public access. This network contains NOS servers that provide the World Wide Web, e-mail, and other services to the public Internet. This public network is sometimes called a "dirty LAN" or "sacrificial LAN" because public requests are allowed on it. It is commonly called the Demilitarized Zone (DMZ). The DMZ acts as a buffer area. The boundary router should include an IP filter that protects against obvious vulnerabilities. For example, the management protocol, SNMP, should not be allowed into the network from the outside. The NOS servers in the DMZ should be tightly configured. The boundary router should allow only specific types of traffic to these servers. In Figure 14-12, the boundary router should allow only HTTP-, FTP-, mail-, and DNS-related traffic.

A dedicated firewall solution, such as a Cisco Private Internet eXchange (PIX) Firewall, connects the DMZ to the protected LAN. This device performs additional IP filtering (including stateful filtering), proxy services, NAT, or a combination of these functions.

The DMZ is designed to keep the inside network "clean." The example shown in Figure 14-12 is a simple configuration. Complex variations on the principles discussed here are common.

Common Firewall Solutions

There are several common firewall solutions:

- **Appliances**—A device that is standalone and easy to configure is often called an *appliance*. The most popular firewall appliance is the Cisco PIX, which includes NAT and stateful packet-filtering capability in an all-in-one appliance. The PIX Firewall is rack-mountable. The model you choose determines how much RAM and Flash memory you get. Figure 14-13 shows PIX Firewall 515. The 515 model uses TFTP for image download and upgrade. It has a low-profile design, 128,000 simultaneous sessions, and 170 Mbps throughput. Figure 14-14 shows the PIX Firewall 520. This model uses a 3.5-inch floppy disk drive to load the image and upgrade. It has an enterprise chassis design, 256,000 simultaneous sessions, and 240 Mbps throughput.

  The PIX Firewall is secure right out of the box. The PIX Firewall default settings allow all connections from the inside interface access to the outside interface and block all connections from the outside interface to the inside interface. After a few installation procedures and an initial configuration of six general commands, the PIX Firewall is operational and protects the network. Cisco PIXs also offer support for IPSec and VPN.

- **Router configured for packet filtering or NAT**—Most routers can be configured to filter packets and run NAT. The Cisco IOS Firewall Feature Set provides stateful packet filtering. Figure 14-15 shows a Cisco 3600 series router that has some firewall capabilities.

- **UNIX host**—Essentially, this solution is a UNIX host that serves as a router, running packet-filtering software (such as ipfw) and/or NAT. A potential drawback of this solution is that the hardware and software involved are not necessarily optimized for switching and filtering packets. Therefore, this option might be unsuitable for an enterprise that cannot tolerate high latency.

- **Proxy service software**—Dozens of proxy service software packages are available. One of the most popular is Microsoft Proxy Services 2.0.

Home users have a variety of firewall options available, such as ZoneAlarm from Zonelabs, McAfee Firewall, and Norton Firewall from Symantec. These are software firewalls, which are installed on the home machine.

Figure 14-13   PIX Firewall 515 Model

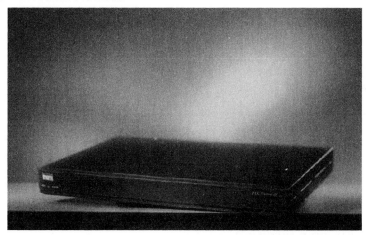

Figure 14-14   PIX Firewall 520 Model

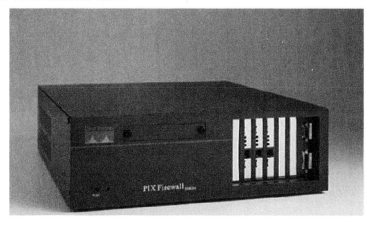

Figure 14-15 Cisco 3600 Series Router

Using a NOS as a Firewall

This chapter explained that the NOS can function as part of a firewall solution by filtering packets, running NAT, or acting as a proxy server. In high-traffic environments, a specialized packet-filtering-and-NAT solution is recommended. A specialized device such as a router or firewall appliance is designed to switch packets and manipulate them quickly. A NOS running on ordinary hardware might be able to do the job, but not without adding latency and overhead on the server.

In low-traffic environments, such as small offices and home networks, a NOS firewall solution is a good choice.

Summary

The Microsoft Press *Computer and Internet Dictionary* defines network security as "the steps taken to protect a computer and the information it contains." Some of the important concepts to retain from this chapter include the following:

- A first step when creating a security policy for a company network is to define an acceptable-use policy, which defines what is acceptable and allowed on the company network.

- Policies regarding passwords should be strictly enforced. They include a specific expiration date, lockout rules, and the use of letter and number combinations. Passwords should never be left where they can be found and used.

- Security threats from the Internet include hackers, crackers, viruses, and worms. Although a hacker can cause damage, a cracker breaks into a system to do specific damage or to steal. A virus and a worm can both do considerable damage. However, a worm attaches not to files but to active memory, and it is self-replicating.

- Well-defined security policies help minimize inside threats. Employees and trusted users are likely to have critical information about the network, including passwords, and they can facilitate corporate espionage.

- The system administrator must guard against data theft, data destruction, and denial of service (DoS) attacks. Distributed denial of service (DDoS) attacks originate from multiple hosts and can be extremely difficult to defend against.

- To keep the NOS current, apply software security patches and upgrades as they become available.

- The most important defense against outside security threats is an Internet firewall. An Internet firewall solution can consist of several components, including IP packet filtering, proxy services, and NAT.

Check Your Understanding

The following review questions help you assess what you learned in this chapter. Answers can be found in Appendix A, "Answers to Check Your Understanding Questions."

1. Match the types of DoS attacks with their descriptions.

Type of Attack	Description
Teardrop	Sends more data than the target system can hold
TCP SYN	Spoofs the IP headers of multiple ping requests so that replies are all sent to the target
Smurf	Sends packet fragments with overlapping reassembly information
Buffer overflow	Leaves a large number of half-open connections

2. Which software option included in Windows 2000 and XP periodically checks for software patches and upgrades by contacting Microsoft via the Internet?

3. Based on the following choices, at which layer can the following protocols be filtered? (Choices might be used more than once.)

   Layer 3

   Layer 4

   Layer 7

Protocol	Filtering Layer
HTTP	
TCP	
FTP	
IP	
UDP	

4. Using the following options, label the components in the network shown in Figure 14-16.

   Internet

   Intranet

   Boundary router

   Firewall

   DMZ

Figure 14-16 Network Components

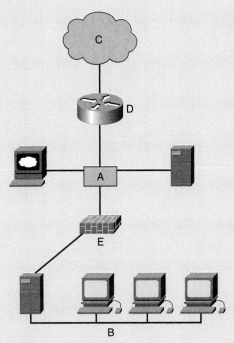

5. The first step in developing a viable plan for protecting network data is to assess its security needs. Which of the following are factors to consider?

  A. The type of data stored on the network

  B. Geographic location

  C. The type of business in which the company engages

  D. The organization's management philosophy

  E. Demand analysis

6. Developing secure password standards is usually a system administrator's first line of defense against an intruder. What are some of the best practices to implement to keep passwords secure?

  A. Passwords should expire after a specific period of time.

  B. Password standards should prevent users from writing down passwords and leaving them unprotected from public view.

  C. Passwords should be easy to remember.

  D. Rules about password expiration and lockout should be defined.

  E. Users should be able to change their passwords whenever they want.

7. Many methods can be used to implement security measures. What form of encryption is a way of encrypting data stored on a computer disk so that it is unreadable to anyone but the data's creator?

   A. Secure Sockets Layer (SSL)

   B. Public/private key encryption

   C. File encryption

   D. IPSec

8. Many methods can be used to implement security measures. What form of encryption is another way of securing communications on the network by providing encryption within the user's application layer?

   A. Secure Sockets Layer (SSL)

   B. Public/private key encryption

   C. File encryption

   D. IPSec

Key Terms

acceptable-use policy   A statement that informs the users what is acceptable and allowed on the company network.

buffer overflow   A kind of attack that is designed to overwhelm the software running on the target system.

CERT Coordination Center (CERT/CC)   The purpose of CERT/CC is to discover and study Internet-related security vulnerabilities.

computer security   The steps taken to protect a computer and the information it contains. No guarantees are implied in this definition.

cracker   A person who breaks into computer systems to tamper with, steal, or destroy data.

denial of service (DoS)   A type of attack in which the targeted system cannot service legitimate network requests effectively because it is overloaded with illegitimate messages.

distributed denial of service (DDoS)   A type of attack that originates from hundreds or even thousands of coordinated hosts. The classic DDoS attack begins with weeks or even months of hacking. Before the hacker can attack the ultimate target, a fleet of systems must be coordinated for the attack.

file encryption   A way to convert data stored on a computer disk so that it is unreadable to anyone but the data's creator.

hacker   Someone who dissects systems and programs to see how they work.

Internet firewall   Specialized software, hardware, or a combination of the two that prevents unwanted or malicious IP packets from reaching a secure network.

Network Address Translation (NAT)   A process that runs on a router (typically a router that acts as a gateway to Internet). A router running NAT rewrites the addressing information contained in IP packets. Administrators use NAT to alter the source address of packets originating from a secure LAN.

patch   A fix to existing software code. A NOS manufacturer typically provides security patches when vulnerabilities or potential vulnerabilities are discovered and fixed.

proxy service   A proxy is software that interacts with outside networks on behalf of a client host. By using the services of a proxy, the client never interacts directly with outside hosts. This protects clients from potential Internet threats.

public/private key encryption   Uses two keys—one that is published and widely available and one that is private and known only to the user. Both keys are required to complete the secure communication.

Secure Sockets Layer (SSL)   A way to secure communications on the network by providing encryption.

Smurf   A kind of attack that spoofs the IP packet header using ICMP or ping.

TCP SYN attack   Exploits the TCP protocol three-way handshake.

Teardrop   A program that takes advantage of how IP handles fragmentation. Teardrop sends fragments that have overlapping reassembly information, which confuses the target software, causing a crash.

Trojan horse   A program that presents itself as another program to obtain information.

virus   A piece of programming code that is usually disguised as something else. It causes an unexpected and usually undesirable event.

worm   A self-replicating virus that does not alter files but resides in active memory. It duplicates itself to produce uncontrolled replication that consumes system resources, slowing or halting other tasks.

Answers to Check Your Understanding Questions

This appendix contains the answers to the Check Your Understanding questions at the end of each chapter.

Chapter 1

1. What are three reasons to use MS-DOS?

    A. Simple, low-overhead operating system

    B. Inexpensive

    C. User-friendly

    D. Stable and reliable

    E. Runs on all platforms

    Answers: **A, B, D**

2. Match each operating system with its description.

    Answers:

Operating System	Description
Windows 95a	Original release of Microsoft's 32-bit operating system
Windows 95b	OSR2, FAT32 enhancement
Windows 98	Added Active Desktop and USB support
Windows 98 Second Edition (SE)	IE 5.0 and stronger encryption and Internet connection sharing
Windows Millennium Edition (Me)	Built-in disaster recovery and faster startup and shutdown

3. Enter the command that accomplishes the result.

Answers (the commands can be uppercase or lowercase):

Command	Result
dir	Lists the files in the current directory
cd	Changes to a different directory
Time	Displays or sets the system time
Date	Displays or sets the date
Copy	Copies files to another location
Diskcopy	Copies the contents of one floppy disk to another
Attrib	Displays or changes file attributes
Find	Searches for a text string in a file
Help	Displays a list of other available commands and their functions

4. Which of the following are distinguishing characteristics of a workstation?

A. Standalone computer

B. Must be configured for network access

C. Runs a Graphical User Interface

D. The system typically has speakers/sound card

E. Multiple processors

Answers: A, C, D

5. What are the two most important features that a server must contain?

Answer: Reliability and fault-tolerant hard disks

6. Give three examples of a Linux server that is considered a dedicated appliance.

Answer: Router, firewall, print server

7. Select all of the following that are a consideration in determining customer resources.

A. Evaluating existing hardware

B. Inexpensive

C. User-friendly

D. End-user support

E. Budgetary concerns

Answers: A, D, E

8. Explain why most servers and other network operating systems are configured to use the TCP/IP protocol.

Answer: The TCP/IP protocol is the standard protocol that the Internet runs on. It is generally universal in that just about any operating system can be configured to use it. Because of the importance of the Internet, the majority of network services and client programs use TCP/IP to exchange data.

9. Whether designed for a standalone desktop computer or a multiuser network server, all operating system software includes which of the following components?

A. Sound card

B. File system

C. Kernel

D. Multimedia support

E. User interface

Answers: B, C, E

10. Fill in the following chart with the appropriate type of file system that can be used on the operating system in the left column.

Answers:

Operating System	Supported File System(s)
DOS	FAT
Windows 3.x	FAT16
Windows 95/98/Me	FAT16, FAT32

Operating System	Supported File System(s)
Windows NT/2000	FAT16, FAT32, NTFS
Windows XP	FAT32, NTFS
IBM OS/2	High Performance File System (HPFS)
Linux	Ext2, Ext3, Journaling File System (JFS)

Chapter 2

1. Match the definitions to the following networking terms.

Answers:

Term	Definition
Star	All computers are connected to a central point
Topology	A network's general shape or layout
WAN	A network separated by a large geographic area
LAN	Many interconnected users and systems in close proximity
Bus	Computers attached to a single long cable

2. Which type of communication lines are used by point-to-point WAN connections? (Select two.)

   A. Serial

   B. Ethernet

   C. Leased

   D. Parallel

   E. Ring

   F. Coaxial

   Answers: A, C

3. Correctly order the layers of the OSI model by name.

Answers:

Layer 7	**Application**
Layer 6	**Presentation**
Layer 5	**Session**
Layer 4	**Transport**
Layer 3	**Network**
Layer 2	**Data Link**
Layer 1	**Physical**

4. Select the five items that are part of the TCP/IP protocol suite.

   A. FTP

   B. SMTP

   C. IPX

   D. SPX

   E. SAP

   F. Telnet

   G. DNS

   H. RIP

   I. UDP

Answers: A, B, F, G, I

5. Fill in the blank with the maximum allowable cable distance between the switches for this type of network.

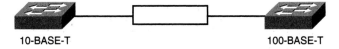

10-BASE-T   100-BASE-T

Options

100 meters
1000 meters
100 feet
1000 feet

Answer: 100 meters

6. Which of the following are not advantages of using FDDI Token Ring over basic Token Ring?

   A. Faster transmission speeds

   B. Fault tolerance

   C. Transmission of synchronous data

   D. Transmission of asynchronous data

   E. Costs

   Answers: D, E

7. Describe the difference between half-duplex and full-duplex transmission modes.

   Answer: Half-duplex mode allows for one-way directional transmission. Full-duplex mode allows for data transmissions in both directions at the same time. This process allows for much faster transmission speeds in full-duplex mode.

8. Which of the following Ethernet standards are used in linear bus topologies?

   A. 100BASE-T

   B. 1000BASE-TX

   C. 10BASE-T

   D. 10BASE2

   E. 1000BASE-T

   F. 10BASE5

   Answers: D, F

9. Fill in the following chart.

Answers:

Network Architecture	Cabling Type(s)	Transfer Speed
Ethernet 10BASE2	Thin coaxial	10 Mbps
Ethernet 10BASE5	Thick coaxial	10 Mbps
Ethernet 10BASE-T	UTP Categories 3 to 5	10 Mbps
Ethernet 100BASE-T	UTP Category 5	100 Mbps
Ethernet 100BASE-FX	Fiber-optic	100 Mbps
Ethernet 1000BASE-T	UTP Category 7	1 Gbps
Token Ring	STP or UTP	4 Mbps or 16 Mbps
FDDI	Fiber-optic	100 Mbps

10. Which of the following are not characteristics of UTP cabling?

   A. Flexible and easy to work with

   B. Not susceptible to EMI

   C. RJ-45 connector

   D. Operates at only 10 Mbps

   E. Maximum cable length without repeaters is 100 meters

   F. Fast Ethernet-compatible

   Answers: B, D

Chapter 3

1. Which three of the following are advantages of a star topology?

   A. It's easy to add more nodes

   B. It requires less cable to connect computers

   C. It has a flexible topology

   D. It's less expensive to build than a bus topology

   E. It's easier to diagnose problems

   Answers: A, C, E

2. Which topology provides connections for each node to every other node?

   Answer: mesh

3. When selecting a NIC, which three of the following features must you consider?

   A. Network type

   B. Serial connection

   C. Medium

   D. Parallel connection

   E. System bus

   F. IRQ

   Answers: A, C, E

4. Which component allows a computer to connect directly with the physical medium to connect to the LAN?

   A. Hub

   B. Active hub

   C. Network Interface Card (NIC)

   D. Modem

   E. Ethernet cable

   Answer: A

5. You must consider three things when selecting an appropriate NIC to install. Which of the following choices do you *not* need to consider?

   A. Type of network

   B. Type of medium

   C. Type of protocol used

   D. Type of system bus

   E. Type of operating system

   Answers: C, E

6. Select the options that are available to assign IP addresses for hosts on a LAN.

   A. Manual

   B. Static

   C. DNS

   D. Automatic

   E. Dynamic

   Answers: B, D, E

7. Explain the difference between physical and logical topology.

   Answer: Physical topology relates to the network's layout, where all nodes and other network hardware can be seen exactly how it is. Logical topology relates to a layout of the nodes and network devices in a manner that shows the path that data travels from one point on the network to the next.

8. The following definition is an example of what type of hub?

   It must be plugged into an electrical outlet, because it needs power to amplify the incoming signal before passing it back out to the other ports. It can manipulate and view the traffic that crosses it.

   A. Passive

   B. Intelligent

   C. Active

   Answer: C

9. All the following choices are advantages of a star topology except which one?

   A. The star topology is flexible. The layout is easy to modify, and new hosts or devices can be added quickly.

   B. It is upgradeable. Adding a new computer is as easy as plugging the cable that is connected to the new workstation into the hub.

   C. It requires additional costly devices, such as hubs and switches, which are needed to run between the central device and each computer.

   D. It makes diagnosing problems relatively easy, because the problem is localized to one computer or device.

   Answer: C

10. Fill in the following chart.

Answers:

UTP Category	Maximum Transmission Speed	Characteristics and Uses
1	Voice only	Used in old telephone installations
2	4 Mbps	Not recommended for data transmission
3	16 Mbps	Lowest recognized data grade; used for most telephone wiring
4	20 Mbps	Suitable for networking 10 Mbps Ethernet networks
5	100 Mbps	Most popular grade for LAN networking; used for Fast Ethernet/100

11. All the following choices are advantages of a cable Internet service over DSL service except which one?

A. Existing cable TV systems offer plenty of available bandwidth for both upstream and downstream traffic.

B. Much faster upstream data rates.

C. Cable TV infrastructure upgrade with HFC has addressed many of the existing service bottlenecks.

D. Backward-compatible with conventional analog phones.

Answer: D

Chapter 4

1. Enter the layers of the OSI reference model and map them to the corresponding layers of the TCP/IP network model. Layer names may be used more than once.

Answers:

OSI Reference Model	TCP/IP Network Model
Application	Application
Presentation	
Session	
Transport	Transport
Network	Internet
Data Link	Network Interface
Physical	

2. Enter the *well-known* port number for each protocol.

Answers:

Protocol	Port Number
DNS	53
FTP	21
RIP	520
SMTP	25
SNMP	161
Telnet	23
TFTP	69

3. Convert the decimal number 206 to binary.

Answer:

1	1	0	0	1	1	1	0

4. ARP is used to find a host's _____ given its _____.

Answers: MAC address, IP address

5. Match the dotted-decimal number with the appropriate term.

   Answers:

Term	Number
Host address	192.168.140.11
Subnet mask	255.255.255.0
Broadcast address	192.168.140.255
Network address	192.168.140.0

6. Which layer of the TCP/IP network model determines protocol and data syntax rules; ensures agreement at both ends on error-recovery procedures, data integrity, and privacy; and maintains session control?

   A. Network interface

   B. Internet

   C. Application

   D. Transport

   Answer: C

7. Which layer of the TCP/IP network model defines addressing and path selection? Routers use the protocols that function at this layer to identify an appropriate path for data packets as they travel from network to network.

   A. Network interface

   B. Internet

   C. Application

   D. Transport

   Answer: B

8. What formula helps you determine the number of available host addresses?

   Answer: 2^N-2 (2 to the Nth power minus 2), where 2 is the number of bits in the host portion of the address.

9. Determine the address class and calculate the subnet of the given network address in the following IP address and subnet mask:

15.5.6.18

255.255.255.240

Answer: It's a Class A address (0 to 126 in the first octet).

The network address is 15.5.6.16.

The Class C subnet mask 255.255.255.240 uses 4 bits of the fourth octet for subnetting, leaving 4 bits available for host addresses. The host IP address 15.5.6.18, therefore, must belong to the 15.5.6.16 network.

15.5.6.18 = 00001111.00000101.00000110.0001 I 0010

255.255.255.240 = 11111111.11111111.11111111.1111 I 0000

15.5.6.16 = 00001111.00000101.00000110.0001 I 0000

10. Determine the address class and calculate the subnet of the given network address in the following IP address and subnet mask:

108.163.211.115

255.255.128.0

Answer: It's a Class A address (0 to 126 in the first octet).

The network address is 108.163.128.0.

The Class B subnet mask 255.255.128.0 uses 1 bit of the third octet for subnetting, leaving 15 bits available for host addresses. The host IP address 108.163.211.115, therefore, must belong to the 108.163.128.0 network.

108.163.211.115 = 01101100.10100011.1 I 1010011.01110011

255.255.128.0 = 11111111.11111111.1 I 0000000.00000000

108.163.128.0 = 01101100.10100011.1 I 0000000.00000000

Chapter 5

1. Match the protocols with the function they represent.

   Answers:

Service	TCP/IP Protocol
World Wide Web server	HTTP
File transfer	FTP
File sharing	NFS
Internet mail	SMTP
Remote administration	Telnet
Automatic network address configuration	DHCP
Network administration	SNMP
Directory services (Internet)	DNS

2. Which two of the following are standard CLI commands to open a Telnet connection to a remote computer?

   telnet candy.company.com

   connect candy.company.com

   telnet 204.45.55.90

   connect 204.45.55.90

   Answers: telnet candy.company.com, telnet 204.45.55.90

3. Many companies, both large and small, have deployed private networks called intranets. Select the five best reasons for a company to create an intranet.

   Internal information, memoranda, and reports

   Staff and employee directories

   Store backup files

   Calendars and appointment schedules

   Purchase items securely

   Application and software deployment

   Conduct research on competitors

   Employee services

Answers:

Internal information, memoranda, and reports

Staff and employee directories

Calendars and appointment schedules

Application and software deployment

Employee services

4. DNS translates _____ into _____, and DHCP assigns _____ to computers.

Options are as follows (they may be used more than once):

Internet names

NetBIOS names

IP addresses

MAC addresses

Answers:

DNS translates Internet names into IP addresses, and DHCP assigns IP addresses to computers.

Chapter 6

1. Of the following, which three are the main functions that the operating system performs?

A. Store security information

B. Control the computer hardware

C. Make changes to the database

D. Program the execution environment

E. Provide a user interface

F. Establish network control

Answers: B, D, E

2. There are a number of differences between a standalone client operating system and a network operating system. Decide whether each of the following statements refers to a standalone client, a NOS client, or both.

   Answers:
   Access resources that are local to the PC: both
   Access devices that are directly attached: standalone client
   Access nonlocal or remote resources: NOS client
   A single account is active on the system: standalone client
   Multiple user accounts at the same time: NOS client
   Concurrent access to shared resources: NOS client
   Specialized software and additional hardware: NOS client

3. Provide an example of a multiuser system, and state why it is a multiuser system.

   Answer: Examples of multiuser systems include UNIX, Linux, and Windows NT/2000/XP. They are considered multiuser systems because they can support multiple users concurrently. The user account on the server lets the server authenticate that user and allocate the resources that the user is allowed to access.

4. There are many different areas of concern when choosing a specific NOS to install. Which of the following are points to consider?

   A. Management and monitoring

   B. E-mail settings

   C. Security

   D. Robustness/fault tolerance

   E. Bandwidth

   F. Scalability

   Answers: A, C, D, F

5. Windows server-based networks that run Windows NT Server or Windows 2000 Server are based on the concept of a group of computers and users that serves as a boundary of administrative authority called _____.

   A. NDS

   B. Workgroups

   C. Domains

   D. NIS

   Answer: C

6. Microsoft's Windows 2000 is an upgrade from the previous Windows NT operating system. It includes many new features and advantages. Which of the following are advantages of using Windows 2000 as opposed to Windows NT?

   A. Support for mobile users through APM and ACPI

   B. Secure virtual private networking with L2TP and IPSec

   C. Directory replication using PDCs and BDCs

   D. IPP lets users print to a URL and manage printers through a web browser interface.

   Answers: A, B, D

7. Several different distributions of Linux are available. Of the following, which are key elements that are included in these distributions to make them different?

   A. Startup scripts

   B. Kernel

   C. Configuration files

   D. NIS structure

   E. Support software

   Answers: A, B, C, E

8. Which client systems can connect to a Linux file server running Samba?

   A. Windows

   B. Novell

   C. UNIX

   D. Macintosh

   E. OS/2

   F. All of the above

   Answer: F

Chapter 7

1. When formatting a partition on a Windows NOS, which three file systems can you select?

   A. NTFS

   B. UFS

   C. FAT32

   D. EXT3

   E. FAT

   F. HFS

   Answers: A, C, E

2. List the steps in the Windows 2000 boot process.

   Answers:

Step 1	**Preboot sequence**
Step 2	**Boot sequence**
Step 3	**Kernel load**
Step 4	**Kernel initialization**
Step 5	**Logon process**

3. Match each file with its default location on a Windows 2000 client.

   Answers:

File	Default Location
NTLDR	**Root of the active partition (C:\)**
Ntoskrnl.exe	**C:\Winnt\System32**
SYSTEM Registry key	**C:\Winnt\System32\Config**
Device drivers	**C:\Winnt\System32\Drivers**

4. Which two of the following are types of physical partitions?

   A. Secondary

   B. Primary

   C. Logical

   D. Extended

   E. Volume

   Answers: B, D

5. It is recommended that you perform some verification activities before installing any hardware in a server. Which of the following would you *not* do?

   A. Verify that the power outlet for the network server is available and active. (Test with a volt/ohm meter.)

   B. Verify that the network connection is available and active.

   C. Verify the release version of the operating system that the hardware will be installed in.

   D. Verify that the location where the server is to be installed is ready for the installation.

   E. Verify that all the hardware for the network server has arrived and that the hardware is as specified in the installation plan.

   Answer: C

6. What approximate server room temperature tells you that you need to install a secondary cooling device for the room?

   A. 65 degrees

   B. 68 degrees

   C. 70 degrees

   D. 72 degrees

   E. 75 degrees

   Answer: D

7. Complete the following table by filling in the minimum system requirements for installing Linux.

Answers:

Component	Description
Computer/processor	**x86 processor or higher CPU. Recommended minimum is a Pentium-class or better CPU.**
Memory	**32 MB of RAM recommended minimum**
Hard disk	**300 MB minimum free hard disk space; 1.2 GB disk space for a full workstation**
Drive	**CD-ROM drive or 3 1/2-inch floppy drive**
Display	**VGA or higher-resolution monitor**
Peripheral	**Keyboard and mouse or a compatible pointing device (optional)**

8. Fill in the blanks in the following sentences.

To view or change the network configuration for a Windows system, use the _____ command.

To view or change the network configuration for a Linux system, use the _____ command.

Answers: ipconfig, ifconfig

9. Which of the following are advantages of partitioning a disk before installing an operating system?

A. You can create a swap partition to supplement the system RAM and enhance performance.

B. You can install multiple operating systems on the same disk.

C. You can physically separate data from the system files to provide security, file management, and fault tolerance.

D. You can exchange files between operating systems that are installed on the separate partitions.

Answers: A, B, C

10. When you partition a hard drive that has Linux installed on it, numbers are assigned to each partition. The partition numbers 1, 2, and 3 are reserved for what kind of partition?

    A. Extended

    B. Logical

    C. Primary

    D. DOS

    Answer: C

Chapter 8

1. Order the four main steps in the Windows 2000 installation process, starting with the first step.

   Answers:

   The Setup program

   The Setup wizard

   Installing Windows networking

   Completing the Setup program

2. Complete this table using the following options. Choose whether each password is good or bad, and indicate two reasons that support your choice. You may use some of the options more than once.

   Answers:

Password	Good or Bad?	Reason 1	Reason 2
Sco	Bad	Too short	Contains no numbers or special characters
cisco	Bad	Uses a complete English word	Contains no numbers or special characters
C!isco98	Good	Not an English word	Contains a number or a special character

3. In the following table, match the permission level to the correct description.

Answers:

Permission	Description
Write	Allows the user to edit and save changes to a file and add files to and delete files from a directory
Execute	Allows the user to run a file or enter a directory
Read	Allows the user to read the contents of a file or directory

4. The administrator wants to allow a user to only look at and run a program in Windows 2000. Which of the following permissions should be set? (Select two.)

   A. Write

   B. Read

   C. Execute

   D. Full control

   E. Modify

   Answers: B, C

5. What command is used to redirect print jobs from the local port to the network printer?

   A. net send

   B. net use

   C. redirect

   D. port print

   Answer: B

6. What protocol is used to transfer files to other network devices?

   A. Telnet

   B. HTTP

   C. HTML

   D. FTP

   Answer: D

7. What tool allows the system administrator to manage all areas of a computer?

    A. IIS

    B. Taskbar

    C. Computer Management

    D. Windows Explorer

    Answer: C

8. Which of the following is not a type of group in Windows 2000?

    A. Global

    B. Local

    C. Universal

    D. Remote

    Answer: D

9. In Windows, what is the name of a graphical pane that displays system or program information?

    A. Window

    B. Button

    C. Icon

    D. Menu

    Answer: A

10. What tool is used to verify hardware compatibility with Windows?

    A. Device Manager

    B. HCL

    C. Computer Management

    D. Hardware Profiler

    Answer: B

Chapter 9

1. A variety of installation media can be used to install Linux. List all of them.

    Answers: CD, network server, floppy disks, a hard disk that has the CD files copied to it

2. Three main types of file systems that a disk can be formatted with are supported by Linux. What are they?

    A. ext2

    B. Reiser

    C. NTFS

    D. ext3

    E. FAT

    Answers: **A, B, D**

3. Two types of formatting can be performed. What are they, and in which situations do you perform them?

    Answers:

    High-level formatting is used when the entire file system needs to be re-created.

    Low-level formatting is used when only the physical sectors on the disk need to be rewritten.

4. During the installation process, three main security configurations are made. What are they?

    A. Root account options

    B. Hardware access control

    C. Defining user accounts

    D. Password options

    Answers: **A, B, D**

5. Although both LILO and GRUB can be used as the Linux boot loader, there is a specific instance in which LILO must be used instead of GRUB. What is this instance?

    Answer: LILO must be used if you're dual-booting a Linux system with a Windows system.

6. What are the three main configuration tools used to configure XFree86 3.3.X?

    A. XFree65cfg

    B. Xconfigurator

C. Xf86config

D. XF86Setup

Answers: B, C, D

7. What are the four main types of window managers used with Linux?

Answers: **KWM, Sawfish, Enlightenment, IceWM**

8. What are the four main types of desktop environments used with Linux?

Answers: **KDE, GNOME, CDE, Xfce**

9. What are the three main types of package managers that Linux systems use?

Answers: **Red Hat Package Manager (RPM), Debian packages, tarballs**

10. RPM uses a database to store information about the packages that are installed. What four types of information are stored in the database?

Answers: **package information, file information, dependencies, provision information**

Chapter 10

1. What Linux xterm CLI command would display a calendar for March 2015?

Answer:

cal -y 3 2015

2. Match each task with the Linux command used to perform it.

Answers:

Task	Command
Add a user	**useradd**
Change a username	**usermod**
Change a password	**passwd**
Delete an account	**userdel**

3. Which two tasks can be accomplished using the **cp** command?

A. Change the working directory

B. Copy a directory

C. Capture a file

D. Copy a user account

E. Copy a file

Answers: B, E

4. The following two commands have just been executed at the Linux command prompt:

```
chown jose.executives script2
chmod 770 script2
```

Which two of the following have permission to execute script2?

A. User jose

B. User executives

C. User 770

D. All users in the group executives

E. All users in the group jose

F. All users in the group 770

Answers: A, D

5. What is the web-hosting program used with Linux?

Answer: Apache

6. What command can you use to start a second X Window System session in a virtual terminal?

A. **startx** and press Ctrl-Alt-*F1 through F6*

B. **startx --:1 vt8**

C. **startx --:F1**

D. **startx :2 vt8**

Answer: B

7. What command can you issue on a Linux system to view all the files that are in the current directory, including hidden user files and system configuration files?

A. dir

B. ls -l

C. ls -a

D. dir -a

Answer: C

8. Fill in the following chart.

Answers:

vi Editor Command Mode	Functions/Characteristics
Command	The initial default mode for creating and editing files, positioning the cursor, and modifying existing text. All commands are initiated from this mode. Pressing Esc in either of the other modes returns you to command mode.
Entry	Used for the entry of new text. Entering an insert command such as I (insert), a (append), or o (open new line) takes you from command mode to entry mode. Pressing Esc returns you to command mode. You enter entry mode commands without pressing the Enter key.
Last-line	Used for saving your work and quitting vi. Type a colon (:) to get to this mode. Pressing the Enter key returns you to command mode.

9. Which two Linux commands control file and directory permissions?

Answers: chown, chmod

10. If you want to change to a different runlevel, what two commands do you enter at the shell prompt?

Answers: telinit, init

Chapter 11

1. Backup storage devices do not need to be extremely fast or easily accessible. Instead, there are more relevant considerations when you're implementing a backup scenario. What are these four concerns?

   Answers: Cost, size, manageability, reliability

2. Only the files that have changed since the last backup are selected to be backed up. These files are selected based on whether they have changed recently, instead of an arbitrary selection based on directory names or filenames. This describes what kind of backup?

   A. Partial

   B. Differential

   C. Incremental

   D. Full

   Answer: C

3. Backup files have been created or have changed since the last normal backup. Files are not marked as having been backed up, and the markers are not cleared. All files, even those that have not changed since the last backup, are backed up. This describes what kind of backup?

   A. Partial

   B. Differential

   C. Incremental

   D. Full

   Answer: B

4. What two main tools are used in Linux to perform backups?

   Answers: tar, cpio

5. When mapping a drive in a Linux system, you can use two methods. Which method do you use when mapping a network drive to a Linux server from a Windows workstation, and how do you go about doing this?

   Answer: You first properly configure the Linux server to run Samba, and then you connect to the network share by mapping a drive from the Windows OS.

6. What is the correct command syntax to use when mapping a drive from a Linux workstation to a Linux server?

Answer:

mount *servername:/directory/ subdirectory/ localdirectory*

7. What are the three main tools in a Linux system that are used to manage disk partitions?

A. fdisk

B. mkdir

C. mkfs

D. fsck

Answers: A, C, D

8. What program do you use to schedule tasks to run at regular intervals on a Linux system?

A. Core dump

B. Log rotation

C. cron

D. Find

Answer: C

9. The **top** command is one of the most useful commands you can use on a Linux system. You can find much useful information by studying this command's output. Which of the following are facts you can obtain with this command?

A. The number of users currently logged on to the system

B. The amount of available memory

C. The percentage of the CPU being used for various tasks

D. The amount of available virtual memory the system has left

Answers: A, B, C

10. Approximately 63 different parameters can be entered for a signal that is sent to a process. Each of these terminates the process differently. What command can you use to display this entire list of parameter options at the Linux command prompt?

    A. kill -i

    B. ps -i

    C. kill -l

    D. ps -l

    Answer: C

Chapter 12

1. In Linux, what program is used to remove drivers or modules?

    A. lsmod

    B. rmmod

    C. modprobe

    D. insmod

    Answer: B

2. What Linux program is used to list all modules that are currently loaded on the system?

    A. rmmod

    B. insmod

    C. modprobe

    D. lsmod

    Answer: D

3. What type of PCMCIA card is the smallest and thinnest?

    A. Type I

    B. Type II

    C. Type III

    D. Type IV

    Answer: A

4. What IEEE standard is supported by firewire?

   A. 1918

   B. 1386

   C. 1394

   D. 1905

   Answer: C

5. As the system loads, what operation produces a series of beeps?

   A. BIOS loading

   B. CMOS loading

   C. POST

   D. OS loading

   Answer: C

6. What value is used to compare processors from different manufacturers?

   A. MIPS

   B. Clock rate

   C. Clock speed

   D. TDR

   Answer: A

7. What tool displays the output of voltage readings to a monitor as a waveform?

   A. Multimeter

   B. Oscilloscope

   C. Cable tester

   D. LAN meter

   Answer: B

8. What component enables a device to send data directly to motherboard memory without the intervention of the processor?

   A. IRQ

   B. I/O

   C. CMOS

D. DMA

Answer: D

9. What type of port is commonly used with a printer?

A. Parallel

B. Serial

C. RS-232

D. USB

Answer: A

10. In Linux, what file would you edit to change the assigned IRQ and I/O settings?

A. /etc/rc.d/rc.local

B. /etc/lilo.conf

C. /etc/pcmcia

D. /etc/fstab

Answer: B

Chapter 13

1. Many things can cause errors in a computer system. What are the five main areas of concern in which most computer problems occur?

Answers: Hardware, kernel, application software, configuration errors, user errors

2. If you experience an issue related to a hardware failure, it is a good idea to check some of the log files to find out what piece of hardware is causing the problem. What specific log file do you check, and what specifically are you looking for?

Answer: The log file to check is /var/log/messages. You look for any message that begins with oops. This indicates that the hardware is malfunctioning.

3. There are four specific instances in which common signs of application bugs are apparent. Which of the following is *not* one of them?

A. Resource exhaustion

B. Program crash

C. Failure to execute

D. Incompatible driver

E. Program-specific misbehavior

Answer: D

4. Log files are a very important and useful component of Linux servers. Which of the following are activities on a server that are recorded in log files?

A. Monitoring system loads

B. Intrusion attempts and detection

C. Normal system functioning

D. Server bandwidth

E. Missing entries

Answers: A, B, C, E

5. What three methods can you use to boot a Linux system without using LILO?

Answers: LOADLIN, raw kernel on a floppy, LILO on a floppy

6. What are the three key issues to keep in mind when installing a package in a Linux system to avoid package dependency issues?

Answers: Missing libraries or support programs, incompatible libraries or support programs, duplicate files or features

7. List some of the solutions to package dependency problems.

Answers: Find a different version, rebuild the problem package from source code, modify the system, force the installation

8. One of the most important tasks for any system administrator is ensuring that employees have network and Internet access at all times. Any network downtime can lead to serious monetary losses for the company. List the steps you follow when testing for TCP/IP errors.

Answers: Ping the host name, enter the ipconfig command, ping 127.0.0.1, ping your own IP address, ping the default gateway, ping the remote host, ping your own IP name, ping the remote host's IP name

9. Fill in the descriptions for the Windows 2000 Server **netdiag** command flags.

Answers:

Command Flag	Description
/q	Quiet output (errors only).
/v	Provides verbose output. More-detailed information is provided.
/l	Logs output to Netdiag.log.
/debug	Provides even more verbose output.
/d:*DomainName*	Finds a DC in the specified domain.
/fix	Fixes trivial problems.
/DcAccountEnum	Enumerates DC machine accounts.
/test:*test name*	Tests only this test. Nonskippable tests are still run.

10. Fill in the descriptions for the Windows 2000 Server **pathping** command flags.

Answers:

Command Flag	Description
-n	Specifies to not resolve addresses to host names.
-h *maximum-hops*	Specifies the maximum number of hops to search for.
-g *host-list*	Specifies the loose source route along *host-list*.
-p *period*	Specifies the wait period in milliseconds between pings.
-q *num-queries*	Specifies the number of queries per hop.
-w *timeout*	Specifies the wait timeout in milliseconds for each reply.
-T	Tests connectivity to each hop with Layer 2 priority tags.
-R	Tests whether each hop is RSVP-aware.

Chapter 14

1. Match the types of DoS attacks with their descriptions.

   Answers:

Type of Attack	Description
Buffer overflow	Sends more data than the target system can hold
Smurf	Spoofs the IP headers of multiple ping requests so that replies are all sent to the target
Teardrop	Sends packet fragments with overlapping reassembly information
TCP SYN	Leaves a large number of half-open connections

2. Which software option included in Windows 2000 and XP periodically checks for software patches and upgrades by contacting Microsoft via the Internet?

   Answer: Windows Update

3. Based on the following choices, at which layer can the following protocols be filtered? (Choices may be used more than once.)

   Layer 3

   Layer 4

   Layer 7

   Answers:

Protocol	Filtering Layer
HTTP	Layer 7
TCP	Layer 4
FTP	Layer 7
IP	Layer 3
UDP	Layer 4

4. Using the following options, label the components in the network shown in Figure 14-16.

Internet

Intranet

Boundary router

Firewall

DMZ

Figure 14-16 Network Components

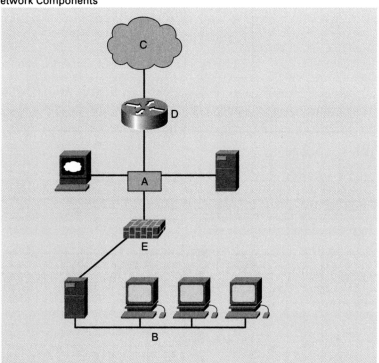

Answers:

A. DMZ

B. Intranet

C. Internet

D. Boundary router

E. Firewall

5. The first step in developing a viable plan for protecting network data is to assess its security needs. Which of the following are factors to consider?

   A. The type of data stored on the network

   B. Geographic location

   C. The type of business in which the company engages

   D. The organization's management philosophy

   E. Supply and demand analysis

   Answers: A, C, D

6. Developing secure password standards is usually a system administrator's first line of defense against an intruder. What are some of the best practices to implement to keep passwords secure?

   A. Passwords should expire after a specific period of time.

   B. Password standards should prevent users from writing down passwords and leaving them unprotected from public view.

   C. Passwords should be easy to remember.

   D. Rules about password expiration and lockout should be defined.

   E. Users should be able to change their passwords whenever they want.

   Answers: A, B, D

7. Many methods can be used to implement security measures. What form of encryption is a way of encrypting data stored on a computer disk so that it is unreadable to anyone but the data's creator?

   A. Secure Sockets Layer (SSL)

   B. Public/private key encryption

   C. File encryption

   D. IPSec

   Answer: C

8. Many methods can be used to implement security measures. What form of encryption is another way of securing communications on the network by providing encryption within the user's application layer?

   A. Secure Sockets Layer (SSL)

   B. Public/private key encryption

   C. File encryption

   D. IPSec

   Answer: A

Glossary of Key Terms

acceptable-use policy A statement that informs the users what is acceptable and allowed on the company network.

Active Directory Microsoft's distributed directory implementation that is used to manage all objects, computers, and user accounts.

active hub A hub that must be plugged into an electrical outlet because it needs power to amplify the incoming signal before passing it back out to the other ports.

Address Resolution Protocol (ARP) A discovery protocol that helps a server or other network device, such as a router, locate where other systems are on the network.

advanced intelligent tape (AIT) Uses 8mm tapes that use helical scan recording hardware (much like a VCR). AIT tapes have memory in the tape cartridge, known as Memory-In-Cassette (MIC), which stores the tape log to facilitate locating a file during a restoration.

agent station The piece of equipment from which you are trying to extract data.

AppleTalk Data Stream Protocol (ADSP) Supports the flow of unstructured data between Macintosh systems.

AppleTalk Filing Protocol (AFP) Allows Macintosh desktop workstations to share files.

AppleTalk Session Protocol (ASP) Establishes connections between clients and the server so that sequences of messages can be associated with each other in Macintosh systems.

AppleTalk Transaction Protocol (ATP) Provides reliable, connection-oriented transport in Macintosh systems.

application layer   Specifies the details of how an application makes requests and how the application on another machine responds.

assigned permission   A permission explicitly granted by an authorized user.

Asymmetric DSL (ADSL)   The most common DSL implementation. It has speeds that vary from 384 kbps to more than 6 Mbps downstream.

asynchronous serial transmission   Data bits are sent without a synchronizing clock pulse. This transmission method uses a start bit at the beginning of each message.

autorepeat value   A line in the configuration file whose value determines the rate at which keys repeat when they are pressed on the keyboard.

backup   The process of copying data from one computer to some other reliable storage medium for safekeeping.

baseline   The level of performance that is acceptable when the system is handling a typical workload. This involves comparing various measurements to the same measurements taken earlier.

Basic Input/Output System (BIOS)   A software program running at the computer's lowest level. As the computer boots up, the BIOS is loaded to configure basic aspects of the computer before the operating system loads.

bottleneck   The point in the system that limits data throughput, which is the amount of data that can flow through the network.

Bourne Again shell   This shell was created as an enhanced extension of the Bourne shell. It is also called the bash shell and is used for many "UNIX-like" systems, such as Linux.

Bourne shell   Known as the original UNIX shell. Provides all the (sh) functions as well as shell programming using shell script files.

bridge   Makes intelligent decisions about whether to pass signals on to the next segment of a network.

broadband remote access   The name that is given to high-speed DSL and cable Internet connections.

broadcast domain   A logical area in a computer network where any computer connected to the computer network can directly transmit to any other computer in the domain without having to go through a routing device.

buffer overflow   A kind of attack that is designed to overwhelm the software running on the target system.

cracker   A person who breaks into computer systems to tamper with, steal, or destroy data.

cron program   The way to schedule tasks to run at regular intervals on a Linux system.

crond   This daemon runs scripts at a specified time.

crossover cable   A cable that has reverse pin settings on each end. Used to connect like devices in a network environment.

CSMA/CA   Reduces network collisions by listening to the network before broadcasting.

Custom installation   Chosen if customized selections for the device configurations are needed.

daemon   Allows the operating system to provide functions such as the Internet, file sharing, mail exchange, directory services, remote management, and print services.

daemon list   Specifies the names of servers that appear in /etc/services. These are the servers to which access is either granted or denied.

daily backup   A useful partial backup method that an administrator can perform to select all the files and folders that have changed during the day.

data cable   A cable that lets devices transmit data.

data link layer   Specifies how packets of data are organized into frames on a particular type of network and the rules for inserting frames onto the network media.

datagram   Another name for a packet of data.

de facto   Something has become the industry standard just because the majority has chosen to implement it.

Debian package   A package system that is similar to RPM packages. One main difference between Debian packages and RPM packages is that they are not interchangeable. Another main difference is that certain distributions use RPMs and others use Debian packages. A Debian package looks similar to an RPM package and is installed in much the same way.

dedicated appliance   A Linux system running as a router, print server, or firewall, for example.

default gateway   The router's near-side interface. It is the interface on the router to which the local computer network segment or wire is attached.

default shell   The shell presented to the user when he or she logs in.

delay value   The time (in milliseconds) that the system waits until the key that was pressed is repeated.

denial of service (DoS)   A type of attack in which the targeted system cannot service legitimate network requests effectively because it is overloaded with illegitimate messages.

dependency   A package that requires other packages to be installed for them to function.

differential backup   Backs up files created or changed since the last normal or incremental backup. It does not mark files as having been backed up. All files, even those that have not changed since the last backup, are backed up.

Digital Audio Tape (DAT)   Uses 4mm digital audiotapes to store data in the Digital Data Storage (DSS) format.

Digital Linear Tape (DLT)   Offers high-capacity and relatively high-speed tape backup capabilities. DLT tapes record information in a linear format, unlike 8mm tape technologies, which use helical scan recording techniques.

Digital Subscriber Line (DSL)   An always-on technology that provides Internet access over regular telephone lines.

digital volt-ohm meter   Also called a voltmeter. Used to measure electronic pulses through cable and determine if the cable has any shorts or breaks.

direct memory access (DMA) channel   Allows attached devices to send data directly to the motherboard's memory.

Directory Access Protocol (DAP)   Lets the Directory User Agent (DUA) communicate with the Directory System Agent (DSA). DAP defines the means by which the user can search the directory to read, add, delete, and modify directory entries.

Directory Information Base   Acts as the central data store, or database, in which directory information is kept.

directory service   Provides system administrators with centralized control of all users and resources across the entire network to simplify network management by providing a standard interface for common system administration tasks.

Directory System Agent   An X.500 Electronic Directory Service (EDS) standard that manages directory data.

Directory User Agent   An X.500 Electronic Directory Service (EDS) standard that gives users access to directory services.

disk cluster   The basic unit of logical storage on a disk.

distributed denial of service (DDoS)   A type of attack that originates from hundreds or even thousands of coordinated hosts. The classic DDoS attack begins with weeks or even months of hacking. Before the hacker can attack the ultimate target, a fleet of systems must be coordinated for the attack.

distributed lock manager (DLM)   Handles the arbitration of resources in the event of a conflict. The coordination of the access adds significant overhead to the cluster and makes it much more complex to design, configure, and maintain.

Domain Name System (DNS)   Provides access to name servers where network names are translated to the addresses used by Layer 3 network protocols.

Domain Name System (DNS)   The process of assigning and associating a name with an IP address to help identify and locate other client and server systems throughout the network.

drive mapping   A useful tool that allows an administrator to share resources that are stored on a server. The client computers that are connected to the network assign a drive letter that acts as a direct path to access over the network those resources stored on a server.

dual ring   Two rings allow data to be sent in both directions, which creates redundancy.

Dynamic Host Configuration Protocol (DHCP)   A protocol that allows individual computers on an IP network to extract their IP address configurations from a DHCP server automatically when they start up without having to manually configure them.

EIDE device   Enhanced Integrated Drive Electronics device. Usually hard drives, floppy drives, CD-ROMs, and other types of disk and tape drives. EIDE technologies enable mass-storage devices to address drive space above 528 MB.

emergency boot disk   A disk that enables you to boot the system without using any part of the main partition. This is useful when there are errors on the boot partition.

emergency boot system   Linux provides an emergency system copy of LILO that you can use to boot Linux if the original LILO boot loader has errors or is not working.

encapsulation   Data is passed down the OSI reference model layers, and these layers prepare the data for transmission.

environment variable   Contains information about the computer system that programs use to get a status report on the computer's current state. These variables contain information such as the location of a user's home directory, how much disk space is on the system, the system's Internet host name, the name of the shell that is currently being used, and what resources are available on the system.

Ethernet cable   The unshielded twisted-pair (UTP) cabling generally used in the 10BASE-X architecture.

execute permission   A permission that allows a user to run a file or enter a directory.

extended partition   A variation of a primary partition that acts as a placeholder for a logical partition.

extended star topology   A topology in which a star network is expanded to include an additional networking device, such as a hub or switch, connected to the main networking device.

extranet   A technology that allows employees and customers to access the private network or intranet via the Internet.

FDISK   A program that manipulates a hard disk's partition table by creating partitions, deleting partitions, and setting partitions as active.

Fiber Distributed Data Interface (FDDI)   A network that runs on fiber-optic cable and combines high-speed performance with the advantages of the token-passing ring topology.

fiber-optic cable   A networking medium that can conduct modulated light transmissions. Fiber-optic cable is cabling that has a core made of strands of glass or plastic (instead of copper), through which light pulses carry signals.

Fibre Channel-Arbitrated Loop (FC-AL)   Fibre Channel can use either fiber-optic cable or copper wire as the connection medium.

File Allocation Table (FAT)   The type of file system that is used on Windows operating systems.

file encryption   A way to convert data stored on a computer disk so that it is unreadable to anyone but the data's creator.

file information   Information on all the files that are installed on the system using RPM.

File Transfer Protocol (FTP)   A general-purpose protocol that can be used to copy all types of files from one computer to another.

firewall   A barrier between one network, such as the Internet, and another network. It controls security and traffic that is allowed into and out of the network.

FireWire   A faster successor to USB. FireWire devices support IEEE-1394 and speeds up to 400 Mbps.

forest   A Microsoft term for the collection of all the different domain trees in the Active Directory hierarchical structure.

formatting   The process that defines the partition's file system.

frame   A packet is passed to the data link layer, where it gets packaged into a Layer 2 header and trailer.

frequency-division multiplexing (FDM)   The process of splitting bandwidth to create multiple channels. This ability is why a user with DSL can surf the Internet while using the telephone to call a friend.

full backup   Also called a normal backup. Backs up everything on the hard drive at the scheduled point in the day, every day.

full duplex   Allows for two simultaneous directions of data flow.

Get Nearest Server (GNS)   Makes services known to NetWare clients and lets clients locate the services they require, such as print or file services.

Ghostscript   Part of the Linux print queue. Acts as a translator that allows Linux and UNIX systems, which use the PostScript printing language, to print to non-PostScript printers.

Grand Unified Boot loader (GRUB)   One of the boot loaders that a Linux system uses to boot the operating system. This boot loader can be used on systems that only have Linux installed.

graphical user interface (GUI)   Allows the user to manipulate software using visual objects such as windows, pull-down menus, pointers, and icons.

hacker   Someone who dissects systems and programs to see how they work.

half duplex   Allows for only one direction that can be used at a time when data is transmitted over the lines.

hardware compatibility list   A support page that you can view or download from an operating system vendor's website. You use it to find compatibility information on specific third-party hardware that you will install.

Hardware Compatibility List (HCL)   A tool that can be used to verify that the hardware will actually work with Windows 2000.

hardware loopback   A device that is connected to the serial port to send data, which is then looped back to be received by the same computer.

hierarchal file system   A system of arranging the directory and file structure so that they are placed in logical containers that are arranged in a tree structure. The file system starts at the tree's root.

hierarchical address   A naming system in which the name consists of multiple parts, with each part of the address being an identifier.

High Data Rate DSL (HDSL)   Provides bandwidth of 768 kbps in both directions.

high-level formatting   Creates or recreates the entire file system, including redefining the physical sectors on the hard drive.

home directory   The directory that the user has complete access to. The user can add files to and delete files from this directory or just use it to store files.

host table   A list that can be configured in each computer, associating the names of the computers in the network with the IP address host table.

hot site   A commercial facility available for system backup. For a fee, a vendor provides a facility with server hardware, telecommunications hardware, and personnel to help your company restore critical business applications and services in the event of an interruption in normal operations.

HTTPD   This daemon is responsible for web browser requests.

Hub   A multiport repeater. In many cases, the difference between hubs and repeaters is the number of ports that each provides.

hybrid topology   Combines more than one type of topology. When a bus joins two hubs of different topologies, the configuration is called a star bus.

Hypertext Transport Protocol (HTTP)   The protocol that is used to transfer World Wide Web pages between web browser client programs, such as Netscape Communicator and Internet Explorer, and web servers, where web pages are stored.

icon   A small image used to represent a program, service, file, or application.

ifconfig   This command can be entered at the shell to return the system's current network interface configuration.

inconsistent error   A problem that occurs only sporadically or under indeterminate conditions.

incremental backup   Only the files that have changed since the last backup are backed up.

inetd   This daemon waits for an incoming request to be made and then forwards that request to the appropriate daemon.

inherited permission   A permission that applies to child objects because they were inherited from a parent object.

init program   The main program that is used to run the startup configuration files.

input/output (I/O) port   A port that allows a device to be connected that transfers data to or from a computer.

insmod   A Linux program that inserts a single module into the kernel.

Institute of Electrical and Electronic Engineers (IEEE)   The group that has been the most active in defining LAN standards. Through its "802" working groups, which began meeting in February 1980, the IEEE has published standards for the most widely implemented LANs.

intelligent hub   Basically functions as an active hub but also includes a microprocessor chip and diagnostic capabilities.

Internet   A worldwide public network, interconnecting thousands of other networks to form one large "web" for communication.

Internet Control Message Protocol (ICMP)   An error correction and control protocol that provides a set of error and control messages to help track and resolve network problems. The ping application uses ICMP echo messages to test remote devices.

Internet firewall   Specialized software, hardware, or a combination of the two that prevents unwanted or malicious IP packets from reaching a secure network.

Internet Information Services (IIS)   Services that can be activated when using FTP or Web Server services.

Internet Message Access Protocol (IMAP)   A newer e-mail protocol that is more robust than POP3. IMAP is a method of accessing e-mail or bulletin board messages that are kept on a mail server.

Internet name   A naming system that uses additional strings of letters, or suffixes, after the names to guarantee that the full names of any two computers will be different.

Internet Package Exchange (IPX)   Controls network addressing and forwards packets from one network to another toward a destination in Novell networks.

Internet Printing Protocol (IPP)   Allows users to print to a URL and manage printers through a web browser interface.

Internet Protocol (IP)   Provides source and destination addressing and, in conjunction with routing protocols, packet forwarding from one network to another toward a destination.

Internet service provider (ISP)   A company that provides Internet access to homes and businesses.

interrupt request (IRQ)   A value of allocated space that signals or interrupts the CPU with a specific operation from a particular device.

intranet   Organizations build web servers to create a private network to prevent information and services from being made public on the Internet.

IP address   A 32-bit binary number that is divided into four groups of 8 bits known as octets, each of which is represented by a decimal number in the range of 0 to 255. These addresses give computers that are attached to the network the ability to locate each other.

ipchains and iptables   Tools you use when configuring a Linux system as a firewall. These tools are security tools that can block access to the server based on IP addresses or port numbers.

IPSec   A set of protocols developed to support secure exchange of packets at the IP layer.

IR (infrared) technology   A common wireless technology in which workstations and digital devices must be in the transmitter's line of sight to operate.

ISDN DSL (IDSL)   Has a top speed of 144 kbps but is available in areas that do not qualify for other DSL implementations.

JavaScript   A popular scripting language that is based on the Java programming language most often used in web pages.

K Desktop Environment (KDE)   One of the most popular desktop environments used in Linux today. KDE is built on its own window manager, KWM.

kernel   The core of the operating system. This is a small piece of code that is loaded into memory when the computer boots. It contains instructions that allow it to manage hardware devices such as disk drives, memory allocation, system processes, and other programs.

kernel   The engine that runs the operating system.

kernel ring buffer   The process of using the **dmesg** command to display recent kernel messages.

kernel startup message   Contains important information about the drivers and the hardware installed in the system. The information relates to whether the drivers are being loaded successfully and what devices they control, such as EIDE or SCSI controllers.

Korn shell   Combines the interactive features that make the C shell popular with the easier-to-use shell programming syntax of the Bourne shell.

LAN meter   Used to test broadcasts, collisions, usage levels, and errors on Ethernet and Token Ring LANs. Can measure throughput across WANs and can identify devices connected to the network.

Layer 2 Tunneling Protocol (L2TP)   An extension to the PPP protocol that lets ISPs operate virtual private networks (VPNs).

library   A set of routines that are used by software. Every Linux system relies on a library called the C library (libc). Linux systems rely on the C library for the routines that are necessary for C programs to run in Linux.

Lightweight Directory Access Protocol (LDAP)   Developed as a subset of DAP to simplify access to X.500-type directories. LDAP is designed to use fewer system resources than DAP, and it is easier to implement.

line printer daemon (lpd)   A program that manages print queues on a Linux print server. The lpd program accepts the print job and directs it to the correct printer. It also monitors print queues and directs print jobs from print queues to multiple printers.

Linear Tape-Open (LTO)   Comes in two distinct forms: one designed for high storage capacity (Ultrium), and one designed for fast access (Accelis).

Linux   An open-source operating system that looks and feels like UNIX. By the late 1990s, Linux had become a viable alternative to UNIX on servers and Windows on the desktop.

Linux Loader (LILO)   One of the boot loaders that a Linux system uses to boot the operating system. This boot loader can be used on systems that only have Linux, or it can be used to dual-boot Linux with another OS, such as Windows.

Linux shell   Operates as a command interpreter and takes the input that the administrator enters and uses it to launch commands and control the operating system.

Linux shell scripting   Specific to the Linux NOS, these shell scripts consist of many Linux commands and programming logic to perform a series of commands at once.

local group   A group comprised of various users on a single computer.

local-area network (LAN)   Connects many computers in a relatively small geographic area, such as a home, an office, a building, or a campus.

Logical Link Control (LLC)   An IEEE-defined standard for providing error and flow control over different LAN types. Defined in the IEEE's 802.2 specification.

logical partition   A partition that is created in an extended partition.

logical topology   The paths that signals travel from one point in the network to another.

login privilege   A rule that states what kind of rights a user is granted when he accesses the system.

low-level formatting   Redefines the physical sectors on the hard drive.

lpq   This command is useful to help resolve printing problems. It displays all the jobs that are waiting to be printed.

lsmod   A Linux program that lists all the modules that are currently loaded on the system.

mail server   A system that is configured with programs and services that let it handle the exchange of e-mail from one client to another.

main console   Functions identically to a terminal window, except that it runs in the background, which allows users to switch their displays to the full-screen main console when running X.

man page   A help file that displays detailed information about any Linux command available to the user.

Management Information Base (MIB)   The data that the management system requests from an agent. This is a list of questions that the management system can ask.

management interface   The part of the NOS that provides the tools for server monitoring, client administration, file and print management, and disk-storage management.

Management Service Provider (MSP)   A company subscribes to an MSP service, which provides performance monitoring and network management. This saves the organization the cost of buying, installing, and learning to use monitoring and management software.

management system   The centralized location from which you can manage SNMP.

Media Access Control (MAC)   Rules for coordinating the use of the medium.

medium   The communications channel that all the computers on a LAN share.

menu   A collection of program-specific functions grouped based on like characteristics.

mesh topology   Connects all devices (nodes) to each other for redundancy and fault tolerance.

Microsoft Management Console (MMC)   This tool uses snap-ins, which are modules that contain the tools for specific administrative functions.

Millions of Instructions Per Second (MIPS)   The MIPS number is a general rating of the CPU's performance. This rating is usually based on a series of benchmark tests.

modem   An electronic device that is used for computer communications through telephone lines by converting digital data to analog signals and analog signals back to digital data.

modprobe   A Linux program that reduces administrative overhead by automatically loading any module dependencies.

multimeter   A device for checking the voltage of a power source.

Multistation Access Unit (MSAU)   The central device to which systems are connected in a Token Ring network.

multitasking system   A system that can execute multiple tasks or processes at the same time.

multiuser system   A system that can support multiple users concurrently.

Name Binding Protocol (NBP)   Associates network names for services with their addresses in Macintosh systems.

name resolution   The process of translating names to addresses that is done by the DNS server.

Network Address Translation (NAT)   A process that runs on a router (typically a router that acts as a gateway to Internet). A router running NAT rewrites the addressing information contained in IP packets. Administrators use NAT to alter the source address of packets originating from a secure LAN. This technique enables companies to keep their private addresses secure and unknown to the public by translating all the incoming and outgoing traffic through "known" or public IP addresses.

Network Basic Input/Output System (NetBIOS)   A widely used service for communicating between client applications and network services in older, small, native Windows networks.

Network Directory Service (NDS)   Novell's distributed directory implementation that is used to manage all objects, computers, and user accounts. It is a global database that is replicated between servers on the network.

network interface card (NIC)   A device that plugs into a motherboard and provides ports for the network media connections. It is the component of the computer that interfaces with the LAN.

network layer   Specifies how addresses are assigned and how packets of data are forwarded from one network to another toward the destination.

network operating system (NOS)   The software foundation on which the computer's applications and services run. A NOS has extra features that enable communication between multiple devices and the sharing of resources and services across a network. Network services include the World Wide Web (WWW), file sharing, mail exchange, directory services, remote management, and print services.

networking medium   The means by which signals (data) are sent from one computer to another.

NFS   Used to share files between multiple computer systems connected on a network. However, the main difference with NFS is that it is designed to work on UNIX systems.

Novell Link-State Protocol (NLSP)   Functions like OSPF in a TCP/IP environment to build and maintain routing tables.

Novell Routing Information Protocol (NRIP)   The Novell version of RIP operates much like RIP in a TCP/IP environment, but with variations that make it unique to NetWare networks.

Open Shortest Path First (OSPF)   Lets routers build forwarding tables. Unlike RIP, OSPF selects routes based on other characteristics of the links between networks, such as bandwidth and delay.

Open System Interconnection (OSI) reference model   Designed to promote interoperability in networking. This model is an overall description of the functions performed in a computer network and the relationships between them. The intent of the model is to provide a framework within which more-detailed standards can be developed for each function.

open-source   A noncommercial alternative means of software distribution in which the source code is open for anyone to copy or change. Usually, open-source means that the software is distributed and available for free.

operating system (OS) The software foundation on which the computer's applications and services run.

organizational unit (OU) Combining groups of the same user accounts or computers for easier administration to organize resources within domains.

OS Loader The boot loader that is found on Windows and DOS systems. It is also called NTLDR.

oscilloscope Measures how much voltage passes through a cable over a set period of time. The output is displayed on a monitor and can indicate breaks, attenuation, crimped wire, or shorts in the cable.

package information Stores all the information about a package after it is installed on the system.

packet A segment becomes a packet when the transport layer passes the segment to the network layer, where a protocol header is added.

packet filter A type of firewall that restricts traffic based on port assignments.

page fault The condition encountered when an attempt is made to access a program page but the page is no longer in memory, so it must be retrieved from disk.

paging function Allows users to have multiple workspaces or desktops open that can be switched back and forth with one mouse click or by selecting the appropriate screen from a menu.

partial backup Backs up only selected files. Partial backup types include copy and daily backup.

partition table The section on the hard drive that contains the partition information and the MBR.

passive hub Serves as a physical connection point only. It does not manipulate or view the traffic that crosses it.

password A secret series of characters used by the user to gain access to restricted areas.

Password Authentication Protocol (PAP) A protocol that presents the user's username and password in an unencrypted form when used for authentication.

patch A fix to existing software code. A NOS manufacturer typically provides security patches when vulnerabilities or potential vulnerabilities are discovered and fixed.

pathping   Combines the features of ping with those of tracert and provides additional information that is not displayed by either utility. With pathping, you can detect which routers are causing problems on the network and measure how many packets are lost at a particular router.

peer-to-peer network   Networked computers act as equal partners, or peers, to each other. As a peer, a computer can take on the client function or the server function.

peer-to-peer networking   A set of calls for each network device to run both client and server portions of an application. Also describes communication between implementations of the same OSI reference model layer in two different network devices.

percent processor utilization   The percentage of time that the processor is busy.

peripheral device   A device that connects to the computer through an external or internal port and that is controlled by the computer. Examples of external peripheral devices are mice, keyboards, monitors, printers, and scanners.

permission   A set of restrictions and privileges that disable or enable user actions.

permission   The file system controls who has permission to access files and run programs.

Personal Computer Memory Card International Association (PCMCIA)   A standard for credit card-sized memory or I/O devices that fit into computers—mostly laptops. There are three types of PCMCIA cards: Type I, Type II, and Type III. Type I is the smallest and thinnest of the PCMCIA cards. They are also called PC Cards.

physical layer   Corresponds to the network hardware (cabling, media). This layer determines how binary data is translated into electrical, optical, or other types of physical signals transmitted between systems.

physical topology   The layout of the devices and media.

ping   A simple utility that sends a message called an echo request to a designated destination computer using ICMP.

ping time   The amount of time that elapses between the sending of the echo request and the receipt of the echo reply.

point-to-point link   A direct connection from one computer to another.

Portable installation   Installs the options that might be needed with a portable computer, such as a laptop.

Post Office Protocol version 3 (POP3)   A common mail service protocol that is used by ISPs that provide Internet and e-mail service to home customers. POP3 permits a workstation to retrieve mail that the server is holding.

post-office box   The place on the e-mail server that is created to store incoming e-mail messages until the user downloads them from the server. Each user with an e-mail account has his or her own post-office box.

power cable   A cable, either internal or external, that provides an electric current for devices or components to use.

Power-On Self Test (POST)   The point during the boot process when the computer tests its memory and verifies that it has all the necessary hardware, such as a keyboard and a mouse.

preemptive multitasking   The operating system controls the allocation of processor time, and 32-bit programs run in their own separate address spaces. With preemptive multitasking, an unruly program cannot take over the system, and if a program crashes, it does not affect the others.

presentation layer   Specifies the arrangement, or syntax, of the data that the application expects. The presentation layer may include translations from one format to another and also includes security and efficiency functions (encryption and compression).

primary partition   The same as an original partition. It is usually the partition that contains the MBR and the default operating system files.

print server   A computer dedicated to handling client print jobs.

Printer Access Protocol (PAP)   Lets clients locate printers and controls the execution of print jobs on the network in Macintosh systems.

printtool   A GUI tool that can be used to set up printers and print queues in Red Hat.

processor queue length   The number of processes waiting for the processor.

proprietary technology   Hardware and software that are owned by one company and are generally incompatible with equipment sold by other vendors.

protocol   A set of messages and rules that is exchanged between systems in a defined sequence to accomplish a specific networking task.

provision information   Installed packages provide features for other installed packages.

proxy service   A proxy is software that interacts with outside networks on behalf of a client host. By using the services of a proxy, the client never interacts directly with outside hosts. This protects clients from potential Internet threats.

public/private key encryption   Uses two keys—one that is published and widely available and one that is private and known only to the user. Both keys are required to complete the secure communication.

quarter-inch cartridge (QIC)   Tapes used in QIC drives are one-quarter inch wide. The QIC standard has limited storage capacity and is used only in entry-level network servers.

RAID 0   Also called disk striping. Writes data across two or more physical drives. This type of RAID has no redundancy. If one of the drives fails, all the data is lost.

RAID 0+1   Has the performance of RAID 0 and the redundancy of RAID 1. Four disk drives and a disk controller are required to implement RAID 0+1.

RAID 1   Also called disk mirroring. Requires the use of two disk drives and one disk controller to provide redundancy. Each drive is completely mirrored, an exact copy of the other. This provides 100% redundancy. If one of the disk drives fails, put in a replacement, and the data is copied to the new drive.

RAID 5   Also called disk striping with parity. Parity is an encoding scheme that represents where the information is stored on each drive. It writes data across disks and adds a parity bit for redundancy. Three drives are required to implement this type of RAID.

RAIT (redundant array of independent tapes)   Can be used for mirroring of tape drives or (with at least three tape drives) implemented as data striping with parity.

Read permission   A permission allowing a file to be read or the contents of a directory to be displayed.

Red Hat Package Manager (RPM)   Provides all the tools that are needed to efficiently install and remove programs, such as a package database.

remote access   Lets employees access the corporate remote-access server and log in to the network with their regular user account. Employees can then use all the resources that would be available from the office desktop computer.

repeater   Receives the signal, regenerates it, and passes it on.

replication   The process of copying data from one computer to one or more other computers and synchronizing that data so that it is identical on all systems.

RF (radio frequency) technology   Allows devices to be in different rooms or even buildings. The limited range of the radio signals still restricts the use of this kind of network.

ring topology   Connects computers in a closed loop, in which a cable is run from one computer to the next until the last one is connected to the first.

rmmod   A Linux program that removes drivers or modules.

route   This command displays or sets the information on the system's routing, which the system uses to send information to a particular IP addresses.

router   The most sophisticated internetworking device. It operates at the network layer of the OSI reference model. It is slower than a bridge or switch but makes "smart" decisions on how to route packets received on one port to a network on another port.

Routing Information Protocol (RIP)   Operates between router devices to discover paths between networks to build and maintain information about how to forward packets toward their destination.

runlevel   Controls what predetermined set of programs will run on the computer when the system starts up. Some programs run only at specific runlevels. What runlevel the system is booted up in determines what programs are loaded on the system.

Samba   A program that uses the Server Message Block (SMB) application layer protocol, which gives Windows computers access to the Linux file system over the network.

scalability   How well a hardware or software system can adapt to increased demands.

script   A simple text program, written in a specific programming language, that allows the user to perform many automated tasks at once.

SCSI configuration   The process of installing SCSI devices and configuring SCSI parameters.

SCSI Configured Automatically (SCAM) protocol   A protocol that automatically allocates SCSI IDs to SCSI devices.

SCSI ID   An ID used by the computer to identify a SCSI device.

SCSI interface   An ANSI interface that allows communication with peripheral devices at much faster rates than traditional interfaces.

Secure Sockets Layer (SSL)   A way to secure communications on the network by providing encryption.

security   When referring to a NOS, this includes authenticating user access to services to prevent unauthorized access to the network resources.

Security Accounts Management Database (SAM)   Controls the authentication process when a user logs on to the domain.

segment   Results when a header is added to a data unit for sequencing and error checking.

Sequenced Packet Exchange (SPX)   Functions much like TCP to provide a reliable, connection-oriented transport between client and server systems.

serial line   A line that transmits bits of information one after another in a series, like cars traveling on a single-lane highway.

server   Servers generally look very different from workstation systems. They have no need for user-oriented features such as large monitors, speakers, or a sound card. Servers consist of things such as very reliable and fault-tolerant hard disks.

server chassis   The casing that houses the server hardware.

Service Advertisement Protocol (SAP)   Makes services known to NetWare clients and helps clients locate the services they require, such as print or file services.

session layer   Allows a number of copies of an application to communicate with other applications at the same time. Also establishes the rules of the conversation between two applications.

setserial   This utility provides information and sets options for the system's serial ports.

shadow password   A password that is stored in a file other than /etc/passwd so that it is not accessible by all users. This greatly improves security.

shadowing   A BIOS setting configured so that parts of the information or information stored on other devices can be copied to RAM. This process speeds up the system's access to DOS, because it can access it straight from RAM.

shielded twisted-pair   Combines the techniques of cancellation and twisting of wires with shielding. Each pair of wires is wrapped in metallic foil to further shield the wires from noise.

Simple Mail Transport Protocol (SMTP)   A protocol that provides messaging services over TCP/IP and supports most Internet e-mail programs.

single ring   All the devices on the network share a single cable, and the data travels in one direction only.

Smurf   A kind of attack that spoofs the IP packet header using ICMP or ping.

sniffer   Any program that "eavesdrops" on network traffic.

SNMP (Simple Network Management Protocol)   Lets network administrators remotely troubleshoot and monitor hubs and routers. Using SNMP, you can find out information about these remote devices without having to physically be at the device itself.

SSH   A secure means of authenticating users to a server by storing a special key on the server and another one on the client. The client uses this key, and not a password, to authenticate to the server.

standby mode   A mode in which the system leaves devices powered up so that the system can recover power more quickly.

star topology   A network topology that resembles spokes in a bicycle wheel. It is made up of a central connection point that is a device (such as a hub, switch, or router) where all the cabling segments meet.

subnet mask   A 32-bit dotted-decimal number that is assigned to networks and used to differentiate between networks that are subnetted. This number determines whether a particular host IP address is local (on the same network segment) or remote (on another segment).

subnetting   Using the subnet mask to divide the network and break a large or extremely large network into smaller, more efficient, more manageable segments, or subnets.

superserver   A server that listens for requests for any of the daemons and services on the server. It loads the daemon or service into memory only when a request has been made and it is in use.

superuser account   Also called the root account. The account that the system administrator uses to perform administrative tasks on a Linux system.

support package   Works in much the same way as a library. For example, all KDE programs rely on a support program called Qt. If the Qt support package is not installed, no KDE packages will be able to be installed using RPMs.

suspend mode   A mode in which the system shuts down programs and powers off devices except for the CPU and memory.

swap file   An area of the hard disk that is used for virtual memory.

switch   Also called a multiport bridge. Although a typical bridge might have just two ports (linking two network segments), a switch can have multiple ports, depending on how many network segments are to be linked.

Symmetric DSL (SDSL)   Provides the same speed, up to 3 Mbps, for uploads and downloads.

symmetric multiprocessing (SMP) A computer architecture that provides high performance by making multiple CPUs available to individual processes.

synchronous serial transmissions Data bits are sent together with a synchronizing clock pulse. In this transmission method, a built-in timing mechanism coordinates the clocks of the sending and receiving devices.

Sys V script A script that is used to automatically start, stop, or restart Linux daemons when the system is booted.

syslogd This daemon records information about currently running programs to the system log file.

System Commander A very advanced boot loader with many advanced features and configurations. Like NTLDR, it cannot boot Linux directly, but it can boot it indirectly.

system configuration file Controls settings for the entire system. A file that controls services that are set to run for each user who logs in to the system.

system files The files that allow the operating system to function. NOS installation involves creating and copying NOS system files to a hard disk.

tape backup drive Most commonly used as the device for backing up the data on a network server's disk drives. Tape devices are known for their long-lasting performance, which is partly due to the tape drive mechanics that some systems include.

tape library Usually an external system that has multiple tape drives, tens or hundreds of tapes, and an automatic mechanism for locating the tapes, loading them into the tape drives, and returning the tapes to the proper location.

tar A utility that combines multiple files into a single file that can be copied to the medium.

tarball The most widely supported type of package available with Linux. Tarballs, like RPM and Debian packages, are a collection of compressed files that can be uncompressed and installed on a Linux or UNIX system.

Taskbar A management tool located at the bottom of the screen on Windows operating systems. It maintains a list of open programs, quick launch icons, and the Start menu.

TCP SYN attack Exploits the TCP protocol three-way handshake.

TCP/IP A set of public standards that specifies how packets of information are exchanged between computers over one or more networks.

Teardrop   A program that takes advantage of how IP handles fragmentation. Teardrop sends fragments that have overlapping reassembly information, which confuses the target software, causing a crash.

Telnet   A terminal emulation protocol used for remote terminal connection. It lets users log into remote systems and use resources as if they were connected to a local system. The Telnet application is used to access remote devices for configuration, control, and troubleshooting.

terminal emulation   The process of accessing a remote system via a local computer terminal. The local terminal runs software that emulates, or mimics, the look of the remote system terminal.

terminal window   Also called xterm. Displays a standard Linux command prompt in a small window on the screen so that a command can be entered.

termination   A device or technique used to properly bring to an end a cable or signal.

Thicknet   A very large version of coaxial cable in which the diameter is rigid and difficult to install. In addition, the maximum transmission rate is only 100 Mbps.

Thinnet   A thinner and more flexible version of coaxial cable that is occasionally used in Ethernet networks. Thinnet has the same transmission rate as Thicknet.

thread   A program that can execute independently of other parts. This lets programmers design programs whose threaded parts can execute concurrently.

Time Domain Reflectometer (TDR)   A tool that tests shorts or breaks in a cable. It works by analyzing a sonar-type pulse that is injected through the cable.

time stamp   The information that is marked on an e-mail message to indicate the time at which the e-mail was sent by an individual and received by the e-mail server.

tone generator/locator   A tool that identifies a cable. It consists of two components— the tone generated and the locator.

traceroute   Shows all the routers through which the packet passes as it travels through the network from sending computer to destination computer.

Transmission Control Protocol (TCP)   A connection-oriented protocol that is the primary Internet protocol for reliable delivery of data which guarantees that messages arrive at their destination or, if they cannot be delivered, informs the application programs of the failure. TCP includes facilities for end-to-end connection establishment, error detection and recovery, and metering the rate of data flow into the network.

transport layer   Provides delivery services for each session. Provides a reliable delivery service that guarantees that data arrives at its destination, or an "unreliable" best-effort delivery service that transports the data without checking for errors.

Travan cartridge tape   Based on QIC technology. In many cases, it is either read/write-compatible with some QIC tape cartridges or read-compatible with QIC cartridges. Travan tape drives have a higher storage capacity than the older QIC tape drives. Travan tape drives have the capacity to back up low-end network servers but are relatively slow.

Trojan horse   A program that presents itself as another program to obtain information.

Typical installation   The basic type of installation that is configured for a standard standalone desktop computer.

uninterruptible power supply (UPS)   A backup power supply system that is commonly found on servers. It provides power for a short period of time if a power loss occurs in the building where the server is located.

Universal Serial Bus (USB)   A Plug and Play interface that connects the system to peripheral devices. USB interfaces support data transfer rates up to 12 Mbps.

universal service   How long it takes almost all households in the technologically advanced world to use and depend on access to a certain technology.

UNIX   An operating system designed to support multiple users and multitasking. UNIX was one of the first operating systems to include support for Internet networking protocols.

unshielded twisted-pair   Used in a variety of networks. It has two or four pairs of wires and is the most commonly used cabling in Ethernet networks.

user and group IDs   Numbers that the Linux operating system uses to identify a user or group.

user configuration file   Stores information that is specific to an individual user, such as desktop icon placements, window manager preferences, and scripts that are set to run automatically.

User Datagram Protocol (UDP)   A connectionless, "unreliable" service to applications that can tolerate a loss of some messages but still function.

user interface (UI)   The component of the OS that the user interacts with.

username   The name that identifies the person logged on to the system.

VBScript (Visual Basic Script)   A popular Microsoft scripting language based on the Visual Basic programming language.

Very High Data Rate DSL (VDSL)   DSL that is capable of bandwidths from 13 Mbps to 52 Mbps.

vi Editor   A powerful editing tool with which you can edit configuration and script files and create some configuration and script files.

virtual memory   Hard disk space that is used to supplement RAM.

virtual private network (VPN)   A technology developed by extranet designers that allows employees and customers to access the private network over the Internet in a secure manner.

virus   A piece of programming code that is usually disguised as something else. It causes an unexpected and usually undesirable event.

volt/ohm meter   A device that verifies that a power outlet is available and active.

volt-amp (VA) rating   A unit of measure for a UPS that specifies how long the UPS can keep the network server running in the event of a power failure.

Volume Table of Contents (VTOC)   The first sector of the hard drive on BSD and Sun UNIX systems. Also called a disk label.

web server   A system that uses Hypertext Transfer Protocol (HTTP) to deliver files to users who request them using a web browser from their workstation.

wide-area network (WAN)   Usually segmented into multiple LANs. A WAN uses dedicated point-to-point or serial communications lines to connect the various LANs to make up the WAN.

window   A graphical pane that displays system or program information.

window manager   Linux and UNIX software responsible for providing borders and control around windows and desktop environments, which include several additional utilities that help users customize and control their working environment.

Windows Internet Naming Service (WINS)   An addition to DNS that native Windows systems use to translate the names used by NetBIOS applications into IP addresses.

Windows Script Host (WSH)   A component of Windows 2000 and XP that lets users create scripts using VBScript or JavaScript languages.

wireless network   An alternative method of connecting a LAN in which there are no cables to run and computers can be easily moved. Radio frequency (RF), laser, infrared (IR), and satellite/microwaves are used to carry signals from one computer to another without a permanent cable connection.

workstation   A system that is typically a standalone computer consisting of one monitor, keyboard, and mouse. Most often, a workstation is configured with a network connection.

worm   A self-replicating virus that does not alter files but resides in active memory. It duplicates itself to produce uncontrolled replication that consumes system resources, slowing or halting other tasks.

Write permission   A permission allowing a user to edit and save changes to a file or add files to and delete files from a directory.

X server   The main component that establishes the GUI mode on a Linux system.

X Window System   The set of programs that comprise the Linux GUI environment.

Xconfigurator   A configuration tool used to configure the X Window GUI. Can be used in either text mode or GUI mode.

xf86cfg   Works much like XF86Setup, but the user interface works a little differently. The xf86cfg interface has graphical pictures of the different hardware that is attached to the system.

xf86config   A configuration tool used to configure the X Window System GUI. It operates entirely in text mode. Its basic process is to ask a series of questions about the hardware in your system and your configuration preferences.

XF86Setup   A configuration tool used to configure the X Window System GUI that can be used only from GUI mode. It is used to reconfigure the X environment while it is in a nonoperational mode. You can make changes at any time without having to start over if you make a mistake.

Xfce   A desktop environment that is very similar to CDE. Unlike CDE, which is used for commercial UNIX systems, Xfce is entirely open-source.

XFree86   The free X server that comes with every major distribution of Linux that supports a GUI interface.

Zone Information Protocol (ZIP)   Maintains a correspondence between networks and the names of partitions, called zones, between Macintosh systems.

Index

Symbols

$ cd /home command (Linux), 457
$ cd command (Linux), 457
$ cd user2/dir1 command (Linux), 457
/etc/fstab file, editing, 487
/etc/hosts.allow file, configuring TCP wrappers, 219
/etc/hosts.deny file, configuring TCP wrappers, 219
/etc/inittab file, editing, 485–486
/etc/printcap configuration file, 507

Numerics

1000BASE-T Ethernet, 84
100BASE-X Ethernet, 84
10BASE-T Ethernet, 83
32-bit processing, Windows 9.x, 21
8mm system backup tape, 527

A

acceptable-use policies, 722
access control. *See* MAC
accessibility versus security, 720
accessing
    command console from X Windows System, 456
    man pages, 458
account administration, Windows 2000, 274
ACLs (access control lists), 748
ACPI (Advanced Configuration and Power Interface), 642
active hubs, 128
adding
    Linux user accounts, 469
        creating passwords, 471
        useradd command, 469
    swap space to swap files, 341
    user accounts
        to groups, 473
        Windows 2000 Professional, 376
add-on options, Windows 2000 Professional, 368
ADSL (Asymmetric DSL), 143

ADSP (AppleTalk Data Stream Protocol), 81
AFP (AppleTalk Filing Protocol), 81
agents (SNMP), 584
AIT (Advanced Intelligent Tape), performing system backups, 527–528
Anaconda, 329
ANSI standards, 77
antitheft devices, securing server rooms, 728–729
Apache web servers, 498, 500
APM (Advanced Power Management), 642
AppleTalk protocol suite, 81
appliances, 754
application errors, troubleshooting on Linux servers, 687–688
application layer
    OSI model, 70
    TCP/IP networking model, 158
application protocols (TCP/IP suite), 79
applications, identifying problems with, 655–656
applying patches and upgrades, 747
ARP (Address Resolution Protocol), 80, 160, 185–186
ARPANET (Advanced Research Projects Agency Network), 75
assessing security needs, 720
    management philosophy, 722
    type of business, 721
    type of data, 721
assigned permissions (Active Directory), 233
assigning
    IP addresses
        name resolution, 105
        to network hosts, 101–102
        via DHCP, 102–104
    permissions to processes, 551–552
asynchronous serial transmission, 135
AT commands, 139
ATP (AppleTalk Transaction Protocol), 81
attacks
    buffer overflow, 733
    DDoS, 735–736
    DoS, 733

exploits, 737
Smurf, 734
TCP SYN, 733
teardrops, 734
attenuation, 84
audiovisual programs, Linux, 290
authentication, text-based PPP client configuration, 210
automating system backups, 533

B

backup system
verifying NOS preinstallation checklist, 315
backups, 519
automating, 533
differential, 522
documenting, 532
errors, troubleshooting, 684–687
full, 521
grandfather-father-son method, 531
hardware
8mm tape, 527
AIT, 527–528
DAT, 528
disk drives, 530
DLT, 528
LTO, 529
QIC, 525
tape arrays, 529
tape autochangers, 529
tape drives, 525
tape libraries, 530
Travan cartridge tape, 526
incremental, 522
partial, 521
performing in Linux, 523–525
configuration files, 492
performing in Windows 2000, 522–523
six-cartridge weekly method, 531–532
tape backups, 521
Tower of Hanoi method, 532
verifying, 533
baseline measurements, 569
basic CLI commands (Linux), 457
beaconing, 87
biometrics, securing server rooms, 728
BIOS (Basic Input/Output System)
boot process, 347
configuring, 328
verifying settings in Linux systems, 629–631

boot process, 348
BIOS interaction, 347
boot files, 346
emergency boot disks (Linux)
creating, 674–675
locating, 673–674
kernel initialization, 349
kernel load, 349
LILO boot loader
booting without, 670–671
configuring, 440–442
installing, 442
reconfiguring, 439
troubleshooting, 667–669
Linux systems, 350
configuring options during installation,
414–415
runlevels, 488–490
logon, 350
preboot sequence, 346–348
Windows 2000 versus Windows 9x, 345
bottlenecks, 564
disk subsystem bottlenecks, 567
memory bottlenecks, 566–567
network subsystem bottlenecks, 568
processor bottlenecks, 566
Bourne Again shell, 463
Bourne shell, 462
bridges, 129
filtering, 130
broadband remote access, DSL client configuration,
216–218
broadcast domains, 133
browsing distributed directory database, 228
BSD UNIX partition tables, 334
buffer overflow attacks, 733
buffers, 566
built-in modems, 136
bus topologies, 58, 111–112
buttons, Windows 2000 Professional, 370

C

C shell, 462
cable modems, 144–145
remote access client configuration, 216–218
versus DSL, 145–146
cabling
attenuation, 84
coaxial, 118, 120
fiber-optic, 123

plenum, 118
PVC jacket, 118
twisted-pair, 120
    STP, 121
    UTP, 83, 122–123
cal command (Linux), 457
Caldera Linux, 282
card readers, securing server rooms, 727
categories of UTP cabling, 123
cd command (Linux), 457
CDE (Common Desktop Environment), 431
changing runlevels, 489–490
CHAP (Challenge Handshake Authentication Protocol),
   text-based PPP client configuration, 210
characteristics of NOSs, 263–264
child processes, 546
chmod command (Linux), 476
chown command (Linux), 476
CIFS (Common Internet File Systems), 504–505
Class A addresses (IPv4), 167
Class B addresses (IPv4), 168
Class C addresses (IPv4), 168
CLI (command-line interface), 9
   Linux, 32–33
      basic commands, 457
      ls command, 460–461
      man command, 459
      man pages, 458–460
      switching to X Windows, 456
   MS-DOS commands, 25–26
   UNIX, 32–33
   Windows 2000 Professional, 373–375
client configuration (remote access), 210
   cable modems, 216, 218
   DSL, 216–218
   ISDN, 215
   PPP, 210
      GUI dialing utilities, 213–215
      text-based, 210, 213
client/server networks, 38–39, 65–66
   versus peer-to-peer, 66
clients, Linux, 286
clock speed, 601
clustering, 10, 704
CMIP (Common Management Information
   Protocol), 582
coaxial cable, 118–120
cold sites, 711
collision domains, 128, 132
command console, accessing from X Windows
   System, 456

command interpreters, Linux shell, 462
command modes (vi Editor), 465
commands
   Linux
      chmod, 476
      chown, 476
      cpio, performing backups, 525
      df, 478
      du, 479–481
      kill, 498
      ls, 460–461
      man, 459
      passwd, 471
      shutdown, 490
      unmount, 478
      useradd, 469
   MS-DOS, 26
   dsmg, 664–665
   FTP, 244
   netdiag, 696
   pathping, 697
   ps, 546–548
   RPM, 436–437
   top, 548
   traceroute, 693
common carriers, 60
communities (SNMP), 586–587
comparing LANs and WANs, 57
compatibility
   of Active Directory with other directory services, 234
   Linux hardware support, 595
      RPM and multiple Linux distributions, 435–436
   of NDS with other platforms, 236
completing NOS installation, 344
components
   of Linux printing environment, 507
   of mail services, 239–240
   of network servers, 310
      backup system, 315
      FC-AL, 316
      KVM switch, 317
      memory, 314
      monitors, 314
      NICs, 316
      RAID controllers, 316
      SCSI adapter, 316
      SCSI cable, 315
      server chassis, 310
      server rack, 311, 314
      UPS, 315
      video adapter, 317

of OSs
  CLIs, 9
  file system, 10–11
  GUIs, 9–10
  kernel, 7
  UI, 7
of X.500 directory services, 230
Computer Management tool (Windows 2000), 556
configuration files, 481
  /etc/printcap, 507
  backing up, 492
  documenting, 490–491
  editing, 485
    /etc/fstab file, 487
    /etc/inittab file, 485–486
    control lines, 485
  for specific servers, 484
  runlevels, 488–490
  startup, 483
  system, 483–484
  system maintenance logs, 491
  user, 482
configuration tools, UNIX, 33
configuring
  BIOS settings, 328
  boot options for Linux systems, 414–415
  IP addresses, default gateway, 108
  LILO boot loader, 440
    for two operating systems, 442
  Linux
    network settings, 412
    printing system, 414
    remote access clients, 223–226
    security settings, 410–411
    services, 414
    time zone, 413
  network protocol, 324–326
  NIC IP address, 101–104
  NIS clients, 238
  remote access clients, 210
    cable modems, 216–218
    DSL, 216–218
    GUI-dialing utilities, 213–215
    ISDN, 215
    PPP, 210
    rights, 218
    text-based PPP, 210, 213
  remote access servers
    file permissions, 223
    firewall services, 218

passwords, 222–223
    TCP wrappers, 219, 221
  swap files
    Linux, 339
    Windows 2000 Server, 339
  X server, 419–420
    hardware, 423–426
connection speed (Internet), verifying, 571
connectivity
  loss of, troubleshooting, 689
  ping utility, 690–693
  testing, 325
control lines, editing, 485
Control Panel (Windows), 27
cooperative multitasking, 17
core dumps, Linux, 543–545
core system hardware, troubleshooting in Linux systems, 640–641
Corel Linux, 283
corporate espionage, 739
cost-benefit analysis of network administration requirements, 56
counters, monitoring system performance, 566
cpio command, performing backups in Linux, 525
CPU, 596
  clock speed, 601
  monitoring, 555
  selecting for Linux systems, 599–601
crackers, 732
crashed Linux servers, troubleshooting, 688
creating
  administrator user account, 343–344
  cron jobs
    system cron jobs, 541–542
    user cron jobs, 543
  directories in Linux, 474–475
  disk partitions, 334–335
    FDISK, 335
    FIPS, 337
    Linux, 336
    third-party tools, 336
  emergency boot disks, 674–675
  folders in Windows 2000, 379
  Linux file system, 406
  Linux groups, 472–473
  local groups in Windows 2000, 380
  pre-installation hardware inventory, 320–322
  security policies
    acceptable-use policies, 722
    network access rules, 723

online security resources, 725
securing removable media, 729
server room security, 725–729
username/password standards, 722–723
virus protection standards, 724
waste disposal, 723
critical processes, 545
cron jobs, 540
system cron jobs, creating, 541–542
user cron jobs, creating, 543
CSMA/CA (carrier sense multiple access collision avoidance), 81
CSU/DSU (channel service unit/data service unit), 61
customer resources, evaluating, 43–44

D

daemons, 493
FTP, 501–502
HTTP, Apache, 498–500
lpd, 507
mail client, 506
NFS, 505–506
pppd, 210
scripts, 511
SMB protocol, 504–505
starting and stopping, 494–497
superservers, 496–497
Telnet, 502–504
DAP (Directory Access Protocol), 230
DAT (Digital Audio Tape) for system backups, 528
data overrun protection, 334
datagrams, 81
data link layer (OSI model), 73
date command (Linux), 457
DDNS (Dynamic DNS), 232
DDoS (distributed denial of service) attacks, 733–736
Debian GNU/Linux, 283
packages, 437–438
dedicated appliances, evaluating requirements for, 43
default gateways, configuring, 108
default runlevels, changing, 490
default shell (Linux), 467
defragmenting disk subsystem, 567
delecting core files, 544–545
dependencies, 409
troubleshooting, 679–684
depletion of available IPv4 addresses, 169–170
DESCRIPTION heading (man pages), 460

desktop computers, evaluating requirements for, 41
desktop environments (Linux), 429–432
"Destination Unreachable" messages, 186
developing security policies
acceptable use policies, 722
considerations, 720
management philosophy, 722
type of business, 721
type of data, 721
disaster recovery plan based on fault tolerance, 709–711
network access rules, 723
online security, 725
securing removable media, 729
server room policies, 725
antitheft devices, 728–729
biometrics, 728
card readers, 727
combination locking mechanisms, 726
lock and key, 725–726
username/password standards, 722–723
virus protection standards, 724
waste disposal policies, 723
development of Linux, 29–30
Device Manager, identifying hardware, 322–323
devices
bridges, 129–130
cable modems, 144–146
clustering, 704
CSU/DSU, 61
drivers, loading on Linux systems, 614–615
hubs, 127–128
ISDN modems, 216
jumper configurations, 613
modems, 135, 137
NICs, 99
IP address configuration, 101–104
selecting, 101
PnP configurations, 614
repeaters, 127
resource allocation on Linux systems, 612
routers, 132–134
switches, 130
terminal adapters, 216
transmitters, 125
UARTs, 135
df command (Linux), 478
DHCP (Dynamic Host Configuration Protocol), 189, 254
IP address assignment, 102–104

diagnostic tools for Windows 2000
  netdiag command, 696
  pathping command, 697
differential backups, 522
directories, 10
  Linux
    creating, 474–475
    symbolic links, 496
directory services, 54, 227–228
  Active Directory, 231
    compatibility with other directory services, 234
    database structure, 231
    DNS integration, 232
    domains, 231
    OUs, 232
    permissions, 233
    replication, 233
    servers, 232–233
  DAP, 230
  LDAP, 230
  NDS, 235
    database structure, 235
    platform compability, 236
    security, 236
  NIS, 237
    client configuration, 238
    database structure, 237
  root, 227
  X.500 standard, 229–230
disabling
  FTPD, 501
  Linux user accounts, 471
disaster recovery, 698
  cold sites, 711
  developing plan based on fault tolerance, 709–711
  hot sites, 711
  risk analysis, 699–700
disk clusters, 10
disk drives
  for system backups, 530
  verifying NOS preinstallation checklist, 314
disk labels, 334
disk management, 552–554
disk partitioning, 331, 334–336
  data overrun protection, 334
  FIPS, 337
  Linux systems, 332
  on multiple disks, 333
  third-party tools, 336

disk subsystem bottlenecks, 567
DISPLAY environment variable, 444
displaying
  kernel messages, 664–665
  man pages, 459–460
distributed directory database, 227
distributed networking, client/server networks, 66
distributions of Linux, 281, 285
DLM (distributed lock manager), 705
DLT (Digital Linear Tape) for system backups, 528
DMAs, verifying configuration in Linux systems, 624
DMZ (demilitarized zone), 754
DNS (Domain Name System), 79
  host names, 252–254
  integration with Active Directory, 232
  name resolution, 105, 180–181
documenting
  Linux configuration files, 490–491
  system backups, 532
DoD model, 75
domain structure, Windows NT 4.0, 272–273
domains, 254
  Active Directory, 231
  Internet, 253
DOS (Disk Operating System), 14
  commands, 26
DoS (denial of service) attacks, 733
dotted-decimal format, 165
  IP addresses, 101
downstream data transfer, 143
drive mapping, 534
  in Linux, 537
  in Novell, 537
  with net use command, 536–537
  with Windows Explorer, 535
drivers, 676
  Linux, locating, 609–610
  loading on Linux systems, 614–615
DSL (digital subscriber line), 142–144
  remote access client configuration, 216–218
  transfer rates, 143
  versus cable modems, 145–146
dsmg command, 664–665
du command (Linux), 479–481
dual ring topology, 115
  FDDI, 89
DUN (dialup networking), 138–139

E

echo cancellation, 144
editing configuration files, 485
    /etc/fstab file, 487
    /etc/inittab file, 485–486
    control lines, 485
    vi Editor, 464–465
EDS (Electronic Directory Service) standards, 229–230
EIDE devices, verifying configuration in Linux systems, 626
e-mail
    IMAP, 195
    Linux mail client, 506
    POP3, 195
    security, 742–743
    services, 52
        post-office boxes, 52
        Windows 2000, 389–390
emergency boot disks, 672–673
    creating, 674–675
    locating, 673–674
encapsulation, 74
encryption, 740
enterprise servers, 267
entry mode, vi Editor, 465
environment variables (Linux), 444
environmental conditions, verifying server room temperature, 309
Ethernet, 82
    1000BASE-T, 84
    100BASE-X, 84
    10BASE-T, 83
    full-duplex transmission, 85
    half-duplex transmission, 85
evaluating
    customer resources, 43–44
    requirements
        for dedicated appliances, 43
        for servers, 41
        for workstations, 41
evolution of networking, 5
examining log files, 662–664
    kernel startup messages, 664–665
exiting X Window System, 457
exploits, 737
extended partitions, 331
extended star topologies, 113
External devices, replacing on Linux systems, 611
external modems, 136
external security, 730
extranets, 249

F

FAT (file allocation table), 10–11
fault-tolerant systems, 268
    high availability, 707
FC-AL (Fibre Channel-Arbitrated Loop), verifying NOS preinstallation checklist, 316
FDDI (Fiber Distributed Data Interface), 87–89
fdformat command (Linux), 408
FDISK, creating disk partitions, 335
FDM (frequency-division multiplexing), 144
fiber-optic networks, FDDI, 87–89
file access servers, Linux, 292
file sharing, 241
    CIFS, 504
    NFS, 505–506
file systems, 10
    checking for errors, 539–540
    FAT, 11
    formatting process, 343
    Linux
        configuration files, 481, 485–492
        creating, 406
        directories, 474–475
        managing, 478
        mounting, 477–478
        startup configuration files, 483
        system configuration files, 483
        system function configuration files, 484
        user configuration files, 482
    naming conventions, 12
    NTFS, 21
    partitions
        fdisk utility, 538
        formatting, 539
file transfers, configuring for Linux systems, 225
files
    boot files, 346
    permissions, configuring on remote access servers, 223
    system files, 305
filtering, 130
final NOS installation procedures, 344
FIPS (First Nondestructive Interactive Partitioning Splitting), 337
firewalls, 748
    ACLs, 748
    configuring on remote access servers, 218
    NAT, 750
    packet filters, 748–753
    placement, 753–754
    proxy services, 748–750
    solutions, 754–755

flavors of DSL, 143
folders (Windows 2000), managing, 379
forests (Active Directory), 231
forked chains, 634
formatting hard disks, 342
    high-level, 408
    low-level, 408
    partitions, 539
frames, 74
    tokens, 114
fsck utility, checking file system for errors, 539–540
FTP (File Transfer Protocol), 79, 192
    services, 242
        CLI commands, 244
        DoS attacks, 244
        Windows 2000, 385–386
FTPD, 501–502
full backups, 521
full-duplex data transmission, 85

G

GNOME (GNU Network Object Model Environment), 31–32
    desktop environment, 431
GNS (Get Nearest Server), 80
grandfather-father-son method of system backups, 531
group accounts, Linux, 469
group IDs, Linux, 467
groups (Linux)
    adding user accounts, 473
    creating, 472–473
    SGID, 551
GRUB (Grand Unified Boot loader), 414
GUI dialer PPP configuration, 213–215
GUIs, 9–10
    Linux, 31
    logins, configuring, 224
    printtool, 509
    UNIX, 31
    Windows, 24
        Control Panel, 27
    X Window System, 454
        accessing command console, 456
        exiting, 457
        similarities to Windows 2000, 455

H

hackers, 732
half-duplex data transmission, 85
handshaking sequence (DUN), 138
hard drives
    formatting, 342
    partitions
        creating, 334–337
        data overrun protection, 334
        NOS installation, 331–332
        on multiple diskd, 333
hardware
    CPUs, 596
    identifying problems with, 654
    identifying with Device Manager, 322–323
    jumper configurations, 613
    Linux, 597
        compatibility issues, 595
        kernel modules, 616, 619
        loading drivers, 614–615
        locating drivers, 609–610
        replacing, 610–611
        requirements for installation, 409
        resource allocation, 612
        selecting CPUs, 599–601
        selecting internal modems, 603
        selecting monitoring devices, 605
        selecting sound cards, 603
        selecting USB devices, 603
        selecting video capture cards, 603
        selecting video hardware, 601–602
        troubleshooting, 633, 636–641
        verifying configurations, 621, 624–631
    memory, 596
    motherboards, 596
    on NOS servers, 267
    PnP configurations, 614
hardware inventory
    creating, 320–322
    verifying against HCL, 323
HCL (hardware compatibility list), verifying hardware compatibility, 323
HDSL (High Data Rate DSL), 143
headers, 74
headings (man pages), displaying, 458–460
Hewlett-Packard OpenView, 581
hexadecimal format of IPv6 addresses, 172–173

hierarchical addresses, 165
hierarchical file systems, 10
    Active Directory domains, 231
high availability, 707
high usage, identifying, 570
high-level formatting, 408
high-speed remote access, 216
history
    of Linux, 29–30, 278–280
    of TCP/IP, 155–156
    of UNIX, 28
home directory (Linux), 467
host names (DNS), 252–254
host tables, 178–179
HOSTNAME environment variable, 444
hosts.allow file, configuring TCP wrappers, 219
hosts.deny file, configuring TCP wrappers, 219
hot sites, 711
hot-swap components, 708
HTTP, 190, 246
    Apache web servers, 498–500
    Windows 2000 services, 384
hubs, 127–128
hybrid topology, 117

I

I/O settings, verifying configuration in Linux
    systems, 625
IBM Tivoli Enterprise, 579
ICMP (Internet Control Message Protocol), 79, 186–187
    echo requests, 188
icons, Windows 2000 Professional, 370
identifying
    application problems, 655–656
    configuration problems, 656
    hardware problems, 654
        Device Manager, 322–323
    high usage, 570
    kernel problems, 655
    problems based on user feedback, 665–667
    user error problems, 657–658
IDSL (ISDN DSL), 143
IEEE (Institute of Electrical and Electronic Engineers), 76–77
IEEE 802.3 standard. *See* Ethernet
IEEE 802.5 standard. *See* Token Ring
ifconfig utility, 659–660, 694
IMAP (Internet Message Access Protocol), 195, 240
implementing security measures
    e-mail security, 742–743
    file encryption, 740

    IPSec, 741
    public/private key encryption, 744–745
    SSL, 742
incremental backups, 522
information superhighway, 55
inherited permissions (Active Directory), 233
init program (Linux), 483
insmod program, loading kernel modules, 617
installing NOSs, 305
    administrator user account, creating, 343–344
    BIOS configuration, 328
    disk partitioning, 331, 334–335
        data overrun protection, 334
        FDISK, 335
        Linux, 336–337
        Linux systems, 332
        multiple disks, 333
    final configuration procedure, 344
    formatting process, 342
    hardware compatibility, verifying, 323
    hardware components, 310
        backup system, 315
        disk drives, 314
        FC-AL, 316
        KVM switch, 317
        memory, 314
        monitors, 314
        NICs, 316
        peripherals, 314
        processors, 314
        RAID controllers, 316
        SCSI adapter, 316
        SCSI cable, 315
        server chassis, 310
        server rack, 311
        UPS, 315
        video adapter, 317
    hardware inventory, creating, 320–322
    hardware requirements, 317–319
    installation program, 328
    Linux
        boot loader, 439
        configuring boot options, 414–415
        configuring network settings, 412
        configuring printing system, 414
        configuring security settings, 410–411
        configuring services, 414
        configuring time zone, 413
        file system creation, 406
        hardware requirements, 409

license terms, *405*
LILO boot loader, *442*
pre-installation procedures, *401–402*
selecting installation class, *405*
selecting installation media, *403–404*
selecting keyboard/mouse, *405*
selecting language parameter, *404*
selecting packages, *408*
verifying system functionality, *445–447*
network configuration, 324, 326
planning for, 306
verifying installation site, *308*
verifying network connection, *310*
verifying power source, *308*
verifying server room temperature, *309*
verifying UPS size, *308*
selecting installation method, 327–328
swap files, 338, 341
Linux configuration, *339*
Windows 2000 server configuration, *339*
troubleshooting
post-installation problems, *353*
unable to boot, *351–352*
Windows 2000 Professional, 361–368
X server, 418–419
instant messaging, 53
Intel systems, boot process, 347–348
kernel initialization, 349
kernel load, 349
logon, 350
preboot sequence, 348
intelligent hubs, 128
internal devices, replacing on Linux systems, 611
internal modems, selecting for Linux systems, 603
internal security, 731
internal security threats, 738–739
corporate espionage, 739
rebellious users, 739–740
Internet, 55
connecting to
cable modems, *144–146*
DSL, *142–144*
connection speed, verifying, 571
DNS, 252
host names, *252–254*
domains, structure, 253
firewalls, 748
ACLs, *748*
NAT, *750*

packet filters, *748, 751–753*
placement, *753–754*
proxy services, *748–750*
solutions, *754–755*
ISPs, 140–141
web services, 244–246
zones, 106
Internet layer (TCP/IP networking model), 160
Internet protocols (TCP/IP suite), 79–80
intranets, 246–248
IP addresses
name resolution, 105
NIC configuration, 101–102
via DHCP, *102–104*
IPP (Internet Printing Protocol), 274
IPSec, 741
IPv4 addressing, 163–165
Class A addresses, 167
Class B addresses, 168
Class C addresses, 168
depletion of available addresses, 169–170
dotted-decimal notation, 165
hierarchical addresses, 165
host tables, 178–179
NAT, 171
name resolution, 178
DNS, *180–181*
NetBIOS, *181*
WINS, *182*
network classes, 166
private IP addresses, 170–171
subnetting, 169, 173
subnet masks, *175–177*
IPv6 addressing, 172–173
IPX (Internet Packet Exchange), 80
IPX/SPX protocol suite, 80
IR technology, 125
IRQs (interrupt requests), verifying configuration in Linux systems, 624
ISDN remote access client configuration, 215
ISPs, 55, 140–141
ITU (International Telecommunications Union), 77

J–K

JavaScript, 251
journaling systems, 540
jumper configurations, 613

KDE (K Desktop Environment), 430
kernel, 7
    boot process
        initialization phase (boot process), 349
        load phase (boot process), 349
    identifying problems with, 655
    Linux, 442–443
        drivers, locating, 609–610
        numbering, 443
        recompiling, 443
    modules
        loading, 616, 619
        unloading, 619
    oopses, 558
    startup messages, 664–665
kill command, 498
killing Linux processes, 549–551
Korn shell, 463
KPPP dialer, configuring, 213–215
KVM switches, verifying NOS preinstallation
    checklist, 317

L

LANalyzer (Novell), 576
land attacks, 734
LANs, 5, 57
    bus topology, 111
    default gateway, configuring, 108
    devices
        bridges, 129–130
        hubs, 127–128
        repeaters, 127
        routers, 132–134
        switches, 130
    DUN, 138–139
    Ethernet, 82
        1000BASE-T, 84
        100BASE-X, 84
        10BASE-T, 83
        full-duplex transmission, 85
        half-duplex transmission, 85
    FDDI, 87
        dual rings, 89
    hybrid topology, 117
    IEEE standards, 76–77
    MAC, 58
    media, 58

mesh topology, 116
modems, AT commands, 139
near-side interface, 108
NICs, 99
    configuring IP address, 101–104
    selecting, 101
point-to-point links, 57
ring topology, 114
star topology, 112–113
Token Ring, 86
    beaconing, 87
    MSAU, 86
versus WANs, 57
wireless, 125
laptops, Linux systems
    PC card devices, 644–645
    power management, 641, 643
last-line mode (vi Editor), 465
layers
    of DoD model, 75
    of OSI model
        encapsulation, 74
    of TCP/IP model
        application layer, 158
        Internet layer, 160
        network interface layer, 161
        transport layer, 158–160
LD_LIBRARY_PATH environment variable, 444
LDAP (Lightweight Directory Access Protocol), 230
legacy applications, 16, 307
legal issues, proprietary networking standards, 69
libraries, Linux, 296
license terms for Linux installation, 405
LILO boot loader, *414–415*
    booting without, 670–671
    configuring, 440
        for two operating systems, 442
    emergency boot system, 672–673
    installing, 442
    troubleshooting, 667–669
linear bus topologies, 111–112
Linux, 29–30, 37, 281
    Apache web servers, 498, 500
    audiovisual programs, 290
    backups
        errors, troubleshooting, 684–687
        performing, 523–525
    boot loader, reconfiguring, 439
    boot process, 350

broadband remote access, compatibility issues, 217

Caldera, 282

checking system resources, 561–563

CIFS, 505

CLI, 32–33, 453, 457
- *basic commands, 457*
- *ls command, 460–461*
- *man command, 459*
- *man pages, 458–460*

clients, 286

compatibility issues, 595

configuration tools, 33

core dumps, 543–545

core system hardware, troubleshooting, 640–641

creating disk partitions, 336

critical processes, 545

cron jobs, 540

customer resources, evaluating, 43–44

daemons, 203, 493
- *pppd, 210*
- *starting and stopping, 494–497*
- *superservers, 496–497*

dedicated appliances, evaluating requirements for, 43

DHCP clients, 254

distributions, 281, 285

drive mapping, 537

emergency boot disks
- *creating, 674–675*
- *locating, 673–674*

emergency boot system, 672–673

environment variables, 444

fdisk utility, 538

file access servers, 292

file systems
- *configuration files, 481, 485–492*
- *creating, 406*
- *directory management, 474–475*
- *managing, 478*
- *mounting, 477–478*
- *startup configuration files, 483*
- *symbolic links, 496*
- *system configuration files, 483*
- *system function configuration files, 484*
- *user configuration files, 482*

FTP, 501–502

GNOME, 32

groups, creating, 472–473

GUI, 31

hardware
- *jumper configurations, 613*
- *kernel modules, 616, 619*
- *loading drivers, 614–615*
- *locating drivers, 609–610*
- *PnP configurations, 614*
- *replacing, 610–611*
- *resource allocation, 612*
- *selecting, 597–605*
- *troubleshooting, 633, 636–639*
- *verifying configurations, 621, 624–631*

history of, 278–280

installation procedure
- *configuring boot options, 414–415*
- *configuring network settings, 412*
- *configuring printing system, 414*
- *configuring security settings, 410–411*
- *configuring services, 414*
- *configuring time zone, 413*
- *hardware requirements, 409*
- *package selection, 408*

kernel issues, 442–443
- *numbering, 443*
- *recompiling, 443*

laptops
- *PC card devices, 644–645*
- *power management, 641–643*

libraries, 296

LILO boot loader
- *booting without, 670–671*
- *configuring, 440, 442*
- *installing, 442*
- *troubleshooting, 667–669*

log files, examining, 662–664

lpq, 659

mail client, 506

mail servers, 291

Mandrake, 281

networking, 30

NFS, 505–506

NIS, 237
- *client configuration, 238*
- *database structure, 237*

offic tools, 288

packages
- *Debian, 437–438*
- *dependency problems, troubleshooting, 679–684*
- *RPM, 434–437*
- *tarballs, 438–439*

partitions, 332
  formatting, 539
pre-installation procedures, 401
  boot method, 402
  keyboard/mouse selection, 405
  language parameter, selecting, 404
  license terms, 405
  selecting installation class, 405
  selecting installation media, 403–404
printing, 506
  /etc/printcap configuration file, 507–509
  components of, 507
  Ghostscript Translator, 510
processes
  assigning permissions, 551–552
  killing, 549–551
  managing, 546–548
programming tools, 295–296
recovery tools, 676
Red Hat, 281
  printtool, 509
remote access, 223
  file transfers, 225
  GUI logins, 224
  remote administration protocols, 225–226
  server configuration, TCP wrappers, 219–221
  text-mode logins, 223
remote login servers, 292
scripts, 511
servers
  application failures, troubleshooting, 687–688
  evaluating requirements for, 41
setserial, 658
shadow files, 471
shadow passwords, 411
shell scripting, 251
shells, 462
SMB protocol, 504–505
swap files, configuring, 339
System Activity Reporter, 565
system cron jobs, creating, 541–542
system logging, 557
  log file analysis tools, 558–559
Telnet, 502–504
text editors, 293
user accounts, 466–467
  adding, 469
  creating passwords, 471
  disabling, 471
  group accounts, 469

  in multitasking environment, 467
  managing, 471–472
  permissions, 476
  superuser account, 468
user cron jobs, creating, 543
verifying software compatibility, 297–298
verifying system functionality, 445
  in production environment, 446–447
  in test environment, 445
vi Editor, 464
  command modes, 465
workstations, evaluating requirements for, 41
X Server
  configuring, 419–425
  desktop environments, 429–430, 432
  installing, 418–419
  options, 418
  selecting video card chipset, 416–417
  verifying configuration, 421
  window manager, 427–429
  XFree86 3.3.X configuration tools, 421
  XFree86 4.0.X configuration tools, 423
X Window System, 288, 454
  accessing command console, 456
  exiting, 457
  similarities to Windows 2000, 455
Linux Mandrake, 281
LinuxPPC, 284
LLC (Logical Link Control), 76
loading
  hardware drivers on Linux systems, 614–615
  kernel modules, 616, 619
local groups, Windows 2000
  managing, 380
  permissions, 381–383
locating
  emergency boot disks, 673–674
  hardware drivers for Linux, 609–610
lock and key security, 725–726
lock files, 661
log files
  examining, 662–664
  kernel startup messages, 664–665
  Linux analysis tools, 556–559
log rotation, cron jobs, 541
logical partitions, 331
logical topology, 109
login procedure
  Linux via FTP, 501
  Windows 2000 Professional, 369

logins
    GUI, 224
    Linux privileges, 466
    text-mode, 223
Logon screen, 350
loss of connectivity, troubleshooting, 689
low-level formatting, 408
lpd (line printer daemon), 507
lpq, 659
ls command (Linux), 460–461
lsmod program, viewing kernel module information, 620
lsof, 694
LTO (Linear Tape Open) for system backups, 529

M

MAC (media access control)
    CSMA/CA, 81
    CSMA/CD, 82
    LANs, 58
Mac OS, 13
machine names, 253
MAEs (Metropolitan Area Exchanges), 141
mail servers, Linux, 291
mail services, 52
    components of, 239–240
    Linux mail client, 506
    post-office boxes, 52
man command, 459
man pages, 458–460
management system (SNMP), 583–584
managing
    Linux file systems, 478
    Linux processes, 546–548
    Linux user accounts, 471–472
        groups, 472–473
        permissions, 476
    network services, 577
        for small and medium-sized networks, 581–582
        Hewlett-Packard OpenView, 581
        Microsoft SMS, 577
        MSPs, 582
        Novell Managewise, 578–579
        SNMP, 582–585, 587–588
        Tivoli Enterprise, 579
    Windows 2000 Professional user accounts, 377
many-to-one NAT, 751
mapping utilization patterns, 570
mapping network drives, 534
    in Linux systems, 537
    on Novell networks, 537

    with net use command, 536–537
    with Windows Explorer, 535
Master Boot Record, 331
MDA (Mail Delivery Agent), 239
measuring performance
    baseline performance, 569
    CPUs, 601
    usage, 570
media, 117
    coaxial cable, 118–120
    fiber-optic cable, 123
    LANs, 58
    twisted-pair cable, 120
        STP, 121
        UTP, 122–123
    wireless, 125
memory, 596
    bottlenecks, 566–567
    buffers, 566
    core dumps, 544–545
    RAM, monitoring, 554
    swap files, 338
        adding, 341
        Linux configuration, 339
        Windows 2000 server configuration, 339
    verifying NOS preinstallation checklist, 314
menus, Windows 2000 Professional, 372
mesh topology, 116
methods of system backups
    grandfather-father-son method, 531
    six-cartridge weekly method, 531–532
    Tower of Hanoi method, 532
MIBs (management information bases), 585
MIC (memory in cassette), 527
Microsoft SMS, 577
minimum hardware requirements, 307
    for NOS installation, 317–319
MIPS (Millions of Instructions Per Second), 601
mkfs command (Linux), 408
    formatting partitions, 539
mobile users, 207
modems, 135, 137
    AT commands, 139
    DUN, 138–139
modprobe program, loading kernel modules, 618
monitoring
    network performance, 573–576
    system performance, 564–565, 576
    system resources, 556
monitoring devices, selecting for Linux systems, 605
monitors, verifying NOS preinstallation checklist, 314

motherboards, 596
mounting Linux file systems, 477–478
MSAU (Multistation Access Unit), 86
MS-DOS, 13–16. *See also* DOS
    CLI, 25
MSPs (Management Services Providers), 582
MTA (Mail Transfer Agent), 239
MUA (Mail User Agent), 239
multimaster replication model (Active Directory), 233
multiple disk partitions, 333
multiprocessing systems, 267
multitasking systems, 266
multiuser systems, 266

N
NAME heading (man pages), 460
name resolution, 105, 178
name services, 54
NAT (Network Address Translation), 171, 750
NAUN (Nearest Active Upstream Neighbor), 87
NBP (Name Binding Protocol), 81
NDS (Network Directory Service), 235
    database structure, 235
    platform compability, 236
    security, 236
near-side interfaces, 108
net use command, drive mapping, 536–537
NetBIOS, resolving IP addresses to computer names, 181
netconfig utility, 694
netdiag command, 696
network administration, 55
network connections, verifying NOS pre-installation
    requirements, 310
network interface layer (TCP/IP networking model), 161
network layer (OSI model), 72
network monitoring software, 577
    for small to medium-sized networks, 581–582
    Hewlett-Packard OpenView, 581
    Microsoft SMS, 577
    MSPs, 582
    Novell ManageWise, 578–579
    Tivoli Enterprise, 579
network protocols, configuring, 324–326
network services
    remote access, 205
        client configuration, 210, 213–218
        mobile users, 207
        on Linux systems, 223–226
        rights, 218–223
        telecommuting, 206
        terminal emulation services, 207–208
network subsystem bottlenecks, 568
networking
    ANSI standards, 77
    AppleTalk protocol suite, 81
    client/server, 65–66
    client/server model, 38–39
    devices
        bridges, 129
        hubs, 127–128
        repeaters, 127
        routers, 132–134
        switches, 130
    directory services, 54
    DoD model, 75
    DSL, 142–144
    DUN, 138–139
    IEEE standards, 76–77
    Internet, 55
    IPX/SPX protocol suite, 80
    ISPs, 140–141
    ITU standards, 77
    LANs, 57
        Ethernet, 82–85
        FDDI, 87–89
        MAC, 58
        media, 58
        NICs, 99–104
        point-to-point links, 57
        Token Ring, 86–87
        topologies, 58
    loss of connectivity, troubleshooting, 689
    mail services, 52
    media, 117
        attenuation, 84
        coaxial cable, 118, 120
        fiber-optic, 123
        twisted-pair cable, 120–123
        wireless, 125
    modems, AT commands, 139
    name services, 54
    open-source standards, 68
    OSI reference model, 69
        application layer, 70
        data link layer, 73
        encapsulation, 74
        network layer, 72
        physical layer, 73
        presentation layer, 71

session layer, 71
transport layer, 72
peer-to-peer, 63
proprietary standards, 68
protocol suites, 78
TCP/IP protocol suite, 78
   application protocols, 79
   ARP, 185–186
   DHCP, 189
   FTP, 192
   HTTP, 190
   ICMP, 186–188
   IMAP, 195
   Internet protocols, 79–80
   POP3, 195
   SMTP, 193–194
   TCP, 188
   Telnet, 192
   transport protocols, 79
   UDP, 189
topologies, 108
   bus, 111–112
   hybrid, 117
   logical, 109
   mesh, 116
   physical, 109
   ring, 114
   star, 112, 114
user error, troubleshooting, 689–690
WANs, 59
   asynchronous serial transmission, 135
   common carriers, 60
   connection types, 61
   CSU/DSU, 61
   modems, 135–137
   serial lines, 60
   synchronous serial transmission, 135
networking with Linux, 30
networking with Windows 3.x, 18–19
NICs (network interface cards), 99
   IP address configuration, 101–102
      via DHCP, 102–104
   selecting, 101
   verifying NOS preinstallation checklist, 316
   WOL, 698
NIS (Network Information Service), 237
   client configuration, 238
   database structure, 237
NLMs (NetWare Loadable Modules), 203
NLSP (Novell Link-State Protocol), 80
noncritical processes, 545
non-Intel-based systems, boot process, 347

Novell LANalyzer, 576
Novell NDS, 235
   database structure, 235
   platform compability, 236
   security, 236
Novell NLMs, 203
Novell Managewise, 578–579
Novell NetWare, 36
   drive mapping, 537
Novell RIP (Routing Information Protocol), 80
NTFS (New Technology File System), 21
numbering Linux kernel, 443

O

octets, 101, 165
office tools, Linux, 288
online security policies, creating, 725
Open Source Initiative, 279
open-source networking standards 30, 68
   versus proprietary, 69
OPERANDS heading (man pages), 460
options for ls command, 461
OPTIONS heading (man pages), 460
origins
   of Linux, 29–30
   of UNIX, 28
OSI reference model, 69
   application layer, 70
   data link layer, 73
   encapsulation, 74
   network layer, 72
   physical layer, 73
   presentation layer, 71
   session layer, 71
   transport layer, 72
OSPF (Open Shortest Path First), 80
OUs (organizational units), 232

P

packages
   Debian, 437–438
   dependencies, 409
      troubleshooting, 679–684
   RPM, 434–435
      commands, 436–437
      compability issues, 435–436
      upgrading, 436

selecting for installation, 408
tarball, 438–439
packet filters, 748–753
stateful packet filtering, 752
packets, 74
page faults, 567
paging functions (window managers), 428
PAP (Password Authentication Protocol), text-based PPP client configuration, 210
PAP (Printer Access Protocol), 81
parent processes, 546
partial backups, 521
partition table, 331
partitions. *See also* **formatting hard disks**
checking for errors, 539–540
creating, 334–336
with FIPS, 337
with third-party tools, 336
fdisk utility, 538
formatting, mkfs utility, 539
logical, 331
NOS installation, 331
data overrun protection, 334
Linux systems, 332
on multiple disks, 333
passive hubs, 128
passwd command (Linux), creating passwords, 471
password protection, Linux, 466
passwords
configuring on remote access servers, 222–223
shadow passwords, 411
patches, 745
applying, 747
selecting, 746
PATH environment variable, 444
pathping command, 690–693, 697
PC card devices, Linux laptops, 644–645
PC-based LANs, 5
PCMCIA modems, 136
PCs versus NOSs, 265
peer-to-peer networks, 18, 63
versus client/server, 66
percent processor utilization, 566
performance
bottlenecks, 564
baseline measurments, 569
disk subsystem bottlenecks, 567
memory bottlenecks, 566–567
network subsystem bottlenecks, 568
processor bottlenecks, 566

Internet connection speed, verifying, 571
monitoring, 565
monitoring tools, 564, 573–576
of CPUs, measuring, 601
usage
mapping patterns, 570
measuring, 570
protocol-specific patterns, 570
Performance Monitor, 573–574
Performance tool (Windows 2000/XP), 559–560
performing backups
in Linux, 523–525
in Windows 2000, 522–523
peripherals
troubleshooting in Linux systems, 636–639
verifying NOS preinstallation checklist, 314
permissions
Active Directory, 233
assigning to processes, 551–552
Linux, 467
Windows 2000, managing, 381–383
persistent problems, troubleshooting, 661
physical layer (OSI model), 73
physical topology, 109
pico, 471
ping, 187, 690, 692–693
placement of firewalls, 753–754
planning for NOS installation, 306
verifying installation site, 308
verifying network connection, 310
verifying power source site, 308
verifying server room temperature, 309
verifying UPS size, 308
plenum, 118
Plug and Play technology, 273
PnP configurations, 614
point-to-point links, 57
POP3 (Post Office Protocol version 3), 195, 240
port numbers, 159–160
POST, 347
post-installation problems, troubleshooting, 353
post-office boxes, 52
power cables, verifying configuration in Linux systems, 621, 624
power management, Linux laptops, 641–643
power supplies, VA rating, 309
PPP (Point-to-Point Protocol), remote access client configuration, 210, 213
GUI dialing utilities, 213–215
pppd (PPP daemon), 210

preboot sequence, 345, 348
preemptive multitasking, 18
    Windows 9.x, 21
pre-installation procedures
    hardware inventory
        creating, 320–322
        verifying against HCL, 323
    Linux, 401
        boot method, 402
        license terms, 405
        selecting installation class, 405
        selecting installation media, 403–404
        selecting keyboard/mouse, 405
        selecting language parameter, 404
preinstalled NOSs, drawbacks of, 306
presentation layer (OSI model), 71
primary partitions, 331
printing in Linux environment, 506–507
    configuring during installation, 414
    /etc/printcap configuration file, 507, 509
    Ghostscript translator, 510
    printtool, 509
printing services, 240–241
    Windows 2000, 390–392
printtool utility, 509
private IP addresses, 170–171
problem-solving guidelines, 695–696
processes, 546
    unresponsive, troubleshooting, 660–661
processors
    bottlenecks, 566
    verifying NOS pre-installation checklist, 314
programming tools, Linux, 295–296
proprietary networking standards, 68
    versus open-source, 69
protocol analyzers, 570
protocol suites
    AppleTalk, 81
    IPX/SPX, 80
    TCP/IP, 78
        application layer, 158
        application protocols, 79
        ARP, 185–186
        DHCP, 189
        FTP, 192
        history of, 155–156
        HTTP, 190
        ICMP, 186–188
        IMAP, 195

Internet layer, 160
Internet protocols, 79–80
network interface layer, 161
POP3, 195
SMTP, 193–194
TCP, 188
Telnet, 192
transport layer, 158–160
transport protocols, 79
UDP, 189
protocols, 78
protocol-specific utilization patterns, pinpointing, 570
proxy services, 748, 750
ps command, 546–548
PS1 environment variable, 444
public/private key encryption, implementing, 744–745
PWD environment variable, 444

Q–R

QIC (quarter-inch cartridge)
    for system backups, 525
quotas, 553

rack-mount servers, verifying NOS preinstallation checklist, 311
RAID (redundant array of inexpensive disks), 700, 703
    controllers, verifying NOS preinstallation checklist, 316
RAIT (redundant array of independent tapes), 529
RAM, 596
    monitoring, 554
read permission (Linux), 475
rebellious users as internal security threat, 739–740
recompiling Linux kernel, 443
reconfiguring Linux boot loader, 439
recovery tools, 676
recurring problems, troubleshooting, 661
Red Hat Linux 7.x, 281
    Anaconda, 329
    minimum system requirements, 319
    printtool, 509
redundancy. *See* RAID
regional providers, 141
remote access, 205
    client configuration, 210
        cable modems, 216–218
        DSL, 216–218

ISDN, 215
PPP, 210, 213–215
directory services, 227–228
   Active Directory, 231–234
   DAP, 230
   LDAP, 230
   NDS, 235–236
   NIS, 237–238
   X.500 standard, 229–230
file sharing, 241
FTP web services, 242
   CLI commands, 244
   DoS attacks, 244
mobile users, 207
on Linux systems, 223
   file transfers, 225
   GUI logins, 224
   remote administration protocols, 225–226
   text-mode logins, 223
rights, configuring, 218
   file permissions, 223
   firewall services, 218
   passwords, 222–223
   TCP wrappers, 219–221
telecommuting, 206
terminal emulation services, 207
   Telnet, 208
web services, 244–246
   extranets, 249
   intranets, 247–248
remote login servers, Linux, 292
remote management, 203
remote notification, SNMP, 588
removable media, securing, 729
removing core files, 544–545
repeaters, 127
replacing hardware on Linux systems, 610–611
replication, Active Directory, 233
request/response protocols, peer-to-peer networks, 63
requirements for Linux installation, 409
resolving
   IP addresses to computer names
      DNS, 180–181
      host tables, 178–179
      NetBIOS, 181
   NetBIOS names to IP addresses, WINS, 182
resource allocation on Linux devices, 612
resource management on Linux systems, 561
responsibilities of network administrators, 56
restore errors, troubleshooting, 684–687
reviewing daily logs, 556

RF technology, 126
rights, controlling remote-access policies, 218
   file permissions, 223
   firewall services, 218
   passwords, 222–223
   TCP wrappers, 219–221
ring topologies, 58, 114
RIP (Routing Information Protocol), 79
risk analysis, 699–700
rmmod program, unloading kernel modules, 619
root account (Linux), configuring, 410
root object (directory services), 227
route utility, 660
routers, 132–134
   default gateway, configuring, 108
RPM (Red Hat Package Manager), 434–435
   commands, 436–437
   compatibility issues, 435–436
   upgrading, 436
rules-based forwarding, 748
runlevels, 488
   changing, 489–490
   changing default, 490
running window managers, 429

S

safe waste disposal security policy, 723
Samba, 286, 504–505
SAP (Service Advertisement Protocol), 80
scalability, 706
   of NOSs, 269
scarcity of available IPv4 addresses, 169–170
script kiddies, 736
script services, 250–251
scripting languages, 250
scripts, 250
   Linux, 511
   Sys V scripts, starting and stopping daemons, 494–496
   text-based PPP client configuration, 212–213
   Windows 2000, 393–394
SCSI (small computer system interface) devices
   cables, verifying NOS preinstallation checklist, 315–316
   terminations, 628
   troubleshooting in Linux systems, 633
   verifying configuration in Linux systems, 627
SCSI IDs, 627
SDSL (Symmetric DSL), 143

sectors, Master Boot Record, 331
security
    assessing needs, 720–722
    attacks
        buffer overflow, 733
        DDoS, 735–736
        DoS, 733
        exploits, 737
        Smurf, 734
        TCP SYN, 733
        teardrops, 734
    authentication, text-based PPP client
        configuration, 210
    creating security policies
        acceptable use policies, 722
        network access rules, 723
        online security resources, 725
        securing removable media, 729
        server room security, 725–729
        username/password standards, 722–723
        virus protection standards, 724
        waste disposal, 723
    e-mail, 742–743
    external threats, 732
    file encryption, implementing, 740
    firewalls, 748
        ACLs, 748
        NAT, 750
        packet filter, 748, 751–753
        placement, 753–754
        proxy services, 748–750
        solutions, 754–755
    internal threats, 738–739
        corporate espionage, 739
        rebellious users, 739–740
    IPSec, implementing, 741
    Linux, configuring during installation process,
        410–411
    NDS permissions, 236
    passwords, remote access configuration, 222
    patches, 745
        applying, 747
        selecting, 746
    public/private key encryption, implementing, 744–745
    SNMP, 587
    SSL, implementing, 742
    Trojan horse programs, 738
    upgrades, 745
        applying, 747
        selecting, 746
    versus accessibility, 720

Security Accounts Management Database, 273
segments, 74
selecting
    hardware for Linux systems, 597
        CPU, 599, 601
        internal modems, 603
        monitoring devices, 605
        packages, 408
        sound cards, 603
        USB devices, 603
        video capture cards, 603
        video hardware, 601–602
    installation media, 327–328
    Linux installation class, 405
    Linux installation media, 403–404
    NICs, 101
    NOSs
        performance criteria, 268
        security criteria, 269
    patches, 746
    upgrades, 746
    video card chipset for X server, 416–417
    window managers, 428–429
Sendmail, 240
serial transmission, 135
**server chassis, verifying NOS pre-installation
  checklist, 310**
server racks
    securing, 728
    verifying NOS pre-installation checklist, 311
server rooms, securing, 725
    antitheft devices, 728–729
    biometrics, 728
    card readers, 727
    combination locking mechanisms, 726
    lock and key, 725–726
server-based networks, NOSs, 5
servers, 38
    Active Directory, 232–233
    client/server networks, 65–66
    DHCP, 254
    drive mapping, 534
        in Linux systems, 537
        on Novell networks, 537
        with net use command, 536–537
        with Windows Explorer, 535
    evaluating requirements for, 41
    hardware components, 310
        backup system, 315
        disk drives, 314

FC-AL, 316
KVM switch, 317
memory, 314
monitors, 314
NICs, 316
peripherals, 314
processors, 314
RAID controllers, 316
SCSI adapter, 316
SCSI cable, 315
server chassis, 310
server rack, 311
UPS, 315
video adapter, 317
Linux application errors, troubleshooting, 687–688
services. *See also* daemons
    configuring during Linux installation, 414
    network administration, 55
    printing, 240–241
    TCP/IP-based, 204
    Windows 2000
        e-mail, 389–390
        FTP, 385–386
        HTTP, 384
        print, 390–392
        Telnet, 387–388
session layer (OSI model), 71
setserial, 658
Setup program, Windows 2000 Professional, 363–367
setup.exe, 329
SGID (set group ID), 551
shadow files, 471
shadow passwords, 411
shadowing, 631
shared network technology, 88
sharing folders in Windows 2000, 379
shell sites, 711
shells, 32
    Linux, 462
shutdown command (Linux), 490
single ring topology, 115
six-cartridge weekly method of system backups, 531–532
Slackware, 285
slow connection speeds
    causes of, 572
    EIDE/ATA devices, troubleshooting, 632
SMB (Server Message Block) protocol, 504–505
smbclient, 504
smbmount, 504
SMP (symmetric multiprocessing), 276
SMTP (Simple Mail Transport Protocol), 79, 193–194

Smurf attacks, 734
Sniffer protocol tools, 575–576
SNMP (Simple Network Management Protocol), 225, 581–583
    agents, 584
    communities, 587
    installing, 585
    management system, 583–584
    MIBs, 585
    remote notification, 588
    security, 587
    traps, 584
software
    open-source, 68
    patches, 745
        applying, 747
        selecting, 746
    upgrades, 745
        applying, 747
        selecting, 746
sound cards, selecting for Linux systems, 603
spoofing, 734
spread spectrum transmission (WLANs), 126
SPX (Sequenced Packet Exchange), 80
SSH protocol, password encryption, 222
SSL (Secure Sockets Layer), 742
star bus, 117
star topologies, 58, 112–114
starting
    daemons, 494–497
    MS-DOS command-line, 26
startup configuration files, 483
stateful packet filtering, 752
stopping daemons, 494–497
storage-and-retrieval applications, e-mail, 52
store-and-forward applications, e-mail, 390
Storm Linux, 285
STP (shielded twisted pair), 121
structure
    of Internet domains, 253
    of NDS database, 235
    of NIS databases, 237
    of Windows 2000 Active Directory database, 231
subdirectories, 10
subnetting, 169, 173
    subnet masks, 101, 170, 175–177
SUID (set user ID), 551
Sun UNIX partition tables, 334
superservers, 496
    xinetd.d file, configuring, 497

superuser account, 468
   creating, 343–344
   managing groups, 472–473
SuSE Linux, 285
swap files, 338
   adding, 341
   Linux configuration, 339
   Windows 2000 server configuration, 339
SWAT (Samba Web Administration Tool), 225
switches, 130
switching between X Window System and CLI, 456
symbolic links, 496
symptoms
   of application software problems, 655–656
   of configuration problems, 656
   of hardware problems, 654
of kernel problems, 655
   of user error problems, 657–658
synchronous serial transmission, 135
SYNOPSIS heading (man pages), 460
syntax, ls command, 461
Sys V scripts, starting and stopping daemons, 494–496
system administration
   CPU usage, 555
   disk management, 552–554
   Linux, checking system resources, 561–563
   logging, 556–557
      log file analysis tools, 558–559
   memory usage, 554
   reviewing daily logs, 556
   Windows 2000
      creating folders, 379
      local groups, 380
      permissions, 381–383
system backups, 519
   automating, 533
   differential backups, 522
   documenting, 532
   full backups, 521
   grandfather-father-son method, 531
   hardware
      8mm tape, 527
      AIT, 527–528
      DAT, 528
      disk drives, 530
      DLT, 528
      LTO, 529
      QIC, 525
      tape arrays, 529

tape autochangers, 529
      tape drives, 525
      tape libraries, 530
      Travan cartridge tape, 526
   incremental backups, 522
   partial backups, 521
   performing in Linux, 523–525
   performing in Windows 2000, 522–523
   six-cartridge weekly method, 531–532
   tape backups, 521
   Tower of Hanoi method, 532
   verifying, 533
system configuration files, 483
system cron jobs, 541
   creating, 541–542
system files, 305
system function configuration files, 484
system maintenance logs, 491
System Monitor, 573–574

T

Tab completion key, recalling filenames in Linux, 457
tape arrays for system backups, 529
tape autochangers for system backups, 529
tape drives for system backups, 521, 525
tape libraries for system backups, 530
tar program, performing backups in Linux, 523
tarball packages, 438–439
taskbar (Windows 2000 Professional), 372
TCP (Transmission Control Protocol), 79, 188
   port numbers, 159–160
   wrappers, configuring on remote access servers, 219–221
TCP SYN attacks, 733
TCP/IP (Transmission Control Protocol/Internet Protocol)
   protocol suite, 39, 78
   application layer, 158
   application protocols, 79
   ARP, 185–186
   DHCP, 189
   FTP, 192
   history of, 155–156
   HTTP, 190
   ICMP, 186, 188
   IMAP, 195
   Internet layer, 160
   Internet protocols, 79–80

IPv4, 163–165
    Class A addresses, 167
    Class B addresses, 168
    Class C addresses, 168
    depletion of available addresses, 169–170
    DNS name resolution, 180–181
    dotted-decimal notation, 165
    hierarchical addresses, 165
    host tables, 178–179
    name resolution, 178
    NAT, 171
    NetBIOS name resolution, 181
    network classes, 166
    private IP addresses, 170–171
    subnetting, 169, 173
    WINS name resolution, 182
IPv6 addressing, 172
    hexadecimal format, 172–173
network interface layer, 161
NOSs, 161
ping, 690–693
POP3, 195
security threats, 731
services, 204
SMTP, 193–194
TCP, 188
Telnet, 192
transport layer, 158, 160
transport protocols, 79
UDP, 189
verifying network connectivity, 325
teardrops, **734**
telecommuting, 206
Telnet, 79, 192, 208, 502–504
    Windows 2000 services, 387–388
temperature of server room, verifying, 309
TERM environment variable, **444**
terminal adapters, configuring remote access clients with ISDN, 215
terminal emulation services, 207–208
terminations, **628**
testing network connectivity, 325
text editors, 676
    Linux, 293
    pico, 471
text-based PPP configuration, 210, 213
text-mode logins, configuring, 223
third-party partitioning tools, 336
threads, 267

threats to security
    buffer overflow attacks, 733
    DDoS attacks, 735–736
    DoS attacks, 733
    exploits, 737
    internal threats, 738–739
        corporate espionage, 739
        rebellious users, 739–740
    outside sources, 732
    Smurf attacks, 734
    TCP SYN attacks, 733
    TCP/IP services, 731
    teardrops, 734
    Trojan horse programs, 738
throughput, bottlenecks, 564
time slicing, 17
time zones, configuring during Linux installation, 413
Tivoli Enterprise, 579
Token Ring, 86
    beacons, 87
    MSAU, 86
    versus FDDI, 88
tokens, 114
Tom's Root/Boot Disk, 674
top command, 548
topologies, 58, 108
    bus, 111–112
    hybrid, 117
    logical, 109
    mesh, 116
    physical, 109
    ring, 114
    star, 112–114
Torvalds, Linus, 29
Tower of Hanoi method of system backups, 532
traceroute command, 693
transfer rates of DSL, 143
transmitters, 125
transport layer
    OSI model, 72
    TCP/IP networking model, 158–160
transport protocols (TCP/IP suite), 79
traps, 584
Travan cartridge tape for system backups, 526
Trojan horse programs, 738
troubleshooting
    application problems, 655–656
        on Linux servers, 687–688
    backup and restore errors, 684–687

based on user feedback, 665–667
configuration problems, 656
hardware in Linux systems
 core system hardware, 640–641
 peripherals, 636–639
 SCSI devices, 633
hardware problems, 654
kernel problems, 655
LILO boot loader, 667–669
network problems, 689
 loss of connectivity, 689
 operator error, 689–690
NOS installation
 post-installation problems, 353
 unable to boot, 351–352
package dependency problems, 679, 681–684
persistent problems, 661
unresponsive programs, 660–661
user error problems, 657–658
Turbo Linux, 285
twisted-pair cable, 120
STP, 121
UTP, 83, 122–123
types of NOSs, 269

U

UARTs (Universal Asynchronous Receiver/Transmitters), 135
UDP (User Datagram Protocol), 79, 189
port numbers, 159–160
UIs (user interfaces), 7
CLIs, 9, 32–33
GUIs, 9–10, 31
UNIX, 37, 279
CLI, 32–33
configuration tools, 33
GUI, 31
origins of, 28
UNIX/Linux System Activity Reporter, 565
unloading kernel modules, 616, 619
unmount command, 478
unmounting Linux file systems, 477–478
unresponsive programs, troubleshooting, 660–661
updates, 745
Upgrade Advisor tool website, 319
upgrades, 745
applying, 747
selecting, 746

upgrading RPM, 436
UPSs
VA rating, 309
verifying NOS preinstallation checklist, 315
upstream data transfer, 143
USB devices, selecting for Linux systems, 603
user accounts
administrator, creating, 343–344
Linux, 466–467
 adding, 469
 creating passwords, 471
 disabling, 471
 group accounts, 469
 groups, 472–473
 in multitasking environment, 467
 managing, 472
 permissions, 476
 superuser account, 468
quotas, 553
Windows 2000
 adding, 376
 managing, 377
 permissions, 382
user configuration files, 482
user cron jobs, 541
creating, 543
USER environment variable, 444
user feedback as source of problem identification, 665–667
useradd command (Linux), adding users, 469
UTC (Coordinated Universal Time), 413
utilities
crontab, 543
fdisk, 538
ifconfig, 694
ipconfig, 659–660
Linux
 Debian, 437–438
 lpq, 659
 RPM, 434–437
 setserial, 658
mkfs, 539
netconfig, 694
ping, 690–693
printtool, 509
recovery tools, 676
route, 660
SWAT, 225
TCP/IP, 160
UTP (unshielded twisted-pair) cabling, 83, 122–123